THE REMINISCENCES OF

Admiral Carlisle A. H. Trost
U.S. Navy (Retired)

INTERVIEWED BY

Paul Stillwell

U.S. Naval Institute • Annapolis, Maryland

Copyright © 2018

Preface

This candid oral history traces the career of an individual who grew up in the farm country of Western Illinois and eventually ascended to the top uniformed position in his service, Chief of Naval Operations. His period in uniform included all but the first few years of the Cold War that pitted the United States against the Soviet Union. During that time he was involved in the conclusion of the important Incidents at Sea agreement between the U.S. and Soviet navies and exchanges of visits between top-ranking U.S. and Soviet officers. Along the way, he was one of the pioneers of the U.S. Navy's nuclear power program. In the case of the first nuclear submarine in which he served, USS *Swordfish* (SSN-579), he and other early crew members were more knowledgeable about the propulsion plant than the personnel in the yard that built the ship. He was a pioneer as well in being one of the first Olmsted Scholars, a program that exists to this day to send promising junior officers overseas for postgraduate study. Trost was studying in Germany when the Berlin Wall was erected in 1961. He was Chief of Naval Operations when the wall came down in 1989. The Cold War ended during his watch as CNO.

The memoir contains many revealing descriptions of Trost's relationships with such individuals as Commander Jack English, skipper of his first ship, the destroyer *Robert A. Owens* (DDE-827); Admiral Hyman G. Rickover, head of the naval nuclear power program for many years; Vice Admiral Shannon Cramer; Admiral Donald "Red Dog" Davis; Admiral James A. "Ace" Lyons; Admiral William Crowe and General Colin Powell, Chairmen of the Joint Chiefs of Staff; Deputy Secretaries of Defense Cyrus Vance and Paul Nitze; Secretaries of the Navy John Warner, William Middendorf, John Lehman, and James Webb; Dr. David Chu, systems analyst for the Defense Department; and Chiefs of Naval Operations, Admiral Elmo Zumwalt and Admiral James Holloway.

For a variety of reasons, it took far too long to complete this oral history. The first interview was in 1991 and the final one in 2017. Too many competing priorities and other circumstances caused the interruptions. The drawback is that Admiral Trost's once-phenomenal memory has faded somewhat in recent years. The result is that the details eluded him in responding to some questions. On the other hand, he does still remember a great deal, as evidenced by the nearly 700 pages of transcript that follow. In a number of cases, the memories came out in a stream-of-consciousness format, with a topic moving forward or backward in terms of chronology. In order to make the sequence flow in a more coherent form for the benefit of readers, I have sometimes rearranged the sequence to produce an essentially chronological flow. That has involved moving some text from one interview to another. Another factor was my unfortunate difficulty in mastering the art of audio recording in digital format. Some material thus went unrecorded. As a remedy, I did one additional follow-up interview to fill in some of the gaps that went unrecorded. The original versions of the transcripts exist in the Naval Institute files. Admiral Trost edited them by hand to make sure the final version expressed his desires.

One constant throughout my relationship with the admiral was his frequent expressions of affection for his late wife Pauline and his discussion of the many contributions she made to his successful career and to the raising of their four children. Many of the interviews in this volume took place within a few months of his wife's passing, and that energized his recall. Throughout I have been impressed by Admiral Trost's sense of integrity and his graciousness. He endured with patience my sometimes-fumbling operation of the recorder. Things worked better when I had technical assistance from Brian Rehill of the Naval Academy faculty and Jonathan Hoppe of the Naval Institute staff. Scot Christenson of the Naval Institute recorded a video interview with Admiral Trost that constitutes a condensed version of the overall oral history.

As this project comes to a close, I thank Susan Corrado. managing editor of the Naval Institute Press; she coordinated the printing and binding of the finished history. Janis Jorgensen of the heritage division has been a strong supporter throughout the process. Deborah Lattimore, now head of Techni-Type, did the excellent initial transcription of the interview audio files. Debbie is a long-time friend who introduced the Naval Institute to the digital age in the 1980s, not long before this project began.

Paul Stillwell
U.S. Naval Institute
November 2017

The U.S. Naval Institute Oral History Program

Researchers and authors have been drawing on the Naval Institute's Oral History Program since 1969, the year it was established by Dr. John T. Mason Jr. He and his successor, author and historian Paul Stillwell, sought to capture, preserve, and disseminate a permanent record of the stories of significant figures in naval history. Under the leadership of Vice Adm. Peter H. Daly, U.S. Navy (Ret.), CEO of the Institute, the program has expanded, with increasing numbers of historians conducting more interviews.

These oral histories are carefully fact-checked and reviewed by both historians and interview subjects before being made available. The Naval Institute is known for this high level of editorial intervention and polishing. The reader is reminded, as with all oral history interviews, that this is a record of the spoken word.

The Naval Institute wishes to acknowledge the many donors who make this program possible, in particular the generous support of the Pritzker Military Foundation of Chicago and the late Jack C. Taylor of St. Louis.

ADMIRAL CARLISLE ALBERT HERMAN TROST
UNITED STATES NAVY (RETIRED)

Carlisle Albert Herman Trost, the son of the late Elmer H. and Luella (Hoffman) Trost, was born April 24, 1930, in Valmeyer, Illinois. He attended Washington University, St. Louis, Missouri, for one academic year prior to entering the U.S. Naval Academy, Annapolis, Maryland, in 1949. On 5 June 1953, he was commissioned an ensign, graduating first in his class from the Naval Academy.

Following graduation, Trost first reported to the destroyer *Robert A. Owens* (DDE-827) and in December 1954 was detached to attend the Submarine School, New London, Connecticut. In June 1955 he reported to the diesel submarine *Sirago* (SS-485), where he qualified as a submariner in July 1956. From January to June 1957, he attended the Advanced Nuclear Power course at the Submarine Base, New London, Connecticut, followed by training at the Naval Nuclear Power Training Unit, Idaho Falls, Idaho, until September 1957.

In November 1957, Trost reported to the nuclear-powered attack submarine *Swordfish* (SSN-579) and in December 1959 qualified to command submarines. From January until June 1960 he studied German at the Army Language School, Monterey, California, and was then assigned temporary duty in the Bureau of Naval Personnel, Navy Department, Washington, D.C. In September 1960 he reported to the University of Freiburg, Federal Republic of Germany, serving until January 1962, when he reported as executive officer of the nuclear-powered attack submarine *Scorpion* (SSN-589).

From May to July 1963, Trost attended the Polaris command course at the Fleet Anti-Air Warfare Training Center, Dan Neck, Virginia. He then reported as executive officer of the Blue crew of the nuclear-powered ballistic missile submarine *Von Steuben* (SSBN-632). In March 1965 he reported as military assistant to the Deputy Secretary of Defense, Washington, D.C.

In January 1968 Trost assumed command of the Blue crew of the nuclear-powered ballistic missile submarine *Sam Rayburn* (SSBN-635). In September 1969 he was assigned as Assistant Chief of Staff for Personnel and Administration on the staff of Commander Submarine Force, U.S. Atlantic Fleet. He reported in August 1970 as executive assistant and naval aide to the Under Secretary of the Navy, and later Secretary of the Navy, John W. Warner, serving until June 1973. In March 1973, his selection to flag rank was approved by the President. In June 1973, he assumed command of Submarine Flotilla One (later renamed Submarine Group Five) in San Diego, California, with additional duties as Commander Submarine Force Pacific Representative, West Coast.

In December 1974, Trost reported to the Bureau of Naval Personnel as the Assistant Chief for Officer Development and Distribution. In January 1976, he was assigned to the Office of the Chief of Naval Operations as Director, Systems Analysis

Division, OP-96. On 22 August 1978, he was promoted to vice admiral and reported as Deputy Commander in Chief, U.S. Pacific Fleet, Pearl Harbor, Hawaii.

On 14 February 1980, Trost assumed command of the U.S. Seventh Fleet and served in that position until 15 September 1981. For his service he was awarded the Government of Japan's Order of the Rising Sun (Second Class) and the Republic of Korea's Order of National Merit. His next assignment was as Director, Navy Program Planning, OP-090, on the staff of the Chief of Naval Operations. On 4 October 1985 he was promoted to the rank of four-star admiral and became Commander in Chief U.S. Atlantic Fleet and Deputy Commander in Chief U.S. Atlantic Command.

Admiral Trost served as Chief of Naval Operations from 1 July 1986 to 29 June 1990. His personal awards, in addition to those listed above, include the Defense Distinguished Service Medal, Navy Distinguished Service Medal, Army Distinguished Service Medal, Air Force Distinguished Service Medal, the Legion of Merit, the Navy and Marine Corps Achievement Medal, Navy Unit Commendation, Navy Meritorious Unit Commendation, the Navy Expeditionary Medal, Navy Occupation Service Medal (European Clasp), the National Defense Service Medal with bronze star, the Antarctica Service Medal, the Humanitarian Service Medal, Navy Sea Service Deployment Ribbon.

Trost was married to the former Pauline Haley of Cottage City, Maryland, from 1954 until her death in 2015. Their four children are Carl Michael, Laura Lee, Steven Glenn, and Kathleen Susan.

Deed of Gift

The U.S. Naval Institute is hereby authorized to make available in any format it chooses, from bound-book hard copy to electronic/digital Internet access, the audio recordings, transcripts, and videorecordings of the oral-history interview series conducted concerning the life and career of the undersigned. Disposition, repositories, and access shall be at the discretion of the Naval Institute.

The undersigned does hereby release and assign to the U.S. Naval Institute the rights and title to these interviews, with the exception that the undersigned and heirs retain the right to use the material for personal, noncommercial purposes. The copyright in the oral, transcribed, and videorecorded versions shall be held by the U.S. Naval Institute. All recordings, transcriptions, and videorecordings of the interviews shall remain the property of the U.S. Naval Institute.

Signed and sealed this _1st_ day of ___July___ 2015.

_____
ADM Carlisle A. H. Trost, U.S. Navy (Retired)

Interview Number 1 with Admiral Carlisle A. H. Trost, U.S. Navy (Retired)

Place: Admiral Trost's home in Potomac, Maryland

Date: Tuesday, 23 July 1991

Paul Stillwell: Just to begin at the beginning, Admiral, could you talk, please, about your ancestors as far back as you're aware of, and then your immediate family, with your parents?

Admiral Trost: Okay, I'll try that. Unfortunately, I know less about my ancestors than I'd like to, but I'm in the process, as soon as I clear up some of my other paperwork, of getting started with some bits and pieces I've been collecting over the years.

My ancestors were farmers who came from Germany, as best I can determine, in the 1870s time frame. They came to Illinois. We think we have located some of the paperwork that shows when they came through Ellis Island. But they settled in downstate Illinois, just across the river and about 20 or 30 miles south of St. Louis, which is on the Missouri side. They were all farmers, and it wasn't really until my father's generation that people started going out elsewhere, because there wasn't room for all the kids, especially during the Depression, to stay on the farm as adults and earn a livelihood.

I was born in 1930, during the Depression, on my grandparents' farm, where my parents were living at the time.* My mother was also from a farm family. She lived about two miles down the road and had gone to school with my father. My dad, at that time, was working for room and board for himself and his wife, basically for his father, who had determined that he really couldn't keep all of the then five boys gainfully employed, and the three girls, who were my dad's sisters. So he apparently worked to get the girls married off—those who were old enough. Actually, the oldest one went off to become a domestic worker in St. Louis. The oldest son went off to learn a trade for a period of time. He became a linoleum and tile layer; later, after the death of my grandfather, he came back and ran the farm until his death.

In the meantime, having to find other means of livelihood, my dad managed to get a job as a farm manager in a little town outside the town of Columbia, where I was raised.

---

* Trost was born 24 April 1930. His parents were Elmer H. and Luella (Hoffman) Trost.

My birthplace was actually south of Valmeyer, Illinois. Valmeyer, at that time, and even today, is a community of about 350 people. The most prominent things in the region were the grain elevator; about five taverns, in the days when I was growing up; and a couple of grocery stores, one of which purported to be a department store; and, of course, houses for the people who lived there. It was primarily a farm-support area—farm implements, granaries, and things of that nature.

Paul Stillwell: What were the main products produced by your grandfather's farm?

Admiral Trost: Primarily the staples were wheat and corn. They grew some oats, mostly to mix their own feed. In later years—later years being, really, the early '40s—they started raising soybeans as a very good cash crop. Soybeans, during the war years, were extremely important, both as a food source and also as an oil source, as I remember.

Paul Stillwell: Did they have any livestock?

Admiral Trost: They had livestock. These were the days of farming with horses and mules. As I was growing up, they raised primarily cows, for both milk and some beef cattle, but not very many beef cattle; and a lot of hogs and a lot of chickens. So the farm communities of those days were the ones where if the farmer went off somewhere on a Sunday to enjoy himself, he was back by 5:00 in the afternoon to milk cows and feed his stock.

There was really that kind of environment that I was raised in as a little kid, because I spent a lot of time, even after my parents moved into town, on my grandparents' and uncle's farms. My dad, as I remember, worked for several years for the gentleman who owned this small farm place outside Columbia. He was a man who was the first to bear the title that I later heard called quite frequently, city farmer, meaning he lived in St. Louis and owned this land, and other people took care of it for him.

Paul Stillwell: Absentee landlord.

Admiral Trost: Absentee landlord, absolutely. But he came out, apparently on weekends, and used the main house that was on this farm. My parents lived in a smaller place next door to it. My dad was able in the early '30s—and I think the time frame was '32-'33—to get a job with Midwest Rubber Reclaiming Company, up in Monsanto, Illinois, to the north of where we lived. At that time, they moved into the town of Columbia, where I was raised, and where I lived until I went to the Naval Academy.

My formative years were spent, as I said, in a small town. Columbia had a population of about 1,800. It, too, was a farm community with the grain elevator—one of two, as a matter of fact being the most prominent features in town, farm implement stores, two department stores, several grocery stores. I think, at one time, the count was 15 taverns. People had to have a place to wet their whistles when they came to town. Since Budweiser beer was brewed just 15 miles away at that time, there was a ready availability of lots of good draft beer—at a nickel a glass, of course.

Paul Stillwell: Prohibition was repealed in late '33.[*]

Admiral Trost: Yeah, it was, and it was before my memory. As I was growing up in that time, I remember, as a matter of fact, being sent up on rare occasions, usually by one of my neighbors, with a little gallon bucket to the nearest tavern, which was a block away, to bring home a bucket of beer. That was a pretty standard thing to do. Usually on a Saturday evening, or Sunday evening, they sat around and had some beer in the yard and enjoyed themselves.

But it was very much a rural community environment, even though we were less than 20 miles from the heart of St. Louis at the time. I do recall going over to St. Louis for shopping from time to time. There were areas on South Broadway in St. Louis, which was then sort of the five-and-dime strip—the area where the name brands weren't sold. You could get almost anything you needed at a price that some of the people could afford.

---

[*] The 18th Amendment to the Constitution was ratified in 1919 and went into effect in 1920, prohibiting the consumption of alcoholic beverages in the United States. The Volstead Act, enacted by Congress in 1919, spelled out the penalties for violations. In December 1933 the ratification of the 21st Amendment to the Constitution repealed the 18th Amendment and thus ended national prohibition.

Paul Stillwell: As you describe it, it sounds like there were not a lot of luxuries in the Trost family.

Admiral Trost: There were very few luxuries. I can recall things like dessert on Saturday evening, and only on Saturday evening, being a pint of ice cream cut into four blocks—it came in a pint box—cut into four blocks for the family. That used to be my thrill. As a matter of fact, I'm still an ice cream lover, even though people say it's bad for your cholesterol.

But it was a relatively austere environment as we were growing up. We had no extras at all. My dad's salary wasn't very high, and people didn't live that high. I've often commented that we didn't know we were poor at the time, because we had a roof over our heads and good solid food to eat. My mother made clothes. She repaired everything that got damaged or was wearing out.

Paul Stillwell: When you divided the ice cream into fours, does that mean you had a brother or sister?

Admiral Trost: I had one sister. And the ice cream was always divided four equal ways.

Paul Stillwell: What's her name?

Admiral Trost: Her name is Mardell. She lives in a little town, Waterloo, which is just to the south of Columbia.* It's the county seat of the county where I was raised, also a farm-support community, predominantly—slightly larger than the town in which I lived. As a matter of fact, the population of the three towns in our county together was less than 6,000 people. So it was predominantly rural.

Columbia itself is an interesting place. It's very green; it used to be known as the garden town, probably still is, by the people that used to come there on weekends from St. Louis to visit. They liked two things. They liked the good restaurants they found, because the cooking was good; they also liked the fact that the taverns in Columbia could

---

* She died subsequent to this interview.

be open on Sundays, and in St. Louis they could not. And the gas stations were open. So they'd come over to buy gasoline and drink their beer and have a good meal and then go back home.

But the town itself lay between the very flat, rolling farmland to the east and the Mississippi River Valley. We were sitting up on a bluff, about three miles to the east of the river. The bluff is sort of a woody, craggy area with lots of sinkholes and lots of woods. Then it fell off into the very flat river bottom, which was some of the most fertile farmland I think in this country. It was to the south, in that river bottom, that my aunts and uncles and grandparents farmed, and where I spent an awful lot of time when I was growing up.

Also, when I was living in the town, I worked for some of the local farmers. So I'd really have to say that during my elementary and high school years I spent a lot of time on farms. I learned to drive a team of mules when I was about five years old; drove a tractor for the first time when I was six—could barely push down the clutch pedal because of the heavy spring on it. That tractor was a very old thing that my grandfather got at my uncle's behest—my uncle farmed with him at the time—and it was quite the pride of the family. But I spent a lot of time cultivating corn with mules. I spent time driving a team, hauling wheat that was sacked after the threshing machines had finished with it then hauling it off to the local grain elevator with my grandfather. I actually participated in the wheat harvest, which at that time consisted of using a binder, which cut and tied the bales, which were then stacked into shocks to dry. After they dried, the so-called threshing machine run would start.

Paul Stillwell: Did you enjoy the out-of-door life?

Admiral Trost: Oh, I really did. As a matter of fact, when I was a kid, I thought that I was probably going to be a farmer, because I really did enjoy working out there. I enjoyed working around animals—learned what to do. I guess as a teenager I could have been a competent farmer, or at least I could have learned to be. Today I'm afraid I'm a little past that; I remember a lot of things, but not enough. I'd probably plant everything at the wrong time.

Paul Stillwell: Were there are special pleasures you remember from that period?

Admiral Trost: Well, I just enjoyed roaming around. My grandparents lived at the edge of the woods, which was right at the edge of the river valley—I'm talking now about maternal grandparents, with whom I spent more time. As for my father's parents, my grandfather died a year after I was born, and my grandmother when I was eight years old. Although I spent time on that farm then and later, when my uncle—who was dad's oldest brother took over, it was my mother's parents that I spent more of the time with—and her oldest brother. She was one of three children; my dad was one of eight.

My mother's oldest brother, who was the oldest member of the family, was a bachelor until he was 40 years old. He farmed with my grandparents for a period of time. I spent a lot of time with him, not only learning about the farm and enjoying it, but he's the one who taught me to curse and got my mouth washed out for the first time. As a matter of fact, I used some words around my mother that he'd use routinely, and I couldn't understand why I was being punished. Because it seemed so much a part of his vocabulary. But I did spend a lot of time there.

I think my favorite periods during that time were, in fact, the so-called threshing runs, when they'd bring this huge machine along, with the big steam engine that both hauled it along the road and powered it when it was sitting there doing its job. But they'd bring the shocks in out of the fields on big wagons. That was the glamour thing those were the cowboys. If you had any horse teams at all, they were always hitched to the wagons that brought the wheat shocks in from the fields. Then they'd pitch them in, and grain came out the other end. It was sacked by guys like me—when we were old enough to hold the sack up without spilling all the wheat—and put in the box wagons, and generally hauled off to the local grain elevator, which in our case was just about a mile away.

Paul Stillwell: The combine must have seemed a marvelous invention.

Admiral Trost: The combine was a fantastic invention. I thought it was one of the greatest things around, and it did come in during my time working on the farm, right after

World War II. Once it did, the early ones were liked for their efficiency and for their manpower savings, and disliked because they cut about a 3- to 4-foot swath in a time that took forever. It's like mowing a several-acre lawn with a 19-inch lawn mower. But it was a great time saver. But it was during that time, when I was still a teenager, that the farms were making their transition to tractors, from horse- and mule-drawn equipment. I guess what really impressed me, and probably influenced me a great deal, was the self-sufficiency of farmers. If something broke, they fixed it. It didn't make any difference what it was, they fixed it. If they needed something built, they built it.

Paul Stillwell: And grew a lot of their own food.

Admiral Trost: And grew their own food. You know, there was everything there to eat. There was always the butchering season, when a cow, if you were going to butcher beef, or certainly several hogs were butchered. People would get together, generally the family, and do the slaughtering, and do the preparation of the meat—the canning of things to put away. Hanging things in the smokehouse was a very, very standard thing. If you wanted a chicken, you went out and caught one and chopped its head off and cleaned it. It was as simple as that. If you wanted vegetables during the growing season, you went out—they always had big gardens. And they canned the food that they didn't use then, for winter use. There was really never any shortage of good food. There was very, very little money. I can remember my grandparents one year being proud of the fact I think I was about eight years old, and they gave me my first watch. It was a little Ingraham pocket watch that I think cost a dollar. That was almost a splurge for them to have that kind of free cash, because they were also giving gifts to my sister and small things to my parents. It was an austere environment, and yet a very, very good family environment.

Paul Stillwell: Did your family benefit from any of the Depression relief measures?

Admiral Trost: Relief measures were considered to be a very bad thing. Anybody who was on any form of relief was viewed with distaste by my family and by most of the people out there.

Paul Stillwell: So there was a stigma.

Admiral Trost: There was a stigma, very definitely. I can recall a family—after we lived in town, during the time when I was, oh, in the age range of about six to 12 we had neighbors whose son was a schoolmate of mine, who had been on extended relief. Now, I guess it was sort of like a welfare payment is today, because I didn't know the details. All I know is that I was taught that that was very bad; that you should never do that, because it was not something one did with dignity; one went out and worked.

Paul Stillwell: It implied a lack of character on the part of the person.

Admiral Trost: It really did. During that time frame, prior to World War II, a lot of people were scrambling. But there were very few people unemployed for very long, even if the employment was fairly menial in nature.

Paul Stillwell: Well, there was also an informal system, where people would help an individual who was willing to work.

Admiral Trost: That's right. So they did not have any of these measures, or would not have taken advantage of them just would not have considered doing it.

Paul Stillwell: What other values did your parents impart to you?

Admiral Trost: Well, first of all, that you never buy anything unless you can pay for it. My parents made only one, I guess what I'd have to say, charge purchase in my recollection. That was a kit to build a house. My dad and my mother, one of my uncles, and I built a house when I was 16 and 17 years old. They bought a lot, waited several years, and saved money, and then at that time, shortly after World War II—this was in '46-'47 when we built this—they went off and ordered a home. Liberty Homes, Bay City, Michigan, sent precut kits. The first thing that came was the blueprints. We contracted. Dad and I dug the basement with a mule team and scoop that had handles on it. We put in the footings. We dug the sewer line by hand. Then we hired a man who built the concrete-block basement, who objected to the fact that the plans said he was to be within a quarter inch on the dimensions they'd given, so the precut home would fit it. He said, "That's not the way we do it. People build to fit my foundations, not the other way around."

Well, we finally persuaded him to build to suit our plans, and he did. And he did a good job for us. Then one day a railroad car showed up at the grain elevator siding, and we had three days to unload it. It had all the lumber, the doors, the windows, the shingles, the siding, the paint—everything you needed to do it, except to finish the interior of the house. We unloaded the things we needed first off onto the lot, and the rest went into the garage of the house we were renting at the time.

Then we built the house. My dad, with our help, as directed labor, did almost everything. We couldn't hook up the plumbing, because that was against code; that required a plumber, to do the final hookup to put the sewer line out to the street. He could wire the house, but not hook up the panel. He did that. He had the furnace and the ductwork installed by people. We put up all the lath for the plaster, and had a plasterer come in and do that. We put in the hardwood floors. We did all the painting and all the finishing. And it still sits—very well built. But it was a good experience to me. My parents, I can recall, fretted over the fact that they actually had to borrow some money to buy that house, which cost $3,000. My mother went to work, since her kids were all old enough to take care of themselves; we were teenagers. She went to work in a department store over in St. Louis to help pay off. I think it took them three or four years to pay off the house, which let them breathe more freely again, and enjoy it.

So their sense of values was, I'd say, twofold: honesty—and I'll give you an example of that, that's always stuck with me—and frugality. They just didn't spend on things they didn't need, and they didn't spend it if they didn't have it. I can't envision their having ever applied for a credit card, for example.

I learned the value of sticking to the truth when I was about ten years old. I had done something; I can't remember the details. I do remember my dad calling me in to talk to him when he came home from work and asking me something about what I'd done. My first reaction was, ""How'd he find out about that?" My second reaction was, "Well, he can't know too much about that." So I gave him a story.

He said, "Okay."

I thought, "By Gosh, I got away with that one."

About two days later, he asked me the same thing, and I'd forgotten what it was I'd told him. So the story I thought I'd told him wasn't quite the same, and he said, "That's not what you told me the other day. You're going to find out that if you tell the truth, it's easy to remember what you said, because that sticks with you. You tell a story, you're not going to remember what you said."

So I thought that was a good lesson in life.

Paul Stillwell: And he was probably one who believed in the idea that one's word was one's bond.

Admiral Trost: Very, very definitely.

Paul Stillwell: How well educated were your parents?

Admiral Trost: Both had eighth-grade educations, in the small, one-room schoolhouse, in a little store junction near where they lived. I say near; it was about a mile from my dad's home and about two miles from where my mother was raised. Both were raised on the farms where their parents lived, obviously—the ones I've been referring to.

Paul Stillwell: What sort of school experience did you have yourself?

Admiral Trost: I went to elementary school in Columbia, the town where I was living. We didn't have kindergarten in those days. I just went to the regular elementary school. I went to a high school in a neighboring town, five miles away, called Dupo. Dupo was a

Missouri Pacific rail yard and engine-repair place—about 2,000 people, most of them associated with that railroad operation. But it had a community high school, which was very well financed.

It had a student population of around 800 students at the time. They came from surrounding farm communities. But they also came out of the suburbs just to the south of East St. Louis, an area that was very heavily—and still is very heavily—industrialized. The school had the advantage of a very heavy tax base. Its taxable constituents included a Phillips Petroleum terminal on the river; it included one of Monsanto Chemicals' main plants and still one of their main plants; a zinc refinery, Lewin Metals; the place where my dad worked, the rubber-reclaiming company; Darling Fertilizer plant; goodness, several other major industries. And, of course, the railroad operation was there. So it was one of the richest high schools in Southern Illinois and offered a lot of facilities. The high school in my hometown was not state accredited for entrance into the University of Illinois at that time, and for some reason I thought I might want to go to college. So, with my folks' concurrence, I went to school in the neighboring town. I had to work throughout my high school years, because I had to pay my own tuition to go there.

Paul Stillwell: It was accredited, I take it?

Admiral Trost: It was accredited, yes. It, for example, offered a full range of science and math courses, which my local school did not. The local school had two years of math in high school, that was it, and no physics, no biology; it had a general science course, no chemistry.

Paul Stillwell: What about the humanities?

Admiral Trost: The humanities, I'd say, were probably stronger in the school I went to, simply because they had much more. They had a fantastic library and very, very good literature courses, both American and English literature, which were mandatory courses; a very good history department. The history department was a husband-and-wife teaching team, who were absolutely superb.

It offered not only a very sound academic arrangement, but also had other things. For example, we had a wood shop and a metal shop that would have put most apprentice schools to shame. We learned to build furniture in wood shop. In metal shop we learned to do just about anything you could with metal. I took both those courses. I did not take their automotive course, but we had an eight-stall automotive repair shop in high school. You could come in and modify a car; you could overhaul it. Of course, in the latter stages of World War II, teenagers were looking for anything they could make run in any possible way. The cars were simple enough for teenagers to learn them pretty well. For example, they taught body repair work. We had kids who graduated from high school who went immediately to work in shops that repaired cars, and they were qualified to do it.

The school also, at the time, because of its size, had a very well supported athletic arrangement. So they had teams that were well outfitted and well equipped. Where in my hometown, the mothers would sew the uniforms the jerseys and things for their sons—in Dupo they bought them. So that was really uptown.

Paul Stillwell: So you were the beneficiary of this tax base.

Admiral Trost: I was the beneficiary of that, and it cost me $125.00 a semester to go to school there, which was expensive for me, but very cheap when you look at the opportunity it provided.

Paul Stillwell: What sort of jobs did you take to earn that tuition?

Admiral Trost: Well, I had worked on farms, as I mentioned. I did work for one friend of my father's, who was a farmer down in the river bottom, about seven miles out of town. We used to harvest potatoes—and he grew quite a few by a machine that went along and dug up one row at a time, essentially, and they came shaking out the back with the dirt off, and the potatoes wound up on top of the ground. It was stoop labor. They hired young kids to come in and pick them up. We picked them up in a bucket, dumped the bucket into sacks, which were then hauled off to market. I had done that. I had worked for that gentleman and another one, making hay. I worked for another guy, out at the edge of town, one year, milking his cows morning and evening. And, of course, you got paid for that.

I worked in a department store where you had groceries here, and dry goods in another section, and then hardware in another section, and farm implements out back. I think I was 10 or 12 years old when I went to work there. I was sort of a jack of all trades there. I stocked shelves in the grocery department. Sometimes I took care of customers when the other two people who worked there were busy. I stocked hardware items and sold hardware items. I swept floors. I did whatever I was told, for 25 cents an hour. I'm not sure that was minimum wage, but it was about as good as we could do. And I did that into high school.

About my sophomore year in high school, I got a job in the post office, as an assistant letter carrier. But that meant for the balance of my high school years I carried one mail route during the week. My town was divided into four routes, and I carried one of the four in the afternoon, after school. On Saturday, the regular carrier had his day off, and I carried all four routes. So I was a letter carrier for about three years, as I recall, and that took care of my high school tuition.

The summer before I started college, I worked at two things. I was part of a labor gang for a while, until I got cement poisoning one day working in a very hot sun and being the guy who split open bags and dumped them into a cement mixer. I got cement dust all over myself—I didn't have a shirt on. The combination of perspiration and cement dust and an oily mist that the mixer gave off, ended up with a mess on my skin that I couldn't get out. I did that for about a week. At the end of the week I got very sick. It was cement poisoning in the pores of my skin. So I got different jobs. I went to work at the grain elevator, and unloaded trucks and railroad cars, and helped mix feed and sack feed, and did things like that.

Paul Stillwell: So jobs were available for people who were willing to work.

Admiral Trost: Yes, jobs were available. They didn't pay very much, but if you were willing to work, and especially if you could go out and help farmers. For example, the one guy, when I milked cows, my pay for that was usually bringing home a bucket of milk. It didn't net me anything, but it certainly netted the family something. And whenever they had something extra, you know, then they'd send it in. When he butchered a cow, he gave my folks some meat. With the man for whom I picked up potatoes, one week my pay was a bushel of potatoes. Most of the rest of the time he paid 25 cents a day for his labor. One summer, when I was the oldest of the kids he had out there working, I got paid a nickel a day extra to sort of set the pace and show the young kids what to do. So I guess I was the Judas goat there, leading them along.

But things were available. People really worked hard for not very much; it was mostly a self-sustaining type of environment when I was growing up.

Paul Stillwell: That was literally the early-to-bed, early-to-rise environment.

Admiral Trost: That's right. Well, my grandparents, for example, when I was with them—when the sun came up, it was time to be up. And the roosters did crow; they really do things like that. But you'd hear the rooster, and if the rooster crowed and you weren't up, it was time. In the evening, we'd come home after a pretty long day of working, and then have our evening meal after all the animals had been fed and the cows were milked. After supper they could sit and listen to the radio for a little while, but certainly by 9:00 o'clock everybody was in bed. Of course, my grandparents didn't have electricity till after World War II, so we had little kerosene lanterns. If you were a reader, you couldn't see very well—at least not for very long.

Paul Stillwell: How did you power the radio?

Admiral Trost: Ah, the radio was battery powered. We used to have one of those big old things with the terminals on top; you still see something like that. And that was a luxury. That belonged to my uncle. He had bought that, and so it was there, and that was kind of nice. At home we could plug in; we had electricity in town. I guess it was the Rural Electrification Act that finally carried through. But my grandparents weren't hooked up until either during or just after the war.

Paul Stillwell: How much did you keep track of the events of the wider world?

Admiral Trost: I can remember sitting and listening in about 1937 to events in Europe, and finding it very frightening, because it was difficult to understand what was going on and why. I can recall when Germany invaded Poland—I guess it was '39—listening to the radio news.[*] We listened to "Captain Midnight" and some of the other soap opera serials of the time. I guess "soap opera" is not the right term, but radio adventure stories: "The Shadow," "Captain Midnight," and things of that nature.

I guess I kept up with world events reasonably well. During World War II, of course, I was a little older, and I kept up quite well. I used to keep scrapbooks of things from the newspapers. We learned something about geography. One of the things I bemoan is that my children don't have the grasp of geography that we were taught when we were kids. I think it's true of this country in general, and maybe it's true of the world. I don't know.

I recall hosting the Swedish CNO down here several years ago. He's now retired, but he was a very personable gentleman. One of the things that Rear Admiral Walt Davis, who was then Commander Naval District Washington, had done, in our partnership-with-schools efforts, was to bring young children from inner-city schools out to see some of these ceremonial events.[†] So on the day we had the ceremonial welcoming with honors—every time we did this, we had a group of children—usually junior high, sometimes high school, but usually the junior-high-age groups. We'd have 40 or 50 young kids there, and they'd be watching the events. Well, the Swedish CNO thought this was quite good. So he walked over after the ceremony and said to this group that he was pleased that they were there, and did they know he was a foreigner? Well, there were a few nods. He said, "I'm from Sweden. Does anybody know where that is?"

One little black girl put her hand up and said, "I know. Swedes come from Minnesota." That was the nearest we got to Sweden, and I don't think that's unusual. I

---

[*] World War II began on 1 September 1939, when German ground forces invaded Poland. Two days later Great Britain and France declared war on Germany.
[†] Rear Admiral Walter J. Davis, USN, served as Commander Naval District Washington in the late 1980s.

think you could have done that in just about any age group of that size across the country.

Paul Stillwell: We had an article by Admiral Carter in the *Proceedings* recently along those lines.[*]

Admiral Trost: I saw that—yeah, Ed Carter, and I agree fully with him; he's absolutely right.

Paul Stillwell: My own favorite radio serial was "The Lone Ranger."

Admiral Trost: I liked "The Lone Ranger" too. I listened to "The Lone Ranger" all the time.

Paul Stillwell: And apparently the St. Louis Cardinals games too.

Admiral Trost: Oh, we never missed the games if we could. We were Cardinals fans. Of course, St. Louis had the Browns at that time, as well. But for some reason I grew up knowing, based on my upbringing, that the American League fielded inferior teams, and that the National League had the really good ones. I think I made my first trip to Sportsman's Park, the old ballpark in St. Louis, when I was six years old, with a neighbor boy, who was about four years older than me. We were given permission to ride the bus to St. Louis. Then we caught a trolley out to Sportsman's Park. He knew how to get there, and we went out and saw the Cardinals play a ball game. It was really a thrill. I got to an occasional ball game later on with my parents, and a couple of times on my own. But it was an expensive proposition. As I remember it, it cost us 25 cents to ride the bus to St. Louis; it cost another nickel to take the trolley out, another nickel to take it back, and 25 cents to go to the game. And so it was an expensive day when you did things like that, and a real treat.

---

[*] Rear Admiral Edward W. Carter III, USN, "Our Military is Geographically Illiterate," *U.S. Naval* Institute *Proceedings*, April 1991.

Paul Stillwell: I went to my first game there, and I remember as you'd go up Grand Avenue you'd look for the light towers on the ballpark. I guess it didn't even have light towers when you got started.

Admiral Trost: No, it did not. They weren't playing night games then. I don't know when those were put in, as a matter of fact.

Paul Stillwell: About 1940.

Admiral Trost: But when I first went I know they weren't there, and they didn't play night games. I never saw a night game in that park, I don't think, but they must have played. And I was picking the Cardinals—oh, what was it, '44 or '45, I think, when the Browns and Cardinals had an in-city World Series?

Paul Stillwell: Forty-four.[*]

Admiral Trost: Forty-four. That was quite an interesting thrill for everybody out there.

Paul Stillwell: I've seen a picture that was taken at that series, and it showed a husband and wife sitting together; one had a Cardinals button, and one had a Browns button on.

Admiral Trost: Well, you know, I remember one time being given these little baseball bats that were about a foot and a half long; they were really just little souvenirs. We got two. One had the Cardinals' imprint, and the other had the Browns' insignia on it. They were given to me, and I gave my sister the Browns' bat, because I knew that one wasn't as good as the Cardinals' bat. But those were great things. You know, the Cardinal ball players were the heroes of that area. Every kid wanted to play like—well, if you were a shortstop you wanted to play like Marty Marion, and if you were a hitter you wanted to hit like Johnny Mize. And, later on, when Slaughter and Musial and those guys were playing, they were the heroes. I remember Enos Slaughter and the fact that he never

_____

[*] The Cardinals won the 1944 World Series, four games to two.

walked anywhere on the field; he always ran out to his right-field position; he always ran in at the inning change—he was always jogging, always moving, which is probably why he enjoyed as long a game-life as he did.

Paul Stillwell: Well, Cardinal baseball was practically a religion in the area.

Admiral Trost: Oh, it was, and interestingly it still is. When St. Louis lost the football Cardinals, there wasn't too much hand wringing about it. A lot of people said, "Gee, we've lost our team." But they weren't being supported. The baseball Cardinals are still pretty well supported. As a matter of fact, they've been talking about building a new stadium. I don't know how they can support that, because they've got that beautiful Busch Stadium in the heart of downtown. I don't know what its total seating capacity is, but having been in the stadium several times, it's pretty doggone big.[*]

Paul Stillwell: It's about 50,000.

Well, the real religion, how much did your family participate in that?

Admiral Trost: The real religion—church going, very steadily church going. If you didn't go to church on Sunday, there was something wrong. We were Sunday school attendees. We went to an Evangelical and Reformed church. And we attended Sunday school first, then went to church, every Sunday. When we were away from home on Sunday, we went to church. If we were down visiting the grandparents, we went to a little town called Maeystown, where they were baptized, where they were confirmed, and—as a matter of fact, the cemetery there is where most of my relatives are buried, and we'd go down there. So we really got to know a lot of people down there as well.

Once a year, for a while, while I was young, we used to go down to the Lake of the Ozarks for a week's vacation, and rent a cabin down there that had been built by the

---

[*] Sportsman's Park, which Trost attended as a boy, was renamed Busch Stadium in 1953. A second Busch Stadium opened as home of the Cardinals in 1966. A third Busch Stadium, still in use, opened in 2006.

CCC guys.* We'd spend a week. We hauled all our food, everything else along.

Paul Stillwell: That's a beautiful area.

Admiral Trost: Oh, it really is, and we'd go down there. I can remember that we always went to—I think it was Wentzville, Missouri, to church. It was on the way to where we were going, and we would leave very, very early on Sunday morning to be in Wentzville in time to go to church and Sunday school, and get our Sunday school certificate from them so we could take it back to our church the next week. We'd go to church on the way; we didn't miss it, even though we were off on vacation. I don't remember missing many times.

Paul Stillwell: You probably took highway 40 out there.

Admiral Trost: I think so. I think so.

Paul Stillwell: It was the main route.

Admiral Trost: I don't remember that area too well anymore, but I think we did: 40, and I want to say 61 or something like that. Then we'd go down—I know on a number of occasions we went to Springfield. I toured the Illinois state capitol in Springfield. We went to several places in the Ozarks, with the Bagnell Dam area—greater vicinity—being one of the favorites; it seemed like a real fine resort. The big thrills there were getting to go out on a speedboat, which was—I don't know how fast they were, but they were speedboats then, and something that had a motor it was a great thrill. Because what we did around home was row on the ponds or on the lake.

Paul Stillwell: That Evangelical and Reformed denomination had strong Germanic roots.

---

* CCC – Civilian Conservation Corps, which began in 1933 as an agency authorized by the U.S. Government to hire unemployed young men for public conservation work. Among other things, the men planted trees, built dams, and fought forest fires. More than two million men served in the CCC before it was abolished in 1942.

Admiral Trost: Very strong Germanic roots.

Paul Stillwell: My father was a preacher in that denomination, so I know it well.

Admiral Trost: It and the Missouri Synod Lutheran Church were very strong in that area, in terms of numbers. We had three churches in town at that time. The Catholic Church was the biggest and the wealthiest. You learn biases even then; you learn that Catholics have money, and Protestants don't, you see. The lessons one learns as children are interesting. But the Catholic Church had the largest church. The Evangelical and Reformed had—I'm not sure the congregation was all that much smaller, but the church wasn't quite as massive. The Lutheran church was fairly small, but there was a small Lutheran church in every one of the towns around there. And they were very, very active churchgoers.

Paul Stillwell: And very, very fundamentalist.

Admiral Trost: Oh, very, very definitely, very definitely. I can recall on occasion we'd attend Presbyterian churches if we were traveling. We generally went to Methodist or Presbyterian if we couldn't find any E and R. And I guess the Methodist is probably the closest in terms of worship services, or at least was at that time.

Paul Stillwell: And Presbyterian is pretty close.

Admiral Trost: Yes, it is very close.

Paul Stillwell: What sorts of things did you enjoy reading when you had the opportunity?

Admiral Trost: Almost everything. I really liked to read history; I've always enjoyed history. I wish I could go back and study history from scratch; it would make a lot more sense now, because I'm convinced that the way history is taught doesn't make sense. One year you may be told you're going to study European history, so you start from scratch and go through it. But you don't relate what happened, or at least we didn't, to what's happening in the rest of the world at the time. So it's sort of a disjointed conglomeration. I think the reason a lot of students dislike history is just that; it doesn't relate to other things. You're learning in parallel columns with no interface between them.

One of the things I've enjoyed since then, when I've had the time to read—for example, when I had command of the Seventh Fleet, I used to read a lot of the World War II history. Now I could relate things to each other. Even though the historian himself might not tie all events together, you read half a dozen books on what happened in World War II, if they're the right books, you very quickly learn how to correlate in your own mind what's happening around the world. I found it far more meaningful after I was 50 years old than I did when I was 10. But I used to read a lot of adventure stories too.

Paul Stillwell: Nancy Drew and the Hardy Boys.

Admiral Trost: Nancy Drew, the adventure stories. Nancy Drew always did everything to perfection, as I recall, and always solved everything. The Hardy Boys, and—oh, Lord, I don't know. I read everything on *Tom Sawyer* and *Huck Finn* I could find.

Paul Stillwell: Did you get up to Hannibal?*

Admiral Trost: One time, when I was fairly small, and that was a real thrill. But if Mark Twain wrote it, we knew it was good—Mark Twain and the things under O'Henry's moniker. I read a lot of the adventure stories. I read a lot of English literature in high school and rather enjoyed it. I think in part because I had a really superb teacher, Mrs. McGuire, who was just—she lived history, and she really communicated very well.

---

* Hannibal, Missouri, on the Mississippi north of St. Louis, was the town where Samuel Clemens (better known as Mark Twain) grew up. *The Adventures of Tom Sawyer*, published in 1876, included a fictional town named St. Petersburg, Missouri.

Paul Stillwell: The best teachers are the ones who inspire as well as educate.

Admiral Trost: Yes. You know, it's interesting. I've been back for two reunions at my high school, the most recent one being in '88, my 40th high school reunion. We had a fairly good turnout, and they invited people from the class before and the class after. So we had just one heck of a big reunion and a very fine evening. That evening was attended by the Bollerjacks, who were the history teachers. I think she also taught typing and business. They retired from teaching, but they stayed in that one school their entire teaching career. The widow of a guy named Moss—Mr. Moss was the chemistry teacher. He made chemistry and biology live to kids. He had been at the reunion five years previously, and had made a model of a molecule. Then he connected it with paper, so you had these nodes out here, but you had faces on it—on which he had written the names of every student he had taught out of our class, which was probably half the class. Wherever he remembered some little something about it, it was written very finely. Unfortunately, he died in the interim, but you can imagine a guy like that; when he was teaching, you learned because he showed you.

We had a physics teacher; his name was Faulkner, and from him you were learning physics hands-on. We had beautiful labs in both those things. I did not study biology, but the biology lab was also superb. But you had hands-on experiences; the equipment was there. We did experiments. If you said this thing is going to start here, and it's going to slide down there, and it's going to run about that fast, first of all you computed it, and then you went and did it. That's a remarkable way to get a feel for what goes on.

Paul Stillwell: And that was the advantage of going to Dupo.

Admiral Trost: That was the advantage of going to Dupo. None of that existed in my hometown, which has a new and much larger school system now, but did not at that time. It was a smart move on my part, because that school experience resulted in my getting a one-year academic scholarship to Washington University in St. Louis, which I did accept. I took that over going to the University of Illinois, which I could have done, simply because at U of I, I had to live on campus. I'd have had to travel there and send things like dirty laundry back and forth. This way I could live at home. My parents didn't help me with college, but I could live at home free. And somebody was taking care of my laundry and helping out.

We joke a lot, and I have to share this with you. I press suits and uniforms—not because my wife can't, but because my mother taught me in a very good way. I was probably a high school freshman when I came home one day. Now, some of the kids in my class dressed much better than others; I was not one of those. But I noted that some of these guys came in with very nicely pressed trousers. I said to my mother, "Could you put a little sharper crease in my pants?"

She said, "Sure. Come here, let me show you how to do that." She ironed this pair of pants and put a sharper crease in them. I thought it was very nice.

The next time I said, "Mom, how about doing that again?"

She said, "You know how to do it." And from that time on I pressed my own trousers."

Now, I made the mistake of saying something to Pauline when we were first married about, "Maybe you could press this for me, and kind of get these wrinkles out."

She said, "Your mother said you know how to do it." [Chuckle] So that's been my task, which I don't mind at all, as a matter of fact. But you learn some things in interesting ways.

Paul Stillwell: What ambitions did you develop along in these years for a career you might want to pursue? You, at some point, must have gotten beyond farmer.

Admiral Trost: Well, I did, as a matter of fact. I think it was when I was in high school. I have always enjoyed science and had a relatively good capability in it. I didn't have much problem in any courses, as a matter of fact, but I enjoyed math and science courses quite a bit. I decided while I was in high school that I really wanted to be an engineer. After more thinking on that, decided I wanted to be a mechanical engineer. My goal, at the time, was to be a guy who designed things to be built—automotive, or machinery, or things of that nature. So when I did have the scholarship opportunity to go to college, I did go as a mechanical engineering major. That was my goal.

I had had an opportunity to do a little work; I did some drawing work for a civil engineering firm in St. Louis. They offered an opportunity to people who were enrolled in the descriptive geometry and mechanical drawing courses, the engineers, to do some really off-hour work for them—drawings and things for them. This was back in the days before cad/cam and everything else, and everything was done mechanically. The professors would take several of us—I think there were five of us—who were doing well in the course, and we got this opportunity to earn extra money by coming in on Saturdays, or on afternoons when we didn't have classes, and doing drawings for this firm, which paid the university to do it, and paid us as individuals.

So there was a period of time there, also, where I had some interest in civil engineering, when I was doing both drawings for equipment, and then also doing scale sketches on things like—you're going to cut through this hillside to fill in this area over here and build a road through. That sounded pretty interesting to me. We had a large construction company, Luhr Brothers, which was based in my little hometown. At that time, it also did work in, I think, just about every state along the Mississippi River. And they still are in existence, still based there, still a very large—almost a national-level construction firm—earthmovers, dam builders, road builders—that kind of thing.

Paul Stillwell: What had inspired this interest on your part?

Admiral Trost: I don't know if I can tell you that. It just evolved. I enjoyed things mechanical. I enjoyed both learning the technical background of things and the application. I was very interested in applied mathematics at one time, simply because it's an—you know, instead of just learning a bunch of stuff that people say—you know, "What am I going to do with this junk?" You were actually seeing what you were going to do with this junk, and it made good sense. I took a shop course, I think, all four years, except maybe the year I took typing, and I didn't have time for shop. I'm not sure.

But I enjoyed, and still do enjoy, working with my hands. I enjoyed building and repairing. I had worked with my Uncle Herman, the bachelor I was telling you about earlier. Herman could fix anything. So could my dad. These guys were simply taught that when you needed something done, you did it. They were very, very conversant with tools. And they overhauled cars. They did all their own mechanical work. They fixed farm machinery. They could do some passable welding. And I had learned to weld. So those kinds of things appealed to me—just wanted to work with things.

Paul Stillwell: And the equipment was not so sophisticated that you had to be a specialist.

Admiral Trost: That's right. I enjoyed the logic, for example, of taking apart the hitch from a combine, which had broken and had to be welded. You had to take the plate off, and to find all the places that you were going to take things apart without this whole machine coming apart—that was rather fascinating. I learned how to get inside the place where the straw got separated and kicked out, and take it apart, because it used to jam up. That kind of thing appealed to me.

Frankly, I enjoyed building. I think I'd have enjoyed almost anything that had to do with my hands, and I probably would have been happy at that, as long as somebody gave me books to read in my spare time. I don't know quite how that interest developed, but it did. It was fostered at Washington University, whose engineering department was absolutely superb, and had really outstanding professors, including one who was really my first introduction to anything to do with the Naval Academy.

All I knew was that he was a professor. His name was Zellmer, and I encountered him in later years. Zellmer taught mechanical drawing. He was a graduate student at the time, working on his PhD. He was a Naval Academy graduate.[*] I think he came out of the Naval Academy right about the end of World War II and served his initial obligation and then went back to the academic field. I encountered him later on, here in Washington, when he was working out at the CIA. In fact, as a Navy captain I ran into this guy who had taught me mechanical drawing.

---

[*] Midshipman Ernest J. Zellmer, USN, was in the Naval Academy class of 1944, which graduated in 1943, and qualified in submarines. He resigned his regular commission in 1947 and eventually retired as a Naval Reserve captain in 1967.

But they were very dedicated people. We had a Professor Van Shock, and I think he was the head of the math department, assistant head or head. He took one class, a group of five of us, all of whom had had calculus up to or into differential equations, and said, "You guys are going to be a guinea pig math class." He took us, and we just got pushed along, as I did when I was in high school. He said, "As fast as you guys can work, I'll teach you." It was really rather fascinating. He was extremely dedicated and another guy who made things very interesting.

I had a high school teacher who was very much like that, Mr. Willis, whom I met initially as the gym coach. Mr. Willis was also the advanced mathematics professor. He taught advanced algebra normally. He offered, our junior year, second semester, to take a group of us from my class to go in the advanced algebra courses. Again, I think he took five or six students, and we were split out of the regular classes. We started a progress-as-you-will-type course, and it worked very well. He carried us through senior year on that; otherwise, we'd never have been taught calculus or got into differential equations. People like that spark your interest. They're very dedicated. They're very devoted. They're very good.

Paul Stillwell: It must have been a bright group, because you usually don't get into those things in high school.

Admiral Trost: No, but I was amazed when I got to college that there was a group— probably about a dozen kids in this freshman engineering bunch how many there were in our class, I don't even know. I think the college had a daytime enrollment of about 6,500 at that time, but that was the total university, not just the engineering department. I have no idea how many engineers there were, but there were probably at least a dozen who'd had some calculus, as a minimum. I'd had almost a year at that point. As a matter of fact, through my freshman year in college I had more math than was taught at the Naval Academy at that time, and had gone further, by far, than I went at the academy. Unfortunately, we could not validate at that time; you took the courses. All we could validate at the Naval Academy were things like—if you'd had a composition or rhetoric college course, then you could validate that and go on into a literature course. And there was one other thing, as I remember, but I don't recall it. I think there were two things that could be validated, and gave you some slight variance from the standard. But the major was the same, no matter who you were. So you didn't vary very far from the standard course.

Paul Stillwell: As you describe those various things you were interested in—the math, the science, engineering, and so forth—I can see why you would have been very appealing to Admiral Rickover.

Admiral Trost: Well, I can tell you Rickover stories that are—

Paul Stillwell: We'll get to him eventually. But I see the basis for that, even as you describe these school experiences. Anything else to say about your relationship with your parents or your sister?

Admiral Trost: Well, we had a very close relationship. You know, when I think back on it, my wife always says I am somewhat akin to my father. I never became quite as much of a buddy of my children as somebody who was always the father figure. He was that. He was also a very hard-working guy. He was a good teacher, a good person to watch and to emulate. Had a lot of patience—let me do things. If I messed up, he showed me what I'd done wrong. That was very, very useful. I think he probably had more patience than I had when my children were growing up. In large part, probably, I blame that on the demands of a naval officer who goes to sea part time and is home occasionally. But I'm probably a different personality, different person.

My parents were very, very solid citizens. They were very community minded, very good supporters of things that were going on. Taught you things like you don't litter, because it's wrong. Their rationale for things was usually, "It's not right," or "It is right." And you can accept that. And my parents were both very willing to help other people. I can recall my dad pitching in and helping people, farmers who'd been hurt—you know, going down and helping harvest their crop, or build something. He was always going off and helping somebody build a new shed or do something of this nature.

My mother just liked people as much as anybody I've ever known. And she loved children. She was always helping. She was one of the best women I knew, really, growing up. You feel that way because she's your mother, yes, but you feel that way because in retrospect you look back, and she was just a person who helped people and never expected anything in return—did it with her parents when they were growing older; did it with her sister when her sister needed something. In the years prior to about the '43-'44 time frame, when the so-called big levee was built along our side of the Mississippi River, the farms that my aunts and uncles lived on were generally flooded out just about every spring from the Mississippi. I can recall going down there, and I'd see my parents down there scrubbing walls, shoveling mud out, and helping people get their places back in order; or going down to help them move things to high ground before the water came up. They just sort of did this; it was just sort of family not a duty as much as an obligation that you willingly undertook. I was always impressed by that attitude, that willingness to help.

I can recall one summer, for example, on this threshing run that I was talking about earlier. I think there were about 12 farms in a given run of the thresher machine. Of course, they all moved from one to the other—they did them in sequence. That's where you got your labor; everybody got together. And one year there was a man who'd been pretty badly hurt in a farm accident. So the neighbors got together, and they cut his wheat, and they stacked the shocks, and they threshed his wheat. It was just the accepted thing to do.

Paul Stillwell: Sort of equivalent to insurance.

Admiral Trost: Yes, the insurance was people. It was not a no-risk society, as so many want to make ours today. I think no-risk societies are a hazard to people, very frankly, because they lose their sense of values and their sense of obligation to others; their sense of responsibility, even for themselves. I think what we are doing today is generating a very large number of people in our society who are basically not self-responsible. You know, "Somebody else is going to take care of me. If I screw this up, they'll take care of me." That's a terrible attitude.

Paul Stillwell: Anything specific to add about your sister?

Admiral Trost: No. We had a fairly close relationship growing up. We were two years apart in age; she was younger. Of course, she had her group of friends as she got older in school, as did I. So we weren't the tightest pair, I suspect. But we got along fairly well. The usual competition among kids—I want this, I want that; the big one picks on the little one; the little one blames the big one for what he did or what he might have done, just in case he had the opportunity. But a pretty good relationship.

Paul Stillwell: Did your parents have ambitions for you, or did they pretty well leave that up to you?

Admiral Trost: They pretty well left it up to me. One of the things that I told my dad one time was, "Tell me what to do." This was when I was getting ready for college.

He said, "I can't tell you what to do. I haven't been there." He felt very acutely, I think, especially in those years, the fact that he hadn't gone beyond the eighth grade because he had to work. On the other hand, if you looked at the handwriting or the letters of either my father or my mother, their penmanship was superb; their grammar was perfect. Their vocabulary was pretty good, and they were very smart people, in terms of what they did in life. My dad's family is the only family that had anybody go to high school. His youngest two brothers and the youngest sister went to high school, because they weren't needed on the farm; the others were working. Then the youngest sister went on to what was then a teachers' college and became a schoolteacher. But she was the only one of that group to go to college, and the three were the only ones who went to high school.

She later married. She married another schoolteacher, who died just within the last several years. And they went on. He was the superintendent of schools—first of all an elementary school principal, then a high school principal, then the superintendent of schools. Then finally I think he was the registrar at Illinois Normal University in Bloomington, Illinois. He was always the academic of the bunch. I used to recall listening to him and my dad and his brothers argue politics. He was a good debater and generally had a deeper background than they did, but they had a gut feeling of what was right and wrong. They used to get into some real wingding arguments on political matters.

Paul Stillwell: What was the perception of Roosevelt in your household?[*]

Admiral Trost: Not all that good. Not all that good, although he was sort of the father figure of the country. But not necessarily that good. My dad, and I think most of my relatives, were registered Republicans, and Roosevelt just—you know, those guys—the welfare thing was a bad thing. He did all sorts of things—welfare. What he did with the banks was pretty good. They didn't bother about that. They knew he was going to get us into war, long before he did. He liked the English too well. It was not generally a very, very strong pro feeling, other than the fact that he was sort of big father image up there, for the country.

Paul Stillwell: The Midwest was a very isolationist area in the prewar era.

Admiral Trost: Um-hmm, very conservative, very conservative and very isolationist.

Paul Stillwell: Even though he could not give you guidance on some of these things, I have a feeling that he was very supportive once you'd chosen.

Admiral Trost: Oh, he was, he was. And I must say, he made me think, more than I might otherwise have thought, about a lot of things. I'd do all my research, come back and talk to him, and he'd say, "Yes, that makes sense," or "That doesn't make sense." Or sometimes, "You decide what you want to do." He'd say, "I'm not going to tell you what to do." And there's nothing wrong with that.

Paul Stillwell: It sounds as if these ventures to Wentzville and the Lake of the Ozarks were very isolated, that the family did not have a lot of joint recreation.

---

[*] Franklin D. Roosevelt served as President of the United States from 4 March 1933 until his death on 12 April 1945.

Admiral Trost: Well, these were the family vacations. We went down to—I've forgotten the name of the lake—Lake Kentucky, I think it is, down in Kentucky, one summer. It might have been more than one summer. I enjoyed that. The family times together—you know, the recreational ones—were the weekends down on the farm, sometimes staying overnight, sometimes just going down for the day, sometimes going down Sunday and going down again Monday, because my grandparents' farm was just over 20 miles from where we were living—visiting relatives. They got together on holidays. We always played ball and that sort. So there were a lot of those kinds of things, with family and—you know, aunts and uncles and cousins getting together.

I have a batch of cousins, some of whom I don't know very well, because they were two who were older than me. One girl, who I think   she was in high school when I was, so I'd say she was probably about two years older; and her brother, her older brother, who was probably four years older. He served in the latter stages of World War II. He was probably four years older than I was. Then there are groups that are well—lots younger than me. Once I left to go to the Naval Academy, many of them I did not see with any frequency.

But even up until well after I was married, my dad and his surviving brothers and their families would get together every Fourth of July. We used to go out to Illinois, try to get out there for the Fourth of July, because one of the uncles owned a small farm, and we cleared one cow pasture of cows for the event, and that was the ball field. And they put up volleyball nets. So there was quite a bit of that kind of recreation. We'd go over to the—I'm trying to think of the name—is it the Meramec River, just south of St. Louis?

Paul Stillwell: Yes.

Admiral Trost: And the caves there—Onondaga Caverns was one, and I guess the Meramec Caverns are the other. We'd go over there for Sunday picnics and go to the caves. So there was really quite a bit of weekend, primarily recreation.

Paul Stillwell: I see.

Admiral Trost: But my dad was up and off to work bright and early every morning, and home 4:00-4:30 every day. And we always had a big garden. And he'd do the work around the house and take care of the garden. When I got older, that was my chore, to take care of the yard; and work on his car, that was required.

Paul Stillwell: How frequently did you go to the movies?

Admiral Trost: Not very frequently until high school years. There was a small movie theater in town. My recollection is that Saturday matinees, as we were growing up, we were permitted to go to. They were Tom Mix and Roy Rogers, the Lone Ranger, movies like that primarily. Except for one time when we were in high school, when they sponsored locally, for educational purposes, for all the teenagers, the horror movies about sexual diseases. And they segregated the audience so you weren't sitting there being embarrassed. These movies were supposed to keep you safe—teaching you all about what you shouldn't do, because, "Here's what you're going to look like if you do." But we couldn't go to the movies very often.

Paul Stillwell: How much did you take part in sports when you were coming up in school?

Paul Stillwell: Quite a bit. I played baseball and softball, primarily. I started playing basketball, but in high school I worked every afternoon, so I couldn't be a regular participant. I'm not sure I would have been good enough had I, but what I did during high school was played in a softball league, which practiced and played on weekends—there was time for that—about the only thing you could do part time. I did that the year I was in college, as well. But I was not an organized sports participant after elementary school. And that was not on the level of little league today, by any means; it was just plain intramural and casual, and not heavily organized.

Interestingly, even the little towns we lived in had numbers of baseball teams, mostly high school and adult players. Baseball was a big sport, and so was softball.

Paul Stillwell: Semi-pro?

Admiral Trost: They weren't semi-pro; they were town teams, but some of them went on and played semi-pro. Our towns, with fewer than 2,000 people, with a fairly good rural environment, fielded two adult baseball teams, and they played a regular series. We had a place called Meramec on the Illinois side, probably across from the Meramec River. Meramec was just a little settlement—a grain elevator along the railroad tracks and a store and a couple of houses. Meramec Tavern fielded the best baseball team in the county. They were all guys, farm boys, and some darn good baseball players. Basketball and baseball were the two big sports—baseball and softball. But basketball and baseball were the two big sports in the high school. They could not afford a football team till later on, just because of the equipment costs.

So the baseball/softball leagues were really big things. I can remember when we got lights on what was then the high school diamond. It was also the local ball field. And there was always the big controversy about using it for softball because you were going to mess it up for baseball. They'd simply relocate the mound and scrape it up, and put everything back to battery. But it worked well. There was a lot of activity, and it was the standard weekend activity.

Paul Stillwell: How much of a social life could you have with all the after-school work?

Admiral Trost: Well, enough, enough. During high school I was generally home by around 6:00-6:15 at night, and then did my homework. When I was working, I'd try to do my homework, if we had study periods, during the day at high school. I'd try to get my homework done before I went home, because I knew I was going to be working, so I didn't have too much to do in the evening. Although I did have things to do most evenings. We generally had homework assignments every day in most subjects. I usually did my math assignment at school, because that always went so quickly, and took the reading home.

I had enough. We probably didn't run around as much as teenagers would like to do today. Whether or not they actually do as much as they'd like, I don't know. But we really were discouraged from doing anything social during the week. The social life was normally Friday night, Saturday night, and maybe something on Sunday. That's usually whenever we did whatever dating we did.

My little town had a—it was a gymnasium, really. It was the Turner Organization, which is the German Turnverein, which is German background. In fact, it originated as a big, two-story hall with a full basement, which was the Turnverein's place where they did exercises. They had a gym instructor there for people of all ages. I participated in that when I was a kid. The hall also had a big floor, which was where basketball was played before the new high school was built after my time. It was also where dances were held. It's where stage productions were held. It had a U-shaped balcony that came around the upper level, where you could sit. And you could sit around the sides down below, during the dances. The lower level had a great big bar and tables and served sandwiches and beer and soft drinks. There was a dance there every weekend, sometimes twice on a weekend. It drew people from all over the county.

Paul Stillwell: Were there still a fair number of German-speaking people in the area?

Admiral Trost: Quite a few. As a matter of fact, my grandparents, parents, and other relatives spoke German at home into World War II. They really continued to speak it, but after about 1942 it was an unpopular thing to do openly, so people didn't speak it. But if we were at home—I learned to speak a German dialect, I think, probably before I spoke English. And it continued. Our church had, and still has, German services, or did last time I was out there. They continued their German-language worship services throughout the war. Most of the attendees were elderly folks, but they continued that. My parents' confirmation classes were in German. We still have some of the certificates of confirmation and their confirmation booklets up there. They're in German, the old German script, so it's very difficult to read.

Paul Stillwell: My parents came up in that background also, and yet they were completely loyal Americans.

Admiral Trost: Yes, so was everybody out there. It would be very annoying to them that people would criticize them for speaking German, when that was simply the language of their ancestry, not of their political belief. But it became very controversial during World War II.

Then there was a period of time a lot of German prisoners from World War II were brought over to the U.S. and used as foreign labor in a lot of areas. We had quite a few in our region. We have a couple places that were pretty large tomato-growing areas, and the POWs were used there to harvest tomatoes. They were used on other crops. A fairly good number of them came back after the war, to the U.S., after they were repatriated, and married people and settled down out there. As a matter of fact, the gent who was our family doctor from about the early '50s on—I'd say '54-'55 time frame on—had been a German Army doctor—a very young guy—during World War II. He came to this country in '48 and worked until he could get licensed as a doctor, and then proceeded to become a very wealthy man.

Paul Stillwell: It certainly beat getting shot at.

Admiral Trost: It really did. Well, the German POWs loved it, because they came into an area where people could talk to them and understand them. And they loved the cooking, which was predominantly German in flavor and in recipe. So they were very, very happy with all of it.

Paul Stillwell: How many blacks were there in the area?

Admiral Trost: Very few. In our town there was an ordinance that a black couldn't be in town after sunset or before sunrise. The only ones that we saw routinely were a black couple who worked for one of the farmers down on the river bottom. The guy actually ran that farm for the old gentleman who owned it, and he and his wife would come in— I'd see them in the store quite a bit, when I was working in the store, because they did all the grocery shopping and all the farm supply shopping. They were very well liked, very well respected. But even that guy couldn't be in town after dark, even though he was part of the community.

I had several blacks in the high school I attended in the next town, because there were a fair number of blacks living in the industrialized areas south of East St. Louis. Again, it was neither   it was they were black, and yes, they were discriminated against, without question. In the high school environment everybody got along very well. My dad worked with quite a few black men, many of whom I met on company picnics and all. I'd play ball. And they had a very, very good relationship. Yet they couldn't come into our town after dark, which was sort of an interesting commentary on society at that time. It was without question a discriminatory society.

Paul Stillwell: And both sides had no choice but to accept it.

Admiral Trost: Yeah, they simply didn't. And in the work environment and the school environment, we got along very well. That's not to say there wasn't any, but I don't remember racial tension in the region, nothing of the '60s nature, for example. It just simply wasn't there. But there was definitely a keep-them-in-their-place type of mentality. What their place was, nobody ever talked about.

Paul Stillwell: Well, and also in these work and school situations, you were dealing with individuals, rather than stereotypes.

Admiral Trost: Oh, yes, you knew people. They were names; they were faces you knew.

Paul Stillwell: What are your recollections of keeping track of the events during the war as it went along?

Admiral Trost: Well, I followed very closely. We got the *St. Louis Globe-Democrat* as our morning newspaper. As I mentioned earlier, I had maintained a scrapbook, and I did throughout the war. I kept up, I think, perhaps even more so than my parents did, with day-to-day events, because I was maintaining the scrapbook of things as they unfolded. I had a couple different books. I wish I had kept them, as a matter of fact. They're probably all pitched out. I was particularly interested in equipping airplanes. I built airplane models incessantly and built some ship models. Most of my ship models, though, were hand built. I'd carve boards and make them look like ships, and built battleships and things. So I followed it, from that standpoint, fairly closely.

Paul Stillwell: Did the Navy have any special appeal to you at that point?

Admiral Trost: Not particularly. I didn't really know much about it. As a matter of fact, my recollection of the Navy and its potential appeal was limited, because there were some people from our area who enlisted in the Navy. The great majority of them went in the Army when they were drafted. We had a couple of our young people in town—men I played softball with, as a matter of fact, and who played with my dad—who joined the Marine Corps. I played, as just a little kid, only when I had a mixed group. When they had the organized teams, they were of an age where they were old enough to have played on the team that my dad played on. I can recall one of those guys being killed in '42 on Guadalcanal, and that really brought the war home. He was one of the first from the town.

The Navy was lightly represented. I remember some of the people who joined the Navy, and they were some of the older people—older meaning probably mid- to late-20s at the time. They went off and enlisted in the Navy very early on, and served in the Navy. We had one guy, in '45—the one I went to the ball game with, Walt Giffhorn, who left high school with about a semester go to, but with most of his work completed, to join the Navy in about January or February of '45. I recall his coming home from boot camp. Of course, he was the local hero; he was now in the Navy and wearing that neat uniform. He lived just a block from us. I remember his comments when people said, "Well, why did you join the Navy?" Well, he was still 17, and he really wanted to get off and do things. And he said, besides that, he had seen that if you're a foot soldier you carry everything you eat and everything you're going to sleep with and everything else on your back. And he said, "In the Navy they use tablecloths and they have plates and things, and you don't have to carry it around." I've never forgotten that. But that in itself wasn't an incentive to join the Navy, to me; my Navy incentive was totally different.

Paul Stillwell: Scott Field was not too far from there, so there was some Army Air Forces representation.

Admiral Trost: There was that. Scott Field is 13 miles away. We became very, very aware of it, because this little town, as you noted, was in an isolationist environment by nature. I can recall Air Force people for the first time, about the time the war started: when obviously the President and Scott started building up, and the people who came there were branching out. Those who were married were looking for places to live, and some of these folks showed up in our hometown. They were not only strangers, they were foreigners as far as most people were concerned. The reception to anybody who wasn't part of the local community was not that good at first. They always had an attitude of, "You prove yourself, and then we'll decide whether or not we're going to like you."

Paul Stillwell: On the other hand, it was an economic boon to the area. So that was welcome.

Admiral Trost: Yes, and that's something that didn't show to me at the time. Although there was not a lot of available housing, because generally, when somebody got married, they moved into an area locally. Something their parents owned if they were lucky, or something they could get into. People would carve up houses into apartments to accommodate more couples. There was not a lot available. But we had people who moved in, couples who rented rooms, couples who rented apartments, whole houses. That was really the first involvement of somebody coming in.

Of course, if you read about the war, and listened to what was going on, you got a heavy involvement of all the services, although I thought that the Army moved everything. That's probably because, as a Boy Scout I felt more kinship with them than anything else. When I went to college, I was in Army ROTC in—to me—a very new and challenging environment called the coast artillery, which was already dead, but they just hadn't recognized it yet.

Paul Stillwell: [Laughter] Along with the cavalry.

Admiral Trost: Yes.

Paul Stillwell: You haven't talked about the Boy Scouts. Could you talk a little more about that, please?

Admiral Trost: Yeah, we had a longstanding Boy Scout troop in town, which was very active. When I was about ten and a half years old, they started a Cub Scout pack, so I became a Cub Scout. Those of us who were already ten and a half at that time—age 9 through 12 was considered Cub years, and you had to be 12 to be a Boy Scout. That's changed now. But I was a Cub and enjoyed that. I had a very fine den mother. Mrs. Schorb. Her son was my age group, and he was in the group with her. She made things very interesting. We built models and did lots of things; learned lots from the lady.

Then as soon as I was 12, I became a Boy Scout. I enjoyed that very, very much, because we had a couple of really fine scoutmasters during my time. We also had the advantage of being in an area where you could see and learn a lot. I still have some of my arrowhead collection, for example. I've got flint arrowheads that came from the hillside of my grandfather's farm, that I actually dug up or found. As he was plowing, I was walking along behind him as a little kid. The Kaskaskia Indians had roamed that area, so you could teach young kids a lot about the environment, but also how people abused the environment. And you could go off to places—Fort Kaskaskia being one—and a couple of state parks that were within reach for trips when you wanted to make a field trip.

But the biggest benefit we had, I think, was an old quarry that had been abandoned about 1929, by the company that still ran a stone quarry operation near town. The scoutmaster who was there during much of my scout time was a quarry employee, management type; he was also a great outdoorsman. The quarry company had given the scouts authority to use the old abandoned quarry, which was about a mile out of town, as a scout area. It was restricted to everybody else. This place—if you can envision driving in on a road—had a flat floor covered with old concrete foundations for stone-crushing equipment; trees growing up through what remained; very rugged; puddles of water; springs; and then getting up to the base of about a 100-foot cliff, which was about three sides of this quarry, where the rocks had been carved out of the side. This was our area, and it was a great place to play. It was a great place to learn.

We built pioneer bridges and did projects like that. We built our lean-tos. We had one place where we built a trail up one side of one cliff face. And there was a big flat area on top that was about 30 feet below the crest. We made that our campsite, cleaned it up, and leveled it out a little more. So we used to sleep there. We'd sleep on rocks, little rocks. Little rocks, like peas, can have a big impact after you rolled on them all night. But it was just a great area to learn things. We'd go out there. We'd do our own cooking. We'd camp out for the weekends and then go back. From the standpoint of learning handicrafts, it was really quite good.

We also had a Boy Scout camp, Camp Vandeventer, which was about 15 miles away, south of the neighboring town of Waterloo. It was, again, a very rugged area—this band between the Mississippi River bluffs and where the good farm country started again, which was just wild. It was just creeks running along, big trees, hills. It was an ideal place. Vandeventer had a swimming pool where Boy Scouts were taught to swim. You had to learn to swim.

The quarry company's current operation had its own pool, which was spring fed, and gravel sides and bottom. They simply built the gravel levees on three sides against the hillside and ran a pipe in from a spring that dumped right nearby. That was their recreation pool for the quarry employees. And that, too, was used by the Boy Scouts. It was like being part of the polar bear club. [Laughter] We did a lot of swimming there. That's where we had all our swimming tests during the year.

So it was good environment, again with some very dedicated people. Interestingly, the boys Scouts then, as I'm sure it is today—you know, "Don't tell me you really want to be a Boy Scout? Why do you want to do all that stuff? They tell you when to show up."

But it was interesting. Some of my classmates, who either didn't at all or didn't initially go in the scouts, would be obviously a little envious sometimes if you said, "Well, I've got to go."

They'd say, "Oh, you mean you can't stay and do this? Gee, what are you going to do?" When they found out what you did, they were always, I thought, a little envious of what we did. We thought we had a pretty good operation, had good community support. A lot of fun.

By contrast, I'm going to tell you about a guy back home. His first name was Bob, and I don't remember his last name, but he came from a family that was sort of dysfunctional. His dad didn't spend much time around the family, and this kid was always getting into trouble and always fighting. He was a much better fighter than I was, and I knew that. I wasn't much of a fighter. He jumped me one day as I was going from the Scout outing heading home. He jumped me about a block away on the corner, and beat me pretty thoroughly. I held my own to a degree, but not to a total degree, and finally forgot about it. I steered clear of him as much as I could and didn't get beat up anymore.

Years later, I encountered this guy again. In the meantime, he had served as an enlisted Marine and had retired as a Marine captain. He came to a yard sale that I had after my dad died. He was looking at a riding lawnmower that my father had bought from Bob. I didn't know that at the time.

He said, "Do you still have that lawnmower that your dad bought from me?"

I said, "I still have a lawnmower. I didn't know he bought it from you."

"Well, I was selling lawnmowers at the time, and I sold him that lawnmower, and I'd like to buy it from you." I figured he was going to low-ball me on it. But he said, "And I'll pay you what he paid me."

I said, "But when he bought it, he bought it new."

"Yeah, he did, and I'll pay you that."

I said, "Well, that doesn't seem fair." He bought it for what my dad had paid him. Very congenial, nice guy, and I thought he'd learned an awful lot in the Marine Corps. He became sort of a hell-raiser to a gentleman and turned out to be a nice guy.

Paul Stillwell: Then you said he apologized for what he'd done earlier.

Admiral Trost: He apologized for what kind of a person he was, which really threw me.

Paul Stillwell: You said also that you had a deterrent, that after he beat you that one time, you told him you would come armed the next time. [Laughter]

Admiral Trost: Yeah, I would. I'd fight any way I could, dirty or clean, but I was going to fight him. And we never had another fight.

Paul Stillwell: Well, you've got a funeral to go to. Maybe this is a logical breaking point. We can get into the Navy the next one.

Admiral Trost: Okay.

Paul Stillwell: Well, thank you very much for a good start.

Interview Number 2 with Admiral Carlisle A. H. Trost, U.S. Navy (Retired)

Place: Admiral Trost's home in Potomac, Maryland

Date: Thursday, 8 August 1991

Paul Stillwell: Well, Admiral, since we got together last, I wrote to you with some suggested topics just to fill in from the first interview, so I'd appreciate if you would start there please. We talked about, for one thing, your Boy Scout experience and whether you had made Eagle Scout.

Admiral Trost: I did make Eagle Scout. I became an Eagle Scout in 1947 and remained active in the scouting movement through the balance of my high school time, with some assistance provided when I was in my freshman year of college. I then was relatively inactive, although I did assist my boys later on when they were Cub Scouts and Boy Scouts, but mostly with the kinds of things that dads could do. My only major activity in the scouting movement, where I thought I made a significant contribution, was when my neighbor and I down in Norfolk served as the den masters or cub masters for a cub pack that had about more than 30 boys. It seemed the only two fathers we could get actively involved were the two of us who used to alternate taking over the job when neither one of us was deployed. We did that because both of our oldest sons at that time were Cub Scouts.

I have subsequently become re-engaged with the Boy Scout movement here in the area. Last October, the National Capital Region Council awarded to several people their Distinguished Eagle Award, which is a national Eagle Scout Award to scouts who served subsequently in various walks of life and had been successful in that endeavor. Bill Marriott and I were two.[*] I can't think of the third gentleman right offhand who received the award last fall. There were about 800 distinguished Eagles in the country. Some rather well-known names among them, including, as I recall, Gerald Ford, Ross Perot,

---

[*] John William "Bill" Marriott Jr. is executive chairman and chairman of the board of Marriott International hotel chain.

and quite a number of others.[*] I have since agreed to serve on the executive committee of the National Capital Region, which will entail some time on my part and some financial support for the scouting movement, which I have continued over the years.

Paul Stillwell: I seem to recall hearing that the Naval Academy considers that being an Eagle Scout is the most reliable predictor of success as a midshipman.

Admiral Trost: They really do, and they have an Eagle Scout chapter at the Naval Academy, which is in itself rather unusual. The National Eagle Scout Association had limited its chapter affiliation to chapters themselves, chapters sponsoring Eagle Scouts. There was a great interest in establishing an Eagle Scout chapter at the Naval Academy when Chuck Larson was the superintendent.[†] Chuck was able to persuade the national authorities to let him start a chapter at the Naval Academy, and it is a very active group. I spoke to them this past winter. They have, as I remember, 300 to 400 members. There were more than 200 at a banquet up in Memorial Hall the night I spoke. It's quite an impressive group. As a matter of fact, one of my themes was that having been successful as an Eagle Scout is a good predictor of somebody who has the gumption and the perseverance to stick to things and has the interest in meeting the challenges required of advancement in almost any field.

Paul Stillwell: Did you get to travel to jamborees or anything like that in Scouts?

Admiral Trost: Not very much. We did have activities in our vicinity. I mentioned earlier Camp Vandeventer, which was a place where we did have both the camping opportunity for a week, sometimes two weeks at a time, and opportunity to learn more skills. They did have some scouting jamborees, but I never went to one of the large ones. My boys

---

[*] Gerald R. Ford served as President of the United States from 9 August 1974 to 20 January 1977. Midshipman H. Ross Perot, USN, was president of the Naval Academy class of 1953. He resigned from the active Navy in 1957 and became a successful businessman. He founded Electronic Data Systems (EDS) in 1962. In 1992 he ran unsuccessfully for President.
[†] Rear Admiral Charles R. Larson, USN, served as superintendent of the Naval Academy from 31 August 1983 to 19 August 1986. As a retired four-star admiral he again served as superintendent, from 1984 to 1988, in the wake of a midshipman cheating scandal.

went down here to Goshen while we were living in this area.[*] They were active in the Scout movement. Goshen, of course, is quite a big operation and doing very well right now to my knowledge.

Paul Stillwell: Did your family, except for these trips to Missouri, get to travel much? Or were you pretty much confined to a two-state area?

Admiral Trost: We were pretty well confined to that area. The longest distance travelled, other than going over to the Ozarks for summer vacation, was up to portions of northern Illinois, as far north as Bloomington, to visit my aunt and uncle who were both educators. They moved around among various small towns in Illinois and then gradually larger towns as they became more senior in the school principal-school superintendent business. As a matter of fact, I had never been on a train. My first train ride was going to the Naval Academy. It was quite an experience.

Paul Stillwell: You really had your horizons expanded.

Admiral Trost: I really did. I rode, I think it was the Baltimore-Ohio from St. Louis Union Station to Baltimore and then got on that Toonerville Trolley, the Baltimore-Annapolis railway I think it was, which existed then and brought us down. I think it dumped us right in the vicinity of the governor's mansion, where some of the new state buildings are located now. I say new, new since I became a midshipman.

Paul Stillwell: Well, one other thing that we didn't talk about was the origin of your three first names.

Admiral Trost: Well, Carlisle, of course, is an English name, rather unusual in a German family, but it was a name that my mother liked because the minister of the little Evangelical and Reformed Church in Maeystown, Illinois, was named Carlisle C. B. King or C. D. King, I don't remember the spelling of his name exactly. She thought that was a pretty name, so she selected that as the first name. Albert was my dad's oldest

---

[*] Goshen Scout Reservation, Goshen, Virginia. Included in the complex is Camp Goshen, named for Major General George H. Olmsted, USA (Ret.), who had an impact on the career of Trost, who was an Olmsted scholar in the early 1960s.

brother, and Herman was my mother's oldest brother, so very logically they became my godparents and my two godfathers, and I was named after them. It has an advantage if you've got two middle initials; it's hard to get lost or to get mis-addressed mail.

Paul Stillwell: We were going to talk some more about your time at Washington University, where you got involved in the Army ROTC, which is interesting.[*]

Admiral Trost: Well, it was. When I originally had thought about going to the University of Illinois, I was interested in getting an ROTC scholarship if I couldn't get an academic scholarship, to help defray expenses. I have to put that in perspective too. I graduated from high school in 1948, and although we had to register for the draft when we reached age 18, there was no draft, so throughout that period and until after the start of the Korean War, there was no draft pressure on people in that portion of my generation. But when I made the decision to go to Washington University, the options were ROTC or physical education classes. Well, the physical education classes appealed to me, except that they were generally late in the afternoon, at which time I had to get myself downtown to catch a bus home, unless I wanted to wait until late at night to go home. So that reduced the options somewhat. The ROTC classes and drills were held during the academic day, as a matter of fact, usually around lunchtime.

So I joined the Army ROTC, which, unlike the Navy program, was not a scholarship program but was simply an affiliation. They did issue one uniform to each individual: one shirt, one blouse, one pair of trousers, one cap, and you brought your own shoes to the game. We had both the military drilling and lectures on the subject. It happened to be a coast artillery unit, which I guess at that time even the people in the coast artillery didn't realize how obsolescent they would become. Because I can recall studying about big guns that popped up over a parapet and fired, then dropped back down for reloading. It seemed relevant at the time, since I didn't know any better. But, it, of course, was already beyond its demise at that time. I'm not certain that the knowledge I gained was all that significant, but it was rather interesting. A good bunch of people to

[*] ROTC – reserve officers' training corps.

deal with.

Paul Stillwell: That would have been your first introduction to military-type discipline.

Admiral Trost: With the exception of the Boy Scouts. You know, the Boy Scouts actually taught people how to stand in line and dress right and form up properly and march, although it was somewhat looser discipline by far than that particular ROTC unit was. We were drilled there by a gnarly old sergeant under the eyes of a very watchful, very young, Army captain. I think he was very young, even though I was obviously considerably younger. But they were both World War II veterans.

Paul Stillwell: That combination almost sounds like a stereotype.

Admiral Trost: It does. It does. I think it is standard staffing.

Paul Stillwell: After we turned off the recorder last time, you provided an interesting vignette on the meals that were provided in the farm situations in connection with threshing and so forth. If you could put that on the tape, please.

Admiral Trost: Well, I don't recall whether we described what threshing runs were all about on the tape, but in the days before combines, wheat was cut by a machine called a binder-tractor—or horse drawn, in my early days—and actually cut and tied in bundles. They were then stacked in the fields to dry further. It was cut much earlier than it would be if you were combining. And, those bundles, after they dried, were threshed through a great big machine with a steam engine driving the thing with a big belt. In the particular threshing run that my grandparents were part of, there were, my reflection about either 10 or 12 families involved. One man owned the equipment, and so he got a certain cut of the grain from any particular run, and everybody else simply went together to provide labor.

They came either with their so-called bundle wagons, which hauled the bundles of things from the field, the bundles of wheat to the threshing machine and threw them in, or they provided a regular box-type wagon. Those were the people who bagged the grain as it came out in the sacks and hauled it off either to the farmers' storage or into the local granary next door to the railroad track. So it was usually a pretty manpower-intensive evolution. In my experience at that time, everything was drawn by horses or by teams of mules, and so we learned early on how to handle them. It was bread and butter to any young kid working on or around the farm. The highlight to me, though, was always the meals, because the ladies would also come together. The person at whose farm the work was being done was responsible for the food, and there was lots of it—all kinds—and these people worked hard and ate heartily. They always had their big meal in the middle of the day. Everything would stop, and the ladies would have everything all laid out with lots of fried chicken and beef and pork and all kinds of vegetables and mashed potatoes and gravy and lots of different pies, which was sort of the highlight of the whole thing. The other good thing was that if you were a little kid and you were out there working, you got to eat with the men, instead of waiting to eat with the ladies and that had the fringe benefits of as much pie as you wanted and also gave an opportunity to drink coffee. I drank coffee not because I liked it, but because it showed that I was one of the big guys, even when I was eight years old. So that was my introduction to coffee, as a matter of fact.

Paul Stillwell: Was homemade ice cream part of the menu?

Admiral Trost: Not usually. That was usually a Sunday afternoon treat that was relatively rare, because you had to get the ice to make that homemade ice cream. And the ice and rock salt were not that readily available, not that plentiful on the farms at that time. When we had ice, of course, it was a block that had been brought, usually packed in straw and burlap, from town out and very carefully preserved as long as possible in an old ice box, which was also relatively rare. The way of cooling things was normally to either put them in a cellar dug into the ground under the house, where things were kept at a reasonably cool temperature or, if you had butter and milk and things of that nature, we put them in little gallon tin buckets with handles and lowered them into the well. We let them sit there just above the cold water, and that's where they would be until you needed them.

Paul Stillwell: Did your home in town have a refrigerator?

Admiral Trost: No, I don't recall a refrigerator until maybe just about the start of the war, when my folks bought a used little refrigerator that was in our kitchen and ran occasionally. I think it was out of commission as much as it ran. Most of my early existence, my recollection was iceboxes, with the metal-lined boxes and the men who would come by and deliver ice.

Paul Stillwell: And the ice would gradually melt into the drip pan.

Admiral Trost: Oh, yeah. And we were disciplined early on not to open the icebox unless you really needed to, in order to make sure you didn't draw off all that cool air.

Paul Stillwell: What do you remember about the Sunday afternoon atmosphere for relaxation from the six days of labor?

Admiral Trost: Well, Sunday afternoons were always sort of the highlight. We always went to church, no matter where we were, even when we were off visiting somewhere. And we very frequently went down to visit with my grandparents while they were still alive. Sunday afternoons generally meant big meals, people sitting around under the shade trees swapping stories and experiences. And there were enough of the younger, more active people around, more active who hadn't worked so hard all week; there were usually volleyball games or softball games. We seemed to be able to improvise a softball diamond out of just about any kind of surface area and people didn't mind. Sometimes the bases, which were comprised of what we refer to as cow pies, weren't quite dry, so you would be awfully careful. You didn't slide into the bases too vigorously without regretting it.

Paul Stillwell: It was probably also a time just to sit around and talk.

Admiral Trost: It really was, it really was. One of the highlights when we were little kids was to be permitted to sit close enough to listen to what the men were talking about. It was usually talking about business. I recall in later years, after I became a naval officer, my wife and other wives saying, "All you guys ever do is sit around and talk shop." But that's all the farmers ever did. If you sit around with a couple of lawyers, all they do is talk shop, so it's a question of which shop you're interested in.

Paul Stillwell: I remember interviewing Chaplain Neil Stevenson, who grew up in New York City and then went out to a small college in Missouri.[*] It was almost like a foreign country to him, he said.

Admiral Trost: I can imagine; it's a totally different environment and totally different lifestyle.

Paul Stillwell: Well, anything else to include about that phase before you get to the Naval Academy?

Admiral Trost: No. I think that pretty well covers that time frame. Life in a small town at that time was rather interesting. One of the things I notice today, when people bemoan the lack of activity of young people who have television to occupy the time, we didn't have television to attract us. We talked earlier about listening to some of our favorite radio programs in the afternoon while we were sitting around, but we didn't do that much sitting around after school. I also noted that from the time I was seven years old, I had a bicycle. My sister had a bicycle. We rode bicycles everywhere. We rode bicycles extensively, and I don't see children doing much walking or biking these days. When they get a little older and decide they need exercise or something, they go out and learn all of these new habits that people used to have because of necessity.

There was never such a thing as saying, "Mom or dad, will you run me up to such-and-such?" If you wanted to get there, you biked or you walked. It was a pretty standard routine. But life in a small town was good. It was interesting and especially since we had a rather varied topography around us, we could go out. Both as Boy Scouts and individually, we could take a bicycle ride out seven or eight miles along country roads. And there was an area where there was a pretty good-size spring coming out of a hillside that we used to go to and have our lunch and climb around in the woods for a while and then ride back to town. That was a pretty good day for us.

We had an area right on the edge of town, but only about a quarter of a mile from where my parents lived, that there was a creek running along the base of a hill, and we

---

[*] See the Naval Institute oral history of Rear Admiral Neil M. Stevenson, CHC, USN (Ret.).

used to go down there. That's where I learned to swim. We had an area that we dammed up with rocks and any other kind of debris we could find and got the creek partially dammed up and created an area that was about six feet deep. There was an old tree that had fallen across that part of the area. That was the springboard, if you will, to jump in. The way to teach people to swim was to push them off the log into the water and let them splutter until they managed to keep themselves up as they were learning to swim. I can't call it real swimming. It was dog-paddle survival, but a good introduction to the water. And the scouts subsequently had some good swimming training programs.

Paul Stillwell: Of course, another difference that made walking more feasible was that things were a lot more compact.

Admiral Trost: Oh yeah, they were. Well, my town was over a mile long and about a half-mile wide, so that didn't go too far in any direction before you ran out of town.

Paul Stillwell: How did the Navy come into your life?

Admiral Trost: Well, very, very much by accident. I don't know if I had gone over this with you previously, but it was really an economic necessity. I had a one-year academic scholarship to Washington University, and that covered my tuition and my books, not in total as I recall. I think I had a certain something about $500.00 a semester in additional cost, plus my living expenses to take care of. In the spring of my freshman year I applied for a scholarship for the following three years with no assurance of getting it. About the same time the mayor of our hometown also had mentioned to my father that he had heard from our local congressman about competitive examinations for the service academies. I knew nothing about them, but it sounded like an opportunity, so I did take the competitive examination for the Naval Academy. Congressman Bishop of our district subsequently notified me that I was the only college student in the group that had also done well on the examinations, and I had one of his appointments.[*]

---

[*] Cecil W. Bishop, a Republican from Illinois, served in the House of Representatives from 3 January 1941 to 3 January 1955.

So, by pure chance, I went to the Naval Academy. I knew very little; I knew nothing about the Naval Academy, could find no books on the Naval Academy in either my old high school or my college libraries. There was one in the college library that was sort of a "Dick and Jane Go to School"-type of presentation that showed people in midshipman working uniform with a sailboat and very, very little concrete information about what to expect. So, really, my decision was made on the basis of the Naval Academy catalogue and the fact that if I wanted to stay in school I didn't think I was going to be able to stay where I was.

Paul Stillwell: Did your family have any political connections?

Admiral Trost: They had none. The mayor of the town worked in the same factory as my dad. It was a part-time job for him in that old town, although he had held it at that time for I think about 18 years. It was strictly his having gotten a notice in the mail and knowing that my parents couldn't afford to help me in school, and I was trying to get another scholarship, and so he mentioned it. No political connections. I couldn't have told you who the congressman from my district was until I wrote to him and asked to compete for his appointment.

Paul Stillwell: Did you do any specific cramming or preparation for the exam?

Admiral Trost: No, I didn't. I really had no idea what to expect of the exam. There was a standard examination, which was administered at that time in federal centers, and I believe it was for the military academies alone. And it was, as I recall, very much similar to what the SATs are today, just a very comprehensive series of exams on different topics.* I didn't cram because I didn't know what to work for. I don't recall at that time there being these books that people have now saying, "Do the following to prepare for your SATs," for example.

---

* At various times, the SAT, administered by the College Board, has been known as the Scholastic Aptitude Test and the Scholastic Assessment Test. Now known only as SAT, it is widely used in measuring the ability of high school students to do college work.

Paul Stillwell: Well, there was a specialized breed, usually academy graduates, who set up cram schools. They had the old exams, and they would teach specifically from those. But it sounds as if you had a good education at Dupo.

Admiral Trost: Well, I had a good education at Dupo. I think that's really what carried me through. It was a very solid education in math and sciences and fairly good in humanities area. So it did carry through. I was not aware of the thing that helped people at that time. I didn't know what a prep school was, so I struck out on my own.

Paul Stillwell: Please describe the process of arriving in Annapolis and getting started.

Admiral Trost: Well, I got on the train, as I noted, dressed in my only complete suit, non-sport coat and non-matching slacks, but this was my own suit. We were told whatever luggage we brought would be shipped home or would have to be shipped and whatever clothing we brought would be shipped home. So I arrived after an overnight trip on the train about 19 hours, as I recall, to get to Baltimore. I got to Baltimore mid-morning, got on the Toonerville Trolley and got to Annapolis. Walked through the area past Tecumseh Court there and into the court in front of Bancroft Hall and thought, "My gosh, what a big place this is, and do I really want to be here?"*

I went on up to the check-in desk. At that time, instead of bringing the entire class in at one time, as they do today, they staggered us. So I was actually one of the later arrivals. I came in just after the middle of July. I think the initial group that arrived was there before the first of July and was, of course, the people that came from the Naval Academy prep school, most all of whom had prior military service, not just ten months up there, but prior military service before they went in. They were there as sort of the cadre, if you will, to get the various boat crews organized, and we got in.

---

* Bancroft Hall is the large multi-wing dormitory that houses Naval Academy midshipmen. It also contains the offices of members of the executive department, including the commandant, executive officer, and battalion and company officers. Tecumseh is the nickname of an American Indian pictured in a prominent bust near the entrance to Bancroft Hall. It is a prominent Naval Academy landmark, often decorated in different colors to celebrate sporting events.

My recollection of the first couple of days is going through the check-in process, which included getting all our hair shorn. I never realized it could be that short. That's a good introduction to the quality of haircuts that were given throughout my time at the Naval Academy. Then going down for follow-on physical. We all had the preliminary screening physicals. I had a momentary setback when I went through the dental examination. I was told that my mouth was full of cavities, which surprised me since our family dentist had just finished certifying me the month previously. He himself had been a Navy dentist throughout World War II, and I still have some concerns about that. I'm not sure the integrity was quite what it should have been or who they were examining, because to my surprise, I and several other people were sent out to a dentist in town who seemed to be expecting us by name and who seemed to know exactly how much cash we had in our pocket. I think that's what determined the amount of work we got done. Fortunately, I didn't have too much money with me, so I didn't have too many teeth ground out. But we then went in the following morning and were certified as fixed, with no further examination on the basis of this doctor's certification.

Paul Stillwell: That does sound pretty shady.

Admiral Trost: Yeah, and that day I was sworn in as a midshipman up in Memorial Hall in civilian clothes with my fuzzy hair. Then we went through the business of being issued uniforms and clothing, and it was done very much in boot camp fashion: "What size are you? Here, catch it if you can and get it into your duffel bag before it hits the deck." The initial orientation, I think, was rather interesting. We were organized into boat crews. I'm not certain how that's done today, but they called us boat crews. There were 14 of us, which was the manning required for a pulling whaleboat, which was used both to get us accustomed to teamwork and help build us up physically, I was quite certain. But the people that were in that initial crew, a lot of them were long-time friends. Both of my Naval Academy roommates were in that initial crew with me, as was Freddie Franco, who became quite a good football player while at the Naval Academy.[*] He took the five-year course there and graduated with the class of '54.

_____

[*] Midshipman Frederick J. Franco, USN.

But I can recall a number of us getting together, getting accustomed to things going on. Bob Raffaele, who is a retired Navy captain and who's retired here in the Washington area, made a comment.[*] "My God," he said, "look at that guy Franco. The guys are out there drawing football uniforms, and look, he got a brand-new one instead of one of those scruffy old ones." That's when we realized that Freddie Franco was there as an already recognized, very capable football player, and Freddie had his new uniform on. I also noticed that when a few of us thought that maybe we would go out and get a little exercise and try out for the football team, we put on our old pads and uniforms and went out there. We got worked over by guys who really knew what they were doing. And guys like Freddie were off in their uniforms, didn't get quite as dirty as ours, because they were ahead of us and cared for pretty nicely.

Paul Stillwell: Who were those roommates that you've kept in touch with?

Admiral Trost: Bob Woods was one.[†] Bob was from Minnesota and Walt Lake, who was from New York, upper New York State and Brooklyn both.[‡] His stepfather was a realtor or banker who lived normally in an apartment in Brooklyn but who also had a place up near Pawling, New York.

Paul Stillwell: That was one real value of the Naval Academy at that time, probably more so than civilian schools, bringing in people from all over the country.

Admiral Trost: Oh, yeah. Well, it really was fascinating, because communications weren't as open, nor was knowledge about the other parts of the country what it is today. It really wasn't until World War II that people really started travelling and migrating and even considered moving to other areas or settling in other areas of the country. So the knowledge about the rest of the country was not that great. I can still recall, for example, as a midshipman step up a few years—going to New York City one time. It was not my first visit, but it was the first visit of one of my friends, a classmate who was from Nebraska. I remember our getting off the train in Penn Station and walking out into the

---

[*] Captain Robert J. Raffaele, USN (Ret.).
[†] Midshipman Robert C. Woods, USN.
[‡] Midshipman Walter W. Lake, USN.

open world after about a block underground, and suddenly he just stopped dead in his tracks and looked at all of these towering buildings. He had never seen anything like it. The biggest thing he'd seen I think was 12 stories in Washington, D.C., and that after he had become a midshipman, quite an astounding thing. I must admit, it was quite an impression on me when I came in on my first summer cruise in New York City. It was the first time I had ever been there, and it was fascinating.

Paul Stillwell: And black midshipmen were still an amazing rarity. I guess Larry Chambers out of '52 was there.[*]

Admiral Trost: Yeah, Larry was there. A fellow named Brown had been there.[†] Then we had, what the devil was his name—Taylor?[‡] I think there was perhaps one black in our class, and of course, then we had several Asian and South American midshipmen. Yeah, they were quite a rarity at the Naval Academy—very, very unusual.

Paul Stillwell: Do you remember how they were treated?

Admiral Trost: I don't really. It seemed to me that with the foreign students, at least those I became acquainted with, they got an awful lot of assistance. They spoke English, but the whole culture was different to them. You know, for all of us it was a considerable change. Of course, the Naval Academy plebe summer is intended to shell shock the individual into recognizing the difference and the uniqueness of his new environment and also trying to make sure that you are willing to tolerate the discipline and the challenges lying before you.[§] It was very difficult for a number of these young people.

I remember one young gentleman from Peru who had a considerable amount of education. He was about our age, but he had been educated in the Navy at the Peruvian

---

[*] Midshipman Lawrence C. Chambers, USN, graduated in the class of 1952 and later became a rear admiral. He was the first African American Naval Academy graduate to reach flag rank.
[†] Ensign Wesley A. Brown, USN, became the first black graduate of the Naval Academy in 1949, then entered the Civil Engineer Corps. He retired as a lieutenant commander in 1969. His oral history is in the Naval Institute collection.
[‡] Midshipman Reeves R. Taylor, USN, an African American, graduated in the class of 1953. He became a naval aviator and eventually retired as a captain in 1975.
[§] A midshipman in his or her first year is called a plebe; second year, youngster or third classman; third year, second classman; fourth year, first classman.

Naval Academy. And, as was the case with all of those people, especially selected to come to the U.S. Naval Academy, it was a different life. But for him it was simpler than for others, because even plebe year a limousine from the Peruvian embassy in Washington used to come over and pick him up, because the daughter of one of the senior Peruvian officials was apparently a girlfriend of time past. He lived a considerably better life than most of the rest of us did.

But the initial entry was sort of a good experience in building discipline and acceptance. But I have to admit that I did entertain thoughts of leaving after two weeks. Not because of the discipline, but because my father forwarded a letter from Washington University. It advised me that I had been awarded the scholarship for my final three years. I thought, "Why should I start over and face four years here when I can go back there and do what I was doing—and enjoying—three more years?"

I called my dad to tell him what was in the letter and told him I was coming home. He said, "You can't do that. You've taken somebody else's place. You made a decision; you've got to stick by it." Good advice, very sound advice.

Paul Stillwell: Did you feel any sense of culture shock that you were sort of overwhelmed by all of these things that were being thrown at you?

Admiral Trost: I really didn't. I took it pretty much in stride, I think, because my attitude was, "I'm not the first guy to come here. An awful lot of people have been here before me." I also had the advantage, throughout plebe year, of facing very little new academically, and so because academics came to me fairly easily to begin with and because I was essentially repeating the year, I could focus on the harassment, if you will, of plebes. And it was harassment. If they found that you could memorize things rapidly, you were just simply given more to memorize. If you did a good job in one area, the reward was to be given more to do. Whereas that was a burden on some people, because it interfered with their time for academics, it wasn't to me, because I didn't need the time for academics. So I didn't mind it as much. I have to admit that I would go out of my way on occasion to escape some of these first classmen who I thought were a bunch of witch hunters and really shit birds.

Paul Stillwell: What were some examples of things they would do?

Admiral Trost: Well, other than the mental harassment, it was the business that the uniform raises, for example. Calling you in after dinner, telling you to report in a certain uniform and then telling you, "Okay, you've got 30 seconds to come back in a different uniform." By the time you were finished, you'd essentially torn up everything you had, everything was scattered about in your room, and then they would come in and give you a room inspection and put you on report for having a sloppy room. The physical part of it included doing pushups. I did a lot of pushups, but they weren't that difficult at that time and a lot of things of that nature intended to get you charging up and down four flights of stairs as fast as you could go. The thing that I think was most trying was the business of sitting on the chair that wasn't there with your back against the wall. There is a point where your body simply collapses, and it's difficult to get out of there. That was harassment. Charging from the sixth wing to the first wing to deliver a message to somebody's buddy and getting back within a set period of time was a challenge, but that wasn't bad. So life was interesting.

Paul Stillwell: My observation is that people always remember these things from being on the receiving end, but never the delivery.

Admiral Trost: Well, I'd like to think that sometimes we were more humane in our delivery.

Paul Stillwell: Anything else about plebe summer? It's no bargain to do all that exercising in the Maryland heat.

Admiral Trost: No, it really wasn't. Yeah, I remember plebe summer well. I rather enjoyed the pulling whaleboat business, mostly because we had a well-coordinated crew as it turned out and we did very well on the races, which gave some spice to the summer. I can remember going out in my first sailing dingy and turning it over about ten feet from the pier and getting chewed out by the old chief who was watching and would immediately proceed to tell me all of the dumb things I had done. It being my first experience in a sailboat, I thought, "Well, I've got a lot to learn."

Fortunately, I could swim, and swimming was something that stood me a good stead. I felt sorry for the young people who came in who had never had any introduction to swimming, because for some of them it became quite difficult. They were on what we called sub squad for quite some time. I had very vivid recollections of the rifle range and the pistol ranges that were on Greenbury Point, over by where the radio towers are.* And at that time, of course, the old air facility there was still in operation, and they used second-class summer for flight introduction in N3Ns.† But I remember going over there in the big launches. Being introduced to the Marines, usually at the PFC and corporal level, considered plebes about the lowest level of humanity, which I think was the goal.‡

And introduced us to M1s and to the, what was the carbine? I don't remember the designation anymore—M2A1 and .45 caliber pistols. I had an introduction to all of them through the Army ROTC, so I was familiar with the weapon. I knew how to field strip. I knew how to clean, so that to me was fun, but it was hot over there. And I recall they would get you down in the prone position with the rifle, and to make sure that you understood that you were supposed to be as flat as possible so that the enemy wouldn't shoot your head off, the Marine normally put his big boot right in the middle of your shoulder blades and shoved you down at least once while you were busily sighting in. But it was fairly interesting. It was challenging also.

I can recall my one roommate, Bob Woods, who had been in the Minnesota National Guard for a year before he came to the Naval Academy and also was familiar with weapons and had as a kid also learned to shoot, standing there with the .45 pistol that was handed to him by the Marine. He very carefully sighted in, and when he pulled the trigger and shot, the slide went shooting back over his shoulder and landed at the feet of a couple of us who were watching. Well, there was a moral there, too, because what was missing—I don't know if you are familiar with .45s, but there is a little pin that goes through to secure the barrel and the slide so that neither one separates. In the field-

---

* Greenbury Point is on the opposite side of the Severn River from the Naval Academy itself.
† "Yellow Peril" was the nickname for the yellow-painted N3N trainer, a biplane equipped with a centerline pontoon. It was 26 feet long, had a wingspan of 34 feet, gross weight of 2,792 pounds, and a top speed of 126 miles per hour.
‡ PFC – private first class.

stripping process you take that out, and that's one of the final things to go into the weapon on reassembly. The instructor had intentionally removed it. The moral of the lesson was never accept a weapon that you haven't personally checked. They made quite a point of things like taking an M1 and sticking it barrel first into the dirt and then handing it back to you and saying, "Your weapon is dirty; clean it." Good training, I suppose.

Paul Stillwell: He could have been hurt, though.

Admiral Trost: Yeah, he could have been. He could have been. It was a very, very dangerous thing to do, because fortunately it went just right past his ear behind him.

Paul Stillwell: In general, do you think that was a useful type of process to find out who can hack it and who can't?

Admiral Trost: The plebe summer?

Paul Stillwell: The whole thing, yes.

Admiral Trost: I think we do a lot better today in the prescreening because of the indicators of success that are being used by the Naval Academy. I give Bob McNitt an awful lot of credit as dean of admissions for having inaugurated what I think was one of the best screening processes for any military academy, as a matter of fact, that matter perhaps for almost any major school in the country when you look at the results.[*] And Jack Renard has certainly carried that on very well.[†] The Naval Academy does an exceptional job of their preliminary screening and then, emphasizing earlier on, as one should do in plebe summer, that, "You're here. If this isn't for you, now is the time to get out of here before you waste a lot of our money and time and your own." I think it was done pretty well.

---

[*] Rear Admiral Robert W. McNitt, USN (Ret.), served from 1972 to 1985 in the civilian post of dean of admissions at the Naval Academy. His Naval Institute oral history discusses the admissions process in great detail.
[†] Captain John W. Renard, USN (Ret.).

I don't recall what our attrition rate was. Plebe summer it was several hundred. We came in, my recollection, was about 1,250, and we graduated 925, which was the second largest class that graduated at the time, not by today's standards.* And I think we probably lost about 150 or 200 right in plebe summer. That seemed to be the big attrition. There were a relatively small number of people who turned back. At that time you turned back one full academic year instead of just having to make up the courses in which you were unsuccessful, or you were kicked out if you didn't appear to have the motivation. I think the screening was probably pretty good, and I do think it's the right thing to do. I think the intensiveness of the disciplinary process is necessary to weed people out.

We do the same thing at the Naval Academy Prep School. I recall my son's reaction up there. He was there because he wanted to be, because he wanted to get into the Naval Academy, and we were in Japan at the time.† I remember hearing from him about three months after he had left, saying, "We were given five minutes' free time today and told to write a letter, and it will be short, because I've got several other things I better do." We got a letter from him, but he was heavily engaged, and when he came home at Christmas, I'd say he had matured markedly. I think he would agree today. We were a little bit surprised.

We saw this skinny kid who just had an appendectomy just before he left. I was very concerned about it, because when he got to Newport he was on a physically restricted list for a while. Of course, that didn't help him in the eyes of a lot of people, but he had the appendectomy on the Fourth of July and left for Newport. I think he had to be there mid-July or thereabouts, beginning of August I've forgotten which. But the physical conditioning—he was bigger, stronger, more mature in his every attitude and overlooking, and he had said subsequently it was just a very, very good process. They just get you right down and focus on what you are there for. Make you work hard, and it was good.

---

* The Naval Academy Alumni Register indicates that the class of 1953 comprised 925 graduates and 216 non-graduates.

† Midshipman Steven Glenn Trost, USN, born in 1962, graduated from the Naval Academy in 1985.

Paul Stillwell: Well, a lot of what you encountered was just Navy tradition too, such as the pulling whaleboats. This was the way you brought a man into the Navy.

Admiral Trost: That's right, that's right. Well, I think the intensity was absolutely necessary. Of course, the fear instilled by the pending return of the upper class was interesting, but wasn't anywhere nearly as bad as people led us to believe.

Paul Stillwell: That's a thing I remember from boot camp, is that sense of fear that the chief was trying to instill.

Admiral Trost: I heard incidentally an interesting comment yesterday from a civilian businessman, of German extraction, who has been a U.S. citizen since '72. He said, "I looked at that guy and I said to him, 'You look like one of those guys who only shines the front of his shoes.'" I thought, "Here is a man who never had any military background that I've heard that kind of term from chief petty officers inspecting their troops: "You look like a guy who only shines the front of your shoes." [Laughter]

Paul Stillwell: Well, how was it once the academics started for you?

Admiral Trost: Well, considerably better because you're in part of the routine now, and you're starting to encounter it. I cannot say in all honesty that I enjoyed plebe year. I didn't enjoy the harassment. You had the need to learn some things that were viable and others that were pure nonsense. Amazingly, some of the pure nonsense you were required to learn stuck with you longer than some of the factual information that came out. But academics, as I said, for me were relatively an easy thing. We looked forward to any holiday that gave us time off. We looked forward to a win over Army so we could get some time off. If we lost, of course, plebe year redoubled in its intensity as a result of the loss to Army that first year. Of course, the plebes did not date, except in the spring of plebe year when some of the academy presentations put on by the academy groups like the Masqueraders required that plebes buy tickets in order to provide necessary fiscal support. We were told we could date because then we had to buy two tickets.

I can recall looking forward to getting home for Christmas, because this was really my first extended period away from home, and that was quite a thrill going home.

We were riding trains that the Baltimore and Ohio Railroad kept in storage only for use when midshipmen had to ride them, either for the Army-Navy game or for trips out there. That meant the heat didn't work, the windows leaked, the coal engines—soot from those things came streaming in. I can recall going home, again an overnight trip with my big heavy midshipman overcoat on, wrapped up as snugly as I could possibly get. I had long johns on under my uniform trousers just to stay warm, because there was no heat in those darn things. It didn't seem to bother the train crew at all.

We were there. We were being given a good rate to ride home, and that time most of the midshipmen who were on leave traveled by train. So the train to St. Louis was quite full with people both going partway and those going all the way to St. Louis and then catching other things out from there. So quite a few cars, and we were forbidden from leaving our section of the train and going into the place where the real human beings were travelling. So that was a rather miserable trip, but I think ameliorated somewhat by the excitement of going home. And everybody's attention was focused on the new guy, and the girl I was dating liked uniforms.

Paul Stillwell: Well, that was a very prestigious thing, to get into the Naval Academy.

Admiral Trost: Yeah, it was. And, of course, your comment earlier about did you have any political connections is exactly what I heard all the time: "Well, gee, how did you do this because your folks don't have any money and your dad doesn't know anybody politically? How did you do that?" And it's a misperception. My in-laws had that feeling when Pauline first dated at the Naval Academy, "Well, those are all rich people over there, people from rich families." The perception was around even for the people who lived within striking distance of Annapolis.

Paul Stillwell: More on this ease of getting the academic material. You finished first in your class.

Admiral Trost: Yes.

Paul Stillwell: How does one go about that? Is it a matter of having a very good memory?

Admiral Trost: I don't know. I would be a smart aleck and say without even trying. I was able to retain things well. I guess I had good study habits. I could read and seemed to have an ability to look at things when I was reading a text and see what was important and what wasn't. And I had a good retention capability for figures, and I had and have a good mechanical mind, so I could figure out the kinds of things so that if somebody showed me an ordnance publication I could figure it out. I could read it and understand why it worked the way it did. That basically made life simple for me. I had a good capability in things like mechanical drawing and design drawing; that wasn't a problem. Math was absolutely no problem, so it just came fairly readily.

Paul Stillwell: A lot of it was native ability then.

Admiral Trost: I think native ability. I think I was blessed in that sense, and I found that I'd do my preparations for exams by just sort of scanning through my notes and making another set of notes on a pad. By the time I finished, I'd write quite half a dozen pages for a particular subject that was sort of my crib sheet, which I would then review one more time. Then they became very popular. I used to help some of my classmates who had more difficulty than I did with those things, and they liked to read my notes and get a little extra instruction from time to time.

Paul Stillwell: How are you at analytical type problems?

Admiral Trost: Good. Good. I think that's why I enjoyed math so much. I just enjoyed word problems, for example, figuring out how to set something up to solve it.

Paul Stillwell: You were really rare I think at finishing number one and getting four stars. Often I look at those number-one guys, and they retired as lieutenant commanders or something like that.

Admiral Trost: That was told to me by a number of people: "Well, you know, that's all very nice. You graduated number one, but I've never known anybody who graduated number one who was worth a damn." I've heard that lots of times. [Laughter]

Paul Stillwell: "Welcome to the Navy."

Admiral Trost: Yeah.

Paul Stillwell: What do you remember about the class routine itself? I've heard it was not very imaginative. It was pretty much a rote thing.

Admiral Trost: It was too much by rote, I think. Of course, the physical setup was that you marched to classes at that time because everybody was essentially on the same basic curriculum with some minor modifications. Because I'd had composition and rhetoric in college, I got a literature course plebe year, so that was one difference. I don't remember anything else that was really different. I think I noted earlier while at the Naval Academy the entirety of the math courses offered was less than I had had by the end of that first year of participation in college in that advanced course. The physics course was for me essentially a repeat, as was chemistry from what I had had previously.

There were times when one had the feeling, I think rightly so, that the instructor was just about one day's lesson ahead of you because if you got too much into detail or attempted to probe on a subject, he would say, "We'll cover that later." That meant usually he hadn't read the book that far yet. I really think the faculty caliber has improved markedly since we were there. I think the overall curriculum has without question. Today is a more challenging academic environment. The Naval Academy as an academic environment was less challenging by far than my freshman year in college, where I was privileged by having several courses where you proceeded at the pace that you could proceed at, and that made it rather interesting. The Naval Academy offered more potential, individual attention in some areas than did a college class.

If you went into a college chemistry course, for example, and sat in a lecture hall with 300 other people, there was not an opportunity to ask questions. There were never, never question periods. That was done in the lab sessions, taught usually by graduate assistants and there again, even the lab sessions there were 30 to 50 people and that's an awful lot. The labs I recall were two or three hours, twice a week, and that simply wasn't enough time to get into a lot of the things that you could pursue more deeply. The interest level in pursuing other than let's just get today's material out of the way at the Naval Academy varied markedly among instructors. I think I would have put as a group the greatest credence in long-term civilian faculty who were very dedicated bunch. This was especially true in the fields of math and English, history and government department.

Paul Stillwell: Slipstick Willie is a legend in that regard.[*]

Admiral Trost: Well, there were some fascinating people there. There were some naval officers who seemed to be serving there almost as a penance. There were others who were there because they wanted to be, and I would say there was that same variation on the part of many of the company officers, people in the executive department in general. I had three company officers during my four years there. The guy who stands out is Lando Zech, who was a standout who was there in the last year, year and a half of my time.[†] He made a point of being a leader. He made a point of getting to know the midshipmen in his company—he asked me about them—and providing guidance. Some of those guys were just sort of there. Some delighted in the cat-and-mouse aspects of being a company officer when they had the duty, and others were truly helpful to other people.

I can recall one guy; I do know his name, but I'll leave him unnamed. He was there as a Navy lieutenant, teaching navigation. He was a good nav instructor, because he was a good navigator; he knew his business. But he was at the Naval Academy because he had been divorced, and by being at the Naval Academy, I don't recall where officers stayed, but he apparently was able to get a place to stay that didn't cost him very much. This was a lifestyle that was affordable for him because he was paying some pretty heavy alimony. He was also a very bitter guy. You couldn't be a student of his without knowing all his personal problems. On the other hand, he brought occasional light moments to things. We had these navigation P-works, which were famous or infamous, but good, enjoyable, and they really tested your ability in both piloting and doing celestial navigation problems and finding out whether or not you understood what you were doing.

---

[*] "Slipstick Willie" was the nickname given Professor Earl W. Thomson because of his prowess with a slide rule. He taught at the Naval Academy from 1919 to 1959. For details see *Shipmate* magazine, published by the Naval Academy Alumni Association, June 1982, page 13.

[†] Lieutenant Lando W. Zech Jr., USN. As a vice admiral, Zech served as Chief of Naval Personnel from August 1980 to 28 September 1983.

I can recall one particularly famous statement that was attributable to him. We were in this particular exercise, and the exercise involved getting under way from a West Coast port, San Diego or Long Beach, and going out and, of course, you had to determine your fixes from the raw data presented to you, and you had to identify lights and other navigational aids. The intent was to navigate into Puget Sound and then down to the Naval Station Seattle and moor at the Navy pier there. I got into Puget Sound, so I was one of the luckier ones. My pencil ship was making it in the right direction. It was a very, very complex and comprehensive one, and a lot of people didn't finish at all because there was a lot to work out.

Paul Stillwell: It had both coastal and celestial, sounds like.

Admiral Trost: Yes, both coastal and celestial. So you had to navigate and you had to pilot both, and it included things like radar fixes. It included star sights, moon lines, sun lines, a bit of everything, and it was the final nav P-work. Well, one of the guys in my class, actually my company, ended up, he did the whole thing and he completed, but his final location was somewhere on the other side of Richmond, Washington, desert area, kind of high and dry. I can recall we got a critique a couple of days after this thing, and this guy had said, "You know, I did everything right. All of my procedures were right." He said to the lieutenant, "You know, in a lot of courses you get correct for data. If you work a problem out and use the right procedure, but you make a mathematical error and you get a CFD, and that's part credit."

I remember this lieutenant sitting there and just looking at him saying, "Son, ain't no CFD in the fleet. You ran your ship aground." That was a good lesson, good moral. But they varied. The intensity of people varied. I recall the electrical lab that we had that was, I guess, very good instruction even though it was probably obsolescent even at that time. But we did an awful lot of wiring up of different things, and they taught us how to wire up things to measure as well as wire up things to make motors run, do different things. It cost the Navy a few fine instruments from time to time when they were hooked up wrong and got burned up. But I can still recall the guy—again, in my battalion over there, and he was not unique in any sense—who was doing the hookup with these leads.

The leads were plugged in with big wooden handles on them, lead on the end of these copper cables going off rubber-coated copper cables and the power trenches were in the decks. You would plug in there, and you would energize your board after you had everything fixed up. He was getting ready to energize the board, having just gotten everything on his board hooked up and his partner said something to him and he, with a lead in each hand, turned like this and these things got close enough together to actually—we vaporized some copper and, of course, that blew the power for the whole lab. It tripped everything off the line. Fortunately he hadn't plugged in yet, so he didn't destroy his experiment, but it ended that day's teaching activity.

Paul Stillwell: What did it do to him? Was he injured?

Admiral Trost: He was not seriously injured. He had his blue service uniform on; that's when we wore the blues or the white works to class. We didn't have blue drill shirts for that purpose. We had them for other reasons, infantry drill, but he had a lot of copper plated out on him, but those things tripped pretty fast, so all that was left—he had blackened wooden handles in his hands. He had some minor burns, and the copper inserts which were about what I recall that long were totally gone.

Paul Stillwell: About two inches?

Admiral Trost: Yeah, they were about two inches. They were vaporized. But it's a vivid demonstration of what electricity can do.

Paul Stillwell: Do you recall any specific examples of Lieutenant Zech's leadership?

Admiral Trost: Well, I can give you examples of his counseling. Nobody got into trouble without sitting down with him and talking about it. They automatically got in there. He gave people the impression of, "I'm on your side, and I support you, but, by God, you've got to do things right." He and his wife made quite a point of getting to know people. For example, Jo Zech's brownies were famous in my company, because they would invite the people over   I don't think more than six or eight of us at a time. They had one of those Perry Circle sets of quarters, which weren't all that large, those apartments, and they had several daughters at that time. We would be invited over on Sunday afternoon, and Jo Zech would serve brownies and hot chocolate, I think, and we would sit and talk.

As a midshipman, it was sort of rare to be able to sit down with an officer with a grade of lieutenant. They were rather God-like in our eyes and have him actually talk to you and display an interest. He was very much there. He was always the common-sense guy. When he inspected his company, it wasn't, "There is a nit there that I'm going to take care of." Or no little small stuff. It was, "You can do a lot better with your shoes, or the next time you wear that uniform to an inspection, make sure you get it pressed first." It was always logic. It was maturity, I think, that came across more than anything else. I don't recall if I mentioned to you or not, I attribute his influence as the major factor in six out of the 39 first classmen who graduated in my company going to Submarine School the following year. No question in my mind that he influenced us. He himself was always sort of picture perfect in his uniform and set one heck of a good example.

Most of the people who were on duty over there were pretty good, but there were others. There was a man known as "The Hat." He was known as "The Hat," because he wore a hat that was several sizes too large for him and he would pull it down in the back so that his head actually came out of it in sort of a point at the top, and his ears were folded down a little bit by the thing. It was ludicrous. He was a lieutenant commander, and his pride in uniform was not that great and, as a matter of fact, he was not that great as a company officer. He happened to be my company officer. He was less an object of admiration then an object of ridicule, because the guy just didn't seem to care. I don't know if that was a fair appraisal of him or not, but there were some marked distinctions in some people there

Paul Stillwell: Another future Chief of Naval Personnel who was there then was David Bagley.[*] Did you encounter him at all?

---

[*] Vice Admiral David H. Bagley, USN, served as Chief of Naval Personnel from 1 February 1972 to 10 April 1975.

Admiral Trost: Sure did, sure did. He was a company officer. That's where I first got to meet him. I've seen him but once since he's retired, but I used to know him quite well and worked for him when he was the Chief of Naval Personnel.

Paul Stillwell: Any memories of him from the Naval Academy?

Admiral Trost: Yeah. Always, you know, a guy who really enjoyed the hunt and was sort of feared by the midshipmen, because he was going to get you if you did something wrong. But, on the other hand, always an immaculate and rather impressive person.

Paul Stillwell: Do you remember any examples of these "cat-and-mouse" games you mentioned?

Admiral Trost: I remember two or three Marines and several Navy people who liked to stand behind the bush with the messenger and then watch a group of people in ranks coming who were unaware of the duty officer's presence and chitchatting as they are not supposed to, but as one logically might do walking back to class, marching back from class. Suddenly a messenger would come flashing at you and get that man's name. This was a big game we used to enjoy watching it. It was a "cat-and-mouse" game. Who could spot the duty officer before he spotted you doing something wrong. I can recall a dispute between another Navy lieutenant and Lando Zech on some subject, and this other lieutenant coming over and visiting our company area on the basis of every time he had duty, and just putting all sorts of people on report.

That ended when Lando had a personal talk with the guy and said. "Knock it off." I can recall one guy, in first class year when I was the brigade sub commander in the middle set, and the brigade commander's room had safes for locking mostly ordnance pubs we had at that time. Bill Leftwich, who was the brigade commander, and I agreed that I would be the custodian of the safe.* I'd be the guy responsible for the safe, and my name was on it. We just moved in. We went down to get the safe combination from the admin office, and they didn't have it. I've forgotten who the brigade sub commander was preceding me. Anyway, they didn't have the combination, so we went to ask him. While I

---

* Midshipman William G. Leftwich, USN.

was trying to get the combination from that guy, another company officer inspected the room in which the brigade commander and brigade sub commander lived together. He put me on report for an open safe. Of course, it was locked open; I remember that one. That was also one where Lando Zech got rather annoyed because this guy refused to back off. I had an opportunity to reclama. I forget how we did that now, but you have an opportunity to submit a statement, and I did that and this guy backed off and I said, "Okay." I left it at that. And word got back to Lando somehow, and after a little while I was called in again by this guy. He said, "I hope you've learned your lesson. I have pulled the form 2." So, anyway, there was some—

Paul Stillwell: Pettiness?

Admiral Trost: Pettiness, yeah, little stuff.

Paul Stillwell: Well, the unfortunate part of a thing like that is you get a squabble between two officers, but it is the midshipmen who are the pawns and the victims.

Admiral Trost: Yeah, the midshipmen get it. Once when I was the brigade commander, I got put on report for a burned towel. Jimmy Mahony was my sub commander, and one morning I don't even remember which one of us, but one of us got up before reveille and before the other one and draped a towel over a light fixture.* It used to be some little ceramic globe over a bulb over the medicine cabinet, and many times I would drape a towel over it, just to keep from waking the other guy up with the light. I think I'm the guy who did it, as a matter of fact, and scorched the towel and folded the towel back up. It was hanging neatly and the scorched thing was hidden. One of the company officers came in on his duty day to inspect our room and pulled the towel off and saw the burn spot and put me on report for a burned towel. I thought, "What the hell difference does that make? It's my towel. I'm the guy who is going to have to replace that sucker." And, of course, it was obviously my towel because it had my name on it. But I thought that was little pettiness sometimes in that business too, as if they were coming in just to— brigade commanders didn't have much free time. You know, if you kept up with the

_____

* Midshipman Wilbur James Mahony, USN.

academics and all of the other stuff you were busy well past the normal waking hours. It always annoyed me to see us be the focus. We had a pretty squared-away room to start with.

Paul Stillwell: Well, a guy, if he's determined to find something can, and it sounds like Zech had a good sense of proportion on things.

Admiral Trost: He really was very commonsense in his approach. When the company was involved in any kind of competition, he was always out there. He was there either cheering you on if you needed that or giving comments. We went over to the ordnance and gunnery competition. The company competition used to include gunnery problems back in the days when we learned how to use the—what were they? The Mark 1A computers that were used for the 5-inch gun control on most ships at that time and one had a problem. It had the sort of platform that was called a puff board. It had terrain, and it had coordinates and you had to determine the fire control settings. You had to go through the routine of designating that target and getting that information into the ship's fire-control system. The navigation party had to maneuver the ship, so you got precise nav input, and the fire control party had to get everything set up. Then you fired, because when you fired, the analog computer that was in this thing would drive under the table a little cart, and it would position to where the following shot was going to come, based on what you put in. It made a little puff of smoke up through the board, which was porous, and you could see where your shells would have landed. But we occasionally wiped out a few front-line troops from the firing on friendly forces. It taught a good lesson, however, and he would come over for things like that. They were important—we'd really compete. I think we had about three teams per company that had to participate in this thing and give an average score. He was always there with his moral support. He was always out when we had some company athletic competition, and he was visible—always visible.

Paul Stillwell: I never heard of that training device. That sounds neat.

Admiral Trost: Oh, it was fascinating. I'm sure it doesn't exist anymore, because it is so totally obsolescent, but it was fun. On this one time—actually the team I was a member of we were going through, and we had everything set up and also got graded on time, and we had done it in record time. We were really proud of ourselves, and the first command may have been fire for effect; I think it was. We got three puffs of smoke, all of them behind friendly lines. What have we done? We quickly went through everything: "Nav team checked all your stuff, and target guys checked all of their stuff and fire control guys checked all this stuff. We went through everything, and we said, "We've got it right." Did it again, same result. Time ran out, and we couldn't find the problem. Well, the problem was one guy who was responsible for the target elevation being cranked into the computer. The knob turned clockwise to increase elevation, counter-clockwise to decrease. He had cranked in the wrong direction the right number of turns and put in a negative elevation corresponding to the height of the target, which means your fire's gone off a little short. We never found it. It was pointed out to us by the fire controlman who was the supervisor.

Paul Stillwell: He did it both times wrong?

Admiral Trost: He did it both times wrong, yeah. Set it up, just cranked the wrong direction. It was just a pure error, and he was so hyped up, everybody was.

Paul Stillwell: You came into the Naval Academy as a bunch of individuals. How did the teamwork and camaraderie develop?

Admiral Trost: Well, I think it started out plebe year by surviving a common experience and thereafter, by the fact that you marched together. You went to class together. You really got to know best the people in your battalion, your company obviously, but in the battalion because the class groups were made up of people within the companies of a battalion. So I think it's the sharing of common experiences in a common environment. You get to know each other both professionally and socially. You see people performing in class. You see people doing their things in the military training aspect. You see who responds, who seems to accept challenge, and who just works to get by. There are those who become very successful, but all they've done is gotten by. They've done the minimum necessary to do whatever it takes to stay around. On the other hand, you've got people who come out as the anchorman.[*] Our anchorman was Frankie Scolpino, a very much-admired classmate who entered the Naval Academy with the class ahead of us, and his five-year course ended with our graduation.[†] Of course, the anchorman, then and I believe still, gets money from his classmates, so Frankie collected his money and somebody said to him, "Gosh it must feel terrible to be the anchorman in the class."

He said, "I'm senior to the number-one guy in the next class." Which I thought that was a good attitude. Frank was an example of one of those guys who worked very, very hard to get through and was a very successful naval officer. Retired captain, never lost his sense of humor.

Paul Stillwell: I've heard some guys say with tongue in cheek that it's more difficult to finish at the anchor then at the top, because you had to calculate to a hair's breadth so you don't flunk out.

Admiral Trost: Very small margin of error will have you flunk out. Well, at that point, you're not going to turn back the next class in all likelihood. You are probably just not going to get commissioned.

Paul Stillwell: I've heard Admiral Hill, one of the superintendents while you were there, described as a very enthusiastic gentleman.[‡] What are your memories of him?

Admiral Trost: Very enthusiastic. He would come over—my greatest recollection—first of all, he was very much the venerable father figure as the superintendent, because he was much older than today's breed, I don't know. He was gray-haired. He had been an experienced flag officer in World War II. He was there as a vice admiral. His focus seemed to be less on the day-to-day administration, but I say that, knowing that it may be that that was simply something outside of our scope, the day-to-day administration at the academy. Our contact with him was predominantly either seeing him as the

---

[*] "Anchorman" is the slang term for a midshipman who finishes at the bottom of his class at the Naval Academy.
[†] Midshipman Frank J. Scolpino Jr, USN.
[‡] Vice Admiral Harry W. Hill, USN, was superintendent of the Naval Academy from April 1950 to August 1952.

representative figure off in the distance there at a functions, or most often, he was the head cheerleader over in Dahlgren Hall for football rallies.

I still remember Tom Bakke out of '52 was the captain of the football team, I think, as a second classman.* Tom was a standout individual, but we used to mimic Admiral Hill, who would get up there and stand up on the railing—the way Dahlgren was configured at that time, the railing went along the lounge area that is on the landward end now.† It was not that large a deck. It was much smaller deck, and he got up there on the railing and would be looking over at all the mids down below at that time still surrounded by all of the M1s in the rifle racks on the wall. And, he would say, "We are going to play So-and-so this weekend." He put his arm around Tom Bakke in his letter sweater and said, "Tom Bakke and I are going to be out there leading this thing." He was the self-ordained head cheerleader. He got really enthusiastic and really trying to get everybody all fired up.

Paul Stillwell: Well, that kind of enthusiasm is contagious.

Admiral Trost: Yeah. But he was really an interesting guy.

Paul Stillwell: Were there any receptions or anything at the superintendent's quarters so that the midshipmen got to get to know him better?

Admiral Trost: Well, there were receptions for the first class. They were predominantly those at the end of the graduation, the supe had a reception then. When Admiral Joy, who succeeded Admiral Hill, was the superintendent, I was invited one time to a reception at the supe's quarters, but it was as the brigade commander, and that was prior to graduation week.‡ There were receptions over there, to take our families into the garden. I was invited a number of times to the commandant's quarters when Charlie Buchanan was the

---

* Midshipman Thomas N. Bakke, USN.
† Dahlgren Hall is a former armory that has been converted for use as an ice rink and snack bar. For many years it was the site of Naval Academy graduation ceremonies.
‡ Vice Admiral C. Turner Joy, USN, was superintendent of the Naval Academy from August 1952 to August 1954.

commandant.[*] That was once or twice as a first classman with groups of first classman coming in. Once he had the brigade officers in, and on other occasions I was there because I knew Mary Gale, his daughter, quite well. So I got to the house over there.

Paul Stillwell: Any recollections of Buchanan as an individual?

Admiral Trost: Yes, quite a few. He and Captain Pirie were the two commandants during my time.[†] I liked Admiral Buchanan very much. I thought he was a very straightforward guy, moderate, straight-shooter type of individual, the kind who was much feared by the mids, because if you got called in to see the commandant, it was usually trouble. Except I got called in once, that was by Buchanan, telling me that I was going to be the next brigade commander. It was rather pleasant. I walked in; I didn't know what the devil he wanted me for, although I had a fair amount of contact with him as the brigade sub commander, but we dealt mostly with the assistant commandant on most of the matters having to do with the administration of the brigade. But Buchannan was very pleasant. I remember in those days I would always think these guys looked so relaxed just sitting back there, and they are real big shots. They seemed very much at ease. That always impressed me. I found out later on that to be comfortable within one's environment isn't all that difficult.

Paul Stillwell: Well, Pirie, I got the impression, was a more volatile-type individual.

Admiral Trost: He really was and much-feared reputation as a man with a—"volatile" is a good term, man with a temper. On the other hand, very highly respected. When he detached, my class bought him flag officer shoulder boards. He had been selected for flag rank, and it was a mark of respect. It was a spontaneous thing. People said, "Let's do something for this guy." It was a very small thing, shoulder boards, which I think was a meaningful gesture. It would have been to me. And they were presented by the class president, Ross Perot. Pirie had the reputation for being tough; he was volatile, often impatient, and yet respected as a very professional guy.

---

[*] Captain/Rear Admiral Charles A. Buchanan, USN, served from 1952 to 1954 as the Naval Academy's commandant of midshipmen.
[†] Captain Robert B. Pirie, USN, served from 1949 to 1952 as the commandant of midshipmen.

Paul Stillwell: Joy on the other hand, I gather, was a very dignified, diplomatic gentleman.

Admiral Trost: Very dignified, very diplomatic and a man in poor health when he came there. He'd been our senior U.N. negotiator, in Korea, and I'm told it had broken his health.[*] He came to the Naval Academy for recuperation, I think. A fine gentleman, very dignified, very impressive, interesting to listen to.

Paul Stillwell: In what ways?

Admiral Trost: He would relate experiences from his U.N. days when he was in armistice negotiations. He seemed to have this tremendous grasp of politico-military, which to most of us at that time was still a field we were learning something about, but certainly didn't have this kind of broad grasp. Then again, it was the kind of thing that impresses you when you yourself are not very knowledgeable. You look back on it later on and say, "Well, gee, sure, he should have known that because of his position," but I didn't know that at the time. I would say that was a problem with any senior military officer who didn't have a grasp of politico-military matters at this point, but I didn't know that as a midshipman.

Paul Stillwell: He did not live all that much longer.

Admiral Trost: No, he did not.[†] He did not. His son was class of '47, C. Turner Joy Jr. He stayed pretty active after he left the Navy, Navy league functions and alumni matters.

Paul Stillwell: Another submariner.

Admiral Trost: Is he?

Paul Stillwell: I talked to an officer who was in the USS *Macon*, I guess about '49, and he said they had a skipper named Olin Scoggins, who recruited virtually every JO in that

---

[*] Vice Admiral C. Turner Joy, USN, served as Commander U.S. Naval Forces Far East from 27 August 1949 to 4 June 1952. In 1951-52 he was also senior U.N. delegate in the Korean War truce talks. He covered that experience in his memoir *How Communists Negotiate* (New York, Macmillan, 1955).
[†] Admiral Joy died 6 June 1956.

ship for submarine duty.*

Admiral Trost: There were a few like that.

Paul Stillwell: You mentioned being called in and told you would be the brigade commander. What was that selection based on?

Admiral Trost: Well, I guess it was to be based on the aptitude marks, which I had at the time. I think it was a combination of aptitude, academics, leadership performance, involvement in brigade and class matters. I think in part I had the advantage of having been the brigade sub commander. We had three sets of stripers; I don't know if it is two or three now. I was the mid-term brigade sub commander. I had been the vice president of the class for the period from my youngster year onward. And I was I guess pretty well known and involved in things that were happening within the brigade. I was one of the class officers, along with Ross Perot and Bill Lawrence, who spearheaded the formation of the honor concept his first-class year when he was brigade commander.† I know it was based on the recommendations of company and battalion officers, but I don't really know what the total process entailed.

Paul Stillwell: Well, the selection as class vice president had preceded that. Was that by your peers?

Admiral Trost: That was. The way you became vice president was to get the second most votes in the run for president.

Paul Stillwell: Was that something that you actively campaigned for?

Admiral Trost: Yeah, I did. I did not the first time. I did subsequently. As a matter of fact, in the final effort I tried to beat out Ross Perot, but I didn't succeed.

Paul Stillwell: What motivated you to seek that office?

---

* Captain Olin Scoggins, USN, commanded the heavy cruiser *Macon* (CA-132) from May 1948 to May 1949. The recollection of his recruiting for submarine service was in the Naval Institute oral history of Vice Admiral Thomas R. Weschler, USN (Ret.).

† The Naval Academy honor concept was devised in the early 1950s. For details see the Naval Institute oral history of Vice Admiral William P. Lawrence, USN (Ret.), who was president of the class of 1951.

Admiral Trost: That's a hard one to say. I don't know. I just thought there was a role for leadership, and I must say that first-class year, when I subsequently had the opportunity to serve both as a five-striper and six-striper, I felt I had more of the leadership role and responsibility by far than I would have had I been the class president.[*] But it was really an interest in, I guess, trying to influence things and get involved in the direction we were headed.

Paul Stillwell: Well, please describe those responsibilities as brigade commander.

Admiral Trost: Well, they were perhaps almost not, certainly not unique, but different, our first-class year, in part because of the reaction of the academy administration to some of the antics of the class of '52 at the tail end of their time at the Naval Academy. If I need to put those in perspective. I can. I don't know if you are familiar them, but the class of '52 was threatened   I'm sure it was Turner Joy who made the comment. There was question on the eve of '52's graduation as to whether or not the superintendent would let them be commissioned. That was based on the fact that there were a lot of good-natured high jinks during the week preceding graduation. But at the color parade, the class of '52, the stripers, not all, but most, when they unsheathed their swords for pass in review, they were painted red, as if they were bloody. The majority of the class stepped out of their shoes when they stepped off from their parade positions to start passing in review, so what remained was a lot of shoes. That was what gave birth to the statement that is on one of the scoreboards in the stadium at the Naval Academy—on the scoreboard presented by the class of '52 it says, "Hard shoes to fill." That's the basis for that.

The last people—squad leaders, usually—at the tail end of each company had lanterns hanging from their bayonets as they passed in review. From a military perspective, it was a little bit of a debacle. They had a big kick out of doing it, and they carried a reputation with them into the fleet for many years afterwards. People I can recall made an appeal and would say, "Oh, are you that class that left your shoes on the parade field?"

---

[*] The midshipman in the top leadership position within the brigade was designated as the six-striper, indicated by the narrow stripes he wore around each sleeve of his uniform blouse. The brigade sub-commander had five stripes.

I said, "No, no, no, we're not that class." But the reaction to that was that our class leadership was told by the commandant and by the superintendent, "You run the brigade, by God, or I will take it away from you." So we faced quite a challenge. We went out of our way to make sure that we did everything in a professional military way and motivated the entire class to do it. And, as always in every group, there were those who like to go out and cut up, and we simply motivated them not to.

Paul Stillwell: What techniques did you use for that?

Admiral Trost: Threats, cajoling. When I was brigade commander, at one point, the commandant, Captain Buchanan, told me, "If you don't like what they are doing, come back and see me, and I'll take away a weekend. That will get everybody's attention." And it would have, but I didn't feel that was the way to do it. I spent a lot of time trying to motivate people to do well. And we had a good class for that. We had a class that seemed to be well geared to doing things the right way and had pride in themselves, and I think that helped. I don't know that '52 didn't, but our class came in with about 75% of the class having at least one year of college. We had some people who had a full college term. We had two ensigns who gave up their commissions to join our class. A guy named Jim Webster, who was a surface officer.* I think Jimmy, who was from the Eastern Shore, came from a destroyer out off of China to enter the Naval Academy as a plebe. There had been an ensign in one of the short programs at the latter stages of the war, a guy named Tom Schaaf, who was a qualified designated naval aviator.† I guess he came in through the aviation OCS program.

Paul Stillwell: Surprising they were still young enough to get in.

Admiral Trost: Well, they were young enough, and at the time we went in the age requirement was either 23 or 23½ maximum by July of the year of entry. And so we had people graduate who were 27 years old. The average age was considerably higher than anything near what it is now. I don't remember exactly what it was anymore, but I had turned 23 at graduation, and I was by no means part of the older bunch. We had an awful

---

* Midshipman James M. Webster, USN.
† Midshipman Thomas W. Schaaf, USN.

lot of people who had more than a year of college and a considerable number who had had two or three years of active enlisted service before they came. So it was an interesting group.

Paul Stillwell: Well, all of that would be a help to you as brigade commander, because you had a pretty mature group.

Admiral Trost: Yeah, you had a mature group and, as graduation approached, Jimmy Mahony as my sub commander and the other brigade leaders, the battalion commanders and regimental commanders, spent an awful lot of time one on one and sitting with small groups and talking about what we were going to do and came out very nicely—to all of our great satisfactions, as a matter of fact.

Paul Stillwell: Well, it's a tradition among midshipman, though, of trying to beat the system or pull their imaginative pranks. You didn't want to stifle that completely.

Admiral Trost: No, you didn't. On the other hand, there was a time and a place for things of that nature. The time wasn't when you had the whole world looking at you out there, and when your reputation as you went off to the fleet depended on your performance. So we were fortunate. We had a good week. The general military administration of the brigade, the administration of the honor concept was left to the midshipman leadership.

Paul Stillwell: Please describe that.

Admiral Trost: Well, you know, the honor concept and the honor committees were probably not as active then as they are today, the administration, because it was a relatively new thing. The business of determining modifications to the conduct system, to the administrative rules, was something that we as class leaders had a chance to sit down and make recommendations on to the commandant. Charlie Buchanan, as the commandant, was very good about referring things to us, and I wish I could recall the name of the assistant commandant at that time, because he was an absolute jewel to work with.

They would say, "Hey, we've got the following problem. We've got the following thing coming up." Sometimes it was we had to host an awful lot of official visitors, and the brigade commander got involved in just about every one of those things. It was up to me as the brigade commander to determine what was required and who else should be involved and make sure that everything procedurally and training-wise was scheduled for those. It was rather interesting, because we met some interesting people. For example, I got a chance to sit in on visits from people like Field Marshal Montgomery of El Alamein fame.[*] He was a rather interesting man. Everything I've ever read subsequently about his mountainous ego was borne out when he was there for an official visit and to review the parade. When Eisenhower was our President, Eisenhower was over there, and I had a chance to be his formal host for Sunday chapel and had been invited to join in a sort of a pre-lunch reception at the supe's house for him.[†] It was a pleasant thing. He was quite, quite impressive. Very warm, very warm, which was surprising. I thought, "Why should this guy who has been a five-star general have anything to do with me?" He just treated midshipmen very nicely. Very courteous, very warm and outgoing guy.

Paul Stillwell: I read his memoir, and you get that sense from it—very down to earth.[‡]

Admiral Trost: Very much a people man. Very down to earth. Very definitely a people man. I don't really recall the others. We had congressional dignitaries; I remember Senator Saltonstall coming over.[§] Thought he was a rather pleasant gentleman to talk to. He would speak to a midshipman as if he really were of some import to the world and would sit and talk to us as an adult, which was not always the mode of some of our company officers when we were with them.

---

[*] Field Marshal Sir Bernard Law Montgomery (1887-1976) was a controversial British Army officer. In 1942 he commanded the Eighth Army during victorious operations in North Africa. He later commanded Allied armies in Northern Europe and commanded the British-occupied zone in Germany after victory was achieved in World War II.

[†] Dwight D. Eisenhower served as President of the United States from 20 January 1953 to 20 January 1961. During World War II he had been Supreme Commander of the Allied Expeditionary Force for the invasion of Europe. In the early 1950s, as a five-star general, he served as Supreme Allied Commander in Europe in 1951-52 when the military portion of the North Atlantic Treaty Organization (NATO) was established.

[‡] Dwight E. Eisenhower, *At Ease: Stories I Tell to Friends* (Garden City, NY: Doubleday, 1967).

[§] Leverett Saltonstall, a Republican from Massachusetts, served in the Senate from 4 January 1945 to 3 January 1967. His son Peter was killed on the island of Guam in 1944.

Paul Stillwell: He had a son killed on Guam, I think, so he had a special place in his heart for the military.

Admiral Trost: He was quite impressive, quite impressive.

Paul Stillwell: You mentioned Ross Perot. The *Lucky Bag* says that he had an unusual combination of administrative talent and a warm personality. How do you remember him?

Admiral Trost: Well, Ross was, my gosh, what a spark plug. Ross just seemed to have boundless energy. Very articulate, loved to debate. Very, very active. I think Ross has a pretty good-sized ego, but he had reason to have it. He was a very successful person in just about everything he did and very much a class activist and well known. You know, he would just come around and with that big Texas smile and a handshake and born politician was the way I would have characterized him. He was very enthusiastic about everything, very capable.

Paul Stillwell: Well, not just the shallow politician approach, he obviously mastered the subject matter.

Admiral Trost: He really was. He was a competitor, and he knew what he was talking about. Very good.

Paul Stillwell: One thing that's unusual is for a brigade commander to finish top in the class because that takes up enough time that it could eat into your studying.

Admiral Trost: I didn't study much as brigade commander. I really didn't. We still had lights out at 10:15 at night, I think, and I spent many a night sitting reading and I did get away. I think I could stay up to 11:00 or 11:15. Of course, my lights were visible from right around the corner of the company officer's office, but we had special dispensation to allow us to be able to spend more time studying, and you needed it. It was not enough time to study. I can recall even the final week, June week, was exceptionally busy. There was so much going on.

I and my wife, I should say my current wife my one and only wife—came over the last half of that week. We were still determining whether or not we were really serious about each other. But my parents and my sister were there, and my wife stayed with them in a very nice private home out in town. But I remember that my time with them was much less than I had expected it to be, just because of the demands that were put on us. We had to get ready for every parade. We had to sit down and brief the senior officers on what was going to happen and what we were going to be doing. There were so many events that it was just a very full week.

I remember after graduation, I drove my family and my date back out to the house, dropped them off, came back and started packing my cruise box to ship out, because I didn't have a chance to do it during the week. It involved stuff that was going to be shipped out to Illinois and then making the arrangements that afternoon to get the thing shipped and finally packing up the things that I was going to be carrying with mc. I didn't even get a chance to do that until after graduation. I don't think it was because I was ineffective at time management. There was so much to try to manage in the given time. But it was a fascinating, satisfying experience. You had to feel that you really did have control of events and what you were doing and could make a difference in how it was done.

Paul Stillwell: You would hear about some guys that have almost an obsession with finishing first in the class, and they grind away. It sounds like you didn't have that opportunity.

Admiral Trost: I didn't have the obsession. I really have never had that obsession. I had finished first in everything I had ever done academically, because I studied as hard as I felt I had to to learn what I want to learn, and it just came out that way. It's a God-given capability that I had the opportunity to use. But no, I didn't have an obsession in finishing first in the class; it just happened. After plebe year, when I saw these things posted and I saw that I was first in my class I really had a little trouble accepting that. It can't be. Then in my youngster year I don't know if I was first in my class or not, I was second, but first overall through the two years. I'm not sure how that worked. I think it may have been youngster year, and if I had been obsessed by it I would have had a real problem first-class year, because I wouldn't have had time to do the studying.

Paul Stillwell: You mentioned this brief interlude you had in football with the not-so-great uniform. What was sports participation throughout your four years?

Admiral Trost: Well, I was not a football player to begin with, and I was never destined to be one. I went out, and interestingly they kept cutting the plebe squad back. They made the first several cuts and I survived. I was out there. I said, "I want to be a guard." I really didn't know. I knew what a guard was supposed to do, basically. I didn't know how to do it, because I had not played in high school. I had been working. I survived, and I really did it to get in shape and didn't expect to be surviving. But I remember when the list came out, and they cut the squad to 88 my name was still on it, and my two roommates were off. They looked at me and said, "Something is wrong here," because both of them knew a lot more about football and what to do than I did. Both had played, but I dropped the next cut. They saw through me, and I got eliminated.

Then, what I did then was go out for soccer, which I had never played before, which looked like an interesting sport. What really always appealed to me about soccer was that you go out there, and you do an awful lot of scrimmaging, so it's an awful lot of—the training was playing, and I enjoyed that. I in fact played soccer for all four years until about midway through the fall season, first-class year, when the JV coach and I was still JV, said, "You guys who are first class are wasting your time here, and there is no point in our investing further in you. If you want to do something else, fine."[*] So I went off and ran company steeplechase. Our company steeplechase team needed a boost, and so several of us who had been playing soccer went on that and took advantage of the fact that we were in better shape than most of the people we were running against and added more points than they were able to get before. I played an intramural sport called field ball. Played some tennis. Did a lot of sailing. Outside the soccer field, I probably spent more time sailing than anything else.

---

[*] JV – junior varsity.

Paul Stillwell: Was sailing something that you enjoyed?

Admiral Trost: I really enjoyed it. I went out plebe year. They taught us to sail, and I had never been in a sailboat. As a matter of fact, I had never been in anything other than a rowboat before. I got involved plebe year in sailing as a crew of one of the 44-foot yawls. I really enjoyed that. I qualified my youngster year for yawl command and sailed, obviously mostly in the fall and spring series races and some weekends, a number of nights. I really did enjoy and still do enjoy sailing.

Paul Stillwell: This kind of appealed to this outdoor-type life you had enjoyed before.

Admiral Trost: Well, it really did, and it was something when I was first was introduced it was totally different. There is a sense of peace, calm, serenity when you are out on a sailboat that isn't matched by anything else, and I really love it. And you can be challenged on the Chesapeake Bay by storms too. There were times when I wondered whether we were going to make it back in, but it's nice to see that proper training and skill and common sense get you home.

Paul Stillwell: You went to sea during the summers. What do you remember of your cruises?

Paul Stillwell: Well, our initial cruise was the summer that the Korean War actually started.* At that time, they were still making up cruise squadrons. I know we had the *Missouri*, quite a few destroyers, a light carrier back in the days of CVLs, and cruisers. The Naval Academy and ROTC people were scattered across these ships. It was going to be a U.S. cruise, not going overseas to Europe, and that was for money reasons.

But I can recall going down at the old seawall at the Naval Academy, tossing our duffel bags over into the landing craft and being taken out to the *Bexar*, named after Bexar County, Texas.† She was an APA, and I was introduced to the dirtiest living space

---

* The Korean War began on 25 June 1950, when six North Korean infantry division and three border constabulary brigades invaded South Korea. The troops were supported by approximately 100 Russian-made T-34 tanks. In New York that same day the United Nations Security Council adopted a resolution condemning the invasion.
† USS *Bexar* (APA-237), a *Haskell*-class attack transport, was commissioned 9 October 1945.

that I've ever been in. The troop compartments were in holds, and I remember being assigned to a bunk that was the fifth one up, a pipe-frame bunk with canvas on it. We had life rafts, and for years afterwards I thought that in the amphibious Navy they soaked their life jackets in diesel oil, just to give them the proper odor to stink up the berthing spaces. But that was our transportation down to Norfolk and just overnight.

We loaded up overnight, and then we were held down there, because I think we got down two days or so before the cruise was to commence when the ships would sail. We were being taken on very orderly fashion and sent to our ships. I envy the several classmates of mine whose fathers were senior naval officers. One of them was the skipper of the air station in Norfolk, and a black sedan pulled up on the pier and picked up this character while all of the rest of us up on the ship jeering at him: "What are you trying to pull?" But we were kept in that hot monster without liberty for, as I remember, two days and then finally I was to go aboard a destroyer for the cruise, and we were mustered and sent over to the ship.

Of course, what they would do at that time was draw down the ship's company by a certain amount by sending people on leave and to school. We were filling in as the labor force, the deck force and they needed us as watch standers in the engineering spaces, junior watch standers. So it was informative and educational. That third class cruise was intended to introduce you to the duties of the enlisted watch stations, to get a flavor for shipboard life, and it did so. I was aboard the USS *Brownson*, which was a relatively modern destroyer at that time. High number—I think she was 868. *Brownson* was an interesting ship.[*]

Brownson was a long hull.[†] She would have had to be with that number. *Brownson* had been down involved in antarctic operations, we were told, and had come

---

[*] USS *Brownson* (DD-868) was a *Gearing*-class destroyer commissioned 17 November 1945. She had a full-load displacement of 3,460 tons, was 390 feet long, 41 feet in the beam, and maximum draft of 18 feet, 6 inches. Her top speed was 36.8 knots. She was armed with six 5-inch guns and ten 21-inch torpedo tubes. One of the officers in the *Brownson*'s crew in 1949 was Ensign William L. Read, USN. The oral history of Read, who retired as a vice admiral, is in the Naval Institute collection.

[†] The 2,200-ton destroyers were those of the short-hull *Allen M. Sumner* (DD-692) and long-hull *Gearing* (DD-710) classes, both built during World War II. The ships of the former class were 376 feet long, versus 390 for the latter. The extra length provided added fuel capacity.

back. She was based in Boston at the time. As we were getting ready to go aboard, the rumors were that she was not permitted to enter homeport. That they had put her at anchor for three days while they were cleaning her up so that their squadron commander would let her come in port. If they did all of that, they should have spent a lot more than three days cleaning her up, because she was a ship that needed a lot of tender care. The engineer officer on board prided himself on spending a minimal amount of money. He literally used wire, and if they were missing a bolt, they would wire flanges together, and it was a just a gross example of malpractice in an engineering plant.

Her most notable characteristic was that she was considered by the midshipmen to serve the worst food that any of them had ever been exposed to. We would go through the breakfast line, and this was in the days that the steam line went down to the old first platform deck, just forward—well, really under the main superstructure and through the serving line. The midshipmen were always served separately and secondly, after the crew ate. The midshipmen went through the line and my recollections are still very distinct that breakfast, for example, it was trays of grease with eggs floating back and forth. Sometimes the grease wasn't very hot anymore, and the eggs were greasy but cold with greasy bacon, greasy sausage, and cold toast. That was standard practice on the *Brownson*.

Still, it was one hell of a good introduction. I learned how to use chipping hammers. I learned later on how much people appreciate these crawlers to chip paint, because it's a lot better than doing everything by hand. It's like painting an automobile with a little tiny artist's brush. But we got good experience. We had some good liberty ports. We went up to Halifax, Nova Scotia. My first visit up there in Halifax was a superb place to visit in the summertime. There was a festival of some sort going on in town while we were there, so we had a good opportunity, we did liberty, people were very friendly. Many of us were invited out to homes for dinner. I went out to a home of a family that had a young daughter who wanted to meet midshipmen, and several of us were invited out. They had a sailboat. We went sailing in some of the coldest water I've ever been in, but good experience. They were extremely friendly to us and a good stop.

We then went to New York City, our second liberty port. It was my first exposure to New York City. I would say it was rather impressive. I also note that we walked from the piers, which were I guess, the lower west side where we berthed, all over the city because we didn't have much money, and we rode the subways when we could. We walked around—we walked everywhere. We were never thinking of any kind of street danger, places down there that I wouldn't even drive through now that we walked through with no concerns. I guess that's a demonstration of what's changed in our society. The pier areas were pretty decent at that time.

Paul Stillwell: Did you get to the Polo Grounds or Yankee Stadium?

Admiral Trost: I got to Yankee Stadium to see one game and got to Rockefeller Center, and we got to the United Nations. As a matter of fact, I met Admiral Nimitz, who was our senior military U.S. military representative to the U.N.[*] A group of us signed up for a session over there, and a busload of us who went over. He greeted us and told us all about the United Nations and what his job was about and then took us into a room where they had set up cookies and coffee and soft drinks, and he talked to individuals. Very pleasant, very distinguished gentleman. Very impressive. I would say at one point in my highlights in meeting people, very, very pleasant gentleman.

We had a very enjoyable time in New York, and we got under way from New York. We were out conducting exercises off of the Jersey coast when all of the sudden somebody said, "Hey, where's the *Missouri* going?" All we saw was the fantail of the *Missouri* as it receded into the distance. That's when the Korean War started. The *Missouri* was broken out and went independently to Norfolk, off-loaded midshipman and on-loaded ammunition, and started heading for Korea.

We continued on the rest of the cruise and went down to Guantánamo Bay and did training down in that area.[†] My first exposure to Gitmo with a lot of recollections.

---

[*] Admiral Chester W. Nimitz, USN, Commander in Chief Pacific Fleet and Pacific Ocean Areas, 1941-45. In December 1944 he was promoted to fleet admiral, a five-star rank. From 1945 to 1947 he was Chief of Naval Operations, and from 1949 to 1953 worked with the United Nations.
[†] Guantánamo Bay, on the south coast of Cuba, near the eastern end of the island, for many years provided a fleet anchorage and training area for U.S. Navy ships. The area also included a support facility ashore.

That's where I first saw the intense competition on liberty between Navy and Marine Corps personnel. Unbelievable. Fights in beer gardens and clubs, just because these guys had been cooped up for a long time, and they just loved to fight. I also recall several of us getting sick on canned pineapple juice, because we hadn't had juice or fresh fruit or anything else on our ship. Milk was frozen or canned, and when we got down to Gitmo the milk was frozen and not all that good, but we were buying these great big cans of pineapple juice to slake our desires for fruit juice, and you can get sick on pineapple juice. I did. But very, very pleasant time, good training. It was a good cruise in terms of good indoctrination of what the Navy was all about.

My first-class cruise was also aboard a destroyer, *Haynsworth.*[*] She was totally a different ship, smartly run, good ship, and a very pleasant environment. That was a cruise to Northern Europe, so it was fortunate. We went to Brest, France, and to Scotland. We went into Brodick, Scotland, Firth of Clyde. Of course, our time in Scotland was my first in a latitude that was so far north that I came back to the ship at midnight and the sun was still out. If you went to bed and didn't get up until 4:00 o'clock in the morning, you missed the night totally. But, it was very pleasant. Again, very pleasant and at that time, it was in the summer of '52, people in Scotland in that region still remembered all the Americans. That was sort of the main entry point for most of the U.S. troops when they came in. They brought them around to the north of Ireland and into the Firth of Clyde, and they off-loaded there in Scotland at Brodick and Glasgow. Then they were sent by train down to southern England, so a lot of families there had had very direct interface with Americans, and we were treated very, very well.

Then we went to Brest, France, which was most interesting in the destruction of the submarine pens and things that were still very visible there. The Germans built submarine pens. We had a chance to go to Paris and spent several days in Paris. Again, very interesting place.

Paul Stillwell: What do you remember specifically about the submarine pens?

[*] USS *Haynsworth* (DD-700) was an *Allen M. Sumner*-class destroyer commissioned 22 June 1944. She had a standard displacement of 2,200 tons, was 376 feet long, 41 feet in the beam, and a draft of 16 feet. Her design speed was 34 knots. She was armed with six 5-inch guns and ten 21-inch torpedo tubes.

Admiral Trost: Well, I remember, first, the massive nature of them. They had been built right into a hillside. It was huge, massive, I would say 12- to 20-foot-thick concrete covering over them. What had probably been almost impervious to bombing was largely damaged, I think, by the placement of explosives after the war. Because I don't think we ever knocked out those things by overhead bombing. We could not go in. You could see it as you went by, but we were anchored out and went by in boats and could look into them and see, and just the massive nature of it was very impressive.

In Brest itself, the area down around the waterfront still was largely un-rebuilt after wartime destruction. I remember it as a very drab place and not a very particularly friendly place. Those who did not get a chance or did not sign up for one of the Paris tours, which everybody had an option to do, did not have the most enjoyable liberty. There was not that much to do, and the people weren't all that friendly. There was available a lot of very cheap rotgut wine that people bought and drank too much of, in absence of anything else to do. That was not the best liberty port. As a matter of fact, the highlight of it I remember going aboard *Wisconsin*. I know *Wisconsin* was there because my ship went alongside *Wisconsin*, and I don't remember the reason. We went alongside and moored alongside her at anchor. We were there for the better part of the working day, and of course for the tin can sailors it was a great opportunity to visit all the gedunk stands on *Wisconsin*.* I can recall some of my classmates showing us around this huge ship. One of my roommates was on board, and a couple of the guys from the company were on board. Quite an impressive thing. It was my first real direct fact to face with a battleship. They are impressive.

Paul Stillwell: Any specifics from the *Wisconsin*?

Admiral Trost: Well, what I remember then, and reaffirmed when I was CNO on the same ship, was how indestructible they appeared. Went down to the engineering alley, where you could then go out into the engineering spaces from both sides.

Paul Stillwell: Broadway, they called it.

---

* Gedunk is a Navy slang term for candy, ice cream, and sodas—snack-type food.

Admiral Trost: Broadway—and walking down there and then going down in the spaces and looking at just the massive nature of everything. Looking at the uptakes and the girdering and the protection. You could take a bomb right down the stack, and it might scratch the sheet metal. And you had the feeling of going below the armored decks and looking at how thick those things are as you go down through a hatch. It was just the massive nature of going up in the armored conning tower and seeing the bridge. Of course, it was massive compared to a destroyer. Crawled into a turret. Of course, we had studied computers and the guns, and so all of that stuff was essentially reasonably familiar. It was quite interesting.

I went aboard *Wisconsin* several times during her pre-commissioning and after she was recommissioned this last time.* What impressed me during the pre-commissioning period—she was taken into Avondale Shipyard down the Mississippi River near New Orleans to have bottom work done. She was up high and dry, and the warrant officer who was responsible for her engineering spaces, the Navy guy that was kind of watching all the coordination of the work, took me down to some spaces that were opened up the previous day. She had been so well preserved you walked into a space, and it was just really impressive. There was preservative to be removed, but there wasn't any deterioration apparent. Just unbelievably well preserved. Then I went through her later on when she was at Ingalls, as I remember it, for the rest of the work. I went through her there, and then I saw her again in Norfolk, and those ships are superb. It's a shame to take them out of commission, because they do have a utility in today's military. It's just a shame to see them go away.

Paul Stillwell: Did you get to Portugal? I know that *New Jersey* was on that cruise. She went to Cherbourg and then down Lisbon.

Admiral Trost: I did not, did not. It was Scotland and Brest, and some ships went into Torquay, England. Some of them went to Le Havre, France. I thought that someone went

---

* The *Wisconsin* (BB-64) was recommissioned 22 October 1988 at Pascagoula, Mississippi, site of the Ingalls shipyard where she was modernized. She was decommissioned 30 September 1991, the month after this interview.

up also to Norway. For some reason, I think somebody went to Bergen, but I don't remember what ships.

Paul Stillwell: What was the difference in your responsibilities and duties on these two cruises?

Admiral Trost: Well, the first-class cruise, we were treated more as prospective officers, and the watches we stood reflected that. We were away from being the grunts down in the firerooms and introduced to engineering supervisor watches. We were up on the bridge. We actually did real-world navigation problems separately from the navigator but with the ship's navigator overseeing what we were doing and the Naval Academy escort officer supervising what we were doing. It was more of an introduction. It was not wardroom living yet, but we were brought in two at a time to have meals in the wardroom and introduced to the wardroom environment. We were also given a lot more administrative and leadership responsibilities for the third-class midshipmen, so it was a good hands-on opportunity.

Paul Stillwell: I think that youngster cruise, though, was extremely valuable just to experience for yourself how the enlisted man lived.

Admiral Trost: It really was.

Paul Stillwell: Anything else about the cruises to mention? I'm interested in how you reacted just to the business of going to sea itself.

Admiral Trost: Well, I was one of the fortunate ones. I never got seasick on any of the cruises. Whether that was just inherent in my nature or partly the result of all of the sailing I had done prior even to the first cruise I don't know. But I felt very fortunate, because I saw the wretched nature of those who did. Bud Whittemore, classmate, was one of those who knew early on—I think that's correct.[*] He was told before he was half through the Naval Academy that he would be permitted to go into the Air Force, because he had chronic seasickness. He was on the ship I was on on one of these cruises—I've

_____

[*] Midshipman Albert Burton Whittemore, USN.

forgotten which one—got so wildly ill they transferred him to another ship off of the destroyer, because he just couldn't stop retching. He was just a very, very miserable human being. I saw others who would spend the first couple of days at sea every time sick.

I was seasick on several occasions. All of those occasions took place when I was executive officer of *Scorpion*, which was the *Skipjack* class. When that sucker would get under way from Norfolk and we hadn't been out for a while, I would get queasiness in my stomach—just the round bottom and the way it rolled. It wouldn't go away until we submerged and started operating. But I've never had a problem with a surface ship.

Paul Stillwell: I saw a story recently—some passenger liner skipper was asked, "Well how do you help your passengers with seasickness?"

He said, "We don't have to help them. They know what to do on their own."

Admiral Trost: Of course, now they have a combination of Dramamine and these patches that supposedly go on, and I guess they are much more effective. I don't know.

Paul Stillwell: It must have been a pleasant contrast, though, to the way of life in Bancroft Hall.

Admiral Trost: It was really—I enjoyed it because it was sort of hands on. Of course, with the instruction we had—for example, by the time I went to sea first class year on that destroyer, I knew that ship. We knew what every piece of engineering equipment looked like because it was over there in Isherwood Hall, I guess was the place, where the brigade activities center now stands, where Alumni Hall now stands. You could walk inside an M-type boiler, you could look at cut-apart turbines; you could look at pumps. You could understand how they worked, and to stand a watch in the engineering space was a breeze because there wasn't anything unfamiliar. They were just learning how it was integrated in its operation. We knew how to navigate. We were turned to on that. We had had our YP training, so we knew how to handle ships.* We weren't given much

---

* The YP is a yard patrol craft used for training of ship handling and seamanship.

opportunity for that, but a little bit. It was sort of applying in the real world what you were learning.

The focus of education at the Naval Academy was more on the professional side at that time than I think it is today, more than could be today, because of the diversity of the equipment. At that time, if you went aboard a destroyer, every one of them had a common propulsion plant. Most of them had very similar fire control and gun systems. The radars were similar, and the sonars were similar, so if you knew one, you were at home in most. We had been taught enough of the details about battleship-peculiar items, primarily guns and fire control, that we weren't strangers to that. We had done damage control problems that was interesting to be taught by the ship's DCA, by some of the "how you really do some of this stuff."[*]

I can recall they had the floodable models over at the Naval Academy where you did your calculations and then you, in fact, could flood. They had little relay-operated valves, and you could flood a space to see whether the result was what you had calculated it would be. We would sit there and calculate, and we learned also how to sink that sucker when we wanted to by just calculating and figuring out how much more to do and then just hitting another button and watching it either turn turtle or sink in place.

Paul Stillwell: But, again, very practical education—sort of like that shore-bombardment exercise.

Admiral Trost: Yeah, it was.

Paul Stillwell: Was the engineering plant in the *Haynsworth* better maintained than in the *Brownson*?

Admiral Trost: Far better maintained, yeah. Far better, fewer leaks. On the other hand, one of the advantages of *Brownson* was learning some real-world practicalities, like how to make coffee in an engineering space. In the firerooms, my first watch, I was asked—I

---

[*] DCA – damage control assistant.

don't remember what the rank of the individual was, but one of the enlisted watch standers said, "Do you know how to make coffee?"

I thought about that, and I said, "Yeah."

He said, "Okay, make some coffee."

I looked around and didn't see any coffee pot. I said, "Where's the coffee pot?"

He said, "Right here." And he reached up, and there hanging over a valve was this sort of a dis-credible bucket with a wire handle on it. He handed me that, and he handed me a big asbestos glove that went halfway up to my elbow. He said, "You'll need that. I'm going to show you how." First of all, there was a 20-pound tin of coffee there, and there was a coffee cup in there and scooped some coffee out and threw it into the bucket, just a cupful. And then he hung it back up. And then he had a glove on, and this was a low-point drain on one of the steam lines. And, of course, there was all this water, and he opened that valve. He cracked that valve, and hot water went shooting in. Some coffee went splattering out, and then as steam started issuing out, he cranked it back up and said, "Okay now, let that sit for a while." And that's what we did. That's how we made coffee. I thought, pretty practical and if the same guy did it all the time, with the same amount of coffee and got some consistency, it was pretty good. The biggest problem was that you had to strain the grounds out. And they way they did that, they just took an oily rag and poured the coffee through it into the cup, and you served it. When I say oily rag, they were the working rags down there, and that got the grounds out of your coffee, and a little surface oil effect wasn't that bad.

Paul Stillwell: I've heard using a sock for that. I think that might even work a little better.

Admiral Trost: These guys just took something out of the ragbag; sometimes the rag was already used, and they just put it over the end of the can. The guy had both of these asbestos gloves on to keep from burning himself, and he was pouring the coffee.

Paul Stillwell: In general, what was the attitude of the petty officers in those ships toward the midshipmen?

Admiral Trost: I don't know that it was all that positive. I didn't sense that it was. I thought that we were kind of in the way. We made work harder for them, because their contemporaries were off doing other things, and they are the guys that would rather be off on the beach instead of babysitting these midshipmen and teaching them things. But that was variable also. There were some very, very good ones. Some very positive attitudes. Some really did a great job with us, and I think overall it was a positive experience, but I think it was a resentment, certainly at the outset of cruises, the fact that we were in port and were kind of in the way and taking up their time, cluttering up the mess decks. And, of course, we weren't permitted to stay down there. We had to eat and get the hell out of there as rapidly as possible. But I think most of the midshipmen saw the training cruise as a very positive experience. Of course, the liberty ports were the icing on the cake. They were fun.

Paul Stillwell: How was the food at the Naval Academy contrasted to that which described in the destroyer?

Admiral Trost: Far superior. I recall some complaints about food, but I thought the food was generally quite good. I thought—and I still think—having eaten there from time to time, sometimes we may have eaten better when I was a midshipman than I do today. I attribute that in part to the fact that there were a lot of Navy people there in continuity in the mess operation. They had Navy stewards who did the serving. They were an insubordinate bunch, but they were humorous. But, I remember the food by and large was pretty good. On the other hand, I'm probably biased, because I was taught as a kid to eat whatever was put on my plate, and you didn't say, "I think I will have so-and-so." You said, "I think I will have whatever is available." That does train one into liking food. Now, the Naval Academy I thought did well. The dairy products were always superb, and the meat was good for two years of my time as a midshipman.

We had a midshipman mess officer, Navy lieutenant; he was a jaygee when he got there. He had been a football player at Navy, I think, Supply Corps Officer and his big coup, as I remember it, was buying a huge amount of Argentine beef which I think came up in a Navy ship and manifested itself by a Navy meal where we all sat down. The steaks came out, and the steak was the size of your plate, and we ate steak for about six months like kings. Of course, that guy could do no wrong from that point onward. But we had good quality food at the Naval Academy.

Paul Stillwell: Did you have any encounters with the *Reina Mercedes*, where those stewards lived?*

Admiral Trost: Well, no. We weren't putting midshipmen over there anymore. When I say that midshipmen were walking off their extra duty, and if they were confined I don't think they went over there. I don't recall anybody being physically confined. Those stewards lived over there, and, of course, you knew they were around because you would hear them in the morning singing in this singsong chant as they marched along. They would come into Smoke Park there before that new wing was added to the midshipmen's mess. Living in the old sixth wing, we would be awakened every morning by these guys marching in about 5:30 in the morning. I'm going to say they were a congenial lot, by and large. Whether it was because they enjoyed it or made the best of it, I don't know.

Paul Stillwell: Were they mostly black?

Admiral Trost: They were mostly black or Filipino.

Paul Stillwell: Did you have any sense of racism in Annapolis as a city then?

Admiral Trost: No. Less so than I observed really in places like East St. Louis and St. Louis growing up. But there were clearly areas in Annapolis that were black residential and, by and large, poor. If there was then an open problem, other than the fact that there was a disadvantaged group of people there, I do not know. Hard to tell.

Paul Stillwell: How much chance did you get to get out in town?

---

* USS *Reina Mercedes* (IX-25), captured during the Spanish-American War, served as a station ship at the Naval Academy from 1912 to 1957. Until 1940, midshipmen being punished for various disciplinary infractions slept and took meals on board the ship but continued to go to classes ashore.

Admiral Trost: Plebe year, very little. Plebe year I think we were permitted out in town Saturday afternoons, and we would go out and walk around, usually go out to a movie or something and come back in. Subsequently, a lot more but only on weekends. We could not go out there during the week. Even first-class year, it seems to me that right at the end of first-class year there were several times we were given a Friday night opportunity to go out in town, but by and large, it was noon Saturday to evening mealtime Sunday was the liberty window.

Paul Stillwell: Was there any opportunity to drive at all?

Admiral Trost: No opportunity to drive. We could not legally drive at the Naval Academy until June in the first class year and could not legally own a car. A number of people did. I had one for my last four months there. That was an economic necessity. It was available, and if I didn't buy it I wasn't going to be able to get it at that price, and I couldn't afford to buy a new one. So I had to buy it and find a garage to put it in. But we couldn't drive within a seven-mile limit. You couldn't drink anything within a seven-mile limit, including beer. And you couldn't go outside of the seven-mile limit, except on weekend liberty so that sort of took care of boxing people in pretty nicely. I think today's regulations may be a little more logical.

Paul Stillwell: How much social life did you have as a midshipman?

Admiral Trost: I dated a fair amount. I took advantage of the dating opportunities plebe year when we had to buy tickets and go somewhere, and actually I dated a girl whom I had met after a football game in Baltimore plebe year. Our home games were being played in Baltimore at that time. Not much social life plebe year. Thereafter, I was not a steady dater. I was as the occasion presented itself.

Paul Stillwell: How did you meet your future wife?

Admiral Trost: I met her when I was asked one Saturday by a classmate to take care of his date from start of liberty, noon or 12:30, until he got off with the watch section on Saturday evening meal. I agreed to do that. It was, as I remember it, approaching Christmas, probably sometime in December. It was our youngster year, and the date that I was minding for him and my wife Pauline were over there together dating two classmates of mine. Pauline had on several occasions dated another guy from my company who was class of '51, but I had not met her then.

At any rate, this was the first time we met, and she continued to date another guy from my company for a period of time. We got to know each other pretty well, since we were either mutually dating or at the same functions. We used to dance together at "hops." We got along quite nicely. Didn't in fact date until spring break of my first-class year. We tried it and weren't sure we liked it. I invited her over for June Week, for that last half of June Week, and we got along extremely well. She subsequently came out to Illinois a couple of weeks later and spent a week out there while I was on my graduation leave. I got called back, and that's when I decided I was going to marry her, but I figured she was going to need a little persuading. We continued to date, but I deployed shortly after I went aboard my ship. When I came back it was spring of '54, we found that we were still very, very compatible and got married a couple of months later.

Paul Stillwell: Where was her home?

Admiral Trost: She lived in and was raised in Cottage City, Maryland, just outside the district, right near the peace cross in Bladensburg—29 miles from the Naval Academy.

Paul Stillwell: You would know that very specifically.

Admiral Trost: Very definitely.

Paul Stillwell: Another of your fellow midshipmen, a couple of years ahead and in the class of '51, was Bill Lawrence. What were your recollections of him from then?

Admiral Trost: Bill I remember was a very impressive leader. Very conscientious guy, as he has always been throughout his lifetime. Very dedicated to doing things right, and I guess Bill was both his class president and he was a six-striper. Just very, very much the leader in that group. Good man.

Paul Stillwell: Any specific examples you remember from his time as a midshipman?

Admiral Trost: Well, I remember when we started talking about the honor concept, and he was the guy who had sort of visualized this thing. If there were others, I was unaware at the time. I've since read that Ross Perot had this diagram of how it should work. I didn't realize that we were other than followers at that time of Bill Lawrence. In the meeting I attended, he was the guy who appeared to have the most fully formulated thoughts and the guy who led all of the discussions that we had. I remember him as the brigade commander just watching him interface with visitors. I was very impressed. He seemed very much at ease, and he was very sincere and personable guy. He was also a varsity basketball star and one hell of a good basketball player. Just an impressive midshipman.

Paul Stillwell: Sincere.

Admiral Trost: Sincerity was his key. Sincerity and integrity, absolutely.

Paul Stillwell: He described to me growing up in the South, and some of his role models were people like Robert E. Lee and a sense of honor that was like an internal compass.

Admiral Trost: He did have a sense of honor, and that was what caused his departure from the Navy. I say that because that is what Bill has told me. He just felt frustrated by his inability to do and to accomplish what he knew had to be done, so he felt thwarted.

Paul Stillwell: One of the supreme ironies then was that one of his antagonists, James Webb, wrote a novel called *Sense of Honor.*[*] What other extracurricular activities were you in besides sports and brigade leadership?

Admiral Trost: I was in the marching band my first year there, and then I didn't stay with that. I didn't do a hell of a lot else. I was not a club member or anything else. I didn't sing much in the glee club, even though I enjoyed that. I didn't participate though in any of those activities. We had a fledgling photo club which I visited a couple of times but

---

[*] James H. Webb, *A Sense of Honor* (Englewood Cliffs, New Jersey: Prentice-Hall, 1981). Webb, a graduate of the Naval Academy class of 1968, served as a Marine in Vietnam. He was later Secretary of the Navy and a U.S. Senator from Virginia.

didn't join. I really didn't have the time. If you were involved in sports and if you sailed, there was not much extra time. Most of the guys who were having these club activities did that in lieu of their afternoon sports participation.

Paul Stillwell: Would sailing qualify as your "hobby" from that period?

Admiral Trost: Yeah, very definitely, very definitely. Sailing and reading. I would say sailing was a hobby, but I sailed just every opportunity I got. And, we had a rather water-oriented group in my company in my class. We would race. I recall there were five of us in a seven-man crew who had our yawl commands. I thought it was sort of fun to sail with these guys. We would take turns skippering the thing, and you knew you had a really hotshot bunch of qualified guys when you went out and raced, because every one of them had gone through all of the wickets and knew what to do. So it's sort of like running a ship with a bunch of commanding officers on board to help you out, although that may not be the best deal. But, this worked out quite well in midshipman days.

Paul Stillwell: Another impressive individual in your class was Bill Leftwich. What do you recall of him?

Admiral Trost: I knew Bill well. I guess I really got to know him well on second-class summer because our second-class summer was at that time devoted to aviation training and amphibious training. I don't remember the sequence anymore. We started the summer with aviation training. We visited a number of different people. We had places— we went down to Patuxent River as a group and went through the test center and their activities down there. We went down to Norfolk and went to sea aboard the *FDR* for a week to observe carrier flight operations and briefed on carrier ops.[*] We went down to Eglin AFB, where they had great static display at that time.[†] That was back in the days of

---

[*] USS *Franklin D. Roosevelt* (CVB-42) was an aircraft carrier commissioned in 1945.
[†] Eglin Air Force Base is near the towns of Valparaiso and Niceville in the panhandle region of western Florida.

the B-36.[*] I remember the big multi-engine B-36 sitting in one of those climate hangars where they had the temperature down way below freezing. We walked on a very hot, humid summer day in our summer khaki uniforms and the perspiration became icy as soon as we stepped inside this hangar. No one was around this thing that would tell us how they were testing different climate conditions. We had a chance to crawl around and get lectured on a lot of things, but the most memorable portion of it was the afternoon beach party down on the gulf where most people got too much sun.

We went to Naval Air Station Jacksonville again to be introduced to different kinds of airplanes that were down there. But there we stopped. The social life was very pleasant, and then we went to Memphis and went through the training center there. I recall there staying in the old wooden World War II barracks—these big long rooms with the heads were as I recall all down on the lower floor and we were berthed up on the second floor, so you had a long hike to make it to the head, but that too was a very pleasant town. We went through the McCormick-Deering or International Harvester, one of the other factories. There we saw them taking regular tractors and putting cotton pickers on them. That wasn't a great naval aviation training process for us, but it occupied us for several hours, which I was suppose was the intent.

Lots of social activity, and one of my most pleasant memories of that was going out to Bill Leftwich's parents' home in the Memphis suburbs. They had a pleasant lawn party that evening and included us among of their guests. I guess I got to know Bill quite well that summer, because we also were in the same group then when we went to Little Creek for the amphibious portion of the training. Then Bill was the first-class year the middle set brigade commander. I was the sub commander, so we were roommates for that time. So we got to know each other quite well. We stayed in touch over the years, to and including his first return from Vietnam. He had been John Warner's Marine assistant and Marine aide in the Under Secretary's office. Shortly before returning to Vietnam

---

[*] Consolidated Vultee, based in San Diego, built the Air Force's B-36 bomber, known as the Peacemaker. The B-36D model was equipped with four J-47 jet engines in under-wing nacelles and six piston engines that drove propellers. The jet engines enhanced the plane's maximum speed from 376 miles per hour to 435 miles per hour. It first flew in 1946 and subsequently was operational in the Strategic Air Command from 1948 through 1959.

again, I had gone in as Warner's naval aide shortly after Bill left. I was there when Bill was killed over there.* So I knew him quite well. Fine guy.

Paul Stillwell: What qualities in him do you remember?

Admiral Trost: Bill, very conscientious, hard-working, energetic, perfectionist in doing right in mastering things. Very warm person. Very strong as a leader, both as a role model and as one directing the efforts of others. I can see why he was such a fine Marine, and I would concur with all of those who say that he would certainly have been the Commandant of the Marine Corps if his career continued to progress the way it was. Remarkable quality to motivate people and the kind of guy who would talk to somebody and say, "Okay, now let's charge. You and me are all going to charge."

Paul Stillwell: Why did he choose the Marine Corps? Do you know?

Admiral Trost: No I don't. I don't know what sent him in that area. Bill had been an all-state football player and a superb tennis player. Liked outdoor activities; that may well have been the driving factor. I don't know what specific motivation it was, but I know it was something he decided on fairly early.

Paul Stillwell: Well, all of this was really a recruiting tour for the Marine Corps and aviation and such. Were you swayed in any direction?

Admiral Trost: Well, no I really wasn't. I had at one time thought I would like to be a naval aviator, but by the time that summer training took place, I already knew that I had an eye defect which would keep me from flying for the Navy, and I could have been an Air Force pilot. I had a defect that showed up only when my eyes were dilated and they did certain tests. What I had was over-accommodation. I used to read 20-15 routinely. It was because my eyes were over accommodating for muscle weakness, and I'm nearsighted and have been for a number of years, as a result of that. So, even though it was interesting, I knew I wouldn't be doing it. And in the time with the Marines, we were exposed to amphibious operations. I would not have any problem with that, because

---

* Lieutenant Colonel William G. Leftwich, USMC, who was subsequently killed in Vietnam in November 1970. The destroyer *Leftwich* (DD-984) was named in his honor.

the Marines to me did the same kind of outdoor activity that I enjoyed as a Boy Scout and on the farm, and it didn't look bad at all. But I was more intrigued by shipboard life than I was by sleeping in the mud. I guess that's it, more than anything else.

Paul Stillwell: Why was Eglin included? Was that because a number of people from class were going to the Air Force?

Admiral Trost: Twenty-five percent of our class went to the Air Force, and that was pre-ordained. It was not mandatory but there were more than 25% volunteers, so they had no trouble filling that quota. But I don't know that. The motivation I thought was to introduce us to the Air Force, and as I said, they had this huge static display set up for us which introduced different types of Air Force airplanes. I think it was their shot in the recruiting pitch, because it was an aviation summer. Everything else was naval aviation-oriented. That portion of the summer was a very pleasant one for us, because my group traveled in two of these—we used to call them flot wings—fleet logistics air wings. We had two multi-engine airplanes, and they hauled us around. They were with us the entire time, and it was very pleasant. There was a lot of social activity, a lot of social interface. In Jacksonville at the air station they put us in a barracks which were separated by a swimming pool from the WAVES barracks, and so every afternoon we had lots of company out at the pool—wasn't all bad. They had parties for us in the officers' clubs in every one of these places where we went, and they were quite pleasant. Social functions in places like Memphis were one of the country clubs where a number of I guess they were civilian leadership who had Navy affiliation were members and they had a very, very nice reception for us.

The period aboard the *Roosevelt* at sea was non-motivational for me, other than learning some of the carrier aviation, because they lost a couple of pilots in the process. They had an unusual series of accidents, and of course that puts a damper on thing. Some of the people who were very much inclined toward aviation saying, "Do I really want to do this? By gosh, that looks kind of dangerous out there." Kept reminding us that it was really an anomaly, and it was. The safety we have today is far superior with a higher-performance airplane than it was then.

Paul Stillwell: There seem to be some people who just have an almost inherent desire to fly and love of flying. I guess you didn't come equipped with that.

Admiral Trost: I don't think it looked interesting to me, but I didn't have that absolute, you know, you've got to do this. I had an opportunity to go up in an airplane when I was about 16 years old with my next-door neighbor who had been an Army Air Forces pilot during World War II. And there was a small airfield across the river in a place called Meramac, Missouri, that had received a bunch of Army single-engine observation airplanes. They had a bunch of Piper Cubs over there and he had this airplane that had been used in the Army, and my neighbor used to go over there on weekends to fly, just to fly around. He invited me to join him one weekend and we flew all over. We buzzed the cornfields near home, and I thought that was pretty great. He took us out over the Mississippi River about 2,000 feet and started to set this airplane on its side and did a very tight circle with it. I looked down and thought, "Oh, gee, if I fall down I'm sure going to hit that water down there."

But I really enjoyed that, and then we had our introduction second-class year to the N3Ns, the Yellow Perils, over there at the naval air facility, and that was rather pleasant. The company officers and the people stationed at the Naval Academy, the instructors who were qualified pilots getting their flight time in they did it in part by taking us up in the air and introducing us to those airplanes. We got to take them off and land them, and they were fairly docile if you just followed directions. I must say that wasn't something that would have stimulated me to become an aviator, because it was like flying a rock. But it was a good introduction.

Paul Stillwell: One of your classmates who, like you, became a submariner was Brad Mooney.[*] Did you know him as a midshipman?

Admiral Trost: Yeah, I did.

Paul Stillwell: What do you recall of him?

---

[*] Midshipman James Bradford Mooney Jr., USN, later a rear admiral.

Admiral Trost: Oh, very congenial, very jovial. Guy that enjoyed having fun.

Paul Stillwell: Well, he had a lot of respect when he was board chairman at the Naval Institute.

Admiral Trost: Yeah. I knew Brad well. We marched to a lot of classes together.

Paul Stillwell: Well, I guess the culmination of all of this is the graduation and the payoff for all this effort that you put in for four years. What are your recollections of the graduation and the events leading up to it?

Admiral Trost: Well, one has this tremendous feeling of accomplishment as you approach graduation. I think it's true of whether standard college graduation or graduation from the Naval Academy. The feeling of finally having completed what you had set out to do. Sort of a sense of loss right toward the tail end, realizing there are people you are never going to see again and you come from this very close-knit society. You go out, and you don't yet have the appreciation for the fact that you are going to have a lifelong relationship with many of them and that they are in many respects are the people with whom you will have your closest personal associations as well as your professional associations. One of the things that I think that is probably the greatest value of the academy is the personal association that you carry away with you. My kids, one is a Naval Academy graduate. Two are graduates of civilian universities, and one was an attendee, but not a graduate. But one of the things they noted over the years in observing us is this close relationship and this natural liaison that exists among people who were classmates at the Naval Academy or acquaintances over there, and it's something that those who graduate from civilian universities don't feel and don't have. They don't have that sense of institutional loyalty or certainly that large sense of camaraderie that we were able to carry away.

Paul Stillwell: And it's reinforced by the fact that so many graduates go into the same business.

Admiral Trost: That's right. That's right. When I look today at the people who are the leadership element in our class alumni business, our affairs, it is in many respects people that have been close friends for many, many years. You could almost say that there are those that who have consistently taken on leadership roles, service roles. They just seem to be the same people who are always the volunteers to go out and do things and they do it well.

Paul Stillwell: That June week is a lot of pomp and ceremony at a place that has a lot of it to begin with. What value does that have?

Admiral Trost: Oh, I think it's a chance to show off a little bit to families. The place you have, where you've been, what you've been doing, how you can do it. I think the pomp and circumstance adds to the excitement of the occasion and to the thrill of graduation. The graduation ceremony itself, as a spectator I can say it was awfully long. As a participant under a slightly different system, it was long, and there was a great feeling of accomplishment and also that sense of, "My God, it's over," and here you are about to enter on a brand-new world on your own. But it was a graduation not only from a university environment but into the real world of adult life. So it was quite an experience.

Paul Stillwell: Did your parents come out from Illinois for the graduation?

Admiral Trost: My parents came and my younger sister came out there for the entire period. Of course, it's a thrill there, especially if you are one of the people receiving awards. Your parents are out there, and you see the look on their face, and they look at you.

Paul Stillwell: It's intriguing to think that they were then pretty close to the same people they were four years earlier, and you were vastly different.

Admiral Trost: That's right, you really were. My parents were very proud of the fact that I had that opportunity to go to the Naval Academy, and I did well while I was there. It was great pleasure for me to be able to make them feel that way. They felt very strongly about the value of an education, which neither one of them had much of an opportunity for.

Paul Stillwell: Well any other things to add about the Naval Academy—either specifics or some broad generalization?

Admiral Trost: Well, I would make one broad generalization. I repeat something that I've said to many people. If I were to look at any one aspect or period of my life, that period probably influenced me more than any other single period. There were instances and other educational opportunities where people influenced me very considerably, but the Naval Academy, the influence of that institution for the standards and what it stands for, I think made a greater influence on me than any single element. I feel a sense of loyalty and real love for that place, despite the fact that I was never one to say, "Gee, I really want to be a naval officer. I really want to go to the Naval Academy." Just quite a hold on me. I still get a thrill when I walk into Memorial Hall.[*] I still have the sense of awe that I had when I first walked into that place. I have been in it many, many times, but it's always been a special place for me. I walk into the middle of the Bancroft Hall rotunda and I can't help but just look up and look around and Lord knows how many times I've been in there. So, it's a feeling for a place that's very, very special. When I look back on it, I think I've told a number of people in response to this, "Gee, you must have always have been a naval officer. You must always have wanted to be CNO."

My answer is "No and no." I've told several civilians I became a naval officer by accident, and they give me a puzzled look. They can't quite figure out how that could possibly be. How could be a naval officer, and how could you stay in the Navy unless that's what you always wanted to do?

Paul Stillwell: Well, and that's part of what the Naval Academy tries to accomplish and those first years in the fleet—to sell this as a career.

Admiral Trost: Yeah, well now I've told an awful lot of young people over the years that when I interview somebody for as a Naval Academy candidate—now I'm on the screening committee for Congresswoman Morella, who is the congresswoman from this

---

[*] Memorial Hall is a large, ornate space in Bancroft Hall, the Naval Academy dormitory.

district.[*] But I have over the years talked to a lot of young people, counseled young people and I've never been a proponent of this philosophy that you have to want to be a career military officer to go to a military academy. As a matter of fact, I found that many of the people who say, "Well, I really want to be a career military officer," but they didn't know what they were talking about. I would rather see the individual who goes and says, "I will serve that period of time which I'm required to pay back as I evaluate what I'm seeing. If it's for me and I'm for them, then I will be there." That is really what gives you the people, and they perform.

Paul Stillwell: And, in your case, it obviously was for you.

Admiral Trost: It was for me. I didn't know it at the time. But I think it takes a certain motivation and dedication to be successful at the Naval Academy—be successful meaning complete the four years. And if you don't have that, it's not a wise idea to stick around. As a matter of fact, I upset at least one set of parents by telling their youngster who was at NAPS prior to entering the Naval Academy, which they dearly wanted, that I thought that based on his feelings and his observation and his reaction he would be better off getting out as early as he possibly could and get on with his civilian education.[†] He did, and he's been very successful, very happy with him, but they weren't very happy with me at the time for that advice, because the father was saying, "Damn it, you stay here and make it work." That would have been a major mistake. The young fellow would admit to me, but not to his father, that he was there because his parents wanted him to be and not what he wanted to do at all. That kind of individual is not going to be successful at the Naval Academy and would be a lousy naval officer.

Paul Stillwell: Well, I thank you for a fine interview, and I look forward to the next one.

Admiral Trost: I look forward to that.

---

[*] Constance A. Morella, a Republican from Maryland, served in the House of Representatives from 3 January 1987 to 3 January 2003.
[†] NAPS – Naval Academy Prep School.

Interview Number 3 with Admiral Carlisle A. H. Trost, U.S. Navy (Retired)

Place: Admiral Trost's home in Potomac, Maryland

Date: Thursday, 19 September 1991

Paul Stillwell: Admiral, last time we pretty much concluded talking about your experiences at the Naval Academy. After we finished up, you mentioned something about your association with Captain Otie Gregg—if you could put that on the record, please.

Admiral Trost: Captain Gregg was a department head at the Naval Academy in my latter stages there.[*] Otis Gregg was a naval aviator. He went from the Naval Academy, as I recall, to command *Princeton*.[†] At the time he was there, he lived in one half of one of the large sets of quarters adjacent to the commandant's house. Captain Gregg had two nieces, the Harvey sisters, who were resident with him and his wife at the time. They were quite an attraction for the midshipmen. So Jean and Joan were the targets of a lot of the mids who were looking for pretty girls to date, and I dated Jean for a period of time. I got to know the Greggs quite well as a result.

Paul Stillwell: That's how your association started, through the niece?

Admiral Trost: That's how the association started, and then we maintained contact by letter while he was the commanding officer of the *Princeton*. Then I saw them again when they settled down in the Virginia Beach area. I think it's out in the Great Neck area of Virginia Beach.

Paul Stillwell: What do you remember about the association from your time as a midshipman?

Admiral Trost: Well, he was always, of course, as any department head there, a fearsome individual. Also a senior Navy captain, graying hair—but also a very pleasant demeanor. He was quite a pleasant gentleman, a very enjoyable man to sit and talk to. He would take

---

[*] Captain Otis C. Gregg, USN, head of the department of aviation.
[†] Captain Gregg commanded the aircraft carrier *Princeton* (CVA-37) 18 May 1953 to 15 February 1954.

time to sit in the living room and chitchat with the midshipmen who were gathered over there. There were generally more midshipman than there were nieces in his case to go on a date, but he'd sit and talk, tell us about the Navy. He would tell sea stories. Very pleasant gentleman. His wife was a very warm, cordial individual. It was always very pleasant. It was a very homey environment and one we enjoyed, because we would go over on Saturday or Sunday afternoon and just sit around, relax and have a Coke and chit-chat with them, chit-chat with the girls.

Paul Stillwell: There was a Gary Cooper movie that came out around that time called *Task Force*, in which Cooper was a naval aviator at the academy and trying to recruit people for naval aviation.* Did Captain Gregg do that?

Admiral Trost: I think all the naval aviators were good recruiters over there. They always looked to try to capture some of the best of the students, as well as the best of the athletes, for the naval aviation program. I can't say that Captain Gregg overtly worked on it, but he was certainly a role model who would have attracted a lot of people. And it was that role model influence, I think, that affected many of us. I mentioned in our prior session the fact that Lando Zech was my company officer my last two years and as a submariner was so impressive to so many people that a number of the first classmen in my graduating company actually went into the submarine force. I attribute that, in large part, to his influence as a submariner.

Paul Stillwell: So in your case, his influence was stronger than Captain Gregg's.

Admiral Trost: His influence was stronger, but I also had the disadvantage of not having eyes that qualified for the naval aviation physical exam, so it was an easy choice. Would I have gone into aviation otherwise? I really don't know.

Paul Stillwell: Another thing you mentioned when we were talking last time was a refuge you had out in the town of Annapolis. What did that consist of?

---

* Gary Cooper, Jane Wyatt, and naval aviator/actor Wayne Morris starred in the 1949 Warner Brothers film *Task Force* about the development of naval aviation and its association with the Naval Academy.

Admiral Trost: Well, it was actually a pretty light basement, look out the windows, had an outside entrance that was rented to a group of us in my company at the Naval Academy. It was sort of a place to come when we had liberty in the afternoon or on weekends and a place where the owner had several spare refrigerators in the basement in which we could keep soft drinks or our beer, which was prohibited at that time—or the consumption was prohibited inside a seven-mile limit. It was a place we could take dates, listen to music, watch TV, watch football games, generally relax. Sort of the treasured spot by most of the first classmen in my company, who used it to enjoy things before or after a game or an athletic event. Also a place to just go out and relax, let off steam.

Paul Stillwell: Did the Naval Academy have any view toward places of this sort?

Admiral Trost: I believe they were probably considered out of bounds and non-regulation.

Paul Stillwell: Well, you told me also that your classmates protected you when you were chosen as brigade commander.

Admiral Trost: When I became the brigade commander, they said, "Hey, this won't do. If we ever got caught, it would certainly not be good to have the brigade commander listed on this." So they basically disowned me and invited me to take my membership away. It was a non-controversial thing on their part and non-discriminatory also. They simply wanted to protect me—to make sure that if anything happened, I wouldn't be one of them.

Paul Stillwell: Well, could there have been self-interest on their part to protect them?

Admiral Trost: Well, perhaps so. I don't think my continuing membership would have been detrimental to their interests, but it would have been to mine.

Paul Stillwell: Anything else about the Naval Academy?

Admiral Trost: Not that I can think of offhand. I think back, and all of us were influenced very heavily, I think by a place like the Naval Academy. I certainly was. I think the standards they instilled were things that guided many of us through our lives; it certainly maintained my interest. After that first year of saying, "Well, I'm going to do away with the rigors of plebe year," which can be as much of an annoyance as beneficial in some cases—from that point on, I found it a rather enjoyable place to be. I would've liked to have had more freedom. I think today's midshipman are fortunate to be treated more like the mature college students they are. I think there was a disadvantage in our time there—for some people, in that you were on your own, yet you weren't. You were in sort of a protected society, but I think they taught very fine standards of discipline. The education was good, but could have been a lot better at that time, because everybody taking the same course without any recognition of prior accomplishments academically resulted in sort of the lowest common denominator form of college education. We were well capable, well equipped to go out and join the Navy and being able to pull our weight.

I was, for example, certainly qualified to go out to become a destroyer navigator.[*] Fortunately, I had a very fine chief quartermaster who made sure I stayed out of trouble. We were also equipped to go out, in the case of destroyers, and take an immediate billet, an engineering billet, and know what the equipment looked like, what its parameters were, how it should operate. So I think we were well equipped from a professional standpoint to go out and enter the Navy.

As we've seen, as the academic rigors have increased in the Naval Academy's curriculum, we've seen the need for the subsequent training of officers in professional skills after they're commissioned. There were two reasons for that: one is the people are better fitted academically and less fitted, I think, in professional traits, but, in part because of the wide variety of ships or aircraft to which they're assigned. Also, the increase in complexity of today's Navy has dictated some further professional training for everyone going to the various platforms.

---

[*] Ensign Trost's first ship was the destroyer *Robert A. Owens* (DD-827). She was a *Gearing*-class destroyer that served as a test platform to evaluate the hunter-killer concept for antisubmarine warfare. Her keel was laid 29 October 1945; she was not commissioned until 5 November 1949. She was originally armed with two Weapon Able ASW rocket launchers, four 3-inch guns, and four 21-inch torpedo tubes. She was reclassified DDK-827 on 28 January 1948 and as DDE-827 on 4 March 1950.

There was a time, of course, when as now all naval aviators went through basic flight training, they have a lot more schools they have to attend now to be able master all the complex equipment that they have. Submariners always had the six-month Submarine School. With the advent of nuclear power, the one year's nuclear power training program took such a bite of available time from a junior officer that the submarine course itself was reduced in length, but now, instead of focusing on all aspects of submarining, it focuses on the ship-driving aspects. You learn the principles of the submarine as opposed to the power plant, which was already something that the young officer had had extensive grounding in.

In the case of the surface Navy, they came somewhat belatedly into the rest of the Navy's—I shouldn't say standards, I should say practices. Basically in the late '70s the Navy established a requirement for an officer going to a surface ship also to go through a basic surface warfare officers course, which I think has been a tremendous improvement. The surface Navy's professionalism increased markedly in the last two decades, in large part because of that requirement and because they imposed qualification requirements on their officers, very much akin to those of the submarine force has historically used. Not only is the professionalism higher, the sense of professionalism is much higher as a result.

Paul Stillwell: Part of that is to make up for the fact that that training wasn't provided as much as it was prior to commissioning.

Admiral Trost: That is correct. I found, when I came aboard a destroyer as a junior officer, I had the advantage of having had two training cruises aboard destroyers, so I was familiar with the basic ship, plus the various courses at the Naval Academy made you very familiar with the engineering department, fire control, weapons systems, operations, and ability to navigate, and so it was relatively easy to qualify as a watch stander, both as an officer of the deck and as a CIC watch officer at the time, and as an engineering officer of the watch for most of us coming out from that background.[*]

---

[*] CIC – combat information center.

Paul Stillwell: Well, you could expect to find a 600-pound steam plant almost anywhere you went.

Admiral Trost: That's right, any place you went. Now, many of the officers from commissioning sources, at that time predominantly OCS and contract ROTC, had had less grounding in some of the professional subjects, and they were, unfortunately, pretty well left on their own.* It was sort of up to them to get to know what they had to know. Today's more formal program, I think, is a very definite assist to commanding officers in running better ships. Skills and practices were basically assumed. You walked aboard, you were assumed to be competent as a division officer, competent as a watch officer trainee, if you will, capable of navigating a ship, things of that nature. Today we have a much more professional approach to those qualifications.

Paul Stillwell: Well, I think perhaps another change is that the Navy was more "all encompassing" in a man's life back then too. Fewer people were married, so a lot more people lived on board ship, and that was the whole thing. There wasn't that much freedom overall in the Navy.

Admiral Trost: We did just a quick mental survey about a little over year ago when the first ship I was on had a reunion of people who served on it. The predominant number of people who served on that ship that came to the reunion, were those with whom I had served in my relatively brief time on it. But one of the things that we found interesting was that we counted up who was married and who was not. The six officers who attended from the group of 19 that were aboard during my time, all were married or got married in that time frame. But we had, I would say two or three, probably three other officers, exclusive of the captain and the executive officer, the rest were bachelors. Half of the wardroom, basically, was not married.

Among the crew we decided about one in six was a married man, and this was very evident. I spent nearly my first year aboard that ship as a bachelor officer. After hours, the bulk of the people were aboard ship. Having a 6:00 o'clock or 5:45 A.M.

---

* OCS – officer candidate school.

reveille didn't disturb too many people. It was having an early morning call to quarters, if it was before, let's say 7:30 or quarter to 8:00, that worked its hardship on the married people. They had to get up and come in, but then traffic was much lighter in the Norfolk area for that very reason at that time. The great majority of the people were bachelors, went on liberty together, so in some respects the social cohesiveness of crews was probably greater than it is today.

Paul Stillwell: In a sense, the Navy back then treated the enlisted men like children. And in a sense they did the midshipmen.

Admiral Trost: They really did. They were young fellows. They were given a pipe-frame bunk, food on board the ship, and that was it. Of course, they also weren't paid very much; nobody was.

Paul Stillwell: So they couldn't afford to be married.

Admiral Trost: Well, they couldn't afford to be married and couldn't afford to do one heck of a lot. Pay might mean liberty money for the next two weeks or something of that nature. But it certainly didn't mean a lot of money to invest. The young guys would go out and buy a car, and their car payments would frequently totally strap their ability to do much of anything else.

Paul Stillwell: What specifically led you from the Naval Academy to the *Robert A. Owens*?

Admiral Trost: Well, we, as they do now, chose preference numbers for order of selection of available ships.

Paul Stillwell: Essentially a lottery.

Admiral Trost: A lottery. Of the 925 who graduated, my number was either in the high 600s or low 700s; I don't recall exactly. So I had a long wait, and even though I had determined that I wanted to go to a destroyer, because I thought that offered more opportunity for responsible assignment early in a career than a large ship would, I had my hopes dashed when I saw the destroyers rapidly disappearing. Of course, out of that first

700 or whatever they were that preceded me, there were also 225 who chose Air Force and a large number of the men—I think we had roughly 100 or just over 100—who became Marine officers and many of them, of course, were also off. So, in a sense, I was probably roughly in the middle or just past the middle of those who actually went into the Navy unrestricted line. At the time, we had the watches, things were chosen. Somebody was keeping score and writing down what was there and what had already been taken.

At the time my number came up, there were three destroyer-type ships available, remaining; *Robert A. Owens* was one. She and *Carpenter* were unique in that they were built as DDKs (hunter-killer destroyers) for ASW work in 1949 on a long-hull destroyer design. They were different in that they had no 5-inch guns; they had open twin-mount 3-inch/50s forward and aft to replace the old mount 51 and 53. They had a Weapon Alfa—Weapon Able, it was called at that time—which was an antisubmarine rocket. It fired about a 12-inch rocket with a rotatable mount and a big tube sticking out of it that shot patterns of three depth bombs, basically out to ranges, I recall, of about 2,000 yards, maybe a little less than that. And we had trainable Hedgehogs for antisubmarine warfare, and we had some 20-millimeter guns which would be mounted on the bridge wings, and that was it.* So she was lightly armed from a standpoint of a combatant compared to her sisters and yet much more heavily equipped for antisubmarine warfare, including prototype computers and underwater battery fire-control systems.

Paul Stillwell: Did she have better sonar than the others?

Admiral Trost: She had better sonar. What resulted in my choosing her, as opposed to the other two, was, as I remember, one was in yard overhaul, and one was about to enter. *Owens* was going to deploy just a few months after my graduation. That intrigued me much more than going into a shipyard overhaul and staying ashore, because I thought the opportunities to qualify were certainly much more limited if you were sitting on land than when you go to sea. So I opted for *Owens* on that basis.

---

* Hedgehog, developed in World War II, was a British-designed spigot mortar that fired its weapons out ahead of the attacking ship. It was the first ASW weapon that could be fired while the surface ship remained in sonar contact with the target. Its name came from the collection of spigots in the launcher; they stuck up like porcupine quills.

Paul Stillwell: I see by the log that your first skipper was Commander Dawson.* What do you recall of him?

Admiral Trost: My first contact with George Dawson was a phone call I received. We were granted 30 days' graduation leave before reporting to our ships. Some of our class was directed to ships that were deployed off Korea, and some of those, in fact, had their leave curtailed so they could catch available transportation to head west and join their ships. Since my ship was to be home-ported in Norfolk, I went back home to Illinois after having stayed on the East Coast for a couple of days for a wedding of a good friend of mine down in the Norfolk area, expecting to have another three and a half weeks roughly of graduation leave.

I'd been out there probably two weeks roughly, when I received a phone call one evening, and the voice said, "This is George Dawson, your commanding officer." That was my first contact with him. I thought it was rather unusual. I thought how nice of him to call me and welcome me to the ship. He said, "You start school in Key West Monday morning," this being Thursday night.

I thought, "Gee that's unusual. I still have leave left. How can he do that?"

He said, "You're going to be the antisubmarine warfare officer. I noticed in your background sheet that you played in a band, and people who have played music have good ears for sonar, so you're going to be the ASW officer."

I thought, "What a wonderful way to choose somebody."

He said, "You've got to go through an eight-week course so that you're back before the ship deploys."

So I rogered that. I was told to report in via the ship to pick up my orders, the ship being in port in Norfolk. I got off the phone, told my parents about that, and my mother said, "Can he do that?" I had the same question, but I figured he probably could, so I decided to comply. So, early the next morning, I packed my gear and tossed stuff into my

---

* Commander George Ely Dawson, USN, commanded *Robert A. Owens* 12 June 1952 to 24 October 1953.

car, which I had bought a few months earlier, a used car, and hit the road for the East Coast. I got to Washington late Saturday afternoon and stopped and spent the evening at Pauline's parents' home to see her and then drove down to Norfolk on Sunday morning. Reported to the ship at about 10:00 in the morning and was met by Ensign Harvey who had been aboard a week.[*] He was an old-timer. He was in the duty section. He said, "I'm supposed to meet you and take you over to the airport. You've got a flight at 1:00 o'clock. The exec would like to talk to you, but he's out at the beach with his family."

"Well," I said, "okay. What kind of uniforms do I need down there?"

He said, "Oh, not very much, just your summer stuff." So I pulled my summer things out. I left a footlocker full of uniforms, including my blues, in the trunk of my car. Ensign Harvey told me that he was advised to take my car and park it at the exec's house where it would be safe. I reluctantly gave him my keys, and I got on a flight to Jacksonville, Florida. Upon arriving in Jacksonville I found that the flight to Key West wasn't until Tuesday, which wouldn't get me there for my Monday morning class. So I got to a bus station, got a bus to Miami, another bus to Key West. I arrived at Key West about 5:00 o'clock in the morning of the day I was to report in prior to 8:00. I did report in and then spent the next eight weeks down in Key West as an ASW officer trainee. In barracks at that time, BOQs, were the old frame World War II type with the screens, no windows, on the outside. The fans kept us sleeping in cool sweat, rather than hot sweat. But we had the advantage of a swimming pool right across the street. I did have an opportunity to go to Havana several times during that time frame, which I found enjoyable. Havana, in that day, was not Castro's Cuba.[†] One of the things that Mr. Batista had in his Havana was a lot of tourism and a lot of amenities for tourists.

Paul Stillwell: What specifically do you remember?

---

[*] Ensign Andrew C. Harvey, USN.
[†] Fulgencio Batista was the dictator and military leader who was President of Cuba from 10 October 1940 to 10 October 1944 and from 10 March 1952 to 1 January 1959. His government was overthrown by rebels under the leadership of Fidel Castro.

Admiral Trost: We'd catch rides on minesweepers. The minesweepers and the PCs that were assigned to Key West seemed to get over to Cuba frequently on weekends.* It was about a 90-mile sail, as I recall. They would shove off shortly after noon on Friday and then shove off again Sunday evening to come back. We could sign up for rides on those, and that's the way a friend of mine and I went over on two occasions. What I remember was staying in the Hotel Nacional, which was a tall, beautiful place and real oasis of an area around the swimming pool. I think our special rates were $10.00 a night because we were military, and they gave discounts to U.S. military.

We rented a car at the behest of my buddy, who had been there once before me. We basically rented a car and driver, who was ours for the weekend. I think he cost us $5.00 a day. He was an American expatriate who had come over to Cuba in the early '30s and knew the area well. He was a little disappointed in that we seemed to have a lack of interest in finding prostitutes and were more interested in seeing some of the nightclubs and what they were like. But you could go to a nightclub, which with their gambling establishment. The set prices were so low that any standard tourist could go and really have an enjoyable dinner and a few drinks for a very, very low price. So we basically had a sightseeing and fun weekend. This guy took us all over the Havana environs and went sightseeing to the castle—Morro Castle, I guess it was—across the harbor. We got to know the place quite well.

When I went back later to Cuba as a submarine officer for a weekend visit, I felt very much the old hand, because I knew my way around so well. That was really the highlight, I think, of the time in Cuba. It's that and about midway through my ASW course, I went to sea on *Corporal*, which was one of the diesel submarines based in Key West.† I took the opportunity to just go out on an overnight with them while my fellow officers were up above in surface combatants trying to find him. I must admit that during that time, I came to the conclusion that maybe the guy under the water, at that point in time, had a better advantage than the guy up above. I also was impressed very much by

---

* PCs – patrol craft.
† USS *Corporal* (SS-346) was a *Balao*-class submarine commissioned 9 November 1945. She underwent GUPPY conversion in 1947-48.

the camaraderie of the submarine crews—the closeness and the informal, yet very disciplined nature of their activity. That may have been something of an impetus for submarine duty also, because I remember telling Pauline when she and some girlfriends of hers came down for a visit while I was down there, that I was really sort of interested in submarines. After looking at one from topside, she thought that it was certainly not the thing to do. [Laughter]

Paul Stillwell: What do you remember about the course itself?

Admiral Trost: The course itself very much attuned toward both the physics of sound and the philosophy of construction of systems. Systems were pretty basic then compared to what they are now, as was our knowledge of underwater sound transmission.

Paul Stillwell: And still a pretty short range too.

Admiral Trost: Very short range. Active sonar, short range. No or little emphasis on any passive listening, primarily active sonar with ranges 800 to 2,000 yards max. If you've got a 4,000-yard range on a contact because sound conditions were such that you could get it, it was quite a rarity. You could literally go right over the top of a submarine pinging away and not know he was there. Under certain sound conditions, you still can't for that matter. It was a different world. We came out well qualified in the operation and utilization of that time frame's sound systems. I did not have an introduction into the kind of systems on *Owens*. I did on the sonar, but *Owens* had an underwater battery fire control system, Mark 100, built by Librascope, one of two of a kind or one of three of a kind, I've forgotten which. Built as prototypes with no spare parts support, which was a rather interesting challenge.

I still recall I had one fire control technician named Paul Thompson. He was a young FTSN who made third class during my time on board, one of the brightest young men I ever knew. Paul subsequently left the Navy, got his college degree, I think got an advanced degree, and went to work for Librascope as an engineer. I ran into him once just a few years back. He did quite well for himself. Paul was ingenious in his ability to make that system operate. We had an entire bank of automatic switches across the after bulkhead of the fire control system room. It was a control console, really two control consoles, on which one could set up the system for the kind of attack and the kind of weapons to be used, simply by positioning several selector switches. When one did that, all of the automatic switches behind were supposed to roll and position everything and provide power to the right equipment, put everything in the right mode. It was so unreliable that we would have to go through and manually check and frequently position switches, as a matter of fact, normally position switches.

Paul Stillwell: Were these just bugs from the newness of it?

Admiral Trost: It was a combination of bugs from the newness but primarily equipment failures, where there was no support. For example, there were small positioning relays that we were supposed to pick up. The relay itself looked very much like—as a matter of fact, I think some were spools of thread, except the windings were copper instead of thread. Of course, the spool itself was metallic, and it was supposed to pick up on the relay, which had a multi-pull switch on the other end of it, which would then line things up. When they didn't pick up, they didn't pick up, and they didn't roll. Some of these were designed to roll, rotary switches as opposed to linear. One of the things that Paul Thompson did was he took these things and he rebuilt them. You would see him there with a little spool of copper wire rewinding and cleaning with toothbrushes and doing all sorts of things. We had, at any given time, I'd say roughly two-thirds of the automatic portion of the system operational. Never the same two-thirds, which meant it was quite a chore.

Paul Stillwell: So it was an electro-mechanical system?

Admiral Trost: It was an electro-mechanical, fully analog system, and the other part— the other unforgettable memory of that system was the spaces in which they were located. We were deep down in the bowels of the ship, forward of amidships. We were basically directly under the bridge, but down in the bottom of the ship with just one either storeroom or void space beneath us—storeroom or tank space, I guess.

The sonar room was just forward of us athwartships, and the two spaces were air-cooled for equipment comfort with a ventilation system, a fan that was just a constantly recirculating system. After several hours of smokers being there, with the ship being buttoned up for general quarters, the air was so rancid that people got sick who had never gotten seasick before. As a matter of fact, I got seasick in that space twice at general quarters going out of port in the Mediterranean when there was just a bare swell. It was simply the poor quality of the air.

The guys were young; this was the time when the Navy had let many people go after Korea.[*] It was letting people go during my tour there. So we had a lot of very good, smart young people doing a good job, but very little mid-grade experience, because people were not staying around. We had a lot of good senior petty officers for supervision well through my first deployment, because they were people with World War II background that had been recalled for Korea and had been in the Navy on average three years and were really quite sharp and very capable, but we lost most of those after our deployment, after the Korean War wound down.

Paul Stillwell: The typical stereotype has the young ensign going aboard and coming under the influence of a senior petty officer. Was that your case also?

Admiral Trost: That happened to me. I didn't come under the influence as soon as I should have, in all likelihood. I came aboard and was initially to be the ASW and sonar and third division officer, third division having the fire control technicians, the gunner's mates, everybody in the gunnery department, except for the deck hands in the first and second divisions. I was greeted when I came aboard in the passageway right outside the ship's office. There was a photo that had been published at graduation. It was a photo of me as the brigade commander standing with a sword salute at one of the parades during June Week.[†] Underneath it said, "our new Ensign!" I thought, "Whoops, behind the eight ball for starters."

---

[*] On 27 July 1953 negotiators for the United Nations and the Communist North Koreans signed an armistice agreement at Panmunjom, Korea, to end the Korean War. It took effect at 10:00 that same date.
[†] The photo appeared on page 20 of the September 1953 issue of *All Hands* magazine, published by the Bureau of Naval Personnel. It was in an article titled "White Hats Add a Ring of Blue."

But I found people generally receptive. We had seven new ensigns who came aboard within a few weeks of each other from various commissioning sources. I was the only Naval Academy graduate in that bunch. We had another seven ensigns from the preceding year's crop on board. We had about another four jaygees who were the "old hands," having been aboard two or three years. We later received a lieutenant who came aboard as gun boss. The exec was a newly promoted lieutenant commander and then Commander Dawson, the CO. So we had a relatively junior wardroom, relatively inexperienced, and yet the four jaygees were pretty heavy load carriers. A few of the ensigns eventually became people who'd start to carry their load.

But I was sort of secure in my knowledge that I knew a lot about this kind of ship, and I was buzzing along doing my job. The ship deployed two weeks after I got back from sonar school and went initially on a North Atlantic operation and then over to the Mediterranean for the balance of its deployment. I thought I was doing pretty well, because I was qualified as an officer of the deck within a matter of about two or three months of arrival. I was qualified on arrival as a CIC watch officer.

The ship's exec, Jerry Pounders, had been the previous engineering officer and had been a chief motor machinists' mate at the start of World War II and finished World War II as a lieutenant.[*] Not too very long after our arrival, I was told that he was not qualified to navigate, and therefore would be the navigator "in name" only. But I would be the navigator "in fact" as long as I listened to Chief Glasgow, the chief quartermaster, which I was smart enough to do. He was a gent I thought kind of an old grizzled hand at the time, but Glasgow probably had about 17 years in the Navy. Very professional. Sort of a glum personality—a droll personality is a better description. But a very fine Navy man and very helpful. I learned all sorts of techniques from him, just practical navigation techniques that I hadn't picked up before. He was superb.

Paul Stillwell: What about dealing with enlisted men? Did he give you some guidance in hat area too?

---

[*] Lieutenant Jerry K. Pounders, USN.

Admiral Trost: No, he did not. We didn't have too much problem in that division.

My problems came with the chief gunner's mate in third division, who was my senior petty officer, a gentleman named Czarcyki, who's retired now as an E-8 living up in New Jersey. Chief Czarcyki one morning, after I had been aboard a couple of months, told me at morning quarters that he would like to see me up in the gunnery shack after quarters. Our quarters were back on the 01 level aft, and the gunnery shack was just forward of the number-two stack, a little tiny cubicle that had a desk and a chair and bookshelves. So I followed him in, and he sat down on the desk and said, "Sit down," which I thought was rather a brusque way to treat an officer. So I sat down, because he seemed serious about it.

His opening words were, "One of us is going to have to go." It turned out that in his view I had been getting in his hair, doing many of his jobs, going around him directly to the senior petty officers on job assignments. I was hands on to the extent that I liked to be present when significant jobs were done, and if I had read the book and somebody else hadn't, I damn well intended to supervise, and he thought that I was cutting into his responsibilities. He reviewed with me, in a very nice way, the principles of leadership and the responsibilities of an officer and the role of a senior petty officer.

After I listened to him, I decided that, "Yep, you're right, Chief. I've been doing some things that you ought to be doing, including some of the reports that are really yours to do and give to me instead of mine to take and carry out." So we came to a meeting of the minds, and it was clear to me that if one of us had to go, it was probably going to have to be me, because I'd be the one who wasn't conforming to his desires, and he seemed to be rather well situated at the time. But it was extremely helpful and something that I have always found very useful. It's a story I've told many times, because I think he embodied the elements of practical leadership to a degree that few of us were able to appreciate as young officers.

Paul Stillwell: Well, did you both survive after that?

Admiral Trost: We both survived. I can't say we became good friends. We became good workers with a lot of respect for each other. I contacted him. I found him when I was Chief of Naval Operations early in my tour and wrote a letter to him. I wanted to get him to come to Washington if I could. He was a retired New Jerseyan and was never able to get down. But it was good to make contact with him and know that he was still around. He retired as a senior chief petty officer some years back, a very fine gentleman.

He and Chief Glasgow, the chief quartermaster, who was the assistant navigator, were probably two of the most solid petty officers I encountered in my time on that ship. But there were a number of good ones. We had a chief boiler technician named Larry, whom I saw last year at the reunion. Larry, when he retired from the Navy, became one of the fuel kings on the piers at the Naval Base Norfolk, so we got to see him a lot after that. I saw him when I was a submarine officer while he was refueling destroyers down there. He also was a very, very solid citizen. There were a number of people, again people I saw last year, Chief Carlson, who was a machinery repairman who was absolutely solid. Just very sound guy. We had DiPietro, who was a chief boatswain's mate, a native of Naples who joined the U.S. Navy long before World War II, his parents having come to this country. But DiPietro was just a good solid citizen. He took no guff from the young deck hands and had a lot of respect and really did his job extremely well.

Paul Stillwell: So the idea was that these are good people, let them do their jobs.

Admiral Trost: That's right. That's right. We had an interesting command environment in *Owens*. I think George Dawson had been commissioned from enlisted status—I don't recall what pay grade as a gunner's mate. He had served during World War II and made commander after the war.[*] He had previously had command of a DE prior to getting command of *Owens* and was the officer in charge of the sonar school in Key West, and that was an interesting path. Command of a DE to running that sonar school down there

[*] Dawson's date of rank as commander was 1 July 1949.

to one of the new DDEs. That was quite a plum assignment. Jack English, who succeeded him, followed the same path.*

So it was rather interesting. Dawson had a lot of good background. He was, in appearance, the epitome of the naval officer. In a set of service dress khakis he just looked like he walked out of a recruiting poster. He was a tall, well-built gentleman, graying temples, very nice-looking gent of very impressive, almost awesome appearance. I think he, in my evaluation, was grossly lacking in self-confidence. My first introduction other than the phone call was almost two weeks after I came back from Key West, when I was finally granted an audience and the opportunity to call on the captain. He did not eat in the wardroom. He ate in his cabin, so we didn't see him at meals.

Paul Stillwell: Was it because he was shy, perhaps?

Admiral Trost: I don't know. Either that or because he felt that it was his prerogative and his place.

Paul Stillwell: That's unusual for a destroyer.

Admiral Trost: Well, it is unusual. And, it's a practice that I have always, throughout my naval career, thought was the perfect way to basically avoid leadership responsibility by getting to know your people, on an other than a direct watch-standing basis. But Dawson was an interesting man. When he finally agreed to see me, his first words were to me, "You're a Naval Academy graduate. I don't like Naval Academy graduates and don't ever forget that." Well, that was a fine introduction. I don't remember any other substance from the conversation; it was very brief.

On the other hand, I have to say that he seemed to have a lot of confidence in me as a watch stander, because he had an interesting way of doing business. We got under way from Norfolk to go to Newport to pick up a staff. It was a destroyer flotilla staff, and Rear Admiral Whitey Taylor was the commander.† I had met him on one occasion

---

* Commander Jack Raymond English, USN, commanded the *Robert A. Owens* from 24 October 1953 to 29 November 1955.
† Rear Admiral Edmund B. Taylor, USN, Commander Destroyer Flotilla Two.

previously, because his son Ted was a classmate of mine.[*] Admiral Taylor and his staff came aboard, and they were going to be the screen commanders for the task group with which we were deploying. We went up to Newport; we came alongside a tender at anchorage. On our first pass, we slammed the side of the tender at a rather oblique angle and bent our forward jackstaff, which was higher than many, over about 60 degrees. We backed off and tried it again, and following our second collision, we got the lines over.

We then loaded the staff, which had been on board the tender—I think a total of 19 people all told—onto the ship. Most of us were immediately displaced from the berthing we'd enjoyed up to that point in time. The chief of staff, who was Captain Andy Nisewaner, who is retired and lives in Bethesda now.[†] Fine gentleman. He had, as I remember, three other officers aboard, and the balance were radiomen and operations-type enlisted personnel. *Owens* was outfitted with a group commander's cabin adjacent to the commanding officer's cabin. It also had two additional cabins on the additional 02 level on the ship, which was unusual on those classes. There were two large cabins, one of which the XO used, and the other was the chief of staff's cabin. So we had room for the chief of staff and for the flag officer, but the other lieutenant commanders basically bounced the rest of us downward a few steps. So most of the news guys like me ended up in a makeshift JO bunkroom that had been built back in the aft main deck torpedo room. It had, unfortunately, no toilet facilities, just a bunk and very limited storage space.

Dawson's ship handling came into question that day. I was up on the bridge, and I was surprised that, as junior officer of the deck, I was assigned to wear the JA phones. Normally, the JA was the command circuit. The phones would have been worn by junior enlisted man, because he was a phone talker and relayer, but Captain Dawson didn't trust enlisted personnel. Phone talkers of battle stations and sea detail in the surface Navy were always officers.

Paul Stillwell: Especially curious for a mustang that he wouldn't trust enlisted people.[‡]

---

[*] Captain Edmund B. Taylor Jr., USN, was later killed in a helicopter crash off Vietnam on 8 May 1972.
[†] Captain Terrell Andrew Nisewaner, USN.
[‡] "Mustang" is Navy slang for a former enlisted man or woman who has risen through the ranks to become an officer.

Admiral Trost: Absolutely, but he did not. I learned that he was a lousy ship handler. He was a screamer, and those characteristics remained with him. We did leave from there. We deployed, and we were off in the north Atlantic for just shy of a month in a NATO exercise. It was in the vicinity of Iceland, my recollection being to the southeast and north of Iceland primarily, where we operated against another group. At one point in time, we had a British battleship, several British cruisers and a British carrier, with a U.S. carrier task force. We had no battleships with us. We had several heavy cruisers and some light AAW cruisers with us.[*]

It was quite an exercise, but it was hampered by very, very bad weather.[†] We went for a period of three or four days being unable to cook anything other than soup in the big deep kettles, and we subsisted on soup and crackers for that period of time. We would have our soup and crackers in the wardroom—not at the table but sitting wedged against the bulkhead somewhere with your feet spread out so that you wouldn't roll with the ship. I remember watching *Bennington*, one of two carriers that was with us, lose airplanes. I was up on the bridge and was the JOOD one afternoon when *Bennington* took an unusually heavy roll, and about five airplanes went sliding off the deck, went over the side.[‡] It was very difficult for them in flight ops of any kind. We then went on into the Mediterranean, and our initial port of call was—

Paul Stillwell: They're all here on this sheet.

Admiral Trost: Okay, Palermo, Sicily. Okay, they're all here. Well, I can go through here, and I can also pick up some of these other items here.

Paul Stillwell: I'd be interested in your recollections of Admiral Taylor too. He was a colorful destroyer veteran.

Admiral Trost: He was. I liked him because he was always calm. He was approachable. He'd chitchat. He liked to come out on the bridge, especially at night, and he'd chitchat with the bridge watches. Incidentally, the way I became a bridge watch early on—when I

---

[*] AAW – antiair warfare.
[†] This was Exercise Mariner in the North Atlantic in September 1953.
[‡] JOOD – junior officer of the deck.

came aboard I was told I was a qualified CIC watch officer, even though I hadn't been in that ship's CIC yet. But, again, I guess my Naval Academy training prepared me to do the job. And we had a first class electrician named Bennett who ran the CIC, who was just absolutely superb. He was extremely helpful. But I became the CIC watch officer, and then as we got under way from Newport, Captain Dawson started firing OODs and JOODs. The normal progression was when they were fired from the bridge, somebody else went up there, and they became members of the crypto board. Of course, cryptography was very much a manual operation at that time. We started with, I guess, Bob Cross, who was the communicator and had been the officer of the deck and was also the guy in charge of that board.[*] But he had two other JOs assigned to the crypto board.

By the time we'd been under way for about two weeks, the crypto board was nine officers, which was a pretty good chunk out of the wardroom at that time, because these were people being fired. I was in CIC, I can't tell you the time frame, but one day, only a few days out, I was told to go to the bridge and relieve So-and-so, who was the junior officer of the deck. He'd just been kicked off the bridge by the captain. I got up there and stood my watch and became the JOOD. I felt rather comfortable in that role. There was no big problem. I had been there, on the bridge as a watch stander, only a few days when the officer of the deck, on my watch, was thrown off the bridge by the captain and told to go up and wake up his relief. The captain left the bridge, and that left me.

I thought, "Well, I guess I'm the OOD. So I told the quartermaster that I had the bridge and the conn, and he said, "Roger that." About 30 minutes later, the relief OOD came up and relieved me and took the watch. Not too very long after that, I was designated qualified OOD, so my watch standing in CIC was rather foreshortened. I never made the crypto board, because by the time I got to the bridge he'd fired so many people off the bridge that there wasn't anybody left, and he couldn't afford to get rid of them anymore. But it was a rather interesting experience in watching the man operate.

Paul Stillwell: What kind of sins did these officers commit to get fired?

---

[*] Lieutenant (junior grade) Robert C. Cross, USN.

Admiral Trost: It could be any number of things. Not executing quickly enough when a signal was flashed. Being out of station. Those were the days—maybe we still do that in the surface Navy, although I don't know that as an observer—when it seemed that the watch officers, for example, some of Admiral Taylor's guys, specifically his lieutenant commander operations officer, had as the sole function checking the radar ranges and things and telling people that they were off station by 100 yards, which in heavy weather is easy to do. As a matter of fact, even in good weather, it was probably at the limits of the radar's ability to discriminate in that day. But if somebody called a signal and said your call sign station, that meant, "You're off station, buddy, get back on." The captain didn't like that. He thought that was a "black mark" on him. The guy responsible might get bounced off the bridge. Or an announcement might be goofed up by the man that passed it on the general announcing system, and the nearest officer, the junior officer of the deck or the officer of the deck, got bounced off the bridge. The captain would come out to the bridge and find something he didn't like and throw people off the bridge.

Paul Stillwell: Well, as a screen flagship, you were probably less off station than anybody.

Admiral Trost: We didn't reorient the formation very often except when the axis needed to be reoriented, so we had a relatively easy time.

Paul Stillwell: Because of his background was the captain pretty good at ASW tactics?

Admiral Trost: Fair. Fairly good, fairly good. I remember one day being on the bridge during an exercise. It was in the Mediterranean, and I was the officer of the deck. We were exercising. We knew there were submarines, U.S. and Italian, out there. We were down south of Taranto, and we were operating, and I remember somebody said we had a sonar contact: "Conn, sonar, I've got a contact." And the guy was about 800 yards off our bow. That's what I had been trained to do, so I immediately turned and executed an urgent depth charge attack on him. His bubble came up for marking purposes and then basically enveloped the green dye that we dropped over the fantail as we passed over the point.

The captain was absolutely delighted with that. That helped my stock rather considerably, but he himself was good. He also was very good at using his team. I know that when I was down below as the sonar supervisor in the underwater battery fire control center, he was good about taking the coaching from down below on where to go and recommended tactics and approach courses and all. He was good to work with in that sense. He was very much apart, though, from the wardroom and from the crew in essence. But a very impressive man in appearance all the time.

Paul Stillwell: How would you describe the morale in the ship?

Admiral Trost: Not bad, in part because there was a degree of, "Don't give a shit, I'm a short-timer." Most of our senior enlisted personnel were going to be leaving the ship at the end of that deployment, out of the Navy. They were the guys who had been recalled for Korea. A number of the officers this was back in the days where a contract ROTC officer had two years of active service obligation. A regular ROTC candidate had three years, and they had reserve commissions. With a reserve commission, they received a letter about six months in advance, not saying, "Would you like to stay in the Navy?" But, "Your release from active duty will occur on the following date." So there wasn't much career orientation in the way we handled our people at that time. So we had several of these two-year jaygees on board, who were good officers, who were going to be leaving also within a few months after the deployment. We had some of the other three-year guys who were also going to be leaving at the end of their third year. So it was rather a fascinating business.

A lot of people said, "Well, I'm going to be gone." And, besides that, they were looking forward to it. The Med cruises were fun in those days. We were at sea a fair amount of time, but we hit a lot of ports. When you were at sea, things were pretty busy. All night long the staffs would be rotating screens and doing other things just to keep people occupied. I frankly preferred that to steaming on station. It gave you something to do to make the watches pass much more quickly. It was a fairly active life, and people enjoyed it.

Paul Stillwell: Did the staff serve as a useful backstop for the skipper?

Admiral Trost: I didn't think they did. I thought, as a matter of fact, the watch standing staff, the three junior people, were there to show how smart they were and how dumb all the ship's were. Captain Nisewaner was a breath of fresh air with them. Very pragmatic, commonsense guy, very pleasant guy. And I think was probably the balance wheel for Admiral Taylor. Admiral Taylor was very, very pleasant, professional and pleasant, but something now—

I'd like to just digress for a minute while I'm thinking about it, that some of the things that I remember about that tour specifically. We and several other ships came into Palermo, Sicily, and we were basically a cripple. Other ships went into other ports for their first stop. The intent was to repair us after that North Atlantic voyage. We had not a single topside weapon system that was operational, having suffered from saltwater leakage and other types of damage. We had amplidyne motors that had gotten saltwater into their oil systems and had just basically clogged up. We opened up one motor and pump, and it was as if they had Vaseline inside. It was congealed lube oil with saltwater mixed in. We had several protective low bulkheads on the main deck forward which had been hit hard enough by waves to deform them, but they also cracked the welds where they went to the deck. In a couple of cases, actually ruptured the seam going down below, so we had welding work and other requirements. There was, as I remember, a tender that came in to Palermo at the time we were there to do some of this work.

Paul Stillwell: Had the ship taken water through these cracks?

Admiral Trost: Some yes, but most of them had been stuffed temporarily as best they could be from underneath. So we had quite a task ahead of us. We were in, I don't believe for more than maybe six days or so, but it was a rather heavy schedule. We had a lot of work done. We also got the ship painted, and that was my first introduction to practical cumshaw. Chief DiPietro spoke Italian like a native, and there was a local ship-chandler sort of organization, a group of people. Our first day in port I saw DiPietro on the pier, and he had about a dozen worn foul-weather jackets and a few other things like a 20-pound tin of coffee. He was out there talking with his hands to another Italian gentleman in close. Later on that day, not very much later, the Italian left with all this stuff, and back came an army of people who painted our ship, completely top to bottom in about two days, externally. That was the price, so we looked good, and we were ready to be part of the Sixth Fleet.

The captain had accepted from the ship that we were turning over with, not only the publications and the other things, but also an old jeep that lacked headlights and a few other amenities that this other ship had found somewhere the Mediterranean. This was going to be the captain's jeep. That jeep was hoisted aboard and parked up on the 01 level above our torpedo house, aft of the number-two stack. The machinery repair division and the electricians went to work on it. They took battle lanterns and made headlights for it. The repair guys did some welding. They reworked the brake system. They did some engine work on it, and then it was repainted haze gray. That became the CO's car.

Well, on the first outing in the CO's car after it had been taken out for a test drive by one of the enlisted men, the car was hoisted off onto the pier. Captain Nisewaner, the chief of staff, and Captain Dawson were going to go off for a trip. For some reason, I was along. It was not because Captain Dawson wanted my company, but rather because there was a utilitarian reason. I don't remember what it is. I do remember his driving us down a nice date palm-lined road with concrete road markers every tenth of a mile. And I remember that we hit two to the extent that Captain Nisewaner, who'd been riding with his foot outside on the little step on the passenger side, decided to keep his feet inside the jeep from that point onward. I sat back there hoping that I wouldn't be bounced out of the rear end, because I thought I was riding with one of the craziest drivers I've ever been with. We'd hit bumps, and I would bounce up in the air and come back down. It was almost like living in a cartoon world. That was a rather fascinating experience with Dawson.

We drove all over the island, including up into one village, up in the foothills of Sicily, where I'm convinced we were lucky to escape with our skins. He just kind of drove through at very high speed and up into the village square. There was a little taverna place off to the side—I forgot the Italian name for it, but just a little place on the side of the square. He said, "Let's get something to drink." So we went up there, and he said to me, "You get something to drink." Well, at that time I spoke fairly fluent Spanish, but only a few words of Italian. But I managed to get across that we were looking for some soft drinks, and I was able to buy us three soft drinks. In the meantime, a bunch of kids had climbed into the jeep, and Captain Dawson was out there shooing them away from the jeep. Some mother came over and scolded him in Italian for fussing at her children, and he was having an argument with her. He was arguing in English, and she was arguing in Italian. Neither one knew what the other was saying. So we got our soft drinks and started to drive away, and the owner of the shop came running after us, because he was supposed to get those bottles back. This was true recycling, so we finished our soft drinks, gave the bottles back, and exited the town. I told him I thought we ought to get out of this as soon as we could because the looks of the people around didn't appear to be too friendly towards us. But we got out, and we went out.

I remember going with Lou Oberle, who was my roommate during much of my tour on *Owens*, another one of the ensigns who had come aboard when I did.[*] We went out one evening with Chief DiPietro, the chief boatswain's mate, who said, "Do you want an Italian dinner? I've got a place with some friends and have a good time." We wandered out into the city of Palermo, which was a fairly nice place, with a lot of the war damage having been repaired or cleaned up. We got off the main part of the town and into this area where one shouldn't normally walk alone at night. It was probably perfectly safe. At any rate, we turned down a narrow alley with the chief, and we said, "Are you sure you know where you're going?"

"Oh, yeah." Well, we didn't see any restaurant signs or anything down there, just big stone walls and about a three-story-high building. We walked down this alleyway which also served as a local drainage gutter, water running down the middle of it and got down to a little hole in the wall that was about four feet high. There was an entryway through the wall on the right, and there was a wooden door which was open. And we descended about three steps, and we were on the dirt floor of a restaurant. Candles on the tables in little jars and red-and-white checkered tablecloths. It was an honest-to-goodness

[*] Ensign Louis A. Oberle, USN.

Italian restaurant. We went in and had one of the best Italian meals I think I've ever had at a very, very inexpensive rate. Everybody there knew him. He'd been out there on liberty about two nights before that, and they all knew him. And, of course, he took care of everything, introducing us in Italian. People were very friendly, and we met all sorts of people and listened to him jabber, but it added to the environment. It was a lot of fun. A lot more fun than going out to the local hotel and having lunch or dinner.

Paul Stillwell: Sounds like the skipper couldn't drive a jeep any better than he could a ship.

Admiral Trost: The skipper didn't drive the jeep very well, and he didn't drive the ship very well. We participated in the exercises, and he was always very antsy. It was a blessing to have us in station one, because it required the least of the commanding officer, and we were in station one all the time when Admiral Taylor was with us during that tour. I think he debarked about two-thirds the way through the Med deployment and shifted his flag. During the time he was aboard, we were busy, but not doing as many things as we might have otherwise had.

But the CO also was a very stubborn man. One night, he walked to the bridge, and I had the deck. A signal had just come over the tactical radio circuit, and that's why he was out there. I had just notified him of it. It required a screen reorientation, and it was one of these things where we weren't going to do anything. We were going to stay right where we were. He was shifting things, but that particular screen left unit one right where he was, offset from the axis. So the execute came over just as he came up, while I was doing nothing. He said, "Move Goddamn it, move." I thought he meant get out of the way, so I moved over. Then he said, "When are you going to do something?"

I said, "There's nothing to do, Captain; we don't move."

"Goddamn it, move." He yelled, "Right full rudder," and we put on right full rudder, and we did a full circle, at full speed, and he left the bridge. So I settled back down, and I reported to him when we were on station. He said, "Good, do it more smartly next time." He settled down. But he was an interesting man to go to sea with.

Paul Stillwell: Did you have submarine opposition in any of these exercises?

Admiral Trost: We did, infrequently. The main exercise of submarine opposition was one that took place in the Gulf of Taranto. We went into Taranto, Italy, for a period and were at anchor. I guess we initially went inside the harbor, which was rather a scenic thing. Because I remember we went through a rather narrow slot with one bridge overhead into an inner harbor which was quite large. It was a major Italian fleet base. Taranto at that time was also a Communist stronghold, and there was no unescorted liberty in town, although they did have some functions for visiting ships—the several of us that went in there.

We departed from there and went out on ASW exercise in the gulf. For submarine opposition I think there were one or two U.S. diesels, a British boat, there were some British destroyer types there, and an Italian submarine that was ex-U.S. World War II diesel, and we had ASW exercise out there. One of the things I remember well about that was that I was assigned one day as a liaison officer to the senior of the two Italian ships that were participating. I was transferred over by high-line. The captain said, "Well, you know, they probably want to learn a little bit more about our tactics. Be careful what you tell them now. Don't tell them too much."

So I got over to the ship, and I was greeted by an Italian officer. He was actually the squadron commander of the people based there. Very pleasant, spoke only a few words of English, but he had one officer who did speak English fairly well. I explained to him that I really couldn't speak Italian, and I could speak enough Spanish if anybody spoke Spanish. "Oh," he said, "that's not the problem. All you have to do is speak English. We wanted to have you on board because we're having great difficulty understanding the Brits. So we wanted an English speaker on board to communicate, to handle radio communications." [Laughter] And I must admit, I had almost as much difficulty understanding the Brits speaking English as did the Italians speaking English. But I had an interesting day on board the ship, just observing the difference in the way the ships were operated. Much more professionally casual, I would have placed it.

Paul Stillwell: What does that mean?

Admiral Trost: That means, things that I thought, "Is anybody going to worry about that guy over there?" They were driving like Italian sport car drivers as they went about. But they handled the tactics very nicely. The tactics were fairly standardized as NATO tactics adopted in large number from those that we had used. So when two ships were operating together, you had a pretty good idea what the other guy was doing.

Of course, I went down for lunch, and the fare is somewhat different they what we would normally expect, including the glass of red wine that was part of the lunch, which we wouldn't have seen. It was a rather pleasant experience. We operated with a number of ships. We operated with carriers for about the—my recollection, the early part of the time over there we operated as part of a surface action group with several cruisers being the nucleus of that group for a period of time. Then we did some operations where there were just groups of destroyers, as in this ASW exercise. We also made a couple of port visits where we were one of just two or three. We went into Cagliari, Sardinia, on one of our early port visits but never got ashore because the winds were high, and our anchors wouldn't hold. *Owens* had two lightweight anchors—I've forgotten the proper designation. I think they were Danforth type, and they didn't hold in anything above about two knots of current and some breeze. So we steamed to the anchor the entire time we at Cagliari and never got anybody ashore.

We also had anchoring problems in Souda Bay Crete, where we, in fact, did ultimately get ashore. We came into Souda Bay in the evening as part of a group of ships and anchored. I was the duty officer the following morning, and I had gone around the ship. I had gone up to the bridge to look at the final position of the duty quartermaster. We were anchored about 2,000 yards from the destroyer tender that was also anchored in Souda Bay. While I was looking at that guy and checking the bearing on him and on the land things, the bearings changed, and I said, "We're dragging anchor." We had about a ten-knot breeze and, by golly, we were.

We sounded the collision alarm, directed the engineering spaces to get up propulsion steam. All we had was a boiler on the line for hotel load at the time. I got turns to the engines about 20 seconds before we hit the tender. And we simply drug back with both anchors dragging at the same time, never getting enough propulsion. Never got enough turns to get any power on them. We hit at probably about two or three knots and hit dead on the bow of the tender with the after port quarter of the ship. We put a big gash almost down to the waterline in the ship, which resulted in our being brought alongside the tender and much better liberty. Because the tender had a lot more boats than we did. So we got ashore in Souda Bay to see some of the old ruins in Crete—a rather fascinating place to go.

Paul Stillwell: Sounds like that ship had an affinity for hitting tenders.

Admiral Trost: Well interestingly, we subsequently, I believe it was in Naples, had another repair availability where we got one standard destroyer anchor installed on the starboard side which meant they had to, in fact, put in a big hawsepipe on the starboard side. Where it came from, Lord knows, but we suddenly had this great big thing on one side and on the other side was almost like letting the anchor free from a scupper. It did make a big difference, because from that point on we had no more problems. We also drug anchor in Greece, Piraeus, off Athens. When we had winds of any kind before we got the heavyweight anchor, we always had a steaming watch anytime we were anchored, and after that it was not necessary.

Paul Stillwell: Did you have any idea why she was equipped with such inadequate anchors?

Admiral Trost: Apparently, people thought they were going to be adequate. Whether it was a weight consideration, I don't know. I would think not since one of the factors had to do with the very large sonar dome that she had. It wasn't like some of the later ships, where you didn't have anchors on one side where you always tried to put a bow anchor, side anchor down so the ship would tend away and protect the sonar dome. We had one in the normal position on each side, but they were the lightweight type. They were the same anchors that we used on LSTs at that time. That's the old LSTs. I guess their displacement wasn't significantly less, if it was. They were lightweight anchors. We just simply sailed around on the wind many a time. The ship also had a very high superstructure on it and was much more boxy than the standard destroyer superstructure, so she had a lot more wind resistance than the standard, in my opinion.

Admiral Trost: How well did you do vis-à-vis those submarines when you were opposed?

Admiral Trost: I'd say fair. They got their shots off against us, and we got an occasional attack off against them. It was more a question of finding them than it was making a successful attack once found. Once found, we did pretty well. As I recall, the sonar conditions were not the best in the Gulf of Taranto at that time. This must have been mid-fall we did that. Sonar conditions in the Med are never optimum, but there was a relatively shallow layer, as I recall, and the submarines could sort of pop through with impunity.* Of course, they couldn't hear us when they were below the layer, and when they got above the layer they were in danger of being detected. By that time, they were usually in close enough, if they saw you further out and made an approach on you and ducked below the layer, you didn't pick them up coming in, until they popped up at maybe 600 or 800 yards to shoot you, which made detection a little difficult, made countering them a little difficult.

Paul Stillwell: Well, I've heard the generalization that submariners have a much better knowledge of the layers and how to use them than surface officers.

Admiral Trost: I think it's only been, well, say within the last 20 years, maybe even less time than that, that the surface Navy has appreciated the need to know more about sonar systems in close.

We had an interesting time in the Mediterranean. I guess in addition to the operational things, you remember ports. There was a tremendous opportunity, educational experience, for us because I had never been to the Mediterranean before and we, as I said, had been in Palermo, Sicily. We, as I recall, went in and out of Naples several times, and that was rather interesting. During time in Naples we got a chance to

---

* Thermocline layers of differing temperatures underwater can prevent or degrade active sonar signals from being detected.

go to Rome and play tourist in Rome for several days. Went up to Florence. Went to Pisa and saw the Leaning Tower. As a matter of fact, we spent New Year's Eve in Florence in an Italian hotel, and I was not a consumer of very much alcohol. And, unfortunately, my roommate and I should have been heavy drinkers because we would not have gotten as cold or felt as cold. It was a very frigid night. The hotel we were in had no heat. It had a number of tourists, and everybody was partying, so it was hard to sleep, and we were freezing our tails off. Very memorable New Year's Eve. What a way to spend it.

Paul Stillwell: Did you see vestiges of the war in any of these places?

Admiral Trost: Oh, you bet. We did in many places in Italy, especially. We went in to the Cannes, France, area for Christmas holidays. And that, of course, was a lovely resort that showed no signs of ever having been involved in any sense. The areas around it—I was able while we were there to take a drive again in the company of the commanding officer. I think I was there as a backup driver maybe or somebody to blame if something went wrong. We went to a small town—I can't think of the name now—within probably about 30 or 40 miles of Nice to go to a place that the captain had heard about that was a great place to have lunch. We did see war damage still from that. Of course, war damage from World War II, war damage from the time of the Romans and a few other things, but some rather spectacular, beautiful country. But war damage, not too much visible in most places we went. It was hard in some of the places and some of the old towns to know what was war damage and what was just stuff that had fallen down.

Paul Stillwell: How well had the economies come back in these places?

Admiral Trost: Not sure I was a good judge of that. My recollection is that our money stretched quite well. We didn't go anyplace that we felt was expensive, even though we had rather meager incomes ourselves. I can't say that I have a recollection of a lot of poor people. There were a lot of poor. You saw poor people in the villages of Sicily, but not people who looked like they weren't eating and being adequately clothed—the same with Greece. I would say that of all the places, Greece seemed to be one of the poorer places at that time. We did have a good opportunity in Greece to tour Athens, and did not get much beyond Athens and Piraeus for sightseeing, but it was rather pleasant. We went to

Iskenderun Bay, Turkey, at the eastern end of the Mediterranean for a ceremony marking the opening of a NATO storage depot, as I remember. It became a NATO supply depot. The commanding officer was the only person permitted ashore as part of the delegation.

There were ships from various nationalities there for this particular ceremony. Several of us—matter of fact, my roommate and I—decided that we would make a wardroom call on a Turkish destroyer that was anchored not too very far away from us. We got our ship's whaleboat and crew in the water and went over about 10:00 o'clock in the morning to the ship. Came alongside, lots of steering when our boat came alongside. Went up, and there was a young petty officer of the deck who spoke no English, but he made it known he wanted us to wait a minute. About five minutes later, an unshaven, hurriedly dressed officer wearing the equivalent of jaygee stripes came up, and he spoke English. We explained to him that we were making a wardroom call. He didn't quite know what that was. So we explained to him what our book said it was. We hadn't made one either, and this was our first try at it.

He smiled and apologized for his appearance. They had a big party the night before and had been up pretty late. He had just been awakened, and he was the only officer awake. He took us back down to the wardroom; this was an old British ship that had a beautifully paneled wardroom. We sat down and within a few minutes, three or four other stragglers appeared, equally unshaven, hurriedly dressed. We sat and, using this guy as our interpreter, we had a nice conversation. We were served strong coffee and some sort of a syrupy white lightning liqueur and little tiny chocolate bars that were rather bitter and tasted like they were meant to go with the liqueur. The combination—it took one to kill the other, I'm not sure which was which. But we made our wardroom call.

Based on the experience, we didn't try that again in the Mediterranean, but it at least gave us something to do while we were there. We were the only other two people who got off the ship other than the boat crews and the captain.

While we were in the Med, we also went into Beirut, Lebanon, which was at that time a very pleasant place. There were three ships, and I think we were joined by an oiler when we went into Beirut. Again, it was, for me, a very pleasant experience. Lou Oberle, who was my roommate during that assignment, and I were two of the new ensigns who were basically qualified for anything on board. I think we were the only two officer-of-the-deck-qualified guys out of that group, which gave us a good leg up with the exec, who seemed rather willing to let us go almost anytime on liberty and would keep other guys around—sometimes, we thought, just for the hell of it. We got in, and Lou and I were told that there was going to be a dance for the sailors sponsored by the local—I don't think they called themselves USO, but it was the American Wives group, and these were primarily wives of oil company employees, TAP Line, the Trans-Arabian Pipe Line, being the predominant one at that time. I think we had some 4,000 U.S. citizens in Beirut employed by the oil industry at that time. We were told that they needed a couple of officers to assist the ladies and sort of be in informal civilian clothes, shore patrol clothes—they sent shore patrol out there.

So Lou and I got the directions, and we walked out through a part of town again, that we probably shouldn't have been in, through market areas, looking at various cuts of meat, including chickens hanging there and we were impressed by the fact that they were very heavily preserved by pepper all around them. We got to the big hall where this was going to take place, and among other things, I made a comment on our observations to one of the hostesses and she said, "Pepper?" She said, "No, they don't use pepper." She said, "Flies." She said, "That's why I don't shop. I have a Lebanese woman who does my shopping." At any rate, we did our duty that evening. We were with probably a dozen U.S. wives, who had done a very nice job. They had hors d'oeuvres and soft drinks and hostesses, French, American, Greek young ladies who were there. I think the sailors, by and large, had a good time.

We did our duties and were preparing to go back to the ship, and one of the ladies said, "Well, wouldn't you like to go out and have dinner with us? We're going out to dinner, our husbands are picking us up, several couples, and we are going down to a very nice restaurant." We went down with them to the waterfront. My recollection was the King George Hotel, was right on the water, and this was almost across the street from that restaurant, which was a French restaurant owned by a Greek owner. One of the young ladies was the singer at this restaurant, and she had come back with us from the function. We had a very nice dinner that night, spent time with them, and then they took us back down to the ship. And they said, "Well, wouldn't you like to go sightseeing tomorrow?"

Well, we thought, "We better call you because we've got to check to see if we can get liberty or not." We did check with the exec first thing in the morning, and he thought this was very good people-to-people relations, and we kind of laid on that pretty heavily ourselves. So Lou and I, once again, got off the ship. These people picked us up. We had met a Lebanese businessman the night before, never forget his name, Reyad Hamadi, he was a 1936 Olympic swimmer from Lebanon. He was, in 1953, a junk dealer. He and a couple other guys after the war had bought a couple of surplus LSTs and had gone around the littoral Mediterranean, picking up tanks, trucks, you name it, and they sold a lot of the stuff that was in working shape or that they could get into working shape. Trucks especially were a premium right after the war. Trucks and jeeps. The rest of it, they scrapped.

They were just big on junk—he made a lot of money. He took us out that day. He was the tour guide. He took us out in his open Ford convertible to his Mediterranean villa, which was just down the coast from the Saint George, to the north of the airport. He had this beautiful place right across the coastal highway stretching back. We met his mother and his wife, neither of whom ever went out with him at night, just their custom, and about nine children. And he took us off; we went all over the city. He was going to show us the airport. We did see the airport. We got to one point as we were approaching the airport where there was a roadblock and a couple of guys with weapons, and he started flashing his lights and blowing his horn, and they moved the roadblock, but he didn't slow down. They leveled their weapons down at us, and he said, "Don't worry about it—local militia," and we went zooming right through, and they didn't shoot.

We got an interesting look at the country. We drove a little bit off to the east of Lebanon, up into the hills and saw some of the very few remaining Lebanese cedars that are still up there growing and generally had a good time. We spent the majority of the several days we were in port with these folks; we were with them all day long. We had dinner in several homes; all of them employed Lebanese shoppers and cooks and housekeepers because the cook had to see what the food you were going to eat looked like before you got it prepared. But it was rather nice. We ate there, we ate in the restaurants, we had drinks, Cokes in our case, out on the pretty patio of the Saint George, looking out over the Mediterranean. It was a rather pleasant time.

I guess the most memorable event, though, was when we had our change of command.* Jack English came in by plane into Beirut to relieve Dawson. We didn't know at the time that they knew each other, but I mentioned that their backgrounds were similar. In fact, English, my recollection is, relieved Dawson in each of those three jobs. DE—same DE—sonar school, he was the successor in sonar school, and now he was getting *Robert A. Owens*. None of us had seen English. We went through the normal preparations for the change of command, the inventories, and the various things. We heard the—I don't remember where I was—I heard the new "Commander, USN," being bonged aboard, being piped aboard, and then within about 30 minutes we heard, "Commander, USN, departing." I didn't know what was happening. It was English coming aboard, and 30 minutes later George Dawson left. It was a very brief change of command. No formalities. They signed things over. I didn't know until then that they didn't like each other much, and they didn't plan to spend any time together on the ship.

Paul Stillwell: No big ceremony.

Admiral Trost: No big ceremony, none whatsoever. We had a new commanding officer, and we hadn't even met him yet. As a matter of fact, I think I was involved with probably Bob Cross inventorying crypto material when the old CO left and the new CO came aboard, and we hadn't even finished the inventory yet for these two guys to sign. I'm not sure how we handled that, but it was a rather interesting changeover.

Jack English was a totally different type of person. Very outgoing, very, almost a brash, outgoing personality. Dawson was a tall, distinguished-looking gentleman. English was a much shorter man, bright red hair with a very bright red mustache, medium build

---

* Commander English relieved Commander Dawson on 24 October 1953.

and very, sort of dapper looking. His movements and everything were sort of flashy. It was quite interesting, whereas Dawson was the world's worst ship handler, English was one of the best I've seen. He had lots of confidence. His standard comment was, to an officer of the deck, "You can't screw up anything bad enough that I can't get you out of it safely." And I think that was probably right. He had very short patience with officers. He didn't seem to particularly like officers. He didn't engender loyalty in his actions.

He was always catering to the crew in the eyes of the wardroom. One specific example, at Christmastime, which was, I guess, about a month and a half or two after he had taken over, less than two months, I had received from home a package, and it included, among other things, a cake that my mother had baked, which arrived with a very tasty package of crumbs. But it was a good spice cake, and it was still edible. She'd also sent several other things in the package. I'd opened the package, and I had left these things on my bunk in the two-man room that I was sharing with Lou Oberle. By this time, the staff had departed, and we had our room back.

Lou also had gotten something and had left it there and, by Golly, things left our bunks. In the meantime, we had a history of people saying, "You know, I thought I had more money than this," just little things. We were down in a little complex where there were three two-man rooms and a four-man bunkroom in this one little segment of the first platform deck. So we did an investigation, very casual at first and finally found that one of the things—I have no idea now what it was—my mother had sent me, and one of the things from the other guys had been offered to one of our steward's mates, by the TN, the non-rated steward who had took care of the particular part of the officers' country there, in exchange to cover a debt.

When that came to light, we said to the exec, "Hey, you know, this guy has taken these things out of our room. We can identify him, and we have these other problems."

So the exec said, "Okay, put him on report." So we did. We took him to captain's mast, and the captain dismissed it, out of hand, then called the crew to muster. We had nothing, no loading machines or anything else between the two stacks on the 01 level on that ship, just a 5-inch gun and the torpedo tubes. So he called the crew up there. He got up on the signal bridge and said, "I just want to talk to you about this ship. You, the crew, and I can run this ship, no matter how incompetent the officers on this ship may be." Then he called up Torney, this TN, and said, "Here's a man who's been put on report unjustly, but I dismissed that." He put his arm around the guy's shoulder. Well, that was our indication of what kind of leadership we got from the captain.

Well, we later, as our last port call in Spain, went into Cartagena. We were one of three destroyers. He was the senior commanding officer, and he was SOPA.[*] This was a port that had had no U.S. port visits since 1945, so there were no SOPA instructions. So, again, I was one of a two-man team to prepare SOPA instructions for them, which we did. We couldn't do the normal delineating of out-of-bounds districts, because we didn't know where they were, and there was no such indication. But when we did get in, we met with the police chief, who told us the areas that should be out of bounds. So we put out that word to the ships. Jim Moore, who was the gunnery officer then—Jim was a full lieutenant—was assigned as the senior shore patrol officer for the visit.[†] And, because I spoke Spanish I was both the liaison with the pilot coming in and also with the shore patrol. We found out that the first man apprehended in the red-light district for being charged with failure to pay by the madam of the place was our commanding officer. So he set the stage all the way.

That was a rather interesting port visit also. I was up on the bridge, and we were going into this port, which had a breakwater off the port. We picked up the pilot just outside the breakwater and then headed for the pier. I don't think we were much more than a mile or a mile and a half from the pier at the time. The first order from the pilot in Spanish was, "All ahead full." I turned to the captain and said, "He has just given an all ahead full order, Captain." The captain said, "All ahead one-third; balance him out." He had never handled a warship in his life. So we went one-third speed, and the captain said "You better give whatever orders you think are the right orders and let me know what you're doing." I said, "Okay." So this man went in very happily, conning us in, and the ship never did anything he said. The biggest problem was that I'd never Med-moored a

---

[*] SOPA – senior officer present afloat.
[†] Lieutenant James A. Moore, USN.

ship before, and that was a Med moor, but that was a good experience. The captain was there, and he said, "Don't worry about it. I'll tell you what to do when." We did, and we moored, and everything went fine.

Paul Stillwell: What were the peculiarities involved in achieving a Med moor?

Admiral Trost: Well, you're moored stern first to the seawall with no pier. What you have to do obviously is put the ship in position so that you're backing toward the seawall.

Paul Stillwell: Straight in?

Admiral Trost: Straight in. You don't want to hit it. You have to drop both anchors, just right, so that you're held off enough and use the anchors forward to hold you out and a line to the pier. You use quarter lines to be able to hold you back. If you drop your anchors in the right location and get your lines over smartly aft and stop the ship before it hits the pier, you're in good shape. The biggest problem in many of the Mediterranean ports was that there was debris on the bottom near the quay walls that could very easily be kicked up by screws turning over.

We had an experience in our brief visit in Taranto where we kicked up some debris astern when we Med moored there and then, when we were preparing to get under way the next morning, the Italian ship immediately adjacent to ours got under way first. Since our anchors went down after his, our anchor lines were crossed. We had our starboard anchor chain across his port anchor chain. He slipped out very silently without having said anything to anybody about 6:00 o'clock in the morning. He didn't slip very far because he got under way to about—he was heaving in on his anchor line, and it didn't come in anymore. His ship started swinging around, and he very hastily redropped the other anchor, re-moored, and then we had to get a platform crane—actually a barge with a crane on it—to go down and untangle and lift the two anchors up and separate them so that we could get under way. We were held up a little bit. So there can be hazards to it.

Once you're moored—of course, our ships don't normally moor that way. Our people are not necessarily so adept at making that kind of mooring, but we did it quite frequently in the Mediterranean. English himself, when he handled it, could just do it beautifully. He had a tremendous feel for it. But it's so difficult when you're standing on the bridge to judge precisely how much room you have remaining aft, even when you've got a talker back there. We usually had the exec back there as the best judge of distance to tell us how far back we could come.

Paul Stillwell: Was the purpose of this to get more ships into a given space?

Admiral Trost: Yes. It's a combination. What you've really got is just a flat seawall with no piers out from it. So everything just moves in, and you get a lot of ships in there that way, of course. It means everything comes over the fantail of the ship, all the stores and garbage going off and everything else. It's more difficult to fuel and to take water aboard.

Paul Stillwell: So you had a brow directly from the seawall to the fantail?

Admiral Trost: That's right.

Paul Stillwell: Speaking of the exec, where was he in all this, with these captains that were bizarre?

Admiral Trost: Interestingly, and I want to come back to the ship for a minute. Let me just give you one other recollection from Cartagena, Spain, in that port visit. One of the things that was fascinating was that we went out, and we called on the mayor, the captain with me as his interpreter and senior shore patrol officer along with us and the chief of police. The mayor was a very, very outgoing guy, very congenial. The hospitality in that port was tremendous. They were just so pleased to see us, because here was an opportunity to make money. There was a poor city in a poor country.

We found a very nice restaurant right across from the police station which served good food, fairly good size, had a big cappuccino-type machine on the side that was kept going full time. But, interestingly, we went in there I guess I was among the first U.S. customers to go in there because the police chief took us over and introduced us to the owners. We had a lunch for less than a dollar, considerably less than a dollar. The sailors found the place, and they found you could order a good big full steak dinner and pay less than a dollar. So they were walking out leaving one-dollar tips. By the time we left three days later, steak dinners were going to $2.50, and they were still leaving dollar tips. The owners learned quickly. Prices escalated rather markedly during our stay, probably not making us too popular with the other people in town, but it was a good visit, a very interesting one.

It was also the period of time during which some of the other ships from our surface action group had gone into Barcelona, and the crew members of one of the cruisers had gone to a bullfight and caused a near riot because they thought the bull was being taken unfair advantage of and started cheering for the bull. The Spaniards would probably have strung them up had they been able to get them all, but they were escorted out of the ring and back to the ship. We all got the word that we don't do things like this in Spain.

Paul Stillwell: Interesting difference in cultures.

Admiral Trost: Very much so. Very much so. The executive officer—it's interesting, the executive officer who was there when I first reported to the ship was Joe Ady.[*] Joe was detached during the time I was in school, and Jerry Pounders, who had been the ship's engineer, became the executive officer. Jerry is the one I mentioned earlier who had been a chief motor machinist's mate at the start of the war and a lieutenant at the end of the war. He was promoted to lieutenant commander during my tour on board. Jerry was an interesting personality. A very good professional, primarily engineering oriented because of his background. Not comfortable with navigation, but a good ship handler. He later commanded an APD and had a good successful tour.[†] I think Jerry probably ran the ship for the captain very, very well.

As I said, there were people who became clearly his favorites, and Lou and I were among those people. You became his favorites because you sort of earned your way. If you were a good, serious professional guy doing your job, that was fine. You were one of Jerry's boys. If not, he would sort of screw up his face and look at a guy—he was

---

[*] Lieutenant Commander Joseph W. Ady, USN.
[†] APD – high-speed amphibious transport.

referred to—his nickname was the "Black Look," because he had slicked-down black hair and he had a black mustache, a narrow face. He could adopt a very stern countenance. Jerry would look at some JO, and he could really strike the fear of God into him. Crew members would rather go to mast with the captain than have Jerry call them into his room to chew them out if they were one of the troops getting into trouble.

When George Dawson was the commanding officer, any time we went alongside a ship, under way or in port or made a landing—as I said, I was a JA phone talker for quite a period of time. Jerry would stand on the engaged side, a couple of people behind the captain, and his role was to relay the captain's orders. He did that. Chief Glasgow, the chief quartermaster, was the only person the captain would trust on that wheel when we were in a close situation. Between Chief Glasgow and his seaman's eye and Jerry's hand signals after the voice signal, they would bring us safely alongside for refueling and transfers and all. We seldom followed the commanding officer's commands. I realize that sounds way out, but that's the way it worked.

There were times when Chief Glasgow, if we had a distance line over—they always put the distance line high so that Glasgow could see the markings. He would simply steer the ship, to keep the distance proper, and Jerry Pounders would add and subtract turns to keep us alongside. It worked well. Of course, with English as a good ship handler, Jerry sort of stayed out of the way and used the enlisted phone talkers, because they were more trustworthy than the officers were in English's domain. Jerry was definitely part of the picture.

[Break for change of tape]

Admiral Trost: . . . recollections of some of the officers on board. I talked about the executive officer, Jerry Pounders, and two commanding officers. Jim Moore, who was a lieutenant when he reported aboard—he came aboard not too very long after me—Jim was also a Naval Academy graduate—became the gunnery officer, a very professional man. Jim, as I recall, retired after having commanded a destroyer. He retired as a commander some years ago. Jim was an interesting guy. Very much respected by the crew. Very fine condition physically. He used to impress people when something really ticked him off, he'd just ball up his fist and slam it into the nearest bulkhead. And you used to wonder if it was going to dent before he did, very frankly. He also was a man who was known for his like of Texas Pete hot sauce. Jim's taste buds must have been gone, because he'd sit down, and if he had a plate of eggs in front of him, he'd smother it with Texas Pete hot sauce first, and then he'd taste it. So put Texas Pete and pepper on everything he ate, sort of branded him as a guy who liked hot foods.

Some of the other people who were on board when I came in, Mort Briggs was the operations officer, and Mort was one of those three-year jaygees, very fun, very competent guy, good officer of the deck, good ops officer. Another was Sig Redelsheimer.[*] Sig was the ASW officer before me, and then I guess initially I was sonar officer under him as ASW officer, I think that's the way the assignment worked out, although I ultimately became the ASW officer. But Sig, likewise, was a very solid citizen, and he and Mort were both married. Sig was in many respects the old sea daddy, even though he was probably no more than two maybe three years older than I was at the time. Probably three years older. Sig was the guy that gave good advice, very solid, pragmatic individual, including, "Okay, you're going to get married, let me give you some tips to stay out of trouble on your honeymoon. How not to get your wife pregnant the first week you're married," those kinds of things. So he was a fine gent.

I ran into Sig once since that time. He was working, as I recall, for McDonnell Douglas. I was in Washington during my tour as CNO and he dropped by one day to say hello. We had a chance to reminisce a little bit. Bob Cross was another man in that group. Bob was a communicator. Bob was a real fine gent, solid citizen, also married. The guy I probably knew best was Lou Oberle, my roommate. We maintained in touch over the years. He and Harry Davidson—Lou was a graduate of Villanova, regular ROTC.[†] Harry, as I remember, was a contract ROTC graduate from Yale. Harry and Lou are both retired reserve captains, and we've kept in touch with both families over the years. Dick Simcoe

---

[*] Lieutenant (junior grade) Sigmund Redelsheimer, USNR.
[†] Lieutenant (junior grade) Harry A. Davidson, USNR.

was the first lieutenant during most of the time there.[*] Dick, as I remember, was a year ahead of me. Dick was a very fine, very conscientious officer. Good man.

Al Mumma came aboard after I reported.[†] I think Al may have been Jerry Pounders's relief, so he came aboard after I first checked in, but was on board before I got there. Al, as I recall, was a Merchant Marine Academy graduate either Kings Point or one of the other state maritime academies. A very fine engineer, a very competent guy. It used to be a standing joke with Al, neither George Dawson nor Jack English set foot in anything below the main deck. Neither of them knew very much about engineering, including operations. For example, if you wanted to go above 27 knots in those destroyers, you needed super-heated steam. When you fired off the super heaters, you also had to remember that you couldn't just stop and not have steam flow, or it would blow up your boilers. So the normal practice was if you had to, in an emergency situation come to a stop bell, then sat there and rocked turbines alternately opening the throttles ahead and astern to keep steam flowing until you could cool down after you secured the burners, secure the burners and cool down the super-heater by running steam through them on a continuing basis.

The one who really didn't appreciate that was Jack English. Dawson didn't either. I can recall one time when, I don't remember which skipper now, we came to "all stop" with super heat, having been running at about 29 or 30 knots. The engineers immediately, without orders, started rocking the turbines. The commanding officer looked aft and saw the swirl and the screws turning over and called down and said, "God damn it, I said 'all stop.'" The engineer, Mumma, got on the PA system, the MC system and said, "You know, Captain, we can't stop. We will burn up our super heaters."

"God damn it, when I say 'all stop,' I mean 'all stop.'"

"Yes, sir." They continued to rock, and the captain looked back periodically and called down and chewed him out again, and they continued to do it until they got the

---

[*] Lieutenanr (unior grade) Richard O. Simcoe, USNR.
[†] Lieutenant (junior grade) Albert H. Mumma, USNR.

things cooled down. Had they not done it, they would have suffered millions of dollars' worth of damage.

But, subsequent to that, I went down—I used to do the engineering below-decks inspections on the periodic zone inspections at the direction of the XO. He said, "You and I are the best qualified guys, other than the engineers, to go down there and inspect, and I'm not going to go down and do it; you're going to do it." So I'd get the zone inspection for all the engineering spaces. But I got a kick out of it. After that incident, I got down to main control, and there in the engine room, mounted right below the MC system was a little cartoon of an MC system with the captain's neck coming out of a very thin pipe and then growing into a big head, yelling, "I said 'all stop.'" That was there for the enjoyment of all the engineering watch standers, secure in the knowledge that the captain would never go down there and see it.

Paul Stillwell: How clean was the plant?

Admiral Trost: Pretty clean. It was a pretty good plant. We had some very good senior people. I mentioned Larry, the chief BT. His boiler spaces were in superb shape. We had good senior petty officers at the mid-term, mid-level, mid-experience level until we came back from the Mediterranean. We lost an awful lot of them. But, by and large, clean. Generally, a very well-functioning ship, good functioning ship. We had some very good, competent people. The good officers and the ones I've named were good officers, really did their jobs very, very well. So those were the guys that were important when I got there and, gosh, I just lost Jack's name—looking here for a Jack. Jack came aboard the next year as one of that group's officers. He and Simcoe and Davidson, Oberle, Mumma, and I are the six from that group that made that last reunion and I've kept in touch with over the years. We got along well.

As a matter of fact, Jack and his wife Joyce and the two of us, Pauline and I, made our one and only call on the commanding officer, because this was the day that formal calls were very much the vogue, as compared to today's practices. We had come back from the Mediterranean and had been in our homeport for several months before, finally, one Friday the executive officer said, "You two guys and your wives are going to call on the captain, Sunday at 1400."

Cheery, "Aye, aye." So Jerry and I and the gals got all dressed up, had their white gloves on, and we were dressed in a suit and tie. It was a very hot day in Norfolk. We went out to the Ocean View area where the captain was renting a house. We were greeted at the door by our commanding officer wearing bathing trunks—not what the book said. He invited us in, and his wife came out, and she was in a bathing suit. And we sat down, and he said, "I make good whiskey sours [or something]. We'll have a whiskey sour." The book said a call is 15 minutes, and we had our prescribed number of calling cards and put them into the tray. Then we sat down, and we made sort of strained conversation, periodically interrupted by kids popping in in their bathing suits saying, "Daddy, Daddy, you said we were going to the beach."

At the end of 15 minutes, I said, "Well, we'd better be going so you can go to the beach."

"No, no, no," he said. "I'm going to fix another drink. I've got some more out there." So he went out there and fixed another drink and after about 20 minutes, we were getting a little uncomfortable that we were really overstaying. I think our total call was about 30 uncomfortable minutes in duration, but it was rather interesting and quite a difference from the much more relaxed atmosphere that we would see at most of that type of social life today.

Paul Stillwell: Well, an explanation might be that he had not been a junior officer when that kind of calling was very much in the vogue.

Admiral Trost: That's probably true; that's probably true. Because he was commissioned in, I believe in 1940 from Columbia University through the OCS courses that were conducted there. So he was a 90-day wonder, 120-day wonder and came in, and by the end of the war, he was a lieutenant commander. And here it was, eight years later or nine years later, he was a young commander. So that may well be.

Paul Stillwell: Did you have much other experience with the engineering plant?

Admiral Trost: We did not routinely have an engineering officer of the watch, except at battle stations. So I did not stand watches down there at any time. I went down periodically. I toured the plant periodically and got myself sort of requalified on what I knew about it before, and, as I said, I made inspections on almost a weekly basis down in the engineering spaces. So I was fairly familiar with it.

Paul Stillwell: The *Owens*'s sister, the *Timmerman*, had that experimental high-pressure plant.

Admiral Trost: She did. She was the experimental forerunner, I guess, of the 1,200-pound plants and had a few problems, too, as I remember.

Paul Stillwell: Right. We didn't talk about your stops in Greece. Anything memorable there?

Admiral Trost: I just remember the dragging anchor in Greece, as we had in so many other places. Then the chance to see the ruins in Athens and visit Athens was really quite good. Again, I learned that there were things you don't volunteer for, and I learned there were things you did volunteer for. By this time, I had become an experienced volunteer, so when the exec said, "I need two officers to go to the naval attaché's garden party," everybody said, "Ah, you know, we're going sightseeing." I think it was Lou, again, and I who said, "We'll go." So we got transportation. We went with the commanding officer; we were the due representatives and went to this very, very nice place. Large grounds, the naval attaché's home.

Captain Williams was the attaché at that time, and we were part of the group. We had a lot of Greek, Navy, and civilian people there, members of the U.S. diplomatic community and other dignitaries. Quite a big garden party. We had a very pleasant time. I had a rather memorable, unforgettable experience there. I got locked into a bathroom. This place was one where you entered on the ground level, and a large portion of the area under the house was open and screened off. That was sort of a big reception area. It was open air in many respects, except for the screens. The entryway was a very good, solid door and one went in. And inside I remember this had a built-in bar area. It had a cloakroom area, receiving area, and there was a bathroom that sort of butted up to the right from the front door.

The bathroom had a small, high window leading outside, and I had gone in rather routinely. When I tried to come out the knob turned, but the door wouldn't open. The door was a very heavy thick wooden door. I looked up at the screen in the window. There was a screen, there was a window, and there were iron bars on the outside of the window. So I wasn't going to go out that way. So I spent about 15 or 20 minutes knocking on the door trying to get somebody's attention and finally did, including the attention of the hostess, who was very embarrassed that somebody would be locked inside. They freed me by literally destroying the area of the door around the lock, because they couldn't get this thing open. It was so sound that nobody could open it. So they chipped and chiseled away with a hammer and chisel on the door. This was not the kind of attention that a young officer wants to have in such a situation, but it had a major advantage. The Williamses had a young daughter, Nancy, whom I had seen several times. Subsequently she married a naval officer. Nancy was probably 18 years old, and she had a young Greek friend whose father was a naval officer. They were there, and they were directed by the mother to take care of these two dumb new ensigns. And they did very nicely.

They went out that night with us. Took us to dinner and went out and showed us a little bit of the nightlife in Athens. So there were good things about volunteering, and there were bad things. It was, by and large, a very, very pleasant experience. We did take one trip out of Athens to the countryside. We did have a chance to see villagers living, literally, among the rocks in some of those areas. Made you wonder how they could even get enough stuff growing there to feed the goats who were so prevalent in their places. Of course, the houses with the animals coming in under the house to provide heat in the winter and shelter other times. That was only a degree of poverty greater than we saw anywhere else.

Paul Stillwell: This was not long after the period when President Truman had a specific policy to counter Communism in those areas.[*] Did you see evidence of that?

Admiral Trost: I can't say we saw evidence of it at that time. This was after the Truman efforts. Greece was not a Communist state, but it was also not an openly pro-U.S. environment in my view. Athens at that time seemed to have quite a few tourists. We saw a lot of tour ships going in and out of the harbor at Piraeus. I would say, not much evidence directly of the Communist influence, but no real strong shift over.

Paul Stillwell: Were there worries anywhere in the Mediterranean area about Communists?

Admiral Trost: We were told about that background there. The only place there were warnings was in Taranto, Italy, where we were specifically precluded from going ashore. The only people of ours that went ashore there were the commanding officers to make their calls on the mayor. They were the only ones who went ashore.

Paul Stillwell: How much evidence or awareness did you have during that period of Senator McCarthy and his efforts to find Communists?[†]

Admiral Trost: Some. I can't recall how much. I was very aware of McCarthy's efforts during the time he was carrying them on, because you couldn't help but read about them and listen to them. But I don't recall any particular awareness in that particular timeframe.

Paul Stillwell: Well, you mentioned your honeymoon. At what point in the sequence did you get married?

Admiral Trost: We returned from deployment in February. When I saw Pauline, I decided, again, that she was the woman I was going to marry, and all I had to do was

---

[*] On 12 March 1947 U.S. President Harry S. Truman announced a doctrine of international resistance to Communist aggression. It guaranteed aid to free nations that resisted Communism.

[†] A senator from Wisconsin in the early 1950s, Joseph R. McCarthy went on an anti-Communist witch-hunt that came to be dubbed by the pejorative term "McCarthyism." The Senate eventually censured him.

make sure she felt the same way. We were married on the first of May 1954, with several of my shipmates as ushers in my wedding party. I was permitted to leave the ship a week before my wedding, because the ship was due to get under way on Monday morning, with my wedding on Saturday with no guarantee that it would be back in Friday, which meant that I would lose my ushers, and so we were a little concerned about that. As it turned out, the ship did get in Friday, and the guys all got up to the wedding. I just got an extra week's leave, which was very nice. Things worked out quite well.

Paul Stillwell: Where were you married?

Admiral Trost: Married in College Park, Maryland. Pauline is from this area. She was living over in Cottage City, Maryland, at the time, and we were married at the Episcopal church near the University of Maryland.

Paul Stillwell: Where was the honeymoon that you had been given directions on?

Admiral Trost: The honeymoon—we left our reception at the Cheverly Legion Hall and changed clothes and we got out of town, sort of heading south. We went down through Fredericksburg and Richmond and over to Wilmington, North Carolina, and on down—destination Daytona Beach. We spent about five days in Daytona Beach, the time being governed by the amount of money we had, which wasn't very much. We rented a place in a little cottage type of motel on the ocean. We had a very enjoyable five days and then meandered from there through Nashville, Chattanooga, up to my home in Illinois and spent a couple of days there.

Came back to this area, dropped Pauline at her parents' house, and I went to the ship and got under way. The next time we came into port a couple weeks later, I came up and got my wife, and by this time a friend of ours had helped locate a house for us down in Norfolk, furnished and ready to be rented. We moved in and lived as husband and wife and got acquainted with Navy things. Pauline was rather astounded the first morning that I had a duty day when I said, "I'll see you tomorrow night."

She said, "What do you mean tomorrow night? What about tonight?"

I said, "I have time in the duty section."

"Yeah, but you'll be home?"

I said, "No, I won't be home. I have to be aboard ship." That was her introduction to why somebody's aboard ship all the time. It was a rather pleasant time for us.

Paul Stillwell: How much camaraderie was there in that wardroom?

Admiral Trost: A fair amount among most of the people. The executive officer, Jerry Pounders—I'll have to admit that Jerry liked liberty, and he liked to party. But he and his wife Loretta hosted several nice parties in their home for the wardroom. They were always very congenial. The only sour point on them was Captain English's appearance at one, he and his wife. The exec, I think, was convinced that the captain wouldn't be coming. The captain himself never entertained to my recollection. The captain and his wife came, stayed a relatively brief time, and departed. They were barely out the front door when there was a loud cheer from all the guys there who'd had several beers under their belt. I'm sure he heard it, but he didn't come back in. I was waiting for the door to reopen. But, outside of that, most of the people in the wardroom got along quite well. There were several who were constantly in trouble with the exec, usually for not having met qualification requirements and getting on with things. I guess I'll withhold the name of one guy who seemed to be the butt of almost everything because he earned it. He almost went out of his way, it seemed, to screw things up. But, by and large, it was a very compatible group of people in the wardroom.

Paul Stillwell: Well, having a common enemy would sort of draw you together.

Admiral Trost: It does. We had one interesting officer report aboard. He came to the ship, new supply officer replacing a very popular supply officer, who was also a Naval Academy graduate. This supply officer came aboard, and he was aboard the ship for four days before we knew he was there. Everybody was expecting him. The exec kept saying, "Hey, this guy's due." Well, he was down in that four-man JO bunkroom, which during that in-port period was—the other occupants were guys who were married, and they weren't on board ship at night and didn't go down there very much. This guy was down there in a bunk for four days. One of the stewards knew about it and was supplying him with food. He kind of rested up before he came up and reported. [Laughter] Rather fascinating. He did not last a real long time. He was aboard the ship, as I recall, for about three or four months and got into trouble on his disbursing accounts. A noticeable shortage of funds caused him to depart early. We had a true cross section of people. A lot of Ivy League college graduates, which I always thought was a darn good influence on the Navy. It bothered me during Vietnam that the Ivy Leagues shut down their ROTC systems in many cases.

Paul Stillwell: Why do you say that?

Admiral Trost: I thought they brought a perspective. They brought a somewhat different educational background than the Midwesterner or the guy from the Far West or West Coast. I always thought that the mix of Naval Academy and non-Naval Academy officers from various commissioning sources gave you a good background. You saw the melding of officers into a community over a period of time. The speed at which they became functioning naval officers depended to some degree on the background they had and the training, the length of training they had, the depth of it, and also very much so on the individual. Some people just got in and started digging right away and were productive and others seemed to have to be prodded to make every move. We had a few of those.

We had a couple of playboys on board. We had one gent who received a monthly allowance from his parents, his mother actually, which matched his base pay, which wasn't much, so that was very nice. Of course, he lived rather more highly as a bachelor than the rest of us bachelors did. His parents also, as a welcome-home present when we returned from the Mediterranean, gave him a brand-new Ford convertible so he would have something to drive around the area. We had a couple of playboys on board in addition to him. One of whom—I think he was a University of Pennsylvania graduate—he was the most carefree human being about everything I've ever known. He enjoyed life on the town. He also drove a convertible, but it was an old convertible whose top wouldn't go up anymore. It used to be parked out at the piers down there. Of course, in those days ships were burning black oil and blowing tubes nightly, and any car down there was covered with soot all the time. This thing was always just black on the inside, and it never dawned on him. He'd just jump in and take off. He was usually alone, because nobody else wanted to ride in the car. They were interesting people.

Paul Stillwell: You said when you reported aboard you saw that your picture as a midshipman had been posted. Were you, in any sense, a marked man when you got there?

Admiral Trost: Probably to a degree at least they were certainly going to wonder what the hell this guy was. This picture had been in *All Hands* magazine. I guess it was pretty widely published, but probably was to a degree, hard to tell.

Paul Stillwell: But I take it that probably that feeling evaporated after you had that confrontation with the chief.

Admiral Trost: Oh, yeah. I never really felt any problem or any distance or any problem at all in relations. My problem was not being a good division officer until I got squared away, and it made quite a big difference. As a matter of fact, I've told all of the young officers that story just to remind them that it's better to ask the people who know than go off and go the wrong direction yourself. It was a good experience.

Paul Stillwell: I've got another sheet on your post-deployment experiences.

Admiral Trost: We did go to a lot of places here that I'd forgotten about. Toulon, France, we went in, and I remember one of the French battleships in dry dock, and that seemed almost to be the mark of the French major combatant Navy at that time. It was in dry dock for several years. And it saved money, and they did whatever conversion they wanted to at a rather leisurely pace. When we went in there, we were challenged to a soccer game, and we went out and played. I had played soccer at the Naval Academy, but I had never played on cinders. The field was paved with cinders and the portions of our legs that weren't covered with the bruises from the French kicking the devil out of us, were covered with scabs of having fallen in the ashes and sliced ourselves open. We lost rather badly in that game.

We had Tangier, Morocco. I remember Tangier well. I've been back to Tangier one time since then, just a year ago, aboard a cruise ship. We went in; it was our final port of call having department the Straits of Gibraltar part of the way home. Really what happened was that the going-home fleet that was sailing together was mustered off Tangier early on to sail home. We went in, as I remember about three destroyers; there was an LST in there. I don't remember any other ships or not. Morocco at that time was a rather pleasant place. It's a town and what you see or sightsee is really seeing that part of the world, as opposed to seeing other things. We did not get out of the city very far. Great shopping mecca. It's got that shopping area is just   you can get lost in it, in the maze of it, and we saw that again while we were there this last time. But it was called the souk, I think it is.

Paul Stillwell: Right.

Admiral Trost: Winding down through that was rather fascinating, and of course, that's where also our guys bought all sorts of things, camel saddles and leather stuffed animals and things which had to be gutted and all the stuffing taken out when we got back to Norfolk because you couldn't take those things ashore.

Paul Stillwell: Why was that?

Admiral Trost: It was some form of insect, like a beetle that was in the straw that they used to stuff this up there. They would hatch, and then they would be in the stuff when it came back. And so for the guys out there, there was a big bin out on the quarterdeck and those guys went ashore and they would take them into customs, the inspector sliced these things open and dumped everything out and handed the remnants back to guys. It was a rather interesting place.

I'll tell one of the sea stories on Captain English on that particular one. We were due to get under way from there at anchor about midnight. Liberty had expired at about 2000, and we had everybody back, except the commanding officer. The commanding officer had told the exec that he was going out with some friends. Well, at about 11:00 o'clock at night, we got the word that the commanding officer was en route back with the whaleboat, really the gig, which we still had to lift. He said that he had some friends with him, and that he wanted sandwiches and coffee and things ready when he got back to show his friends the ship. We looked at that, because we were making our underway preparations at the time. The stewards, not knowing how many people were with him, had prepared this huge platter of sandwiches, and he'd brought back an American couple to visit the ship. They were people who lived in Tangier; he was a businessman, and they'd been very nice to him. And it was clear that all three of them had had a fair amount to drink before they came back out. So he sat, sort of shooting the bull with these people, and it was getting to be underway time. And the exec reminded him that we were getting under way shortly.

He said, "Oh yes." He said, "We'll send the people back in." Well, it was about a 20-minute boat ride in and a 20-minute boat ride back, and the people left. We got ready to get under way, reporting to the commanding officer that we were ready to get under way, but still awaiting the return of the whaleboat. He came to the bridge in fresh khakis and said, "Let's get under way."

I was the navigator, and I said, "Captain, we're ready to get under way, but we don't have our whaleboat back."

He said, "Tell him to follow us." Well, we did have walkie-talkie communications with the whaleboat, and he was still about ten minutes away from us. He was heading for the LST, which he thought was us, and so we got him headed in the right direction. We weighed anchor, and we started out. I kept recommending to the captain that we keep a very slow speed, since that whaleboat wasn't going very fast. We finally stopped to pick up the whaleboat, and we got it just before we came abreast of the breakwater, which juts out from the west to the east. We were being set down on the breakwater, so as soon as we got the whaleboat up, I said, "Captain, we are being set down. We need some turns, and we need to go due north."

So he cranked on speed and headed north, and all of the sudden he said, "Left standard rudder." And, hell "left standard rudder" would put us right into shoal water, quickly. I said, "Captain, recommend hold your course and speed."

He said, "No," he said, "I want the searchlight manned. I promised these people I'd illuminate their house up on the hill as we went by."

I said, "You can't do it here. You're going to run aground."

He said, "I'm the commanding officer."

Well, he was the commanding officer, and I could see the green table in front of me at my court-martial as the navigator. I said, "Yes, sir." I said, "Quartermaster, please log that the commanding officer has disregarded the recommendations of the navigator that he is standing into shoal water."

He turned around and said, "What?" And then he gave a right-rudder order and steamed out. Another reason, I guess, that I was one of his real favorites. [Laughter]. We got away from that anyway and then did steam back. We had rather rough steaming coming back, and there was some question—we were all hoping that we'd run out of fuel and therefore would have to go into Bermuda, because we were told we would have to fuel in Bermuda if we were short of fuel. But we managed to eke it out and get into Norfolk on schedule. The only remaining navigational event being that we were coming up—we had crossed on the southerly course about 34° North all the way across because of winter weather and then come up. So we were approaching Norfolk from the southeast, and as one approaches, off Dam Neck, as a matter of fact, off Sand Bridge, off where we had our cottage, there is a navigational buoy. It is well south of Cape Henry, where you turn to go into Norfolk.

We were steaming up, and the captain said, "It's time to turn."

I said, "No, sir, we've got another 20 minutes on this course before we alter course."

"No," he said, "I see the buoy." Well, he saw that buoy—what he thought he was seeing was another one up off Virginia Beach where we should legitimately have been getting ready to turn. We had another argument there about navigational accuracy until the chief quartermaster, very diplomatically, stepped in and looked at the radar repeater and noted that the direction which he wanted to go appeared to be solid land on the radar and, in fact, we could see the opening, the channel opening between the two capes. So, again, we didn't run aground, but not because we didn't have a very stubborn gentleman there. We came back in, let's see—early February 1954.

Paul Stillwell: We haven't really talked too much about the operations you were involved in in the Sixth Fleet. Any comments on that? You were with the *Bennington* a long time it appeared in the log.

Admiral Trost: With *Bennington* a long time. They were rather routine exercises for the sake of exercising more than anything else. I didn't see any big effort to work this thing up. My recollections at the time were that we spent one hell of a lot of time just maneuvering. As a matter of fact, it was fun from the standpoint of being an OOD, because you could go alongside other ships; every one of us got a shot at landings and approaches alongside of ships. We were the volunteer mail ship periodically, and we'd get all of the mail transferred to the other ships in the group. If you were in the surface group, for example, with several cruisers and about eight destroyers you made a lot of alongsides. It was great ship handling for everybody. But I almost had the sense that it was make-work under way and enjoy liberty and show your presence, of course, which you were there for. We had a lot of liberty time. We had a lot of time in port.

Paul Stillwell: Do you have any observations on Weapon Able?

Admiral Trost: I saw one weapon fired. I had no good feeling for how effective it would have been. There was enough explosive in that head that had it hit the submarine it would clearly have done very, very substantial damage, probably sunk it. The tactics for its use were good. We practiced tactics for its use quite a bit. They would try to lay a triangular pattern with those things, and I would say that if you had a fairly good sonar solution, you were standing a reasonably good chance to hit the target. But I'm not certain whether those were contact fuzed; I think they were.[*]

Paul Stillwell: That was going to be my next question.

---

[*] Weapon Able had a time fuze, set in conjunction with depth-finding sonar.

Admiral Trost: I believe they are contact fuzed; that said, you still need to know exactly where the guy is. I think those are about 60-yard separations, the legs of the triangle.

Paul Stillwell: So it would be like the Hedgehog in that regard.

Admiral Trost: Yeah, except a much more lethal pattern and of course, fewer projectiles. Although I guess if you take a triangle 180 feet on a side, if you've got a good solution, you probably would have a pretty good chance of hitting it. I saw one fired, and my only recollection is that I saw it from the bridge, and the swoosh of that exhaust going back up the mount, sort of looked like a ball with tube sticking out of it that could be elevated. There was a flash deflector on the back that diverted the rocket exhaust back up into the air, and it scorched the paint on the front of the bridge structure. Rather impressive thing to see go off, but that's the only one that I saw shot. There were some sub-caliber munitions of about 5-inch diameter that could be placed in clusters of three inside the barrel. They were used for practice runs. They were plaster loaded, and they were used in there just like the plaster-loaded Hedgehogs. We seemed to have a fair number of Hedgehogs available. We didn't of Weapon Able, because there weren't that many in the fleet. There never were that many.

We also had a Mark 35, Mod 0 electric torpedo, which was an antisubmarine warfare weapon. We had torpedoes on board sometimes, but never fired any. The system did not seem to work very well; apparently it wasn't a very good torpedo. We had this huge main deck torpedo room which was intended to carry a lot of these things, prepare them. And we had two side-firing tubes just above the main deck on both sides back aft and they fired directly out from the ship, perpendicular to the ship. We did shoot some. I remember losing one. I don't remember much about its effectiveness, except that it didn't seem to be much of a weapon at that time. It was probably the forerunner of a lot of the subsequent ASW torpedoes.

Paul Stillwell: Weapon Alfa didn't last very long before ASROC came along and overtook it.[*]

Admiral Trost: Well, that's right.

Paul Stillwell: So there must have been a perceived need already for something better.

Admiral Trost: Yeah, I think there was. Clearly, just a pure contact weapon wasn't going to be enough. It didn't have the legs, although at that time we were still not enjoying the ranges to get a weapon out very far. I don't remember that this was a particularly long-legged torpedo, but it was a pretty good size weapon. It was at least a 19-inch torpedo. It was a long one. It was not a little tiny thing. Probably, in many respects, somewhat similar to the Mark 28 that submarines had right around that time. The Mark 28 was a battery-powered, anti-ship weapon and pretty long range, not especially fast. Not a good warhead.

Paul Stillwell: How much briefing did you as junior officers get on the big picture of the mission of the Sixth Fleet at that point?

Admiral Trost: None that I recall.

Paul Stillwell: It was clearly built around the carriers, and you were there to support the carriers.

Admiral Trost: My evaluation of the use of the surface action groups was a way to split the things up so that you didn't have too many people in the same port at the same time. Go out and give those guys something to do. One particular evolution that I shall never forget was after Jack English took over, and we were doing this mail boy routine—we were going to be the mail boy the next morning, and we were going to go alongside *Des Moines*, the Sixth Fleet flagship.[†] The captain said, the afternoon before, "We are going alongside the flagship tomorrow morning, and I want this ship painted." Of course, we were under way and had been under way for several days, and the ship didn't look bad,

----

[*] The name was changed when the Navy adopted a new phonetic alphabet in the late 1950s.
ASROC – antisubmarine rocket. It entered the fleet in the early 1960s in new-construction ships and in FRAM I destroyer conversions.
[†] The heavy cruiser *Des Moines* (CA-134) was Sixth Fleet flagship from 9 October 1953 to 12 May 1954.

but he directed the first lieutenant to paint the port side superstructure, as there wasn't time to do both. They were going alongside port side to—and paint the main deck. First lieutenant said, "Yes, sir" and went off; the troops painted the main deck.

They painted the 01 level forward, where the Weapon Able sat and the trainable Hedgehogs were sitting. And we had two of those tilt-able, rectangular-type Hedgehog mounts next to Weapon Able. And then one level up was—I think it was one level up, trying to picture it—no, I guess Weapon Able was a level up. Down below we had one trainable Hedgehog mount and two fixed, but you could tilt and adjust the pattern. The 01 level was the handling station for lines. The line forward came over the 01 level just down at the base of the bridge structure, and aft it came to the 01 level aft of number-two stack to a kingpost. There was also our fueling station aft.

But we'd haul in—the fueling trunks were on—at the main deck level they rose up about that high off the deck.

Paul Stillwell: Three feet maybe.

Admiral Trost: At any rate, were painted. At the evening meal, the first lieutenant said, "Captain, the deck's not drying. It's just too humid out here, and that paint's not drying."

The captain said, "God damn it, you should have mixed something with it to dry it faster."

He said, "We did." I don't remember what the paint was, but there was a solvent they used to thin it a little bit to cut drying time. Well, the next morning we are due to go alongside bright and early. I say bright and early, it was maybe 8:00 in the morning going alongside the flagship. So here we are, and at that time in the Mediterranean, in Sixth Fleet, if you were a bridge watch or exposed topside, you had to be in blues. It was especially important when you were alongside the flagship. Alongside the flagship, nobody in dungarees or khakis could be observed from the flagship. So here we were; we were all in blues, including the guys on the deck. Of course, the guys had the working blues without the piping on the collars. I was on the bridge, and when I looked down on the deck, every place a guy had stepped you could see footprints. Even by the time we got alongside and everything prepared, there were guys with paint on their trousers, their footprints all over the place, paint on their shoes and—well, there was nothing we could do about this. The captain said, "Now, I'm going to show these guys a real ship-handling lesson."

Paul Stillwell: This was English?

Admiral Trost: This was English. So English made his approach from astern with a full bell on. The formation speed was about 12 or 14 knots, 12 knots as, I recall. We came up, and we passed the fantail of that cruiser with one hell of an overtaking rate. About the time our bow crossed the stern of the other ship alongside, he put on a backing bell. He backed full. We went sort of ahead full, back full, ahead standard, and adjust the turns, and it was beautiful. We just settled right in alongside in the right place, right there. And he turned around to the exec and said, "We're going to get an 'atta boy' for this."

Well, lines went over, and a few minutes later, flashing light from the flagship, our signalman was taking the message and checking. And he said, "That's it; that's the congratulatory message." Message came up, captain read it and said, "Shit." Crumpled it up, tossed it on the deck, and went to his sea cabin. The exec picked it up and unfolded it, and it said, "Don't ever hazard my flagship again. Use constant speed." [Laughter] So he lost his opportunity for glory. He was a feisty character.

I was looking through some of these other operations. We did a lot of ASW training in that time frame, generally opposed by a single diesel submarine, which didn't give enough—as a matter of fact, the big complaint in that time frame was that the ASW ships didn't have enough submarine services. That's been a complaint throughout my naval career, but I think things were slimmer then than in later years. The planning wasn't good, and they left too many things to chance, and we just didn't get the time to practice as much as we should have.

I was looking in here at these post-deployment operations. We did unload ammunition. I remember about a month after we came back and went up to Brooklyn—New York Naval Shipyard—for a brief period of time. The purpose was a three-week availability to install electronic warfare equipment. I've forgotten which version it was, but it was some of the early versions of intercept equipment to permit you to detect radar signals and other things. We got that and then we went back to Norfolk and became operational again. And then, we were in fact involved in an amphibious exercise that summer, and it was interesting. We were to be participants and do shore bombardment off the coast in support of an amphibious landing.

Paul Stillwell: Without guns?

Admiral Trost: Without guns. That was called to the attention of our squadron commander, who said, "Simulate." So we in fact steamed back and forth off the coast of Virginia Beach, down off Camp Pendleton, between Virginia Beach and Dam Neck, plotting targets and then plotting the courses we'd have to take and then simulating when we should shoot and playing the games. Fortunately, there were several of us on board who had done that in simulators. I had done it at the Naval Academy, where we had been trained to do that. So we played the game, but it was strictly that; it was a mock game. It was always something that struck me as being rather stupid, sort of the least productive employment of the ship in that time frame we could have had.

We did, subsequently, go up to Philadelphia for overhaul. Destroyer overhauls at that time were about three months' duration on average, but again, we off-loaded ammunition. We went up to Fort Mifflin, which is just south of the old Philadelphia Naval Shipyard on the Delaware River. We off-loaded ammunition there and went in and had an overhaul.

I have to admit that my professional competence in getting my stuff done wasn't what it became in later years when I knew my equipment better. It was more of a case at that time it seemed of the shipyard knowing what had to be done. The shipyard was really running the ship, instead of the ship being the driver. We did get things fixed that needed fixing. We did not get our underwater battery fire control problems fixed, because there still weren't any spare parts for the thing. We did get some gun fire control system. We had a Mark 56 system for the 3-inch/50s, and what we got there was a replacement director, one that had been reworked and overhauled that came aboard and replaced the consoles.

We had a hurricane that came through late that summer that roared up and came inland. We were in dry dock at the time with one big hole in the side where the fire control consoles had gone out, a level below the main deck, and several other holes in the hull. I remember the hurried hull patching after that hurricane took a threatening course. We decided that we would flood the dock—have to flood the dock, but leave the gate in place to protect us from any surge and anything else that might take place. The ship, along with there was something else in dock with us, a smaller vessel also being overhauled. So these two ships were moored off the blocks in dock for that period of time, which caused us some time loss.

I was one of several officers who were married, and our wives were over across the river in Paulsboro, New Jersey, living in an apartment complex. There were two-story apartments, upper and lower, and I think there were eight married couples over there. I was designated by the exec as one of—I think there were two or three of us—to go over and make sure the families were all right. Everybody else stayed with the ship. I recall getting over there, and we rode out the hurricane in that apartment, which I thought was going to blow away. It was the kind where if you sneeze in one apartment, you could hear it three doors down. The interesting thing about it was just watching things rock, and I remember that garbage cans that were left outside became missiles. They flew through the air a couple of feet off the ground and were slamming into a house. We were frightened, but not otherwise damaged, and the ship came through it in good shape, although we were set back for several days. But it was a good opportunity. Philadelphia was very popular with the troops at that time.

Paul Stillwell: Why so?

Admiral Trost: Good liberty. They could go out; you could really wander around town, you could really wander around the district between there and downtown, which you can't do today, and do so safely. People were friendly and a lot of the married guys brought their families up. The captain brought his wife and his kids up. We sent a 2½-ton stake-body truck out to his house in Norfolk and a working party, and they packed up and loaded up his things and hauled it to the ship and we put it in the torpedo room, which was empty. It didn't have any torpedoes in it, and his worldly goods went in there. His car, which was an old Cadillac, was picked up from the pier by a pier crane and put up on the old 01 level, covered and lashed down to transport. His wife and kids got up there some way, I don't know. They didn't go aboard ship, but everything else did.

Paul Stillwell: Prerogatives of command.

Admiral Trost: Prerogatives of command, and we reversed the process on the other end and took these out to the place that he had rented up there. The other thing that Captain English had was a phobia about the mess share going down in value during his command tour. I happened to be the mess treasurer during the period of this overhaul, and I was directed to ensure that the mess share didn't go down. He also made that point clear to the leading steward. So when we had to off-load the ship of everything, all our stores and all were going into a warehouse for storage, because the crew's mess was shutting down, and the troops were going to subsist onshore in actually a cafeteria-style environment, where we set up the mess. But he wanted to maintain the wardroom mess on board. The married guys in the wardroom didn't like that because he said, "You know, we're going to serve three meals a day," which only made sense. The duty officers had to eat too, but we were going to do it by going out shopping at the Safeway and having our meals on board. He said, "Okay, well, the Jack-of-the-dust"—I'm sure you've heard of that term.[*]

Paul Stillwell: Right.

Admiral Trost: The Jack-of-the-dust and the leading steward were great buddies. The Jack-of-the-dust arranged not to have to take off anything that had already been opened or some of the stuff that might get damaged in the transition, if the steward would just take it, and he could take it. So it was written off the books. We got this stuff, we had wardroom country—we had a couple of places in wardroom country that were chockablock with sacks of potatoes, flour, sugar, coffee—all sorts of other things that

---

[*] Jack-of-the-dust is an old Navy term for the individual in charge of the provision issue room for the crew's mess.

came from the general mess. In my first month, I was astounded by the high prices, not the individual prices, but the amounts of money that we were spending on groceries to feed this group out of the Safeway. I thought, "Gee, what an expensive way to do business."

Comes to the end of the month, and I get first of all the ration credits for the stewards who were also subsisting on the wardroom mess, and I totaled up all the bills, and after paying all the bills and taking the credits, the mess share had gone up $5.00 without anybody paying anything. I thought, "Hey, this is wrong," so I went to see the exec, and I said, "You know, we got to have the guys at least pay something, and I don't know what happened." I didn't know about this extra food at the time.

"Well," he said, "don't do anything until I tell the captain."

He told the captain, and the captain said, "That's fine. Don't charge anybody anything." So we did this for two months. The third month I found out about all this extra food and where it was coming from. We finally reimbursed. I don't remember how we did that; I guess we wrote a check to the Treasury of the U.S. or something for an amount which didn't cover anywhere near the stuff that we had. But the captain insisted that everybody would show that they had paid something per month, every month, and I think that's something that came out to less than $5.00 a month for up to three meals a day.

Paul Stillwell: Pretty good deal.

Admiral Trost: Pretty good deal. So Uncle Sam helped us out there, recognized our low salaries, and helped out. But we then came from overhaul back down to Norfolk. We moved back down temporarily, because at this time. I had applied for Submarine School, and I hoped to get my orders. I had applied once previously after my mandatory year at sea and qualification, and the commanding officer wouldn't forward the letter. The second time I told him that I thought he had to forward it, because I had read that somewhere, even if he disapproved it. So he forwarded it disapproved, and we went down.

The ship was getting ready then for Gitmo, and I was fully engaged in that. I kept waiting to see what was going to happen, because I found out that I had been selected for Submarine School, but I didn't get any orders. I went to see the exec just before Christmas. We were going to go up and see Pauline's folks on Christmas Day. He said, "Oh, your orders are here, but I'm not authorized to deliver them." I think I had to be in Submarine School on the third of January. My orders were delivered to me on about the 29th of December, at the captain's direction to keep me aboard as long as possible. Then they turned me loose, and we drove on up to New London.

Paul Stillwell: Why did he do that?

Admiral Trost: Spite. He didn't want me to leave the ship. He didn't like submariners. *Cony* was one of the ships in our division. I don't remember the commanding officer's name, but he was one of the most highly regarded guys in the squadron.* And he was a dolphin-wearing guy, had been commander of a submarine, and English really disliked that guy. The guy had a great reputation, good operator, the crew loved him, and he ran a good ship. One of my good buddies from the ASW course was there, and they really had a happy ship.

They operated with us in the Med. I didn't notice them on this particular group here, but *Cony* was in the Med with us. Our entire division was there—*Cony*, *Conway*, and *Waller*, and we got together. We had a Christmas party in Golfe-Juan, adjacent to Cannes. That's where we were actually anchored, and the Christmas party was in a restaurant we leased for the evening, for Christmas Eve. The skippers were all there, and the wardrooms of all of the ships were all represented.

I remember it being characterized by a foot race on the two-block section from the railroad crossing up to a block past the restaurant, which was halfway in between, uphill with my commanding officer being the challenger, challenging different people to race him. Bourbon and chocolate milk were the beverages of the evening, if you can imagine that. That was so that nobody would have too much hard liquor, and the milk was going

---

* Commander Donald A. Dertien, USN, commanded the *Cony* (DDE-508) from 1953 to 1955. He had not been a submariner; all his service was in surface ships.

to coat your stomach. I'll tell you, when you mix bourbon with milk, it looks like it has been regurgitated at least once before you drink it. But we had good food and a very pleasant evening. The commanding officers were very, very much competitors with each other, very much.

Paul Stillwell: How much of an entity was the destroyer division in those days?

Admiral Trost: For this deployment, there was the entity; for some of the ASW exercises it was an entity, but you did not routinely operate as an entity. I would say it was about 50% paper and 50% fact in terms of time cooperation.

Paul Stillwell: Sounds as if you just got the bad luck of the draw in the skippers.

Admiral Trost: Well, I think I did, because I had a lot more regard for all the other skippers. These two men, incidentally, stand out in my mind, as the only two bad COs I've ever had. When I say bad, people with an approach that was hardly leadership. On the other hand, you'd learn a lot of leadership principles by watching these guys totally disregard them. I truly think that had I not been permitted to go off to Submarine School, I would have left the Navy as my obligated tour was up, because I was not a happy warrior on the ship. I got a lot of professional satisfaction out of it, but I didn't like the environment.

Paul Stillwell: It also may well have discouraged some of the shipmate officers of yours who would've stayed in otherwise.

Admiral Trost: I think so. When I think of the group that reported aboard when I did, I'm the only one that stayed in. Of those two sets ahead of me, none of them stayed in. Of course, it was partly this system of automatic out, which, you know, in retrospect, several of these guys, who later continued as very active reservists and then retired from the reserves, thought gee they'd have like to stayed on active duty, but you were told you were going. It doesn't even give you time to think about what you're going to do. It doesn't require you to think, because it's automatic.

Paul Stillwell: So there wasn't even an option of staying?

Admiral Trost: No, there was not really. They were discouraging it, because, see, we were now in the post-Korea time, and the Navy was phasing down. So they weren't looking for more officers. Of course, they weren't keeping enough at that time to keep even the numbers they should have. I don't know what the exact numbers were, but the Navy was decreasing in size.

Paul Stillwell: What do you recall about collateral duties? I notice you were athletic officer, among other things.

Admiral Trost: I think I was boating officer. I was in charge of equipping and training the landing team. We had equipment, but didn't do a hell of a lot of training, because there wasn't an opportunity for it. I was hoping we'd never be put ashore somewhere and left, because I figured they were going to have to worry about coming back and picking us up. We didn't have enough ammunition to be able to go out and practice shooting the weapons we had for example. We did have weapons, but not a hell of a lot of allowance of ammunition.

Paul Stillwell: You had a series of different billets there. Did you feel a sense of growing confidence during this progression?

Admiral Trost: Well, I did. I always felt very good professionally. I can't remember the exact time period, but I was able to serve in the gunnery department, in the operations department as navigator. I think my title was probably assistant navigator throughout that time, because I think the XO actually signed the logs, as I remember. Had a good opportunity—I think the only time I was a department head per se, was when I was the acting gunnery officer during the time in overhaul when Jim Moore went off. He had a family illness problem. He was off for about a month, as I recall. I was the acting gun boss as my only department head tour. But to go to submarines you had to be a qualified department head and qualified officer of the deck under way and in port.

I felt a lot of satisfaction, because I felt very confident about my ability to stand watches, and I got to do that. We got under way from Philadelphia, and I was the navigator, but the commanding officer said, "We're going to go down the river to [I think it was Fort Mifflin] to get our ammo, and you've got the deck."

I said. "Fine," so I got a chance to take the ship down river first under way on a pretty good current running and making a with-the-current landing. And I navigated the rest of the way down there. I always felt I was being given responsible jobs, and I got a lot of satisfaction from that. When I say I was an unhappy warrior, in some respects, it wasn't because I wasn't being able to get in to do the things. It was the command environment, which was disillusioning in many respects. When you're in a ship that returns from a deployment and you have two people being treated for a venereal disease by your corpsmen on the way home, and one of those two is the captain, and the other one is one of the junior officers, that's not a very good leadership environment. When you then see this commanding officer has been behaving like a "tomcat" all over the place, leap off the ship as it still has very minute amount of way on, a couple of lines over the number-two line, which was the spring lay over, head line over, and he leaps off the ship across about three feet of open space between himself and the pier and goes running up the pier to his wife and picks her up and hugs her and swings her around in the air, you're saying he's a phony sucker.

He did take advantage of a lot of things. In addition to moving his things, he used the crew to his advantage, but so did his predecessor. His predecessor owned his house in Norfolk. One day when I was returning aboard after school, before we got under way to go on deployment, I noticed a truck being loaded with a lot of stuff from the ship's basic machinery repair guys, auxiliary gang guys. He got about half a dozen of them with a whole bunch of tools. They were going out to George Dawson's house to build a screened porch on the back of his house, which they did. The charge was, subsequently, that Dawson kept most of the tools. Most all the carpentry tools stayed out there at his house, at his direction. In return, for having done this, he bought them a case of beer. Rather blatant. Now, I've seen examples of that from time to time, but these guys were of that school that you use the people that are there to serve you and use them any way you want. He seemed to have no qualms about it.

Paul Stillwell: The other part about this example he's setting is that you sort of condone misdoings by the enlisted men. Was that a problem for the junior officers?

Admiral Trost: It didn't appear to be, except that discipline in the sense of formal disciplinary action for misdeeds, was lax under English, specifically. Dawson would just hammer the hell out of a guy if something happened. But I didn't have much exposure to Dawson at mast. I had much more with English. With English it became the view of the officers and the chiefs a waste of time to put somebody on report, because the charge against him was going to get thrown out, and the guy who put him on report was the guy that got chewed out.

So there we were fortunate in having an exec who could handle things very nicely. We had a young deck seaman, for example, who didn't like to bathe and didn't like to wash his clothes, and he was rather offensive in bodily odor and appearance. While we were in the Mediterranean, he'd been put on report for not complying with rules of the ship. The captain said, "Well, that's just the failure of you guys to make him do the right thing." So he threw that one out.

What the chief could do, of course, was hold his liberty card, and he did. The chief was finally told one day by the executive officer I happened to be present, so I know this really happened—"You are responsible for that guy, he's in your division, you're the leading chief boatswain's mate. Get him cleaned up. Next time I see him, I want to see him pink and shiny and in a brand-new set of dungarees." Next time the exec saw him, about two hours later, he was pink and shiny; he was scrubbed almost raw. They took this kid, stripped him, threw his clothes over the side and took him into the shower at the after end of the main deck level, the crew's head and shower area. A couple of guys with salt water soap and a salt water shower and hard bristle brushes scrubbed this kid, and, believe me, he was clean. He was raw.

Paul Stillwell: That's an old Navy remedy.

Admiral Trost: Oh, yeah. And then they took him down, and they had bought from ship's service brand-new clothes, which he was going to pay for. They got him dressed up, stenciled properly, took him up for inspection with the exec, and he passed muster. That kid was never dirty again that I saw. It was the kind of lesson in boatswain's mate justice.

We had another guy who was a repeat liberty problem. He'd get his liberty card back, and he would go over and create another problem. Well, he liked to fight, and one day he took a punch at a second class boatswain's mate who'd been first class at least three times in his Navy career. The boatswain's mate he punched was from our ship. He was one of our leading division guys. This guy just kind of picked him up and smashed him around a little bit. The kid came back to the ship and filed a complaint against the boatswain's mate. The commanding officer chewed out the second class boatswain's mate. The next time this kid came down to the boatswain's locker for a cup of coffee, he learned that there is always retribution under that system. They kicked the hell out of him again, and he became a much more squared-away sailor.

We had another guy—he was a gunner's mate striker who was a smart-mouthed kid who'd badmouth everybody, also in third division at that time, but working with the deck force, striking in his spare time. When we were anchored off Taranto, he was assigned as the forecastle sentry, because the quarterdeck was set up on the fantail. That's where we took the boats alongside instead of the regular boat boom to give us a little more room, because we didn't have much walking space on the other side of the deck to receive liberty parties, stores, or anything else. So this was in daylight hours. On this particular day I was the CDO, and as CDO I was in the duty section.[*] At any rate, I went back to see how things were going on the fantail, and we had a second class gunner's mate back there who was on watch. I said, "How are things going?"

He said, "Fine, except that I haven't seen the forecastle sentry. He's supposed to report in to me every half hour, hour."

I said, "Well, I'm going to walk the deck anyway; I'll take a check at it." Made a complete tour of the deck, and I didn't see any sign of the sentry. I did, however, see an

---

[*] CDO – command duty officer.

M1 rifle leaning against the anchor windlass capstan. So I picked it up and took it back to the quarterdeck and said, "Here's the weapon; let's find the guy." So we passed the word for him to report to quarterdeck. Nothing. We did this several times. In the meantime, I sent the petty officer of the watch around while I stayed back aft. He didn't find anybody either, and I sort of thought, "What the hell has happened to this guy? He wouldn't jump over the side; he's not that stupid."

Well, he wasn't that stupid. He'd gone down to the boatswain's locker to get coffee, and he was just sitting down there shooting the shit with his buddies. There was no MC system down there, so he didn't hear the general announcing system when they called his name. He was down there for about 45 minutes and then sauntered back up and the next time he was seen was when he came back to the petty officer's watch station. He said, "I don't know what happened. I set my weapon down for a minute to take a look and adjust the jack, and I turned around and it was gone."

Paul Stillwell: [Laughter] Yeah.

Admiral Trost: So we had a few guys like that. He was handled a little more sternly, but that went to a mast that the XO ran, so his liberty was curtailed rather markedly.

We had another kid who shot himself in the foot while—

Paul Stillwell: Literally?

Admiral Trost: Oh, yeah, literally, because he was unhappy in the Mediterranean. He'd gotten engaged. He was a young, nonrated man, but had got engaged before we deployed, and he was unhappy and wanted to see his girlfriend. He had a buddy on the ship who said, "Hell, you know, the thing to do is get yourself medically evacuated back to the States, and you can be with her."

So he thought about that. He said, "Yeah, that's a good idea." So he was on watch; I don't remember which port we were in. I think it was another time that we were at anchor, as a matter of fact, but he was a sentry, and he was armed with an M1 rifle. They carried one or two clips of those things, but they were not to be inserted into the weapon. He inserted a clip in the weapon and put the barrel of the rifle down on his big toe and pulled the trigger. Well, that splattered his big toe and damaged his foot rather considerably, and I think it hurt a little bit more than he planned on. Also the round went through the deck and down into a berthing compartment. It didn't hit anybody, but he was, in fact, medically evacuated. He was medically evacuated to a hospital in Germany, where he was still reclining in disciplinary status when we returned to the States, so it didn't quite work.

We had an interesting group of guys. When we did come back after deployment, about the second or third day, we started mustering people out, sending them over to the receiving station for discharge, all of them enlisted personnel. I watched literally the enlisted heart of that ship walk across the brow. We transferred 180 people. We deployed with almost 320 as I remember, which was probably wartime allowance, but we were fat after the Korean War. We had a lot of these guys who had volunteered to make this deployment, because they wanted to go to the Mediterranean. We took the heart out. Bennett, our first class electronics technician, who was the leading petty officer of the operations department, went. I can't remember the name of the signalman who left. We lost a first class boiler tender, who was another one of the recallees, one of the real stalwarts. You just saw these guys going off in great numbers, and within three days' time we transferred 180 people. The ship, I don't think, would have been able to get under way right then with the people who remained. There were just too many gaping holes, and then we started receiving replacements. But, of course, the numerical replacements were about half the level of what we lost. We were not getting the petty officer input. We were getting a lot of new guys, some designated strikers, a lot of guys out of boot camp coming in to fill the spots. So we were a pretty lean ship for a while.

Paul Stillwell: Interesting how the CO explained to his wife coming back with this VD case.

Admiral Trost: I don't know how he handled that. I really don't know how he handled that. The corpsman was in his cabin every evening on the way home. It was open knowledge. The captain didn't even particularly hide it. He came back to the ship and picked up the 1MC speaker right next to the quarterdeck, and said, "Doc." Called the corpsman to the quarterdeck about 11:00 at night when he came back on the ship. He talked to the corpsman right there in the presence of the enlisted watch standers on the deck about his problem and how he needs these little tubes, this stuff he was carrying. So it was an open secret.

Paul Stillwell: You mentioned this one Thompson who helped you with the equipment. Who were some of the other bright shining lights among the enlisted crew?

Admiral Trost: Well, one of my best and long-time friends was a fellow named Jack Henrizi. Jack was a second class gunner's mate at the time. A guy who had been recalled for Korea, having served in World War II. In the time he was out of the Navy, I think he had a couple of years of college, and then he was recalled for Korea. He was stymied, because there was no advancement opportunity. GM1 was full and no opportunities for advancement. I got to know him, because I was driving up here to see Pauline whenever I had a weekend liberty. His wife Lorraine was living in Arlington and working in Arlington. He found out or I found out that we were both coming up, and he needed a ride. He started driving up with me on the weekends, and I got to know the man. He was just a superb individual. I talked him into applying for conversion training to fire control technician, which was an open rating. He did that, and he made first class. I'm trying to recall whether he made chief or not. He went from a rated fire control technician to warrant status to LDO status. He was killed while still on active duty as a commander. I knew him over the years as we kept in touch, and we were close friends for a long time.

When I became the commander of Submarine Group Five out in San Diego in roughly mid-'73, I had a submarine base that was then known as a support facility. It became a sub base about a year later, and it needed leadership and guidance because it was a shithouse. The guy who was there was a submarine LDO. It was a submarine commander LDO billet, and the guy wasn't doing much of a job. I took him on a tour of the base one day and said, "Well, now what do you think?"

He said, "Looks good, doesn't it?" What it looked like to me was a place with trash strewn everywhere, weeds that needed cutting, buildings that needed repair work, and so I decided that he had to go. I asked for Jack Henrizi. Jack was, at the time, first lieutenant of the *Enterprise* and had served initially as an officer aboard an ammunition ship. He served under Pete Petersen, who died not too very long ago, retired vice admiral.[*] Under Captain Petersen, Jack as a jaygee, was the OOD training officer. I think he had one or two tours on *Enterprise*. He was first lieutenant for about three years on her. At any rate, I got the screams of submarine detailers who said, "This guy is not a submariner, and this is submarine billet, and we've got lots of good guys."

I said, "But I want this guy." I called him and said, "Jack I would like to have you do this. If I do this, are you willing?" I got him broken loose from the aviation community, who felt they owned him by this time. He did an absolutely 4.0 job for me. Jack was on AirPac staff—gosh, this has been a long time ago, early '80s I guess, about the '82 or '83 time frame.[†] He was killed on his way in to work one morning by a drunk who came down onto a freeway going the wrong direction and hit him head on.[‡] He was an absolutely superb guy. Probably the one guy that stands out more than anybody else in that entire group. We had some good officers in that group that I mentioned sort of the core group that got back together. They're all solid citizens—they are all guys who had done quite well, and a couple of them are now retired, enjoying life.

Paul Stillwell: Looking out beyond the ship and the division, there's much more esprit in the surface force now than then. Did you have a sense of a destroyer force ethic or whatever?

Admiral Trost: Not really. We knew we were part of the surface Navy. We were destroyer sailors and there was, even then, the sort of internal pecking order that the destroyer force thought they were the "cream of the crop." The cruisers knew they were, and the battleships knew they were predominant, but there was a degree of esprit de corps in the destroyers over this guy here pushing the fuel around or hauling ammunition,

---

[*] Vice Admiral Forrest S. Petersen, USN (Ret.), died 8 December 1990. Petersen was executive officer of the nuclear-powered aircraft carrier *Enterprise* (CVAN-65) from 1964 to 1966 and commanding officer from 1969 to 1971.

[†] AirPac – Naval Air Force Pacific Fleet, with headquarters in Coronado, California.

[‡] Commander John T. Henrizi, USN, was killed on 18 November 1981 at the age of 56. He was promoted to lieutenant commander in 1973, the year he joined Trost at SubGru 5.

something of that nature, or part of the amphibs. The amphibs were kind of given the bottom slot, I think, in the hierarchy most of the time then and to a degree later on as well. But I think the increase in professionalism in the surface Navy that we talked about earlier has gone a long way toward making it one hell of a lot better outfit with esprit.

Paul Stillwell: Anything else on the *Robert A. Owens*?

Admiral Trost: Not that comes to mind offhand. She was a good ship; she was relatively new, four years old when I reported aboard. So many of the things that material mishandling could have caused hadn't had an opportunity to really show their effect yet. But the ship was pretty well cared for during that time frame, although we did, as I noted, have a lot of things, especially in the weapon systems area that just plain didn't work. The prototype systems—the 100 was never produced as an operational system, and it's quite good, but it did provide the basic framework in experience for some of the later systems that came out.

Paul Stillwell: Well, the Navy had really come through some lean years then. A previous Secretary of Defense had cut way back, so you were harvesting some of that austerity.[*]

Admiral Trost: Well, we had some of that austerity and we also, of course, were in many respects the beneficiary of the Korean War in terms of the talent that came back to those ships that probably prevented their decline in that time frame. They were good people, and they had very high regard for their equipment. As I've said, our firerooms really impressed me.

I went aboard *Haynsworth*. *Haynsworth* was much more smartly run, good appearance, but *Owens* newer engineering spaces, yes, but not a lot more than the others at that time was just—the boiler rooms were clean, they were sparkling and they were painted. Burner fronts were painted a contrasting color to the boiler front. I have forgotten what that paint is that you put on lagging, but you know that the lagging was always white. We didn't have any gray or stains in the spaces, and we didn't have any

---

[*] Louis A. Johnson served as Secretary of Defense from April 1949 until September 1950. He cut back substantially on defense expenditures, a program that had to be reversed with the beginning of the Korean War in June 1950. He was removed as SecDef a few months after the war started.

verdigris growing on valves, and valve handles were polished daily. It was Chief Larry, but he had a couple of these really, good talented guys who had been recalled who took a lot of pride in their equipment.

Paul Stillwell: That's the key obviously.

Admiral Trost: Things went well. Al Mumma was a good engineer and he kept things running well, and Pounders before him was a very sound engineer. They were real professionals. I don't know if Pounders put the ship in commission as engineer officer or not; he may have. She was certainly well cared in the engineering plant and always very reliable. Much more so than I remember surface combatants being later, older surface combatants, yes.

But my time as a fleet commander, Seventh Fleet then later, LantFlt, these ships routinely did evolutions that people had trouble making. We never questioned the ability to have four boilers on the line and make max speed. Full power was a fairly routine evolution. It really isn't, hasn't been, even with the upgrade program and the materiel upgrade and training upgrade programs we had. In part, a new ship had to be run right to be allowed to have that happen. One of the things that I noticed in contrast later on in the submarine force, we never had any doubt that if you surfaced the diesel submarine with four diesels, if the captain said, as he did on *Sirago*, you know, "Prepare to surface and answer bells on four engines, and, by God, there were four engines on the line the minute you gave them the authority to pop open the exhaust. They rolled over, and they started every time, and they were going to run and we went for homeport full speed all the time. We could've done that with *Owens*. I think they too k care of her quite well.

Paul Stillwell: Well, we are near the end of the tape. Why don't we hear about the *Sirago* and Sub School next time?

Admiral Trost: Okay

Paul Stillwell: Thank you.

Interview Number 4 with Admiral Carlisle A. H. Trost, U.S. Navy (Retired)

Place: Admiral Trost's apartment at Ginger Cove, Annapolis, Maryland

Date: Wednesday, 1 July 2015

Paul Stillwell: Well, Admiral, here we are after a long hiatus. I'm sorry it's so long, but delighted we are back together again. We had concluded in the previous interview, up to the point where you were serving in the destroyer *Robert A. Owens*, and you mentioned getting orders to Submarine School and very short notice on getting there, so if you could resume there please.

Admiral Trost: Well, I had applied for submarine training in the middle of 1954, which was my first year on destroyers. Heard nothing, no orders, no acknowledgement of my application, even though I had all the qualifications required in the instructions. So I encountered Chuck Griffiths, who was quite a bit my senior, class of '46.[*] I knew Chuck; he was a submariner. He was a lieutenant at the time, and I told him I was interested in submarines and told him that I had applied, but I hadn't heard anything.

He said, "Reapply, send a blind copy to the submarine detailer, [his name he gave me], you should hear from him."

Well, I didn't hear from him, so I thought, "Well, I'm turned down again." I think it was on the 29th of December 1954, I was called into his stateroom by the executive officer of the *Owens*. He handed me a set of orders to report to Submarine School four days later. Without a worry, he just handed it to me and then turned around and sat down. I found out later, as I detached, from the ship's yeoman, my first request and my second request had never left the ship. Sending a blind copy was a good ploy, a good thing. I went home and told my wife, in our rental house, "We're moving now."

She said, "What?"

Paul Stillwell: By then you hadn't probably accumulated a lot of possessions.

---

[*] Lieutenant Charles H. Griffiths, USN.

Admiral Trost: We hadn't accumulated; it was fortunate. We didn't have furniture; we were in a furnished house. Everything we had fit in a car. We didn't have a washing machine or anything else. About two mornings later, we set trail for New London. Got to New London; fortunately there were quarters there. They were expecting me, even though they didn't know what happened to my orders. So I had a set of quarters assigned and furnished. We moved in, and I started my submarine career.

Paul Stillwell: Please tell me about the course of instruction at Submarine School.

Admiral Trost: Well, interesting, enjoyable. I thought from an academic perspective it was rather easy. It was very, very interesting and challenging. They had good instructors. The instructors were, by and large, Navy lieutenants qualified submariners, personable— I think selected as much for personality and background, of course. But it was a most enjoyable experience. I think we had 120 people in the class, and about half of them were my classmates from the Naval Academy. So we knew couples and all the guys. It was quite an interesting and enjoyable time.

Paul Stillwell: Any of the Submarine School classmates that stick in your memory?

Admiral Trost: Well, good God, I'll have to go in and look—Gus Hubal, Lee Hebbard, Earl Griggs, Chuck Fellows; that's right offhand.[*] The guys that I've stayed close with over the years, Hank Hukill, probably more if I dredged it up.[†]

Paul Stillwell: What was the balance between classroom instruction and practical work?

Admiral Trost: It was more than half classroom. We went to sea just about every week in one of the local submarines and went out for the day. I don't think we ever went out overnight, because they did not have the accommodations to take, say, eight or ten of us at a time. So it was probably heavily weighted toward the classroom, but a lot of the classroom instruction was hands on. For example, we tore down a diesel engine, put it

---

[*] Lieutenant (junior grade) Augustine E. Hubal Jr., USN; Lieutenant (junior grade) Leroy B. Hebbard Jr., USN; Lieutenant (junior grade) Norman Earl Griggs, USN; Lieutenant (junior grade) Charles D. Fellows, USN.
[†] Lieutenant (junior grade) Henry D. Hukill Jr., USN.

back together, made sure it ran. That was classroom instruction. The gunnery and fire control things were mostly practical, hands-on type of instruction on mockups or actual equipment that was hooked up for example, a fire control console that was hooked up and ran. It could operate just like the regular ones on the ship would have. So it was realistic, hands-on training.

Paul Stillwell: So these were essentially simulators?

Admiral Trost: Yeah.

Paul Stillwell: What was the emphasis there—on making approaches?

Admiral Trost: Emphasis on making approaches. Getting to know the equipment, first of all. For example, from the fire control aspects, every piece of equipment associated with shooting a torpedo had to be mastered. And, then you had actual practical, hands-on approaches, simulator approaches and you could raise a periscope, look through the periscope. You were taught technique; you were graded on technique. You could raise the periscope, you could see through the lens what you would see if you were at sea. It was very realistic simulation—and interesting.

Paul Stillwell: Well, I remember reading during World War II that the optimum firing range meant the submarine had to get awfully close to the target.

Admiral Trost: Yeah.

Paul Stillwell: Had that increased any in the ensuing time?

Admiral Trost: Yes, it had somewhat, but the torpedoes were still basically the same torpedo, so the ranges in which you could shoot in and expect to hit hadn't really expanded that much.

Paul Stillwell: So maybe 1,000 yards or so?

Admiral Trost: I would say that if you shot, I'm guessing now, beyond 2,000 yards, you were scrambling for a hit and not too sure of it. Those runs were generally inside 4,500 yards for the steam torpedoes, and the electric torpedoes were slow, so simulating them was kind of silly and shooting at them and waiting and hoping.

Paul Stillwell: Did this tie in with active-passive sonar during the simulations?

Admiral Trost: It did. But there was a considerable limit placed on active sonar, because that gives you away obviously. You did a lot of learning how to plot with passive bearings only. That was stressed very heavily, as a matter of fact, as was being undetected in your approach, which was hard to simulate, but every once in a while you just throw in a report from the target ship, "You know, saw a periscope at such-and-such a bearing." So they'd say whatever: your plotting technique was sloppy and you were up too long and not careful enough with periscope exposure.

Paul Stillwell: How do you remember applying that knowledge when you went out the school boats?

Admiral Trost: Well, the school boats, they made it as realistic as possible. The targets were either another submarine, very frequently, or a torpedo recovery boat or something of that nature, the small ones. They would watch if they saw a periscope. They'd report it on underwater telephone and of course, that's a negative as you're making an approach, and your grade suffers as a result.

Paul Stillwell: Was there an emphasis on minimum periscope exposure?

Admiral Trost: Absolutely, minimum time, minimum amount.

Paul Stillwell: Are there any of these personable instructors whom you remember specifically?

Admiral Trost: I remember Bob Murrill.[*] Still alive and well—well, not so well, but alive in California in a retirement community. Bob was a lieutenant at the time. He later, when I had Submarine Group Five in San Diego, was my Submarine Development Group Commander and a heck of a fine guy to work with. Gosh, I should remember some of the

---

[*] Lieutenant Robert L. Murrill, USN.

rest; I remember the names when somebody mentions them. Captain M. H. Austin was the guy who was the Submarine School Commander.[*] He died just within the last two or three years on the West Coast.

Paul Stillwell: I remember Mike Rindskopf had that job later, and he died recently.[†]

Admiral Trost: Mike was there. That's where I first met him, and he was amazing. He was a stand-still torpedo fire control computer. He could stand in the conning tower of the simulator when in school, and he had the entire picture in his head. He would comment at the end of the practice run, he'd give his commentary and it's like he recorded it. He never missed a thing. Mike was an amazing guy.

Paul Stillwell: Well, he also fits that description of personable.

Admiral Trost: We moved into Ginger Cove a little over two years ago. That was after we lived downtown for 12 years. Mike lived behind me on Duke of Gloucester Street; we were on Compromise. We did get acquainted over the years. He never changed.

Paul Stillwell: And he was in Bay Woods for a while, which is a counterpart of Ginger Cove as a retirement home.

Paul Stillwell: That's right, he went out there. As a matter of fact, I told him what a dumb move he made, because I've been on the Ginger Cove board for six years, and we looked at both places pretty carefully. I thought this place was much better run and a few other advantages. You don't have to sell your unit here. They buy it back, and you get most of your money back—75%, I think it is—and you don't have to sell it yourself. That's one of the problems that several of the people we know who have been out there at Bay Woods have had. As a matter of fact, I talked to somebody just very recently—it's somebody I know and whose name I would have remembered two years ago. They were bemoaning the fact that they had their place on the market for a year and a half and sold

---

[*] Captain Marshall H. Austin, USN, served as officer in charge of the Navy's Submarine School from July 1953 to July 1955.

[†] Captain Maurice H. Rindskopf, USN, served as officer in charge of the Navy's Submarine School from June 1958 to June 1960. In 1955, when Trost was at the school, Rindskopf was a commander. He subsequently retired as a rear admiral; he died 27 July 2011.

it. The answer, of course, is, "Drop your price, and find somebody who will buy it." That's one thing you're spared here—or your kids are spared here.

Paul Stillwell: How demanding do you remember the pace being at Submarine School?

Admiral Trost: I didn't feel it was very demanding, but I didn't have any academic problem. We had a good social life. The wives got to know each other. We were either out at sea or in school, so the wives had a lot of social contact with their neighbors. We were in so-called T-rows. There were six rows of ten apartments for students. The other poor guys had to be out of town somewhere, but we were lucky to get in, of all places, the T-row. We were one of the ten T's and I think, within about two weeks, my wife knew everybody on our row and everybody on the other side. So they had a pretty nice life, pretty comfortable life in that they had lots of friends. The bridge groups were very active. They did a lot of sightseeing there and between New London and Newport. They probably knew the area pretty thoroughly. Social life was usually constrained pretty much to Friday and Saturday night. Very active club, good club, happy hour on Friday night. I think the most expensive drink was 25 cents.

We sometimes had individual group get-togethers; our classmates, for example, got together. Still remember Ed Worth, whose grandson just graduated as a six-striper and he was a football player.* Ed Worth was a bachelor at the time and lived at the BOQ. Ed was the organizer for one of those parties one night. Our group had one of those private rooms, probably a little bit bigger than this living room here. Ed said, "I propose a cheer for the 100th class." We were the 100th class. He raised his hand with his glass of water, or whatever he had in it went right through the false ceiling and about a 4-foot patch of ceiling came cascading [laughter] down on him. He thought it was pretty funny, so he did it again.

Paul Stillwell: Well, that's how to make an impact.

---

* Lieutenant (junior grade) Edward R. Worth, USN.

Admiral Trost: Yeah, he made an impact and the club made sure they got their money back. All of us got charged on a club bill. All of us who were present and acknowledged our presence paid the extra cost to repair that ceiling. [Chuckle] But we had fun.

Paul Stillwell: How much homework or out-of-class study was there?

Admiral Trost: I would venture it to be anywhere from one to three hours at night, depending on how much you much you understood what happened during the classroom lessons. There were a lot of things you couldn't do. Obviously you can't simulate a simulator, but we brought home reading material and would get ready for the next day's class or refresh what we just learned, what they hoped we learned. It was a good academic environment. We got together often and in different quarters, usually in our row just to get together and discuss what happened during the day or catch up on what the wives were doing when they let us join them [laughter].

I remember there was an active trade. We were all brand-new jaygees, and we didn't have much money. I can recall my wife going next door or going up the block, somebody had a spare light bulb and sub school didn't furnish light bulbs in the quarters. If we needed light bulbs and didn't have the money, we'd pull out somebody's until next payday. We bought gallon wine bottles at a place that was called the New York State Liquor Store, see I remember that [laughter], down under the bridge that approaches on the Groton side. I forgot the name of the wine, but it came in gallon jugs, and it was cheap. It was a $1.80 for a gallon jug of wine, and that's what we drank, except when somebody had a lot of money we bought a case of Schmidt's beer because Schmidt's was $2.20 a case, the cheapest beer that you could buy. We didn't drink anything sophisticated. Didn't drink that much anyway, couldn't afford it.

Paul Stillwell: Was psychological testing any part of this program?

Admiral Trost: There must have been, because there was a lot of stress on the psychological aspects of submarining and how you can't afford to have a guy who's uptight or gets excited easily or doesn't do his homework and doesn't learn the systems. So I guess you'd have to say yes. I don't remember specifics anymore.

Paul Stillwell: Well, claustrophobia might be a thing that would be tested.

Admiral Trost: It's deadly. I had a kid in my division, my first submarine, which was a GUPPY diesel.[*] He was walking from the after battery, where the crew's mess was, and over the after battery, into the control room, and he suddenly panicked. We were underwater. He had been aboard about a month. He just panicked. He felt claustrophobic and, of course, as soon as we got into port he was gone. He had to be. You just can't afford that.

I had another guy in a new-construction SSN who was a fire controlman, new to submarines.[†] He came up one day and said, "I need to get off early today because I lost my glasses, and I can't see without them. Well, he couldn't see with them either because he wasn't there anymore [laughter]. He was a good kid, very dedicated. He had hidden the fact that he couldn't see, he couldn't read very well from a legibility standpoint. He could read, but he had to have his glasses to do it. His eyesight was so poor that he was a hazard, not only to himself, but wouldn't have been able to recognize a tragedy of some sort if he hadn't had his glasses on. So, if he broke his glasses in the process or training or something, he was worthless. So, there was a lot of focus on that.

Paul Stillwell: Was there any stigma in not being able to pass these kinds of tests?

Admiral Trost: He came in shortly before we went on our first sea trials to fill a vacant billet. I have a feeling that we didn't give him quite the screening he should have before he got to the ship. He went through sub school and he must have been wearing his glasses all the time. He was sent up to the shipyard, this new ship, about to get under way, and couldn't see without glasses.

Paul Stillwell: Was there an incentive to finish high in the class standing?

Admiral Trost: Yes, because your order of choice for your first submarine duty was based on your class standing. I stood first, so I got my choice.

---

[*] USS *Sirago* (SS-485), in which he served Trost served 1955-56.
[†] Trost served in the USS *Swordfish* (SSN-579) in 1957-59.

Paul Stillwell: As you had at the Naval Academy.

Admiral Trost: Yes, except the assignments from the Naval Academy were by lot.

Paul Stillwell: How competitive was the atmosphere among classmates at sub school?

Admiral Trost: In some cases, very. A guy named George Sawyer stood second and he worked like hell to stand first.* I didn't, but I didn't have to. I was lucky.

Paul Stillwell: Some people just have more facility at remembering things.

Admiral Trost: Yes. He worked hard at it. He let it be known that he was going to stand first. That was a little bit of a hard pill for him to swallow, I guess. George was later the Assistant Secretary of the Navy for Shipbuilding and Logistics while I was in OpNav.† And he reminded me that he really should have stood first [laughter].

Paul Stillwell: I hope it was a friendly rivalry.

Admiral Trost: Well, it was from my perspective. I didn't really care one way or another. I knew I wanted to go to Norfolk, and if I didn't stand high enough to go to Norfolk, I wouldn't stand high enough to graduate, in all likelihood. Norfolk was basically a last choice, Norfolk and Key West. Hawaii and San Diego were the two prime places everybody wanted. As a matter of fact, I found out later on that I had screwed up the system because the guys near me presumed I would select Hawaii, so they selected some of the alternates, some of the lesser things. If I took that, they wouldn't be screwed up. When I chose Norfolk they were a bit surprised.

Paul Stillwell: What do you recall about the escape tower?

Admiral Trost: I recall going through it. It was interesting. I felt sorry for the guys who were claustrophobic. Some guys clutched, as least initially, when they were down below getting pressurized, getting ready to duck out through the hatch and go up that—as I

---

* Lieutenant (junior grade) George A. Sawyer Jr., USN.
† Sawyer's tenure in that job was from 1981 to 1983, at which point he left to become a vice president for General Dynamics.

recall, we did initially a shallow escape and then I think we did a free escape too, without a mask. We didn't have this breathing system.

Paul Stillwell: The Momsen Lung?[*]

Admiral Trost: Yeah. It seems to me we did a shallow pop out, just to get us used to the idea of rising through the water and also you watch your bubbles and try to maintain pace with the bubbles as they rise. If you go up too fast, you get the bends if you do it from deep enough. If you do it with the lung, you're over-pressurizing the lung if you didn't go fast enough and you're running out of air if you go too fast. It is a good incentive for doing what you should be doing. As I recall, I don't think I did that. Some of us had a buddy who was a regular instructor who went up and made sure we maintained our speed at an appropriate pace. They were very careful, very safety conscious, of course, but we finished that. You also have a lot of confidence on your ability to do it.

Paul Stillwell: That would be the whole point of repetitious training.

Admiral Trost: Yes. That's the whole point of it. You could say, "I did that. I know how to do that."

Paul Stillwell: Did you have any GUPPYs yet as the school boats?[†]

Admiral Trost: They were starting; there were some GUPPYs, both EB and Portsmouth GUPPYs.[‡] My first submarine was a Portsmouth GUPPY. There were a few fleet boats still operating from up there. It really didn't make any difference which one you were on for training purposes, because they were just training you in basic operations, getting you familiar with the routine and the procedures, what people do, what you can expect them to do.

Paul Stillwell: You learn all the systems on board the boat.

---

[*] Invented by submariner Charles B. Momsen, the Momsen lung was a breathing apparatus to be used when ascending from a damaged submarine to the surface. It did not have its own air supply but used the air already in a man's lungs.
[†] The term "GUPPY" grew out of the initials for the postwar modification fitted to World War II fleet submarines to give them greater underwater propulsion power (GUPP).
[‡] EB – Electric Boat Company, Groton, Connecticut; Portsmouth Naval Shipyard, Kittery, Maine.

Admiral Trost: You do. Yes. You learn that in the course of the six months you're up there. You learn all the systems, and that's very helpful. You then had to relearn systems when you got to your ship, because every one was different. You had to know that system on that ship to be able to do the damage control. That year of submarine qualification is a busy year. You have to trace and draw diagrams of every system on the ship, learn to operate and demonstrate their operation as well as demonstrate your proficiency as a watch stander on every watch station in the ship. It was interesting. I found it challenging, but not that difficult. A lot of a submarine's operation is common-sense logic and you learn the system, learn how to operate the system, and there's logic to what you do. As I said, I found it interesting.

Paul Stillwell: Was there any discussion about nuclear submarines at that point?

Admiral Trost: *Nautilus*, in fact, got under way for the first time in January '55, when I was in sub school.[*] We knew she was down there. We couldn't get sub school tours because everybody was so rush-rush, hush-hush. I don't know if that was Rickover saying he didn't want anybody in the way. First time I saw the inside of *Nautilus* was after I graduated from sub school. It was quite interesting, quite a staggering change from what you see. They had a ladder from the top deck to the middle deck, and when I walked down that, it was like going down a stairway. That does pop your eyes open when you see it the first time. But the later ones, the *Skate* class, for example, were a bit smaller, more compact and went back to having up-and-down ladders instead of walking down a grand staircase. They were interesting, interesting to watch. We didn't learn anything about nuclear power in sub school. I went back for nuclear power training a year and a half after I graduated sub school.

Paul Stillwell: I interviewed Admiral Wilkinson, who went through sub school in the early '40s.[†] He said that initially all the Naval Academy graduates who were students

---

[*] USS *Nautilus* (SSN-571), the Navy's first nuclear-powered submarine, was commissioned 30 September 1954. She was 324 feet long, 28 feet in the beam, and displaced 3,533 tons. She had a top speed on the surface of 22 knots and undisclosed speed submerged. She was armed with six 21-inch torpedo tubes. Because she did not have to come to the surface frequently to recharge batteries, the *Nautilus* revolutionized submarine warfare. She first got under way on nuclear power in January 1955.
[†] The first commanding officer of the *Nautilus* was Commander Eugene P. Wilkinson, USN. The oral history of Wilkinson, who retired as a vice admiral, is in the Naval Institute collection.

were ranked above all the reservists, and he complained that he didn't think that was fair. How was the atmosphere when you were there between academy people and others?

Admiral Trost: I didn't really notice much difference. As a matter of fact, I'd say I didn't notice any differentiation. Over half the class were Naval Academy classmates, so we knew the majority of the people there. The Naval Academy class of '52 had maybe 20 guys in our sub school class, as I remember, but 60-some of us were from '53. They were mostly guys we knew or had a familiar background with. We had ten Japanese officers in our class, not included in our numbers, but they went to sea with us, and they were in some of our classes. We were turning over the first of our diesel boats to Japan, and they had sent ten officers to sub school with our class. We had a lot of interface with them. Years later, when I got to Japan to command the Seventh Fleet, the newly appointed head of the Japanese Submarine Force, which had been set up as a separate organization, was one of my sub school classmates.

Paul Stillwell: What an irony from ten years before.

Admiral Trost: What an irony. I had actually met him in a different job when I was in Hawaii, and he came through Hawaii on his way from something to do in Washington, back out to Japan. And of course, we didn't know then he was going to be the head of the Submarine Force, nor did we know that I was going to be commander of the Seventh Fleet. We had a good reunion out there. He came and had dinner with us. We got out to Japan and my wife met his wife, who spoke fluent English, a very personable gal. He's died, but we stayed in touch with her until Pauline died. She was fluent in English, got along, liked the U.S. She was with him in New London, and we didn't know that at the time. She was a lot of fun to have around when we got to Japan, because she helped Pauline with what's where and here's what we do and here's some things that we do. We interfaced our two groups, and so it was great.

Paul Stillwell: One of the great things about the Navy how often you would run into people you've known before.

Admiral Trost: That's for sure.

Paul Stillwell: What was the mission of the submarine force at that time? There was no overt enemy to attack.

Admiral Trost: No. I guess we spent more time training ourselves in our own forces than we did posing a threat. There was no enemy to pose a threat to, as a matter of fact. It was just maintaining the training base and maintaining the number of ships they thought would be necessary in the event of some crisis. What drew me in, frankly, were the attitude of the people and the qualification. I told you before about going to Key West for an eight-week ASW officer course because I thought I would the ASW officer of this destroyer. During the eight weeks, about once a week, we would go to sea. Usually in the destroyer or DE and the purpose of that was to learn how the sonar systems worked, procedures and so forth. Then once about every two weeks, for one day a week, as volunteers we could go to sea in a submarine. I went to sea a couple of times in a submarine, *Corporal*. I was impressed. I had been on two training cruises in destroyers, and what I noticed in the submarines was a difference in atmosphere. It was strictly by the book, but it was low key. It was camaraderie, as opposed to dictatorship.

Paul Stillwell: Not uptight?

Admiral Trost: Yeah. And the fact that they put total faith in the petty officer and weren't constantly standing there looking over his shoulder. He was selected to do his job, he was trained to do his job, and the more informal atmosphere was very attractive, I thought. I rode two weekends from Key West to Havana. I was invited by the ship I rode on Friday to join them at 1600, which was the end of our working day, if I wanted to go to Havana for the weekend. It sounded good to me, I'd never been to Havana.

I reported in, casual clothes and rode aboard to Havana and got over there about midnight. Spent Saturday and most of Sunday there and came back to Key West and went to school again Monday morning. I was very impressed by the underway atmosphere there and the relationship. I did that twice, had two fun liberty weekends in old Havana.

Paul Stillwell: I heard on the radio this morning that the United States and Cuba are setting up diplomatic relations, setting the stage for tourists to go back after all these years.

Admiral Trost: They will go over there and they will see all the 1950s Chevys and Buicks and Fords. It's amazing. It's quite a place. I enjoyed my two visits over there. The third time came later, when I was on *Sirago*. We were running Operation Springboard out of the Caribbean and put into Havana for about three or four days.

Paul Stillwell: Is there anything else to mention about Submarine School before going to your first submarine?

Admiral Trost: I found it very helpful. One of the good things about it was there a weekend visit by *Sirago*, which ended up being my ship, my choice.[*] It had to have had a very major influence on me, because I met Shannon Cramer, who was the CO.[†] I was so impressed by that guy. A friend of mine, Jeff Badgett, who was a class ahead of me at the Naval Academy, was the guy who invited me down to lunch and took me through the boat.[‡] I thought, "Boy this is the kind of guys I'd like to go to sea with." Don Kilmer, class of '51, was on board.[§] He was in my company at the Naval Academy, so I knew two of the wardroom officers.

Shannon was my CO in *Sirago* for a year, and then he left *Sirago* to go to PCO course. He ended up as PCO of *Swordfish*, and when I finished nuclear school I went to *Swordfish* also. So I had good influence from him twice, really good influence. Sort of my hero. Shannon and I stayed friends until he died about two years ago as a three-star.[**]

---

[*] USS *Sirago* (SS-485), a *Tench*-class submarine, was commissioned 13 August 1945. She was 312 feet long, 27 feet in the beam, and displaced 1,835 tons surfaced and 2,400 tons submerged. Her maximum speed on the surface was 20 knots and nine knots submerged. She was armed with ten 21-inch torpedo tubes. In 1948-49 she received a GUPPY II conversion at the Philadelphia Naval Shipyard.

[†] Lieutenant Commander Shannon D. Cramer Jr., USN.

[‡] Lieutenant (junior grade) John Jefferson Badgett, USN.

[§] Lieutenant Donald A. Kilmer, USN.

[**] Vice Admiral Cramer died 15 February 2012 at age 90.

We served together in the Pentagon at the same time, but never the same organization. He and Lando Zech, whom you may have run across—Lando was my company officer first class year.

Paul Stillwell: You mentioned him as a great influence.

Admiral Trost: Those were the two guys I would say were my biggest Navy influence of anybody. They were good people.

Paul Stillwell: I remember when Admiral Cramer was on the Naval Institute board, a real gentleman.

Admiral Trost: Yeah, he was a gentleman, really was, and professional. When he was relieved in *Sirago*, change of command, they lined the crew up outboard, two facing rows.* He went down and said goodbye to everybody. Wasn't a dry eye in the crowd. They worshiped him. He was a people person all the way.

Paul Stillwell: What a contrast to your skippers in the destroyer.

Admiral Trost: Oh, God [laughter]. I talked to somebody who asked me about the destroyer experiences, and I told him about the two destroyer COs. He said, "My God, you must have had the two worst guys in the Navy."

I said, "From my perspective, they were. They really were."

Paul Stillwell: You mentioned that Norfolk was not popular as a destination for the Submarine School graduates. Why did you choose Norfolk?

Admiral Trost: I chose it because my first ship was in Norfolk. My wife's parents were 29 miles from here, and we could get up and see the folks from time to time. It didn't make any difference to me where I went. I did not know what a fun place San Diego was. I'd never been to Hawaii. If I'd known about San Diego, I probably would have gone to

---

* On 6 July 1956 Lieutenant Commander Lionel J. Goulet, USN, relieved Lieutenant Commander Cramer as commanding officer of the *Sirago*.

San Diego. Back then, that was an all-time favorite duty station and went out there once. Just young and dumb.

Paul Stillwell: Well, you go with what you're familiar with.

Admiral Trost: Well, we liked it. We had friends in Norfolk. We had both former shipmates and classmates down there that we knew, and Pauline knew the wives. So it was, I guess, going with the familiar.

Paul Stillwell: What do you remember about the GUPPY package that *Sirago* had?

Admiral Trost: Well, she was pretty fast for a short period of time underwater. That streamlined sail—we had the low-step sail, and that was great, except when you were standing watch on the deck. I had the deck under way and in bad weather. When the water either came over the top, if the waves were high enough, or it came up through the grating from down below, it would hit, crash into us, swell, and the water would come through the free flood and up. If you were the officer of the deck standing there, you were going to get lifted right off your feet, and I was several times. It was a good ship. I liked it. I liked the layout and it was really very similar in some respects to the early nukes, *Skate* class for example, which was a very comfortable ship.[*] Crowded, but comfortable. Crowded in that, comfortable in that things were very logically arranged. It was a little *Nautilus*, basically. Well designed.

Paul Stillwell: And using the teardrop hull, which the *Nautilus* did not have.

Admiral Trost: Yeah, and that made a big difference. That bridge was high enough to be dry most of the time. It had the trunk going all the up from the control room so you could get up and down dry. You had to be awfully carefully though to make sure you shut that hatch at the top of the trunk if the weather was bad, because otherwise you would get water down in the control room. It worked very well.

Paul Stillwell: What was your specific job in *Sirago*?

---

[*] USS *Skate* (SSN-578), commissioned 23 December 1957, was the first ship of her class. Trost served in the sister *Swordfish* (SSN-579).

Admiral Trost: Well, I was the torpedo and gunnery officer. I spent more time than anything else as the auxiliary division officer. I was the assistant engineer for a while. That's about all I remember. Supply officer at one time.

Admiral Trost: Quite a variety.

Admiral Trost: About a year and a half, you shift around. I think my favorite was fire control and gunnery. It was just interesting.

Paul Stillwell: Was it still the Word War II–type torpedo data computer?

Admiral Trost: Yes and we had nothing more advanced. TDC was still the standard. There wasn't anything extra that I recall. We could fire electric torpedoes. They came in late as I remember; I'm not sure of that. I don't think we had anything that unusual, except for the GUPPY, and it could go fast—not very long but fast.

Paul Stillwell: Plus you had the snorkel.

Admiral Trost: Yes. It had the snorkel and it had, basically, our equivalent of a double battery, so you had a lot more capacity. I think we had a speed capability for a brief period of time of about 16 knots, so that was really good. It's good for you if you want to get away from somebody.

Paul Stillwell: Yes [laughter].

Admiral Trost: And blow your capacity for any future operation.

Paul Stillwell: What do you recall about the quality of the enlisted men in the *Sirago*?

Admiral Trost: High quality. As a matter of fact, in the mid-'50s the submarine group was a very talented bunch of people. We still had chiefs who had served at the tail end of World War II, and the ship was relatively new. I think *Sirago* was actually the last submarine commissioned at the end of World War II.[*] They converted to GUPPY in '49,

---

[*] The *Sirago* was commissioned 13 August 1945; the war ended 15 August in the Western Pacific and 14 August in the United States.

and I was aboard in '55-'56, so it was a relatively new ship. It was as up to date as any ship was at the time, except for the—

Paul Stillwell: The Navy had the fast-attack class, like the *Wahoo* and so forth.[*]

Admiral Trost: And they were more up to date, more modern things, but they had drawbacks in that they had things that didn't work the way they were designed to work.

Paul Stillwell: Especially the pancake diesels.

Admiral Trost: Oh, yeah. They were terrible. On one of my ships I had an engineman who served on one of those ships, and he'd almost curse every time he talked about them. Talk about first of all, you'd build a diesel that was mounted upside down, with the oil free to flow through the engine and into the generator on the lower end, which ain't the way you would normally want to do it. We used to have jokes about them. I don't remember the specifics anymore, but they used to joke about what kind of person designed this thing. What was his electrical knowledge when he designed this thing to hang underneath the diesel engine, which is going to leak, sure as hell? It was interesting.

Paul Stillwell: The *Cochino* was a GUPPY that had a fire and explosion a few years earlier.[†] Were there any safety measures brought in as a result of that?

Admiral Trost: I don't know. I had a long discussion with Shannon Cramer, who was my skipper twice. He was in *Cochino* when that happened. I think that was his first submarine, as a matter of fact. He talked a lot about it, but I don't remember any specifics. The emphasis on *Cochino*, well, she had a couple of things, she had flooding. I remember that she had a fire.

Paul Stillwell: She did, yes.

---

[*] USS *Wahoo* (SS-565), a *Tang*-class fast attack submarine, was commissioned 30 May 1952. She had a displacement of 1,560 tons on the surface and 2,260 tons submerged. She was 269 feet long, 27 feet in the beam, and had a draft of 17 feet. Her top speed was 15 knots surfaced and 18 knots submerged. She was armed with eight 21-inch torpedo tubes.

[†] USS *Cochino* (SS-345) was lost off Norway on 26 August 1949 as the result of battery explosions and fires. For details see the Naval Institute oral history of Rear Admiral Roy S. Benson, USN (Ret.), and William J. Lederer, *The Last Voyage* (New York: Henry Holt and Company, 1950).

Admiral Trost: I don't remember enough of the details. I've read about it, but not for years. But, what I remember most is that the transfer they saved almost everybody. They lost just a couple of guys, and Shannon was one of the last of the officers to get off the ship and get transferred over. I guess it was quite a harrowing experience. It would be, certainly.

Paul Stillwell: Yes.

Admiral Trost: There were some guys who did heroic things in the process.

Paul Stillwell: What do you remember about the qualification process to get your dolphins?

Admiral Trost: Well, if you are talking about being thrown overboard or being asked to not have too much alcohol—no.

Paul Stillwell: No [laughter]. What you went through to earn those?

Admiral Trost: Well, I did the qualification process, which I felt very comfortable having done it and having learned. I felt I knew that ship cold when I finished, when I got my qualifications. What I remember about it, more than anything else, is one Monday morning in Norfolk. Across the pier was *Sea Leopard*, commanded by Bob Long.* As the officer of the deck, I called below to the captain, "The ship's ready to get under way, five minutes to go."

He came up to the bridge and said, "Go below, we're going out for two weeks, as you know, with *Sea Leopard* for an exercise. Pack up clothes for two weeks and get over there. You've got five minutes."

I had already gone through my in-port examination with the skipper of the *Cutlass*, and my under way was scheduled a month later with Bob Long. So the captain said, "And this is going to be your underway qualification test."

---

* Lieutenant Commander Robert L. J. Long, USN, commanded the submarine *Sea Leopard* (SS-483) from 1954 to 1956. The oral history of Long, who retired as a four-star admiral, is in the Naval Institute collection.

I thought, "Fine, get it out of the way." So I packed my gear and went across the way. Bob's third officer, a lieutenant commander, had been admitted to the hospital the night before in Portsmouth. I don't remember what the problem was at the time, but he had appendicitis or something. Bob had just shit-canned a lieutenant for non-qualification after a year and a half, which is not light. So I was one of three watch standers, including the exec. And in the course of the two weeks, he examined me. He made every kind of drill that he could have, and it was a pleasant way to do it because things just sort of happened routinely. What I remember about it was it was a very pleasant experience and when it was all over, you know, I was finished, but I had to wait for the 12 months to put on my dolphins. That was a requirement, the 12 months and qualified.

Paul Stillwell: What are your memories of Bob Long?

Admiral Trost: I'm very high on Bob Long. He was fun to go to sea with. He and Shannon Cramer were the greatest of rivals; they were classmates. One time Bob Long called in and announced his position in the channel, knowing he was behind us coming in from an exercise, knowing that their classmate was the ops officer on the tender, on the squadron staff. He also knew that the ops officer didn't pay attention to who was where. He just responded to calls. Bob Long called and said, "This is [whatever his call sign was], and I'm ready to head for my berth; give me a berth assignment."

Well, he got a berth assignment before Shannon got his for *Sirago*. They were rivals to start with, and Shannon was just pissed to the gills. I was the officer of the deck on that occasion too. Coming in, Long passed us in the channel, pulled in, pulled up on the offside of the pier and we were both going to tie up. We were on this side, and he was on that side. We came up and Shannon said, "You make the landing," and I made the landing, got the number-one line over, and he said, "Haul the bow into the pier." So I had it on the winch and hauled the bow; there were no other lines over yet. He ran up to the bow and jumped about three feet over onto the pier. He was running across the pier, shaking his fist at Bob Long saying, "You son of a bitch, you knew I was ahead of you [laughter]." Bob Long was a great guy. In many respects I credit him, along with Shannon for being mentors. Bob Long and I stayed in touch with each other. I worked with him a couple of times in Washington and thought very highly of him there too. Bob was CinCPac when I had Seventh Fleet.[*] It was nice to have your really big boss, not the fleet commander, there. You didn't shiver when he called you. If he was going to chew you out, he was going to do it in a very gentlemanly way. I didn't get chewed out, so it was okay [laughter]. He would call. He would want information on something, and he wanted it from the horse's mouth rather than going through the staff. So he was very good to work with that way.

Paul Stillwell: You mentioned the process of getting the dolphins. What was the ceremony with that?

Admiral Trost: The ceremony was actually a pretty informal one. It was in the control room, where there was room for people to stand. It was crew only, skipper officiating and called me over, took the dolphins, pinned them on me, congratulated me, and that was it.

Paul Stillwell: You weren't thrown overboard?

Admiral Trost: No, I wasn't thrown overboard. I was pleased with that, because somebody in the process of getting thrown overboard had hit his head on a ballast tank top just somewhere within the previous couple of months. So they knocked that off for a while. I think they resumed it later on. I was grateful for that. I was prepared to go overboard. Had on my old skivvies, my old khakis [laughter], and Norfolk harbor was not the cleanest place to moor at the time.

Paul Stillwell: Probably better now than then.

Admiral Trost: It probably is. But there was always garbage floating between the ships and lots of crap, little skin of oil here and there.

Paul Stillwell: What do you recall about division officer duties in that boat about working with the enlisted men in your division?

Admiral Trost: Well, I think, Paul, I've always been a people-oriented person. I tried to

---

[*] Admiral Robert L. J. Long, USN, served as Commander in Chief Pacific from 31 October 1979 to 1 July 1983.

put a lot of emphasis on advancement, made people study, held lectures on things that I thought they needed to know more about, more professional stuff than the stuff that was specific to their particular rating. I enjoyed being a division officer. I thought it was a great responsibility, and I liked it.

Paul Stillwell: Well, in some ships it involves dealing with disciplinary problems and personal problems. Probably that wasn't so bad since you had men who had already gone through a screening process to be part of the crew.

Admiral Trost: Not much of a problem there. I had dealt with this very problem on my year and a half on the destroyer, and so I wasn't a neophyte. I was the trial counsel in the destroyer even though DesLant at that time said you couldn't put an ensign in that position.* But I got it. That made me a favorite. Some of the people were bad actors in the destroyer because before I became a trial counsel, I was winning cases as the defense counsel.

Paul Stillwell: [Laughter] That would make you popular with the crew.

Admiral Trost: Mostly because I read the book and stuck with the procedure that you were supposed to use it at mast, and so I was winning cases. I had a guy who shot himself in the foot. I had become the trial counsel, and he asked for me to be his defense counsel, because he figured if I was the trial counsel, I was going to win.† So we knew the guy; when we were out in the Med he shot himself in the foot to get off watch. He wanted to go home with his girlfriend who was back in the States.

Paul Stillwell: You talked about him in one of the earlier interviews.

Admiral Trost: I rather enjoyed it. I thought being a defense counsel was sort of fun, because you get almost always the guy who is prosecuting didn't do his homework. It was easy to do things right, and win, even though sometimes I wish I'd lost [laughter]. If somebody asked for you as a defense counsel, that's what he got. That was an interesting ship. Unlike what I would say about my submarine wardrooms, which were invariably

---

* DesLant – Destroyer Force Atlantic Fleet, the type commander.
† The trial counsel is the prosecutor.

very good, very knowledgeable, very conscientious—that destroyer wardroom was loose. We had a couple of guys, how they ever got commissioned, I don't know. Most of them didn't stay. And a couple of the good ones left because of the skipper.

Paul Stillwell: You suggested that you might have done so, if not for the salvation of submarines.

Admiral Trost: I think I would have. If I'd ever kept on there, I don't think I would have stayed. And it wasn't that I didn't like the Navy. I liked what I was doing and I was— well, on the destroyer, I'd served as the ASW officer, third division officer, the gun boss. I was the navigator for my last eight months. I was a sea detail OOD, so I had good jobs, and they were satisfying jobs in terms of—well, I did a lot to drive the ship, which I happened to like. It was the people you worked for.

Paul Stillwell: How would you describe a typical underway watch in the *Sirago*?

Admiral Trost: Well, submerged or surfaced?

Paul Stillwell: Either, both [laughter].

Admiral Trost: Orderly, calm. We were by the book, on the bridge, on the surface. We were quiet submerged. The captain wouldn't brook any noise in the control room or in the conning tower. So, unless it was something that was an order or response to an order, it was quiet, which was good. The way it should be. I stood a couple of engineering officer of the watch watches as part of my qualification requirement, and I liked that because I liked engineering. Normal, under way, submerged—[ringing phone].

Paul Stillwell: [After phone call] Well, we talked about the war games, submarine versus submarine. You couldn't take a periscope picture necessarily. How would you evaluate the results of those?

Admiral Trost: You did your best to analyze what you had, what you did and what you responded to. That's doable. Usually you had sonar tapes with the nukes at least and didn't on *Sirago*. But, you got tapes that you could replay to analyze what you had, what you were listening to and they were annotated so you had some idea of what you did.

Paul Stillwell: Did you make any deployments in that submarine?

Admiral Trost: Not in *Sirago*.

Paul Stillwell: Anything else to remember about your duty in *Sirago*?

Admiral Trost: I don't think so. Didn't deploy. She came off a Med deployment shortly before I got aboard, and we did not go out of the Western Atlantic. We deployed to the Caribbean, but that was for training and did two of those.

Paul Stillwell: How did you then make the transition into nuclear power? Did you apply for that specifically?

Admiral Trost: I did apply for it, and I'm trying to think what the procedure back then was. I had been qualified in submarines for a couple of months, and I thought that nuclear power was clearly the future. I think the process at that time was to send a letter to your detailer, who I guess sent it over to Rickover's office, and they decided whom they wanted to interview. That's what I did.*

Paul Stillwell: Please tell me about the experience with the admiral.

Admiral Trost: Interesting. Came in, and the groups were still fairly small at that time. Had the usual thing—I can't tell you whether the front legs were sawed off on the chair or not. I didn't notice that. The first part of my interview lasted about a minute and a half. He said, "Why didn't you do better at the Naval Academy?" [Laughter]

Paul Stillwell: How could you?

Admiral Trost: I said, "Well, I did my best."

"You probably did other things; it says here you played tennis and you sailed." He said, "sail" with sort of a sniff. I sailed for all four years and had my yawl command and

---

* On 27 December 1956 Lieutenant (junior grade) Trost was detached from the *Sirago* with orders to report to the commanding officer of the Naval Submarine Base New London for duty with the Nuclear Power Division.

enjoyed it and learned a hell of a lot. You learn a lot sailing yawls. You learn a lot about wind, weather, and handling something that's in the water.

Next question was, "I guess you think you did better academically than I did at the Naval Academy?"

I knew I had, so I said, "Yes, sir."

He said, "Get out of here."

So one of his henchmen took me and put me in the broom closet, they called it, not even a closet, but that's where you went. It had a little chair in the middle of a bunch of cleaning stuff, and that's where you cooled your heels. I sat out there for about an hour and a half, I guess. Nothing to read, just sitting there. He called me back in, chewed me out again for not having done better, and said, "That's it; get out of here."

So after they released us about 1800, on a Friday, I went to Pauline's parents' home, and Pauline said, "How did it go?"

I said, "Very poor. I have to report back in tomorrow morning, but they're not going to take me." So the next morning at 8:00 I showed up downtown at Main Navy, down the mall, and sat while he talked to people.* About 4:00 in the afternoon my turn came. I came in, and his response was, "Oh, you again [laughter]. Get out of here."

So I went home, had a drink, and said, "Well, Pauline that's it; we're going to Norfolk tomorrow," and then I waited. I forget how long it took. I think about a week. I got a phone call from a submarine detailer saying, "You'll be getting orders to Nuclear Power School in New London" in whatever the time frame was. That was it.

Paul Stillwell: Did he ask you any substantive questions during the interview?

Admiral Trost: No, not really. I expected to be quizzed about math or physics or something—no. Just interesting.

Paul Stillwell: Sounds like typical compared to other people's experience.

---

* Main Navy was the popular name for the old Navy Department building at 17th Street and Constitution Avenue in Washington, D.C. The building remained in use from its opening in 1918 until the early 1970s, when President Richard Nixon directed that it be demolished. The adjacent Munitions Building was long occupied by the War Department. In 1943, with the opening of the Pentagon, the Army moved out and transferred the Munitions Building to the Navy.

Admiral Trost: It was. I got to know him later. Went through nuclear training. Only time I saw him was in Idaho when he came out, the guys used to say he came out to see if there was any dust on the ventilation system. He came out to look at the plant out there about every six months. I was one of the trainees at the time. As a matter of fact, I had the watch running the plant at the time. That was the *Nautilus* prototype. We were all introduced to him as a group, but no personal interface with him.

The next time I saw him was when I was on the *Swordfish* pre-comm detail up in Portsmouth, New Hampshire. He came up with his henchmen to give us sort of our pre-critical exam where he or his guys talked to every one of the officers who was in nuclear training, which was all of us. He had to make his decision on whether or not we were knowledgeable enough to go to sea on sea trials or before sea trials to take the plant critical and start the pre-critical operations. So each one of us got interviewed, would be a term. I'm not sure it would be accurate, but we got quizzed by him, one on one.

Paul Stillwell: Well, getting back to your time at Nuclear Power School at New London, what do you remember about the curriculum or how that went?

Admiral Trost: I remember it requiring full days and full nights and full Saturdays and at least I tried to leave half-Sundays for my family. It was a busy damn period. Challenging, people worked hard at it. Got together periodically on Sunday. Somebody would be having trouble. There were 13 of us in the class and somebody would have trouble or something. We'd arrange for 1400 on Sunday we would all get together, come back to the base from wherever we were living and go through the problems, go through and toil. Whoever didn't understand it got tutored, basically. It was a very close group. Nine of the thirteen ended up going out to Idaho, the prototype, and the other four went up to Schenectady and they were in the *Seawolf.* So it was an interesting experience. You got to know the people you were studying with very well. We got out to Idaho, and the prototype was due to shut down for refueling early, earlier than planned. So we got six weeks chopped off our schooling in New London, but we didn't miss any courses, because they simply doubled up, and we had Saturday and Sunday classes.

Paul Stillwell: Ooh [laughter].

Admiral Trost: We were given "proceed" time. I don't know if you're familiar with "proceed and travel." Proceed time is four days between stations. So we got the four days plus travel, however many miles that there was from New London to Idaho Falls, and I remember getting in the car in New London the morning after classes ended, driving down to Pauline's folks here, and spending about a day or two stopping in Illinois with my folks. Heading for Idaho, getting to Idaho. One of my classmates had a house that he rented from somebody in the previous class that they had retained or he rented early, and so Pauline and the one child we had at the time stayed with his wife.* Because we got out there, got on a bus the next morning out to the site of the prototype and spent the next two weeks, 24 hours a day, out at the site.

We didn't know that when we went out there. Pauline started house hunting and had been unsuccessful by the time I got back after two weeks. I had a weekend to find a house and get my wife settled and get back out to school and we started shift work rotating every week. It was an interesting time. Loved Idaho; it's a great place.

Paul Stillwell: It was pretty remote, from what I've heard.

Admiral Trost: Very remote. We lived in Idaho Falls, got on a bus in the morning in Idaho Falls and rode 50 miles out to the site. Got on the bus after an eight-hour shift and came back. Had time to eat dinner and sleep, then back out in the morning. It was interesting. Weekends were great. Every four weeks, we got off shift at 1600 on Friday afternoon. Didn't have to be back on until Monday afternoon, so you had that long weekend. We had next-door neighbors who were Idaho natives and were wonderful people. They had two kids, 10 and 14, and they loved to camp, and so every weekend we would go up into the country, up there on the Yellowstone, we went up in there, the Teton Mountain chain is to the east of Idaho Falls and coming out of the Tetons is the Warm River, which flows down into the Snake north of Idaho Falls.

_____

* Son Carl was born in 1955.

They had a place they liked to pitch a tent and camp on the Warm River. They had a station wagon, so did I, so we'd take the two wagons. He'd take his wife and two kids, I took my one child and one wife, and we slept inside the station wagons most of the time after we had bears scratching on the tent. My wife went ballistic and ran out, opened the tailgate on our station wagon and slammed it behind her as she went with her son in front of her.

Paul Stillwell: He wasn't your son at that point?

Admiral Trost: Oh, he was my son too. But she was worried about him and getting him in. I was on my own [laughter].

Paul Stillwell: That seems like an uncomfortable place to sleep.

Admiral Trost: We had a great time. We went into Yellowstone several times and went to Jackson Hole. We had fun out there. We went deer hunting totally unsuccessfully a couple of times, and it was fun. Went up and visited a place where one of the neighbors had been born on the farm. When you stepped outside of this two-story house, you saw a platform outside the second floor with a door and nothing coming down. They said in the wintertime you step right out into the snow from up there.

Paul Stillwell: That's amazing.

Admiral Trost: It was really unbelievable. And, they farmed. They raised crops. They were experts at the area. They knew the area, and we had a good time with them.

Paul Stillwell: What was the content of the course work in New London?

Admiral Trost: Very heavy on water chemistry and physics. Understanding the fusion and fission processes, understanding the mechanical principles of a reactor, understanding safety above all. Rickover was just something on safety. He was successful in never having an incident. There was no accident with problems; that's why he was such a stickler on training, and rightly so. Hopefully, that will never cease, because if it does, that's the end of the nuclear power program for the Navy. But we went through chemistry, physics, biology, mechanics. By the time we finished—it turned out to be five and a half months—we could have designed a reactor and a plant and known all the mechanics of the operation and controls. And you knew why you did certain things. You knew the whys of water chemistry and the whys of certain kinds of controls, what to do if you had a failure of any portion of the control system. The answer was generally to shut it down as fast as you could to avoid a problem. You learned the need for very meticulous water chemistry control and very careful control of any kind of contamination from the plant itself. You came out being pretty smart in some areas. I forget which one it was, but one of our U.S. universities gave credits for nuclear power for people who went to postgraduate school in the engineering area. I have forgotten how much credit you got, but it was substantial. It surprised me when I heard about it. When I went to the Olmsted program, the German university that I went to credited me with a—[*]

[Telephone interruption]

Admiral Trost: I had the four years of college here, obviously I had a year of college before I went into the program and then they credited me with another year and half, because of my nuclear power training, which I found interesting.

Paul Stillwell: Yes.

Admiral Trost: I didn't consider a year of training to be a year and a half of college, but it was the German university system, and they are usually sticklers on accreditation. But it was enjoyable. I learned a lot.

Paul Stillwell: Did you have to do any math refresher going into this study?

Admiral Trost: On the side, yes. There were a lot of things that came back after I spent a couple of nights looking through the book. And from within they gave extra instruction. One of our instructors gave extra instruction in mathematics and anything people had trouble with. We had one non-engineering type major, non-technical major and that was an experiment on Rickover's part. He took a guy who was a Princeton graduate and had a

---

[*] Trost was an Olmsted scholar in Germany in 1960-61.

good record to see if he could make it. He got a lot of extra instruction, but he made it. He did not stay in the Navy. He spent a couple of years as a nuke and then left. I don't know if it was feeling unsuited for the duty or just wasn't for him.

Paul Stillwell: Who were the instructors?

Admiral Trost: Some of Rickover's staff lectured. We had one guy who was a physics instructor, PhD in physics. We had a couple of guys who were involved with Rickover in the early program that were sent to New London to be instructors. People with the technical qualifications to teach what they were teaching—preaching is the right term, I guess [laughter]. We had about ten class hours a day, including Saturday. Sunday was free. That was the catchup time.

Paul Stillwell: That's demanding, wow.

Admiral Trost: It was demanding. After the class I'd come home, and my wife and I drank a Manhattan every night at that time in our lives. I'd have my Manhattan and have my dinner. Get to work and study until about 11:00 o'clock, get up at 6:00 and sometimes do a little studying before I went to school, and as I said, Saturday was just a regular day. Sunday was catchup day. They demanded it.

Paul Stillwell: Well, I remember talking to Admiral Train who was in BuPers, and he said there was almost a one-to-one match between nuclear billets and qualified officers, so Admiral Rickover had to take some people to fill those billets.[*] No matter how he treated them.

Admiral Trost: He drafted some people by asking for people with certain qualifications. My friend Jeff Badgett, class of '52 was in that category. He and I were shipmates in *Sirago*. He was turned down for nuclear power the first time because he had five kids and according to him, Rickover said, what else do you do? He was qualified in submarines, on schedule, on time, and one hell of a good shipmate. I think Jeff was department head in a diesel boat, and this was his first submarine when he was interviewed the first time.

---

[*] See the Naval Institute oral history of Admiral Harry D. Train II, USN (Ret.)

Then he was in another tour and had a great reputation. The second time around, he was drafted by Rickover because he was qualified in everything he could have been. And we had a couple of guys who opted to go to PG school instead of nuclear power school, when told they were going to be ordered for interview, they turned it down and got drafted out of PG school when they finished if they had the right documentation, right major and came into the nuclear program. And most of them became volunteers after they got drafted [laughter].

Paul Stillwell: As if they had any choice.

Admiral Trost: Well, you know, it was interesting because there were some guys who would probably not have gotten command if they hadn't gone through the nuclear power program and done well at it. There were some guys who, had they not gone into the nuclear power program, and some who came from surface into submarines because of the nuclear power program because they were drafted into it, they would have retired more junior then they did. Some guys made out quite well and earned it. They didn't get it for free. I know one guy specifically who was a commander when he got drafted out of PG school. He was going to command of a surface ship, and then all of the sudden he was drafted for nuclear power school. "Oh shit," he said. Well, he got one of the nuclear cruisers as his next command. So he said one day, "You know, maybe I made the right choice after all."

I said, "You weren't making the choice; you were chosen [laughter]."

Paul Stillwell: Is there a name you want to attach to that story?

Admiral Trost: No. He'd be embarrassed.

Paul Stillwell: What specifically did you do at Idaho Falls?

Admiral Trost: Well, the whole idea was to get qualified on the various systems that support a nuclear reactor and stand watches initially in the plant itself, which was a mockup of *Nautilus* plant. They built the plant out there, trained the *Nautilus* crew, built *Nautilus* making corrections as they found things that they should have thought about or didn't know about, or something like that. So we stood watches initially as watch standers in the plant, and then in the control room as what was called, the chief operator; it was engineering officer of the watch, basically. We'd run the plant. We ran a lot of experiments. Since it was end of core time, there were a lot of things they wanted to see what the core would behave like in its situation. We ran some things that you would never do with operation of a propulsion plant because you might just burn it out.

I stood watches where I had all control rods fully withdrawn, which you'd never do on a ship; you'd probably burn out the core. They were fully withdrawn because it was at the point where the poisons from the operation were shutting the core down and had shut it down. You were kind of waiting for regeneration, and I can't explain that exactly. I can't because I'm not sure I understand it anymore. I stood watches with the plant at 100% power and cut all cooling pumps off. Now you had cooling water circulating to cool the plant and keep from burning the thing up.

Some of these experiments were pretty daring, but they were very well planned, and they were very carefully done. You'd end up just running that plant to its limits. One of the things it did—at least in my case, it gave me much more confidence as an operator, because I knew what the plant would do under certain circumstances I hoped never to see in actual operating time. It was worth doing. We came out, those of us who were out there just before the shutdown. It shut down right after we finished up. It shut down actually a month after they had programmed or expected it to.

We did things that we will never do again, but they gave you insight into what to expect, and it was very helpful. So I was always very confident when we went to new construction. That was the other thing about new construction. The ship's crew ran all the tests on the power plant to get it operational because the shipyard didn't have anybody qualified to do that. We were the ship's engineers, if you will, for all the tests and all that were run in the process of getting this second of a kind because *Skate* was in operation, but the first thing that the Portsmouth ever built that was nuclear.[*] So we were the engineers for both the ship and for the shipyard.

---

[*] In December 1957 Trost reported to the submarine *Scorpion* (SSN-589), then under construction at the Portsmouth Naval Shipyard.

Paul Stillwell: That's intriguing.

Admiral Trost: It was interesting because when we would override the ship's supervisor for the power plant, he couldn't tell us what to do, and if he did something or ran something that we didn't think was right, we had the power to stop it, get it checked out. If it looked like it was satisfactory, we could say, "Okay, go." If it wasn't, we could say, "You've got to do the following to fix it." So that made the life very interesting because you were sort of a little bit more important than the average ship worker. There were five of us who were qualified to run the power plant from our prototype experience so we were part of the builder crew. It was interesting.

Paul Stillwell: Who were the instructors out in Idaho?

Admiral Trost: I'm not sure who they all were. I'm trying to think. Some were enlisted instructors who had been with *Nautilus* or *Seawolf* pre-commission detail, or they had been there when the prototype was built, or they worked for one of the labs like Bettis in Pittsburgh. They were all people who were very highly qualified for the job, including some who had served in one of the first two nukes. They were guys who knew what they were doing. They were guys who should know all the same procedures, except for two guys who decided to take a swim after a shift one day in the "spent" fuel pool, which is like a swimming pool where you put expended fuel rods that had been lifted out of the core. You put them in the fuel pool. You don't dive into radioactive water like they did. This had happened before I got there. The entire time I was out there for almost six months, they were bringing their stool sample and their urine samples on the bus every morning. I'm not sure whether all that was necessary or was just to teach them a lesson.

Paul Stillwell: Probably the latter.

Admiral Trost: It might have been the latter. It was interesting. They had to keep a log of everything they did. They had to write sort of a thesis on why what they did was wrong. It was graded with the shift supervisors out there. So they were given a hard time—rightfully so.

Paul Stillwell: Was there any kind of final exam in this process?

Admiral Trost: There was. You had a final oral and I think we had a written as well. I had my oral in the control room, power plant while operating doing certain procedures. You had to be on your toes, because you had to remember what you were doing and not get thrown off by a theoretical question, but it was well done. You did that to get your chief operator designation. I think the written preceded the oral, as I recall, and by this time you'd been observed enough times as an understudy or under training chief operator that the guys who were watching you knew you pretty well. They know what you could do and what you would do. It's a strenuous process and a good one, so when they put their stamp of approval on people, they were qualified to run the plant.

Paul Stillwell: Do you remember any kind of graduation ceremony?

Admiral Trost: No, I do not. I remember detachment. I think we were handed orders and went from there to Portsmouth for the new construction that was being compressed at the time. So those of us who were, there were three of us in the same class in Idaho all went to the same ship. Joe Synhorst, who had been with *Nautilus*, went directly.[*] Jeff Metzel, the exec, went with the three of us out there.[†] Shannon Cramer ran a separate course with the PCO group, and so Shannon, the exec, the engineer, and three more of us all showed up right about the same time and of course, in advance of any of the testing while the construction was going on.[‡]

It was an interesting experience, because we got the first nuclear ship built in Portsmouth. They were totally relying on us for supervision of anything that had anything to do with radioactivity. We knew the power plant in Idaho, knew the basics of the construction, so, in fact, on any particular ship we were the go-to guys when the people doing the building had questions, which was an interesting position to be in. Now we all had basic engineering degrees and, as a matter of fact, if you were Naval Academy basically a combination of electrical and mechanical background. The only guy who wasn't that I've ever known was this guy Pettis from Princeton. He came in with liberal arts, which everybody kind of sniffed at, but he was a pretty smart guy. He survived very

---

[*] Lieutenant Gerald E. Synhorst, USN.
[†] Lieutenant Commander Jeffrey C. Metzel Jr., USN.
[‡] Cramer was promoted to commander a few months prior to reporting to the shipyard.

nicely. He had a hard time with it, but—and they took a couple more guys, I knew a couple more who said they were not technical graduates, but that came a little later in the program.

Paul Stillwell: The people at Portsmouth had built dozens and dozens of submarines, but now it was you who had more expertise than they.

Admiral Trost: Well, we did. They did not have that expertise at all. I'm trying to think—the skipper had a special license, if you will. The shipyard commander was a two-star, but he wasn't in charge of construction on *Swordfish*. It was kind of interesting. He may have had a responsibility, but it wasn't to come down and tell people what to do on this ship, especially in the power plant. We had a good engineer who was the ship's supe who was a senior commander and it was his ship that sat on the power plant. It was sort of interesting. Of course, the engineering duty officers who were not nuclear trained, but had a responsibility to the shipyard for various things, got pissed very easily if they got told by some JO lieutenant what to do, but they had no option because they couldn't run the tests and we could. It was interesting.

Paul Stillwell: Is this a convenient place to break?

Admiral Trost: It's up to you. If you want to convene it, fine.

Paul Stillwell: Well, we've covered everything up to the ship getting into action, so we could pick that up at the next visit.

Interview Number 5 with Admiral Carlisle A.H. Trost, U.S. Navy (Retired)

Date: Wednesday, 8 July 2015

Place: Admiral Trost's apartment in Ginger Cove, south of Annapolis, Maryland

Paul Stillwell: Admiral, it's a pleasure to see you again today and resume our series. Last time we had gotten into the *Swordfish*. You also talked about your time out in Idaho and mentioned that you had gone camping while you were in Idaho and mentioned a child or two. Please tell me about the children and when they came.

Admiral Trost: Well, the child out in Idaho was our oldest son Carl, who will be 60 years old this coming September. He was, by the time we got out there, about a year old, very adventuresome, adventurous, and loved to camp. We went up on the Warm River, just outside the Snake River complex north of Idaho Falls. And we camped on the river with our neighbors, who were natives of Idaho, and we had a great time, just walking, hiking, and being out in the open with mountains off to the east of us and more off to the west and a river in between going by. Went fishing. Cooked some of our fish that we caught for dinner and cleaned the rest and took them home. Several of us went up in the Yellowstone Park quite frequently, because that was just a few miles further up the road. We did that about once a month, because every fourth week I had a long weekend off from the prototype training. And so we had a very good time. Saw a lot of the area; went over to Jackson Hole periodically and got familiar with that side of the mountains, the Tetons, and enjoyed outdoor living.

Paul Stillwell: Then you had a daughter a few years after that.

Admiral Trost: Older daughter is Laura Lee. She was born in '57 and has just had her 58th birthday. Laura Lee was born in Portsmouth, New Hampshire, while the *Swordfish* was being built. I saw her for about five minutes before I went on shift work during the new-construction period. And she's been a stalwart. She's a Mary Washington graduate, majored in economics and business, and currently serves as the office manager for her husband's accounting firm—good common sense, wonderful lady.

Paul Stillwell: Please talk about your duties in the *Swordfish.*[*]

Admiral Trost: Well, I was a little bit of a jack of all trades eventually. I was one of the initial four or five nuclear-trained watch officers during the construction period. We did all the construction supervision that had anything to do with the nuclear power plant, because the shipyard did not have anyone qualified. It was their first nuclear ship, so we were sort of a jack of all trades. I served as electrical officer; I served as torpedo and gunnery officer, auxiliary division officer, supply officer. We had a busy time. It was SSN number four; it was second of the *Skate* class. Our only assets experience-wise were in the *Skate* wardroom, which was down at EB.[†] And they were ahead of us by, I guess, about a year schedule-wise.

So we used to make trips down to Groton periodically when we had problems, because they didn't always correct the blueprints when they felt something didn't work and had to be changed. We'd go down and find something totally different from our installation, which supposedly mimicked theirs. Whether that was EB's way of getting ahead competitively or just oversight on their part, I was never quite sure. I spent a lot of time traveling back and forth on my various jobs. Spent a couple of days in Groton, finding out what they had done and why. I'd carry the information back up and help with the changes in prints and procedures.

Paul Stillwell: Do you remember any specific examples of things you learned?

Admiral Trost: Most of them had to do with the auxiliary systems, where they did modifications to piping, or, more specifically, valve placement and control placement, so

---

[*] USS *Swordfish* (SSN-579), a *Skate*-class nuclear submarine, was commissioned 15 September 1958 with Commander Shannon D. Cramer Jr., USN, in command. She was 268 feet long, 25 feet in the beam, and displaced 2,570 tons surfaced and 2,861 submerged. . She had a top speed on the surface of 15.5 knots and a speed in excess of 20 knots submerged. She was armed with eight 21-inch torpedo tubes.
[†] Electric Boat Division of the General Dynamics Corporation, Groton, Connecticut.

that from an operational perspective they were more accessible and less likely to be pulled by somebody and knocked out of line or things of that nature.

Paul Stillwell: What do you remember about your duties once you got to sea?

Admiral Trost: Watch stander, of course, in the control room as the ship's diving officer or officer of the deck and watch standing back in the power plant. We shifted back and forth. When we went to sea for the initial time, the skipper and exec, of course, were nuclear trained, and there were five or us who were. So we sort of shared the watch load, depending on what we were doing and where we going.

Paul Stillwell: What do you remember about some of the other officers in the ship?

Admiral Trost: Well, I remember the exec, Jeff Metzel, very capable guy.

Joe Synhorst was our engineer, had come from a tour in *Nautilus*, very competent guy. One of the brightest and best engineers I ever met. He seemed to have a knack for being out ahead of the problem when there was a problem. He had the ability when you were going to do a test, which we did lots of, to sort of forecast what might go wrong and brief you to make sure you were alert to what might go wrong. And very frequently it did, and he was just ahead of the curve all the time. Dick Lewis was the next senior guy, very, very capable guy.[*] He was assistant engineer and electrical officer. I don't know where Dick went to school, but he was one of the brightest guys. Practical operationally bright guy, good man.

Joe Fuller, class of '51, Naval Academy, one of the nuclear-trained guys who had gone through the prototype with me, was a very capable guy.[†] Good officer, good solid officer. He screwed up, somewhere along the line, as a new construction engineer officer and got fired from the program. I don't know what he did.

---

[*] Lieutenant James R. Lewis, USN.
[†] Lieutenant Joe Ed Fuller, USN.

Glen Merritt was a graduate of one of the New England universities, and I've forgotten which one.[*] Overall, I'd say he was drifty. He did the dumb things that you shouldn't do. He liked to experiment, and in the nuclear program, especially at that time, it was very much by the book. If it's not written, you don't do it. If it is written and you do it, you record what you've done. He just free-lanced and then forgot what he had done. That was definitely trouble.

He did nonsense things like right after the control room was freshly painted with its final coat of paint, he wrote such things as, "Battle lantern here," "Such and such here" in black magic marker on fresh paint [laughter]. It didn't endear him to the people who just did the painting [laughter]. It got put there eventually, but they had to repaint the wall before they could put the brackets up for them. So he was not our favorite. Dick Lewis. We had a limited duty officer, Dave Johnson.[†] He was my next-door neighbor up there. A very capable guy and a very solid guy. Been a former enlisted engineman and was commissioned, a very reliable watch stander. He retired as a lieutenant commander. Very common sense guy, good man.

Oh, and Dave Smith, a class behind me at the Naval Academy, good officer, good, solid guy.[‡] We had a good wardroom, reliable watch standers, well trained, and good experience. Of course, all the officers were qualified in submarines, so we didn't start out with any trainees. We were all nuclear trained and capable watch standers at the time. So there was no excess talent when it came to watch standers, but we had good watch standers. Had a good enlisted crew too.

Paul Stillwell: Any of the enlisted men that you remember specifically?

Admiral Trost: Yeah, Harry Harmon was my leading petty officer in the auxiliary division, and I can't think of the name of the guy; his last name was Clark. These guys were both first-class enginemen, very experienced submariners, made my job very easy because they had the ability to, again, forecast problems. They were experienced guys

---

[*] Lieutenant Glen C. Merritt, USN.
[†] Lieutenant David E. Johnson, USN.
[‡] Lieutenant David G. Smith, USN.

who knew what might go wrong, and we generally wrote our procedures up and briefed our people before tests and things, and were generally ahead of the curve on keeping things from going wrong. Both of those guys made officer. Matter of fact, my first three petty officers in the auxiliary division were all commissioned within about two years of the commissioning of the ship.

[Telephone interruption]

Paul Stillwell: We were talking about the petty officers who were so helpful in anticipating problems. You must have had a tremendous learning experience during this whole time.

Admiral Trost: Oh, it was—learning the nuclear program, the nuclear plant operation, shipyard operations. I had been through short overhauls in a diesel submarine, been through one in a destroyer, so I knew shipyard procedures and what you had to do. But we were the guys. We were in charge of an awful lot of the program, and that was a different experience, and interesting. We had a very talented group of people. Of course, that was true of the nuclear people, most of whom came to us from *Nautilus* and a couple from the *Seawolf* program.* They were quality people with good experience, good background, good leadership capability, so we had a dynamite crew. They were fun to be with.

Paul Stillwell: How much did you get acquainted with the front end of the submarine and the weapon system?

Admiral Trost: Thoroughly, because I was the weapons officer at one point in time too. I

---

* USS *Seawolf* (SSN-575), commissioned 30 March 1957, was the Navy's second nuclear-powered submarine. The first, USS *Nautilus* (SSN-571) had a pressurized water reactor. The *Seawolf* served as a test bed for a reactor cooled by liquid sodium. The latter was not deemed a success, so the *Seawolf* was later equipped with the pressurized water type. For the first skipper's view, see Richard B. Laning, "The *Seawolf*'s Sodium-Cooled Power Plant," *Naval History*, Spring 1992, pages 45-48.

had almost every job except engineer, exec, and CO. But very well acquainted.

Paul Stillwell: What do you recall about the *Swordfish* getting into operation?

Admiral Trost: That was when I almost got out of the Navy.

Paul Stillwell: Let's have that on the record.

Admiral Trost: The ship got built, did the sea trials, got commissioned, and then it did workups. Our pre-shakedown—shakeup in some respect—was about a three-month period. We operated on the East Coast out of Portsmouth and out of New London. We participated in a bunch of exercises and basically made sure the ship was ready for post-shakedown availability, which was an eight-week period as I recall, to correct any deficiencies found in that operating period.

We were due to leave Portsmouth in February of '59 to go to Hawaii, our new homeport. We were going to be the first SSN in the Pacific. We were to go to New London, load up orders and paperwork for the Pacific, and load torpedoes. Go down to Canaveral and stop in Canaveral for five days to check out their ability to support a nuclear plant and provide pure water and things like that in preparation for getting the first of the Polaris submarines to come down there and stop. They were to hit there before they deployed the first time. After we went there, we were to go through the Panama Canal and out to Hawaii. We left Portsmouth as scheduled. My family was heading for Hawaii. They were on the housing list out there. When we got to New London, I got called into the captain's stateroom. Shannon Cramer and the exec, Jeff Metzel, were there with a guy that I didn't recognize, a commander.

We were being told that we were going to deploy on a special operation for 60 days in the Atlantic, and then we were going to go to Hawaii. I think we had either three or seven days to do whatever we had to do to get ready. So we shoved off from New London, came back to New London 60 days later. In the meantime, we had families scattered all across the country. Some got to Hawaii and were told, "The ship's not coming, so you're canceled off the housing lists." Some got partway across the country and ran out of money, couldn't get in touch with their husbands, so unless they could reach their families and get some money, they were kind of hanging out in left field. I was able to get hold of Pauline when we were told we could tell anybody we could reach we were going to sea and the schedule would be provided later on. So I told her, "Stay with your folks until you hear from me again."

She said, "When will that be?"

I said, "Maybe two months." So she went semi-ballistic, and we shoved off for two months. As for communications, you receive, but you don't send. We came back to New London 60 days to the mark later and loaded the sub as we should have loaded two months previously, went down and stopped at Canaveral. I found my family still ready to carry out orders. Pauline had flight reservations from San Francisco out to Hawaii, but ended up being put on an MSTS ship, where it turned out she met some good people and some good friends that were friends for years afterwards.[*] So it worked out all right. But I was stewing because of my people and all of the above. Families, couldn't find them, couldn't contact them. They were out of money, or they got to Hawaii and couldn't get any quarters.

So I brooded about this, and one night I came off watch about, oh, I guess about midnight and wrote my letter of resignation and dropped it on the skipper's desk. The next day I was the in-port duty officer. One of my shipmates, Joe Fuller, came and said, "I was told to relieve you for a little while." It was like midnight, and I was the duty officer. So the skipper stuck his head in my stateroom and said, "Meet me on the pier at 2:00 o'clock." So I got relieved as the duty officer and went out on the pier. I was staying in Canaveral, and Shannon's brother-in-law was riding the ship, as was Jake Laboon. I don't know if you know Jake or not.

Paul Stillwell: I know of him.

---

[*] MSTS – Military Sea Transportation Service, a part of the Navy that operated ships for support functions. In some cases it chartered the ships, and it some cases it ran the ships directly with civil service mariners. In 1970 MSTS was renamed Military Sealift Command (MSC), the current title for the command.

Admiral Trost: Well, Jake and Shannon were classmates, and Jake was a World War II submariner before he became a priest.[*] He had ridden the ship down and been aboard ship for little less than a week. Great guy and great shipmate to have, and so I went out on the pier, and I was standing out there. There were Shannon, his brother-in-law, and Jake Laboon. "Let's walk and talk." It started off with the brother-in-law saying, "Carl, what is this shit about resigning?"

I said, "Well, I don't like the Navy I'm in today," and I told him why.

"I understand that," he said, "but you've got a good future. It's a dumb thing to do."

I said, "It's not a dumb thing for those families who are out there scattered across the country. I don't want to be part of this outfit anymore."

So all three of them took turns haranguing me. They said, "We're going to stop in the Canal Zone for three days. First night in we will take a walk on the pier down there. Think about it."

About an hour later I got back to the ship. Now I was having trouble sleeping. I was thinking. We got to the Canal Zone, and on the first night in, they took me out on the pier and walked me and talked to me. By the time we got to Hawaii I thought, "Maybe I won't submit this right now."

Shannon said, "It will be in my safe."

I said, "Okay." So I ended up not sending it and glad that I didn't. I was so pissed off at the Navy at that time I was just going to get the hell out and say, "You guys want to tolerate this kind of thing, fine, but we don't treat people like that."

Paul Stillwell: What a difference they made with those walks on the pier.

Admiral Trost: Yes. They were persuasive.

Paul Stillwell: What happened during the 60 days? Can you talk about that?

---

[*] Lieutenant John F. Laboon Jr., CHC, USN, had graduated from the Naval Academy in the class of 1944 and served as a line officer before becoming a chaplain. The guided missile destroyer *Laboon* (DDG-58) is named in his honor.

Admiral Trost: We operated off foreign coasts to see what was going on. That's all I can talk about.

Paul Stillwell: How did things eventually settle out for the families?

Admiral Trost: Well, the first of our people got out there and were basically rejected, and they had no one to turn to at that point in time. By the time we got back, there had been enough squawking by wives who'd gotten there and had found a voice and who—I guess somebody on the SubPac staff started looking into it and found out what happened and said, "Oh, God, we really screwed that one up."[*]

So by the time we got there, for example, my wife was one of the latecomers, having been tipped off to sit tight till we got back. She and the gals who went out with her were on the housing list, and a lot of the other women who'd gotten out there early and were stranded managed to get into housing after about a month. So things were starting to settle down, and with the arrival of the ship and the husbands, everything went back to normal pretty quickly. Took a couple of weeks.

The problem was that we were at sea. We got out there, and three weeks after we got there, we commenced all sorts of—we were the first SSN in PacFlt, and it was everybody's toy. Five weeks after we got there, we sailed for the West Coast and spent six weeks on the West Coast doing torpedo and sound trials up in the Pacific Northwest. So it was a hectic period.

I left the ship just before the first of the year, and *Sargo*, which was the sister ship, had come out, having been built on the West Coast. She had come out two or three months after we did and was due to deploy about the first of the year. *Swordfish* deployed three days after I left it in December 1959 and was due to be relieved by *Sargo*. *Sargo* had an oxygen fire while charging oxygen, and to put out the fire they sank the stern of the submarine.[†]

---

[*] SubPac – Submarine Force Pacific Fleet.
[†] On 14 June 1960, while under the command of Lieutenant Commander John H. Nicholson, USN, the nuclear attack submarine *Sargo* (SSN-583) was charging her oxygen tanks while at Pearl Harbor. A leak developed, and fire broke out in her after torpedo room; it was made worse by the detonation of two torpedo warheads. The ship's officers then made a shallow dive with the torpedo room hatch open to put out the fire. Machinist's Mate Third Class James E. Smallwood was killed in the fire.

Paul Stillwell: Commander Nicholson.

Admiral Trost: Yep, Jack Nicholson. Which saved the ship. *Swordfish* came back from deployment, turned around about a week or ten days later, and made another six-month deployment. Luckily, I was gone.

Paul Stillwell: Yes. [Laughter]

Admiral Trost: So we started out with a bang. We started out operating and operating and operating. As I said, it was everybody's play toy. Everybody wanted to do something with it.

Paul Stillwell: What were some of the things they wanted you to do?

Admiral Trost: Well, go out and do ASW trials with destroyers to see whether we were any harder to detect than any other submarine, which, of course, if you're looking for a piece of metal in the ocean, it doesn't make any difference what's driving it. It's still a piece of metal in the ocean. And then checked our ability to get in undetected and make simulated torpedo attacks on destroyers. And we did sound trials. We had a lot of VIP tours. I think every flag officer in the Pacific who was in Hawaii rode us for a couple days as a minimum, and they kept us busy, a lot of in-port tours, and just busy.

Paul Stillwell: How well did you do in those attacks on destroyers?

Admiral Trost: Oh, very disappointingly from the destroyer perspective, because, well, first of all, we could relocate. We weren't the three-knot diesel boat that creeps around and tries to do things the old way. They might detect us out there, but by the time we shoot them, we're back here, and they haven't detected us going by. So that was of interest to us and probably of dismay to them, but fact of life. They were developing tactics to counter nuclear submarines, which were new, so it was helpful in that respect.

Paul Stillwell: Do you remember any inputs from ComSubPac?

Admiral Trost: Well, a lot of interest, a lot of riders from SubPac staff. They were with the nuclear boats, and the same thing with *Sargo* when she got out there finally. And I'd say curiosity in how do we handle these things and what was different. They were so geared up for diesel boats, and when they planned an exercise, it didn't take into account the added capability that nuclear power gave ships like ours. So they were learning, learning how to handle and employ the ships.

Paul Stillwell: It's an interesting phenomenon. You've got senior officers in a given period who have to command technology that wasn't available when they were in submarines.

Admiral Trost: That's right. That's right. There was a lot of curiosity and a lot of well, a combination of failure to have the knowledge—understandable—and a degree of jealousy over the attention that the new technology was grabbing. The attention of the VIPs who wanted to see the ship would come through, and SubPac staff, for example, would have us drop everything. "You've got so-and-so coming. Take care of him." So I think a little bit of jealousy, a little bit of annoyance. We were the new kid on the block, but we were getting all the attention.

Paul Stillwell: Jealousy on the part of whom?

Admiral Trost: The staff members who were not nuclear trained and couldn't answer the questions about the nuclear training and what advantages that gave you, and they saw the attention being focused on us. I think that annoyed them.

Paul Stillwell: What do you remember about family life in the area?

Admiral Trost: What I had of it was great. [Laughter] By the time we got out there, we had our two children, and they loved it, loved the weather, loved playing outside. Our daughter Laura Lee was a year or a year and a half. She was fascinated by bugs, which abound in Hawaii. She used to bring bugs into the house and drive Pauline batty. "Look what I found!" [Laughter] But it was good, and it was our first time out in Hawaii, and so we enjoyed that very much. It was sort of great having the opportunity to be out there.

Paul Stillwell: Any specific memories?

Admiral Trost: Well, I remember one specifically. I remember being rocked out of bed one morning on a Saturday morning when the Air Force Thunderbirds—the Blue Angels' equivalent—were out there flying out of Hickam, and we lived about half a mile from Hickam.[*] I'd been at sea all week, and I didn't read the paper to catch up, and so I didn't know they were there. I was in bed, sleeping in on Saturday morning, and I heard this thing go over our heads probably 100 or 200 feet, doing their demonstration with Hickam as the focal point, and it rocked me right out of bed. Woke everybody up in the neighborhood, I think.

We enjoyed touring the island. That was fascinating. I remember going down to Waikiki, which was much simpler a place than it is now, and walking the beach and seeing all these places we'd read about and hadn't seen before and hadn't been familiar with. It was interesting. Hickam had a great beach, and we loved the beach, kids loved the beach, so we spent a lot of time over there. It was fun. And going aboard the *Arizona* Memorial and things we'd read about and never seen before—it was all fascinating.[†]

Paul Stillwell: What do you recall about the command qualification process?

Admiral Trost: Well, you know, I guess, now that I think about it, not too very much. I remember what we did. There was an academic process, and I don't remember much about that. There was going to sea with another ship, being judged on your capability to make approaches and things by the skipper of the ship taking you out.

---

[*] Blue Angels is the name of the Navy's flight demonstration team, which has done close formation flying for air shows and other events since 1946. Hickam Air Force Base, adjacent to Pearl Harbor.
[†] USS *Arizona* (BB-39), a *Pennsylvania*-class battleship, was commissioned 17 October 1916. She was sunk by Japanese air attack on 7 December 1941. A memorial was built over her hull in the 1960s.

When *Sargo* came out, I went to sea with Jack Nicholson for sort of an underway observation period. I don't remember what else we did, to tell you the truth. I qualified for command while I was out there, and I don't really remember much about it. Must have done something.

Paul Stillwell: You talked about Commander Cramer putting your resignation letter on ice. What do you remember about him as an operator?

Admiral Trost: He was sharp as an operator. He was—I'd use the term "professionally aggressive." He was the aggressor when he was making an attack on somebody, but also very capable professionally, and we did well in exercises as a result. He was very competent.

Paul Stillwell: Anything else to say about that submarine?

Admiral Trost: Great experience for my first nuke. That deployment that I complained about, that two-month deployment, was trying on the crew, but it made the crew early in the life of the ship professionally very, very much more competent than we would have been otherwise, because we had mud on our shoes by the time we got back. We had done the kinds of things that we were supposed to be built for and trained for and never had any experience in. When we came off those 60 days, we were a well-trained, qualified crew, and so it gives you a good feeling that we can handle anything that comes up, and it was a good shakedown, unexpectedly.

Paul Stillwell: And I'm guessing it was a great bonding experience.

Admiral Trost: It was, it really was, and despite the setbacks to our families and the fact that we had a shipload of pissed-off people, they pulled together. It unified the crew. Maybe it was "We'll show those bastards." There was certainly that attitude. When they ran us in the Pacific after we got out there, the attitude was "We can do anything." And we did everything.

Paul Stillwell: Well, that tour came to an end with the Olmsted Scholarship.

Admiral Trost: It did, yes.

Paul Stillwell: How did you get into that program?

Admiral Trost: Well, I was called by a General Aurand, who was retired from the Army and lived in Hawaii.* Aurand said that George Olmsted, a West Point graduate of '22, was a retired Army two-star and had been on active duty in World War II as a logistician.† First of all, Olmsted felt very strongly that military officers should be more broadly educated and should have a sense of geography, government, and foreign relations that he didn't feel they had as a group. And he was right. So he wanted to establish a scholarship, which was at that time still awaiting approval by the Secretary of Defense, which would send as an initial group two officers from each service overseas to study in the language of the country they were sent to.

I had been nominated by the Navy to be one of the two naval officers. So General Aurand was telling me all about this, kind of, "Are you interested?" I didn't even know I was available to be interested. It sounded interesting, and I thought at the time, "Does this mean if I take that, I'm out of the nuclear program?" Because I was told I was slated at that point in time to go as engineer of a new-construction submarine, which was the next professional step in the nuclear business.

So he described what they wanted to do, told me he recommended it highly because he believed in the concept. We talked about it. Pauline wasn't too keen about it, because she didn't speak German, and my German was old Plattdeutsch from Illinois as a kid. We spoke that German in my hometown before World War II. Pauline and I talked about it, and we thought it could be interesting, and so I told Aurand I was interested, appreciated his input. So I responded then to my detailer and said I would be interested if selected for it, and he said, "You're selected."

---

* Lieutenant General Henry S. Aurand, USA (Ret.), West Point class of 1915. He served from 1947 to 1949 as Director of Logistics, Department of the Army.
† Olmsted was the first captain, i.e., top-ranking cadet, and he finished second in class standing in 1922.

So we got orders to Monterey, left Hawaii just before New Year's Day 1960, reported in the first week of January to Monterey, to the then Army Language School, and they were teaching German to Army officers. I learned how to command troops in an MP unit, I learned how to do exercises in a sandbox, and my vocabulary wasn't academic in its nature.[*] It was more geared toward the military requirements of people who were going over there for a tour of duty. We had two German professors who were native Germans, who'd come to the U.S. after World War II, and both of them worked with me at night and talked to me and developed my language capability so I was speaking modern German, not old German.

So I spent six months out there, came back to Washington for two weeks, and spent the two weeks with the Navy Intelligence people. Frau Maria Wilhelm was my instructor. [Laughter] She was a lady probably in her 60s, native German, and tough. She was a slave driver. [Laughs] And I learned a lot from her, a lot of academic capability in German. Then I got intel briefings of limited utility, and then we went over to Germany.

Paul Stillwell: How readily did you pick up the language?

Admiral Trost: Very. It turned out to be very easy, and by the time I got there, I was a self-sustaining student. And when I got to the school, I could speak well enough that my German colleagues thought I was Swedish or Norwegian because I had something of an accent, apparently, but my German was okay.

Also, I was a Navy lieutenant when I got over there, and I was brought in Arnold Bergstraesser was the head of the political science department at the University of Freiberg. He was, with Adenauer, one of the founders of modern Germany, really.[†]

Paul Stillwell: Chancellor.

Admiral Trost: Yeah. I met him, and because I was a U.S. naval officer and because he'd

---

[*] MP – military police.
[†] Konrad H. J. Adenauer was the first post-World War II Chancellor of West Germany. He served in that post from 1949 to 1963.

been in the U.S. for an extended period of time at Princeton, as I recall, and because the head of the political science department was a Princeton graduate, native German, he basically opened the door for me. I sat in on all sorts of things that I'd had to have been at the university for two years at least to get into. So I got immediate access, so it was quite nice and interesting, got to participate in a lot of things that I wouldn't have been qualified for. Maybe I wasn't qualified when I did it!

So the time was interesting and productive. The German university system, you go to school, you go to class, and then you have what I would consider a very early break for the semester break. You have a long semester break, and you're given a book list that would choke a horse, and you're expected to read that while you're off, which keeps you pretty busy. The summer, the summer break, I think it was about four months, same type of thing, lots of books to read, but we could travel because you can read anywhere. So we did.

So I had a good experience and met a lot of young Germans, some close to my age—I was 30-31—and had a lot of guys who had finished high school, who for one reason or another didn't go on to college right away, even though they were qualified. So they were latecomers. So I had classmates who were in their late 20s, and, interestingly, they were a conservative group and anti-Nazi, and some of them hadn't spoken to their fathers since the war was over because they didn't agree with what the fathers did during the war.

So we used to run what was called the Little America House. We had an apartment, and I had German students who'd come by, I had a couple of American Fulbrighters who came by.[*] We had a guy who was a high school professor who'd been a Fulbright scholar in the U.S., had gotten his basic degree in London, so he spoke fluent English like a Brit and spoke English with an American twinge or Kansas accent. He had stayed on at Kansas after his Fulbright scholarship for three years as an instructor at Kansas. He was teaching there, and he sort of took us under his wing, he and his wife. So we saw a lot of them.

---

[*] The Fulbright Scholarship Program for international study was established in 1946 by J. William Fulbright, a Democrat from Arkansas, who served in the U.S. Senate from 3 January 1945 until his resignation 31 December 31 1974.

We had company a couple nights a week. I never did know whether it was because we had food, because we could shop at the commissary in Karlsruhe. We had food that they couldn't get. [Laughs] But we had some good sessions, great sessions, and I think the American Fulbrighters benefited from it. We have one that we still stay in touch with. He's a retired IBM executive, and we got to know him and his wife quite well, got to know his kids after we came back to the States after they had children.

So, interesting life. Language was never a problem. Pauline took some night classes when they were available in Monterey, but didn't speak the language and didn't have quite the learning ability for the language. She got to the point where she could understand a lot of conversation but couldn't participate as a conversant.

One of our big jokes was before we left Germany, the week before, she was going to prove to me that she could understand as well as I could. So she went up to a local bakery to buy different things, different breads and sweets. She came home with a dozen hard rolls, *brotchen.*

I said, "I didn't think you went for hard rolls."

She said, "I didn't." [Laughter] That's what the guy gave her when she told him what she wanted in German, and that's been a standing joke for, well, 60 years.

Paul Stillwell: And she didn't want to admit that that wasn't what she asked for.

Admiral Trost: That's right. It wasn't what she asked for.

Our son Carl, who was five when we got there, went both to a German kindergarten and to half of the first grade, and he was fluent in German by the time we left. Our daughter Laura Lee was three. She picked up some French because we had French military neighbors with little kids, and she played with them. So we were a conglomerate of language capability, but it was interesting.

Paul Stillwell: Did you find out how you particularly came to be nominated? This was a first for the Navy.

Admiral Trost: I never did, really. I never did. The other nominee was a guy named Pat Lockwood.[*] Pat was a year ahead of me at the Naval Academy, surface warfare. Neither one of us had any specific special qualifications that I could see, other than we both did well at the academy. So I don't know.

Paul Stillwell: How much freedom did you have in picking a curriculum?

Admiral Trost: Total, total. That was the other thing. I wasn't qualified for a lot of the things that I participated it, because it's one of these—the Germans are very rigid in their standards: "You have to do this and have done this and done this to be eligible for this." Well, I wasn't eligible for any of those things because I wasn't in the German school system and hadn't been. So they were very good about that. They waived all these things. Bergstraesser just said, "Whatever."

So I sat down with this head of this political science curriculum, and we decided what I should take and what I could do. I did take a "German for Foreign Students" to polish up my German, and my German instructor for the two years is one of those who thought I was Norwegian. So it was interesting.

Paul Stillwell: Could you cite benefits from later in your career that came from that experience?

Admiral Trost: Well, I'd say that having been exposed to Europe and to a lot of Europeans, including some military, was helpful, certainly. When I was more senior, when I went overseas, I had an ability to relate on a slightly different professional level than had I not had that background. So I think that was extremely helpful.

The German language itself was useful. I made a couple of visits to Germany at their invitation—well, as a senior officer but before I became CNO. Then I went over as CNO, and the German equivalent, the first one when I went over there became their Chairman of Joint Chiefs equivalent, so he and I had a great relationship. Then his

---

[*] Lieutenant Forrest Patterson Lockwood, USN.

successor, whom I met over there, we still correspond at Christmas. So, yeah, in that sense it was very valuable.

I went on my visit as CNO, went to Bonn, and actually was the principal in a press conference in German and could handle it then yet. So, yeah, that was beneficial. At the press conference, my audience was German professors at Bonn at the university, and so it opened a lot of doors.

Paul Stillwell: During your tenure as CNO is when the Berlin Wall came down.[*]

Admiral Trost: That's right.

Paul Stillwell: So what do you remember about that specific experience?

Admiral Trost: And it went up while we were over there. [Laughter]

Paul Stillwell: Interesting.

Admiral Trost: Yeah. What I remember about it was that, first of all, going back to when it went up. I had ordered a Mercedes 220 sedan to replace my VW Beetle when we came back to the States. The wall went up. I got a call from the salesman who I'd been working with, who had told me initially I probably had a two-year wait, and it probably wouldn't come in while I lived in Germany. So I was resigned to the fact that I was never going to see the car.

The wall went up. Two days later, he called me and said, "Would you like your car next week?" Germans were cancelling or deferring their purchases because of the wall.

---

[*] In 1961 the East German regime built a wall that separated the Soviet- and NATO-controlled sectors of the city of Berlin. It was a symbolic gesture at the height of the Cold War. A number of East Germans were killed in subsequent escape attempts. On the night of 9 November 1989 the East German government suddenly and unexpectedly opened the wall to permit free transit. The wall was subsequently torn down, this time a symbol of the easing of relations between the superpowers.

So I thought, "Well, it's a long shot, and I'm putting $3,200 at risk. I want the car; might not get it otherwise." I said, "Yeah." And I didn't have to pay for it until it came in, so I thought, "Okay."

So we got the car, brought it back with us, and had it in Norfolk. We're talking the beauty of it was with the exchange rate at the time, of the mark to the dollar, the Mercedes 220 cost me less than a stripped Chevy four-door sedan would have.

Paul Stillwell: Sometimes you get lucky. [Laughs]

Admiral Trost: Sometimes you get lucky. But when the wall went down, first of all, I heard from my German counterpart right away, and it was interesting, having been there when it went up and then hearing about it when it went down.

Then we went back a year after I retired. My son Steve, who was class of '85 over here at the Naval Academy, was in Germany, in Stuttgart, as a Navy lieutenant commander on the EuCom staff.* We went to Berlin, which I couldn't do while I was over there because I had too many clearances, so we went over after I retired. So I saw both sides of the wall. We went into East Germany, rode the train that my German professors in Monterey rode when they escaped from East Germany during the Cold War. So it was fascinating.

We saw the wall while we were still in Germany, because one of the other Olmsted scholars, Naval Academy grad, class of '56, an Air Force captain, John Karas, who lived in Göttingen, which is a university town in Central Germany, and we used to visit each other. Göttingen was 12 miles from the wall when it went up. So we went out, used to sneak through the woods, and peer behind trees at this fence and the German Army guys on the other side of the fence. Fascinating.

He had the philosophy that we were in town—their apartment was in a building on a corner of two busy streets, and the road next to their house went out to the fence where the wall was. He said, "If you wake up in the morning or during the night and there are tanks going by either one of these streets, look out. If they're turning right and going that way, they're ours. If they're coming the other way, they're theirs." [Laughter]

---

* EuCom – U.S. European Command.

So we had some interesting times.

Paul Stillwell: What do you recall about the living arrangements while you were there as a student?

Admiral Trost: Difficult, because we were unofficial. The embassy in Germany didn't want anything to do with us because we weren't official. So I was actually attached to the U.S naval attaché's office in London. People in London sent me a paycheck by mail once a month, and I belonged to them officially. There was no arrangement for us. We were on our own to find a place to live.

Now, I had NATO orders, which turned out to be my ace in the hole, because we kept looking at places to rent, and you couldn't rent them either because they didn't want Americans or I had NATO orders, but I was not official, so no, or they had a rule that you had to pay five years' rent in advance.

Paul Stillwell: Wow. [Laughs]

Admiral Trost: This was the standard in Germany at that time to get the capital to rebuild the destroyed parts of Germany. So I couldn't do that, because you got paid back over five years, and that clearly was a loser. They weren't going to pay me after I came back to the States.

So one day, quite by accident, I ran into a guy who worked for the French government, native German, and he had housing in Freiberg. I found him because I inquired, "Who runs this housing and how do I get into it?" Finally, one of the tenants who was French and spoke English gave me this guy's name.

So I found Harold whatever his name was and talked to him, and he listened to my story and what I was. He said, "Well, I report to Baden-Baden, to the French Forces in Germany headquarters. I can call a secretary up there who's my contact, and get her advice."

So he called her, came back to me. "She has set up an appointment for you and your wife to meet the Commanding General, French Forces in Germany."

This is Lieutenant Trost, U.S. Navy, and I thought, "Holy shit." [Laughter]

"Then he's going to interview you to see if they'll rent you one of the French Forces' houses," which were reparations from the Germans to the French after World War II.

So we had a meeting with the guy, very congenial, asked all sorts of questions about my background, was fascinated by the fact that I was a nuclear submariner going to a university in Germany, and he said, "We can do that." He scribbled his signature on a piece of paper, which I couldn't read because it was in French, and gave it to me and said, "Give that to the people back in Freiberg."

So I went back to Freiberg. So this guy gave me the thing, he smiled, he said, "I have an apartment for you, and it's right across the street from the city park. It's a half a block from the start of the Black Forest where the hill goes up and you're now in the Black Forest. It's three blocks from the university, a block from Cathedral Square, nice place, two bedroom."

So we moved in.

Paul Stillwell: Ideal! [Laughs]

Admiral Trost: Yeah, perfect, ideal, couldn't have been better. And the other French housing, there was one block's worth of apartments, three-story, and all occupied by French military officers, and the other big complex they had was on the other side of town. I was, with this one, able to walk to the university in about 10-15 minutes. On the other side I'd have had to drive in and fight for a parking place every day. So it was ideal.

But one thing was the French required me to pay rent to them, which was the equivalent of my housing allowance that they asked for. The people in London insisted on taking my housing allowance, and so I forfeited my housing allowance for two years and paid the Frenchman also. So it was expensive in that sense, but a good experience and worthwhile.

Paul Stillwell: Did you encounter any anti-American feeling in that time?

Admiral Trost: One time. We thought we had a very nice house just outside of town, to the south of town, sort of a German chalet-type place in a little valley. It looked perfect, and the streetcar ran right through the edge of this place, about two blocks away, right into the heart of town, so I could have taken that in to school. We had struck a deal on a lease for the two years I thought I'd be over there for, until the owner found out I was American, and he said no. So, yeah, there was that, but that was minor.

Basically, the Germans we found were generally pro-American and grateful for the fact that we had come in and basically rebuilt or helped rebuild Germany after the war, and especially in Stuttgart. We spent a lot of time in Stuttgart because that was the headquarters for U.S. Forces Germany, and I had to report in to them and keep them advised of travel arrangements and register my car, get my German driver's license from them, and so forth. And the Germans we encountered there were very pro-U.S. because we had both destroyed Stuttgart, along with the Brits, but we'd also rebuilt it, so they were pro-American in their bent. And the young people, the fellow university students, were very pro-U.S. It wasn't bad.

Paul Stillwell: The Marshall Plan was a marvelous thing.[*]

Admiral Trost: It was a great thing, it was a great thing, and it was money well spent.

Paul Stillwell: Did you see any remaining evidence of the destruction?

Admiral Trost: Yeah, most noteworthy in Cologne in the cathedral. Our tour guide showed us damage to the cathedral, which was a big beautiful thing.

Paul Stillwell: Is that the one with two steeples?

Admiral Trost: Yeah. And showed us damage to that from the—you know we came

---

[*] At the Harvard University commencement in 1947, Secretary of State George C. Marshall made an address in which he outlined a plan for the economic rebuilding of war-ravaged Europe. Congress passed the European Recovery Act, and the program of American support came to be known as the Marshall Plan.

across the river at Cologne and blew the hell out of the bridges and destroyed them all. That was to keep the Germans from coming out, but I think we destroyed and they destroyed. I'm not sure who did the most damage. But we had a bombing raid which used the cathedral as the focal point for drops, I was told, and so you'd use that to aim at, but you weren't going to bomb it. But somebody missed his aim a little bit and did some damage to the cathedral. So our guide was soliciting funds from all American tourists because we damaged their cathedral. I said, "Well, your forces did a lot of damage too, " I told him. I argued with him in German. He didn't like that. [Laughter]

But it was interesting. We had that kind of attitude, but generally it was friendly. And down in the—the Black Forest area but

Paul Stillwell: Bavaria?

Admiral Trost: In Bavaria, we went to Garmisch a number of times. That was a great place.

Paul Stillwell: There's a passion play there, I think.

Admiral Trost: They do that. Actually, it's not Garmisch for the passion play; it's just north.

Paul Stillwell: Partenkirchen or something like that.

Admiral Trost: Yeah, it's Partenkirchen. Anyway, we spent a fair amount of time there, and initially went there; there were two U.S. Army-run hotels down there. It's a playground for the U.S. forces in Europe, or was, anyway, and, of course, also commercially it is. We liked the Army places, but one time they were full. We went with our two little kids, got there. I was a member of ADAC, Allgemeiner Deutscher Automobilclub, AAA, and that helped for all sorts of things, but most specifically for reservations at hotels, got special rates, and all the other things you'd only get through AAA or an AAA-like organization.

We got our reservation at this little thing which was on the end of Garmisch and pulled up about 5:30 in the evening, tired, the kids were cranky. A German lady came out and greeted us. I told her we had reservations and my name. "Ah, yes, we've been expecting you." Then she snapped the two kids up and said, "They'll be in your room."

I thought, "Okay." [Laughter]

So Pauline and I grabbed our stuff. They sent somebody out, another woman, to get the suitcases, who insisted on carrying our suitcases in. Guys were standing at the register. We got up to our room, both kids had had a bath, our luggage was up in our room. They were the nicest people. So, thereafter, when we went to Garmisch, we always stayed there instead of the U.S. hotels, which were pretty nice. A great area and very pro-U.S. It was like a little community.

We also stayed outside of town one time. We were out exploring and saw this very nice hotel restaurant, little German one, right next to the railroad tracks that went up to the Alps, and skiers were using that all the time. So we decided one time to stay there, and that was an experience too. It was like staying with your aunt and uncle or something. They were just wonderful people. So we tried that out and liked that.

Then later on when we went back to Germany when our kids were there, we took them down there and went to this hotel, and I swear the guy who ran the place remembered us, and I told him this one son was the little boy that we had with us who they doted over, and he couldn't believe that.

So it was quite an experience. It was a great experience.

Paul Stillwell: What a happy memory.

Admiral Trost: It was a happy memory. It was a good place to be. We got to travel all over Europe while we were there. Our guidelines for how long the trip was going to be, it had to be when there wasn't class, and we'd travel till half our cash was gone, then we'd turn around. I said, "Pauline, seems there's always canned goods back home." So that was our guideline. So we got to see a lot.

Paul Stillwell: What was the teaching method in the classes? Was it mainly lectures? Did you have seminars?

Admiral Trost: Mainly lectures, some seminars, a lot of outside reading. You were expected to have read the material. That was part of it. Sometimes a couple of books per seminar, for example, and that part was hard to keep up with until I figured out that most of the students didn't read most of it. So by reading most of it, I was ahead of the game, and so it worked out pretty well.

I got to know the faculty members. There were probably about five male faculty members that conducted most of the seminars in that department, and I got to go to people who were in the first through fourth year at the university. So they didn't always differentiate this as a first- or second-year class. It was something you had to do. Of course, everything was geared up for a four-year curriculum. So I could almost pick and choose.

I had this guy who ran the political science seminar who was sort of an advisor to me, saying, "You ought to do this and you might want to do this." So it was very helpful. They were very helpful to the program.

Paul Stillwell: Did you have tests, papers to write?

Admiral Trost: Papers to write, papers to write, and I had an occasional oral or there'd be group orals, where maybe four of us would sit down and the professor would introduce a subject and ask for input and comments and see what you'd gotten out of what you read.

Paul Stillwell: Did this lead to a specific degree?

Admiral Trost: No. It was specific that there would not be a degree, nor one required, nor was there the capability of getting a degree.

Now, what we did as a result of the experience of us early guys, set up something with one of the New England universities, either that or one of the Washington, D.C. universities, I'm not sure which, to accept credits from foreign universities and permit a university degree from a U.S. university, or get credit for it anyway. I didn't get that, but I'm not sure what value it would have had.

Paul Stillwell: I know about how fitness reports are usually done from close personal observation, but that certainly wasn't possible. How did your fitness reports get written?

Admiral Trost: They were not observed, so there was a void from a fitness report perspective. Of course, I was expecting to come back and be engineer of a new-construction submarine, one of those. The advent of the Polaris program was just starting, really, so that's what I expected to do. Instead, I got a phone call from Chuck Griffiths, who was my detailer at the time.[*] He said, "I have an attack submarine exec billet opening up that you're qualified for. I'd like to put you in it if you're interested."

Well, shit, who wouldn't be? [Laughter]

He said, "But you'd have to be back by February." And I was due back in May. So he said, "Would you like it?"

I said, "Hell, yes." [Laughter] Pauline would like it, too, because she, not being fluent in the language over there and being a little bit lonely, was ready to come home.

So I came back early, but I finished much of what I would have done in the semester I missed with the help of my mentor, because I had three months' notice, and so it didn't make any difference because I wasn't going to get credit for it anyway. But I could get it done and satisfy him that I'd done everything he wanted me to do.

Paul Stillwell: Were you satisfied with what you got of the experience?

Admiral Trost: I was, very much so, and by that point in time, I think I had gotten just about everything I would have gotten had I stayed another semester. So it worked out well. And besides that, Pauline was pregnant and wanted to have Steve back home, not over there. They were going to put her in the French hospital in Baden-Baden, and she didn't like that idea. So for a number of reasons it worked out quite well.

---

[*] Griffiths, who had helped Trost get into submarines initially, was by this time a commander.

Paul Stillwell: It did indeed. Did you then go through a PXO course?

Admiral Trost: I did not; didn't have time. I went directly to the ship and took over.[*] The guy that I was relieving was going to new construction over at Newport News and had been exec for two years, came aboard during the commissioning period, and so it worked out to his advantage, freed him up in time.

I went with a very experienced CO who had been the commissioning CO, and so I didn't worry about that.[†] Then he was relieved a month and a half later by Yogi Kaufman, who was then my skipper for the balance of the time on *Scorpion*.[‡] So it worked out well in every respect.

When Yogi came aboard, I had the advantage of by this time being the experienced XO, having been there two and a half months when he took over, and he had a reputation for being a hotshot and very professional, and he was every bit. He drove that ship like he was sort of attached to it or born with it or something. But I had the advantage with him because he could be overriding if you let him, but he was very competent. And I had the advantage of being there and being in place, and he had to rely on me [laughter] as the experienced guy because we deployed then about three weeks after he got there, and we were out for 70 days. He needed me and he knew that, so there was an advantage to that.

Paul Stillwell: Who was the first skipper you served with?

Admiral Trost: Buzz Bessac.

Paul Stillwell: He had put her in commission.

---

[*] USS *Scorpion* (SSN-589), a *Skipjack*-class nuclear submarine, was commissioned 29 July 1960. She was 252 feet long, 32 feet in the beam, and displaced 3,075 tons surfaced and 3,500 submerged. . She had a top speed on the surface around 20 knots and a speed in excess of 30 knots submerged. She was armed with six 21-inch torpedo tubes.
[†] Commander Norman B. Bessac, USN.
[‡] Commander Robert Y. Kauffman, USN.

Admiral Trost: He had put her in commission, yeah. Buzz was a very competent guy. We had gone through the Cuban Crisis together, and I can't tell you about those operations, but. I do have a sidelight story.[*] *Scorpion* deployed to the Caribbean during the Cuban Crisis. I came home one evening and told Pauline, "We're getting under way tomorrow morning at 6:00."

She said, "No you're not. You are in for two weeks."

I said, "No, we're not," and we got under way the next morning. We came home five weeks later.

When I got home, I said, "Any big crises?"

She said, "Well, Mrs. So-and-so, wife of a first class petty officer, called me and said, 'My washer doesn't work and I've got three kids. What should I do?'"

Pauline said, "God, I don't know much about washers, but when I have a washer problem, I call Sears."

The lady said, "I've got a Sears washer."

"Well, call them, they'll fix it for you." She said she felt great. She felt like, "Gosh, I'm a leader [laughter]."

Buzz was impressive. When they talk about commanding officers, those two guys were both in command, and everybody knew it. They both were very professional. It was not the first command for either one, and they'd both had a diesel command before that. So they were experienced COs, they were people oriented, and very professional and great guys to work for.

Paul Stillwell: Any specifics on Bessac that you remember?

Admiral Trost: He was very capable, and he loved to tell jokes. Professionally, he was a bit of a flash in that he did things with flair, I should say, and he had the total confidence of the crew, as did Yogi. They were both people people, people came first, and the crew

---

[*] The Cuban Missile Crisis was triggered in mid-October 1962, when a U.S. reconnaissance plane photographed a Soviet nuclear missile site in Cuba and the presence of Soviet bombers. On 22 October President John F. Kennedy went on national television to announce a naval quarantine of Cuba, to be implemented on 24 October. On 28 October Premier Nikita Khrushchev of the Soviet Union notified President Kennedy that he was ordering the withdrawal of Soviet bombers and missiles from Cuba.

knew that. The crew was very well regarded, very highly capable, and well led, and they knew it.

Paul Stillwell: And that creates loyalty.

Admiral Trost: That creates loyalty. That creates competence. I'll tell you a sea story about Yogi, if I may.

Paul Stillwell: Well, of course.

Admiral Trost: I don't think I told you before. Did I tell you about the physical fitness test?

Paul Stillwell: You talked about the sit-up contest.

Admiral Trost: Okay. That's what I was going to tell you. That nut. [Laughter] And I told you probably about his approaching Alzheimer's but having Parkinson's disease.

Paul Stillwell: Yes.

Admiral Trost: But those guys are both great people to work for and with, and I learned a lot from them, and I must say I patterned my own time as XO and CO sort of after what they did. I consider myself a people person, and I think I was, and I think I was a good guy to work for. I enjoyed working with people. I think I treated people right.

Paul Stillwell: You talked about Kaufman being overbearing. I remember visiting him at his house once, and there was a nonstop monologue. It just went on and on. Finally, he paused for breath, and his wife Lucille said, "Bob, do you think you could let Paul talk once in a while?" [Laughter]

Admiral Trost: She used to literally grab him by the nape of the neck and shake him a little bit, and he respected her so highly.

Paul Stillwell: Yes, he did. [Laughter]

Admiral Trost: He was a great guy to work for and very loyal, not only to the Navy, but to his people. I watched him, for example, when I was in OSD.[*] He was in the Joint Staff sometime later. I watched him with people from all services in his JCS unit, and he was—I don't know if the term "dominant," "in charge" is right or not, but he was clearly in charge, but the people he worked with and who worked for him knew they had his respect if they did their job. So the working relationships were outstanding.

People from other services would say to me, "You worked for this guy, didn't you?"

I'd say, "Yeah, I worked for this guy."

"Well, how was he aboard ship?"

And we talked about that. He was the same way in the Joint Staff—just able, capable, approachable, and helpful.

Paul Stillwell: Effervescent. He was just so enthusiastic.

Admiral Trost: Yeah, he was enthusiastic.

Paul Stillwell: What do you remember about him as an operator?

Admiral Trost: Very sharp, very sharp. Buzz was a good operator. Yogi was a very good operator. Well, all these guys had a lot of self-confidence. They were professionally capable and they knew it, so that helped. And deploying with them gives you a tremendous sense of confidence when you're on one of these classified missions and you realize how capable they are and what they bring to the table as commanding officers. They were very good guys. And the crew feels confident when they've got a competent

_____

[*] OSD – Office of the Secretary of Defense, in which Trost served 1965-67.

skipper, and they'll do a lot of things and do them willingly, that they might stop and say, "Do we really want to do that?" They really want to because skipper says do it. So that's a great tribute to a guy like that.

Paul Stillwell: You were now in the *Skipjack* class with the *Albacore* hull.[*]

Admiral Trost: Right.

Paul Stillwell: How did ship handling compare with your previous submarines?

Admiral Trost: Well, first of all, much quicker, much snappier. *Scorpion*, the *Skipjack* class, had what they called a snap roll. If you put the rudder over hard at speed, it would snap into a bank and go in the direction you were pointing it, and that took some getting used to by people when they first experienced it.

It also was very responsive to the controls. You could put that thing into a dive in seconds, so you had to be careful what you did. Yogi Kaufman, just to demonstrate to the crew that he was in charge, on the first deep dive after he took command, went out, and first order was to go down to periscope depth, trim the ship up. Next order was, "Take me to test depth, 30 degrees down." [demonstrates] [Laughter] People were holding on, things were coming out of the overhead. He said, "XO, get this ship properly stowed," because there were things tucked up in the frames, frame base, that came tumbling out at 30-down. But he showed us we could do it, and that became standard. You trimmed the ship, did the 30-down with the test depth, then went about whatever your operation was.

Paul Stillwell: That got the crew's attention.

---

[*] The diesel submarine *Albacore* (AGSS-569) was commissioned in December 1953 as an experimental vessel to test the feasibility of the teardrop-shaped hull. The test was successful, and the hull shape has since become standard in U.S. nuclear-powered submarines. For details on the design of the *Albacore* see the Naval Institute oral history of Captain Harry Jackson, USN (Ret.).

Admiral Trost: It got the crew's attention. They stowed the ship much better after that. As a matter of fact, I'd see a chief petty officer walking through the ship looking at different areas to make sure they were stowed properly.

Paul Stillwell: What was your administrative role as exec?

Admiral Trost: Well, personnel training, anything admin for the ship, basically, but people, people records, training records, training evolutions, doing what we needed to do to get things going, looking at all the reports that had to leave the ship. I was the ultimate arbiter on what was going to go and what wasn't going to fly. A busy job.

Paul Stillwell: What do you remember about relationship with the chief of the boat? That's always a key billet in a submarine.

Admiral Trost: Well, mine was good both my XO tours. The guy I had with *Scorpion* was lost with *Scorpion*. He was commissioning crew, still on board with it eight years later, I guess, and he was a first-class torpedoman when I reported as exec.

I had the commissioning chief of the boat, who was an old-hand quartermaster, as I recall. He and I got along, but that's where I'd leave it. We got along. Came time to replace him, Yogi had taken over as commanding officer, and Yogi said, "Who's the best petty officer we got on board?"

I said, "Wally Bishop, first-class torpedoman."

"Could he handle a COB job [senior chief of the boat]?"

I said, "Yes, I think so."

Well, the chiefs' list had come out, and he was on the chiefs' list. So I said, "Let's try him."

So I called him in to see what he thought about the job. He said, "I'd like to have the job."

So then I got my chiefs' quarters together and said, "You guys have an interest in who's the chief of the boat. Your people are going to be influenced. He's going to be the senior guy here in chiefs' mess as chief of the boat, and the captain and I are thinking of new Chief Bishop."

He got unanimous approval, and so we said, "Okay, he's the guy." And he was great. He's a real people man, very professional torpedoman, and did one hell of a job and was kept on, obviously, till the ship was lost. But he was a great leader. In my relationship, of course, he was sort of my right hand as the exec, for discipline, for training, and for just about everything. Chief of the boat and yeoman, if he's good. If he's not, you're lost. Those two guys are your stalwarts that you have to have good ones, or you don't get there.

Paul Stillwell: The chief of the boat is a useful two-way communications conduit.

Admiral Trost: Very much so, very much so.

Paul Stillwell: Do you remember any specific examples?

Admiral Trost: Oh, gosh, I don't remember specific examples. I remember that he kept me in touch. If we had a morale problem of any sort, which we didn't really have, he'd let me know. If we had an area where he'd see that he thought we needed more training, he'd tell me and we'd schedule it. If he saw anything coming up that he thought needed more focus, he'd tell me. And if he saw something in my doing or something that he didn't approve of, he told me, and that takes guts and professional competence and confidence on the part of the exec, and I had that in him.

Paul Stillwell: But that comes about after you've established a useful relationship.

Admiral Trost: Yeah, yeah. I was going to say he was just a real stalwart. Matter of fact, he was good. I had a good chief of the boat from the *Scorpion* commissioning detail, but Bishop stands out in my time. I had him and his predecessor in *Scorpion*. I had the commissioning chief of the boat in *Von Steuben*. I had the one chief of the boat when I had command of *Rayburn*, and Wally Bishop stood out as the best of the bunch, although

I had no complaints about any of the rest of them either. It's just it's such an important job that the selection is very carefully done, and you don't see many bad ones. Sometimes people make mistakes, but—

Paul Stillwell: You don't see bad ones for very long.

Admiral Trost: Not for very long. You can't afford to have a bad one for very long. Matter of fact, you can hardly afford to have them at all. Their relationship with the crew is absolutely critical to morale, to professional advancement, to ship's performance. They're key.

Paul Stillwell: Any of the other crew members who stand out in your memory?

Admiral Trost: Oh, gosh, lots of them. It'd be hard for me to go back and focus on any one guy. One of my chiefs of the boat was also chief torpedoman. I'm trying to think of his name. I can picture him. Can't think of his name. He told me one time that—I said, "We haven't had many discipline problems."

He said, "No, because they know I'll kick the shit out of them." [Laughter] And he meant that figuratively, not literally. But he had the command. He had one young guy, newly reported seaman, who got in trouble on liberty. I have no idea what the conversation was about between the two of them, but that kid never had a problem again. I'm sure he was threatened with some of skin being missing if he ever did what he did before, and I don't even know what he did. Chief just said, "I'll take care of it." End of problem.

Paul Stillwell: Well, in the old Navy, that sort of petty officer counseling did include physical abuse.

Admiral Trost: Okay. I was going to say there are physical corrective actions taken sometimes.

Paul Stillwell: Did you wind up with mast cases in the *Scorpion*?

Admiral Trost: No, didn't have any. Didn't have any need for them, no. And it's interesting, the chiefs really set the model, and if you've got a good chiefs' quarters, you don't have many mast cases. There's no need for it. I had one guy—I'm trying to remember the specifics—he went over the hill because he fell in love, and the woman he fell in love with, we found out later on, was collecting dependent's checks from three sailors.

Paul Stillwell: Oh, my gosh.

Admiral Trost: And she zeroed in on kids like that, and I don't know what they all did, but clearly she was a sex object, among other things, and treated these guys very, very nicely. She treated him nicely until he was so enamored of her that he decided not to come off liberty and missed a movement for one week's operations out of Norfolk, and that's where all this broke open. I restricted him to the ship for being late coming back and not making that movement.

She came that weekend. We sailed Monday, came back in Friday. She came down to the ship Saturday, demanding his release. She found out through one of the other sailors that he was in the hack.

Topside watch said, "Well, I can't help you."

"Well, I'm going to below and get him."

The response was, "Like hell you are, ma'am. Get off the ship."

But she wouldn't get off the ship, so he called below, asked for the duty officer, who came topside, threatened her with arrest and confinement on the base for breaking and entering. She didn't like that idea, so she left the ship. Then she complained, but she complained to our squadron commander by phone and was pissed off because he wouldn't talk to her.

We finally told this kid, "You'd better just sever your relationship with her, because she's no damn good, and you're going to keep getting in trouble." So to avoid a mast case, he decided he'd rather not go to mast for his missing movement and probably ought to really ditch this gal, so he did.

Paul Stillwell: How did it come out that she had others on the string?

Admiral Trost: I've forgotten. We did an investigation. Don Kilmer, who was one of our officers, did the investigation.[*] Don was formerly a white hat, a Naval Academy grad two years ahead of me, and we had him investigate what happened, because this kid was saying, "She's got a lot of my money and I've given her an allotment." So Don went to cancel the allotment, and that required an investigation on the basis for cancellation. And in the process, he found out there were several other allotments to her. I think there were three others, so she was doing pretty well. She was a war girl, so she had a job.

Paul Stillwell: But she unleashed a chain of events that she probably wished she hadn't. [Laughs]

Admiral Trost: She probably did. She probably did. But at least she didn't have our sailor anymore. We also notified the other people what we'd found out and gave them a copy of the report, so hopefully she didn't have the others either.

Paul Stillwell: What can you say unclassified about the operations when you were in that submarine?

Admiral Trost: Well, our job in *Scorpion* was referred to—you read about special operations, and these special operations are basically keeping an eye on the Soviets, gauging what they're doing, where they're doing it, how they're doing it, and making sure we don't get surprised by anything they do. That was basically it.

Paul Stillwell: Did you get involved in any antisubmarine training?

---

[*] Lieutenant Donald A. Kilmer, USN.

Admiral Trost: Yeah.

Paul Stillwell: Both target and aggressor?

Admiral Trost: We were target and aggressor, yeah, and the targets were always our own in those exercises, but we'd do things to simulate a potential enemy submarine and operate against each other. You tried to stay one up.

Paul Stillwell: Did you ever have training exercises against U.S. submarines?

Admiral Trost: Yeah, we did.

Paul Stillwell: How well did you do? [Laughs]

Admiral Trost: Well.

Paul Stillwell: That sums it up? [Laughs]

Admiral Trost: Well.

Paul Stillwell: Anything else about *Scorpion* to remember?

Admiral Trost: No, except it was a good, sharp submarine, good morale and good crew, very good crew. Being exec of *Scorpion* with Wally Bishop and with those two COs was fun. It really was fun, it wasn't a chore, and I enjoyed that. I enjoyed my time in *Swordfish* as well, but *Scorpion* was probably, from the standpoint of having fun, the most fun I had in any ship, including the other XO tours. Being exec of a missile submarine is dull by comparison. So is being commanding officer of a missile submarine. It can be 70 days of professional boredom at sea.

Paul Stillwell: Interesting term. [Laughs]

Admiral Trost: You have to be on your toes, you have to avoid detection, you have to keep up with what's happening not only in your own area, but what's happening in the world, and you're kept pretty well supplied with information. You were constantly listening, communications-wise, never talking, and so it was like sitting on the sidelines and having CBS on your wardroom TV, hearing what's happening in the world, not being able to do a thing about anything, except stay undetected and ready.

Paul Stillwell: This is good stuff, Admiral.

Admiral Trost: Yeah, if it is good, if it's useful to you, Paul, then it's worth our time.

Paul Stillwell: Well, you don't know what somebody's going to be interested in years in the future, and I've been amazed at some of the ways the oral history things have come out. I wrote a book on the USS *Arizona* and there was an interview with an officer who was serving in the ship back in the 19-teens, and he said, "The aviators on board were just real prima donnas. They'd go out and stick a finger up in the wind and decide whether they wanted to fly that day or not." He said, "After a while, I decided I wanted to be one of the prima donnas." [Laughter] He eventually became an admiral and Commander Sixth Fleet, John Ballentine.* So, a little thing like that can be helpful.

Admiral Trost: That's interesting.

Paul Stillwell: Well, we're on to the *Von Steuben*.† I'm guessing that Commander Metzel asked for you specifically.

---

* Vice Admiral John J. Ballentine, USN, served as Commander Sixth Fleet from 14 November 1949 to 19 March 1951.
† USS *Von Steuben* (SSBN-632), a *Lafayette*-class ballistic missile submarine, was commissioned 30 September 1964. Commander John P. Wise, USN, commanded the Blue crew; Commander Jeffrey C. Metzel, USN, commanded the Gold crew. She was 425 feet long, 33 feet in the beam, and displaced 7,350 tons surfaced and 8,250 submerged. She had a top speed on the surface of 20-plus knots and a top speed of more than 30 knots submerged. She was armed with 16 Polaris ballistic missiles and had four 21-inch torpedo tubes.

Admiral Trost: I don't know. At that time, as I said before, if you were exec of an SSN, whatever orders you had went by the board and you went to new construction. Jeff Metzel had had command of the *Nautilus*. He was due for reassignment. John Wise had had a diesel command, been exec of a new construction missile submarine, and became the Blue CO. So they were coming off. They were obviously assigning experienced people to these ships to get them out early. I'm not sure how many months early we put *Von Steuben* to sea, but quite a bit, and Blue crew got experienced people in all the billets. Our engineer, for example, had been engineer of an attack boat, and so he came as an experienced engineer to put *Von Steuben* in commission.

Paul Stillwell: Metzel was a very energetic individual from what I've heard about him.

Admiral Trost: Very much so. He didn't let any grass grow under his feet. He was a good man, good guy to serve with and work with. A stickler for details. As the Blue crew exec, I was appointed by my CO to be the czar of paperwork and we, at that time, were still writing a lot of our own instructions, which didn't make sense. Later, they shifted and, everybody uses a standard set of instructions once they're approved. He would go through the instructions I gave him to read. I'd say, "Jeff, you've been sitting on that for three weeks."

"Well, I just want to make sure it's carefully reviewed." It used to drive me batty. I think he did it to poke a little bit at me [laughter]. He was a great guy. Great shipmate.

The other exec, Hank Hukill, God, I don't know, eons at sea, had a five-year engineer tour in a missile submarine, including an overhaul, one of the first overhauls, and so he was experienced.[*] My chief of the boat was an experienced chief of the boat. My leading yeoman that I got, I got to pick. I took the guy from *Scorpion*, the first guy, and brought him with me. So we had, the Blue crew especially, the officers were more experienced, about a tour more experienced than you'd expect somebody going to new construction to have. So that was to get them out.

---

[*] Lieutenant Commander Henry D. Hukill Jr., USN.

I reported in. We had a delay. I guess it was the investigation into the loss of *Thresher* that delayed us a little bit because of the institution of the SubSafe program.* That delayed us in *Von Steuben*, I think, by three months, waiting for the results of the investigation, what happened to come out, and the modifications to be drawn up for these ballast and blow valves, which had proven to be part of the problem.

So I was originally due to go directly to the shipyard, and then instead, I was diverted via Dam Neck, where they had a prospective executive officer course. I'd been executive officer, so that didn't really apply, but they had modified that to be a training course for people about the missile program. So I spent I think it was three months at Dam Neck before I went to the shipyard finally.†

We went into commission earlier than planned, even on the accelerated schedule, because the shipyard did one hell of a job of organizing. They were being pushed to get those ships out, and I think we were told one time that President Kennedy personally kept pinging on the Navy about "How are you doing? How are you doing? What's next?" So they probably felt a lot of pressure. But put out with experienced people and it worked. It showed off. It paid off.

Paul Stillwell: What do you remember about the Dam Neck period?

Admiral Trost: We covered a lot of ground. I was the only one in my group with an exec tour under his belt, but the others were all going to new construction, XO also. I remember it actually being quite interesting because that's where I got introduced to Sandbridge, where we've had this place for 38 years. Two of my classmates at Dam Neck, both their families down from New London for a week at the Sandbridge, which I'd never heard of, frankly, and I'd been in Norfolk for a couple of tours, and they invited Pauline and me and our kids out one weekend. We had to bring our water, we had to carry water, water bottles, and they had a water pump. So they had a water tank and you

---

* The nuclear-powered attack submarine *Thresher* (SSN-593) was lost with all hands on 10 April 1963 while operating east of Cape Cod. The presumed cause was a reactor shutdown during a dive. The SubSafe program came about afterward to fix perceived problems in submarine piping systems.
† Fleet Anti-Air Warfare Training Center (FAAWTC), Dam Neck, Virginia Beach, Virginia.

could flush toilets, so that was a big plus.

But it was pretty, and we were in a semi-oceanfront place. The kids had a great time. We thought, "Gee, this was nice." So as soon as I could, I looked into it and decided whether we had enough money to invest there or not, and we did initially, but we bought a lot and sold it later. We actually bought the one we built on. So the relationship goes back quite a few years.

I don't remember much about the course, other than they prepared us well to be knowledgeable about missiles and missile procedures and things that we were going to do. So the operations were not new to us when those who were inexperienced in the missile program took our jobs. We had some feel for what we were going to do. And at that time we were still preparing the paperwork, the instructions and all, for the ship, using some of the earlier boats and then taking the differences in the new ones, the physical differences, incorporating that into instructions and notices and things to get our crew ready and to train our crew accordingly. So it was an interesting period of time. Felt a little bit like pioneers, and we were a little bit like pioneers. Interesting.

Paul Stillwell: Where did the training come on the safety procedures to prevent an inadvertent launch?

Admiral Trost: That had been from day one, I think. Procedures and physical—what should I say—blocks to inadvertent launch were part of the design. It was a very well designed system. An inadvertent launch would have been, I'll say, literally impossible, because nothing is impossible, but literally impossible, given that you've got a well-designed, well-built system, very error-free system, and very well-trained people, in other words, procedural adherence is absolutely essential. So I'd say inadvertent launch wasn't one of my concerns, because it wasn't one of those things that you sat there and worried about on a day-to-day basis.

Paul Stillwell: Was there some sort of screening process on whether crew members would be willing to be involved in a nuclear weapon launch?

Admiral Trost: I would say that would be part of the screening process of people who were assigned. They were very carefully screened, and the critical billets were really hand-screened. So in procedural compliance, procedural adherence was an absolute must in everything, and that's one of the things that kept getting drummed into us.

Paul Stillwell: And that would also apply in the security of the weapons.

Admiral Trost: Yeah, very definitely.

Paul Stillwell: How did the crews get assigned to either Blue or Gold? How were those choices made?

Admiral Trost: Purely random, except the new construction period that I was referring to, the Blue crew was decidedly more experienced. So, for example, the commanding officer that had command of the execs, the exec in my case, I had an excellent tour, and my counterpart would have, except he was retained during that lengthy overhaul as a weapons officer, so he had time-wise the same experience I had, but just as exec less. But he was qualified, and he relieved me when I got jerked off a couple days before the patrol, and he clearly was qualified. He was qualified for command, so that wasn't really a concern.

Paul Stillwell: What do you recall about the shipyard period and interacting during the construction?

Admiral Trost: A very positive experience. Newport News at that time had built a number of missile submarines, and they were under the gun not only to make sure there were no physical problems with the ship as built, but also to get it out fast as they could. So the relationship between the shipyard and the crew was really critical. They needed us, and we needed them to work their ass off to get that ship out on time. And we spent a lot of time in our interface with people who were ahead of us in schedule. We had some of our people ride the ships on sea trials who were ahead of us, and that required some close cooperation with the yard, because those ships are so full of bodies when you go off on sea trials that everybody's in everybody's way, and it requires good discipline, good cooperation between the yard and the Navy guys, and we got that from them.

They were very good about their communications with us, because we needed to witness and sign off on a lot of the tests, the systems tests, before they could be said that this is okay to go. That relationship was good. We had good leadership on the part of the team, the shipyard team that worked on the ship, and they worked hard at not shifting people, getting somebody that was an expert in the missile tube construction or outfitting. You're going to get somebody like that or somebody with the experience as the senior guy in the crew that's working your ship, and that requires very close coordination, and we had that. And we had a good working relationship with the leadership of the shipyard people. Our guys were pretty cooperative, I'd say, because we were under pressure to get this thing out. So everything had a time tag on it, and it took both the ship's crew and the shipyard workers to get it out.

Paul Stillwell: Presumably that sense of urgency had also been communicated to the shipyard.

Admiral Trost: Oh, yeah, very definitely.

Paul Stillwell: One of the things that came along as a management tool for Polaris was PERT.* Did you follow those dictums?

Admiral Trost: We did, yeah. It's a good system. And the tracking of progress and the tracking of critical items was really a key item. It was in every daily summary, it was in every daily meeting, and it required cooperation. We also were lucky we had good people, good supervisors assigned. When we went on sea trials, for example, they would shift over to the next ship in line; then we got them back. When we went off on post-

---

* PERT – Program Evaluation Review Technique, a system of milestones for tracking the progress of a program against its schedule. This was developed in the late 1950s for the Polaris ballistic missile/submarine program.

shakedown availability there, before they went over on sea trials, and then—what did we call it?—the period where we went into commission and operated and trained, then went back for the post-shakedown availability was one where we had no shipyard riders or anybody on board. But the minute we came back in for the short PSA, eight weeks or something like that, to fix anything that was wrong, the shipyard assigned people who'd been with the ship and knew the ship to make sure we didn't spend any more time in PSA than necessary, and we didn't.[*] It went well.

Paul Stillwell: Joe Williams was one of the first skippers of the *Robert E. Lee*, and he said a ship built in Virginia would get especially good treatment from the shipyard.[†] [Laughter]

Admiral Trost: Oh, yeah, it did. Newport News was interested in making a name for themselves to get more business, and they were good. From senior management, you know, the president of the shipyard spent time during the day on the ships in the shipyard touring for visibility from his workers, for one thing, to keep informed himself on what was going on, and to make sure things were moving, because I'm sure he was under the gun from the corporate people to make sure they kept moving.

Paul Stillwell: What do you recall about Admiral Rickover during the trials?

Admiral Trost: [Laughs] A pain in my neck. I was the trial coordinator as the senior exec, and we went out on alfa trials, and, of course, that's his trial because it's propulsion plant-related. But before you do the propulsion plant exercises, you do the simple things like you drop an anchor and recover it, to make sure you've got an anchor if you need it. You do a test dive, you do a trim dive, and every one of those things holds up his propulsion plant tests.

Ours started off with the first thing, which was the anchor, which dropped, and we couldn't get it back up, and we could not haul that thing in, and we finally—for some

---

[*] PSA – Post-shakedown availability.
[†] See the Naval Institute oral history of Vice Admiral Joe Williams Jr., USN (Ret.).

reason, the anchor windlass—I've forgotten what the specific problem was, but you'd run that, then you'd haul the chain up. The chain was stuck; it wouldn't come up. We finally got the chain up by the ingenuity of the chief of the boat, who was a torpedoman, who, with a mooring line and the capstan, hauled the anchor up, length of chain, length of chain, length of chain, one at a time. You'd have to haul it in, stop it off, undo the mooring line, refocus it on something that's six fathoms down the line or something or other, or however far we could reach the end to keep hauling it. Took us two hours to get the anchor in.

Rickover, in the meantime—I was in the control room and he was out there about every ten minutes having my ass and chewing me out, chewing both skippers out, and just, "Let's get this goddamn show on the road!" [Laughter] It was a trial period.

Paul Stillwell: In more ways than one. [Laughs]

Admiral Trost: But we finally got that done. We did the trial. Everything went beautifully thereafter. We did the trial, which was totally focused on propulsion, and finished up and got him up to Lewes, Delaware, and off-loaded so he could make a plane coming in some airport near Lewes, and haul him back to Washington for a meeting, and we got him off on time. So that was the big thing. But he was at his best.

Paul Stillwell: Well, you lent me that book called *Same Date of Rank*, and your counterpart Hank Hukill was quoted as saying that there were letters that Rickover signed.[*]

Admiral Trost: Oh, yeah. He told me later that was why he didn't sign one for me, because he didn't like the way I handled the sea trials.

Paul Stillwell: Hukill implied it was that he was pretending not to know who you were. [Laughter]

---

[*] Christopher. J. Hoppin, *Same Date of Rank: Grads at the Top and Bottom from West Point, Annapolis and the Air Force Academy* (Xlibris Corp, 2009).

Admiral Trost: He knew who I was. At least he knew whom he was chewing out.

Paul Stillwell: Hukill also said he finally found one shortcoming in your overall life experience and capabilities—that you're a Redskins fan. [Laughs]

Admiral Trost: Oh, and he's a Dallas fan because Roger Staubach was a Naval Academy graduate. When Roger played for Dallas, Hank became a Dallas fan, and he and his wife Ginny were really strong vocal Dallas fans. When Roger retired, he wrote him a letter telling him he really shouldn't have retired; he was good for a couple more years.

He was fun to be with. Hank and I were good friends and stayed good friends. Of course, he was pulled off the highway to relieve me when I was pulled off to go to Washington off *Von Steuben.*

Paul Stillwell: He said he was impressed by your remarkable memory for names of crew members and that you made a deliberate effort to do that.

Admiral Trost: Well, I did. I was always able to remember names and details about people, and I found that when you greet people by name, your relationship is different than if you just say, "Hi, Petty Officer." I made a point, when I was both exec and CO, of walking through the ship once a watch and talking to the people who were on watch. You get to know your people that way, and you get input from them sometimes that you wouldn't expect. "Hey, XO, you ought to know that—." And it was often something that I wouldn't have known if he hadn't told me or hadn't been feeling free to tell me. They didn't feel threatened by me.

Paul Stillwell: What do you remember about the commissioning ceremony of *Von Steuben?*

Admiral Trost: Well, a happy day for us, big day in the shipyard. John McCain was our commissioning speaker. He was PhibLant, I think, at the time, and he was a crackerjack.[*] He gave one hell of a speech, I remember that. I remember it being a very positive day. We were all happy because we were in commission and going to get under way and get out of the yard for a change. We'd had our sea trials and everything else, but now we were going to go out, and it was going to be *our* ship, no shipyard workers on board, and that in itself is a very positive, enthusiastic prodding of a crew to go out and do their best. So commissioning was a good day, and we had good weather. I think we were commissioned like 2:00 o'clock in the afternoon and it was September 1964.

Paul Stillwell: What do you recall about the missile test firing?

Admiral Trost: Well, first of all, you sure cross your fingers and hope everything goes well. Fortunately, everything went well.

Paul Stillwell: Well, it had to be another morale booster for your crew on *Von Steuben*.

Admiral Trost: Oh, it was. It was. It really was. We were down at Canaveral and we—I'm trying to think. I'm trying to recall whether that was the one that was inverted schedule-wise with the Gold crew for shooting first. I don't know why I have that in the back of my mind. I'm not sure that's fact. I remember riding with Jeff Metzel when they shot their first missile, but I don't remember the specifics, no. Oh, well, if the brain comes around, I'll let you know.

Paul Stillwell: I guess one more question is what do you recall about the interaction between the two crews in *Von Steuben*.

Admiral Trost: Very good, very good. We operated as a single crew. Hank and I had single quarters for the crew. It was one crew, and we split just before we went into

---

[*] Vice Admiral John S. McCain Jr., USN, served as Commander Amphibious Force Atlantic Fleet from 1963 to 1965.

commission. So people were ordered to a crew, but we did some shuffling in the course of making sure we balanced out, so some people who were in for Gold crew ended up in Blue crew, and some of ours if we had too much talent in a particular area. The tendency of the detailers was to over-crew the Blue crew as the leading crew and under-crew in certain areas some of the Gold crew guys, so the two execs balanced those out after we'd seen people for about a year and made sure. Also we used sea trial experience to watch some guys who might have been different from what we expected, based on their background. It came out pretty well, came out quite balanced.

Paul Stillwell: Okay. Well, I think I've about exhausted my questions, and we're going to a dramatically different type of duty, so why don't we break there?

Admiral Trost: Okay, whatever's convenient.

Paul Stillwell: I look forward to the next time.

Interview Number 6 with Admiral Carlisle A. H. Trost, U.S. Navy (Retired)

Date: Wednesday, 15 July 2015

Place: Admiral Trost's apartment in Ginger Cove, south of Annapolis, Maryland

Paul Stillwell: Admiral, before we got the machines turned on, you told me a delightful story about a midshipman who had come to you even before he was a midshipman. I think it's worth putting on the record to show the interaction with an up-and-coming member of the Navy.

Admiral Trost: Okay. Well, this young fellow—you don't want his name, I don't think, or do you?

Paul Stillwell: Might as well.

Admiral Trost: His name is Sean Fitzmaurice. He is a native of Massachusetts. He's a nephew of a now-deceased former neighbor of mine that I knew quite well since the mid-'60s. This man called me one day and told me about this grand-nephew, I think is the proper term for him, who was very interested in the Naval Academy, who had applied to the Naval Academy as one of six qualified candidates for a seat available to a congressman from Massachusetts. Regrettably, he was not one of the six who got the nod for the nomination for the class of 2010, so the uncle was calling to see what advice could I give this young fellow to better enhance his chances.

So the young man came down from Massachusetts, actually, to visit me, and we had a long conversation, dinner. He struck me as being extremely interested in the Naval Academy, had done his homework, wanted to know what he should do to get in. I spoke to the people in the admissions office at the Naval Academy. First of all, they suggested get into a good university, join the NROTC, do well, and reapply.

He did as told. He reapplied, got an appointment the following year for the class of 2011, and was admitted. I saw him a number of times over lunch, both out in town and at the Naval Academy in the mess hall. He was an obvious leader, based on my observation of how the younger people there reacted to him as he got more senior at the

Naval Academy. So I tracked him very closely. He ended up being the final set brigade commander for the class of 2011. He had wanted to go into aviation. That's all he had talked about for a couple of years. He came to me in the spring of his first-class year, to tell me that he'd opted for nuclear submarines instead. I'd like to think I had an influence on that, but I'm not sure I did.

Paul Stillwell: Well, you mentioned earlier that he asked if you thought he was crazy for dropping aviation.

Admiral Trost: Well, he changed his mind, and for the better, I thought. What was interesting also, his prototype training was aboard the decommissioned *Sam Rayburn* down in Charleston.[*] That was the training ship and also my command years earlier. So I was pleased to see that.

Paul Stillwell: All in the family. [Laughter]

Admiral Trost: All in the family. He completed nuclear power training successfully, reported in to a nuclear attack submarine, and is serving in that ship at the present time. He's qualified in submarines. He wears the submarine insignia that I was given when I qualified in submarines, and it makes me rather proud. He's obviously a frontrunner, and he has decided he wants to be an Olmsted scholar, so I've just endorsed his application to be an Olmsted scholar, which I also was, and he's looking forward to that. More importantly, his wife is looking forward to the challenge of living overseas, despite the fact that Pauline told her what a real pain it was, as the pioneers in the program, to go without really any kind of support and live overseas, and I do mean without support. So it's quite a challenge.[†]

---

[*] The former ballistic missile submarine *Sam Rayburn* (SSBN-635) was decommissioned and stricken from the Navy list in 1989. Her missile compartment was removed, and she was subsequently retained by the Navy as a moored training ship for nuclear propulsion plant operators.
[†] Lieutenant Fitzmaurice is in the class of 2017 in the Olmsted program, studying at the University of Tartu in Estonia.

Paul Stillwell: So even after all those years, there's not more of a support system?

Admiral Trost: There's a much better support system now, but when we went, we were the first ones. The program had not been fully embraced by the Department of Defense, so the support was mediocre. There was no real advance information given us. There was no advance support given us. I actually reported to the naval attaché in London, and I was on duty in Germany. What I got from them was what I demanded two or three times over, and I finally got some mediocre support for my two years over there. It's a lot better now. It's much more organized. But the program at that time, there were actually four of us the first year, with six selected, and the Army decided not to send its candidates because the program wasn't official. The Navy did, but provided no support.

Paul Stillwell: Well, I would say the Navy as a whole is much more supportive of dependents than it was back then.

Admiral Trost: I think so. I think so.

Paul Stillwell: You have ombudsmen and family service centers and what have you.

Admiral Trost: Did I tell you the story of how I got the housing, for example?

Paul Stillwell: I think you did, yes.

Admiral Trost: I think I did, and that was strictly we got absolutely no support. And I've told Sean the problems we had and the things to look out for. Hopefully, he'll be selected.

Paul Stillwell: Yes. We were talking about your tour in *Von Steuben* last time. Is there anything to add to that?

Admiral Trost: I think I told you about the sudden departure to go to my first Washington tour. It was an interesting time, because we had a very compatible leadership team, and we had a good crew. The manning for the early missile program ships was very preferential by the submarine force, so we got good people coming in, a lot of new inexperienced people but good, sharp people who were highly trainable. So it was a busy time, fun time. Hours were lousy, but—

Paul Stillwell: That goes with sea duty. [Laughter]

Admiral Trost: My skipper was an interesting guy. He's now deceased, so I can talk about him. He'd been commanding officer of a diesel submarine, then exec of a recently constructed missile submarine, so he was not inexperienced. He would come into the office, the off-crew barge, about 8:00 o'clock in the morning. We had been there since 5:00. We had access to the ship for training purposes starting at 5:30 in the morning, 5:30 to 7:30. So this wardroom was a little bleary-eyed, ready for the third cup of coffee. By about 5:00 in the evening, after 12-some hours, I was fading. I lived in Norfolk still, so I'd come in from there to Newport News, and I thought I'd go home about 5:30. He didn't. He'd always give me a sort of strange look when I'd tell him I was heading home.

Paul Stillwell: After 12 hours.

Admiral Trost: Yeah, after 12 hours. So my first fitness report noted the fact that I got everything done, but I seemed to leave early every day. And he was right; I did. [Laughter] Didn't hurt too much, but I always got a kick out of that because he'd leave shortly after I did and look at everything, sometimes took stuff home with him to read, but very seldom.

Paul Stillwell: What was this gentleman's name?

Admiral Trost: John Wise. John was an interesting guy. He was very even-mannered, very careful in where he spent his time, what he spent his time on, and, of course, being the experienced missile ship guy of the four team members—my counterpart had been an engineer of a missile submarine through an overhaul, actually engineer for five years, which was a man-killer. So he was very knowledgeable of ship operations and very helpful to me, because I was writing instructions, operating procedures and things from my SSN background, not from a missile ship background. So it was handy to have him there to proofread and edit. But the top four team was an experienced submarine team, so we had no problems in the wardroom, really, about submarine procedures and practices. Interesting life.

Paul Stillwell: Well, from a national point of view, when this is a big part of the strategic deterrent, you do want good people in those slots.

Admiral Trost: Oh, you really do, and we were getting experienced people at the top because the President had said, "We want to get these ships out." So we were actually commissioned probably six or eight months earlier than the initial schedule called for, and Newport News did a superb job with those ships, so I'm a fan of Newport News.

Paul Stillwell: You and many other people.

Admiral Trost: Oh, I tell you, they were great. And we had a good relationship with the working leadership in the shipyards as far as the top guy—I don't remember who the president of Newport News was at the time, but we saw him on board the ship three or four times a week.

Paul Stillwell: There was a man named Bill Blewett, who was down there for quite a while.[*]

Admiral Trost: That name's familiar. I don't know if he was the guy then or not. But they were good, and, of course, the ship's superintendent was visible and on top of things. The relationship with the leadingmen and our senior petty officers and our officers was very

---

[*] William E. Blewett Jr. became president of Newport News Shipbuilding in 1951 and shifted the company's focus to nuclear-powered ships.

was very good also. Matter of fact, I think they worked hard to foster a good relationship, and we weren't the only ones who experienced that.

Paul Stillwell: Well, how did this shipboard duty get interrupted? Why were you pulled out for the Washington job?

Admiral Trost: Well, I'll tell you the story, and it's really the story. The source is Harry Train, who was then Commander Harry Train, working as the administrative assistant to Paul Nitze, who was Secretary of the Navy.[*] Harry said, "Nitze said, 'Cy Vance, Deputy Secretary of Defense, needs a new military assistant. His current military assistant is a rear admiral, newly promoted, and he thinks that naval aviators have too much input to his office because of the seniority of the military system, and so he wants a more junior guy.'"[†]

And Nitze allegedly said, "Who do you know?"

Train said, "Well, I know a guy, but he's got no Washington experience." Me.

Nitze said, "Let me see his record." So they pulled my record. All this allegedly happened; this is secondhand. He looked at his record and said, "Take him."

So that week is when my orders were cut and sent out to the ship as we were getting ready to do our workup for deployment, and that's how I got to Washington. My rear admiral predecessor was being detached on Monday, and he wanted me there for a hand-to-hand turnover, which was two days. So I came to Washington, got checked in, reported in to OSD, and became the military assistant to Deputy SecDef.

Paul Stillwell: Who was your predecessor?

Admiral Trost: Ralph Cousins.[‡]

---

[*] See the Naval Institute oral history of Admiral Harry D. Train II, USN (Ret.). Paul H. Nitze served as Secretary of the Navy from 29 November 1963 to 30 June 1967.

[†] Cyrus R. Vance served as Deputy Secretary of Defense from 28 January 1964 to 30 June 1967.

[‡] Rear Admiral Ralph W. Cousins, USN. Later, as a four-star, he served as Vice Chief of Naval Operations and Supreme Allied Commander Atlantic, Commander in Chief Atlantic Command, and Commander in Chief Atlantic Fleet.

Paul Stillwell: An able individual.

Admiral Trost: A *very* able individual, a very fine gentleman. We stayed friends throughout his career. Matter of fact, he asked for me, he told me, when he became Vice Chief, but I wasn't available. I don't remember what I was doing then. He was a good man, and he had a great reputation at OSD, and he was very effective. Whether he was effective in overselling naval aviation, I don't know. I never heard anybody complain.

Paul Stillwell: Well, that was a time when there were a couple of aviators as CNOs in a row with Anderson and McDonald, so maybe this was looking for a counterpoint.*

Admiral Trost: Could have been.

Paul Stillwell: Had you known Commander Train before that?

Admiral Trost: I had known him, yeah, and I don't recall when we first met, but I had known him because he was my detailer when I was a lieutenant.

Paul Stillwell: As somebody in BuPers, he would know who was available.

Admiral Trost: Yeah. Well, I wasn't available.

Paul Stillwell: You became available. [Laughs]

Admiral Trost: And he wasn't in BuPers anymore. He apparently had known of me as my detailer.

I was more than a little bit annoyed when this happened because I'd gone through this orders change. We had our house in Norfolk on the market, because I was due to go

---

* Admiral George W. Anderson, Jr., USN, was Chief of Naval Operations from 1 August 1961 to 1 August 1963. Admiral David L. McDonald, USN, served as Chief of Naval Operations from 1 August 1963 to 1 August 1967. The oral histories of both are in the Naval Institute collection.

first to command out of Norfolk, but that was changed to go to Idaho instead, which was changed by these orders. So we did that shift.

I had sold my Mercedes, which I'd bought in Germany, because I needed a station wagon to go to Idaho. I had ordered and put a down payment on a Ford station wagon, had to cancel that, bought a very old Ford Falcon station wagon, which caused me more problems than any car I've ever owned. I used to do my own car work, but that stopped about ten years ago. I had worked to get everything all ready to go to Idaho, and then we went to Washington instead. For a period of time when I got my orders cancelled, I said, "The hell with this," then bought a new Ford Mustang, which had just come out in '65, and so I was happy about that, but it was the only thing I was happy about. [Laughter]

Paul Stillwell: That was a hot car at the time.

Admiral Trost: That was a hot car. The Mustang came out in '64. They came out with a V-8, but the following V-8 was hotter by some—I've forgotten the differential. I got number 60 of the second flight of engines, and it was hot. Matter of fact, you had to be careful not to stomp on the gas, because you could spin the wheels. A fun car to drive. Now, Pauline didn't like that car at first, because our first couple of trips to Washington from Norfolk with three children, one being a brand-new baby, were in that car. The baby sat on the center console in a cradle, whatever you call those things, and Pauline didn't like that. But we survived.

Paul Stillwell: It's a digression, but I remember the Steve McQueen movie *Bullitt*, in which he had a long chase, and the sound track piped in the engine sound, which really gets you revving.

Admiral Trost: Yeah, it could roar. It could roar. Matter of fact, I was warned by the salesman who sold it to me not to step on the gas too hard, look around first and make sure no cops were around. [Laughter] So we were careful with it. And my kids loved the car.

Paul Stillwell: You had to fight for it. [Laughs]

Admiral Trost: My oldest son got it with 125,000-130,000 miles on it, and he put about another 15 on it before he smashed it. He was driving when he hit the brakes when he shouldn't have and got hit from the rear, and it folded the trunk in underneath the rear axle, and that was too expensive to repair.

Paul Stillwell: Well, please describe the transition of getting settled in the Washington area.

Admiral Trost: Well, we, of course, had very, very little time. Fortunately, we hadn't sold our house in Norfolk yet, but we did have a buyer coming up for it, and we came up to Pauline's folks right outside of D.C. to house-hunt and looked around, had been told by everybody Northern Virginia is the place to live.

We were going out one Sunday morning to take a second look at a house we'd looked at over—I think it was in Fairfax, as I recall, and Pauline was reading the Sunday morning paper and saw an ad for a place called Fox Hills in Maryland, which is in Potomac, brand-new area built by a company called Pulte, and they were showing their first open house that day.

So we decided we're on our way over, on the new beltway, by the way, and we pulled off on Rockville Pike and made our way over to this new house, looked at it. It was what we were looking for, except for price, and everything was not what we were looking for pricewise compared to Norfolk. So we looked at the place, decided we liked that much better, had many features we liked better than we did the place we were going to look at in Northern Virginia. So I put a deposit on the house, and we were the first occupants of Fox Hills, that development, the first, but there were more coming along within a matter of a month.

We got settled in. The moving truck pulled up on our front yard, up the hill and across the front yard to unload, because there were no finished streets yet, and our driveway hadn't been poured. So we moved in. We were really pioneers in that place, and moved in, got our stuff there, got settled, sold the house in Norfolk, put the rest of the money against this place and settled in for three busy years.

Paul Stillwell: Was that the same house you lived in after retirement?

Admiral Trost: No, it was not. The retirement home was the second one we bought after this one. This one we lived in for three years, and then when I got surprise orders after command and after the SubLant tour in Norfolk, got surprise orders back when I came on to work for John Warner, we called our realtor who was handling the rental and said, "We're coming back. Can our tenant move out?" Because they had a hard lease.

She called the tenant, and the guy was the foreman for that job of building the tunnel under the Mall in front of the Capitol. He said, "Jesus Christ, I'm right at the tail end of this project. I can't move now, can't move my family." That made sense to me.

So we checked around, we found another naval officer who just retired, who was looking for a tenant for a house that was two blocks from where ours was. So we called him, rented the house. He decided not to sell it just then till he decided for sure what he was going to do. He was going to move out to the West Coast, had a job out there, and so we moved into that house.

Then when our tenants moved out, we sold the first house and stayed in the second. Then we came back to the second house after my command tour, and lived in it again for a period of time, bought a new house under construction about a mile away, and that's the one that is still occupied by my son, the one we moved into after I retired. So we found a neighborhood and liked it, and our son liked it, and he's got the house right now.

Paul Stillwell: Good.

Admiral Trost: Going strong.

Paul Stillwell: Well, please tell me about Cyrus Vance.

Admiral Trost: Interesting guy to work for, very bright, very much a procrastinator. He'd been the Secretary of the Army, very successful lawyer with, I think, a New York law firm, as I recall, and would come in early in the morning. To beat him, I had to be in by 6:30 in the morning. I was the screener for the message traffic and all for the day and the intel stuff. I had to get in before 6:00 to screen stuff for him. He showed up usually about 7:00 o'clock in the morning, left the office about 7:30 to 9:00 at night, after his son went to bed. His son was a little kid. So we had some long, long days.

McNamara relied very heavily on him, as the deputy, for technical detail.[*] McNamara, despite his Ford Motor background, was not a guy with a good technical background, in my evaluation. Vance knew nothing about anything technical and used to rely very heavily on me, and probably did on Cousins before me. The other military assistant was an Army colonel initially and then transitioned to an Air Force colonel, but neither one of those guys had a particular technical background.

So Vance was interesting. He was a procrastinator. I used to go in at 6:30 at night, sit down across the desk from him, and hand him paper after paper from the inbox, brief it with a recommendation what to do with it. We got rid of most of our back paperwork that way. Things that interested him he pored over, but he also had a hold box, which we called the "Too Hard" box, and that was often bigger, stacked higher than the inbox was.

Paul Stillwell: How long would things remain in the "Too Hard" box?

Admiral Trost: Until I got them out, insisted he sign them or throw them out, because I was the guy at night who usually had to hand him things. I would rebrief him on what was in it if he hadn't read it, which he usually hadn't. He'd scan something. He was a quick reader, scan something and pitch it back in the "Too Hard" box. Interesting guy.

Paul Stillwell: Sometimes things solve themselves while in the "Too Hard" box. Did that ever happen?

---

[*] Robert S. McNamara served as Secretary of Defense from 21 January 1961 to 29 February 1968.

Admiral Trost: Sometimes they do. That happened very often, and usually it happened after we'd get a call from somebody like the Chairman of the Joint Chiefs saying, "What the hell ever happened to that paper I signed up there for so-and-so?" [Laughter]

If I said, "The Chairman is wondering what happened to this paper," he'd focus on it.

Paul Stillwell: How else would you describe the relationship between Vance and McNamara?

Admiral Trost: Well, they saw each other. They consulted quite a bit. McNamara literally wore out the carpet in front of our desk. It was McNamara's office, and then the next part of his suite was on the other side, and then there was a big conference room. Then the military assistants for the deputy, his outer office, then the deputy. So they were at opposite ends of the complex. And McNamara used to steam through there at high speed. He never walked slowly. He'd nod sometimes to acknowledge our presence, sometimes, and head through to whatever discussion they were having. Then he'd come steaming back through. So they consulted each other quite often.

Paul Stillwell: Sounds as if he was abrupt.

Admiral Trost: He was abrupt. McNamara was not a people guy at all in any sense. To be acknowledged by him meant that you got in his way, you walked in front of him or something, and he was surprised to see somebody, he said hello and kept going. He was a cold fish, my evaluation. I don't know if that was his personality, if it was the job or what it was, because this was during Vietnam, and he was a pretty busy guy. He had an interesting job, I'll say that.

Paul Stillwell: He and the "Whiz Kids" alienated many of the senior uniformed officers.[*]

---

[*] "Whiz Kids" was the nickname for the group of young civilian officials whom McNamara appointed to key positions in the Department of Defense hierarchy.

Admiral Trost: They did that.

Paul Stillwell: Had that improved any by the time you got there?

Admiral Trost: Yes and no. Depends on when I got back there.

Alain Enthoven was a pompous punk, in my book.[*] He didn't take the time to listen to anybody who disagreed with him, because he knew better about almost everything. Those who followed at later times, David Chu, for example, who had the same job later on, David came, spent a day a week in my office when I was the Director of the Navy Systems Analysis Division, because the Deputy Secretary of Defense said, "Enthoven needs to know more about the services."[†] So I got designated as the two-star to brief him.

So we set up every Wednesday he came, spent the day either with me or with my guys when I had other commitments, and we probably taught David something about the Department of the Navy, but if we did, it was never obvious, because he was there a long time. He was there during that two-plus years as Systems Analysis Division and later on for four years as Director of Program Planning, where he did things like, for example, Lee Baggett, who was a fellow three-star in the OpNav staff, and I went down there one time at David's request to talk to him.[‡] I don't remember what the project was, probably had something to do with surface ships, and Chu made a comment to us, "You guys are wasting your time. See that shelf?" There was something very similar to that, as a matter of fact, shelves like that, and they were all full of books. He said, "When you've done enough studies on this subject to fill that cabinet bookshelf, then I'll listen to you." To me, that was just stupid arrogance, and that was David. We didn't teach him much, and he never learned much, as far as I'm concerned. But I am biased against people who close their minds.

---

[*] Alain C. Enthoven served as Deputy Comptroller and Deputy Assistant Secretary of Defense, 1961-65, and as Assistant Secretary of Defense for Systems Analysis, 1965-69.
[†] David S. C. Chu later served from May 1981 to January 1983 as Director of Program Analysis and Evaluation and then as Assistant Secretary of Defense (Program Analysis and Evaluation).
[‡] Vice Admiral Lee Baggett Jr., USN, served as Director, Naval Warfare from August 1982 to April 1985.

Paul Stillwell: I wonder if that kind of personality went with the job. [Laughs]

Admiral Trost: It might. It might. He was a tough guy to deal with, and he wouldn't listen. That was the problem.

Paul Stillwell: I've heard Mr. Vance described as a man of integrity and character.

Admiral Trost: I'll tell you what, he was that. He was that. Right and wrong were very important to him. Now, he was relieved by Paul Nitze six months before my tour ended.[*] Nitze was just the opposite kind of person to work with. He didn't like to leave anything on his desk at night that needed a decision. So he was easy to get things done with. He listened. It doesn't mean he listened and did what we recommended, but he listened. He asked opinions. Vance seldom asked anybody's opinion, or at least any of us. I think it was true of his assistant secretaries as well, because they'd come to us bemoaning the lack of action on something and saying, "Can't you do something to move this?" Sometimes we could. Usually we couldn't.

Paul Stillwell: In his time as a lawyer, he had developed a skill as a negotiator. Was that useful in this job?

Admiral Trost: I can't say yes or no. Whether he did much negotiating, I don't know. He did what McNamara wanted. That was obvious. I never sat down in any of his meetings with the Chairman, who was Bus Wheeler at the time.[†] I thought they had a pretty good relationship, but when things were hard to move, Wheeler would call one of us, my Air Force colonel or me, explain the problem, and say, "Can't you see if you can move this?" So he obviously wasn't able to be persuasive on things that he needed to get done now, so it's hard to tell.

---

[*] Paul H. Nitze served as Deputy Secretary of Defense from 1967 to 1969. He had previously been Secretary of the Navy from 1963 to 1967.
[†] General Earle G. Wheeler, USA, served as Chairman of the Joint Chiefs of Staff from 3 July 1964 to 2 July 1970.

Paul Stillwell: So was your main role as a paper mover?

Admiral Trost: Paper mover, predominantly a paper mover. If it needed amplification or background, we were the ones who had to dig out the background and usually dictate a memo to the boss for him to read and get acquainted with whatever it was, or when we got in, we'd be asked to explain something.

Paul Stillwell: Did you have a screening role to decide what could be decided at a lower level?

Admiral Trost: Sometimes, yes. Very often we could put a recommendation on any document that went inside, and if we thought it needed more background, we were authorized to get it and get it in to him, not to send something in till we were satisfied that the information was there that he needed. So it worked pretty well.

Paul Stillwell: I interviewed Andy Kerr, who worked as a counsel in SecNav's office, and he said very often the issues his office would get were intractable, because if they could have been solved before, they wouldn't have got there.[*] [Laughs]

Admiral Trost: That's right. They would have been.

Paul Stillwell: Was that your sense also?

Admiral Trost: It was. There were instances where stuff came in and he said, "Why the hell didn't they do this?" And they didn't do it either because they couldn't make a decision or didn't want to make a decision. And I'm not sure that didn't want to sometimes outweighed the couldn't.

---

[*] See the Naval Institute oral history of Captain Alex A. Kerr, USN (Ret.).

Paul Stillwell: Was the TFX aircraft still an issue when you got there?[*]

Admiral Trost: Yeah, and I'm trying to remember how long. It was still an issue, and it was resolved while I was there, not in the way McNamara initially wanted it, as I recall.

Paul Stillwell: Well, he made the decision to award the contract to General Dynamics, even though the Navy had recommended Boeing, but then Admiral Connolly later got it killed as a Navy program.[†]

Admiral Trost: Yeah. Connolly was very effective in doing that, by the way. He really stuck with his guns. He was an interesting guy to work with too.

Paul Stillwell: What do you recall of him?

Admiral Trost: Oh, well, first of all, when I came in to work for Warner, Warner was the Under Secretary, and I relieved a guy named Zeb Alford, who was also a submariner.[‡] Zeb had relieved Tom Hayward, a very fine aviator.[§] Tom Connolly came down earlier, like my first week, with Warner and said, "I hope you're more like Hayward than that son-of-a-bitch who relieved him," because he disliked the fact that he had a submariner relieving an aviator who knew what he was talking about. [Laughter] He said to me, "You'd better bone up on aviation programs."

"Yes, sir."

He's an interesting guy to work for. I'll tell you, he was the savior of the F-14

---

[*] The F-111—originally designated TFX—was a controversial fighter plane that Secretary of Defense Robert McNamara tried to develop in the 1960s for use by both the Air Force and the Navy. The Navy was eventually able to thwart its role as a carrier plane and developed the F-14 instead.
[†] Vice Admiral Thomas F. Connolly, USN, served as Deputy Chief of Naval Operations (Air) from 1 November 1966 to 31 August 1971. Admiral Connolly's oral history is in the Naval Institute collection.
[‡] Lieutenant Commander Zeb D. Alford, USN.
[§] Commander Thomas B. Hayward, USN. The oral history of Hayward, who retired as a four-star admiral, is in the Naval Institute collection.

program.[*] He made it happen.

Paul Stillwell: And it has been suggested that that's what cost him a fourth star.

Admiral Trost: It could well be, could well be. He and Warner had a very good relationship. And I liked Connolly. He even condescended to having me sit in on his briefings with the Under Secretary.[†]

Paul Stillwell: How much contact or awareness of did you have of President Johnson's impact?[‡]

Admiral Trost: A lot of awareness of it, not much input. I had one conversation with the President, other than the White House reception. They used to have an annual military reception, so you'd get to say, "Hello, Mr. President," and he'd say, "Hello." [Laughter]

My hotline rang. We had a White House phone sitting on the table between the two military assistants, and the only time we would dare or told to pick it up was if it rang and the boss was out of the office. So that happened once. The phone rang. I was the only one in the office. Picked up the phone, "Yes, sir."

I didn't know who was on the other end, and it's President Johnson, and he said, "Who's this?"

"Commander Trost."

"What's your job?"

"Military assistant."

"You'll do." [Laughter] And he gave me a message to pass on to Vance. That was my contact with power.

---

[*] Grumman F-14 Tomcat fighters first entered training squadrons in late 1972. The F-14A version was 64 feet long, wingspan of 38 feet, normal takeoff weight of 55,000 pounds, and top speed of Mach 2.34. It was equipped with a 20-millimeter cannon and was designed to carry a variety of types of missiles—Sparrow, Sidewinder, and Phoenix—and later equipped to deliver bombs as well.
[†] John W. Warner served as Under Secretary of the Navy from 11 February 1969 to 4 May 1972.
[‡] Lyndon B. Johnson served as President of the United States from 22 November 1963 to 20 January 1969.

Paul Stillwell: What do you recall of the Dominican Republic intervention in that period?[*]

Admiral Trost: What I remember most about it is my Army colonel counterpart calling me from the DomRep saying he was under a table because they were under fire in the hotel, and he was staying under the table as long as there was noise outside, and he could hear it, make damn sure that—they couldn't shoot from above, so he was staying low and staying covered. He was debriefing me because Vance went down and Deputy Smith went with him. That's my recollection of the DomRep intervention.

Paul Stillwell: Anything about the Panama issue during that period?

Admiral Trost: No. Panama, I got more involved in it later on as the CNO from the later Panama issue when we actually overthrew the guy. No, not really.

Paul Stillwell: How much did politics intervene in the process for you?

Admiral Trost: For me, being aware of it was really my job, knowing, for example, what had to get hot attention and what didn't, by my boss. So I was the paper pusher in that area. Now, are we talking about—yeah, we're talking about OSD?

Paul Stillwell: When you were with Secretary Vance and Nitze.

Admiral Trost: Yeah.

---

[*] On 28 April 1965 President Lyndon Johnson dispatched a 400-man expeditionary brigade to the Dominican Republic to protect the lives and property of American citizens caught in a military revolt in that nation. By 29 April, 1,600 Marines had landed, and by 7 May 6,000 Marines were ashore and another 2,000 offshore. They were followed by Army troops, bringing the U.S. combat presence by 11 May to more than 11,000 troops. Navy ships evacuated more than 4,300 civilians during the operation.

Paul Stillwell: Were you on murder boards for congressional testimony?*

Admiral Trost: Yeah.

Paul Stillwell: Any specifics on that you recall?

Admiral Trost: I don't really recall specifics, though the programs, we generally did the research, pulling in from the various secretariat assistants, whatever they needed to get across, making sure all the information was there, then briefing the boss on it, getting answers to questions he might have after he read this stuff. The Chief of Legislative Affairs generally came in with us. We'd be there to answer questions and do further chasing if he had questions. The legislative assistant, who was Jack Stempler most of the time I was there, would answer procedural questions primarily.†

Paul Stillwell: You mentioned briefly Alain Enthoven and the systems analysts. Was that a useful thing to bring to the process?

Admiral Trost: I would say sometimes—it was what I would call bias based on inexperience, in addition to the process. Enthoven's philosophy was that if you can't quantify it, it's not there, and a lot of things you can't quantify. When judgment comes in, I challenged his judgment on a number of occasions, on rare occasion openly, because he was not an easy guy to challenge. He didn't take criticism well. Our job was to make sure we had all the information for our boss, whether it bruised his ego or not, and his ego got bruised anytime anybody challenged anything he put on paper, or orally, for that matter. As a matter of fact, he used to try to bypass us by just coming in and steaming right into the office and saying, "Boss, I got to see you." That was usually because he had a disagreement with somebody, sometimes us, but somebody in OSD who disagreed with

---

* A murder board consists of individuals asking questions of the person who is going to testify so that he or she can mentally prepare practice answers.
† Jack L. Stempler, a civilian, was Assistant to the Secretary of Defense (Legislative Affairs), 1965-70.

what he was doing. You can see I'm not a fan of Alain Enthoven.

Paul Stillwell: Very few in uniform were. [Laughs]

Admiral Trost: Yeah.

Paul Stillwell: And the frustration would be for the uniformed officer who said, "I've been out there. I know what it's like."

Admiral Trost: Yeah, exactly. This guy had no experience, no background, but a lot of judgment.

Paul Stillwell: And a lot of power.

Admiral Trost: Oh, yeah, veto power over almost everything.

Paul Stillwell: Well, please talk more about Vietnam. That was really ratcheting up during your time there—committing ground troops and what have you.

Admiral Trost: It was, yeah. I observed. We observed the decisions being made, recommendations being made, very frequently at odds with what the senior military was recommending. I think the decisions came right out of the White House, frankly. I think Vance and McNamara were executors, as opposed to originators, of much of what went on. I'm fairly certain saying that about Vance. McNamara, I'm not quite sure. He was a major advisor to Lyndon Johnson, and very frequently you couldn't tell whether he was carrying out guidance or initiatives that he'd run by the President and gotten to go with.

I do know that General Wheeler used to be a very, very frustrated guy, and I know that because Bernie Rogers was his EA, and we had lunch together once a week, and he said these guys used to be ready to tear their hair out at some of the things that were coming down as edicts.* So I don't think we were well served in Vietnam by our senior leadership, political. Military guys had no option, except for a few guys. Westmoreland was a "please the boss, don't piss him off." So he's not one of the guys I'd give high marks to.†

Paul Stillwell: Secretary McNamara later came out with a memoir and said he had lost the idea early on that the war could be won militarily, but just kept quiet and followed directives, and it seemed that Secretary Vance apparently had some of those same ideas.

Admiral Trost: I think Vance had a lot of concerns, but didn't speak out against the approved policy. I don't know. I would attribute more decision power to McNamara influencing decisions than he acknowledged later on. You'd think he was a regular peacenik when you see his memoirs and some things he wrote later on. I'm not sure he was. But I was a JO in a big corral. [Laughter]

Paul Stillwell: You saw what the big people did.

Admiral Trost: Yeah, I did. It was enlightening, I'll tell you, for a first Washington tour. It was very, very enlightening.

Paul Stillwell: I would guess somewhat disillusioning also.

Admiral Trost: Well, yeah. You see what's happening and what people are doing and say, why are they doing that or where in the devil did they come from when they came up with that? I guess my expectations for them were higher than they proved to be.

Paul Stillwell: Interesting way to put it. How much awareness did you have of the antiwar

---

* Lieutenant Colonel Bernard W. Rogers, USA, served from 1962 to 1966 as military assistant and executive officer to General Maxwell Taylor, USA, Chairman of the Joint Chiefs of Staff. As a four-star officer Rogers was later Army Chief of Staff and Supreme Allied Commander Europe.
† General William C. Westmoreland, USA, served as Commander U.S. Military Assistance Command Vietnam from 20 June 1964 to 2 July 1968.

movement? I know a man set himself on fire outside of the Pentagon.

Admiral Trost: Well, having been physically confronted, having been grabbed by the sleeve and pulled away from a door as I was going into the Pentagon, I had an awareness that the people out there were pretty serious about it. As a matter of fact, I was put on report by the security people to my boss because I pushed away a guy who grabbed me by the arm and pulled on my uniform sleeve hard enough to pull it partially off my shoulder. I just gave him a big shove and slammed him against the wall and walked past him, and one of the guards put me on report. I was in uniform, unfortunately, that day. "This commander just pushed this civilian."

"Yep, I sure did." I said, "If he does it again, I'll do more than push him; I'll hit him."

The boss said, "Well, I can understand that."

Paul Stillwell: Was that the total resolution?

Admiral Trost: That was the resolution. [Laughter] Normally we wore civilian clothes at that time, and it was one of those rare times when I had my uniform on, and I guess that made me a target for this guy, who was probably antimilitary to start with and didn't expect a reaction, I don't think.

But these guys would clog up the entrance to the building, the Pentagon, yell at people walking in doing their job, sometimes physically accosting them, as they did in my case, and a lot of people were physically grabbed. They liked to grab secretaries too. It's sort of the hunting impulse because they won't hit back. So it was not a happy time in the Pentagon or in Washington.

Paul Stillwell: I'm guessing you didn't have a whole lot of sympathy for the protestors at that point.

Admiral Trost: I didn't have much sympathy for them. I had friends in Vietnam, some who were killed, and it was the U.S. policy. It was we should support those troops, not do things that are contrary to everything they're trying to do and get done. Well, I could second-guess things that happened in Vietnam, but it'd be just that. It wasn't my responsibility. I wasn't the expert on what they were doing. I didn't know how to fight a theater war, so I kept my mouth shut. But lost good friends, lost a couple of Naval Academy company mates over there, one classmate who was one of my predecessors working for Warner, Bill Leftwich, who was a Marine, a very competent Marine, and lost because he was too good a leader, combat leader par excellence.[*] He went out to pick out a couple of his guys who were marooned on a mountaintop in Laos. Their helicopter had been shot down. He got in his helo. He was on his second Vietnam tour. They were his battalion mates. Went out and they picked up the guys. As they lifted off, they got hit by a missile. He was a real loss. He was a guy who I think everybody who knew him had pegged him as a future Commandant of the Marine Corps, and a hell of a fine guy.

Paul Stillwell: He's honored by the visitors' center at the Naval Academy by Ross Perot.

Admiral Trost: Yeah. That was all Perot. What Ross did there, I think he was going to fund the visitors' center with his name on it, and so I talked him out of it. So he took Lyle Armel, who had been his roommate at the Naval Academy, and Leftwich, who was his hero, and named it the Armel-Leftwich Center, which was fitting and very good.[†]

Matter of fact, Ross put money into the Naval Academy. He wanted to fund the Alumni Hall when we were having trouble getting the money through Congress, but only if he could fund it and have it named after him. For some reason, somebody turned that down. Then the visitors' center was the outfall of that, which was okay. The upper deck in Dahlgren Hall, which is the old armory, is named the '53 Deck. He funded that, too, but by this time he'd gotten away from putting his name on things and put the money in.

---

[*] Lieutenant Colonel William G. Leftwich, USMC, who was subsequently killed in Vietnam in November 1970. The destroyer Leftwich (DD-984) was named in his honor.
[†] Captain Lyle O. Armel II, USN (Ret.), who died in 1989.

Paul Stillwell: And he funded statues for Admiral Lawrence and Admiral Stockdale.[*]

Admiral Trost: He did that. He did a lot of things for the Naval Academy, did a lot of good things. Ross has no small ego, no small accomplishments, as a matter of fact. He's quite a successful guy. He has his very human side, as demonstrated with his treatment of Vietnam veterans, Jim Stockdale. What he did with Stockdale was name him as his Vice Presidential running mate without talking to him first, which was not a good thing.[†]

Paul Stillwell: I talked to Admiral Stockdale about that, and he was bitter.

Admiral Trost: He found out when a public announcement was made, apparently.

Paul Stillwell: He thought he would not have to participate in the Vice Presidential debate. That was a public humiliation.

Admiral Trost: Yes, and he did very poorly, wasn't prepared for it. I got to know Stockdale quite well.

Paul Stillwell: There was a nice letter in the *Evening Capital* the other night from Diane Lawrence, saluting a teenager in Arizona who had won a science prize, talking about her husband and his role as a POW and the inspiration that that created. Admiral Lawrence was also a man of great integrity.

Admiral Trost: Oh, he sure was, sure was, and that experience had quite an impact on him. I've known him for years. We served together. He was Chief of Naval Personnel until a few months before I became CNO.[‡] But Bill Lawrence carried the burden of that POW experience, and it sort of broke him, I think, in many respects. He had no tolerance

---

[*] Vice Admiral William P. Lawrence, USN (Ret.); Vice Admiral James B. Stockdale, USN. Both were prisoners of war in Vietnam. The oral history of Lawrence is in the Naval Institute collection.
[†] Perot ran for President in 1992 as a third-party candidate.
[‡] Vice Admiral William P. Lawrence, USN, served as Chief of Naval Personnel from 28 September 1983 to 31 December 1985.

for people who lacked integrity, and came in a number of times with things that, "Do we really have to tolerate this?" It usually was something that, yeah, we had to because it was above us and we couldn't do anything about it. But he took things very, very seriously.

Paul Stillwell: He told me that he was nominated for four stars, VCNO, and he said he had set such high standards for himself that he didn't think that he could live up to them, and that's what sent him into a mental tailspin.

Admiral Trost: Yeah, I think so, and he's right. I heard he was nominated, and it wasn't in my bailiwick at the time, and that would have been earlier. Then he retired.

Paul Stillwell: Well, looking back at Vietnam from this vantage point all these years later, how would you evaluate the U.S. effort there—knowing what we do now about how Vietnam turned out?

Admiral Trost: Well, first of all, we never fought the war to win, in my view. I think it was a political war. Others have said we made a lot of mistakes, tactical mistakes. I think some of our senior military leadership was in it more for the vainglory than to win a war. That's a personal biased opinion, based in part on conversations with contemporaries who served over there. I never served there, so I have no right to comment.

Bud Zumwalt tried to get me ordered over there when I was on SubLant staff, my brief six-month tour, eight-month tour, whatever it was.[*] I found out about it when Joe Williams, who was the chief of staff for Arnie Schade, who was ComSubLant, told me that Shade got a phone call from Chief of Naval Personnel saying Zumwalt was gathering his staff.[†] Zumwalt knew me from my time as commander and had asked for me, among other people, to be assigned to the staff, like now. And Schade's response to the CNP

_____

[*] Vice Admiral Elmo R. Zumwalt, Jr., USN, served as Commander Naval Forces Vietnam/Chief of Naval Advisory Group Vietnam from 30 September 1968 to 14 May 1970. His oral history is in the Naval Institute collection.
[†] Vice Admiral Arnold F. Schade, USN, served as Commander Submarine Force Atlantic Fleet from 19 November 1966 to 12 February 1970. Captain Joe Williams Jr., USN, was his chief of staff.

was, "Tell that f-in' junior admiral to keep his hands off my people."[*] But that's as close as I ever got to Vietnam, and I didn't miss not being there. I was happy not being there.

Paul Stillwell: Admiral Crowe was a submariner who did go on to serve in Vietnam.[†]

Admiral Trost: Yeah.

Paul Stillwell: What had been your interaction with Zumwalt when you were in the Deputy's Office?

Paul Stillwell: Zumwalt was EA to Nitze, who was Secretary of the Navy, so Zumwalt was my sort of big daddy. He and Jerry Miller, who had the same job for the Vice Chief, and Ike Kidd, CNO.[‡] Those three guys were my big daddies when I was on board. If I had a question, I was told to ask them, ask them what kind of advice I needed. So I talked to Zumwalt a couple times a week, and that was my exposure.

Paul Stillwell: Then he got early selected and came back to head Systems Analysis. Were you involved with him then?

Admiral Trost: I was not directly involved with him then. I had the job later on, but not through any direct association. You know, it occurs to me I'm getting a little bit foggy on some of the sequence and timing of billets. It's going.

Paul Stillwell: We can fix that.

Admiral Trost: Brain transplant? [Laughter]

---

[*] CNP – Chief of Naval Personnnel.

[†] See the Naval Historical Foundation oral history of Admiral William J. Crowe, USN (Ret.), who later served as Chairman of the Joint Chiefs of Staff.

[‡] Captain Gerald E. Miller, USN, was executive assistant to the Vice Chief of Naval Operations, and Captain Isaac C. Kidd Jr., USN, was EA to the CNO. Miller's oral history is in the Naval Institute collection.

Paul Stillwell: Editing, it's called. You and I and everybody else have that problem at times.

Admiral Trost: Man, I'll tell you, mine is increasing.

Paul Stillwell: There will be times I'm searching for a name and it just won't come, then five minutes later, it pops into my head.

Admiral Trost: Yeah.

Paul Stillwell: Did you have any contact with the news media in that job in the Pentagon?

Admiral Trost: More as an observer. I can think of about two occasions where I was asked to brief somebody on something after they'd seen my boss in an interview, and I was asked to fill them in on such-and-such, but that was the extent of it.

Paul Stillwell: Secretary Vance had served in the Navy in destroyers in World War II. Did he seem to be able to draw on that experience?

Admiral Trost: Not that I ever saw, no. Drew more, if anything, on experience as Secretary of the Army, and that was really in direct connection with the job he had then, but I didn't see any sign that he had any special knowledge or interest in the Navy.

Paul Stillwell: Well, in a way, then, he was being non-parochial.

Admiral Trost: Yeah.

Paul Stillwell: Any issues about the Soviet Union, Soviet Navy, from that time to recall?

Admiral Trost: Not that I can recall directly. We were, obviously, at odds with the Soviets and concerned about their buildup, and at that point in time, very concerned about their submarine activity and their increasing emphasis on missile submarines. It was in the early days of that effort on their part, but they were already there, so we were concerned about our ability to track them where they deployed, how to keep tabs on them. That's about all I can remember.

Paul Stillwell: Would it be fair to say that Vietnam was the main preoccupation during your time?

Admiral Trost: Yeah, it would be, yeah. Matter of fact, I would say predominantly.

Paul Stillwell: I read that Secretary Vance went out to Detroit when there was a civil unrest out there.

Admiral Trost: He did.

Paul Stillwell: Called in the 82nd Airborne. Quite a change from the role of the military.

Admiral Trost: Quite a change. Well, he reportedly walked down the streets of Detroit with the senior military guy out there in charge of the group we had out there, just walked right down through these mobs. So he had guts or he didn't care what happened to him, I'm not sure which. I wasn't with him, and I'm glad I wasn't.

Paul Stillwell: Right. I remember the '60s as just a tinderbox of racial unrest.

Admiral Trost: It really was. It really was, racial and things like DomRep and, well, in the early '60s, Cuba, Cuban Crisis. And that's something I wish we could talk about someday. We can't right now because I've never been released from clearance. But it was an interesting time, and we did the right thing. As I recall, Kennedy was a brand-new President, and he had the guts to do what he did, and if he hadn't, Cuba probably would have been a Russian suburb for many years, and so what he did was right. Everything he did was not right, but the general thrust of what he did, standing up to the Russians and standing them down, was the right thing to do.

Paul Stillwell: Well, it could certainly be argued that the fiasco at Bay of Pigs prepared him for the crisis the following year.[*]

Admiral Trost: It could be.

Paul Stillwell: And there's also the suggestion that having been humiliated at the Bay of Pigs, he wanted to make a statement elsewhere, and that was Vietnam.

Admiral Trost: Yeah, it could well be. Yeah, because he came into office really as sort of a reputation for easygoing, not blasé, but a man of privilege who was going to take life easy now that he's won the prize of the presidency. I don't think it's the way he wanted to be remembered, and I don't think it's the kind of character he had either. I think he really was a tiger at heart.

Paul Stillwell: Well, and certainly very bright.

Admiral Trost: Yeah.

Paul Stillwell: And being in the job forces the responsibility.

Admiral Trost: Yeah, it does. That's right. Monkey's on your back. And the actions that affected my part of the world at that time and my Navy were the actions of a guy who thought the problem through and was going to take decisive action *now*. Whether it's right or wrong, he's going to take the action, and he did.

---

[*] In mid-April 1961 a force of 1,400 Cuban exiles, secretly trained by U.S. personnel in Guatemala, landed in the Bay of Pigs, on the southwestern coast of Cuba, in an attempt to overthrow Fidel Castro, that nation's Communist dictator. The invasion attempt was a disaster. President John Kennedy decided that U.S. naval intervention would worsen the situation, so ships and aircraft offshore were prohibited from taking part.

Paul Stillwell: Do you recall anything about the Arnheiter affair from Vietnam?[*]

Admiral Trost: Yeah, I do. First of all, I should be honest and say I'm not an Arnheiter fan. Arnheiter graduated the year before I did, having been sent from whatever company he was in to my company at the Naval Academy as a second classman. He was a second classman. He thought third-classmen, which I was one of, were plebes, to be treated accordingly. He was, in short, the biggest horse's ass I think I've ever encountered. I didn't think he was especially competent, although he thought he was an ace at everything he did. So I was predisposed to dislike Arnheiter because I dislike Arnheiter.

So while I was in OSD as a military assistant, Secretary Nitze, who was then Secretary of the Navy, sent down for Vance's review and endorsement action on Arnheiter. I don't remember whether it was denying him promotion or something.[†] I was handed the package and told to review this, which was disciplinary in nature. I reviewed it and I thought, if anything, they were going too light on him, and I told my boss what my background with him was and why I was biased against him. And Arnheiter's appeal was denied. I'd like to think I had a hand in it. I may not have. But I remember a lot about Arnheiter, and I read the testimony of his subordinates who were directed to do dumb things and expose people to death, really, by dumb actions.

Paul Stillwell: Vainglorious.

Admiral Trost: Vainglorious, going to dash in there and be the big hero, shoot up things.

Paul Stillwell: Well, there was a journalist, Neil Sheehan, who did an investigation. He went in sympathetic to Arnheiter, but the more he got into it, the more he felt that the disciplinary action was appropriate.

---

[*] For three months in early 1966 Lieutenant Commander Marcus A. Arnheiter, USN, commanded the radar picket destroyer escort *Vance* (DER-387). During that time she was involved in a number of dubious exploits, including some off Vietnam, and Arnheiter was relieved of command. For details see Neil Sheehan, *The Arnheiter Affair* (New York: Random House, 1971).

[†] Arnheiter's supporters, in Congress and also some naval officers, called for him to be restored to command.

Admiral Trost: Did he write that *Arnheiter Affair*?

Paul Stillwell: Yes, he did. And it cost the prospective commanding officer of the *New Jersey* his job, Captain Alexander, because he was supporting Arnheiter.[*]

Admiral Trost: Yeah, Captain Alexander came in and supported him very strongly, and I never did quite understand that, because I thought anybody who read the actions that Arnheiter was accused of taking would have said, "Gee, that's dumb. What the hell is he doing?" And Alexander was a relatively new CO, as I recall—but he had a good reputation.

Paul Stillwell: He did, yes.

Admiral Trost: So I never did understand that.

Paul Stillwell: There was a really bizarre footnote to all that. Some years ago, I was at the Naval Institute, and among my domain was the library at Beach Hall. This gent came in and he asked for a number of books very specifically. One of them was about naval mutinies and one was about the *Watch Officer's Guide*, and several of them. And he never did give his name. He said that he was in the class of '52. After a while, I went back to my office, and I got a plea from the woman running the library. She said, "He stole the books! He stole the books!" And it turned out to have been Arnheiter. It was an illustration of the phenomenon that he perceived the rules didn't apply to him.

Admiral Trost: Yeah. And did he have a brother at West Point?

Paul Stillwell: That sounds right, yes.[†]

---

[*] Captain Richard G. Alexander, USN, was slated to command the battleship *New Jersey* (BB-62). When Arnheiter's appeal was turned down, Alexander was reassigned to the First Naval District in Boston.
[†] Actually, the only Arnheiter listed in the Military Academy alumni register is Marcus A. himself. He attended West Point for a time before being admitted to the Naval Academy.

Admiral Trost: I think either class of '51 or—I don't think they were the same class. I'm not sure. Interesting guy.

Paul Stillwell: All kinds of people in the Navy.

Admiral Trost: Yeah. "I'm above it all. Rules don't apply to me."

Paul Stillwell: Yeah. [Laughs] I tried to stop him, and he drove up over a curb to escape. [Laughter]

Admiral Trost: I'll be damned.

Paul Stillwell: That was my only encounter with him.

Admiral Trost: Well, you're lucky.

Paul Stillwell: Probably, yeah.

Admiral Trost: I can attest to being treated like a plebe by Arnheiter in the company. He was an absolute asshole. I don't know if he had a friend in the world, certainly didn't have any admirers in my company.

Paul Stillwell: Well, he seemed to have picked up some friends, because Alexander was kind of a patron for him.

Admiral Trost: Yeah, no question.

Paul Stillwell: Then Secretary Nitze came in. How would you compare the working style with Secretary Vance? You mentioned he was more decisive.

Admiral Trost: Yeah. Probably the best way of describing the comparison was to tell you about the first days of his new job. Vance was to retire on the first of July, effective first of July. Of course, the first of July was a Saturday before the Fourth of July on Tuesday. We were to work on Monday. Tuesday was to be a day off.

Nitze came in on Saturday and said, "Cy, I'm supposed to take over on Monday," the third. So he came in to complete the turnover.

Vance said, "I'm not ready. I have to get to this," and he had all these papers on top of his desk he was going to get to. So he called the two of us in and said, "Which of this can you take care of?"

So Nitze said, "I've got a farm on the river," and he said, "I like to spend my weekends at the farm. Call me when you're ready."

Vance stayed, head down, that afternoon. He suggested that since he technically was no longer was in office, that we vacate his office and move across the hall. There was a working office next to Joe Califano, which Vance used to use when he was tired and went over.* It had a bed in there, and he napped in there.

Paul Stillwell: Well, Vance had had back problems also.

Admiral Trost: Yeah, he had back problems. So we moved him Saturday afternoon and Sunday, across the hall, and he continued to work. Monday morning Paul Nitze came in to his new office and said, "Ready to go to work today. At 1500 I'll go back to the farm." At 1500 he left, said, "See you on Wednesday." That's the way it started out, and that was the change in character of the office to all of us. Nitze would come in the office and say, "I don't like to get to the office before 8:00 o'clock in the morning." And he didn't. He'd come in at 8:00 o'clock in the morning, and by 6:00 o'clock he was ready to go home, which was a real enlightenment to us after, in my case, two and half years of Vance. So life got a lot easier for us.

Paul Stillwell: Get reintroduced to your family.

---

* In 1964 Joseph A. Califano Jr. became special assistant to the Secretary of Defense and Deputy Secretary of Defense.

Admiral Trost: Yeah, I could have dinner with them sometimes.

Paul Stillwell: One of the issues back then, and this impacted me personally, was the reactivation of the battleship *New Jersey*. Nitze had approved it while he was SecNav, and then, by the coincidence of moving up to the Deputy Secretary job, he got to approve his own recommendation. Do you remember any of the discussions on bringing back the battleship?

Admiral Trost: I don't. I don't.

Paul Stillwell: Did Nitze bring a different outlook and approach to the job?

Admiral Trost: I really don't recall that. I remember a much easier environment, a lot more conversation with people brought in to talk about things, as opposed to phone conversations, with edicts going out. Nitze was more a collegial leader, and much more people oriented and much more geared toward the farm as a place to relax. [Laughter] We went down one Sunday. He invited our family down—including the kids, and including Bud Zumwalt and his wife—for lunch on a Sunday. As I said, his farm was right on the Potomac River, a sloping green stuff going down about 40 miles to this river from the house—a beautiful place. We had lunch, and he said, "I'll show you around now."

He had a caretaker's—it was actually like a tennis caretaker's residence, and the pigpens are down there; I remember that. So I took my station wagon, and he took my kids and Pauline in his car. He took them down, and he told me about it afterwards. Steve was there; Steve now—he's class of '85 Naval Academy, retired commander. I guess he was about ten years old. They'd get in this little house, and the pigsties were right down next to the house. And my son got out and said, "Mister Nitze, this place sure does stink." [Laughter] And he got a big charge out of that. So he had a ball with my kids. They got a guided tour from the boss.

We were talking about my car. I had an old Ford 6 station wagon at that time, the one I bought when I came up to Washington. It was a mess when I got it, so I got it kind of cleaned up and put in new floor mats. The old ones were rotten. Mrs. Nitze commented on how clean my car was. I said, "My God, this is an old Ford, and it's a mess."

"But," she says, "cleaner than mine." [Chuckle] She was quite a person, quite a character—never minded her tongue about anything.

Paul Stillwell: Well, last night I looked in Nitze's memoir, just to refresh my memory, and there's a picture of him in the pigpen with the pigs.

Admiral Trost: Yeah, he was a serious farm owner. But he had this other guy; he called him the farm manager, and he had the responsibility for the place.

[Interruption for change of tape]

Admiral Trost: Well, Paul, I don't know if you're getting anything useful, but I'm enjoying it.

Paul Stillwell: Well, I am, too, and I'm certainly getting useful material—even the little asides about the working style of these two men that you worked for.

Admiral Trost: They were very different gentlemen, and two, obviously, very competent individuals.

Paul Stillwell: And they had different backgrounds. Vance had been primarily a lawyer, whereas Nitze went way back in national security issues, back to the Strategic Bombing Survey and ISA when McNamara came in, so he brought a great deal of background. How was that manifested? You've mentioned the collegial approach. Anything else?

Admiral Trost: I thought Nitze's interests were obviously more worldly oriented than Vance's, and Vance was a stickler on legal matters and legal niceties and—what should I call it—procedures. Nitze was not unaware of such things. His focus was—well, I'd say on most matters, more on the international side of things, on the operational side more so than Vance was. And Nitze had a pretty good technical background.

Paul Stillwell: What do you remember about the things surrounding the attack on the *Liberty* in 1967?[*]

Admiral Trost: Quite a few things. I think CNO was the acting Chairman. At that time they did a rotation and service chiefs would rotate their responsibilities if the Chairman was out of town.

Paul Stillwell: This was at the tail end of Admiral McDonald's reign.[†]

Admiral Trost: I remember the Vice CNO coming in, asking where the Deputy SecDef was, had to talk to him about it, and it was about *Liberty*.[‡] So maybe it was *Liberty* because a classmate of mine was the exec, and he was killed during the attack.

I remember whoever the acting Chairman was saying, "I've got to get to the—" Was it to the President or the Secretary of Defense? Anyway, the deputy wasn't there, whoever it was. Would have been Vance, I guess.

Paul Stillwell: It was Vance, yes. He left at the end of that month of June.

Admiral Trost: Okay. I'd forgotten the date. It was the Vice Chief who came in, needed to talk about this, what actions to take. I remember reading something about that not too very long ago, and I don't remember what all transpired. I remember helping him locate the deputy. Where he was, I don't recall. And then they started their discussions as to

[*] On 8 June 1967, during the Six-Day War between Israel and Egypt, Israeli aircraft and torpedo boats made a number of attacks on the U.S. communications intelligence ship *Liberty* (AGTR-5). Of the ship's crew of 297, 34 were killed and 171 wounded. Israel claimed that the attack on the *Liberty* was a case of mistaken identity and apologized. Many in the ship's crew were skeptical of the claim.
[†] Admiral David L. McDonald, USN, served as Chief of Naval Operations from 1 August 1963 to 1 August 1967. His oral history is in the Naval Institute collection.
[‡] Admiral Horacio Rivero, USN, served as Vice Chief of Naval Operations from 31 July 1964 to 17 January 1968. His oral history is in the Naval Institute collection.

what to do, and I didn't sit on any of the conferences, so I don't remember specifics of that. So what I know about is what I read afterwards, and I can't pull that out.

Paul Stillwell: Do you remember anything about recriminations or lessons learned?

Admiral Trost: Well, I remember there was a very strong feeling that we had at least a carrier group available, and there was everything from bombing the Israelis—we knew the flights came from Israel, and we felt that had to do something to stop the Israelis right away, make sure the Egyptians didn't attempt to retaliate against mainland Israel right away, and make sure the Israelis didn't take on some Egyptian destroyers that were in the general area. That's about the extent of my recollection, but I think our biggest effort was trying to locate the people who had to make a decision.

Paul Stillwell: What do you remember about the process of Admiral Moorer being selected to relieve Admiral McDonald?[*]

Admiral Trost: Don't really remember.

Paul Stillwell: He was the third straight naval aviator to have that after being surface officers the whole history before that.

Admiral Trost: That's right. Almost everybody was surface. I don't remember, and I don't remember if there was any controversy or not. I guess I was—I don't remember what I was. I was commander, I guess. They didn't ask me. [Laughter]

Paul Stillwell: Well, in a sense, he had been groomed, because he had Seventh Fleet, he had Pacific Fleet, Atlantic Fleet.

Admiral Trost: That's right. He was a natural.

---

[*] Admiral Thomas H. Moorer, USN, served as Chief of Naval Operations from 1 August 1967 to 1 July 1970. His oral history is in the Naval Institute collection.

Paul Stillwell: You left that office in the Pentagon just about the same time McNamara left the Pentagon. Do you remember any events surrounding his departure?

Admiral Trost: I really don't. I really don't, except great shouts of joy when the news first came out. [Laughter]

Paul Stillwell: Clark Clifford came in, and he had been hawkish, but then his views changed.

Admiral Trost: He'd been hawkish, but he was also very political, and I think he had lots of friends and lots of people on his side, and he didn't come in with an idea "I want to change the world tonight," or anything like that, so that probably helped. I met him. I liked the guy. I thought he was a very common-sense guy, very personable. I didn't know him well.

Paul Stillwell: He was a pillar in Washington for years.

Admiral Trost: He was, yeah, very, very well attuned to the nation's politics.

Paul Stillwell: Do you remember any other ways in which politics intruded while you were in that job with the deputies?

Admiral Trost: Not really. Not really. Of course, during the Johnson administration, everything was very political. That was always a major factor in every decision made: "How does it look? How will it sell?"

Paul Stillwell: Including not bringing in a lot of reservists.

Admiral Trost: That's right. That's right. There was an effort to do Vietnam on the cheap,

---

* Clark M. Clifford served as Secretary of Defense from 1 March 1968 to 20 January 1969.

and I really think that's what prompted the Tet Offensive.[*] I think we had visibly let our guard down, and here's Tet, opportunity to really make a big hit with our guys, influence the people of South Vietnam, and they hit and, luckily, our state of preparedness was such that they were able to withstand the assault, but we were lucky, very lucky. That could have been a major disaster.

Paul Stillwell: Bad enough as it was.

Admiral Trost: Bad enough as it was. But there were enough of our guys who were well enough prepared to be able to withstand something like this. I don't think it was great foresight by any means. I think it was good luck.

Paul Stillwell: Well, then that was amplified by the news media reaction, particularly Walter Cronkite.[†] That helped turn the country.

Admiral Trost: Yeah.

Paul Stillwell: Going to the other side of the world, in the mid-'60s, France pulled out of the NATO military structure.[‡] What do you recall about that?

Admiral Trost: Not much, except that the general thought was we haven't given up a lot of strength, based on their political gamesmanship of not getting too involved, not stating what they really wanted, wanting to lead by taking charge without contributing much.

---

[*] On 31 January 1968 the North Vietnamese and Viet Cong launched a massive coordinated attack that came to be known as the Tet offensive because it occurred in conjunction with the lunar new year, a traditional Vietnamese holiday. Attacks were launched simultaneously against cities, towns, and military bases throughout Vietnam and resulted in many casualties. Although the American forces beat back the offensive, the news media at the time reported it as a North Vietnamese victory. Soon afterward, President Lyndon Johnson announced that he would not run for reelection and began scaling back the American commitment in Vietnam.

[†] Walter L. Cronkite Jr. (1916-2009) had a long career in broadcast journalism, highlighted by his tenure from 1962 to 1981 as the managing editor and anchorman of the CBS evening news.

[‡] In 1966 and 1967 French Prime Minister Charles de Gaulle gradually withdrew his nation's naval and military forces from NATO because he believed the United States had too much control over those forces. He also demanded that all NATO headquarters, bases and troops be removed from France by April 1967, which was done. France remained a member of NATO politically but not militarily.

That's about what I remember of it. They really lost NATO Headquarters by default, almost, and lack of interest, desire to run everything but not contribute anything.

Paul Stillwell: A lot of people like that. [Laughs]

Admiral Trost: Yeah, yeah, there are a lot of people like that.

Paul Stillwell: So the upshot was that the NATO Headquarters moved to Belgium.

Admiral Trost: Moved to Brussels, yeah.

Paul Stillwell: The Sixth Fleet flagship moved to Gaeta, Italy.

Admiral Trost: They had a major restructuring change from a basic perspective. And, of course, I think as long as there's a NATO, it'll stay in Brussels. When Bernie Rogers was the Chairman, Joint Chiefs—actually, before that when he was over in Brussels, his feeling was that they had a permanent home there, and I think he was right. Of course, he tried to make himself a permanent resident.[*] He didn't want to retire.

Paul Stillwell: General Goodpaster was over there for a long time too.[†]

Admiral Trost: He was, he was. I liked Goodpaster. I had a chance to sit in a couple times when he was briefing, and he struck me as a very common-sense guy, a senior citizen, a senior diplomat, if you will. "Senior statesman" is the term I want to use. He was quite a guy, a lot of common sense.

Paul Stillwell: That, overall, must have been a very broadening tour of duty for you.

---

[*] General Bernard W. Rogers, USA, was NATO's Supreme Allied Commander Europe, 1979-87.
[†] General Andrew J. Goodpaster, USA, served as U.S. Commander in Chief Europe and NATO Supreme Allied Commander Europe from 1969 to 1974.

Admiral Trost: Oh, it was, you know. I'd never been in Washington. I'd been in the Pentagon once. On my way over to the Olmsted Scholarship, I was told to go in and see this guy named Ernie Barrett, whose widow is right down the hall down here.* I don't remember what job Ernie was in. It was one of the political military jobs in OP-06. He was going to brief me on going to Europe, because I was going——even though I got no support, I was given NATO orders, and so they thought I needed NATO briefings when I got briefed by Ernie Barrett. That was my only time in the Pentagon prior to my assignment there, and I think I was there maybe a half hour. Not really an expert.

Paul Stillwell: Did you have any contact with Admiral Rickover while you were in that Pentagon job?

Admiral Trost: I did. Periodically, when he had something that got hung up, he'd have it traced down, and if it was in OSD, he'd trace it through the Pentagon's Correspondence Control Center, SecDef's Control Center. Those guys took a lot of guidance from us and from McNamara's military assistants. If there was something that should get pushed, we were the guys who got the word that it's got to be pushed, and we'd tell them to track and monitor and tell me where it is.

Well, I don't remember how long I'd been there, but he had a paper that was sort of time-sensitive, and it wasn't going anywhere. And he had his guys track it down and found out it was sitting on the desk of an Air Force three-star. Now, that's *bad* when an Air Force guy is sitting on this thing and it needs to be signed. It's time-sensitive, and it's been there for five weeks, something like that. So he called me personally, which was out of the blue, "Can you find out why this paper isn't being signed?"

So I checked, found out where it was. It turned out this Air Force general and I and two other guys had lunch together just about every day, and so I checked and found out, yes, it was, in fact, in his office, not on his desk. So I asked him if I could talk to him after lunch, and he didn't know anything about it to start with. I explained what was in the document. He said, "That makes sense. When did they send it to me?"

---

* Commander Ernest R. Barrett, USN.

I said, "Well, it's in your office somewhere." So he got his assistants in, and one of them was sitting on it, and so he got the paper and he signed it, and we got it sent out that day. So I made hero in Rickover's book that day. That day.

Paul Stillwell: That day. [Laughs]

Admiral Trost: He would periodically check and call me and say, "See what you can find out about such-and-such. Let me know." And nothing out of order, just stuff that in the normal course of bureaucracy it sat somewhere and didn't get any action. So, yeah, I had some limited phone time with him.

Paul Stillwell: You left that job the same month *Pueblo* was seized.* Was that an issue at all while you were still on the job?

Admiral Trost: It was with me after it was seized, but no. I don't recall what the month was that—

Paul Stillwell: January '68.

Admiral Trost: Okay. I was gone. I was gone. I knew of the basic operation, not the specifics of it, but I knew what she was going to do and what we were doing, and I also knew that we were playing it pretty loose with our potential protection. We had airplanes up there in northern Japan, and that we were standing easy because there was no threat to these operations. So when it happened, it wasn't a surprise. It wasn't a surprise to me, and I'm not sure it was a surprise to the people who ran the operation, and our reaction to it was poor. We let that guy hang out.

---

* USS *Pueblo* (AGER-2), an electronic intelligence ship, was seized on 23 January 1968 in the Sea of Japan by North Korean naval forces. The ship's crew members were held as prisoners until 23 December of that year. Of the 83 officers and men on board, 28 were intelligence specialists. Her commanding officer was Commander Lloyd R. Bucher, USN.

Paul Stillwell: I met Commander Bucher once, and we made small talk for about 15 minutes, and then for a long time the discussion was about the *Pueblo*.

Admiral Trost: Bucher, yeah. I knew Lloyd. He was a submariner, diesel submariner, and he felt he had the rug cut out from under him, and he did. He did.

Paul Stillwell: Well, the irony was that he was not considered good enough to get a submarine command, but put in a job that actually had much more peril.

Admiral Trost: That's right. He, in fact, did not really do everything he might have to prepare his ship. I felt sorry for him and didn't. I knew him not real well, but he was very bitter about having been passed over for submarine command. I always felt he was scapegoat in this event, and he was.

Paul Stillwell: Yes.

Admiral Trost: He really was. Now, during my time in command of Seventh Fleet, I will say that because of *Pueblo*, we would never have done that, and didn't. When we did operations that had a threat to them from the North Koreans, we were ready with backup, and we normally didn't let one guy stand out as the sore thumb beckoning his way out there. I'd like to say that's a lesson learned, and I think it was. But we would have responded immediately. Even had we been that unready, we would have responded immediately.

Paul Stillwell: The concept of the ship being seized was so unlikely, there was no contingency plan.

Admiral Trost: Yeah, that's right. But, again, standard procedure in my time in Seventh Fleet was I was aware of everything going on anywhere around Korea or anywhere else where there was a hazard to the ship. We tracked that, and that's probably because of *Pueblo*. Matter of fact, that was the process before I got there; it wasn't me. We kept track of everything in the Western Pacific and the Indian Ocean, which was also mine, so I knew where every Russian ship was, I knew what the Koreans were doing, so we kept track.

Paul Stillwell: The other night I was flipping through channels and came across a movie called *Hellcats of the Navy* with Ronald Reagan and his future wife, Nancy Davis.

Admiral Trost: I saw that years ago.

Paul Stillwell: Bucher told me it was his submarine that was used for the filming of that movie. [Laughs]

Admiral Trost: Oh, really?

Paul Stillwell: When he was a more junior officer.

Admiral Trost: Well, he was one of many people, because this was the advent of the nuclear program, and a lot of diesel submariners did not get submarine command because the submarine numbers were going down and because these were guys who hadn't made the nuclear program. So downstream we didn't have billets for them in the submarine force.

Now, the guys who ended up being in good shape were the guys who were execs and who were screened and cleared for surface command. Tom Paulsen, who was my EA at LantFlt and again in the CNO Office, was in that category.[*] He was a diesel submariner through exec. I met Tom when he had command of a surface ship in Seventh Fleet in Yokosuka. Then he came to be my surface warfare officer on the Seventh Fleet staff. Tom is one in the category of guys who made out because they were top performers in diesel boats, and ended up going to a surface ship command and kept going. A number of them made two stars. Some of them came into the nuclear program when it expanded. The very senior guys came in and were usually guys with advanced degrees or just top

---

[*] Captain Thomas C. Paulsen, USN.

performers, and they made it into the program, especially with the advent of the missile submarine program. A lot of them came in that way, came in, I think, at XO level.

Paul Stillwell: Admiral Train and Admiral Crowe were two who remained diesel and made four stars anyway.

Admiral Trost: Yeah.

Paul Stillwell: As you say, the top performers.

Admiral Trost: They were the top performers.

Paul Stillwell: You moved from that job to command of one of the crews of *Sam Rayburn*.* Please tell how that came about.

Admiral Trost: Let's see. Well, I had completed a three-year tour in OSD, and I was told I was going to command. I'd been told that twice before and didn't, for various reasons. I went through with the submarine PCO course in New London after I left OSD and then through the Rickover PCO program, which was three months.†

I was originally due to go to a Charleston-based boat, *Simon Bolivar*, and *Bolivar* had a collision, got her scopes and sail nicked by either a destroyer or a cruiser that was running target for them off Charleston. A guy named Skip Orem, who was CO, got relieved.‡ They cut orders for me to go to *Bolivar* while I was still in Rickover's PCO course, and then the flotilla commander said, "Wait a minute. That's not going to work time-wise. It's too late. I want this guy relieved now."

To relieve him now, they had to take somebody. I think he was then just being relieved as exec, a guy named Jeff Badgett, close friend of mine, was already in the

---

* USS *Sam Rayburn* (SSBN-635, a *Lafayette*-class ballistic missile submarine, was commissioned 2 December 1964. She was 425 feet long, 33 feet in the beam, and displaced 7,250 tons surfaced and 8,250 submerged. . She had a top speed on the surface around 20 knots and a top speed of more than 30 knots submerged. She was armed with 16 Polaris A-3 ballistic missiles and four 21-inch torpedo tubes.
† PCO – prospective commanding officer.
‡ Commander Charles A. Orem, USN, was the first commanding officer of the *Simon Bolivar*'s Gold crew.

Charleston area, was immediately available, so he got orders to *Bolivar*.[*] I don't remember the sequence. I don't remember much about it. I remember being told by the detailer, "Sit tight. You'll still go to Charleston." I'd be home-ported in Charleston. So if you planned housing, which we already were looking around for, he said, "You'll still go to Charleston."

So then a little while later, I got orders to *Rayburn*, and since *Rayburn* was the sister to *Von Steuben*, the next ship down the line from Newport News, there were two peas in a pod.

Paul Stillwell: You have talked about waiting around so many times for Admiral Rickover. It's interesting to contemplate how many man-hours were wasted by all that process.

Admiral Trost: Yes. A lot of man-hours were wasted, and I think his modus when we were there as candidates for, either initially for the program or later on as PCOs, was to instill in us the importance of the program, because he really was a bug on safety and procedure and adherence to procedure. I will tell you about that PCO course leading to command USS *Sam Rayburn*. I was one of 13—three of whom were surface, headed for nuclear cruisers, and I was the senior guy. He had weekly get-togethers with the PCOs, and it was always to talk about something that had happened that had a lesson to it that they wanted us all to get. Rickover would say, "I'm going to send something for you to read, but I want to tell you about it first. So pay attention to me."

We always did. At the end, we were sitting in a semi-circle in chairs, and he sat behind a little crusty desk. When he finished his talking, he'd ask, "Do you agree?" Invariably, he got 13 yeses, including me. One day he started in on how a commanding officer of a submarine should have his meals in a stateroom, not in the wardroom, so he wouldn't become buddy-buddy with the young people in the wardroom. I thought it was a dumb-shit idea. So he went along, and he got 12 yeses. He almost choked when I said I disagreed with him [laughter].

He said, "See me after the meeting."

_____

[*] Commander John Jefferson Badgett, USN.

I thought, "Oh no, no."

I walked in his office and he said, "Goddamn it, Trost, you might get away with it, but those dumb shits won't [laughter]. I think it's a lousy idea. Well, you can't influence people if you're buddy-buddy with them."

I said, "You don't become buddy-buddy in the submarine wardroom. You get to know your people and that's important, especially in a small environment like a submarine." I really felt very strongly about that.

He said, "All right, goddamn it, you might get away with it, get out of here." He was interesting and sometimes fun to deal with.

Paul Stillwell: In what way was he fun?

Admiral Trost: He'd come up with these things and you'd think, "God, he's going directly through the overhead. He'd sort of simmer for a while and then say, "All right, get out of here." You know I'd get a kick of it, that he was really conceding the arguments—at least, that was my take on it. Because he was not saying, "All right, you're going to do this, you're going to do that." He never did.

Paul Stillwell: What was the content of the PCO courses? Was that mostly refresher?

Admiral Trost: I'd been through PCO School before my first XO tour for new construction. I was told, "We have a couple guys like you and you're going to get a slightly modified course," and so we did. We spent more time at sea doing attacks and running than some of our accompanying classmates.

Gee, reliving this is interesting. The PCO course in New London was somewhat tailored for us. Matter of fact, mine was cut short two weeks, as I recall, to line me up with the Rickover PCO course, and why that was, I don't remember, because they're normally sequenced, and this was, I guess. The two guys who came in with me were also out of phase, so we came in as a separate little three-men class with Rickover. And interesting, because I think in the course of doing that, they tailored it. We had some stuff cut out because of background and career history kinds of courses we'd had and duty we'd had, and I had actually been to PCO School twice, yeah, because I'd been to PCO course school en route *Von Steuben* pre-commissioning.

Paul Stillwell: Were there separate PCO courses for SSNs versus SSBNs?

Admiral Trost: They were not when I went, no. They were the same.

Paul Stillwell: But having served in *Von Steuben*, you knew what the mission was.

Admiral Trost: I knew what the mission was, yep, and was ready to go.

Paul Stillwell: How did the PCO course wind up?

Admiral Trost: After the first part in New London, I then came down to Washington for period with Rickover. I was with two other submariners, and on a Friday when our course was supposed to be over, they were called in about 1600 and detached. We had been told to turn our books in earlier that day. I turned my books in, and they said, "You can't read any but official books about power plants." So I had nothing to read, and I kept waiting to be detached or told that my tour had been extended for two weeks, like my two coworkers had been.

I sat there and didn't hear anything by 1800. I went up to the front office, and the secretary said, "Well, you're supposed to report back tomorrow."

So I said, "Okay." My coworkers were told to read all their books and get to work. Saturday I got in, nothing. I sat there for eight hours with nothing to read. I wrote things, reminders I think, wrote a couple of letters, and went home.

I was told, "Come back Monday." Monday I came back. I sat in my little classroom all by myself until 1600, when I was told, "The admiral will see you now."

So I went into Rickover's office, and he said, "Sit down. I heard that when you went to Germany, [which I went as an Olmsted scholar, I was the first of the selectees], that you had misgivings, that you were told that you would be kicked out of the nuclear program. Who told you that?"

I didn't remember who told me that, but it was a long time back—two ranks ago, as a matter of fact, in Hawaii. So I told him that I didn't remember. He said, "Well, let me show you something." He got out a German textbook and opened it, and it had margin notes. About two-thirds of the way through, all of the sudden there are no more margin notes. Because he had taught himself to read German by making notes for everything he didn't understand. He said, "I wanted people to learn languages. That's smart. That's why I do it." Okay.

Then he said, "Have you heard about *Scorpion?*"[*] I had been away from her for five and a half years. We were now at the day she was declared lost and missing. He had gotten a call from Yogi Kaufman who was a member of the Joint Staff. Nobody in the CNO's office had called him to tell him that a nuclear submarine was lost or declared lost at sea. So he talked to me for about two and a half hours just as human I ever saw him. Then he said, "Okay, well, enough of that. You can go now, you're finished." That was my detachment. Sent me on my orders back. He had a human side of him.

Paul Stillwell: I suspect that discussion you had after the loss of the *Scorpion* was a time when he felt particularly vulnerable and introspective.

Admiral Trost: Yes, he really was. I felt sorry for him. He took this very personally. He kept talking about those poor guys and those poor families and how many guys that I knew in the crew that were still there. I'd been gone for over five years and I knew five guys, all but two were first class petty officers and three were chief petty officers, including the chief of the boat whom I had selected for the job when I was XO. The other was the chief quartermaster that served there the whole time I was there. I knew the families of those guys, and so it was kind of hard.

At the first get-together of the former crewmembers and surviving wives, we had almost 50 guys who had served on this ship either with me or after me and there are these guys who had been lost. It was emotional, but enlightening. They came together like a

---

[*] The submarine *Scorpion* (SSN-589) was lost with all hands while en route from the Mediterranean to Norfolk. She was last heard from on 21 May 1968. On 27 May she was reported overdue and on 5 June presumed lost with her entire crew of 99 officers and men. The wreckage was located on 30 October of that year. No definitive conclusion has been reached as to cause.

unified crew; they were really great. That impressed me. That's what being a *crew* member means. It's the bond that they form with their guys. They have all been exposed to the same kind of environment, same hazards, and you sense a oneness that you don't see in a surface ship. That may not be true for all surface ships. I can't speak for all of them.

Paul Stillwell: Well they've been through the good times together too.

Admiral Trost: Yeah. They call themselves *Scorpion* survivors now, still get together annually in Norfolk. The families of the former crewmembers and I have not been to the last couple of them because the health of mine or Pauline's, but they still get together.

Paul Stillwell: Well, it was a destroyer sailor who said it, but I remember his quote was, "Friendships come and go, but shipmates are forever."

Admiral Trost: Yeah. *Robert A. Owens*, my first ship, still has an annual reunion. I've been invited every year, but I haven't been to the last couple and they usually are, well they've been held in a variety of places, most of them have been held in Virginia Beach and I think that's the environment and hotel availability more than anything else. They've been to Kansas City, they've been in St. Louis, been on the West Coast and the *Owens* Shipmates Association puts out, it used to be a monthly newsletter and we shifted about a year ago to a semi-annual newsletter. It comes out full page, about eight-page thing and they put out information on what people are doing, deaths of former crewmembers and information that would be of interest to retirees usually. It's interesting, a lot of guys who are subscribers to this again are active in writing for it are guys who guys who were in the Navy for four years, got out, that's their tie with their shipmates. It's sort of interesting.

Paul Stillwell: Well, I've observed that phenomenon in a number of ships—that crew members may not have enjoyed it at the time, but when they get some perspective, they appreciate it that much more. The opportunities, the exposure, the friendships.

Admiral Trost: And the *Sam Rayburn* has an annual get-together. I haven't made the last couple, but they get together and since all of them lived in the Charleston area at one point in time, the reunions are usually in Charleston, and I guess they want to hit old stomping grounds down there. Some of them live there. But that group is very close. The guy who was my leading radioman, my crew, is the head organizer. There are three guys that have been doing this. They've been doing it since the—my gosh, since 1969 they've been getting together. It was a new ship then.

Paul Stillwell: In the late '90s, I saw the *Sam Rayburn* down around Norfolk. The missile compartment had been chopped out and then the bow and stern welded together.

Admiral Trost: The bow and stern put together.[*] She's getting ready now to be re-retired. All I knew is one of the same class being modified to take her place as the afloat training plant. But their crewmembers still get together and have some good reunions.

Paul Stillwell: What do you recall about setting up shop in Charleston and living there?

Admiral Trost: Well, we rented a house from a guy named Bill Roberts, class ahead of me at the Naval Academy, who was exec of another ship.[†] I think they were going into overhaul; either that or he was detaching. I'm not sure which it was anymore. But they wanted to keep the house because they liked Charleston, and so we had a place to go to to rent, which was great.

We moved in on Fourth of July. Temperature was about 105. It was a miserable day. At the movers' request, I had the air conditioning on high because they had to have the door open to come through with stuff, and so we ran the air conditioner for about six hours while these guys came through the front door.

I remember the next day mowing the lawn, which needed it because it had been vacant for maybe three weeks, and discovering these little supersonic flies that hit you. They're called deer flies. I think they're deer flies. Anyway, they hit you and bite before you could swat them, and they're very fast. Pauline liked flowers, so we had these built-in planters out in front of the house, and they were full of weeds, so day two, we pulled the weeds and got bitten by gnats all over the place. Day two, I also mowed the grass and

---

[*] The former ballistic missile submarine *Sam Rayburn* (SSBN-635) was decommissioned and stricken from the Navy list in 1989. Her missile compartment was removed, and she was subsequently retained by the Navy as a moored training ship for nuclear propulsion plant operators.
[†] Commander William E. Roberts, USN.

got bitten by gnats, and deer flies were still there. Big yard, so I did it in two shifts, and that was my initial approach.

Then we went down and we were setting up shop and checking out setting up our new offices. The base in Charleston was an active place at that time, and we had good accommodations. Training facilities were good. The base support was outstanding. I do remember that. So it was a positive experience from that perspective.

I'm trying to recall. It was pretty good. We liked the house we rented, had good neighbors, about half and half Navy and civilian. Did not like the weather. It was hot. The paper plant was across the river to the east of us, but when it was working the odor was horrendous. We were to the west of Charleston. I remember saying, "The one good thing is when the paper mill is running, we don't have as many bugs," because I guess the fumes, they didn't like it any better than we did. But Charleston's an interesting place; weather was lousy no matter what season we had, and we had a good time there. Interesting historical old place, so we enjoyed that.

Paul Stillwell: Fort Sumter.[*] [Laughs]

Admiral Trost: Oh, yeah, we went out to Sumter. Matter of fact, my recollection of Sumter was one time when we had somebody living just south of Sumter, one of our crew people, he invited us over for a swim and a cookout and had little sail things. Anyway, I took my youngest daughter out in this little boat, and coming in, she slipped off. In the process of getting her back on this little sailboat, I slipped off in about waist-deep water and walked her ashore. And when I came out of the water, I left bloody footprints because I was walking on a bed of oyster shells and didn't know it.

I ended up in the hospital that night for a couple hours getting my heels fixed. I had a gash in this heel over here that, right in this part of the heel, and it was about a half-inch deep. When I went into the hospital, they had to clear fragments of shell out of that thing, and that was excruciating. They gave me a shot that I was supposed to not feel

---

[*] Fort Sumter was a Union base on an island at the mouth of the harbor in Charleston, South Carolina. The combat action of the Civil War began on 12 April 1861 when Confederate artillery bombarded the fort. Union forces surrendered the fort 34 hours later.

anything. It didn't work. So I spent a couple of days with a soft boot on my left foot, and the right foot they just bandaged up. So I have some bad memories of Charleston. I guess it was a sailing dinghy I was in with her, and I had done a lot of sailing, so my sailing expertise didn't extend to walking in oyster shells.

So we had good and bad. Bad weather, bad oyster shells, good friends, met a lot of local people, some interesting ones, old Charleston families who are just that, they're old Charleston, and by the time you have spent your first time with them, you know everything about their family, their history, the family's history, and Charleston. Interesting place.

Paul Stillwell: Southern charm.

Admiral Trost: Yeah.

Paul Stillwell: But that would definitely qualify as a freak accident with the oyster shells.

Admiral Trost: Oh, it was very definitely a freak accident. So I was very careful. I never walked, never sailed barefoot again. I always wore sneakers when I sailed just to make sure, and I didn't go swimming for pleasure in the river. I stuck to swimming pools, never out in the harbor again.

Paul Stillwell: Speaking of the river, what do you remember of sea details in and out on the Cooper River?

Admiral Trost: They were interesting. Well, my first time down the river in command, we were going out for five days to get the crew worked up before we took the ship on patrol. You go out and you come back in and you fix anything that's shown to be not operating properly. And it's also a chance to break in new people. Well, I got a new ensign, limited duty officer, former fire control technician, through chief, so he's not a kid. He's an experienced guy. I've taken him out on the little T-boats. Remember those, by chance?

Paul Stillwell: No.

Admiral Trost: I think they were stationed in Key West, small submarines. They were built for training in; I think they built two and gave up. But we had one of those in Charleston, or two of them, maybe. So I took this guy, who was a line officer now, and wanted him to get him as much training experience, so I'd take him out on one of these things. It was like a rent-a-boat, they used to joke. So I took him out and up down the river. We ran the river about four or five times with him as the OOD, and so that worked out quite well. My experienced OODs, if they needed it, we did the same thing with them.

So going off on the first patrol, my second time under way, they sent a pilot up to the site up north Cooper River, where there was a tender. This guy came aboard, and he was one of the Navy yard pilots. He said, "Now, I'm an experienced guy. I don't like commanding officers butting in when I'm giving orders."

I said, "It's my ship. If I sense something under my responsibility needs doing, I'll speak up and I'll take command." Because the Cooper River can be a CO's nightmare, and I used to tell my OODs, the new ones, "When you go down the Cooper River and you're north of the shipyard and the base, you can go aground on both ends at the same time," because an FBM will go across and touch both shores.[*]

So, anyway, this pilot said, "You don't to worry about me. I'm experienced."

"Oh, okay."

So he backed me out around the tender, and he said, "There's a pretty strong current running."

I said, "You told me this is slack water."

"Well, they opened the dam upstream."

I said, "Shouldn't I have been notified about that?"

"Oh, yeah, you should have been." But nobody did.

By this time, we were out past the tender. We were in the middle of the stream, and we were going down the stream sideways. I said, "Give the tug the word to turn my bow around so I can cast off."

---

[*] FBM – fleet ballistic missile submarine.

He said, "I'm the pilot."

I said, "Do what I ask you or get off my ship."

He said, "I'm the pilot."

I said, "Get off my ship."

He climbed down the side rung, cast off the tug, and now I was twisting. You can't twist because you have only one screw, but I'm twisting by going ahead full, maneuvering standby from full bell, because they were one-third back, and they said, "Yes, sir." I got the full bell, left full rudder, and I managed to get the ship turning just before we went around the bend that way and on down the river. So we didn't run aground or hit the floating dry dock that was moored down there.

So on my way down the river, I called my squadron commander and said, "Captain so-and-so was my pilot. I'm going down the river. We're okay. I don't want to ever see that guy on any ship that I'm around again." I told the commodore what had happened.

He said, "I'll take care of that."

The guy got fired and should have been fired, because he'd have run me aground sure as shit. So that was an experience with the Cooper River. I learned to tell all my guys, "You can be aground in both ends."

I learned that merchantmen don't give a damn about a ship with a 32-foot draft. They're going to go where they're going to go when they want to go, and we encountered a lot of those coming up to North Charleston. So I was not a fan of running that river any more often than I had to. [Laughter]

And I was not a fan of the pilots either. They had a couple of good ones, but I generally got under way by myself without a pilot, unless I was inboard of the tender and had to have him to kind of snake me out and turn me around behind it. So it was an interesting place to operate from.

Paul Stillwell: What do you recall about your relationship with the crew?

Admiral Trost: I learned a lot about people. I learned about one guy's love life and why he had put in to leave the ship. His girlfriend, who said she'd be his fiancée officially if he took off and missed the next patrol—well, he could have done that, but he'd have been in the brig. So he told me this on a sea trial before patrol. I said, "When we get back in, you call her and tell her you know that if you follow her advice, you won't be with her during the next patrol; you'll be in the brig in Charleston."

He said, "That's a good idea. Maybe that will get to her." [Laughter] Amazing he hadn't thought of it before. But he was second-class petty officer. He was one of my two trained oxygen generator operators, and I needed that kid. But that was just the result of developing a relationship with him from walking through the ship and talking to him. He was an interesting guy. He was interested in everything. I'd go back out and I'd sit on his watch station for about 15-20 minutes and talk to him, and we covered the world. I enjoyed that too.

Paul Stillwell: That's a strange request to make of someone.

Admiral Trost: Oh, yeah. I don't know what she thought would happen. And he was a good guy. They never got married, by the way. He decided maybe she wasn't for him.

Paul Stillwell: Good choice. [Laughs]

Admiral Trost: So it was interesting, but you get to know your people and you get to know about people. One of my toughest tasks as CO was to keep to myself bad information that had come out to me while I was in the missile submarine about somebody who had a family problem, like a death in the family. You call the guy in, and you don't call him in while you're at sea. You don't want him to stew, in one case for six weeks, over the death of his dad, who the message said he was very close to. You don't want him to know that his wife and kids disappeared from their trailer at Charleston Air Force Base six weeks before the end of the patrol, whereabouts unknown. Nothing you can do about that. Matter of fact, when he got back, there was nothing else he could do about it. He never located them in the time. We broke up the crew right after that patrol, because the other crew was taking it in to overhaul, and he had not located her in the roughly three and a half weeks we were together after the patrol. She was seen with an

Air Force enlisted man by a neighbor, in a neighboring trailer, about a week before she disappeared with the kids.

But that you live with and you keep it to yourself until you're on your way in, at the end of patrol, to try to protect them. Somebody said one time, "That's cruel. They ought to know." It's cruel to tell them, because then they spend the rest of the time out there fretting about it, I think.

Paul Stillwell: And distracted from their work.

Admiral Trost: Yeah, and that's my philosophy, so I just sat on it.

Paul Stillwell: It's a tough life, not for everybody.

Admiral Trost: Yeah, it's not for everybody. We had, fortunately, very few such instances. On two patrols I had a family death, but just one, and that was a blessing. In each case, it was a parent.

So you have to take it as it comes. But the messages come in. The radiomen are forbidden to distribute them to anybody except the CO until he releases them to anybody else. There are some things you want to get out to the whole crew, things of general interest. There are things you want the XO to have and take care of, because they're not deaths, they're not quite that serious. But if the commanding officer calls a guy in, he generally knows it's something serious, and so you have to handle that yourself. One of the chores that go with the job.

I made two patrols on *Rayburn*. After the second one, the ship was due to go in for an overhaul. But the other crew was due to take it in, which means my crew was going to be split, some going with the overhaul crew and the rest would be sent off to other places. So I was not relieved as commanding officer; I was simply disestablished, basically. The other skipper was new, was junior, and he was going to take it through overhaul and then do more patrols.

Paul Stillwell: I think she went up to Portsmouth for that overhaul.

Admiral Trost: She went up to Portsmouth for overhaul.

The reason for my being pulled off was that I was selected for captain, and so BuPers said, "We're not going to send you back to another command," and I got orders to SubLant staff as the N-1, was there for eight months, I think, before I went to Warner and worked for him.

Paul Stillwell: Please tell me about the satisfactions of command.

Admiral Trost: Well, it's nice to be the guy who is responsible, unless you're somebody who doesn't seek responsibility, and I always did. I liked being my own boss, driving my own ship, being responsible for my own crew, a very satisfying kind of assignment.

Paul Stillwell: And not a lot of ability to report what you're doing while you're submerged. [Laughs]

Admiral Trost: You know, when you're told to maintain radio silence, you maintain radio silence. It's nice to be on the receiving end only. Of course, then any decisions you make are yours, and if you've got a personnel problem, you'd better be able to handle it. The toughest ones for me were the bad news messages that would come in, because we were receiving messages constantly, but you couldn't do much about them.

Paul Stillwell: Except if you told the individual, you'd burden him as well.

Admiral Trost: You'd burden him. This way the only person other than me and the radioman who got the message was the exec, whom I kept informed, and we both debriefed the individuals who were affected on our way in. Usually the exec would bring them in, tell them about the message, show them the message, and I'd go in and talk to them. I was sort of the duty chaplain. And that worked well. I think it's a humane way to do it.

It was an interesting life. I enjoyed being commanding officer. I enjoyed being responsible. My ship goes where I want it to go, within orders, of course, and they're my people, I influence their future, their training, their performance. That was very satisfying to me.

Paul Stillwell: Are there any of those crew members that you remember, people who really stood out?

Admiral Trost: There were people throughout my career who really stood out. Well, Wally Bishop, who was the chief of the boat, *Scorpion*, I mentioned him as having selected him as a junior chief. He'd just made chief torpedoman.

It was people like that who really—and there was a guy, last name Smith, hard one to forget. Smith was a first-class electronics technician, reactor operator, and I don't remember which ship. I ran into him again after that ship when I had command of Submarine Group Five out on the West Coast, and he was subsequently a partner with a guy who was my aide out there, former enlisted diesel submariner. They were spooks, obviously, then. They did operations that probably fewer than 50 people in the Navy ever had any knowledge of, but very, very important and required the utmost in competence from guys who were not all that senior.

Matter of fact, my aide in Sub Group Five, Randy McWilliams, as a Navy captain, was later the naval attaché in Japan.[*] I talked to him just recently after Pauline died, and he went with a company that does a lot of spook work for the Navy. He ended up running their Special Navy Operations Group, just a remarkable guy, not a college graduate, never been to college, joined the Navy as a kid on the West Coast in the Los Angeles area, liked motorcycles, like to tinker. Joined the Navy. When I met him he was an LDO. In his career, he shifted from LDO to unrestricted line, to intelligence specialist, back to unrestricted line. Man of many talents, never got a college degree, one of the best mechanics I've ever known, and one hell of a good operator. And he was naval attaché to Japan, which is a diplomatic post, handled it very well. The satisfaction of working with guys like that and seeing them move on is really great.

Paul Stillwell: Fostering their development.

---

[*] Captain George Randolph McWilliams, USN.

Admiral Trost: Yeah, having something to do with their capability.

Paul Stillwell: What do you remember about your relationship with the CO and the alternate crew of *Sam Rayburn*?

Admiral Trost: The CO and I are different personalities. The off-crew relationship was a good one. We had a good relationship between the two.

The CO pissed me off at first meeting when he came in, and I'd just come off patrol. He didn't like the things I had posted on a little corkboard on the desk. I had a desk, bookshelves above it, and there was this area about that big. I had pictures of my family, I had a long-range schedule up there. He took offense with it, so he said, "You get that shit out of there before I relieve you."

I thought, "I don't think I'm ever going to like this guy."

Paul Stillwell: No. [Laughs]

Admiral Trost: And, you know, I didn't. Now, his son was an engineering duty officer that I got to know quite well and purely by coincidence. The son is a retired engineering duty officer at grade rear admiral. Father is a retired navy captain. He and I never really hit it off. We didn't have the same personality. We had a clash of personalities, I'd say, put it that way. So that relationship was not good. The relationship between two crews was outstanding.

Paul Stillwell: How did you keep it from coloring that in the crew's relationship?

Admiral Trost: Well, first of all, limited the time of exposure to each other, because we'd come off patrol and five days later, the other crew relieves you and starts their refit period, and you start your training, retraining, and new member acclimation cycle. I just minimized the time I spent with him. I'd give him his debrief. While I was off-crew, we were in Charleston also, and they were refitting in Charleston, so I had lots of opportunity to go up to the ship, but I stayed clear, and that's probably just as well.

Paul Stillwell: What kind of things would be discussed in the turnover?

Admiral Trost: Well, first of all, ship condition primarily, any problems we encountered operationally. That's primarily it. I had laid out on my relief the things I thought the ship needed work on, and that package was already prepared, so he had that. I had some recommendations for crew training, because we replaced about 20% of the crew each cycle, and I saw the places, some where I thought it was a little excessive in some areas where we'd have to put special attention on, that kind of business.

Paul Stillwell: Was there some kind of automatic record made of the patrol that could be analyzed later?

Admiral Trost: There is. You put in a patrol report. I don't remember what's all in it, but a lot of specifics, including material matters, recommendations on material items, any unusual communications or personnel problems that you might have had, additional training that you think is necessary, mostly equipment-specific where you feel that we're not properly supporting a particular area and need more emphasis on that. That's primarily it.

Paul Stillwell: Were there any mechanical things like tapes of where you'd been or anything like that?

Admiral Trost: Well, you have a record of where you've been, so, yeah. And the likelihood of the new crew taking it on the same route is nil. They're intentionally varied.

Paul Stillwell: One of the mechanisms in World War II on patrol reports that was that seniors would analyze them and give feedback. Did that happen with your reports?

Admiral Trost: Yeah. SP, Special Projects, would analyze their patrol and they would come out with a—not a critique, necessarily; a summary, an analysis of the patrol, with any recommendations they had based on what they read. Sometimes that goes heavily into the material area where they see all these reports, and if there's something that's a recurring problem, then they immediately take steps to correct that.

Paul Stillwell: How could you tell that you were not detected on a patrol?

Admiral Trost: Well, if you were detected, somebody would be taking action to locate you, and you can tell you're not being tracked, unless you don't counterdetect, which is always a possibility, but we have various means of knowing, including communications intercepts, whether or not our activity is observed by others, that you may have been picked up. And so far, we'd been pretty lucky.

Paul Stillwell: So you didn't get any indications that you had been.

Admiral Trost: No, and you do everything you can to stay undetected. You're very careful about contacts, avoidance of close approach to contacts. You've very careful about the periscope exposure, minimize that all the time. Usually if you detect something, instead of going to investigate, you get the hell away and widen the area. You're assigned a geographic area that is big enough to evade anything that comes in the area, unless you're dumb and expose yourself, and haven't been any of those.

Paul Stillwell: Did you have any patrols out of Rota?

Admiral Trost: No. My patrols were both out of Charleston, so I never went overseas. We deployed. Seventy days later, we came back into home port, which from a crew morale standpoint means a few more days at home, no flying overseas. We did our turnovers in Charleston, not in Rota or Holy Loch. So we had probably ten days per cycle more time in homeport.

Now, you're pretty busy during that time frame. Once you take over the ship, it's a 24-hour operation getting everything overhauled and serviced. It has to be. As I said, you have about a 20% crew turnover, so you're making sure you integrate them, and then when you go to sea for that five-day workup, see how you're set watch-wise, make sure you've got the right talent and people are doing what you expect them to do.

Paul Stillwell: What did you as the CO do during those patrols when your order was just go somewhere and hide? [Laughter]

Admiral Trost: Well, you did do something instead of going and hiding. You check on your ship and crew. I lectured, for example, on certain things. I talked about certain things, just the presentations. I sat in on crew training lectures. I inspected the ship. I walked through every four hours and talked to people. You have enough reports and things that you have to pay attention to, that you get the chance to do a lot of reading.

Paul Stillwell: What about contact with Admiral Rickover when you had that ship?

Admiral Trost: Well, first of all, write him a letter about anything you think he should know about at the end of every patrol. I had the one occasion where I had the call from his secretary saying, "The admiral wants to talk to you." I had just come off my ship after patrol. I was in the off-crew office, and we'd been off patrol maybe three days or so—well, within a week, anyway. Rose, the secretary called and said, "The admiral wants to talk to you. Hold for Admiral Rickover."

So I picked up the telephone, said, "Yes, sir." And he started chewing me out, asked me about a problem in my engineering spaces, and I told him, I said, "Frankly, I don't know what you're talking about."

And I got, "That's the trouble with you goddamned commanding officers. You don't get out of your stateroom and see what's happening in your ship. I want you to get out of your stateroom and get back to AMR2," auxiliary machinery room 2, "and then you call me back, tell me what you're going to do about it. Call me back in 30 minutes."

And I said, "Admiral, I can't do that."

And he said, "Why not?"

And I said, "Well, the ship's 90 miles at sea. The other crew's out there, and I can't get a helicopter that fast." [Stillwell laughs.]

He said, "Who is this?"

And I said, "Commander Trost."

Wham! And then 30 seconds later, the secretary called back and said, "Sorry. Wrong commanding officer."

Paul Stillwell: No kidding. [Laughs]

Admiral Trost: That was my only interface.

Oh, and he called me one time to tell me about a commanding officer who was a recreational flier and who had gone flying during his off-crew time, and, "That's a waste of time, it's a hazard to your health. You shouldn't be doing it. I don't want you doing that."

I said, "I'm not a recreational flier."

"Okay." Click.

Paul Stillwell: What sorts of things did you and the crew do during the off-patrol period?

Admiral Trost: Mostly training. We had rating-specific training or job-specific training as a group, and we had a lot of lectures, made sure everybody was up to speed on processes for emergency actions and made sure they were acclimated to the kind of environment they were going to be in, like noise, why you don't drop a wrench, and the kinds of things that can get you counterdetected. So, education and training, and you put a lot of focus on the education for advancement. There were an awful lot of lectures and ship information things as well, mission patrol procedures, operating procedure where the whole crew has to be up to speed.

Paul Stillwell: Any problems with either the plant or the missiles during your time?

Admiral Trost: We had about 99.8% missile readiness, which is really very good, and had no plant problems. Those things are tracked very carefully. Rickover tracked the plant, and SP tracked the weapons readiness. To have 98% missile readiness is considered a little low. "Why don't you have 99?" And the guys are very conscientious about that, making sure nothing wrong.

Paul Stillwell: And the abiding hope that you never have to use the system.

Admiral Trost: That's right, for sure.

Paul Stillwell: Did you wind up during the off-crew period with any recreational activities, even if they didn't involve flying? [Laughs]

Admiral Trost: Well, I spent all the time I could with my family, of course. I played an occasional game of golf, hampered by the fact that I wasn't a good golfer. Occasionally one of my contemporaries would say, "Want to go hit a few?" and do that. Really, it was mostly family oriented.

Paul Stillwell: What do you remember about family life in Charleston?

Admiral Trost: I remember that it was hotter than the devil and that we did quite a bit of sightseeing. We went to a lot of the old plantations around the area. I saw a lot of Charleston itself, went to the beaches with the kids during the summertime, and it was always hot enough during the summer. It's an interesting city to be in, and we had quite a few contemporaries down there since there was a big, big submarine presence. The surface presence was considerably less at that time. But we had a pretty good life, pretty active life centered around the kids and sports and activities they were interested in.

Paul Stillwell: Did the shipyard there in Charleston work on the submarine inventory and patrols?

Admiral Trost: No, the tenders did. We had an occasional need for shipyard work, for example, a stainless steel welder, but we had them on the tender, but they were overloaded with jobs, and shipyard was sending people up for specific jobs, and specifically stainless steel welding and some fire control system expertise that we didn't have on the tender. But by and large, the ship itself is a pretty self-sustaining thing from the standpoint of necessary talent on board to take care of the equipment, so not too much off-crew needed.

Paul Stillwell: Well, if you get a lot of good people, that takes care of it. [Laughs]

Admiral Trost: Yeah, you had good people. Those tenders at that time were preferentially manned, probably still are, so you had good talent on the tenders. They weren't short of people with talent, and so a pretty reliable group.

Paul Stillwell: That's a way for good people to get what amounts to shore duty.

Admiral Trost: Yeah, it is. It is, very definitely. Now, those guys on tenders put in the hours, and they'd have an occasional gap when the workload gets light. When I was in the short refit period between patrols, there was always at least one other SSBN alongside the tender and sometimes two. And on occasion, when the shipyard was overloaded and they couldn't take care of them, they'd send somebody up alongside the tender for specific jobs.

Paul Stillwell: Did you get any missile loadouts or substitutions when you went in there?

Admiral Trost: Yeah, we did. We did. A certain number would be pulled. I don't know anymore how frequently it was, but would be pulled for quality control and inspection. The missile facility was right there north of Charleston where the tender moored, so we were next to the experts.

Paul Stillwell: Did you go through simulated launching drills at sea?

Admiral Trost: We did. We did. You get them triggered by the way they would—you would get it if everything happened, you get the communications alert and then the message starts rolling. The regular broadcast stops, usually with a "ding, ding, ding," "Oops, here it comes." Then the emergency action message comes in and you go through the drill and keep all that information, bunch of specifics, in your report that has to be reported, make sure you're not screwing it up. It's a well very-orchestrated system.

Paul Stillwell: And it's gotten even more established or whatever with—

Admiral Trost: Yeah. I'm sure it's tighter now than when I was out there.

Paul Stillwell: With Kings Bay, that's kind of an isolated enclave, just separated from civilization mostly. [Laughs]

Admiral Trost: It really is. It really is. I will tell you, I was one of the two final examiners at Kings Bay before the decision was made to develop Kings Bay, not because of my importance, but because Warner wanted—it was his decision to make, and he wanted my eyes to see it.[*] His eyes were Charlie Ill, who was Assistant Secretary for Installations and Logistics, and me.[†] We went to see Kings Bay, Quonset Point, Rhode Island, and Mosquito Lagoon down at Cape Canaveral. Those were the three final sites. One of them was going to be the new base, so we went to all three. We kind of sneaked in. "Don't tell anybody we're here, and show us the following." It was sort of interesting, done like a spook.

Paul Stillwell: It was an Army base previously, wasn't it?

Admiral Trost: It was, yeah. It was. Quonset Point had been a naval air station, and Mosquito Lagoon was a marshy area north of Cape Canaveral that had no access to the sea, but it was marshy, and the problem with it, other than the mosquitoes, it was very aptly named, was the fact that it would require a lot of fill dirt, a channel dredging, which

---

[*] Captain Trost served as executive assistant to John W. Warner, who was Under Secretary of the Navy from 11 February 1969 to 4 May 1972 and as Secretary of the Navy from 4 May 1972 to 9 April 1974.
[†] Charles L. Ill.

was going to be some of the fill dirt, a channel dredging and through the beach, which is not easy, I guess, and a whole base built from scratch.

Kings Bay had some warehouses because it was an Army—what was it? Like if we had a NATO contingency. There was a railroad siding, some warehouses, some prepositioning equipment, and the merchant ships would pull in, load up, and haul it to Europe. We surveyed the area. We ran the channels on a tug that came from somewhere, and all this supposedly very quiet, nobody's supposed to know, so they speculate on property. [Laughter]

Quonset Point was fine except there's a bridge at Newport across the channel, and that bridge could be dropped very readily in an emergency contingency, so that's not a good place to have somebody trapped up the bay, and that ruled out Quonset. Mosquito Lagoon was just too much.

And this place had a small airfield at Kings Bay in the little town. I think it was a 6,500-foot strip or something like that, which wasn't too bad. So it had air access, channel didn't need to be deepened except in some areas, and was easily maintainable, not too much drifting in there, and the channel out to the sea was unobstructed and the shortest, except for Mosquito Lagoon. So we saw plenty of land, plenty of room for more buildings than were there then, and it looked like the best place.

We were allowed to talk to the mayor, see what kind of guy he was, was he friendly toward the Navy or not. Turns out he was. Didn't know why we were there, but knew it had something to do with something, and he wanted part of it. [Laughter]

So we came back and we reported to Warner. He used that for the basis for his recommendation then.[*] Then who was it? I'm trying to remember. There was a South Carolina member of Congress who quizzed me as part of—I guess we got called over, Charlie and I. Oh, I know what it was. As CNO, I referred to Kings Bay, before it became a missile base, as a swamp. The response was [with southern accent], "Sir, those are southern wetlands, not swamps." [Laughter]

But it was interesting. We got a good look at it, and, of course, I've seen a lot of it since then.

---

[*] Since July 1979 Kings Bay, Georgia, has been the East Coast base for nuclear-powered ballistic missile submarines.

The other thing was we needed dredging spoil room for the initial channel and for the dry dock, or docks. I forget whether there was one or two. The dredging spoils from the dry dock digging went on land that was marshy and became the golf course. And I was accused of representing the Air Force. When the Air Force builds a new base, the first thing they build is the golf course. [Laughter]

Paul Stillwell: And then an officers' club.

Admiral Trost: Yeah, so I took a little bit of gas. But we pointed out that of the available prospects it was clearly head and shoulders above the rest of them and turned out to be a very good base, well engineered. Navy Seabees built most of it. And my other concern was community relations, which had been excellent; it was a boon for the economy. It would take a while from the economic doldrums. Lots of new residents with money to spend—new schools, new activities.

Paul Stillwell: Well, one of the side benefits I heard was that a number of the officers' wives were schoolteachers, and so they brought in that quality background.

Admiral Trost: That's right. It was a real plus for the community. Matter of fact, I went down while I was CNO. I had a meeting with the community leaders, and they were the most positive people. They were just very, very helpful about the whole thing.

Paul Stillwell: I visited once to Kings Bay, and my impression was, "This is the way God would have made it if God had the money."

Admiral Trost: Or if the Air Force had built it.

Paul Stillwell: [Laughter] Right. Well, it's self-contained. Everything you need is there.

Admiral Trost: Everything is there, and it's convenient. The housing is outstanding. And my former exec in *Rayburn* lives in Groton, Connecticut, but still owns a house in

Kings Bay, because he keeps talking about retiring there someday. Now, he's class of '55, Naval Academy, so I don't think his "someday" is ever going to come. But he's keeping the house because his daughter lives here in Annapolis, and her husband is a retired submariner, hopes to go down there someday and retire there.

Paul Stillwell: Who was your exec?

Admiral Trost: Glenn Arthur.*

Paul Stillwell: What do you remember about him from the submarine?

Admiral Trost: A very good guy, very conscientious guy. He'd served as engineer during overhaul, so he knew everything about the ship. I couldn't have asked for a better guy, and we've been friends ever since.

Paul Stillwell: Anything else to remember about the *Sam Rayburn*?

Admiral Trost: No, except I enjoyed it. And I really didn't like the idea, the circumstances of a shorter command tour. I was looking for about three years in command. It was less than a year and a half. But I got promoted out of it, so I left.

Paul Stillwell: Well, let me suggest this is a convenient breaking point, and we can get ComSubLant next time.

Admiral Trost: Okay.

---

* Lieutenant Commander Glenn N. Arthur, Jr., USN.

Interview Number 7 with Admiral Carlisle A. H. Trost, U.S. Navy (Retired)

Date: Wednesday, 22 July 2015

Place: Admiral Trost's apartment in Ginger Cove, south of Annapolis, Maryland

Paul Stillwell: Well, Admiral, it's good to see you again after we've gone through a technical workshop to get all the microphones working. Last time, we wrapped up when you were about to report to the SubLant staff.[*]

Admiral Trost: That position was initially a puzzle to me because I had just eight months previously left command of *Sam Rayburn*, having expected to be there for at least two years. My explanation of how I got there is that while in command, I challenged the Submarine Force drug policy as recently issued in a directive from ComSubLant. I got a phone call from the then-N1 Assistant Chief of Personnel challenging my thoughts, and I told him why I thought what I thought and why I thought the policy was wrong.

Paul Stillwell: What was the specific objection?

Admiral Trost: As I recall, the objection had to do with the tenure of people who were drug users. I thought that the incentive to stop was inadequate. I thought the punishment was inadequate. I thought that people who were users of any kind of drugs did not belong on submarines.

As I remember and this goes back a long ways, Paul—I argued with Joe Williams, who was the chief of staff, about the contents.[†] He had the then-N1 call me and explain that we were standing to lose too many good people if we were too intolerant of drug users. I pointed out that as a commanding officer, I couldn't tolerate drug users in my crew and couldn't have a policy that appeared to be lenient towards them rather than punitive in nature, which is what they were saying.

---

[*] SubLant – Trost reported to the staff of Commander Submarine Force Atlantic Fleet, one of the fleet's type commanders.
[†] Captain Joe Williams Jr., USN. The oral history of Williams, who retired as a vice admiral, is in the Naval Institute collection.

So, having heard nothing more about that and no new policy having come out, I suddenly received orders to SubLant, and I took that as sort of "You don't agree with what we're doing, you come fix it."

Paul Stillwell: [Laughs] Did you welcome that opportunity?

Admiral Trost: I did not welcome that opportunity. I've forgotten what my orders were to be at the time. I don't recall what it was anymore.

Paul Stillwell: But you had completed a normal tour in *Sam Rayburn.*

Admiral Trost: I completed a normal tour, except that my crew was being disestablished because the *Sam Rayburn* was going into overhaul with the other crew and part of my augment crew was attached to take the ship through overhaul. I was due for reassignment at that point in time.

In the meantime, I had been selected for captain, so instead of going to another command, I was expecting other orders, but I had no idea what they would be at that point in time. So I did go to SubLant; I reported in. I had a very brief, as I recall, about a three-day turnover with my predecessor, who said basically, "It's yours. Fix it." So I took over, had a very, very good staff.

Paul Stillwell: Did you have any guidance from Admiral Schade on what to do?*

Admiral Trost: Not a whole lot, not a whole lot. My only guidance from the chief of staff was, "You're a people person. Fix the problems." So with that broad guidance, I went. Fortunately, the N1 staff was a very good group, including the N11—I guess would have been his code—the personnel officer for the Submarine Force, was a Naval Academy classmate, a Submarine School classmate as well, and a close friend, so we had a very close working relationship.

---

* Vice Admiral Arnold F. Schade, USN, served as Commander Submarine Force Atlantic Fleet from 19 November 1966 to 12 February 1970.

Paul Stillwell: Who was that?

Admiral Trost: Chuck Fellows, now a retired Navy captain.* So we had a very fine working relationship, and he was extremely competent. I'm trying to think of the limited duty officer who was the number-three guy on the staff, also very knowledgeable, been in the personnel field all his life, including as an enlisted man, and knew the business quite well, had a lot of common sense. So we took it from there.

I can't say my tour was eventful, because I can't remember much about it. I remember only that we went through all the policies, revised some, and things were going pretty smoothly when I got a phone call one day saying that I was to report about a day or two later to Washington to see the Under Secretary of the Navy. I didn't even know who the Under Secretary of the Navy was at that point in time, I don't think. And I was to report to the Vice Chief's Office. They said, "Warner is a young guy, he's a good man, he is ambitious, but he's also very conscientious, and he wants a new EA, and you've been selected to be interviewed by him."

Paul Stillwell: Before we get to that, I wonder if you could flesh out a little more the substance of the changes on the drug policy.

Admiral Trost: I really don't remember enough about it to flesh that out. I remember that my thoughts were that we were being a little bit too lenient, too flexible, when we ought to have a hard and fair policy that was stiff, that said, "We can't afford this." You can't have some guy go off the deep end while you're on missile patrol, for example. So my thoughts were, "If somebody's going to voluntarily abuse drugs, they don't belong in the Submarine Force."

Paul Stillwell: And that's a tool that you have, just disqualifying somebody.

Admiral Trost: That's right.

---

* Commander Charles D. Fellows, USN.

Paul Stillwell: You mentioned Joe Williams. He was quite a personality.

Admiral Trost: Joe was quite a personality.

Paul Stillwell: What do you recall of him?

Admiral Trost: Well, Joe started life as a seaman in the Navy, retired as a vice admiral, very professional, strong-willed, strong-minded.

Paul Stillwell: Demanding.

Admiral Trost: Demanding, demanding, intolerant of anything but perfection, and very much in charge. That's the joy, and he never changed. He was personnel oriented, but very demanding in his personnel requirements.

Paul Stillwell: Any specific incidents you recall with him?

Admiral Trost: Only the one time, and I don't remember the issue, when he called me in to chew me out about something that my organization had done, and the final words were, "All right, goddamn it, you might get away with it, but those other guys won't, so don't do it."

Paul Stillwell: Oh, gee. [Laughs]

Admiral Trost: I don't even remember what the issue was. I do remember I spent a lot of time in front of his desk. Now, when I say what I say, I don't mean to be critical. It was his way of doing business. His aims were always for the best interest of the Submarine Force, and I could never challenge that. Interesting man to work with.

Paul Stillwell: Well, he was fascinating to interview also—

Admiral Trost: I'll bet he was.

Paul Stillwell: —because of that personality, and in his quest for perfection, he rewrote the oral history twice. [Laughter]

Admiral Trost: I'm not surprised.

Paul Stillwell: What do you recall about Admiral Wilkinson, the subsequent force commander?

Admiral Trost: Admiral Wilkinson was a very positive guy.[*] I liked Wilkinson. I liked working for him, hated to leave his employ, if you call it that. He relieved Arnie Schade shortly before Zumwalt became CNO, and, of course, well known, good reputation in the Submarine Force, very professional guy.

What I recall him about him, in working for him and working with him later on, when he had an interest in something, he'd tell you what it was, what his interest was, before he asked you what you thought about it or what you recommended. So he was easy to work for in that sense. Guidance was always clear, interested in making sure everything was done right and was very clear, and a hell of a good guy to work for and with.

I worked with him later on when he was the OP-02, the Deputy CNO for Submarine Warfare in OpNav, and we became friends. SubLant was the first time I served with him. I had met him before, but never worked with him or for him. We became good friends on that tour and retained that relationship till well after he retired. I had the command later on of Submarine Group Five on the West Coast, and he had retired on the West Coast just north of San Diego. He used to come down every couple of weeks just to get updated on what was going on, and I'd ask him periodically for his

---

[*] Vice Admiral Eugene P. Wilkinson, USN, served as Commander Submarine Force Atlantic Fleet from 12 February 1970 to 28 June 1972. His oral history is in the Naval Institute collection.

input on things. Quite a nice guy to work with.

Paul Stillwell: I've seldom encountered anyone with so much self-confidence, and it was justified.

Admiral Trost: It was justified. He had a lot of common sense, and he was very professional.

Paul Stillwell: This was the era when more and more nuclear submarines were coming on. What was the balance between nukes and diesel submariners?

Admiral Trost: Oh, you've got me there.

Paul Stillwell: Not numbers, but the interaction and how you picked people for billets.

Admiral Trost: We needed both on the staff, for example, and we were getting more and more nuclear-trained guys available post command. So on the Submarine Force staff, for example, as I recall, most of the N heads, the division heads, were, at that point in time when I went there, nukes. I was the first nuclear-trained N1. I think the N3, the operations guy, was a very senior diesel boat sailor, very competent. The plans guy, I think, changed while I was there from diesel to nuclear, so it was kind of a mix. It was in transition during that time, and we had a good mix of talent. Everybody on that staff was a very talented guy and knew his field well. But you're digging in ancient history to me now.

Paul Stillwell: Was there a sense that diesel guys were in a dead-end career path?

Admiral Trost: Yeah, basically, they were. The diesel guys on the staff were looking at maybe one more promotion if they were commanders, likely to flag rank, low. Some did make it. But nuclear power was becoming, obviously, the propulsion system of choice in the future. So we were on the way to an all-nuclear force.

Paul Stillwell: In the older years, there was an opportunity for submariners to go into surface ships as they got more senior.

Admiral Trost: That's right.

Paul Stillwell: Was that still available?

Admiral Trost: At that point in time, it was. Tom Paulsen was a diesel submariner through exec. I met Tom when he had command of a destroyer, I think, in Yokosuka. The guys who were sort of the top performers as execs of diesel boats, went to a surface command, usually a DE or a DDG. Then he came to be my surface operations officer on the Seventh Fleet staff, which is a good billet and needs good talent. He left my staff on Seventh Fleet and went to command of *Blue Ridge*, which was the Seventh Fleet flagship, as a captain.[*] So that was clearly a competitive billet from a surface warfare perspective. He left that job, was headed for an LHA—or one of the big amphibs, at any rate, when I pulled him off track for that to become my EA when I became CinCLantFlt, and then I brought him with me when I became CNO, made flag out of that job, and had a cruiser-destroyer group in Charleston. I've forgotten what his other assignments were. He got other flag assignments, retired as a two-star. So he is one of the guys who surfaced and had a successful career from that point on, from continuing successful career.

Paul Stillwell: That's an excellent illustration.

Admiral Trost: Yeah, and he was not the only guy that had that happen to him. Some guys surfaced as commanders, were in PG School when Rickover selected them for the nuclear program, and so they came in the nuclear program late, usually at the executive officer level, and that was kind of a rarity, but that opening existed. I don't remember too many specifics or specific guys in that category, but there were people in that category.

---

[*] Captain Thomas D. Paulsen, USN, was commanding officer of the command ship *Blue Ridge* (LCC-19) from 6 January 1984 to 19 November 1985.

Paul Stillwell: Was Admiral Rickover involved in this drug policy you were evolving?

Admiral Trost: No, he was not. He was anti-drug usage, period, and I don't know that he was involved in what was being done down there or in the Navy's policy.

Paul Stillwell: Did you get involved in any of the other areas on the staff, other than personnel?

Admiral Trost: Yeah. We had weekly staff meetings, so, yes, I did. Things that affected the submarine force were discussed, and we all had an opportunity for an input. All the N heads had an opportunity for input.

Paul Stillwell: Was SOSUS becoming more of a factor by then?[*]

Admiral Trost: I'd say it had been a factor for quite some time. Yeah, it was quite a bit of a factor.

Paul Stillwell: You mentioned that you got the call to go be Secretary Warner's EA, and you said you got routed to the VCNO's office.[†] What happened there?

Admiral Trost: He told me that Warner was a young guy, inexperienced in defense, but a good man and very conscientious, and his EA was a very important guy to help him with things that he didn't know about and keep him on track.

I reported in to Warner's office. He got called somewhere and said, "We'll talk later. Come back at lunchtime."

So I came back to his office at lunchtime, and he said, "Let's get in the car." We went down and got in the car. We went over to Metropolitan Club over in D.C., and he

---

[*] SOSUS – sound surveillance system, a seafloor network of listening devices used by the U.S. Navy to detect noises from transiting ships.
[†] Admiral Bernard A. Clarey, USN, served as Vice Chief of Naval Operations from 17 January 1968 to 30 October 1970. His oral history is in the Naval Institute collection.

took me to lunch and we talked. I guess he was feeling me out because we'd never met before, and asked my thoughts on a number of things and said, "Well, I have an EA right now who is going to leave. If he's going to be a flag contender, he's got to get to another billet. I'll call you tomorrow and let you know my decision."

The next morning, in fact, about 10:00 o'clock, he called me and said, "You're it. Can you be here next week?"

That was sort of the story of my life—would I be there next week? So I turned over my job to my N11, Chuck Fellows, and arranged to be in Washington the following week. No place to live, no plans to move, no opportunity to get back into our house, because I'd called my realtor, and we had the place rented, and said, "I've got orders to Washington. Would you check with the tenants [who'd been there three years] and see if they'd like to move?"

The answer came back, "Hell, no." This is the guy, I think I mentioned to you, who was the supervisor for the tunnel under the Mall in front of the Capitol. He said, "I'm in the final stages of this job. No goddamn way am I going to move or be able to move. So, sorry."

Then I got a call from Charlie Ill, who was Assistant SecNav for Installations and Logistics, whom I'd met very briefly during my day up there for the interview, and Charlie said, "My family goes up to [somewhere in New England, whatever place] for the summer, and I've got a house and I'd like somebody trustworthy who'd live in that house for the next three months."

This being, I don't know, June time frame by then, so the kids were not a factor; they were out of school. He said, "When you come up, talk to me and I'll take you out and show you the place." He did, took me. It was out in Potomac Falls, which is not a poor-man's neighborhood, and there is this mansion with this circular driveway in front of it and stables next to it. We pulled around the driveway, down behind the house, pulled into the garage next to the swimming pool, and he said, "This is it."

He took me through the house, and it was it. He had four children, and each child has their own big bedroom. There is a guest suite, which Pauline and I were assigned, and each one of my four kids was told, "That's so-and-so's, that's so-and-so's. The kids will each have their bedroom."

He had a housekeeper who came in daily and took care of all the cleaning, and Pauline did the cooking. Our task was to speak once a week to the grounds guy if I had any problems. The grounds guy also took care of the two horses in the stable, made sure they were fed. So we lived in a very, very nice place for three months.

Paul Stillwell: Your reaction was, "Where can I sign?" [Laughter]

Admiral Trost: Yeah. And in the meantime, we found a place in our old neighborhood that a Navy captain friend of mine was leaving at retirement, didn't know what he was going to do, but he was going to go out to the West Coast for a while, make up his mind, and he wanted to rent his house for a year. So we rented his house actually about three blocks from the one we owned, same model, same builder, and moved into that.

Then when he made up his mind, I bought his house from him and sold the one that had been rented to those people. I got ready to leave a year later. So everything worked out nicely, and we stayed in that house. We stayed in that house and then—I'm trying to remember—went out to the West Coast, came back from the West Coast, moved back into it, then sold it and bought the one that my son's living in now. So we had a few shuffles, which doesn't make wives happy when they've got houses they're accustomed to, but we made out all right.

Paul Stillwell: Did Mr. Warner give you an indication why he had accepted you?

Admiral Trost: Yeah, but I don't want to put it in writing or on the tape.

Paul Stillwell: Okay.

Admiral Trost: He was not satisfied with my predecessor. Let's leave it at that. I can't tell you online because it's taping, but I'll tell you offline.

Paul Stillwell: Please tell me more about his character, personality, and working style.

Admiral Trost: Very conscientious. Working style, very conscious of what his area of responsibility was, worked well with people, including Tom Connolly, who was one of my heroes. Tom Connolly retired as a three-star aviator. We talked about him earlier.

Paul Stillwell: We did, yes, and TFX/F-14.

Admiral Trost: Yes, F-14. Tom liked Warner. I think they liked each other. I should say that. They became good friends. They respected each other. Tom knew he needed good support to get the F-14, and he worked hard on Warner for that, worked hard on me for that, said, "I don't know why they put a goddamned submariner in a job like this. Ought to be an aviator."

I said, "Yes, sir." [Laughter] He worked hard in educating me about aviation matters, and we had a good working relationship.

But Warner worked well. He had a lot of respect for senior Navy guys, worked well with everybody that I know of, and working relationship was good there. Good man to work for if you're on his staff. He was very considerate of his staff, except that occasionally he'd go over to the Metropolitan Club to work out about 5:00 o'clock in the evening and forget to tell us that he was going directly home from there. So there were times when we were there till about 8:00 o'clock at night wondering where the hell the boss was, till finally the driver would check in from home, say, "I'm home. I forgot to tell you guys." [Laughter] So whether that was Warner or the driver, I'm not sure. But he was, in general, a very, very conscientious guy and a very considerate guy of all the people that worked for him.

Paul Stillwell: Well, that sounds quite a contrast to the relationship when McNamara was the Secretary, with the senior uniformed people.

Admiral Trost: Oh, yeah, very different. John Chafee was the Secretary when I came in, and then Warner moved up, and Bill Middendorf relieved him, and that was a contrast in personalities and activity.* Warner got along well with both of those guys, and when Chafee left and Warner moved up, that was, I'd say, as close to a seamless transition as I've ever seen. We didn't lose any ground. We didn't have any hiccups in the process of transferring. Chafee left one day and Warner moved next door and picked up, new desk, new job. Worked out very well.

Paul Stillwell: What can you say about Secretary Chafee and his working style?

Admiral Trost: Well, not too very much. He and Warner worked closely together, and we were always—I say "we" because Warner would debrief me. We were always well briefed on what he was thinking about, what his policies were. I would say Chafee was more liberal in a lot of things than Warner was, different personalities, and difference, I think, between—I don't know if this is accurate or not, but a politician's point of view and a lawyer's point of view on a lot of issues. I can't give you any real examples here to back that up, but we got an awful lot of the "Too Hard" stuff that Chafee would say, "Look into this and tell me what you think," and I'd get some tasking, he'd take some tasking, and we'd debrief the Secretary. So it was a good working relationship.

Paul Stillwell: What was your specific role? What sorts of duties did you carry out?

Admiral Trost: Well, first of all, managing the very considerable paperwork, controlling appointments to a degree, and the scheduling, giving advice when asked, and sometimes when not asked, on topics that came up. I was expected to read everything, put what we called a "buck slip" on things that I had an input I wanted to get to him. I'd just write my own separate little handwritten memo and attach it to the paper that went in with my recommendations. Keep him out of trouble was one of my tasks. "Don't let me get in trouble."

---

* John H. Chafee served as Secretary of the Navy from 31 January 1969 to 4 May 1972. Warner served as Secretary of the Navy from 4 May 1972 to 9 April 1974. J. William Middendorf was Secretary of the Navy from 20 June 1974 to 20 January 1977.

Paul Stillwell: In what ways might he have gotten in trouble?

Admiral Trost: Well, in taking action on something that either he shouldn't have sent forward to Secretary instead of doing himself, or looking at something and not going along with his approach because of something I might know as a military officer that he would not know as a civilian with some military background.

It was a good relationship. My office was right outside of his, and the door opened frequently or the buzzer sounded if he was on the phone and wanted to talk to me. And I will say that he'd listen. You knew when you walked out whether he bought what you said or not. So it was a satisfying thing, in that professionally you knew you were being listened to. Whether or not he agreed with you or not was a different thing, but he had a responsibility for not agreeing if he didn't agree. So it worked pretty good and it was a good working relationship. As a matter of fact, people used to be surprised when they'd walk in the office and see me and he was sitting in the side chair talking to me instead of in his office. [Laughter] It would cut the initial conversation very short.

But we had a very good relationship, an easy relationship. And then that continued. When we moved next door, I moved with him. I spent about half my three years in each of the two offices, and I will say he was very supportive and also a very personable guy to work for. He'd have the staff on certain holidays, with their kids, to his place out in Georgetown or down to Atoka, down in Middleburg, and always had a very, very nice setup. When he had it in Georgetown, the swimming pool would be open. He had a house on—I think it was a corner house on—would that have been Mass Avenue? At any rate, he had a big, big house that he lived in, and then there was about a half a city block in between it and the house on the far corner, which he also had, which his wife used sometimes when she wanted to be alone. And the swimming pool was in between, big swimming pool.

Paul Stillwell: His wife at the time was from the Mellon family.

Admiral Trost: That's right. She was Cathy Mellon. She was a very private person and sometimes, when he had functions, she'd sometimes leave, move next door, stay clear. [Stillwell laughs.]

But he would often have the staff out for, as I said, the holiday things, and he invited us down to Atoka, his estate, which was a very nice place. The kids loved it because there was a barn and inside the barn was a swimming pool.

Paul Stillwell: Oh, my goodness. [Laughs]

Admiral Trost: And you could jump from the hayloft into the swimming pool. And of course you had beautiful stables. He had a couple of horses that were pretty expensive horses, I guess, and the stables were prettier than any stables I've ever been in. So it was quite a nice place, and we'd go out there. We'd swim, play softball, have a holiday cookout. It was fun. So his staff was treated extremely well.

Paul Stillwell: And that creates a lot of loyalty.

Admiral Trost: It does, it does, and he was a very loyal boss, as a matter of fact, as well. I can't say we had any problems that required that, but he was easy to work for. He was considerate of the staff, kept us cut in on what he was thinking and let people know. Very complimentary to the ladies in the office when they did a good job, and easy to work for. I'd say it that way.

Paul Stillwell: Were you involved in monitoring phone calls, scheduling appointments?

Admiral Trost: Scheduling appointments, yes, monitoring phone calls only if requested, and that was occasionally.

Paul Stillwell: How much did you get into budget issues?

Admiral Trost: Quite a bit, quite a bit. Warner was the budget guy at the Secretary for well, I shouldn't say "the budget guy." We obviously had an Assistant Secretary for Financial Management, but Warner, rather than the Secretary, normally got the decision papers. Chafee was the Secretary when I was working for Warner as the under, and he generally passed these things to Warner, who did his homework pretty thoroughly on the things. He was more programmatically oriented that Chafee was.

Paul Stillwell: Was Admiral Rickover a factor in that period?

Admiral Trost: Rickover had a good relationship with Warner. Warner was important to him to get decisions, and he knew it, and he buttered him up. Since I was the EA, I was the intermediary for a lot of messages. He talked to me like a human being.

Paul Stillwell: Both Chafee and Warner at different times served in the Senate, so they've got that gift of relating to people.

Admiral Trost: Yeah. Of course, they both went to the Senate after their Navy time.[*]

Paul Stillwell: Chafee, yes, had been a governor before that.

Admiral Trost: Had been a governor before that, right. They were both easy guys to work with, both considerate of people.

Paul Stillwell: Did Secretary Warner have an agenda, perhaps not so much as Under Secretary, but when he became Secretary?

Admiral Trost: Not as Under Secretary. He was big on readiness and preparedness as Secretary, and people. People programs were probably his top priority, and he did a very

---

[*] John H. Chafee, a Republican from Rhode Island, served in the Senate from 29 December 1976 until his death on 24 October 1999. John W. Warner, a Republican from Virginia, served in the Senate from 2 January 1979 to 3 January 2009.

good job with it. His relationship with key people on the Hill was very well cultivated. He knew the power points, the pressure points, and was very good about cultivating his relationship with them, and he did that in a number of ways, did that both with personal calls, lunch at the Metropolitan Club, which he used very often, and it's a nice tool to have. First of all, it's a ritzy club and people are honored to be invited. I got a lot of luncheons over there as a sit-in note-taker, and food was always good. Had to explain to Pauline when we had a late lunch and I'd had a big lunch and she had fixed a good dinner.

Paul Stillwell: I once was invited to give a Navy birthday talk there, and Secretary Warner was there and Middendorf, and also Will Ball.[*] So it must be attractive to Secretaries of the Navy.

Admiral Trost: Well, yeah, I think they were all members, as a matter of fact.

Paul Stillwell: Well, there's a name we must discuss, and that's Admiral Zumwalt. What do you remember about his impact in that era?[†]

Admiral Trost: In that era? First of all, I have to go back and say I knew him during my OSD tour as a commander, and he was extremely helpful. He was Nitze's EA at the time, and he and—oh, God, just died, senior aviator, three-star, everybody thought should have been a four-star.

Paul Stillwell: Jerry Miller.

Admiral Trost: Jerry Miller. Jerry was the Vice Chief's EA. Ike Kidd was CNO's EA. And between Zumwalt and those two, I had three big brothers looking out for me. Of course, I'd never been in Washington for duty, and they made sure I didn't screw up.

---

[*] William L. Ball served as Secretary of the Navy from 28 March 1988 to 15 May 1989.

[†] Admiral Elmo R. Zumwalt Jr., USN, served as Chief of Naval Operations from 1 July 1970 to 29 June 1974. His oral history is in the Naval Institute collection.

They also made sure that if I had a question, I had somebody to go to. They were extremely helpful.

My relationship with Zumwalt at that time was outstanding. My relationship with Zumwalt later had a couple of glitches. Then I found out later on when—let's see. Let me make sure I've got the right time. It was when I went to work for Warner, Zumwalt was the CNO.

Paul Stillwell: Right.

Admiral Trost: And I found out later that Zumwalt had planned on my becoming the head of his CNO Executive Panel. It was his idea to set us up with senior advisors, some really senior guys names-wise. And I can't think of them right offhand. Isn't that terrible? He wanted an O-6 to be director of that staff, which was going to be a small Navy staff, guiding the efforts and passing on the tasking that he had to these senior civilians, like Johnny Foster and one of the senior missile guys.* I worked with them all, and I can't come back with a name. I found out that he had selected me to be that guy, and when I was interviewed by Warner and accepted by Warner, that, I think, pissed Bud off, and our relationship soured at that point in time.

Paul Stillwell: That's sad.

Admiral Trost: Then later on when Warner became Secretary, I got across Zumwalt's breakers because the guys in OSD correspondence control, whom I'd worked with for three years, would send papers back that Zumwalt had bypassed the Secretary with, that had policy implications. They'd come back to me to get back on to the right route, which was via Warner, and I would send them back to Zumwalt's EA, and say, "These were returned to me because they didn't follow the path via the Secretary." And I think I was blamed for that, so our relationship was cool.

---

* Dr. John S. Foster Jr., served as Director of Defense Research and Engineering, 1965-73.

Then later on when I was CNO, Zumwalt was asked a couple times to testify before various committees on things where his views could be considered controversial or contrary to the official Navy point of view. He'd call me and say, "I'm going to testify before such-and-such committee. I'd like to send my proposed testimony over for you to okay, take a look at, make sure it's okay with your policies." So the relationship got back on track, but I think he was a little whizzed at me for things that I had no control over.

Paul Stillwell: That put you in a tough position.

Admiral Trost: Yeah, put me kind of in the middle. As I think I mentioned to you before, when I was selected for flag, the flag list had come out, and one morning he walked in through the back door between the two suites, and I didn't know he was in there. I was called in by Warner and I walked in, there was Zumwalt, who said, "Oh, by the way, the flag list came out. You just proved that anybody can make it."

Paul Stillwell: Oh, gee. Well, I hope he said that with a smile and tongue-in-cheek. [Laughs]

Admiral Trost: He wasn't smiling.

Paul Stillwell: Oh, no. [Laughs]

Admiral Trost: I was still in "I'm pissed off at you" stage.

Paul Stillwell: Oh. [Laughs] Well, I gathered that he was the deliberate choice of Secretary Chafee to get a revitalization and a younger breed in as CNO.[*]

Admiral Trost: I think that's probably true.

---

[*] Zumwalt was in the class of 1943 at the Naval Academy. His predecessor as CNO, Admiral Thomas H. Moorer, USN, was in the class of 1933.

Paul Stillwell: What is your reaction to the reforms that Admiral Zumwalt brought to the Navy?[*]

Admiral Trost: Well, frankly, I was generally in opposition. I thought too much was too lax. I was asked not to come into a briefing subsequent to one where I opened my mouth and shouldn't have. I was Warner's EA. Zumwalt was having a briefing for fleet petty officers, including chiefs, and made the comment on something he'd come out with that I thought was dumb-shit. Captains aren't supposed to have dumb-shit views of CNOs. [Laughter]

And he said, "Does anybody have any comment?"

I was sitting there as a bystander, and there were no comments. I said, "Admiral, I wonder if I can make a comment." And I did, and it was not favorable to one of his proposals.

I was called in to see him after that meeting. He said, "I want you to know you're not invited as a spectator or a commentator at my meetings," which was pretty black and white. So I didn't go anymore.

Paul Stillwell: Nothing you can say except, "Aye, aye, sir." [Laughs]

Admiral Trost: "Aye, aye, sir." He had something that struck me as absolutely stupid, but it was part of his liberalization of the fleet, and I thought there were a lot of things that he did that were too damned liberal, and a lot of things that didn't make sense from a disciplinary standpoint or from an empowerment standpoint. You don't put a seaman deuce in charge of a program because he might have something new to bring to the table. You invite him to bring to the table his thoughts, but you don't empower him to implement things that he's got no knowledge of.

---

[*] During his tenure as CNO, Zumwalt made a great many dramatic innovations that attempted to deal with such issues as enlisted rights and privileges, equal opportunity, and Navy families. Junior personnel generally viewed the changes much more favorably than did their seniors.

Paul Stillwell: Well, that was a complaint of the Zumwalt years, that you had to sort of guess at the chain of command because it wasn't adhered to.

Admiral Trost: It wasn't adhered to. And a lot of things were liberalized, too much so, including uniforms, I thought. Well, that's another pet peeve of mine.

[Interruption]

Paul Stillwell: We were just talking when the recorder wasn't running, and you mentioned that people who get selected have imperfections, but so do we all.

Admiral Trost: Yeah, so do we all. I served on one flag board and one captain's board. I couldn't find fault with anything anybody did on those boards. People are very conscientious. They recognize they're selecting the future leaders of the Navy, and they do their best. When somebody's got warts that look like they would keep that person from being a more senior performer or more solid performer, they were appropriately not selected for promotion, which is what it takes to keep a Navy young, thinking, performing. So I think this is a method that works very well. Now, could more qualified people be selected? Yeah, there are more qualified people than you have quotas to select. That's life. That's life. It's that way in every business. At least it is on the ones I served on boards for. You're lucky when you've got more talent than you have space for.

Paul Stillwell: Sure.

Admiral Trost: And the Navy in my years, in my observation, had more talent than there was room to move up, but you need that because you need good people at every level.

Paul Stillwell: My sense has been that the SecNav's Office was more reactive than proactive, but did Secretary Warner have things that he was specifically trying to accomplish?

Admiral Trost: He did, and one of them was the quality of people in the flag community, matching the right people with the right job, because there are times when the leadership, like the Secretary, doesn't know these people. There are times when he knows people and says, "Gee, I'm surprised so-and-so wasn't selected." Well, you can generally find somebody who was on that board who will give, like me as an EA, the reason the guy wasn't selected. And that's talking out of school, but not to anybody but the headmaster. So it happens.

Paul Stillwell: Did you get involved with news media any in that job?

Admiral Trost: On a background briefing basis, not very often. It would only be when Warner said, "Let me have you talk to my EA about that. He's knowledgeable." So I'd get interviewed.

Paul Stillwell: One of the things that Secretary Chafee had done in 1969 was essentially end the punishment for Commander Bucher over the *Pueblo* case.* Were there any lingering effects of that when you got there?

Admiral Trost: That was pretty well over, as I recall. My involvement—I'm trying to remember. I'm not sure when that happened now. Was it '70?

Paul Stillwell: The spring of '69 is when Chafee said he would not follow the recommendation of the court of inquiry for a court-martial.

Admiral Trost: Okay. So the spring of '69, I was off. I was in command. I got involved; maybe it was Warner or Chafee's review. I'm not sure. I remember writing a think piece, opinion piece. I thought Bucher got screwed in this way. We were not prepared with backup support because we thought the North Koreans weren't going to do anything.

---

* Commander Lloyd M. Bucher, USN, was commanding officer of the *Pueblo* at the time of her seizure. A court of inquiry in 1969 recommended that he be court-martialed for loss of the ship, but Secretary of the Navy John Chafee decided not to carry out the recommendation, saying that Bucher had suffered enough.

They didn't before, but they did then. I could fault some of his actions, but I would fault the system for lack of support, very frankly. I didn't know Bucher, never met him. He was a decent submariner, one of the guys who didn't get command, surfaced, and went to this ship command. I felt he was not supported by the Navy both operationally and then as a guy who was guilty of losing his ship. He paid a pretty heavy price for that.

Paul Stillwell: Yes, he did. Well, I think that was generally the reason for Secretary Chafee's reaction, that he had already suffered a great deal.

Admiral Trost: What was he, prisoner for a year?

Paul Stillwell: Yes.

Admiral Trost: Of course, that was it for him career-wise, and probably also—"shunned" is not the word I'm seeking, but there were a lot of people who knew him who, because of the event, were really down on him and very critical of him. There are things I would fault him for, and one was readiness for something if it happened. I don't think he was ready with a classified material destruction plan, training of the crew to execute those things. So I think that court-martial was probably warranted, but so should some sort of blame have been placed on the system for not supporting him.

Now, when I was out in Seventh Fleet, if we had somebody on a special mission in that same area, we had people in northern Japan with airplanes on hot alert ready to support on a minute's call. The guy would have had somebody within 30 minutes or less, supporting him, and that would have kept the North Koreans away from that ship. So we sent the guy into a hot area and no support.

Paul Stillwell: Another person who was in SecNav's Office in the early 1970s was Captain Stan Turner.* What do you remember about him?

---

* Captain Stansfield Turner, USN, later a four-star admiral. His oral history is in the Naval Institute collection.

Admiral Trost: Okay. Stan was in SecNav's Office, and Stan was there and left by the time I came to work for Warner. I was interviewed by Chafee for Stan's relief, and that was before the Warner interview. I told him I didn't want the job and had been an EA for three years on the OSD, and he didn't like that. Stan had recommended me, so Chafee was all set to take me. He took Thor Hanson instead.* He interviewed both of us as alternatives. Thor wanted the job, I didn't, and I didn't know I was going to come back and get interviewed by Warner. I thought I was getting free of the monkey on my back. [Stillwell laughs.]

So Chafee was a nice guy. We got along well together, and I didn't know at the time that he'd be leaving when he was. He'd have been a great guy to work for, I think. I think a very congenial man.

Paul Stillwell: Captain Hanson was a solid citizen for the job.

Admiral Trost: He was. He was very definitely, and had a good interview, apparently, and that was great, and did a good job. That's a fascinating job. You have an impact beyond what you realize sometimes, because your words can give a weight, not because of what you said but because of where you're sitting, and that can be dangerous. You have to be awfully careful, and you have to be very careful about your opinions on things, because you don't want to influence something that you have no business influencing.

Paul Stillwell: That takes a real judgment.

Admiral Trost: It does, and doesn't always say you're right. But I looked at the job as the only person that I was there to influence, if at all, was my boss, and that's because I had knowledge of something that he didn't or knew something about the subject that he didn't. I felt it was my responsibility to get him the information, and if he asked for my opinion, he'd get my opinion, but it wasn't my job to promote things or to try to overturn something that somebody who knows more about it than I do believes. And that's sort of a hard thing to do sometimes, but it's interesting. It makes the job interesting.

---

* Captain Carl Thor Hanson, USN, later a vice admiral.

Paul Stillwell: It's curious, then, that you got the call to go see Secretary Warner after you'd already said you didn't want to be an EA.

Admiral Trost: I told Warner I didn't want to be an EA, and it didn't take.

Paul Stillwell: [Laughs] Well, in retrospect, are you glad you had the job?

Admiral Trost: Yeah, I am. I am. I learned a lot. You're sitting there and you're seeing things from the top of the Navy, and I really think it helped prepare me to be CNO. I didn't think of it that way at the time, because I wasn't expecting to be CNO to start with, wasn't my goal. I do think it exposes you to the system, to the decision process and the factors that have to be taken into account when you're sitting at the top. So it was valuable, without question, and you look at things with a different perspective.

Paul Stillwell: I found that on a smaller scale when I was a shipboard officer. Your focus is very narrow. Then I joined the *Proceedings* staff, and I got exposed to the whole Navy. That was very broadening for me.

What do you remember about Secretary Laird, Secretary of Defense?

Admiral Trost: I like Laird.[*] He was decision oriented, a common-sense guy, I thought, and didn't have much personal exposure to him, but I thought he was a good man.

Paul Stillwell: And obviously had a great knowledge of how Congress worked.

Admiral Trost: Very good knowledge of Congress, very effective on the Hill, as a matter of fact, and well regarded because when he said something, they knew he knew what he was talking about, and so he was very good.[†]

I had a lot of exposure to Weinberger and liked him very much. McNamara, the

---

[*] Melvin R. Laird served as Secretary of Defense from 22 January 1969 to 29 January 1973.

[†] Laird, a Republican from Wisconsin, served in the House of Representatives from 3 January 1953 to 21 January 1969, when he resigned to become Secretary of Defense.

exposure wasn't personal; it was exposure from presence. And I was not a McNamara fan. I thought Laird did a great job. I'm trying to remember all the guys who were in there.

Paul Stillwell: His deputy was David Packard.[*]

Admiral Trost: Yeah, and Packard I had a high regard for. He and Warner had a very close relationship. Packard, on one occasion, Warner and I went out to the West Coast for something, and we were up in Packard's home area, Palo Alto. It's where his business was. He had a personal ranch out in the valley. He had a driver, and I think he was still the Deputy Secretary, and he called a conference at his ranch. I remember we were picked up at our hotel. There was a naval air station, in the town, and they had a BOQ. That's where we stayed. It's the south end of San Francisco Bay.

We were picked up and taken out to the ranch, which was yea miles to the east, and he loved that place. He was a great host, took us all around, showed us his ranch. We had a couple of R&D guys. Johnny Foster was there, and so was the Navy R&D guy. I've forgotten what the purpose of the session was, but it was business. He put us up after the first night. We spent two or three nights out at the ranch. I don't know how many bedrooms he had. I know I shared a bedroom with somebody who snored. That's what I remember. [Laughter]

I got up about 5:30 in the morning because we had a pretty busy schedule and I wanted to make sure I had all the paperwork together for Warner, and I walked out in the kitchen to see if there was any instant coffee, I was going to make coffee, and there was David Packard at the stove, preparing breakfast, coffee was already made, and he was the chef of the day.

Paul Stillwell: That's an interesting vignette.

---

[*] David Packard served as Deputy Secretary of Defense from 1969 to 1971.

Admiral Trost: Yeah. And that evening, he cooked the steaks on an outdoor fire and prepared the dinner, and there must have been about eight of us. He put on his old apron and was the duty cook.

Paul Stillwell: A human being.

Admiral Trost: Yeah. Nice guy, very pleasant guy. I ran into him again at Stanford at the Hoover Institute, which I went out for a couple of things, and he was one of the Hoover fellows. It was interesting seeing him there. Then I went out, about six years running, to the Bohemian Club summer encampment, and he came up twice to that. What amazed me was he was getting old and he was sharp as hell mentally, and, as matter of fact, gave a very fine what they call Lakeside Talk up there and made sense all the way, no notes, talked, and very astute. A great guy.

Paul Stillwell: Please tell me about the Incidents at Sea Agreement.[*]

Admiral Trost: Well, we went over and spent two weeks in Russia. All the discussion was in Moscow. We spent the weekend in St. Petersburg, which was—it wasn't called St. Petersburg at the time.

Paul Stillwell: Leningrad.

Admiral Trost: Leningrad. And that was because we out-sped or out-talked or out-negotiated the Russians, and they needed a break, and they needed the weekend to kind of get organized or resettled. We went over. Warner headed the delegation. We had a guy named Herb somebody, a three-star Joint Staff rep. We had another guy named Herb Okun, State Department rep.[†] He was at about the three-star level and stayed. We had a

---

[*] U.S. and Soviet officials signed the Incidents at Sea agreement in Moscow in May 1972. See John Erickson, "The Soviet Naval High Command," *U.S. Naval Institute Proceedings*, May 1973, pages 66-87, and David F. Winkler, *Cold War at Sea: High-Seas Confrontation Between the United States and the Soviet Union* (Annapolis: Naval Institute Press, 2000).
[†] Herbert S. Okun.

surface warfare commander, Ron Kurth, who spoke fluent Russian and had a degree from Tufts in international relations.[*] We had a three-star aviator. Each community was represented.

I was the admin officer for the delegation. I think we had a legal guy; who it was and where he's from, I don't remember. But we went over, first of all, to Copenhagen via an Air Force plane and landed because we had to change airplanes to fly to Moscow. We had to go into what they called a nondescript P-3.[†]

Paul Stillwell: No insignia.

Admiral Trost: Yeah, no insignia, no good paint job, and austere interior, and flown by a Navy crew. Where it was based, I don't know. It was based somewhere in Europe. We flew that in from Copenhagen, landed at Sheremetyevo, an airport in Moscow. We were met by a Russian group, and I don't remember who was senior in that bunch, but they had a welcoming delegation of a sort. We were taken to the terminal and processed and out the door and into limos, and went to our hotel in Moscow.

We operated out of the U.S. Embassy. And I'm trying to remember; it seems to me the meetings were all in our embassy, as I recall. We had morning and afternoon sessions. We were better prepared than they were by far, so there was a daily message back to the SecDef and to the SecState, Chairman Joint Chiefs on progress and any issues that came up. Overnight, they'd get these. It was the middle of the night in Moscow, which was workaday over here.

We had some good sessions. We had plenary sessions. Their delegation was headed by the Vice CNO, Admiral Vladimir Kasatonov.[‡]

Paul Stillwell: Did you get the sense that they were legitimately interested in having a positive outcome?

---

[*] Commander Ronald J. Kurth, USN.
[†] The P-3 Orion was a land-based Navy patrol plane.
[‡] Admiral of the Fleet Vladimir A. Kasatanov, Soviet Navy.

Admiral Trost: I think they were legitimately interested in curtailing our submarine operation. I think that was their prime goal and also finding out what we knew about their operations. They had a very senior Soviet State Department equivalent guy as the number-two guy to the delegation, to their Vice CNO, and he was clearly the guy driving what their group was doing. In addition to their Vice Chief, they had another senior military guy who I thought was probably Politburo because he was more of a politician than he was a military officer, in my view. I don't remember all the people anymore.

We had these daily sessions Monday through Friday. On Friday, Admiral Kasatonov suggested that we would enjoy Leningrad. They'd already made hotel reservations for us, and so Friday afternoon we got aboard a small Soviet military passenger aircraft and flew west. They had a hotel there—I used to remember the name of it, very well known—and put us up in the hotel, had a dinner for us there that night with some Russians from the local area, operational Russians and somebody who was State Department equivalent, and basically wined and dined us for the evening.

Next day, took us around, showed us the—what is the famous museum? And the place where the events took place in 1917, the coup or whatever you call it. The revolution started with a ship.

Paul Stillwell: The cruiser *Aurora*.[*]

Admiral Trost: *Aurora*. Didn't the crew mutiny or something?

Paul Stillwell: I think so, yes.[†]

Admiral Trost: And showed us that, took us out to the Petrograd, St. Peter Palace, and toured that. They toured us, showed us the naval base but sparingly, and poured more

[*] The Russian cruiser *Aurora*, now a museum in St. Petersburg, went into service in 1903. On 25 October 1917 the ship fired a blank shot that signaled the beginning of an attack on the Winter Palace, which had been the official residence of Russian monarchs. That kicked off the October Revolution, which was the beginning of the Soviet Union.
[†] Part of the ship's crew mutinied during the February Revolution, which marked the end of the reign of Tsar Nicholas II. Most of the crew joined the Bolsheviks, who were preparing for the Communist Revolution.

damn vodka than I've ever seen. [Stillwell laughs.] One of our guys was a junior State Department guy, who passed out at lunch, didn't make dinner because of an overload of vodka, and he was still sort of under the weather Sunday. And they did that; they'd double-team you. They'd *"Prosit!"* and *"Prosit!"* and the guy next to you would *"Prosit!"* And if you returned every one of those, of course, they were gulping it down. They're doing it once. And if you do it, you might be doing it six or seven times. So a few of our delegation had a few more than they should have. I felt responsible for Warner, made damn sure I took care of him, so I didn't respond to all of them. I responded to about three of them, and that was enough.

Sunday afternoon, they flew us back to Moscow, and Monday morning we resumed. Their delegation had met all weekend getting ready for the resumption of things. Then Friday of that second week, we had basically reached a concurrence on a draft of what we'd accomplished or what we'd agreed to, and then they arranged for Warner to call on Admiral Gorshkov, who, of course, was a legend to us and to them.[*] We went to his headquarters, and when our escort from the embassy saw the place, he said, "We thought this was a girls' school." This is the Navy Headquarters for the Soviet Union, and they didn't know which building it was in, if you can imagine.

We went inside, went up to the second floor, and Gorshkov dictated that Warner; Herb Okun, the senior State Department guy; our interpreter, who was a native Russian but working for the U.S.; and I would go in to see Gorshkov. Of course, I was happy to do that. He was such a legend in international navies. And he talked to me. He actually acknowledged my presence, and knew my background, knew I was a nuclear submariner, which I found interesting. Of course, he probably had intel on all of us.

Paul Stillwell: At least he paid attention.

Admiral Trost: Yeah. He and Warner, with an occasional input from Okun, the State Department guy, had a very good conversation, and, of course, it was all about the things

---

[*] Admiral of the Fleet of the Soviet Union S. G. Gorshkov served as Commander in Chief of the Soviet Navy from January 1956 to December 1985. He expressed his views in a series of articles on "Navies in War and in Peace." They appeared in the book *Red Star Rising at Sea*, published in 1974 by the Naval Institute Press.

we were doing that caused them concerns and why we should back off. What he really wanted was to know where our submarines were. So this was going to be as more Incidents at Sea, but submarines are blamed for the incidents. So we spent about 45 minutes with him, and he showed us on his map where he thought our submarines were.

At any rate, we had a good session with Gorshkov. Then we went back for a sort of a wrap-up session with their Incidents at Sea group. We had a wrap-up luncheon and then we flew out Saturday afternoon, came back, flew back out to Copenhagen, got in the airplane, flew back to the States. Then six months later, they came over with their delegation to the National War College, and we signed the agreement, which is still in existence, to the best of my knowledge.

Paul Stillwell: And I think it's been beneficial.

Admiral Trost: I think it has. I think it has. We had things like a Soviet Echo II, which is a cruise missile launch submarine in the Mediterranean, make a run at one of our destroyers at periscope depth, throwing a hell of a sail wake, which is not good submarining.* The submarine made what you'd have to call a normal approach course, meaning he was going to hit you. He came at that destroyer and went down after his sail was about six or eight feet out of the water and on a collision course. Finally went down and went underneath and ran out the other side. That kind of thing we wanted them to knock off. We had a number of incidents to talk about. The only things they wanted to talk about were our submarines, which I think we had one collision, and it was not an intentional collision by any means. You don't do that.

So I think the whole thing was beneficial and very good. Before Admiral Kasatanov came over to sign the Incidents at Sea Agreement, they'd had a missile submarine that we detected on the surface north of Iceland. It was a Golf class and it had topside damage.† We were unaware of what had happened because nobody of our guys

---

* Soviet Echo II-class nuclear-powered, guided missile submarines entered active service from 1962 to 1967. They displaced 5,000 tons on the surface and 6,000 tons submerged; length, 377 feet; beam, 30 feet; draft, 25 feet; speed 23 knots. They were armed with torpedoes and surface-to-surface missiles.
† Soviet Golf-class diesel-electric ballistic missile submarines were in service from 1958 to 1990. They displaced 2,794 tons on the surface and 2,820 tons submerged. Length, 323 feet; beam, 27 feet; draft, 26 feet; speed, 17 knots surfaced and 12 knots submerged. They had three missile tubes and six torpedo tubes.

said anything about it. They'd have had to report that they had a collision. And we think it was a collision with a Soviet surface ship somewhere in the North Atlantic where this guy was patrolling, and he was clearly not diveable when we saw him, but that's as much as Admiral Kasatanov would tell me. He said, "You know we sent out an escort."

I said, "Yes, I know. You sent out a submarine to pick him up first, and that submarine ran on the surface ahead of him, so it tells us his sensors weren't working."

"Yeah," he said, "that's right." [Stillwell laughs.]

Paul Stillwell: I remember that one outcome of the Incidents at Sea agreement was an exchange of ship visits. A Soviet ship visited Boston, a U.S. ship went to Leningrad. There was a subsequent article in *Proceedings*, and the title was "There is No Laughter in Leningrad." [Laughs]

Admiral Trost: That's true. That was true. Everything was business that we saw in Leningrad. Interesting place, interesting country, interesting people.

I would say that what was fun was when we had the second Incidents at Sea thing with the treaty signing, they brought along two women secretaries who were crazy to go shopping, and what they wanted was to go to Walmart and wanted to go to one other. There were two specific places that they were told were the best shopping spots, and they loaded up. They had lists of things from their friends back home, things they were supposed to buy. I'm not sure, I don't know if they traveled on an official plane or whether they—they must have, because Kasatonov was part of the delegation, along with a senior State Department guy. I wouldn't think they'd turn them loose on a commercial airline. They may have. So many details I have forgotten.

Paul Stillwell: I recently reread part of Admiral Jerry Miller's oral history when he was Commander Sixth Fleet, and he said he sent out people to get films of these collisions and near-collisions and then sent that reel in to the delegation as information and ammunition.[*]

---

[*] Vice Admiral Gerald E. Miller, USN, commanded the Sixth Fleet from 1 October 1971 to 11 June 1973. His oral history is in the Naval Institute collection.

Admiral Trost: We were well supported. The Joint Staff did a good job of getting things ready for us and helping us, and Warner did a good job of organizing the whole thing. The discussion, sequence of discussions, sequence of events was very good. And their staff was well prepared, and except for a couple of political types who were part of the delegation, the guys were professional, and it worked out well.

Paul Stillwell: Moving back to the United States, was there any impact in SecNav's Office from the Watergate scandal?[*]

Admiral Trost: I think not. Not that I recall. It pretty well stayed clear.

Paul Stillwell: You told me you got picked for flag in that job, and the backhanded compliment or comment from Admiral Zumwalt. What do you remember about your personal reaction, feelings, and those of your family about making flag?

Admiral Trost: Well, surprise, because I was in my 20th year, and you don't make flag in your 20th year, and I didn't expect to make flag at that point in time, if ever. So it was a pleasant surprise.

I was contacted almost immediately about a flag billet. I was told the options were SubMed, which was Sub Group 8, I think. Kin McKee went to that. And Sub Group 5 in San Diego, which was then SubFlot 1 and was going to change to Group Five and Submarines West Coast. I liked both ideas. I'd been to Naples and thought that was a pretty good, interesting operations job.

Then I was told, "Well, McKee made flag at the same time as you did, but he was a year senior to you before, and so he gets his choice." So he chose Med, the Mediterranean, and I chose what was left. [Laughter] It was a great tour. I was out there only a year and a half.

---

[*] In June 1972 operatives working indirectly for the Committee to Re-elect the President broke into the headquarters of the Democratic National Committee in the Watergate complex in Washington, D.C. The resulting cover-up led to the August 1974 resignation of President Richard Nixon.

Paul Stillwell: Why don't we get to that one the next time, Admiral.

Admiral Trost: Okay.

Paul Stillwell: We're near the end of the tape, but I thank you for your great cooperation today. It's very interesting.

Admiral Trost: Well, I probably told you things I won't want to see in print. But let me get that souvenir from the Antarctic and show you that.[*]

---

[*] Admiral Trost did not delete any material when he subsequently edited the transcript.

Interview Number 8 with Admiral Carlisle A. H. Trost, U.S. Navy (Retired)

Date: Wednesday, 29 July 2015

Place: Admiral Trost's apartment in Ginger Cove, south of Annapolis, Maryland

Paul Stillwell: Admiral, we finally got the machine set up, and we're ready to go. Last time when we were together, you talked about your selection for flag rank, deep selection, and then you went out to command a submarine group.

Carlisle Trost: Submarine Group Five.

Paul Stillwell: Were you frocked as a rear admiral in that job?*

Admiral Trost: I was for about the first year.

Paul Stillwell: That's good for wearing insignia. Not so good for pay.

Admiral Trost: Good for wearing insignia, and I had mess specialists in my quarters, so that was good. Just didn't get paid for it.

Warner had a little ceremony in his office. My kids, my wife and my in-laws were invited. Then, all of the sudden Admiral Weisner, who was the Vice Chief, walked in. I was going to get frocked; I was going to get my shoulder boards pinned on. About 15 minutes after Weisner arrived, I felt a little bit uneasy; we were not being very polite to him. So I said to Warner, "Shouldn't we get on with it?"

One more person came in. It was Rickover, who walked in about a half hour late, which was fine. He nodded to everybody and said, "Let's get on with it. Came time to pin my shoulder boards on my summer whites. Pauline put on one of my shoulder boards and gave me a kiss. Rickover took the other shoulder board, put it on the other side, and said, "Don't expect me to kiss you." [Laughter].

---

* "Frocking" a naval officer refers to the practice of allowing him to wear the insignia and assume the title for which he or she was recently selected. The officer does not receive the pay for the higher rank until a vacancy appears on the lineal list so he or she can be officially promoted.

I said, "I don't." Then he became very cordial with my in-laws, talked to them like old friends, and then said, "Well, I'm going." and left.

Paul Stillwell: What a neat memory.

Admiral Trost: Yeah. Well, that was interesting. It blew Pauline's mind. She just couldn't believe it—after all the things she had heard about him. He had a sense of humor.

Paul Stillwell: Occasionally.

Admiral Trost: Occasionally, yeah, and it was usually wry.

Paul Stillwell: Please tell me about your priorities and your agenda when you took up that job.

Admiral Trost: We were in the process of shifting SubFlot 1, which was the predecessor command, which was my command for about five days.[*] Then I transitioned to Submarine Group Five. My job was Sub Group Five/SubPacRep West Coast.[†] If it came within a couple hundred miles of the West Coast, it belonged to me operationally. Ships in Mare Island, ships in Seattle, and occasionally submarines being repaired in Long Beach were mine. I was responsible for them, and was responsible for submarine operations off the West Coast, reserve and regular training. I had a reserve group that worked on our floating dry dock, did overhaul work on my ships. So I had sort of a mixture of people and talent. Interesting job.

Paul Stillwell: Did you have operational control?

Admiral Trost: I did, yeah, operational control I think out to about 800 miles or something like that, for control basically of ships that were on trials, doing workups, getting ready for deployment, that kind of thing.

---

[*] SubFlot 1—Submarine Flotilla One. Trost took command in June 1973.
[†] SubPacRep – Submarine Force Pacific Fleet representative.

Paul Stillwell: Who had operational control of the ones that were deployed?

Admiral Trost: SubPac.

Paul Stillwell: That's sort of the way it was in World War II. Pearl Harbor ran the show.

Admiral Trost: Yeah. He was still the boss. I had opcon for anything operating, as I said, within about 800 miles of the West Coast, which really covered the areas where we did our training workups and got people ready to deploy, basically.

Paul Stillwell: What was your relationship vis-à-vis Commander Third Fleet?

Admiral Trost: It was relatively little except coordination. We coordinated with them for forces available for workups, for pre-deployment workups, and things of that nature.

Paul Stillwell: So then the taskings on deployment would come from SubPac, and where would the input come for that? Like this one's going on an intelligence mission and so-and-so.

Admiral Trost: It came from SubPac directly to me or my staff.

Paul Stillwell: What do you remember about working with the dry dock and the shipyards on repair and overhauls?

Admiral Trost: It was interesting. I spent most of my shipyard time in San Francisco. Hunters Point was still active. Hunters Point was finishing work on a couple of U.S. diesel submarines that were being transferred to the Japanese.* They were getting overhauls. I was responsible for them until they were turned over to Japan. Mare Island

---

* San Francisco Naval Shipyard operated until 1974, when it was inactivated and renamed Hunters Point Naval Shipyard.

worked primarily on our ships, including increasingly nuclear submarines.[*] And I had ships in overhaul in Bremerton, had a submarine captain there full-time.[†] His job was operational, to the extent of getting his ships in, monitoring what was happening to them, and then the workup for pre-deployment when they came out.

So I was required to be at Mare Island and Bremerton about once a month, and, again, monitoring status. It was my ass if they didn't get pushed along. We had a senior captain operational at Mare Island as well as at Bremerton. So I had a senior guy there who was really our pusher guy for SubPac through me, make sure that work got done and monitor, and he was also responsible for the scheduling of workup for getting out of the yard, getting the ship back in operational shape.

Paul Stillwell: And I'm sure Admiral Rickover continued to be interested . . .

Admiral Trost: Oh, yes, he did.

Paul Stillwell: . . . and worked through the reps in the shipyards.

Admiral Trost: He had his senior reps in each one of the yards except Hunters Point, because those were diesel boats and they weren't going to stay with the U.S. Navy. As a matter of fact, I think Hunters Point closed while I was out there. It might still have been open, but the workload was going down quite a bit. And they had done an overhaul on one surface ship, a big one—I forgot what it was—and that was not my responsibility.

Paul Stillwell: Well, Hunters Point did a big rebuild on the *Midway* back in the late '60s, early '70s.

---

[*] Mare Island Navy Yard, Vallejo, California, began operation in September 1854. It was the Navy's first shipyard on the West Coast. Shortly after World War II, the title was changed to Mare Island Naval Shipyard. It was decommissioned in April 1996 as the result of the Base Realignment and Closure process.
[†] Puget Sound Naval Shipyard, Bremerton, Washington.

Admiral Trost: Yeah, but that had been finished. I'm trying to think whether they were carrier repair capable. I seem to think they were, because we had several carriers operating out of Alameda, and I think they did their repair work at Hunters Point.

Paul Stillwell: Did Admiral Rickover have any communication with you in that period?

Admiral Trost: Yeah, he had a lot of communication with me, whenever he wanted it.

Paul Stillwell: What was the nature of it?

Admiral Trost: Well, it was interesting. My predecessor told me, "First of all, I live on the hill on Point Loma, and my tenders and my submarines and my deep-submergence group are all right down there. I can see them on the other side of the trees from my house." He said, "I always try to get in at 5:00 in the morning." That was to our headquarters ship, our flagship. It was one of the two tenders I had out there.

I said, "Why?"

"Well," he said, "it's 8:00 o'clock in Washington, and the admiral's at work, and so you never know when he's going to call."

I decided my working day started at 7:30, and all I had to do was walk down the hill, and a block away was my flagship. So I got in at 7:30, and in the year and a half I was out there, I never got a call in the morning. I got my first call after I'd been out there about six weeks. We were required to report to him once a month about what was going on. I'd been out over there a month. There was nothing unusual going on that I thought should have his attention, so I didn't write a letter. And after about six weeks or so on the job, I got a call from him. The first one I had about 9:00 o'clock in the morning, by the way, and he said, "I haven't heard from you."

I said, "I haven't had anything to tell you."

Phone slammed down.

Got a call from the active duty Navy captain who was—there's a billet for a guy like that—working over in headquarters, who said, "Listen, if you don't want to get in trouble, you'd better write him a letter."

I said, "I don't have anything to tell him." They've got guidelines out on what you're supposed to tell him. I didn't have any of those things happen. I didn't have any problems to discuss with him.

He said, "Well, you might want to do it anyway."

So at the end of the second month, I wrote him a letter and told him there was basically nothing to tell him, had no problems, no support needed that I didn't get. I talked with his guys, even though they were retired Navy, were civilians, super grades, who were his mechanic guys, electrical guys, reactor guy, and I talked to them periodically when we had something going on.

One of these guys called me, I don't remember which one, who said, "You might not have anything to tell him, but tell him something, because he likes to check off that he's heard from you guys." [Laughs]

Matter of fact, it was in that time frame that I met Bill Bass, who lived here until he passed away about a year ago, I guess a year, year and a half ago.* Bill was Rickover's mechanical guy, class of '48 Naval Academy, and he was the guy I had most of the interface with, because in getting people ready to deploy, mechanical things that came up were usually in his bailiwick.

To give you a story, for example, one of my SSNs was due to deploy. On Friday afternoon, my ship repair people and the crew found a leak on a high-pressure drain valve. This is a full reactor systems pressure drain. They're stainless steel. It's a complex valve with a stainless steel cap that is seal-welded in case the internals leak and the water would get out. The valve is located in the forward machinery space just aft of the reactor compartment.

So we had a leak. We couldn't isolate it, couldn't stop it. The only solution was to replace it. That meant cutting it off and welding a new one in place. Before you could cut it off, you had to depressurize the primary system and put what they call a freeze seal on the pipe coming out to where this valve was. The valve's about that big around, the cap is—

Paul Stillwell: Two or three inches.

---

* Commander R. William Bass, USN (Ret.).

Admiral Trost: Yeah, and about that long. So we had to freeze seal, but we had to have a new valve, because it was leaking and there was no way to repair it. So about 4:00 o'clock on a Friday afternoon, I called Bill Bass, told him what my problem was. "I need a valve, and this guy is supposed to deploy at 7:00 o'clock Monday morning."

"Let me call you back."

So I sat back down at my desk waiting for the call. He called me about 7:00 o'clock in the evening—now, this was West Coast time, so it was three hours later in Washington. He said, "Have somebody meet flight so-and-so tomorrow morning, 7:30, and there will be a valve on board," and told me how it would be packaged and labeled.

We did that. The valve was there. We got the valve. By Sunday morning, we were putting a pressure test on everything, re-pressurized the primary plant, checked the valve. Didn't leak. Seven o'clock on Monday morning, the guy reported, ready to deploy.

I tell you that story because it was indicative of the kind of support you got from that organization and the people. They didn't make excuses, didn't chew you out for having a problem that they had to work on over a weekend. They'd just fix it.

Paul Stillwell: And that's a great story to illustrate the point.

Admiral Trost: Yeah, it really was outstanding.

Paul Stillwell: So didn't you have both SSNs and SSBNs?

Admiral Trost: No SSBNs. I had ten SSNs at the time and ten diesel boats in two squadrons, but they were mixed, and I had the Deep Submergence Group for the West Coast for the guys who go down deep and do things. It was an interesting group. We had two tenders. We had a floating dry dock, three piers, one of them being a deep submergence pier. The Deep Submergence Group is a separate group. Interesting job. You didn't get bored.

Paul Stillwell: Please tell me more about the deep submergence.

Admiral Trost: Well, these were the guys that had the little boats that—how do I describe them? They're mini subs, basically, and they could go pretty deep, and they could go to the bottom in most parts of the world and check out things that you wanted to find, they could have been used. We also had the rescue chamber out there and supporting organizations for those guys. So that's about all I can tell you, really.

Paul Stillwell: Who handled the logistic support and so forth for the missile boats, the boomers?

Admiral Trost: They were at the time deploying out of Guam, and homeported in terms of support in Hawaii, in terms of mechanical support for overhaul in the shipyard at Bremerton, and later on, I think, Pearl Harbor started picking up some of that.

Paul Stillwell: Then the Bangor base came later to take on the support role.[*]

Admiral Trost: Bangor base came later, yeah. That came after I was out there and then, of course, they took over.

Paul Stillwell: What can you say about the quality of the work in the tenders?

Admiral Trost: Well, the quality of work was quite good when I was out there because we were manned preferentially. We had the necessary talent to be a nuclear support facility, and since both squadrons had nukes, both my tenders were nuclear support capable, so we had a lot of capability out there. And we had our own floating dry dock, so we could dock a ship if it needed under-hull work or things that required that it be docked to be worked on. So it was a pretty flexible organization.

---

[*] On 1 February 1977 the SSBN base at Bangor, Washington, was officially activated. For a pictorial and description, see Jim Davis, "Building the Tridents' Home," *U.S. Naval Institute Proceedings*, March 1979, pages 62-73.

Paul Stillwell: Did you have any connection with the USS *Dolphin*, the small diesel boat?[*]

Admiral Trost: Yeah, and I'm trying to remember how much. My aide, Randy McWilliams, came from being *Dolphin*'s engineer, for example.[†] He retired as a Navy captain, his last job having been naval attaché in Japan, of all things. He was at times in his career an enlisted machinist's mate, a limited duty officer, engineer of *Dolphin*, aide to me and to my predecessor as well. As an LDO—I'm trying to think—he had a couple different designators. He had an intelligence designator at one point in time because of assignments he got. He was an unrestricted line guy as a captain, and, of all things, attaché to Japan, where he did a hell of a good job.

Paul Stillwell: That's an impressive career.

Admiral Trost: It was quite an impressive career. I talked to him just recently after Pauline died, and he went with a company that does a lot of spook work for the Navy. Randy came from the Los Angeles area, was a kid with motorcycles on his mind, and had a couple scrapes, one leg that was banged up and a shoulder that was banged up from accidents he'd had on the motorcycle. He rode a motorcycle to and from work when he worked for me. He also restored old cars in his spare time and used to get his upholstery repair work in Tijuana, down across the border, and he knew a couple of people down there who did such things. They did a beautiful job.

He, at one point in time, having had another accident on his motorcycle, and at his wife's request, decided to buy a car. So he bought an old '32 Ford coupe and tore all the old rotten upholstery out, took it down to Tijuana, had it reupholstered, totally overhauled the thing, and drove that car as his daily back-and-forth-to-work car. Whenever he wanted to get rid of a car, he had people literally lined up to buy it from him, because

---

[*] USS *Dolphin* (AGSS-555) was commissioned 17 August 1968 as a deep-diving experimental submarine. She was 151 feet long, 20 feet in the beam. She had a top speed of 10 knots surfaced and 7.5 knots submerged. She went out of service on 22 September 2006 and was decommissioned 15 January 2007. She was the last diesel-electric submarine in U.S. Navy service.
[†] Lieutenant George Randolph McWilliams, USN. He was a limited duty officer with a specialty in submarine engineering and repair.

they knew the car was mechanically perfect and he did such a nice job in fixing them up. So, interesting guy. I had some interesting people working for me.

Paul Stillwell: I made a visit to *Dolphin* and it struck me how cramped it was inside, and it had the ability to go deep and to test new equipment. Was that essentially the mission?

Admiral Trost: That's essentially what it was, yeah.

Paul Stillwell: How does a flag lieutenant help the admiral? What things does he do?

Admiral Trost: Well, keeps him out of trouble, first of all. His job is to help the admiral have the time to focus on the prime job and not worry about the things of distraction. He takes care of some of the outside stuff, like the official visitors, the schedule, the social functions that need scheduling, making sure that I know when to go and I know I have to reenlist somebody or I know I have to do something with the ship, and schedules my rides on ships so that I keep up with my job. I had to go to sea. I've forgotten what the time was. I think I had to go to sea once a month, which was easy because I rode the ships in workup for deployment, and I had a lot more days at sea than I had to have, and that was also to keep your sub pay current. I think that was the prime reason for it, but also it gets you out to see what your people do and what life is like.

For example, I rode one ship on its workup for deployment and decided that when they got home from deployment, they were going to have a new skipper because of what I observed on the ship. The skipper's, I'd say, behavior in general was not what I expected. He yelled at people, had three of his senior officers in the wardroom awaiting their okay to get out of the Navy, and crew was unhappy, morale was poor.

So you ride for lots of reasons. I know that one reason came about when I saw the third letter of resignation cross my desk, and it was clear something was wrong on that ship, and it was. For fitness report purposes you have to rank your skippers, and the best way to do that was to go to sea with them and watch them. So I had to get out, and besides that, I wanted to.

So it was a busy assignment, it was satisfying, it was a fun assignment in many respects, because you got to know your people, you got to know your skippers, and you got to know the crews, not individual names, necessarily, but the caliber of the crew and sense of morale, professionalism.

Paul Stillwell: That's what the Navy is for.

Admiral Trost: That's what the Navy is for. That's right. That's right.

I was going to say with the different units you get a good flavor for other across-the-board readiness issues, because I had both tenders and when they went to sea, about once a quarter, I would ride one of them every time they went out. Of course, there wasn't a conflict, because one of them had to stay in anyway. And I had one or two rescue vessels. I guess I had one regular ASR.[*] Of course, the dry dock we didn't ride except when it got moved, which was from this pier to that pier, not too far. So the nice thing about it, it's variety. You don't get bored, and you get lots of different challenges and opportunities to do things. So I think it was one of the best jobs I ever had.

Paul Stillwell: Did you have squadron commanders as subordinates?

Admiral Trost: I had two squadron commanders.

Paul Stillwell: So they probably did the first cut on the fitness reports.

Admiral Trost: They did.

Paul Stillwell: What do you recall of your relationship with Admiral McMullen at ComSubPac?[†]

---

[*] ASR – submarine rescue ship.
[†] Rear Admiral Frank D. McMullen, USN, was Commander Submarine Force Pacific Fleet, 1972-75.

Admiral Trost: I think it would be described by saying from him to me, "You got it." He set the tone and the policy and we talked periodically, but not much. My periodic visit out to Hawaii for updates, he'd get the group and squadron commanders out there about once a quarter and go through policy changes, talk about what he wanted, talk about what he was happy with, what he was unhappy with, and sort of state-of-the-force-type of sessions. Didn't hear from him too often. Touched base with him when I had something to talk to him about.

Paul Stillwell: Remember anything about his personality, working style?

Admiral Trost: A little bit gruff but not with me. Something of a perfectionist, I'd say, but that's not unusual in the nuclear Navy.

Paul Stillwell: No, not at all. [Laughs]

Admiral Trost: Really didn't see much of him. Well, he'd come periodically to the West Coast and visit, and we'd host him. I know he liked to play ping-pong, because Bill Johnson, who was my chief of staff, lived in the end row of eight sets of quarters and had room on his porch for a big ping-pong table.* So we used to have ping-pong tournaments. I think it was Frank McMullen who put his arm through a window on the side of the porch, going back to swing at a ball that was driven hard, and put his arm right through it. Didn't hurt himself; very fortunate.

Paul Stillwell: I'll say.

Admiral Trost: We had glass all over the place. [Laughs]

So we had some good times. We had good social interface. The couples who lived all on the base were Pauline and I, my chief of staff, who was a former squadron commander, the Development Group commander, and Squadron Three commander. We had Mac McKenzie, who was in a surface billet, and I'm trying to remember what Mac's

_____

* Captain Willard E. Johnson, USN.

job was.[*] He wasn't the senior captain in San Diego. Any rate, we had a senior compatible group up there, wives got along, husbands worked together and got along, and so it was quite—oh, I know, one of the tender COs was up there. So it was people who were associated professionally in most cases, except for the one surface captain who was just put there because it was available O-6 quarters and he needed quarters. And we got along quite well together. We had a lot of social interface with the people, saw them all the time.

Paul Stillwell: You mentioned the reservists earlier. How much did you deal with them?

Admiral Trost: I needed engineering support when we got the floating dry dock, and I asked for billets. None available. I asked for support from the 32nd Street Naval Station, which was surface support, not only predominantly, almost totally, and they didn't have the extra support to provide.

So I checked on the reserves and found there was a reserve group that was from Long Beach, and they were ship repair. So I invited their boss—I think he was a commander in the reserves—down to lunch one day during the week, told him what my problem was, what I needed. He said, "I've got guys like that. We'd love to have the task. I keep trying to find things for my guys to do."

Paul Stillwell: I'm sure that's right.

Admiral Trost: So we invited him and his entire group down the following weekend. They all came down, and there were quite a few people. I think he had brought something like 50 guys down for the first visit, and they looked around. They looked at the floating dry dock, which was in a state of disrepair. So before I started docking nuclear submarines, I had to fix the damn dry dock. He had guys who knew something about floating dry docks, and one chief who was a hoss. He worked on floating dry docks, I think, almost since World War II. So they looked, they decided, yeah, they could handle most of the things I had there that needed doing. All they needed was somebody to

---

[*] Captain William W. McKenzie Jr., USN.

authorize them to do it, and I've forgotten what route I took to get them, but I got them assigned, and I had my own reserve group, and these were the guys who not only fixed the floating dry dock, but then manned it.

So they did the dock. They did a lot of the under-hull repair work. I think my tender guys did the equipment repair on board. So we had a bunch of happy campers because they were being utilized, being used in something that they knew about and were talented in respect to the equipment and all. So that was my reserve contact. I don't think that group ever got over about 75, but we utilized a lot of reservists, mostly from the Long Beach-L.A. area. They were happy. I was happy. My tender COs were happy because they had augmented talent that they didn't have in house, and so it worked out well.

Paul Stillwell: Sounds like a great case of need meeting opportunity.

Admiral Trost: It was purely by accident, too, because I met that commander by accident, and he was a go-getter.

Paul Stillwell: I remember when I was in the reserve, and when we would get opportunities to augment regular units, that was much more meaningful.

Admiral Trost: Yeah. Well, it's interesting, I heard from this guy—and if I could put my hand on the letter right now, I'd get it. I heard from this guy, who's no longer active, obviously, but this commander heard that Pauline had died, wrote me a letter. He had met her out there. Well, she'd had him to dinner a couple of times. I haven't heard from him in 40-50 years. This was in the early '70s, when we're talking about, so it was a long time back.

Paul Stillwell: Those bonds stick.

Admiral Trost: Yeah.

Paul Stillwell: What was the role of the ships that you had the operational control of—training, providing services?

Admiral Trost: Mine was training readiness, workup for deployment, so the full gamut of what you might have to do on deployment, making, obviously, approach and attack kind of stuff, but equipment readiness, tactical readiness. I worked them up. I supplied them when they hit Hawaii and got their operations assignment and kept going west. So we were the kickoff, and they went from there.

Paul Stillwell: Did they provide services for ASW exercises?

Admiral Trost: Yeah, yeah.

Paul Stillwell: What do you remember about family life when you were in that job?

Admiral Trost: In that job it was pretty good because I went to sea when I had to. I don't mean to say being driven to. I'm saying when I had to it was workups and going out with the tenders, for example, and seeing how things were going on them, because when they went out, they went out for about a week, as I remember, and when they're going, you have to go and take advantage of the opportunity.

They were scheduled very carefully, because with 20 submarines and a Deep Submergence Group, it takes real schedule juggling sometimes, but I had a good staff. And that was the other thing that was lucky: I had good people. My staff commanders were all former COs, and I had both nuclear and diesel COs because we had both kinds of ships. The materials guys, for example, the head repair officer was a nuke. His number-two guy was a post-diesel command guy, and we had lots of work there too. I had a guy who had been the electrical officer on another tender. All submarines had batteries. All submarines had electrical systems. So we had a real mix of things. My chief of staff was a former nuclear CO and nuclear squadron commander, my ops officer was a post-SSBN commander, and my weapons officer was post-SSN command. I had a very experienced staff. It was a good group.

Paul Stillwell: Any names that pop out that you want to speak to?

Admiral Trost: I'm trying to think. Bill Johnson was my initial chief of staff. Bud Kauderer, who was later a senior submariner in the Navy and a classmate of mine, came out as the CO of my tender, my flagship.[*] The CO of the other tender was post-SSBN command, even though most of his support work was diesel boats, but he did have a couple of nukes. So we had a mixture talent-wise, but when I think back on it, a relatively senior bunch and experienced bunch at the commander level, for example. They were guys with a lot of command experience, and made my life a lot easier.

Paul Stillwell: So they had gone through a lot of screening already to get to that point.

Admiral Trost: Yeah. Yeah. And we were pretty independent. My staff had the responsibility for the things in Mare Island and the other shipyards, so we had guys traveling up and down the coast quite a bit. As I said, I went to Bremerton at least once a month, Mare Island at least once a month, and the Hunters Point was an as-required type of thing. Went into Alameda, but really there to assess repair capability in case we had to divert somebody in there that would normally be based there, because it was basically a couple carriers operating out of there at the time. So the needs varied, but it was still my load. If it went in there, it was mine for repair work. So it was an interesting job.

Paul Stillwell: I visited the old Mare Island yard a couple years ago, and it's almost a ghost town.[†] It's so sad.

Admiral Trost: Oh, it is sad. It was a very capable bunch of people, capable workforce. They were quite good.

---

[*] Captain Bernard M. Kauderer, USN, commanded the submarine tender *Dixon* (AS-37) from 17 August 1973 to 23 May 1975.
[†] The Mare Island Naval Shipyard closed in 1996.

Paul Stillwell: And they built some nuclear submarines there.

Admiral Trost: Oh, yeah, built them, overhauled them, refueled them.

I met future President Reagan up there when he was governor. I got a call one day from McMullen saying, "Got a call from Washington [which meant Rickover] and the governor wants to visit a missile submarine.* We've got *Thomas Edison*, which has just come around from the East Coast to go into overhaul at Mare Island. And I'm worried because Bill McAree is the junior SSBN skipper in the fleet."† He was selected for commander, in command as a lieutenant commander. And he said, "He doesn't have a lot of time in under his belt, so I want you up there when the governor comes, because the governor wants to see *that* submarine, because that submarine fits the description of what he's interested in."

So I said, "Okay." So I hopped on a plane the next morning, got to Mare Island about 10:00 o'clock in the morning, and Reagan showed up about an hour later, I guess, and I greeted him. I was just another fixture there. I was also to accompany him through the *Edison* and then through his tour of the shipyard, so I did. Very congenial guy, very good with the troops. God, he talked to everybody, good politician, and would pause in between and ask me or the skipper questions, and listened while we answered, which impressed the hell out of me, because most guys do this cursory thing and don't understand it either. But he had a good tour and then he had lunch in the shipyard, but that was focused more on the workers, even though I was invited to the luncheon. That was my first meeting with him, and he remembered that when he was President after I became CNO. He said, "I remember that time in Mare Island when we toured the yard together." And I said, "Yeah." So, interesting guy.

Paul Stillwell: That's a great gift for a politician.

Admiral Trost: Oh, yeah.

---

* Ronald W. Reagan served as governor of California from 1969 to 1975.
† Lieutenant Commander William B. McAree II, USN.

Paul Stillwell: Well, back to San Diego. Did you get involved with the community there, make public speeches?

Admiral Trost: Quite a bit, quite a bit. For some occasions, I was the senior guy because I was the junior guy. [Laughs] Bob Baldwin was AirPac.[*] He was the senior military guy out there, and the mayor and the city council met with us periodically, like every couple months, and they met more frequently with him.

One occasion was when Prince Charles was visiting the West Coast as a naval officer.[†] He was a Navy lieutenant. They had a big function up in Los Angeles, a formal dinner for him. Being the junior flag officer, I got the privilege of staying behind in San Diego and minding the store while the other flag officers went up there. So we had an interesting time. We stayed behind and made arrangements for the Prince coming to San Diego. Jim Watkins was designated to be his host. I don't know what Baldwin was doing, but Watkins had also been up in Los Angeles for the formal dinner with him, was hosting a reception at the air station's club, which was quite a good club at that time.[‡] I don't know if it's still open now. But they had this reception for Prince Charles, who got a glimpse of one of Jim Watkins's daughters, and really tumbled.

Paul Stillwell: Laura, I think her name is.

Admiral Trost: Laura. It was Laura. It was Laura.[§] I think that reception took place before our group came back, because I hosted that. I was flag host for that reception, and Pauline and I were the designated parents away for Watkins. So we were in the line, and Laura Watkins stood in the receiving line with us when the Prince came through. And you could see him kind of—eyes popped wide open.[**]

---

[*] Vice Admiral Robert B. Baldwin, USN, served as Commander Naval Air Force Pacific Fleet from 31 May 1973 to 12 July 1976.
[†] Charles, Prince of Wales, is heir apparent to become King of the United Kingdom.
[‡] Rear Admiral James D. Watkins, USN, was then Commander Cruiser-Destroyer Group One. He later served as CNO from 1982 to 1986.
[§] Now Laura Jo Watkins Kauffman.
[**] Laura Jo, then 19, and Prince Charles, 25, met in San Diego in March 1974. He was then serving in HMS *Jupiter*.

That night, we got a call—and I've forgotten just how this worked. There was a complaint about a prowler on North Island Air Station where the Watkins's quarters were. The prowler was Prince Charles, looking for Laura Watkins's home. [Laughter] So we had that minor little incident. I'll never forget that.

Paul Stillwell: Well, I remember they were linked in the media for a while.

Admiral Trost: They were. He invited her to come to England, and she did go. And we were told that the fly in the ointment there was the fact that she was Catholic and he's Church of England, and so that cut the ties very early in the relationship. But it was the Rumor Central for all the wives out there at the time.

He was a very congenial guy, and he kept saying, "Now, you'll have to excuse me, but you know I'm only a Navy lieutenant." Well, yeah, only a Navy lieutenant. [Laughter] The whole town kind of tumbled over his presence. He was a very easy guy to do business with. I shouldn't say "to do business with." I didn't do business with him, just to talk to and to host, very interested in everything, had questions about everything he ran into.

Paul Stillwell: Now he is in his upper 60s and he still hasn't had his real job yet. [Laughs]

Admiral Trost: That's right. That's right.

Paul Stillwell: What sorts of things would you talk about in these public appearances?

Admiral Trost: Well, I was asked to do things like "Why is the Navy doing this? What does the Navy plan for San Diego?" Which really meant I was past my pay grade, but I'd have to get the information and talk to them. The city government was always very interested in what the Navy had planned and what the impact would be on them, and they were generally pretty easy to work with. Sometimes these were just sort of update briefings on what was happening. "We came in from a fishing trip last weekend and we saw such-and-such out at Ballast Point," which is a sub base. "What are you guys doing out there?"

On one occasion, we were cleaning up a mud-hole-filled parking lot and getting ready to repave, that's what we were doing out there. "Why were the trucks and tractors doing out there on the weekend?" That was why they were out there.

So something from the mundane to real business, and, of course, they were always very interested in projects that would bring revenue into the area.

Paul Stillwell: It's a pro-Navy town, so it wasn't a hard sell.

Admiral Trost: No, it wasn't. It wasn't. And we had good business community and Navy League support. The head of the Navy League was a banker, and I thought I'd never forget his name. He was very supportive. We had a great relationship. He was the president of what was, I think, the biggest bank in San Diego, but I don't remember what that was either. They were very, very supportive of almost everything. All they asked for was, "Keep us cut in on what the Navy's going to do out here, so we know, so we can plan accordingly." And their plans were, obviously, they wanted to make money from anything that happens, but they really didn't want to be blindsided with things that they would then have to provide support for, and not knowing what the hell's going on was a negative.

Paul Stillwell: But planning would certainly be useful in that context.

Admiral Trost: Yeah. And they were very good. They had golf tournaments, invited the senior flag officers. Didn't invite me because I didn't play golf at that time. I've maybe played four games in my life. [Laughs] And went out a lot on boats. My friend the bank president had his own 40-footer and invited us out for cocktails and dinner and cruise the harbor in the evening. Very pleasant. And his brother lived on a boat at the San Diego Yacht Club, used to invite us over, stag parties only, on his boat for drinks, and sometimes his favorite new honey, but when he did that, the wives were invited.

Paul Stillwell: Did you have any interaction with the naval district commandant?

Admiral Trost: Not much, no, because we were pretty independent in terms of our operations.

Paul Stillwell: There was a book that came about the submarine operations during the Cold War called *Blind Man's Bluff.** What were your reactions to that book?

Admiral Trost: First of all, annoyance, and let me tell you why. The author and his wife, actually the coauthor was his wife, different name.

Paul Stillwell: The author was Chris Drew.

Admiral Trost: Yeah, it's Chris Drew, but Chris's wife, when she worked for the *Chicago Tribune*, was it? Anyway, I think she was the coauthor on the thing. I knew Chris. He had asked to interview me about this book, and I declined because he wanted answers to things that were really still classified. He wrote things that were classified, as a matter of fact. And what annoyed me about the book was unbeknownst to me at the time it happened, he was standing behind my shoulder at a function and heard me talking to a skipper of one of the ships, and he quoted me as if I'd been interviewed by him, which caused me a lot of heartburn, frankly. Didn't get me into trouble, because I didn't say anything I shouldn't have, but it annoyed me. So I refused to sit down for an interview with him, and I'm not sure he didn't get even with me.

Paul Stillwell: Did you remonstrate with him after it was published?

Admiral Trost: Yeah, I did, and to no avail. I was annoyed by the book because the book really had a lot of things that were still classified, and some of the people talking to him

---

* Sherry Sontag and Christopher Drew, with Annette Lawrence Drew, *Blind Man's Bluff: the Untold Story of American Submarine Espionage* (New York: Public Affairs, 1998).

were doing so just to kind of enhance their status, I think, or their image. So it annoyed me, but we all have to make money, I guess.

Paul Stillwell: I talked to Admiral Larson, and he was pleased by the fact that neither he nor any of his crewmembers talked.[*]

Admiral Trost: And that was fortunate, because Drew tried. He tried. And later on, we had a first-class ET, as I recall, who was on Chuck's crew, who got quoted, but he was out of the Navy when he did it, and, to him, that was excuse enough.[†] But he talked about things he shouldn't have. Whether that hurt is hard to tell. I think it helped the Russians. First of all, it confirmed what they may have suspected but couldn't confirm themselves, and that was the danger of it. That was the cost of it.

Paul Stillwell: You were talking about people who were trying to trumpet their deeds, and I think there was sort of an idea of "We did great things that nobody knew about," they wanted to get it out there.

Admiral Trost: Yeah, but the reason we could do a lot of them is because nobody knew about it. Chuck Larson and his ship worked for me. I was his reporting senior and I was cleared for his program, but I didn't have much to do with it. Matter of fact, I had nothing to do operationally with it except to make sure I had a submarine that was properly maintained at Mare Island and did things.

Paul Stillwell: Any observations about Chuck to offer?

Admiral Trost: He's one of the most competent people I've ever worked with. I knew Chuck quite well. I met him about the time he transitioned from aviation to submarines

_____

[*] Admiral Charles R. Larson, USN (Ret.).
[†] ET – electronics technician. As a commander, Larson was commanding officer of the nuclear submarine _Halibut_ (SSGN-587) from 1973 to 1976. The ship was involved in highly classified intelligence work.

and got to know him quite well, hold him in very high regard. He was a very, very bright guy, very dedicated, conscientious guy, a good man.[*]

Paul Stillwell: Anything else to say about that submarine group job?

Admiral Trost: A couple of personnel sidelights. Jim Stockdale and I were selected for flag at the same time and both went to San Diego on our first flag billets.[†] He used to sit on my front steps over at Ballast Point, the sub base. He and Sybil were at our quarters one night for dinner, and we had a big old house the Army built at the turn of the century up on the hillside. I think there were five sets of flag quarters up there. He came in. We had the end one, and steps going off the front porch down to the street, another set of steps down to the ground level, and I could walk out. He came over that night and we had cocktails out on the screened porch. He said, "This is the most restful place I've ever seen."

So one morning, it was about a week later, I guess, I walked out my front door on my way to work during the week, and there he was, sitting on the top step. He lived over in North Island quarters, so to get there, he had to either drive through Coronado out and around or take a boat across to our landing and walk up there. I don't know which he did; never did find out. But he was sitting there. I said, "What are you doing?"

He said, "Thinking."

I figured he did a lot of that in his time over there as a POW. And after that, it was not unusual, but once or month or so I'd see him sitting out on my front steps, thinking. I don't know how long he stayed. I had to go to work and he had to think. So we used to have him over about once a month, because he liked that location, peaceful. Quite a guy.

Paul Stillwell: Did he share with you some of the things he had reflected on when—

---

[*] Admiral Larson died 26 July 2014.

[†] Commander James B. Stockdale, USN, eventually a vice admiral, was a prisoner of war in Vietnam from September 1965 to February 1973. He was subsequently awarded the Medal of Honor for his heroism while in prison. His wife Sybil was active in publicizing the plight of prisoners in Vietnam and calling for more humane treatment than they had received from their captors. He was Ross Perot's running mate in the 1992 presidential election.

Admiral Trost: Not too much. He was thinking. What was his—wasn't philosophy or morality or something like this. At the time was he at—

Paul Stillwell: He had studied the Stoics.

Admiral Trost: That's what it was. It was the Stoics, and he gave me a short dissertation on stoicism one time, and I said, "Jim, I don't know what the hell you're talking about." That's the last time he tried. [Laughter]

But they used to come over about once a month, either on a weekend for a cup of coffee or during the week for dinner, and he was really a great guy, just liked him, a man of integrity. I was thinking those guys in Vietnam were very fortunate to have him as a leader. His self-sacrifice was very considerable, physical sacrifice, and the mental load on him must just have been immense. He was a man of character, dedication. He was sly, the things he did to embarrass to Vietnamese without their even knowing what was happening. So he did an awful lot, probably eased the burden on a lot of those guys who were over there who otherwise would have been maltreated even more.

Paul Stillwell: And just serving as an inspiration.

Admiral Trost: Yeah. Another person there at the time was my good friend Jack Henrizi, who made commander with no college.[*] He was a second-class gunner's mate in *Robert A. Owens* when I reported in. I told you earlier what a great job he did in cleaning up the sub base. When I got out to Sub Group 5, I had a weak-kneed LDO commander as my base CO, and the base was shitty. So I thought, "Gee, I really wish I had a guy like Henrizi, one of these guys." So I called him, and he liked the idea.

Then I called his CO and said, "I'd like to steal Henrizi." So he agreed to let Henrizi go without squawking too much, and so I got Jack as my base CO. In four months' time, I got all the parking areas paved instead of mud holes. I got the BOQs and BEQs cleaned up, and they needed it. They were relatively new buildings that had never

---

[*] In 1973 John T. Henrizi was promoted to lieutenant commander as a limited duty officer in the ordnance specialty.

had any maintenance. He was just a great leader. And from being the shithouse of the group out there on the base, his guys started becoming the leaders of the base on cleanliness and discipline and so forth. He did a great job.

But there were guys like that that sort of made your day every time you're with them, around them, just great people. And I've lost track of his wife. I don't know if she's still alive. She used to stay in close touch with Pauline, and last time I heard from her was about three years ago, got no response to letters and things, so don't know if she's still around.

Paul Stillwell: Well, from SubGru 5 you moved on to BuPers.* What was your job there?

Admiral Trost: Assistant Chief for Officer Programs, and other than controlling the detailers who control the officer community, I was given the task of downsizing the officer corps post-Vietnam. It had grown by a considerable amount. I don't remember the exact number anymore. For some reason, 7,400 seems like a very high number, and that's what sticks in my mind. I remember we had to take really drastic steps to meet the demands for cutting the size of the force. The first thing we did was release involuntarily all Naval Reserve lieutenants and junior. It was the first three officer grades. If they had reserve commissions, even if they had applied and wanted to go regular, we sent them home. But it was a terrible thing to do, because we gutted some ships by getting rid of four officers from the wardroom of a destroyer, because they were reservists lieutenant or junior, and we just wiped out the wardroom strength. So it was a bad thing to be doing. But that was my first job as Assistant Chief of Personnel. I didn't feel very proud of my actions, but had no choice.

Paul Stillwell: That was draconian.

Admiral Trost: That was draconian. It was the only way we could meet the very, very severe cut that was levied on us. Anybody who had a resignation or retirement request in

---

* Rear Admiral Trost reported to the Bureau of Naval Personnel in December 1974 to serve as Assistant Chief for Officer Development and Distribution.

that was being held because either we needed them or whatever, was automatically let go. Screened lieutenant commanders and commanders whose performance was deemed to be substandard, poor in any way, were sent home.

We had one case that sticks in my mind. I think he was a CEC officer, JAG Corps, or he might have been an intelligence guy.[*] I was approached by the detailer for this commander who was not going to make captain, obviously, who was a substandard performer in his current billet, whose skipper wanted to get rid of him but couldn't, and who has been asked to retire and wouldn't. So the detailer said, "Well, what can I do?"

I said, "Well, find out where he doesn't want to go. He's in Guantanamo right now."

They went through the back door and found out the guy said one day, "Boy, the one place I'm never going is Adak."[†] Adak has had that plus or minus reputation for years. The people who serve there love it. And I can tell you a personal story about that, confirming that.

So I said, "Call this guy and tell him you have a new billet for him. He's going to Adak."

Within two weeks, we had a message request for retirement from this guy. [Laughter] And we granted it. We didn't do that to very many people. We did it through a little bit of housecleaning effort.

And we stopped our reserve. We stopped guys who were called to active duty who were deferred for some reason, like coming out of college and they were not available right now because of an advanced degree or something. We didn't call them in, didn't bring them on active duty. So we did things that were harmful and counterintuitive from the Navy's perspective, just in order to make numbers. I think that was the worst part of that job.

The interesting thing about it was being able to shape certain parts of the officer corps that were sort of out of bounds after Vietnam.

Paul Stillwell: For example?

---

[*] CEC – Civil Engineer Corps. JAG – Judge Advocate General's Corps.
[†] Adak, Alaska, part of the Aleutians chain, is an island in the Bering Sea.

Admiral Trost: Well, I can't remember specific things, but we'd have some specialties where we had built up a specialty expertise, in some cases by calling reservists with that background involuntarily to active duty. Now they were on active duty and we'd tell them, "You have to go home." That's not too good for morale, it's not a way to run an officer corps, but it's something you had to do. Congress controls the budget, and the budget controls what you have to do. So that was a distasteful part of the job.

The good part of the job was being able to influence what happened to people from a detailing standpoint, being able to get rid of some deadwood that should have been gotten rid of a long time ago, either because the detailer or the community sponsoring it didn't want to bite the bullet and say, "Yeah, because they'll point to me and say I'm the guy, and I don't want that to happen." Well, that was life.

So it was a job I enjoyed, even though I had it only about a year and a half, I guess a little less than that.

Paul Stillwell: December '74 to January '76, so only a little more than a year.

Admiral Trost: A little over a year. I came back from San Diego to that job. The reason for the short touring was that I was called by Holloway, who was CNO, one day.[*] He said, "Rumsfeld [this was Rumsfeld's first time to be SecDef] is going to be the SecDef, and he wants a senior military assistant, who is a flag officer who's been in OSD before.[†] There are three guys, Staser Holcomb, you, and Bill Read."[‡] We were all two-stars. "He's going to interview and select one of you." Well, I didn't want to go back to OSD. I had spent three years down there, and I wasn't anxious to go down there. He said, "So sit tight." This was probably in the October time frame before I went to OP-96 in January. And one day in I think it was January, would have been whatever year it was—

Paul Stillwell: Seventy-six.

---

[*] Admiral James L. Holloway III, USN, served as Chief of Naval Operations, 29 June 1974 to 1 July 1978.

[†] Donald H. Rumsfeld served as Secretary of Defense from 20 November 1975 to 20 January 1977.

[‡] Rear Admiral M. Staser Holcomb, USN; Read Admiral William L. Read, USN. The oral history of Read, who retired as a vice admiral, is in the Naval Institute collection.

Admiral Trost: Okay. It was about January, I get a phone call from Admiral Holloway on the phone, no yeoman, Jim Holloway in person, saying, "Could you come see me at 10:00 o'clock?"

My philosophy always was if the CNO wants to see me, it's convenient for me to come see him. So I got a car ordered at the Navy Annex and went over to the Pentagon, reported in, and about ten of 10:00, his prior meeting broke, and he brought me in and said, "I want you to go back and turn your job over to your EA," who was a guy named Al Herberger, "and come over and relieve Staser by 1600 today as OP-96, Systems Analysis Division."*

In the meantime, having been called over, I thought, "He's calling to tell me I'm going to work for Rumsfeld," so I was in the real "Oh, shit" mode. And got over there, so I had time to relieve Staser by 1600 so he could go down the next morning and report in to Rumsfeld's office. So that's how I left the job.

I guess I must not have been smiling when I left Holloway's office, because he said, "Does that make you happy?"

I said, "No, sir, but I'm relieved." [Laughter]

Staser and I actually had part of our turnover driving home from the Pentagon that night. He left his car there and came in with me the next morning because we lived about two miles apart out in Potomac. So we talked for about an hour in this car on the way home, didn't drive that long, but the last part of the turnover took place in his front yard.

Paul Stillwell: And he was a classmate, so you'd known him.

Admiral Trost: He was a classmate, yeah. I'd known him a long time.

Paul Stillwell: He was a real congenial person, from my experience.

Admiral Trost: He was a very congenial guy.

---

* Captain Albert J. Herberger, USN.

Paul Stillwell: Talking about BuPers, that release of lots of officers came about five years after there was another personnel cut. That was in '69, and that was when I got sent home. I was given a choice to extend for two more years of sea duty or go home to grad school. So I said, "I believe I'll take that grad school," and that's when I met my future wife.

Admiral Trost: Oh, great.

Paul Stillwell: So fate is interesting.

Admiral Trost: Well, you know, one of the other guys, while I was in PERS-4, that I was directly responsible for keeping or getting back in the Navy was Tom Lynch.[*] Tom was a lieutenant commander. His resignation had been accepted. He went out and worked for two months, didn't like it, and said, "I made a real mistake."

I don't remember the name of the flag officer that Tom had worked under who called me, and it was a friend of mine. I just don't remember the name anymore. He was a two-star surface warfare guy, and he called me and said, "Do you know Tom Lynch?"

Well, I knew Tom Lynch's name from football days. I said, "Yeah, he played with Staubach."[†]

"Yeah, that's the same guy." Told me the background, said, "He wants to get back in, but the deadline—." And I don't know the specifics of this anymore, I never did really find out, but apparently there was a deadline by which he had to apply to come back in if he wanted to come back in. The deadline was approaching, and his chain of command had been very slow in processing his paperwork. And he said, "He's got to be back in the Navy, accepted back on active duty within—," I think it was ten days or something like that. "Can you do anything about it?"

"Well," I said, "yeah, we can." So I reviewed his record, and he was a superstar on paper. And everybody who talked about him said, "Oh, that guy's great. We ought to

---

[*] Lieutenant Commander Thomas C. Lynch, USN.
[†] Roger Staubach, who won the Heisman Trophy in 1963 and graduated from the Naval Academy in 1965, later played professional football for the Dallas Cowboys from 1969 to 1979.

get him back."

So I talked to CNP, who I think was still Dave Bagley.[*] He said, "Get him. Get his signature on the paper. Get the paper and walk it through SecNav." So we did that, and we got him back in the Navy with three days to spare.

Paul Stillwell: Wow. [Laughs]

Admiral Trost: And Tom did quite well until he got himself in trouble at the Naval Academy.[†]

But it's an interesting job. You do things. Sometimes you had to depart from the normal way of doing business to get it done, but it worked pretty well. It was a satisfying job. One of the things that really satisfied me was Al Herberger, who was Merchant Marine Academy grad.[‡] That's the way he came in, a surface warfare officer, very fine record. Bill Read was my predecessor at PERS-4. Bill said he was the finest naval officer he'd ever met. As an EA, he had no peer. He was just good. He worked with people extremely well and counseled countless people and did a good job at that. I found out that because of his status, he had a reserve commission and he was a Navy captain, which I thought was sort of odd, but this category, for some reason you maintain a reserve commission, and I found out you retired as a captain, independent of your performance. And I said, "That doesn't make sense. I want to keep this guy."

Oh, and the other thing was that his retirement date was the next month. I said, "Bullshit. I'm PERS-4. I'm supposed to control distribution." So I called in the people who knew about this thing, and they explained it all to me and why I didn't have a hand in it, wasn't under my control. I said, "*All* officer assignments are under my control. I know that because I got the piece of paper that tells me that."

---

[*] Vice Admiral David H. Bagley, USN, served as Chief of Naval Personnel from 1 February 1972 to 10 April 1975.

[†] Rear Admiral Lynch was superintendent of the Naval Academy from 15 June 1991 to 1 August 1994. In April 1994 Secretary of the Navy John Dalton ordered the expulsion of 24 Naval Academy midshipmen as the result of widespread cheating on a compromised electrical engineering examination. It was the biggest cheating scandal in the history of the institution; the investigation lasted 16 months and essentially cost Admiral Lynch the opportunity for further promotion.

[‡] Albert J. Herberger graduated from the Merchant Marine Academy at Kings Point in 1955 and became the first graduate of that school to become a Navy vice admiral

So I talked to Bill Read. I said, "Bill, did you know anything about this?"

He said, "Never heard of it. They never mentioned it to me."

So I got it changed. It wasn't a law; it was a policy. I talked to the CNP and said, "Here's the situation. I want to cancel that requirement and keep this guy." So he kept him. Of course, he didn't do very well. He retired as a three-star.

Paul Stillwell: You say that with tongue-in-cheek. [Laughs]

Admiral Trost: I do.

Paul Stillwell: I think he became head of the Maritime Administration after that, didn't he?

Admiral Trost: Yeah, he did. He did.[*] Did a great job, been active in the Navy League of the United States, been on the board. He's done lots of things. I see him once a year. He came down to see Frank Donovan, who commanded MSC during the Gulf War.[†] Frank and Al were big buddies. Frank's gone now.[‡] But we found the place for the Donovans two blocks down from ours at Sandbridge, and Al would come down and spend about three or four days every summer down there, and we'd get together for dinner twice. We stayed in contact. But he's a superstar, just a hell of a great guy.

You find all sorts of dumb things by accident, dumb rules and dumb regulations, and some of these things were made—nobody could tell you why that rule exists. Why was this one group of graduates in this special category expected to leave active duty as captains with no promotion, irrespective of their performance level?

Paul Stillwell: So sometimes common sense has to intrude.

---

[*] As a retired vice admiral, Herberger was administrator of the U.S. Maritime Administration from 14 September 1993 to 30 June 1997.

[†] Vice Admiral Francis R. Donovan, USN, served as Commander Military Sealift Command from March 1990 to August 1992.

[‡] Vice Admiral Donovan died 4 May 2014.

Admiral Trost: You're right.

Paul Stillwell: I interviewed Admiral Read, and the word that sticks in my mind for him is "enthusiasm."[*]

Admiral Trost: Oh, enthusiasm. He had a reputation of being a hardass. I made my first midshipmen cruise on USS *Haynsworth*, straight-stick destroyer, his first duty station, class of '49. So he'd been commissioned one year. That was summer of '50. And Ensign Read, I think he had the deck division. He was a hotshot, got a reputation for being a damn good ship handler and very sharp, very much by the books, and very much in danger of being thrown overboard if he walked the deck at night. [Laughter] This I was told by a first-class petty officer. "If we get that son of a bitch on deck, he's going over." [Laughter] Because Bill was by the book all the way. But, boy, he was a hell of a good naval officer and, you're right, very enthusiastic, everything by the book.

Paul Stillwell: And not only did he work with Secretary Rumsfeld, but he was with Elliot Richardson briefly during Richardson's time.[†]

Admiral Trost: I didn't recall that.

Paul Stillwell: He was with General Goodpaster also.[‡]

Admiral Trost: Could have been. Could have been. Very competent guy, I know that.

Paul Stillwell: This is so interesting, because I've just been looking at his transcript lately.

Admiral Trost: I just wish I could remember more details.

---

[*] Read's oral history is in the Naval Institute collection.
[†] Elliot L. Richardson served as Secretary of Defense from 30 January 1973 to 24 May 1973.
[‡] General Andrew J. Goodpaster, USA, served as NATO's Supreme Allied Commander Europe from 1 July 1969 to 15 December 1974.

Paul Stillwell: Well, you've pulled out a lot of them. There was the story that Admiral Larson told me about he was the XO of *Sculpin* during the Vietnam War, and they had a patrol in which they escorted either a Chinese or North Vietnamese weapons trawler all the way up to Hainan Island, around to the Gulf of Thailand, and then passed the word on to a South Vietnamese destroyer that blew it up. And he was able to get that declassified, so we printed it in *Naval History Magazine.*[*] I think he said a lot of the old patrol reports had been destroyed.

Admiral Trost: I was trying to think. Harry Mathis, who was on my staff in San Diego, came to Washington when I was OP-96, the Systems Analysis Division.[†] I think he went into 02 or 06, but what I remember is sketchy. We needed somebody to be our Tomahawk action officer who knew the Pentagon, who knew the acquisition processes, and who was a hot runner.[‡] They'd been given Harry's name, with no prior Washington background. I've forgotten whom he was going to work for, but whomever he was going to work for said, "I can't use this guy." It was a fellow flag officer, and he was told to see me. I'd written a couple years' worth of fitness reports on this guy. He said, "Is this guy any good?"

I said, "Yeah, he's very good."

"Is he a flag contender?"

I said, "A contender, but not necessarily a shoo-in because of his background, but he's nuclear trained, he's a submariner, and he's a real damn good officer."

"Well, we'll take a chance on him. If he doesn't get really lined up the first couple weeks, we'll just shit-can him and get somebody else."

Okay. Harry and Mary. Anyway, he took over really without a boss knowledgeable in the field, and sold the program and got along beautifully with the people in OSD and the people in Joint Staff. I'll never forget that. He did a great job. I

---

[*] Charles R. Larson, Clinton Wright, and Paul Stillwell, "The *Sculpin*'s *Lost Mission*," *Naval History*, February 2008, pages 28-35.

[†] Captain Harry L. Mathis II, USN.

[‡] Tomahawk is a long-range cruise missile that entered the fleet in the early 1980s, capable of delivering either conventional or nuclear warheads. Originally conceived to have both antiship and land-attack versions, the antiship type is no longer in service. The original guidance system relied on the missile matching its course with the terrain below its path. Navigation now is guided by satellite.

think he might have been skipper of *Sculpin*. I thought he had *Sculpin* about that time frame, and it would be about the right seniority level. I'm not sure of that. But he also told me the story, but that's why I associated him with *Sculpin*.[*]

Paul Stillwell: You mentioned Admiral Bagley as Chief of Personnel. What do you recall about him?

Admiral Trost: Well, first of all, I'm trying to remember when I first met him. I think I met him when he was the Under Secretary's executive assistant when I was in OSD. I'm positive of that, because he was relieved by Bob Long, working for the Under Secretary when I was in OSD.[†] He was one of my big daddies. I had some good parental guidance. He was there. Zumwalt worked for the Secretary of the Navy, Ike Kidd for the CNO, and Jerry Miller for the Vice Chief, and those four guys kept tabs on a new commander down in OSD who has relieved a new rear admiral who's been there for three years and was an aviator. So they were watching me very carefully and were very helpful.

Paul Stillwell: I guess you passed the test.

Admiral Trost: I passed. But that's how I got to know Dave. Matter of fact, I went to BuPers from Sub Group 5 because he asked for me specifically for that job. So we had a good relationship.

One thing that would tell you what the relationship was, we were in this carpooling mode when I was in PERS-4, and Dave was the Chief of Naval Personnel. So I was carpooling with Jim Sagerholm and Jim Hayes, two friends of mine.[‡] We lived within a couple blocks of each other. Jim Hayes was in OSD. Sagerholm was in OpNav somewhere, and so we had roughly equivalent hours, except Dave Bagley. I've forgotten whether he had lost his wife or they didn't live together, one or the other. Dave came in

---

[*] Commander Mathis was indeed the skipper of the *Sculpin* during the Vietnam War mission described in Admiral Larson's article. He later retired as a captain and had a post-Navy career that included service as a San Diego city councilman and deputy mayor.

[†] Captain Robert L. J. Long, USN. The oral history of Long, who retired as a four-star admiral, is in the Naval Institute collection.

[‡] Captain James A. Sagerholm, USN

early and left late. Because a couple times before my wife joined me, he invited me out to have dinner with him, and he and the mess person were the only people in the house. It was very quiet, but we had a very quiet dinner and we'd do business. He gave me some guidance and got opinions and all. So I got to know him even better as PERS-4.

Well, one day we had the morning lineup at 8:00 o'clock, I guess, with the PERS heads, and he started off the meeting by saying to me, "I called you last night at 6:00 o'clock."

I said, "Yes."

He said, "You weren't there."

I said, "I wasn't there. I was on my way home." I said, "Remember, we have this carpooling thing which we're urged to do, and two other guys and I who are friends of mine, both Navy captains, and I carpool, and it wasn't my week to drive, but I got picked up, I think 5:30, quarter to 6:00."

"Hmm."

Next day, same thing. "I called you and you weren't there. See me after the meeting." He said, "Goddamn it, I know you're getting everything done, but when I call you, I want to talk to you."

I said, "Do you want me to tell these guys we're not going to carpool anymore?" I said, "I'm violating *your* guidance about carpooling." [Laughter] So I got exonerated.

Paul Stillwell: He could call earlier. [Laughter]

Admiral Trost: And he never called me anymore at 6:00 o'clock.

Paul Stillwell: That was in the era of the fuel embargo.

Admiral Trost: Fuel embargo, that's right.

Paul Stillwell: Well, other than the long hours, what about his leadership of the bureau?

Admiral Trost: Leadership was very positive, very hands-on. I thought he did a great job. He had a lot common sense, and he took a personal interest in flag detailing, making sure that he had the right guys in the right place and was meeting CNO guidance. So I think he did a hell of a job. Everybody, the flag officers who were there working for him were very satisfied and settled. I was trying to think who some of the guys were. Bill Read was one of them. Joe Metcalf was one.[*] Wes McDonald was one.[†]

Paul Stillwell: That's a talented group.

Admiral Trost: It was a talented group, and it was a group accustomed to doing the job without a lot of hands-on help, and he handled that pretty nicely. He recognized the talent he had. Of course, he had the key to the strongbox, so he got what he wanted, and he put a lot of stress on operational background of his PERS heads. So we were all guys who'd had a two-star command and successful in that way. Matter of fact, every one of us went on to be three-stars, and Wes obviously went to four, and Metcalf retired with three.

Paul Stillwell: Metcalf is another that I would associate with the word "enthusiasm."

Admiral Trost: Oh, yeah. Oh, yeah. He and I served together a couple of times. I'll tell you, he was fun to work with, really fun to work with, and he was the right guy. We had this issue in Grenada with the Cubans trying to move in.[‡] He was just the right guy with the right sense of balance to be the Second Fleet at the time, because he basically came up with a blueprint on what to do before anybody higher up had any idea what they were going to do, and by acting early, he got the jump on the Cubans.[§] The reason we lost some SEALs down there was outside political interference rather than mistaken operator decisions. Those guys were put in a situation where they were pre-doomed because of

---

[*] Rear Admiral Joseph Metcalf III, USN.
[†] Rear Admiral Wesley L. McDonald, USN.
[‡] In October 1983 the United States mounted a joint-service operation to occupy Grenada in the Caribbean after a Marxist military coup overthrew the island's government. The overthrow and subsequent developments led to concern about the safety of approximately 1,000 U.S. citizens on the island.
[§] Vice Admiral Joseph Metcalf III, USN, commanded the Second Fleet July 1983 to September 1984.

poor planning.

Paul Stillwell: When he was OP-03, he preached the surface warfare doctrine up, out, and down.

Admiral Trost: I believe it.

Paul Stillwell: And that logo wound up on his tombstone as well. [Laughs]

Admiral Trost: He was quite a guy.

Paul Stillwell: Admiral Bagley and Admiral Zumwalt went way back, even before the Naval Academy.

Admiral Trost: They did.

Paul Stillwell: So he would be involved in Admiral Zumwalt's personnel issues. Did that emphasis lessen when he left? Admiral Watkins came in.[*]

Admiral Trost: Watkins came. Watkins had a very strong controlling hand on what went on, very much hands-on. I'm trying to think. I don't recall too much changing, because Watkins had been in BuPers, he'd been in PERS-42, submarine side of the house, and knew BuPers well and knew a lot of the people, including a lot of the senior civilians, which could be a real plus. Watkins worked with the CNO. Watkins—well, I shouldn't say this. I will say he looked over his shoulder a lot more than Dave Bagley did. Dave did it and said, "Here's what I did." Watkins checked out and made damn sure he wasn't at cross breakers with the CNO, which is smart anyway.

We had a pretty good bunch. We had our periodic flag conferences, and I found them very useful because you got other people's input on things that you said, "I did

---

[*] Vice Admiral James D. Watkins, USN, was Chief of Naval Personnel, 10 April 1975 to 21 July 1978.

this." Sometimes you wonder, "Did I really take the right tack on this?" That was a good way to sound out other guys whose input you respected on what they would have done. We worked pretty closely together, as a matter of fact.

So that was an enjoyable job but cut short, but I was glad for the background, particularly helpful later on when I was CNO. It was helpful to know how that system worked, because the CNO spends an awful lot of time—I figured one time I spent up 10 to 15% of my time on flag matters, and knowing the system, not having to get educated on how it worked helped. And knowing some of the facts and knowing some of the billets and what the demands of those billets were was helpful.

Paul Stillwell: Admiral Zumwalt had upgraded Navy recruiting to three stars. What do you remember about your relationship with the recruiting command?

Admiral Trost: Not a whole lot, to tell you the truth. I'm digging in my memory. They stood pretty independent. Was Emmett Tidd CruitCom?* I think he was.

Paul Stillwell: Yes.

Admiral Trost: He had total control. I think that sort of got dissipated a bit. They still had a lot of power and a lot of say, and my relationship with the Recruiting Command was more with the recruit training centers and their proper funding than anything else, except we made sure that Recruiting Command got talented people because they needed talented people. That's about as far as current memory takes me.

Paul Stillwell: Everybody wants the best people.

Admiral Trost: Yes, it really does.

---

* Vice Admiral Emmett H. Tidd, USN, Commander Navy Recruiting Command (CruitCom), 1972-75. He began the job as a rear admiral and was promoted to vice admiral in 1974.

Paul Stillwell: It sounds like you were more managing the supply you had than bringing in a new one.

Admiral Trost: That's really true.

Paul Stillwell: What do you remember of your work with detailers?

Admiral Trost: Well, I had a lot of work with detailers, both setting policy, making sure that policy was executed, talking to warfare sponsors, getting their input on what they needed, what they wanted, what they didn't like, working with area sponsors, like recruiting them in. The training centers were low in the priority of some of the detailers, so some of the training centers sometimes—I won't call them dregs. I'll just say not the kind of level of talent that they needed in certain areas.

For example, Great Lakes at one point—I don't know which job I was anymore, but might have been 090—got a reputation for less than motivating talent at the O-6 level.[*] Well, that goes immediately down through the command. We had problems in Great Lakes specifically, before Orlando was closed, with the talent level of people who interfaced with the outside world, like with contractors who maintained facilities under a maintenance contract. And these were Navy captains who had their own little bailiwick and pretty much independence on how to spend the money that they were allocated. We weren't getting the oversight we needed, because we didn't have the talent there. It was a place that was known as a comfortable place to pre-retire in. So there were challenges like that. I remember Bobby Hazard at Great Lakes.[†] Bobby was a very talented lady. Bobby was not always given the full support she needed because she's a woman.

Paul Stillwell: This is when you were CNO?

---

[*] The naval training center at Great Lakes, Illinois, has long been the site of recruit training for the Navy. O-6 is the pay grade for a Navy captain.
[†] Rear Admiral Roberta L. Hazard, USN, commanded the Great Lakes Naval Training Center from July 1985 to August 1987.

Admiral Trost: This is when I was CNO. Actually, it started before that, though. I went out to Great Lakes one time, and she said, "I want to show you some of the places that I don't like and I'm not very proud of." Well, we started with the grounds, broken-up sidewalks, trip hazards all over the place. A big barracks, enlisted barracks, two of ten operable heads, one of which had showers that worked. A couple hundred people in a building, one operational shower, and about four heads in there, but one operational shower. Maintenance of barracks was poor. Classroom buildings were improperly heated or not adequately heated. We had a deal with some outside contractors where if you wanted to have such-and-such fixed, you had to use this guy. I said, "Who said that?"

"It existed when I got here, and I haven't been able to change it." We changed it.

I'm trying to think of one old gymnasium, part of the initial old air station, that was fine but it wasn't heated, and it's a drill hall for new recruits. Well, you imagine you come into the Navy and you say, "What the hell have I gotten into?" Terrible.

I'm not sure we solved this problem yet. We bring recruits in who've been raised in tennis shoes and give them hard shoes and lace them tightly so they get blisters. Then we discharge them because they've got blisters. Stupid. It was things like that.

We had one CruitCom commander who spent $35,000—the number sticks in my mind—renovating his quarters, specifically the kitchen in his quarters, and caused a big damn stink because, one, it was a whole lot of money; two, it was more than adequate for the—oh, what it took to do what he did, which he shouldn't have done, there wasn't a flag kitchen anywhere around as ornate, I can tell you that because I saw it. So, yeah, there were problems in that area that needed fixing and needed attention.

We had problems in Orlando long before we built it up and then closed it.[*] It was probably in the best physical condition of any of the three recruit centers at the time. San Diego was the logical place to close because we had adequate capacity in the other two. Orlando was closed for political reasons because who was it? I guess it was Clinton closed Orlando.[†] It was Clinton, and it had to do with the vote for President in Florida, which went wrong as far as he was concerned, so he shut it down. The Engineering

---

[*] The Orlando Naval Training Center and the primary tenant command, Recruit Training Center Orlando, were established on 1 July 1968. The Navy closed the Orlando facility in the autumn of 1999 as part of the Base Realignment and Closure (BRAC) program.
[†] William J. Clinton served as President of the United States from 20 January 1993 to 20 January 2001.

Experimental Station here in Annapolis closed because of the vote in Maryland for the presidential campaign.

So we had to live with that, we had to try to compensate for that, and it was sort of tough. Demoralizing. You get pissed off for a little while, then you get over it and say, "Well, I can't do anything about that. Let's see how we can fix it." Unfortunately, we haven't fixed this one here yet. That area over there, I think it's still pending whatever they're planning eventually to do.

Paul Stillwell: There's some new structure going up there. I see that when I go to the exchange.

Admiral Trost: Oh, that new structure on the left. It's a new hospital and dispensary. They want to get the other one off where the old naval hospital is on the Naval Academy grounds and move it over there. Now we'll have everything available for support facilities to be over at North Severn.

Paul Stillwell: Well, that explains it. I was wondering about that.

Admiral Trost: That's a plus, and that's taken a long time. That was a full-fledged hospital when I was a midshipman, and then over across the river was the Engineering Experimental Station, which was sort of the cream of the crop as those things go for the Navy. The engineering community fought like hell, but didn't have the political support to overturn.

Paul Stillwell: The story I remember about Admiral Hazard is from 1987, when a building at Great Lakes was named in honor of the Golden 13, the first black naval officers. She specifically wanted to preside at the dedication of that, saying that, "Like them, I've been a pioneer also." So they appreciated that.

Admiral Trost: She worked hard out there. She did a good job out there. She corrected a lot of things that were a mess. She was close to tears. I won't say she broke into tears.

That would be not nice to say about a woman who was that senior, but she was on the verge of tears when she showed me those showers, because she had been trying to do something about it and couldn't do it. Her master chief of the command was trying to take on these personnel-related issues because she was a people person. She also was a very effective leader. When she got stymied up the chain of command, unfortunately, she wasn't a very happy camper, but effective.

Paul Stillwell: That's to her credit.

Admiral Trost: Yeah. She was the right person to put in that job.

Paul Stillwell: You mentioned the cases of Tom Lynch and Al Herberger. Any others that stand out that you got personally involved in?

Admiral Trost: You know the name Dennis Blair? Dennis Blair worked for me as a lieutenant in OP-96.* He remains one of the sharpest people I've ever known in uniform. Denny was selected to be a White House fellow as a lieutenant, went off to that job. He'd been a department head and I think he had been exec of something, like a DE. He came out of the White House fellow tour with glowing reports and he was also an early-select lieutenant commander. He wanted to go to a destroyer XO billet, very operationally oriented, very bright.

His detailer asked me what I thought of Denny Blair. He'd had some job as a lieutenant that would normally have been a lieutenant commander's job, and he'd had the OP-96 job, where he did a super job, and then he had the White House fellowship. I got a call from the detailer saying, "I don't know if you can help me or not, but I've reviewed your fitness reports on Denny Blair, and you obviously think very highly of him. Do you know him personally?"

"Well, shit, yes, I know him personally."

"What do you think of him?"

---

* Lieutenant Dennis C. Blair, USN, stood number two of the 836 midshipmen in the class of 1968. He eventually retired as a four-star admiral.

"Well, I think he ought to go to XO on a destroyer."

"Well, I can't get that to fly because OP-03 himself has taken an interest in it and says he's too junior."

I said, "What prerequisite has he not completed? What hasn't he done?'

"Well, nothing, but we're thinking of sending him—if you insist on his getting an XO billet, he'd be XO of a Naval Reserve destroyer that doesn't get under way very often."

I said, "That's a waste of a good, talented guy."

"Well, you're going to have talk to Admiral Doyle, who's OP-03."[*]

Well, I knew Admiral Doyle, who was a bit senior to me, and talked to him. It was like talking to a stone wall. He was adamant that this guy was not going to get a full-fledged destroyer XO billet because he was too young and too junior. So I argued a little bit and lost, so Denny went to be exec of an NRF destroyer, as I recall, and as I recall, he also did a very good job. Of course, he only made it to four stars.

Paul Stillwell: Director of National Intelligence.[†]

Admiral Trost: Yeah. And still one of the smartest guys I think I've ever known and worked with.

Bill Read was one of the guys I could talk to, because we had the same philosophy on the use of people. If you've got a talented guy, doesn't matter how many stripes are on the sleeve, put him in the job where he can get it done. And I still think that's healthy.

Paul Stillwell: Dennis Blair, as I recall, was the son of a submariner.

Admiral Trost: His dad was a submariner.[‡] Yeah. He was just a bright guy, and not a

---

[*] Vice Admiral James H. Doyle Jr., USN, served as Deputy Chief of Naval Operations (Surface Warfare) from August 1975 to September 1980.
[†] Dennis C. Blair served as Director of National Intelligence from 29 January 2009 to 28 May 2010 during the administration of President Barack H. Obama.
[‡] His father was Captain Carvel Hall Blair, USN.

presumptive or flashy type of person. Just did his job.

Paul Stillwell: There's a name that comes back to discuss every tour, and that's Admiral Rickover. How much impact did he have when you were in PERS-4.

Admiral Trost: He chewed me out on the one selection board I sat on while I was PERS-4. Dave Bagley had me come back from San Diego for a captain's selection board before I got the job but after I got the orders. Bill Cowhill and I were the two on that board.[*] Rickover sent either a note or a phone call, I'm not sure which, to the two of us, telling us that a number of O-5s had been passed over for captain because they were not nuclear trained. Two of them were classmates of mine. One of them had been my deputy down in LantFlt when I was the N-1.[†] He's still one of my close personal friends, a submariner. Well, all these guys were submariners. Rickover said, "These guys were passed over because I'd told him these guys are of no use to us."

Well, both Cowhill and I on the board gave special reviews to these guys, and I think we did not pick up two guys of about eight, voted to promote the rest, and they were promoted. Without our input, they probably would have been left beside, because there was opposition, and if we had sided with Rickover's guidance, they would have fallen by the wayside.

Well, he got very upset about that, called us both, chewed us out mightily, which he could very well. He said, "You just wasted the Navy's money. The salary we pay these guys as captains is going to go to waste." Well, these guys I tracked personally, every one of them, and one of them made flag, and I think there were about four or five who didn't make flag but they were senior captains when they retired. And performers, and that's why selected them, past performance and potential.

He did the same thing when I was on a flag board when I was PERS-4. Oh, God, Ed—Ed's a retired two-star about year group '49, diesel submariner. He was the senior

---

[*] Rear Admiral William J. Cowhill, USN.
[†] His assistant was Commander Charles D. Fellows, USN

financial guy on the SecNav staff for years, and I knew him well, and I can't remember his name. Ed and I were the two submariners on this flag board. And as someone had once said, if you took the last 300 fitness report folders for the flag candidates and threw them up in the air and picked up the first 30, you got as good a group as you could get of any other 30. And I really, after serving on that board, came to that same conclusion, frankly.

Rickover didn't see the point in selecting any diesel submariners for flag, and he had a couple of other guys who had a nonstandard career, that they're out there but they're of no use to the Navy. We picked up two or three guys that were on Rickover's "do not select" list, so then he chewed us out. Of course, you can't do anything about it after the fact, which was probably frustrating as hell to him. And I took my chewing-out because I knew I'd done the right thing and told him. [Laughs] So, yes, you got interference. It's how you took the interference that made the difference.

Paul Stillwell: It was shortly before your time in that job that the all-volunteer force came in.* Did that make a difference in what you were doing?

Admiral Trost: Yeah, it had to. I can't remember specifics of it. It made a difference in retention quality, not that we didn't keep good people before, but we kept people who stayed because they volunteered to stay rather than were kind of urged to stay; let's put it that way. Or in some cases, the salesmanship was sometimes negative, you know, "Boy, you go out and look at the problems you're going to have."

I think the all-volunteer force resulted in a more professional Navy than we'd had before, but I'm reluctant to say that, too, because that was right after Vietnam.

Paul Stillwell: In connection with the all-volunteer force, one of the counterarguments is that the draft impelled a number of really good people to join the Navy who otherwise

---

* In 1972 the Defense Department announced it would end draft calls in mid-1973. Secretary of Defense Melvin Laird announced on 27 January 1973 that the use of the military draft had ended as of then, several months prior to plan. That was the beginning of the current all-volunteer force.

probably wouldn't have.

Admiral Trost: That's probably right. That's probably right. But I don't think the all-volunteer force had a detrimental effect on readiness, so I'm a supporter, was a supporter. It made the force easier to manage in some respect and harder in others. You couldn't go out and focus on a particular talent base to fill a need. You had to attract them, which I think it was healthy from a professional standpoint. I don't know. I'm a fan of the all-volunteer force.

Paul Stillwell: People are there because they want to be.

Admiral Trost: Because they want to be. And I think it's easier to manage an all-volunteer force. Other people would challenge me on that and say you're asking for problems that you don't have to have. Instead of saying, "Do it," you have to say, "We need you to do it." Nothing wrong with that either.

Paul Stillwell: We've talked about surface warfare. It just came into its own during that period with a special designator and breast insignia. Were you involved in getting schools and qualification processes set up?

Admiral Trost: Well, yes, in a way. I think Zumwalt did a good thing by establishing the surface community with the pin and all, although I was annoyed because with my background I was qualified to wear the surface warfare pin when it was brought out, but then he put out if you were also a submariner or aviator, you couldn't wear it. So that kind of annoyed me. That's a petty thing.

Paul Stillwell: That is.

Admiral Trost: And he did that by intent, and I know because I talked to him about it. I was working for Warner at the time. I said, "You know, it's really kind of a slap in the face for people who qualify as surface warfare officers not to wear that pin in addition to dolphins or wings."

He said, "We should have what we've earned last." And I couldn't really counter that. I found it annoying.

Paul Stillwell: The destroyer department head school got upgraded to Surface Warfare Officers School. Were you involved in that upgrade?

Admiral Trost: No, I really wasn't. I really was not, but I did support it.

Paul Stillwell: Also the destroyer force and the cruisers and the amphibious force were consolidated around that time. Did that have an impact in your office?

Admiral Trost: Only in making sure that what I was doing supported it, which is another thing that I think was good, because it spread talent. It also gave some very talented guys with a certain background access to other types of ships, which they improved sometimes and did a good job with. I thought it made sense for a professional Navy group not to differentiate between how the ship looked, but rather how it did. But I've always felt that way. I feel that a good ship commander is going to be a good ship commander, no matter what that ship is.

I was very pleased but had nothing to do with the transition of diesel submariners into the surface Navy because they were not nuclear trained. I've already told you about my association with Tom Paulsen and how he did well once he transitioned to surface. He was my EA down at LantFlt, was my EA in LantFlt for nine months and then at CNO for—I think he had the job for two years. He went from there to a cruiser-destroyer group, which he was certainly qualified to command, and retired as a two-star. I thought he should have been a three-star because he had more common sense than some of the three-stars I had at the time, but it wasn't my say. But guys like that got an opportunity, and the Navy got some very talented people and kept them.

Paul Stillwell: And psychologically the consolidation of the surface force got away from the amphibs and the service force being second-class citizens.

Admiral Trost: It did that.

Paul Stillwell: You mentioned Secretary Middendorf in a previous interview.* How would you compare him with Secretary Warner and Secretary Chafee, whom you had worked closely with?

Admiral Trost: Well, I would say Warner was a more effective Secretary. Middendorf had his pet projects. I don't want to be critical of him, because he was a hardworking guy. His intents, I think, were always good, but he'd get involved in something that attracted his attention, and he'd just go off on a tangent.

One story I'll tell you about him. Bobby Inman and I, as rear admirals, were tapped by Middendorf to come out to Glenview Naval Air Station with him.† I don't remember the occasion. I remember that he was due to speak to a very large group of people and he was bringing us along as sort of combination of window dressing and question answerers. We flew out together. He spent the entire time on the flight from Andrews out there looking at photographic samples of art that he was thinking to buy.‡

When we got there, he hadn't looked at his speech, so he went off and secluded himself in an office, spent about 45 minutes, instead of talking, reading background. Came out 45 minutes late to a gymnasium full of people, and gave a speech for which he was not prepared because he hadn't read the paperwork. So his attention got diverted very easily. He did some good things. He didn't do some good things.

So I would say, first of all, of the three guys—he, Chafee, and Warner—I'd say Chafee was far and away, head and shoulders, the most effective. He was a lawyer, worked like a lawyer. When he focused on something, he focused on it till it was done.

---

* J. William Middendorf served as Secretary of the Navy from 20 June 1974 to 20 January 1977.
† Rear Admiral Bobby Ray Inman, USN, an intelligence specialist. As a three-star he was director of the National Security Agency; as a four-star he was Deputy Director of Central Intelligence.
‡ Andrews Air Force Base, located approximately ten miles southeast of Washington, D.C., in Prince George's County, Maryland.

He also listened to people. I don't know how much Chafee did.

Middendorf depended on what his interests of the hour were, and that's what he'd focus on. So I don't think he was as effective. I know he was not as effective on the Hill, even though he was a very congenial guy. In terms of knowing his business, he did not know it as well, although he made his visits. I was with him on one visit to—was it a carrier or support ship? I've forgotten which, where he did his engineering inspection, but he really didn't know anything about engineering. But it put focus on something that had been neglected for a long time, so it was good in that sense. So I'd say his pluses were primarily in the impact on personnel areas and personnel related, and he was very sincere about that. So it's kind of hard to say. Different focus, different interests.

Paul Stillwell: I gather he liked to visit ships.

Admiral Trost: He did. He did. When I had Submarine Group Five, he came out, visited us, and was very interested in the flagship because it was a submarine tender. He spent a lot of time talking to the kids in the repair department, had tremendous interest and I think it was a sincere interest in what they were doing. He was fascinated by it. Submarines didn't get much interest, even though they were the primary business out there. The repair department got a lot of attention. The engineering support, the things we did as providing services to ships alongside when the equipment was disabled for repair, got a lot of interest. People got a lot of interest.

Women were just coming into the fleet. We'd had a problem, which I really didn't want printed, but I guess it's a matter of record. We got the first four women in our crew aboard *Dixon*, my flagship. The first of them, I think, was either one first class petty officer and one second class or two first class. Then we got two third class. One of the third class asked for a request mast with the CO after about three weeks on board. Her complaint—she was being "recruited" by the first-class, who was lesbian.

The skipper was Bud Kauderer, a classmate of mine, and Bud didn't want a "lesbian ring" on board. So he interviewed the gal, who admitted, yes, she was a lesbian and, yes, she liked this third class, and, yes, she'd made a run on her. So we put more attention into the detailing of small groups of women on a ship that was predominantly male-crewed, and we got a second class who must have been a boatswain's mate before she was born, because she got assigned as the second class in charge of any women assigned to the ship, and we eventually got up—I think by the time I left, we were about 15 or so. And that female boatswain's mate really took charge, and I think had we gotten a woman with lesbian traits, she'd have left the ship. I'm pretty sure of that. I forget how I got on that subject, but it was one of our problems when I was out there, one of the early, early problems in that era.

Paul Stillwell: We were talking about Secretary Middendorf.

Admiral Trost: Oh, yeah. He was interested in the females being assigned, what their talents were, what their ability was.

Paul Stillwell: And he's composed music too.

Admiral Trost: Oh, yeah, he did well at that.

I'm watching the clock because I'm going to have to cut you in about 15 minutes.

Paul Stillwell: Well, I don't have many more in the way of questions, so that might be a suitable breaking point before you go to OP-96.

Admiral Trost: Okay.

Paul Stillwell: When you were PERS-4, did you have any involvement in the manpower side of the job, that is, OP-01, as opposed to detailing, that is, setting forth assignments?

Admiral Trost: No, other than knowing what my target was and what we had to work with CruitCom to get, and if we had new programs that required new talent, make sure that was documented and justified. Other than that, no.

Paul Stillwell: We have not talked about staff officers, flag corps doctors, lawyers—not lawyers.

Admiral Trost: We had their detailers, of course. They worked for me, and so I met with them. And from a recruiting policy and a promotion policy, I had an input, but otherwise, no.

Paul Stillwell: That's the list of my questions on BuPers, unless you've got anything else.

Admiral Trost: I enjoyed the job, actually. The detailers, who take all the gas when somebody's unhappy, I thought were a very professional bunch and a very dedicated bunch, and we had good coordination, except for one, and a guy who was, for most of my time as PERS-4, a surface detailer. We had personality problems. He was a couple classes ahead of me, and I think he might have resented the fact that I was in the job, but he was prone to disregard policy guidance and liked to argue. Unfortunately, we'd known each other for a number of years, and I didn't feel that he could challenge anything he didn't like, and he didn't like a lot of the things I did. Usually his arguments were non-substantive, of the type that, "You put out a directive on such-and-such. I should have done that."

I said, "The policy applied to all areas, all detailers, so, no, you shouldn't have done that."

"Well, I'm the senior detailer."

I said, "You shouldn't have done that. I'm the senior detailer. You work for me."

So I'm not sure we ever really did establish that fact, but we had problems. He had one more job where he got in trouble and got retired.

Paul Stillwell: Was he a captain?

Admiral Trost: Senior, very senior. Got retired for doing something illegal in a command position, and it wasn't something he could challenge.

Paul Stillwell: One general impression on detailing is that the people who are happy with their assignments are less likely to express that happiness than those who complain. [Laughs]

Admiral Trost: That's right. That's right. I still hear about things that happened when I was PERS-4, usually only the positive things or "I know of this case, and thank God you did such-and-such." It's interesting. Depends on what the person's satisfaction is and what the issue is.

I had an intel officer, and, of course, the intelligence detailer is an intel officer. and there is, in that community, or was, occasionally disagreement on things. There are billets that are good billets because people in them have gotten promoted. Now, is that because the billet is something great to get, or is it because the people in it did a good job? I chose to think it's the latter, and I've always felt that way. But there are people who say, "You know, if you'd have assigned me to so-and-so, I'd have done this."

"Well, maybe you would have, and if you had done *this* before, maybe you'd have gotten assigned to this one." So it's hard to tell. And that's true. You want competition because you want the best people to vie for the best jobs.

Paul Stillwell: Thanks for another fine interview.

Admiral Trost: Well, thanks for leading it.

Interview Number 9 with Admiral Carlisle A. H. Trost, U.S. Navy (Retired)

Date: Wednesday, 19 August 2015

Place: Admiral Trost's apartment in Ginger Cove, south of Annapolis, Maryland

Paul Stillwell: Admiral, you mentioned earlier that you had an experience with Admiral Hal Shear when you were head of Systems Analysis.

Admiral Trost: He was the Vice CNO at one point in time, and I enjoyed working with him.[*] He ran that staff very, very well. I'll tell you a sea story, but I don't know if you want to print it or not.

Paul Stillwell: Well, that makes it even more inviting.

Admiral Trost: Hal Shear, a fellow submariner, was the Vice CNO. Bob Long was OP-02, DCNO for submarines. Long had been promoted to four stars to become the Vice Chief.[†] Shear was going to Naples to be CinCSouth.[‡] This story comes from Dave Harlow, who was EA to Shear.[§] I got called up to see Shear, and I knew Shear, so it was not a problem, what the hell? I could take chewing out, and I figured that's what I was going to get. I walked in, and Harlow said, "When you get here, go right on in." So I went in, and coming flying at me was paperwork, a whole bunch of folders full of papers which were now over half the office. Shear said, "Carl, what is this shit? [Laughter]

I said, "Admiral, I can't read it, most of it is upside down [laughter]."

"Well, it's all from your office. Pick it up, sort it out, and tell me what to do with it. So, with Harlow's help, I picked up I estimate a stack about like that—

Paul Stillwell: A foot high.

---

[*] Admiral Harold E. Shear, USN, served as Vice Chief of Naval Operations from 30 June 1975 to 5 July 1977. His oral history is in the Naval Institute collection. Trost was at the time of this incident OP-96, head of Systems Analysis.

[†] Admiral Robert L. J. Long, USN, served as Vice Chief of Naval Operations from 1977 to 1979. His oral history is in the Naval Institute collection.

[‡] Admiral Shear served as Commander in Chief Allied Forces Southern Europe from July 1977 to May 1980.

[§] Captain David L. Harlow, USN.

Admiral Trost: —and took it back to my office. My EA and I sat down and started going through it and trying to figure out what the hell to do with it. We got stuff that left my office more than four months earlier, including right up until just recently, and it was stuff he hadn't gotten to. Some of them should have gone to the CNO several months before, but never got there. So we sorted through, and we wound up with maybe about that much that was useful.

Paul Stillwell: Two inches.

Admiral Trost: So I went back up and checked in. He said, "Put it over there." Well there was a standup desk, and it was full of stuff. So I put it on top, adding my little stack. Shear said, "Now, get the hell out of here." [Laughter]. Well, Long walked in after this— probably quite a few two- and three-stars had been through the same experience. Long came in and saw this standup desk with a couple of feet of paper on it. He saw stacks of paper, some of it on the floor in front of the big desk, and said, "Hal, what the hell is all this stuff?"

"Stuff I'm going to get to."

"Call me when you've got to it," and then he turned around and walked out. What a relief. I always got a kick out of that.

Paul Stillwell: Other people have told me about Admiral Shear's stacks of paper.

Admiral Trost: He said, "I know what is in every pile." He might have known what it was, except some were three months old at least.

Paul Stillwell: He had a gruff exterior, but when he liked you, he really liked you.

Admiral Trost: He was a good guy, a very capable guy. He was J34, I think it was, for CinCLantFlt. He ran all the missile boats and programs and schedule. He kept close tabs on you. I was exec of *Von Steuben*, which was new construction. Shear kept tabs on us because of John Wise, who was my PCO. They had served together somewhere, and they were great buddies. He kept good tabs on the people who'd worked with him and for him.

Paul Stillwell: I suspect you got some talented officers to work in the Systems Analysis Division.

Admiral Trost: Yeah. I mentioned earlier how sharp Dennis Blair is. I still consider him one of the smartest guys I think I've ever known and worked with. I had guys like that in OP-96. That was a fun job. It was the kind of thing where you pointed, "I want you to do this," and you forgot about it, because the next thing you knew, it was done. I had that kind of talent.

Did you know Jerry Smith?

Paul Stillwell: No.

Admiral Trost: He lives over across from Cantler's, across the stream.[*] Jerry is a retired two-star.[†] He stood first in his class of—what class was that—'60 somewhere.[‡] Should have gone beyond two stars. Why he didn't, I don't know. But, again, one of the smartest people around. Jerry was another one of these guys, very bright, and crossed the breakers with somebody in the surface warfare community, and I thought was a three- and probably a four-star candidate, didn't get there, but a good man. It's a disease that infects the surface community predominantly. They eat their young and spit them out. But I had some of the smartest guys around. Jerry was a very early selectee, I think from lieutenant commander through flag, and guys like that are the kind of people who, "Here's my problem. Do it." The next time you see him, it's done. So I was spoiled. I had a couple of jobs where I had really that kind of people, and they're the kind of guys that—Joe Moorer got on my ass when I was OP-96, for sending a lieutenant to chair a meeting.[§]

My action officer on one program—and I don't recall now the subject—was Greg Johnson, a lieutenant at the time.[**] He was later Com6thFlt and retired as a four-star. OP-06's guy was a captain who was not, in the judgment of my people, my deputy and

---

[*] Cantler's Riverside Inn is an Annapolis-area restaurant and crab house.
[†] Rear Admiral Jerome F. Smith Jr., USN.
[‡] Smith was in the Naval Academy class of 1961.
[§] Vice Admiral Joseph P. Moorer, USN, served as Deputy Chief of Naval Operations (Plans and Policy) from March 1975 to August 1977.
[**] Lieutenant Gregory G. Johnson, USN.

my action officer, doing a very good job. So I got the word from the CNO, "I want this, and I want it by such-and-such a time." Well, the only way to do it was to get off top dead center and take charge, so I put out a memo calling a meeting of all interested people and sent Johnson to chair the meeting. Now, we wore civilian clothes in the Pentagon at that time.

It was a very successful meeting. We got the agenda, got the action steps taken, got it off, moving. About two or three days later, I got a call from Joe Moorer, "Come see me."

So I went to see the senior three-star, and he said, "What the hell are you doing sending lieutenants to chair meetings?"

I said, "I send a lieutenant if he's qualified to chair the meeting and knows more about the subject than anybody else who's going to be at the meeting."

"My guy's a captain."

I said, "Yes, and from what I understand, he doesn't know the subject very well."

"Don't ever do that again. Now get out of here." One flag officer to another, curt dismissal. I never heard anything more from him after that. But you had that kind of conflict sometimes, because we had to support the CNO, who was Holloway during my nearly entire time in Systems Analysis. I probably had more face time with Holloway than any of the three-stars in OpNav did.

But Holloway used to, with Red Dog Davis's encouragement—he was the 090, and Red Dog said, "When Holloway calls, don't call me. Get down there and find out what he wants and debrief me."[*] They were buddies from way back, so that worked out well. So I spent a lot of time going directly to the CNO's Office, and I don't think some of the platform sponsors liked that too much, "Why is this junior guy [third two-star billet, but junior nonetheless] going in and getting the ear of CNO on things we'd like to know about?" So that's people.

After my visit with Joe Moorer, my guy Johnson asked, "What do I do next?"

I said, "Do what you're doing"

He said, "The captain says he's not going to come to my meetings."

---

[*] Vice Admiral Donald C. Davis, USN, served as Director of Navy Program Planning, OP-090, from April 1975 to March 1978.

I said, "Do it without him. You're the action officer." We got away with it. [Stillwell laughs.] He was clearly a top performer, one of my several lieutenants who made four stars. So it's interesting. I use this as an example of the not-invented-here syndrome. "If it's not my idea, it must be a lousy idea, so I'm going to criticize anybody who's in it and they're doing it." I have always tried to stomp that out wherever I've been, because it's not making use of talented guys. Our surface warfare community, unfortunately, is the one I point to most, especially in the past, as being guilty of what I call this syndrome.

[Interruption. Some material about Admiral Trost's next duty, Deputy Commander in Chief Pacific Fleet, was unfortunately not recorded. Additional material on that tour is covered in interview 13.]

Paul Stillwell: We were in the midst of talking about supporting the carriers in the North Arabian Sea. It's a very hostile environment because of the heat and the sand and stuff blowing out from the land.

Admiral Trost: It's a tough environment to operate in. I have spent a maximum of five days at a time aboard a carrier in the North Arabian Sea. It's hot out there and those guys are operating in a hot clime, hot environment, and, of course, the airplanes do suffer from the environment. So the maintenance tasks are considerable. But I didn't have the flexibility to give them more time in port because we didn't have the opportunity. We were covering mission packages that demanded that those guys be at sea.

The interesting thing was this governor I started talking about earlier, the ambassador to Singapore I'd say was a political neophyte. I arranged this port visit for *Eisenhower* for five days, and my next call—well, first of all, as the fleet commander, I had to visit each one of these countries every six months, minimum, and stopped in Singapore periodically, just on my way to WestPac and the Indian Ocean.* So I was on a trip to Kuala Lumpur, and I got a message, urgent, from the ambassador in Singapore,

---

* USS *Dwight D. Eisenhower* (CVN-69) made a five-day port visit at Singapore, 17-20 July 1980. It was the only break in a deployment that comprised 254 days at sea. Here Trost refers to a later tour when he was Commander Seventh Fleet, 1980-81.

"Urgent you stop here ASAP." Sounded pretty important. "Will arrange accommodations." He knew where I was. He arranged accommodations for such-and-such a night. "And we'll meet you at the airport." Not "Can you come?" or anything else.

Well, not knowing what the hell was going on, and the implication was that it was related to the Singaporean government and the carrier visit, which had just taken place, so I said, "Oh, God, I wonder what happened. I wonder what did we do? Whose toes did we step on?"

So I cut short my Kuala Lumpur visit and flew to Singapore—fortunately, I had my own airplane. I got there, and I was met by somebody from the embassy, taken right to the embassy and to the ambassador.* What he asked was whether I could get him five more *Eisenhower* ball caps—

Paul Stillwell: Oh, gosh. [Laughs]

Admiral Trost: —because they'd given him a couple sample ball caps, but he needed more for his friends. And that, unfortunately, Paul, is the caliber of some of the people who represented us overseas.

I said, "You know, I was on an official visit to Kuala Lumpur."

He said, "Yeah, how'd that go?"

Paul Stillwell: Couldn't he just send a message, "Send ball caps"? [Laughs]

Admiral Trost: Yeah. So we got him five ball caps. I don't know when they got there. I didn't follow up. [Laughter] So I had problems with some of my ambassadors.

Paul Stillwell: Any others to mention?

Admiral Trost: No, those two guys, that one and the other guy.

---

* Richard F. Kneip was U.S. ambassador to Singapore from 26 May 1978 to 25 September 1980. He had served as governor of South Dakota from 1971 to 1978,

Paul Stillwell: The Oman—

Admiral Trost: The Oman guy, yeah. On the other hand, the ambassador to Pakistan, where I went at least every six months, and I had a very good relationship, as I did with the then-Pakistani Navy Chief of Staff, and their Air Force head, because I needed to arrange for a divert field in Pakistan for my P-3s if they were in the eastern part of the area and had to call an emergency divert. There was a Pakistani Air Force base northwest of Karachi.

My Navy friend introduced me to the head of the Pakistani Air Force, who had arranged for one of my P-3s, which was a non-mission P-3, to fly in on my way out of country and stop at that airbase, and I was met there by the Air Force Chief of Staff. We had a cup of coffee, we talked, he showed me the facilities, and said, "For your first one, never call and ask for permission to come in. Declare an emergency divert, and send me a copy, and then you guys just fly in. I'll take care of the rest." And that's what we did for the balance of my tour. So they were great people to work with.

Our Pakistani relationship, unfortunately, is not that kind of relationship anymore, but they were great. So there were interesting parts to the job, too, and they were very helpful. Our ambassador to Pakistan was a very helpful guy, and later when I was CNO, some years later, made an official visit to Pakistan at their invitation. It was the last official visit I made as CNO, hosted by the then new Pakistani CNO, and Pauline and I had lunch with President Zia of Pakistan and his wife in the palace, which kind of blew my embassy's eyes out because the ambassador was not invited to join me.* [Laughter] But, unfortunately, about five weeks later, Zia was blown out of the air while he was flying between two places, was assassinated. Good guy, retired Army Chief of Staff, pragmatic, a friend of the U.S. as long as we were a friend of his, and made enemies, as everybody does in a country like that.

Paul Stillwell: What role did Diego Garcia play in connection with those carrier deployments?

---

* Muhammad Zia-ul-Haq was President of Pakistan from 16 September 1978 until his death in a plane crash on 17 August 1988. All 31 people on board the C-130 were killed.

Admiral Trost: They were key to my support. We staged P-3s through Diego Garcia, and we used it when we pulled the carrier off station for any reason. We used them for resupply on occasion when we had to bring a hot item in directly. We'd bring it into Diego Garcia via Australia from the West Coast, and they'd send somebody down, usually a COD, down to Diego Garcia. We had a couple of occasions where we used it for logistic support primarily, and primarily P-3s, but it was carrier-capable. It had arresting wires. It had the capability to take anything we could fly off a carrier, as well as B-52s. We were B-52-capable, and that helped. The Air Force loved it because they got good support from the Navy when they flew B-52s, which they did on occasion. So, matter of fact, it was a critical base.

That was an interesting trip too. The Pakistani trip was via a stop in India. Jim Watkins, my predecessor, had been the first Navy CNO to go to India in modern times, and he had hosted the Indian CNO, who was, as I recall, a Naval War College, U.S. Naval War College graduate, or attendee anyway.[*] And that hosting, which was a first after many years, resulted in Watkins being invited as a guest for an official visit, and then prior to my tour, about six months before my tour ended, I was invited to come. We tied that together with the Pakistani visit, and I had a chance to check out Diego Garcia again, which I'd been to many a time.

But because I was going to Pakistan, and India and Pakistan are at odds, the Indians wouldn't let me fly from Diego Garcia directly into India. I went via—I don't think it was Mauritania. It's one of the islands to the west of India in the Indian Ocean, whose relationships with us were congenial, and I was invited by them to fly in, had to spend at least three hours on the ground, had to tour the island so that the head of their limited Navy could host me as an official visit, and that satisfied the Indians that I'd made an official visit to a friendly place. So I went to India. I think we spent almost a week in India, then went to Pakistan for about three days. An interesting sidelight on politics and how it works.

Paul Stillwell: Was that when you were CNO?

---

[*] Admiral James D. Watkins, USN, served as Chief of Naval Operations from 1 July 1982 to 30 June 1986.

Admiral Trost: Yeah, it was about five months before I retired, five and a half months. Both very productive visits. It was very good visit. It was my first and only visit to India. My Pakistani visits were primarily while I was Seventh Fleet.

Another interesting trip I made was to Adak. In BuPers we'd always heard, "If you don't do this, I'll send you to Adak." That was the standard thing. Then I got to Adak the first time when I was the Deputy PacFlt. And because we were deploying regularly a lot of P-3s from Adak, I wanted to see the place, I wanted to see the facilities, and so I hopped one of the P-3s from Hawaii that was going up and then going to deploy and then got one coming back. I made a point of talking to a lot of people, including a lot of the wives, which required pulling some of them out of the classroom because a lot of them were schoolteachers. My take on morale was sky high, happy people, and a lot of E-6s and chiefs who'd been there for long extended tours and didn't want to go anywhere. They were saving money. They wanted to stay there till they retired, take their nest egg and go someplace where they wanted to be and buy a house. And the wives liked it because they could both be employed. They saved lots of money. So my thoughts about Adak colored for the better.

Then when I was CNO, we made a trip to China in 1988. Coming home from a China, Japan, Korea trip, we had one of the P-3s. I think we came from Japan heading back to the States, and I had a speaking engagement on the West Coast, up in Puget Sound, that airbase up there. It was going to be on the night after we left Japan. We left about 10:00 o'clock at night. About 2:00 o'clock in the morning, we started hearing strange sounds. We were in a windstorm and a rainstorm. I thought it was rain. We heard rain. But what we heard was one engine cutting in and out, but you've got four, so didn't worry about it.

So the pilot came back to talk to me and said, "I've lost number-three engine, period. The fuel pump has failed, and we don't have enough fuel with headwinds to make it to Anchorage," which is the divert field on the way to the West Coast. "I'm going to try to make it to Adak, but Adak now is socked in."

I said, "What's the alternative?"

He said, "Well, can you swim?" [Laughter]

About 7:30 in the morning, he said, "We're abreast of Adak right now. It's raining. Visibility is about the length of the runway. They think I can make it if I've got enough fuel, and I've got enough fuel to get that far."

I said, "Let's land." [Laughs] So about 8:00 o'clock in the morning, we landed at Adak. Fuel pump had, in fact, failed. They did, in fact, have a spare fuel pump at Adak, and it would, in fact, put the engine down for about eight hours while they did the repair work.

So we hadn't slept all night, none of us in my group. So they took my wife and Mar Beth Paulsen, who was at the time was my EA's wife, and my female protocol officer, took them, they gave them somebody's apartment who was off the island so they could sleep. Then I got the VIP tour of Adak, of the island, for eight hours with no sleep, and that was hard.

About 1600, we took off. I had by this time missed my West Coast speaking engagement time, and so we took off with a full load of fuel, and I think we went all the way back to Andrews Air Force Base, as I recall. I think we did. So we shortened our time a little bit. I missed my speaking engagement out there.

So I got a different view of Adak. Now it's a community. Again, morale is high, which I found before. It wasn't a place people didn't want to be. The biggest problem was people extending in their billet, somebody else wanting the billet and they can't get it. So I changed my mental approach to Adak and thought the next time I threaten somebody, I'll be more informed. I won't say, "Do this or I'll send you out there," unless I know they don't want to go there. [Laughs]

Paul Stillwell: During that deputy job at CinCPacFlt, what do you remember about Hawaii living for you and your family?

Admiral Trost: Very pleasant. We did quite a bit of official entertainment, so I had a nice set of quarters up on Flag Row. I had about a two-block walk to my office, so that was very convenient, and didn't take too long to get over to Hickam for functions over there, and took maybe 20 minutes to get downtown. It was very convenient.

It was active. From Pauline's perspective, she took up tennis again. She was never a great tennis player, but she liked to play tennis, and we lived half a block from the tennis courts, so they were handy. We were convenient to the sub base and the Navy exchange and commissary there. So from a personal convenience standpoint, it was quite good. She was also a "beach bunny" and liked Hickam Beach.[*] She and the FMFPac wife went to the beach often enough that you could have looked at them and thought they were Hawaiian, darker than the average American.[†] Matter of fact, she paid for that with skin care since we had moved to Annapolis after I retired. But they had a good time. So she played a lot of tennis, went to a lot of beach things. The ladies were a very congenial group and they got along, stayed pretty active in things. They had a lot of wives' activities that were a combination of social and—what should I call it—helping people out, Navy Relief functions and local functions that helped Hawaiians, especially poor Hawaiians, Samoans.

So we enjoyed it when I was Deputy CinCPacFlt. Hawaii is a pretty place to be. We had access to a beach house out at Barbers Point Naval Air Station on the southwest corner of the island. The Barbers Beach was beautiful, and CinCPacFlt had two guest cottages there, one of which could be used by anybody, one of which could be used by the CinC, his guests, and me, and we enjoyed that. That was right on the beach. I could have one of my mess specialists from the quarters go out there and take the food out, make sure everything was ready for the meals, and would cook and could cook, and there were quarters there for him. We normally went out and stayed by ourselves after having him take the food out, and Pauline would do our own cooking. But we loved that, and it was a three-bedroom cottage, one for the MS, and then the master bedroom and a guest bedroom.[‡] We could entertain visitors out there, and it turned out to be a very popular thing. We used that quite a bit.

Of course, I flew in and out of Barbers in my PacFlt P-3, so we used that quite a bit, and it was interesting, nice place. So from a personal perspective, it was a very nice tour, very convenient, very comfortable. Hours were long.

---

[*] Hickam Air Force Base, adjacent to the Pearl Harbor Naval Base on the island of Oahu.
[†] FMFPac – Fleet Marine Force Pacific Fleet.
[‡] MS is the abbreviation for the enlisted rating specialty of mess management specialist.

Paul Stillwell: That seemed to be a characteristic of many of your jobs.

Admiral Trost: Yeah. Well, you're dealing with people on the West Coast who belong to you, people in Japan who belong to you, and people in Washington who don't give a damn what time it is. [Stillwell laughs.] I had one former skipper, Yogi Kaufman. He was skipper of *Scorpion*, I was his exec, and we became, I'd say, lifelong friends. Yogi died a couple of years ago.[*] But he used to call me. He was a three-star in Washington when I had Seventh Fleet.[†] And he used to call me at 2:00 A.M. from his office, and it always started with, "Oh, jeez, I forgot we had a time difference." Shit, we had a 12-hour time difference. He didn't forget that at all. [Laughter] He just called to ring my bell. But it wasn't quite that bad from Hawaii. It was about eight hours. They always called in the afternoon, which meant I was either at a dinner or asleep, and that was typical in Seventh Fleet also.

We had a duty yeoman on the flagship in port. Of course, under way, everybody's on duty, but we'd have a duty yeoman on the flagship to take calls from Washington and direct them to the quarters of whoever the recipient was because they were bound to be asleep. I would say that naval officers are smart enough to know the time zone difference but don't pay attention to it.

Paul Stillwell: I hope you never did that when you were in Washington and calling people. [Laughs]

Admiral Trost: I tried to make sure I never did. Matter of fact, my secretaries and my yeoman had directions *not* to put calls through if they didn't know what time it was on the other end, and we didn't.

Paul Stillwell: One staff member who remembered you fondly from that tour in Hawasii was the chaplain, Neil Stevenson.[‡] What do you recall of him?

---

[*] Kaufman died 26 September 2006 from complications of Parkinson's disease.
[†] Vice Admiral Robert Y. Kaufman, USN.
[‡] See the Naval Institute oral history of Rear Admiral Neil M. Stevenson, Chaplain Corps, USN (Ret.).

Admiral Trost: What do I recall of him? First of all, well, without question, one of the finest chaplains I've ever known, maybe the finest. He was a friend until his death. Neil was the PacFlt chaplain, but he was also the local Pearl Harbor chaplain for the Navy Chapel there. We had a great attendance every Sunday morning at the Protestant services, and especially when the Redskins were playing, because Neil would stop in the middle of the sermon if he'd overrun time-wise and the Redskin game was coming on. We would say "Amen," say a prayer, go out to the lanai, turn on the TV set, watch the rest of the football game. [Laughter] He loved it.

But he was a great guy. We stayed friends. Well, he came back here to be the Deputy Chief of Chaplains, and then later he became Chief of Chaplains. We stayed in touch with Neil until he died a few years ago.[*]

Paul Stillwell: He was so friendly and down-to-earth.

Admiral Trost: Friendly, common sense, loved the people, and they loved him. He was great. But that football game thing was legend out there. And you knew that we had a game day if you hadn't checked beforehand, because the coffee pot was fuller than normal. They had this big urn, and they were about this tall.

Paul Stillwell: Two or three feet.

Admiral Trost: Normal morning, about half full. We always had a reception after the service, and game mornings it was full. And I'm not sure he didn't make the coffee himself. Might have had his religious program specialist do it. You could also tell because all the comfortable chairs were out, including some just folding chairs that were out there to be used in case we overran the comfortable ones. [Stillwell laughs.]

I talked to several people down in Williamsburg after he took over down there, and he was beloved by the people down there at that school.[†] First of all, one guy told me

---

[*] Stevenson died of cancer on 21 November 2009.
[†] After retirement from the Navy, Stevenson became pastor of Williamsburg Presbyterian Church, across the street from the College of William and Mary.

that church increased its membership by a staggering amount when he got down there and word got out what kind of guy he was. He did a hell of a job.

Paul Stillwell: His church was right across the street from William and Mary.

Admiral Trost: Yeah, and he got a lot of students to come to the church, which was great.

Paul Stillwell: He grew up in Brooklyn and went to school, college, in Tarkio, Missouri. He said it was like moving to a foreign country.

Admiral Trost: I bet. [Laughs]

Paul Stillwell: And married the local beauty queen. [Laughs]

Admiral Trost: And his wife is a jewel. She's still living. And his kids, we knew his kids, and I can't remember the names. He had a great family.

Paul Stillwell: Anything else about that job before the segue to Seventh Fleet?

Admiral Trost: I don't think so. We cultivated our relationships with the local government people very carefully and, I'd say, successfully. We had good status. At least twice a year we had major functions where the guests of honor were the Hawaiian local government people, and just to show our ecumenical nature, we invited the senior Air Force guys, the commanders, and, of course, the people from CinCPac staff and our own senior people, but key civilians who were critical to community relations, in addition to the mayor and some other senior staff.

My quarters were very popular because our dining room was the largest of any quarters at Makalapa. We could seat 24, but that's only because we had two 12-man tables in there. We had room for more. I could have put about two more tables in there. It was a huge damn thing, and we had, in addition, a big living room and very nice rear-screened lanai. If that wall were carried straight through to that wall, and this were it, that would be the room. It had jalousie windows, literally floor to ceiling, on the back of the house, so a great view of the garden. Very comfortable, air-conditioned, or most of the time just crank open the jalousies and enjoy the outside.

We had a kitchen which could accommodate three mess specialists at a time working in the kitchen. There was a serving pantry with dishes, and they could pass from the kitchen to the serving pantry to take out to the adjacent dining room. So it was the principal dining area for official entertainment.

The CinCPacFlt's dining room was smaller, matter of fact, less than half the size, and its living room was the same size. So we got to host all the bigwigs that came along, and it was fun because we had help. I got rid of two mess specialists and then we could draw from the CinC's quarters. He had four, and then we had a couple assigned to the headquarters who could be brought in on loan. So we didn't suffer from the activity and didn't have to clean up afterwards, didn't have to dust the furniture beforehand. [Laughs] So it was very pleasant.

Paul Stillwell: Well, I'm guessing that those get-togethers were useful for fostering relationships for business.

Admiral Trost: They were very useful, they were useful, and they were sought after. I recall getting a phone call in the house from a not-to-be-named retired four-star, had moved to Hawaii and settled down there some few years before. And one of the functions where the CinC and I both hosted, it might have been Navy birthday or something. Anyway, the CinC and the DCinC would each host a dinner party, then we'd all get together at the club for—I guess it was like a dance, and ceremony, with usually a couple speeches from the host and then from the local community.

I got a call one day from this guy, "This is Admiral So-and-so."

"Yes, sir."

He said, "I understand you're having the regular [whatever day it was] party on such-and-such a date."

I said, "Yes, sir." I thought he was calling because he didn't have an invitation. I said, "Well, Admiral, you know you and your wife are invited."

"Yeah, but not to the CinC's house; to your house."

I said, "Well, actually, I'm hosting two-thirds of the dinner guests because the difference in size of our dining rooms."

"Well, in the past, I've been invited to the CinC's house."

What do you say? "Listen, you old fart, you're lucky to be invited." [Laughter]

Paul Stillwell: Oh, gee.

Admiral Trost: So we had occasionally things like that. Retired senior officers sometimes feel their oats for a long time afterwards and get slighted if they're not included as the top guy and recognized as such. He wasn't the senior guy to start with, but his ego was. But generally relationships were good, good support from the community reps as well.

Paul Stillwell: Do you remember any specific things where positive business was accomplished in the aftermath of those gatherings?

Admiral Trost: I remember one time, and it had to do with parking down at the Hale Koa.[*] We had an issue with parking down there. Oh, God, I don't remember that well anymore. There was an adjacent area which served in part during the day for community activities and business and was ours off-hours. I think it was Navy property, as a matter of fact. And we had some sort of flap over that, and I called the—I guess he was the deputy mayor of Honolulu, to resolve it, told him, "You know, we need this space to support our tourist visitors, Navy. These are guys, many of them active duty, some with long service who are retired, and we need it to support the Hale Koa."

"Yeah, that makes sense."

I said, "We're having problems." This was like a chamber of commerce subcommittee or something that had arbitrarily kind of preempted some of our parking.

He said, "Who did you guys deal with?" So I told him. He said, "I'll take care of it."

---

[*] Hale Koa is a military hotel on Waikiki Beach.

So, yes, we did have a relationship to be able to do that, and it was very helpful. When we had a problem with the community, we had somebody we could turn to. They were usually pretty responsive. We kept a very close liaison between shore patrol and the Honolulu Police Department, which was necessary, and we did it because they sometimes got a little bit overenthusiastic in law enforcement with sailors who had a little too much to drink, usually guys whose ships were in for a visit, because the guys stationed there didn't really dare do anything to jeopardize relationships. So it helped to have a good relationship with law enforcement, and we did. Was that helped by our social functions? I think so. But it's also common sense.

Paul Stillwell: Well, it helps that you touch base. It's not a cold call at that point.

Admiral Trost: Yeah.

Paul Stillwell: Did you have an agenda laid out for you by Admiral Davis when you moved then to the Seventh Fleet command?[*]

Admiral Trost: Yeah, I had an agenda. It was "Keep me informed." And we talked periodically. We'd worked together for several years and we got along well. His words were, "Keep me cut in." So it was good. I talked to him minimal once a week, and that was usually a pretty long hour session. But he kept tabs and I kept him informed.

It's such a big area geographically, and with the requirement I had to be in Korea once a month because the Korean Navy chopped to me under still-existent U.N. op orders in case of a U.N.-declared contingency if North Korea acted up again. So I actually had an office, a very plush office, in Korean Navy Headquarters in Chinhae, and I was expected to go there once a month. Didn't have to do anything, just had to show up, and they'd brief me and keep me cut in. And that would be my headquarters in case of a contingency.

---

[*] Admiral Donald C. Davis, USN, was Commander in Chief Pacific Fleet, 9 May 1978 to 31 July 1981.

Then I went to Seoul to meet with the head of the Navy and with their Chairman Joint Chiefs, who later became their ambassador to Washington, which helped.* He was an Army general and I knew him well. The first time I met him after he came as the ambassador, it was on the Army-Navy train going up to an Army-Navy game. And having had a drink together in the bar car, our relationship started off as it had left, very good. He was very helpful, but he expected a call, which was common sense and also helpful, because he was interested in what Seventh Fleet did because a lot of his security was dependent on Seventh Fleet and the Marines. So we developed a good relationship.

The geographic nature was exacerbated by the fact that I had to go to Okinawa, visit with the Marines monthly, I had to go to Subic or Cubi Point at least once a month. I had to go to Hong Kong, Singapore, Kuala Lumpur, Manila, and Malaysia.

Paul Stillwell: Thailand?

Admiral Trost: I did go to Thailand; I think that was about every two months, three months, thereabouts.

So I was on the road an awful lot. Matter of fact, I think my aide figured out that of my tour in Seventh Fleet I was either at sea or under way somewhere—I was home 30% of the time of the tour. So it was a mobile existence. Matter of fact, we had one place in my bedroom that was set aside, it had an 8-foot rack, with uniforms and civilian clothes, and that never left there. It went to the closet, because that's from which we took things for trips, which was often.

When I traveled, I normally traveled on official visits, not just to be purely operational, visiting a unit or something. I traveled with a mess specialist in addition to my aide, and my flag writer. So we were operational no matter where we were. And my communicator. So we had an ability to function no matter where we were in my area of responsibility, including Nairobi, Kenya, for example.

I was asked to come after we tried to extend our access to Mombasa for carriers, and that turned out to be a political issue. The Kenyan President at the time was a retired

---

* Lew Byong-hyun served in the Republic of Korea Army from 1948 to 1981. He then served in the Ministry of Foreign Affairs until 1986. He was ambassador to the United States from 1981 to 1985.

Kenyan Army general who had a reputation for being very tough. So I was warned, "Boy, he's going to rake you over the coals, and when you get there, we're going to have the attaché meet you, and the ambassador will want to talk to you and brief you," because the ambassador was not even invited to the meeting with the President, which was odd.

So I went there. We flew into Mombasa on the coast and then flew into Nairobi, and I was met by the attaché, had a meeting about 9:00 o'clock on the night after I got there with the ambassador, who I thought was afraid of the President of the country, which I found interesting.

Next morning, had a 10:00 o'clock meeting with the President, which extended into lunch, which was interesting, until about 2:00 o'clock in the afternoon. And the guy had more questions about the U.S., very interested in the U.S., my Navy operations, other ports I had access to, what we would bring in terms of port fees and all to Mombasa, how long we wanted access, how often. Very detailed. And we got it. We got it at that meeting. He said, "Okay." Fortunately, we were well prepared with the next couple of ships that we wanted to bring in, and he gave us the okay.

Paul Stillwell: Well, liberty was so scarce, that was bound to be helpful.

Admiral Trost: It really helped, and there's a major—I don't know if it was a local, a commercial airport, or military. I think it was commercial. All I know is its runway was long enough for P-3s, because we lost an engine on takeoff on the P-3 I used, and there was room to set the airplane back just after it lifted off and stop before the end of the runway.

Paul Stillwell: Wow.

Admiral Trost: So it was a substantial runway. Of course, a P-3 doesn't use that much space to get off, and we weren't that heavily loaded, so I'm not sure where we were going when we took off. Probably up to Oman.

Everybody there was very accommodating at that time frame. Iran, of course, was a threat to everybody out there, and they made sure they remained a threat. So people were generally opposed to anything the Iranis did, and if anything they did helped us in opposition to Iran, they were in favor of it. So it made my job easier.

Paul Stillwell: Why did you use a P-3 instead of a jet?

Admiral Trost: First of all, availability. We had what was called the nondescript P-3 based on Guam. It used for logistic support for Seventh Fleet in the Indian Ocean, primarily. It was used by Com7thFlt any time he could go somewhere that—well, whether or not it required a carrier was irrelevant. But the availability of jets was limited. We didn't have C-140s, which they probably use today.[*] I would certainly have used that to go to Diego Garcia.

The other thing was the numbers of people and the logistic support we'd have. It was a working thing. The navigator's station was on the port side of a P-3, and on the starboard side they put in two facing bench-type padded seats, with a worktable and shelves to store things in, windows to look out, and that was my workstation. We had berthing for the crew, but I never traveled overnight in the thing, so I didn't need any special berthing. The VIP P-3s that the CNO used when I was CNO had berthing for the staff and all. It's got long legs. You can fly from Japan nonstop to Diego Garcia if you have to. I normally stopped in Singapore to refuel if I was going out there, just for safety. They could be supported readily because we were flying P-3s in theater, operational P-3s, so parts were there, at least no further away than Diego Garcia, and trained people were there to take care of the airplane. So it worked out well. And as I said, you could work on it and get things done.

When I was on an official visit, Pauline established a relationship with wives' clubs everywhere we went, and she'd always have a "We'd sure like to have" list. We went into Malaysia, for example, and the Malaysian staff people, both the military and the State Department staff people, gave her a list after our first visit there which would have choked a horse. She got it all together, took it out there on our next visit. These were things they didn't have access to, nice-to-have stuff, nothing that would stop them from

---

[*] C-140 Jet Star is the Air Force designation for a plane developed as a business jet.

living there, but their embassy and support staff were well supported by my wife. So it helped to have the P-3 because we had room to carry stuff. We had a lot of extra room.

If you fly in a jet, you can't fix food, you carry your box lunch, and here we had a little galley and you could eat on our way, and it worked out well. We had good comm support, better than we'd have had in a jet. In the jet, well, the alternatives weren't there. The C-140s weren't out there, and they weren't there unless my boss came from Hawaii in one, but he normally came via P-3 at that point in time also because of the convenience. You need to carry extra uniforms. You need to have civilian clothes for functions. So it's convenient primarily.

Paul Stillwell: When you took over from Admiral Foley, did he have any unfinished business items he passed on?[*]

Admiral Trost: He had a couple, because we had a three-day turnover, and so a lot of to-dos are left-undones, yeah. But that's pretty standard. You can't stay current on everything. He and I, when I was Deputy CinCPacFlt and he was out there, we talked probably twice a week, so I was current on what Seventh Fleet was doing, what its major issues were, and the turnover was simple.

When we started, we got into Tokyo about mid to late afternoon, got down to Yokosuka, had an arrival welcome party. We arrived there after flying from Hawaii to Japan commercial, so we got to bed about 9:00 o'clock, having been up a long time. Went into the BOQ after the welcome party, went to bed, and Bob and I sat down on the flagship at 7:00 o'clock the next morning to start the turnover over breakfast. And that was our day for turnover.

That evening, the mayor of Yokosuka held a welcome reception, even though he didn't like Seventh Fleet being there. We had all the local businessmen and the local VIPS. Then the following day was the change of command, so no wasted time. But I'd have preferred it that way to sitting around a couple of days not doing anything.

---

[*] Vice Admiral Sylvester R. Foley Jr., USN, served as Commander Seventh Fleet from 31 May 1978 to 14 February 1980.

So when we met with the senior Japanese, I had met them at a cocktail party and then the business meeting was the first time I was sitting down a couple of days later and really getting to start to know them. We were on a Japanese naval base over in Yokosuka.[*] We took it over and then we let the Japanese use it as their fleet support base. It's their sub base, and they had about a dozen destroyers there. So it was a major support and major shipyard support, which we used along with them. So we had a mutual interest in keeping it running right. Good relationship, very good relationship.

Paul Stillwell: You said that the locals didn't welcome Seventh Fleet. Why was that?

Admiral Trost: The locals did; the mayor did not.

Paul Stillwell: I see.

Admiral Trost: The local business community was all for it. We brought business. The local Chamber of Commerce and Industry was headed by a guy named Kosano, who owned the biggest dry goods store in Yokosuka. He had been a one-time mayor of Yokosuka, a much younger man. Kosano was in his late 80s when I got out there, and he was all for the U.S. Navy.

We had quarterly golf tournaments, Seventh Fleet staff and commanders of any ships that were in, and his business community, and we did that over at Atsugi, which was a former Japanese air base that became ours and still is. It's a joint base now, but that was the headquarters for a lot of things that we did.[†] And we'd have a quarterly Chamber of Commerce and Industry and Navy tournament, and every one of their senior businessmen would turn out for that.

Occasionally, I invited a member of the Diet who had been their equivalent of Secretary of Defense, very pro-American.[‡] I invited him down one time for one of our Navy tournaments with the Navy leadership in one of my quarterly conferences there,

---

[*] The Imperial Japanese Navy had been disbanded following World War II. By 1980 the much smaller force was known as the Japanese Maritime Self-Defense Force.

[†] Naval Air Facility Atsugi, operated jointly by the U.S. Navy and the Japanese Maritime Self-Defense Force.

[‡] The National Diet is Japan's bicameral legislature.

and he became the best supporter we had in Tokyo. Matter of fact, the first time he came down, he said, "How often do you do this?"

I said, "Quarterly."

He said, "Wives ever come?"

I said, "Yeah, we have a dinner. Every quarter we have a dinner the first night, and we invite the wives from Korea, from Okinawa, and from Philippines up with the commanders who they're married to."

"Could my wife come?"

I said, "Sure."

"Oh, I come." And he became our buddy. The first time he came, he called his wife. He was in Atsugi, and he called his wife in Tokyo. He told her to get on such-and-such a train—I didn't know what he was talking about—and come to Yokosuka.

I said, "That's tonight's dinner. Tomorrow night is in Atsugi."

"Okay." So he had already arranged for somebody to go to the train station, meet his wife, pick her up, brought her to our quarters so she could get cleaned up and go to the dinner. I got to know all my senior commanders by name, by golf score, because he started joining us for golf, and it was a great relationship. But the businessmen were very much on our side.

Paul Stillwell: What was the mayor's opposition?

Admiral Trost: I think we had authority that he couldn't control. For example, Commander Naval Forces Japan, who was a U.S. Navy two-star, was also based in Yokosuka, had access to the Minister of Defense in Tokyo. The mayor didn't like that because that meant that U.S. Navy leaders at the time could go to Tokyo without a by your leave from him, as could I. We could meet with the Minister of Defense or a member of the Diet, and nobody in his government knew anything about it. And if we made arrangements having to do with our ships' presence, which was our business, he wasn't cut in. He had a liaison guy, an EA, who would meet with my aide weekly, and they'd compare notes on schedule and so forth. So we were doing our best to keep him cut in, but he was not in charge.

On one occasion *Midway*, which was homeported there at the time, was coming back from five-and-a-half month deployment in the Indian Ocean.[*] The mayor asked me to stop her from coming back to port. I said, "Where do you want them to go?"

"Not here."

Paul Stillwell: Oh, jeez. [Laughs]

Admiral Trost: He said, "They're not welcome."

I said, "Well, I have port clearance for her. Your Navy knows they're coming in." Their State Department equivalent, "Your foreign affairs people are aware of it. They've cleared the return." I said, "You can't stop it."

"I will not meet the ship."

I said, "Fine." So that was our relationship, and it never got better than that during my time out there.

With Staser, I don't know. I never compared notes with him.[†] Staser, I don't know whether he played golf or not. But that quarterly golf thing, both the local business quarterly golf and the quarterly commanders' conferences, which were normally held in Yokosuka or in Atsugi, were very big deals for the Japanese who were participants. They really put a big stake in that.

And it helped. If I wanted to meet in Tokyo with my counterpart, their Chairman of Joint Chiefs, or their Minister of Defense, all I had to do is pick up the phone and call, and the odds were if I said I'd like to come that afternoon, I could have. I usually didn't give them short notice, but we had good access and a good relationship. So it paid to be decent.

The mayor couldn't complain about not being cut in, but he could complain about not knowing what was going on because there were things we didn't tell him, and that made him very jealous. He wanted at one point in time to have access to our gate lists

---

[*] The aircraft carrier *Midway* (CV-41) and her escorts arrived in Yokosuka, Japan, on 5 October 1973 to begin the first overseas home-porting of a complete carrier task group. The forward deployment was the result of an accord arrived at on 31 August 1972 between the United States and Japan. In August 1991, after nearly 18 years of service out of the Japanese port, the *Midway* left Yokosuka for the last time and was replaced by the *Independence* (CV-62) as the forward-deployed carrier.
[†] Vice Admiral M. Staser Holcomb, USN, served as Commander Seventh Fleet from 15 September 1981 to 9 May 1983.

which told him who went on the naval base, which were our people and their guys. But we control the base, we control gate access, and he wanted a list. I said, "No, you don't need that. None of your business."

Paul Stillwell: It's interesting that even all the years it's been a U.S. naval base, it's euphemistically called Fleet Activities rather than a base. [Laughs]

Admiral Trost: Yeah. Actually, the basis for all these bases is in the peace treaty. It's a treaty matter, and the mayor of the town doesn't have a damn thing to do with it. And it's a beautiful base, great base.

Paul Stillwell: What do you remember about your flagship *Blue Ridge*?

Admiral Trost: Very good ship. It's one of two of that class. What was the other one? The other one was in Mideast for a long time. They were both built as amphibious command ships, and they were well appointed, well equipped for that job.

Paul Stillwell: *Mount Whitney*.

Admiral Trost: *Mount Whitney*. They could handle helicopters, every size helicopter we flew, including the big SH-3s. And I'm not sure about a CH-53.

At any rate, it had a big hold that could accommodate about 150 vehicles, and we hauled 150 Japanese pickup trucks to the Philippines on one trip to replenish what was on there for the U.S. forces. Now, they were mini trucks. They were the small Toyotas, as I remember, but there were a lot of them. That was a very handy thing to have, because when we went to Hong Kong, the staff and the ship's company liked to shop for furniture. We'd have the vehicles on trips that went to the Philippines, went to Hong Kong with an empty hold, and there was room for people to shop.

I had a big stateroom and a big office. My bedroom was big. I came back from an official visit with the Royal Navy, who was then running Hong Kong, and walked into my stateroom late one afternoon. I could barely move. It was full of stuff that Pauline and her buddies had bought, so they just used the CinC's stateroom, and that's where they put it. To get to my hanging locker, I had to move a couple of pieces of furniture out of the way first so I could get to the doors, and I had to put a little guidance on what not to pack in my room. [Laughs] But they took full advantage of it. And the merchants of Hong Kong did very well.

Paul Stillwell: What about the communications facilities?

Admiral Trost: Outstanding. Worldwide capability. It was built as a command ship, and it had the ability to handle everything, and it was heavily, heavily manned for any kind of ship. We had more comms capability than, as far as I know, any other Navy ship, and it was used pretty widely. We were on several broadcasts and we were in command of a lot of ships. My average fleet size was above 70, and while I was out there, my carrier levels went from two to five, 33,000 Marines. I don't recall how many airplanes total—a lot of airplanes. We had a full Marine air wing between Okinawa and Iwakuni in Japan on the mainland. I don't remember how many airplanes, but a goodly number.

Paul Stillwell: What would decide when you made a visit by airplane versus flagship?

Admiral Trost: The flagship was actually supposed to visit. That was my in-between six-month visits that were normally by plane, and then we tried to put as much into a trip as we could. There again, timesaving was part of it. If you're going down to the southern part of the Western Pacific—well, for example, to go to Australia, I would usually go to Guam, which also was part of my responsibility, for my six-month visit there, then fly down from there to Eastern Australia and sometimes stop in Fiji, because we used Fiji as a stopover from Hawaii to Australia for official business, and we liked to keep the access open. It was not a U.S. base, so we wanted to keep access to that airfield, which was quite good, keep that available.

Then if we went to Western Australia, which we did again every six months, that was best done with the flagship, and we'd go in there and visit two ports. They wanted us in a port south of whatever it is—is it Perth on the west coast? Perth and then—

Paul Stillwell: Fremantle is the port city for Perth.

Admiral Trost: Fremantle. I'd go to Perth to meet with the governor of Western Australia. We'd go into Fremantle and the place south of Fremantle where they developed a submarine base. I forgot what it was. We went in there once to prove that it could accommodate the Seventh Fleet flagship if operations required. I don't know if they ever did.

In Northwestern Australia, we had a communications station for the Indian Ocean, operated jointly by us and the Australians, owned by us, controlled by us until after my time in Seventh Fleet when we turned over opcon to the Australians. But we continued to have a certain amount of manning there, and that was for classified stuff. But we didn't make the east and west coast visits at the same time. The east coast visit on the flagship, I made it twice in my tour. We'd normally go from there back up through the Philippines and through Kuala Lumpur, Malaysia.

Paul Stillwell: Who was the scheduler that figured out your itinerary for all these places?

Admiral Trost: I had an ops officer who was a Navy commander who had a scheduler, and I think he was actually a lieutenant. The guidelines were pretty clear. You almost developed a routine. We knew were going to be in Hong Kong, as I recall, April and September or something like that, or October, just about every year. We were going to be in Singapore—I forgot whether it's the same trip or not. I think Singapore and Kuala Lumpur were on the same trip. Maybe Subic Bay; I'm not sure. I have forgotten so much of the detail of this thing.

But we would have the places we had to visit when, and the places we were supposed to visit when, and occasionally a request from an ambassador in one of these places who wanted a gray hull in port for some national event, and that would be good to show U.S. Navy presence there. So we'd do both complying with requests, with practice, with habit. Operational command, yes, but presence was my primary mission out there, and we were good.

I had an interesting visit with the President of Singapore when Reagan was elected as President.[*] The longtime president/dictator of Singapore said, "Have you heard the news about President-elect Reagan?"[†] He said, "That's very good. Now we can have normal relations out here again." He didn't like Carter.[‡] He was not well received by Carter, apparently, with the dignity he thought he deserved. The Singaporeans were very helpful to me. This was shortly after I took over. He said, "Now we have decent relations. But then you and General—." General, my friend whose name I can't remember. He said, "Keep in close touch with each other. Let us know. We'll support everything you need to our ability," and they did. He said, "Just keep us cut in." Reasonable request.

The Brits in Hong Kong were equally supportive, very supportive. My flagship and staff were very choice duty for sailors because they liked living in Japan, they liked shopping in Korea, Hong Kong, Philippines.

Paul Stillwell: The port visits.

Admiral Trost: Oh, yeah. When we visited the Hong Kong area, for example, we sometimes had wives' groups chartering entire airplanes to go to Hong Kong, because they could buy stuff in Hong Kong, get it on the flagship, get it transported back to Japan with their husbands' labor and their husbands' shipmates' labor. [Stillwell laughs.] And besides, it was a friendly place, a very friendly place. We had very good relations there with the then Hong Kong government and with the British government, and the Hong Kong government hasn't had good relations with the mainland government since they took over.[§]

Paul Stillwell: Interesting.

Admiral Trost: Yeah.

---

[*] Ronald W. Reagan was elected on 4 November 1980.
[†] Benjamin Henry Sheares was President of Singapore from 2 January 1971 to his death on 12 May 1981.
[‡] James E. Carter, Jr., who had graduated from the Naval Academy in the class of 1947, served as President of the United States from 20 January 1977 to 20 January 1981.
[§] In 1898 Great Britain was granted a 99-year lease to the area known as the New Territories, including Hong Kong. The area reverted to China in July 1997.

Paul Stillwell: You mentioned a dual-command relationship on the Middle East Force. Did you get to Bahrain?

Admiral Trost: Oh, yeah, got to Bahrain. Matter of fact, I had a number of visits to Bahrain. I had been to Bahrain with John Warner when he was Secretary of the Navy, and then several times while I had command of Seventh Fleet, because, it was interesting, I had opcon of the ships that operated out of Bahrain, but I didn't have to do anything about maintaining the base or anything else.

I called on the Sheikh Isa, very pro-U.S., when I went there, but I didn't have any official business dealings with him.[*] That was taken care of by the people in London, and I just operated the ships from there, which Commander, Sixth Fleet at the time, Bill Small, whom I knew quite well.[†] Bill was—I don't know if the term would be insulted or pissed off about this relationship because he didn't like it. And it was a little bit awkward and hard to understand it. On the other hand, from an operational perspective, it made lots of sense because before that, Sixth Fleet was responsible for operations in the Persian Gulf, but I think Seventh Fleet's area headed up through the North Arabian Sea. So you had to transfer of command relationships when you went into the North Arabian Sea, which didn't make all that much sense. And when we built up our forces, didn't make sense at all, because I was the force supplier, so it made sense that I have the opcon when you transfer in going through the straits.

Paul Stillwell: But now it's Fifth Fleet and a much more robust operation.

Admiral Trost: Yeah, and with the activity level out there, the current relationship makes good sense, I think. And it gave a little more clout to the Fifth Fleet Commander. He also went up a rank when they became Fifth Fleet, as I recall.

Paul Stillwell: Yes.

---

[*] Sheikh Isa ibn Salman Al Khalifa was the first Emir of Bahrain; he served in that capacity from 2 November 1961 until his death on 6 March 1999.
[†] Vice Admiral William N. Small, USN, served as Commander Sixth Fleet from July 1979 to June 1981.

Admiral Trost: And he doesn't have the dual responsibility. The dual U.S. Navy fleet responsibility, numbered fleet responsibility isn't there like it was before, so it's a cleaner relationship.

Paul Stillwell: Well, Admiral, it's 4:30. Is this a convenient breaking point?

Admiral Trost: Okay. If it is for you, great.

Paul Stillwell: I thank you for another informative session and look forward to the next one.

Interview Number 10 with Admiral Carlisle A. H. Trost, U.S. Navy (Retired)

Date: Wednesday, 9 September 2015

Place: Admiral Trost's apartment in Ginger Cove, south of Annapolis, Maryland

Paul Stillwell: Admiral, before we turned on the recorders, you mentioned a few things in connection with the aircraft carrier *Midway*, and this ties in with the tour of duty we were discussing, your service as Commander Seventh Fleet. Could you tell about the graduation ceremony and your visits to the ship?

Carlisle Trost: I could. *Midway* was homeported in Yokosuka while I had command of Seventh Fleet. The skipper on *Midway* was both a friend and he had a daughter in my son's graduating high school class.[*] He volunteered to set up *Midway* as the platform for the graduation for the Yokosuka High School students, who were all obviously American Navy dependents. Might have had a few Marines in that group. So the kids got an unexpected treat. He set up the hangar deck, decorated it beautifully. It looked like a Navy change of command, and bunting everywhere and had soft drinks set up for the arriving crowd. So they had quite an experience, and well received by the graduates and the parents, a great thing for the Navy to be able to do for its own.

That was my experience with *Midway*. I didn't spend a lot of time at sea in her. I was out a couple of times. I don't remember exactly how many times. But I flew aboard and was catapulted off in a COD.[†] I don't think I got aboard *Midway* while she was deployed to the North Arabian Sea, because I flew off every carrier that went out there, including the ones from the East Coast because they were all under my opcon. But *Midway* was a very familiar site. So I have fond memories of *Midway*'s time out there.

Paul Stillwell: Well, you mentioned a story before we started, about flying a plane on to a ship. You said you were in the copilot's seat.

---

[*] Captain Eddie I. Carmichael, USN, served as commanding officer of the aircraft carrier *Midway* (CV-41) from 7 September 1979 to 17 February 1981.

[†] COD – carrier on-board delivery, an aircraft configured for carrier takeoffs and landings, dedicated to transporting personnel and cargo between ship and shore.

Admiral Trost: I think it was *Constellation.*

Paul Stillwell: It's a good story, so please. [Laughs]

Admiral Trost: I was in Oman and I was due to go out to the battle group, and I think *Constellation* was the carrier, and the cargru commander on board was Bill Ramsey, classmate of mine and a good friend of mine.[*] So he sent a US-3, which was an S-3 with the mission equipment stripped out. It was used for high-priority cargo from Diego Garcia up to the battle group. He sent them up with the squadron exec and the newest jaygee pilot in the squadron as the pilot, and they had me rigged up to sit in the right seat.

When we got airborne, I was told to take the controls and fly the airplane, which I knew you steered with it, and I knew you had pedals that you did things with, so I followed instructions very carefully. I got up to altitude and flew it for about an hour, I guess, heading out to the battle group. They said, "Now take it down in the pattern."

Once I started, I didn't throttle back, so I shook the buddy stores on the wings, and they rattled and scared the exec a little bit behind, in the rear behind me. I got that under control, came down, and then I was flying the downwind leg. That's where you made the carrier approach, which I was doing, when the XO thought it was about time for that jaygee to take over. [Laughter]

So he did and made a successful landing, and got a little bit of a hard time from his squadron commander when he landed. The squadron commander had a few critique comments, and the poor kid's sitting there probably shivering, thinking, "I hope this never happens to me again." It was quite an experience.

Paul Stillwell: So that's one trap in your flight log.

Admiral Trost: That's one trap of many.

---

[*] Rear Admiral William E. Ramsey, USN, served as Commander Carrier Group One from May 1979 to November 1980.

Paul Stillwell: What else do you remember about visiting the support ships that were out in the Indian Ocean, North Arabian Sea?

Admiral Trost: I got aboard both of the real support ships, the LKAs.[*] I don't know if we had any LPAs out there.[†] I don't think we did, but they and the MSC ships that were there. That turned out to be a morale booster for them, because they're normally ignored by people coming out to visit the battle groups. For me, it was learning and quite interesting. I spent quite a bit of time at sea when I was out there. Well, I spent all my time at sea except for when I occasionally went into Oman and occasionally into Bahrain and got familiar with those places because they're both critical to our support. So, interesting tour.

Paul Stillwell: What do you remember about the flagship's travels when you were on board?

Admiral Trost: I was required to make two trips a year with the flagship to Southeast Asia, and we normally hit Hong Kong, Singapore, Subic Bay, Malaysia, and Singapore. What was interesting was that when I would get there, I would meet with the senior Navy people, and usually with their senior diplomatic people, they're usually the Assistant Secretary of State, or in Singapore with the boss himself, the head of government.[‡] He insisted on meeting every six months with me, usually gave me a little bit of guidance, what he wanted Seventh Fleet to be doing, be alert to. And I met with their senior military people in Singapore. It was General Choo, I think was his name, Winston Choo, who was Army, but he was equivalent of their Chairman, Joint Chiefs, an interesting guy and in very close with the head of government. So when he spoke, we listened. So it was quite an interesting tour of duty.

Paul Stillwell: How much of these discussions were substantive and how much

---

[*] LKA – amphibious cargo ship.
[†] LPA – amphibious transport.
[‡] Benjamin Henry Sheares was President of Singapore from 2 January 1971 to his death on 12 May 1981.

ceremonial?

Admiral Trost: I would say over half substantive. It depended on what was going on at the time. I went into Malaysia, for example, as they were looking to expand their presence slightly to the west. They were opening a new port in western Malaysia, and I went there for that. That was ceremonial and substantive, probably more ceremonial because the substantive portion, really answering questions and talking to them about our planning, because they'd invited us to use the spaces that were available, and we could use them from time to time for repair work and a place where their troops could rest and I could bring in ships from the North Arabian Sea around that didn't have the time to get all the way to Singapore or the Philippines, and this gave them a liberty port. I'm not sure how good a liberty port it was, but it was a liberty port, something new and different. So I'd say the meetings were about 50-50.

Paul Stillwell: How much interaction did you have with South Korea?

Admiral Trost: Quite a lot, on a monthly basis. The South Korean Navy, as I may have said before, under the U.N. treaty that ended the Korean War, the South Korean Navy, in the event of a U.N. contingency, chopped to Seventh Fleet for operational control. Actually, I had a headquarters office, Korea Navy headquarters, in Chinhae, and I went to Seoul once a month and met with their head of Navy and their Chairman, Joint Chiefs, at that time, who later became the ambassador to the United States, quite a good guy, very pro-American.

Interesting, interesting place. We kept very current of what they were doing, and we had Commander U.S. Naval Forces Korea, whose only forces would be those that chopped to him in a U.N. contingency. So he and I would meet. He kept his finger on the pulse. He was the U.S. representative to the talks up at the DMZ, and so I had no control over what he did or no guidance responsibility.* But I was kept in the loop by the Commander of our U.S. forces in Korea, who was John Wickham, General, U.S. Army,

---

* DMZ – demilitarized zone.

at the time.* So we'd know what was going on in the discussions and anything that was a hot item that he thought I needed to know about. So it was a very interesting time.

Paul Stillwell: I'm not sure if the timing was quite the same, but General Singlaub got into the media for opposing President Carter's attempts to draw down forces in Korea.† Do you remember that incident?

Admiral Trost: I remember that. That was before my time up there, and I don't even remember any of the details of it, except it was controversial.

John Wickham was the U.S. Forces Korea commander during my entire tour, and then later on, he and I overlapped by a year when I became CNO. He was Army Chief of Staff, and so that relationship carried on very well, matter of fact, carried on as a friendship for several years after that.‡

Paul Stillwell: Were you involved in joint exercises with these various nations?

Admiral Trost: Yes.

Paul Stillwell: What were the objectives?

Admiral Trost: Interoperability, more than anything else, than a contingency, and also show the flag, show that we were there and could be there in whatever numbers needed to be used. For example, when I went to Java, Indonesia, we always set up command-and-control exercises with my flagship, and then if I had somebody accompany me, a Seventh Fleet unit, then we'd set up exercises with their forces. So that really was security of straits and enforcing rights of passages if challenged, and the Chinese at that time

---

* General John A. Wickham Jr., USA, served as Commander U.S. Forces Korea from 19 July 1979 to 4 June 1982.
† In early 1977, when Major General John K. Singlaub, USA, was chief of staff of U.S. forces in South Korea, he publicly criticized President Carter's decision to withdraw some U.S. troops from the Korean peninsula. On 21 March 1977, Carter relieved him of duty.
‡ General Wickham served as Army Chief of Staff from 23 July 1983 to 23 June 1987.

challenged but never carried out their challenge, so we were always sure we were ready in case they got serious.[*]

Paul Stillwell: Were they challenging to the point of being provocative?

Admiral Trost: To the point of putting a presence there whenever they found out we were going to send forces through. They'd have somebody there just to be snooping more than anything else.

Paul Stillwell: Would this be comparable to the Soviets that had tattletails behind U.S. ships in the Med?[†]

Admiral Trost: Yeah, maybe on a more limited basis and not every time somebody went through, but anytime a major group of ships or a major combatant came through the straits, they'd be there. How they found out, must have had our operating schedule. [Laughter]

Paul Stillwell: Well, speaking of those schedules, how did they come about? You're talking about a lot of ships with a lot of missions. I presume you had the quarterly scheduling conferences.

Admiral Trost: We did. We had the quarterly scheduling conference, including the Marines on Okinawa, which were under my opcon. We held those conferences more often than not in Japan, because there were spaces, a briefing theater, for example, and BOQ rooms and things that we needed. So most of our conferences took place there.

Alternatively, we met once in the Philippines, never on Okinawa or Korea, which would have been the other two venues that we'd have used. But we had operational conferences in Korea with the Korean Navy because we had annual exercise with them. I

---

[*] This refers to the strait between Taiwan and mainland China.
[†] "Tattletails" was a nickname for small Soviet ships designated as AGIs. They steamed in proximity to American warships, observing their movements and, presumably, prepared to provide targeting information in the event the Soviets wanted to attack them.

think it was called Team Spirit, as I recall, and that involved Navy and Marine Corps and, to a lesser degree, U.S. Army forces. It was something the North Koreans always propagandized about it, about our warlike intentions, and then, of course, they'd snoop as much as they could and send ships to get in the way from time to time, make an annoyance of themselves, really.

Paul Stillwell: And I know flexibility had to be a hallmark. When I was in a Seventh Fleet ship in the 1960s, we'd get the quarterly schedule and say, "Well, we know it's what we're not going to do," because it would change so often.

Admiral Trost: Yeah, it would.

Paul Stillwell: What types of objectives did you try to carry out in those conferences?

Admiral Trost: Really making sure everybody was on board with the kinds of exercises, we come up with their major exercises, a lot of intelligence exchange on what the Soviet and later the Chinese Navy were doing, made sure everybody knew. We'd review our rules of engagement as they existed or as they'd been changed since the last conference. I think as important as anything else was getting the major commanders to know each other and talk to each other and exchange ideas. There was usually an update, intelligence and operationally, on what's happening and what's coming up and what we expected from the exercises we were running.

Now, exercises became secondary to operational because the North Arabian Sea really drove what happened to my ships. I averaged 75 to 80 ships out there in Seventh Fleet at any given time. Majority of them were in the North Arabian Sea and in the Indian Ocean, so we stayed busy.

Paul Stillwell: That was a challenge, yes.

Admiral Trost: I averaged five carriers in combination, sometimes two in WestPac and three North Arabian Sea. Sometimes when my Yokosuka-based carrier was deployed, all five were in the North Arabian Sea.

Paul Stillwell: Wow.

Admiral Trost: My biggest problem was they were out there, port visits were scarce, so when we got access to Singapore, Singapore's far away. It's across the Indian Ocean. But it was really critical. When you get a carrier and you deploy it for five months and it has one port visit and it's five days in Singapore, those five days are really treasured by the crew.

Paul Stillwell: Yes.

Admiral Trost: I got access to Colombo, Sri Lanka. It's the major port on the southern coast of Sri Lanka, the capital. We got access to Sri Lanka because I sent Marine heavy-lift helicopters down to put a communications tower on one of the peaks in Sri Lanka so they could communicate with their forces, and, in return, I asked for access and they gave it. So we got a carrier in there about every six months, and they'd spend four, five days there, and that was a good liberty port, apparently. I got in there. I stopped there about every few months, usually on my way in and out of the Indian Ocean. So we had a good working relationship with them. Then in Kenya, Nairobi—

Paul Stillwell: You mentioned Mombasa previously.

Admiral Trost: Yeah. So those were kind of critical visits. You could relieve the strain on the guys a little bit, because we'd deploy a carrier from the East Coast, be out for five months and no port visits. So they got a port visit that was on the way in or the way out, South Africa being one of the principal ones, and occasionally back through the Mediterranean. So they didn't get a lot of liberty.

Paul Stillwell: You mentioned that the mayor of Yokosuka was not too happy about having the *Midway* there. How was the general relationship with the local populace?

Admiral Trost: Very good, very good. The local business community supported Seventh Fleet presence very strongly. I'm not sure how much business we added, but we did. With the carrier based there and several other ships and the Seventh Fleet flagship, there were a lot of Navy families over there, and, of course, they were good spenders when they went on the economy. The exchange rate was very favorable when we were over there, so people loved to shop in Yokosuka, and that kept them from straying off north to Tokyo to do shopping. So the business community was very, very friendly and very supportive, and we had a good relationship with them. And they basically overrode the mayor's objections.

So there was a man. I guess he was the president or the chairman of the chamber of commerce. He was about 20 years older than I, but he had power. When he said something, you knew when the message got out by the feedback we got. They made sure there were no liberty incidents that were caused by anything the Japanese did. They were very supportive.

I had an incident one time where about five of our sailors from a visiting ship went out to a bar and thought the guy was shorting them on drinks, and they started raising hell and created quite a stir. We sent shore patrol out to pick them up, bring them in. The next day, I was visited by the chairman of the chamber of commerce to apologize because, "Our people were trying to cheat your sailors." So he came on board my flagship to apologize for the behavior. "People told me it won't happen again."

Paul Stillwell: That's remarkable.

Admiral Trost: Yeah. So they were very supportive, and we had almost zero liberty incidents there. They were accepted by the populace and, of course, they were very carefully briefed to, "You go into town and cause trouble, your ass is in a sling." So they knew that.

Paul Stillwell: I've heard that the Japanese shipyard workers took loving care of the *Midway*, even though it commemorated a Japanese defeat.*

Admiral Trost: That's right. They really did. That ship repair facility at Yokosuka was just outstanding. Well, *Midway*, for example, didn't have regular overhaul schedules because she was taken care of right there. The flagship did not go into overhaul on a regular basis. And one in-port overhaul took place right at the tail end of my tour, and we agreed with them, their ship repair facility had access, with our support, during the working day, because that's when it was their working day, and also we didn't want to pay the overtime fees that would have come otherwise.

But at about 1600, when their workforce left, the ship was sparkling clean, and when they came back to work, they stayed out of our way, we stayed out of theirs. We had an in-port overhaul, and everything we needed fixed was fixed, and the ship was always clean and operational. We were the radio command for Seventh Fleet, and we were online 24 hours a day the whole time. So they were very cooperative and very effective, very efficient.

The Japanese Navy, of course, had ships there. Their fleet headquarters was there, their submarine force was based there. And our relationship was outstanding. I had a good relationship with the submarine force commander, for example, because we found out when I went to sub school in 1955, January, we had ten Japanese officers in our class because we were turning over a boat to them, and he and I were in the same sub school class but didn't know each other in that class. We met for the first time when I was the Deputy PacFlt out in Hawaii and he came through and reminded me of it and had the paperwork, the roster of the people from New London from, at that point in time, 23 years before, something like that.

---

* From 4 to 6 June 1942, U.S. and Japanese naval forces fought a battle northwest of Midway Island in the Pacific. After Japanese bombers had struck the island, carrier-based U.S. dive-bombers attacked and sank the Japanese carriers *Hiryu*, *Soryu*, *Kaga*, and *Akagi* and the cruiser *Mikuma*. U.S. ships lost were the carrier *Yorktown* (CV-5) and the destroyer *Hammann* (DD-412). The battle was both a tactical and strategic victory for U.S. forces.

Paul Stillwell: That's neat.

Admiral Trost: So we had a good working relationship. Our wives got along beautifully. Matter of fact, we corresponded with her as recently as this last Christmas, which we had done very year. She and Pauline were great buddies and wrote to each other regularly. We tracked their family. She had a daughter who was last in Norway in their Foreign Service and had visited the U.S. a number of times. She came over to the U.S. while I was on active duty still and visited with us. So there were some interesting aspects to the tour. It was an interesting tour for us, enjoyable.

Paul Stillwell: What was your relationship with Commander Naval Forces Japan?

Admiral Trost: Very close. First of all, Lando Zech was the first Naval Forces Commander when I got there. He'd been my company officer my last year at the Naval Academy and a friend ever since. Then he was relieved by Linn Felt, who was a classmate of mine, and had been a friend of mine.* We'd gone on training cruise together as midshipmen, and we knew him and his wife, so it was like welcoming home somebody that had been your neighbor before. So we had a very close relationship personally and professionally, but we coordinated. Our staffs had to coordinate very closely, and they were very helpful to us.

Paul Stillwell: Did that commander have any operational duties?

Admiral Trost: He had no operational duties, no. He was really our military diplomat, along with the senior Army guy who was up in Tokyo, but he had responsibility for a number of support things. At Atsugi, I've forgotten exact division of responsibility there, but he had support responsibilities in Atsugi and, of course, in Yokosuka. So it helped to have somebody there that you knew well. It was a good working relationship.

---

* Rear Admiral Lando W. Zech, Jr., USN, was Commander U.S. Naval Forces Japan from 1978 to 1980. Rear Admiral Donald Linn Felt, USN, served in the billet from 1980 to 1982.

Paul Stillwell: Interesting rank relationship with Zech. He had been senior to you for a long time.

Admiral Trost: Oh, yeah, he had been. He had been.

Paul Stillwell: Now you were a three-star and he was two.

Admiral Trost: That's right. But our relationship was always very friendly, professional but friendly, and he was a great help to me.

Paul Stillwell: In what ways?

Admiral Trost: In the sense that he had his ear to the ground. He made very close friends with the senior storeowner that I mentioned, the chamber of commerce guy. They had a very close relationship. They were both very big golfers, and we had our quarterly golf tournaments. We'd alternate hosting responsibilities, but always over at Atsugi. They had, for example, a farewell golf tournament for Zech when he was going to be relieved. And they always started with a breakfast over at Atsugi like at 7:00 in the morning. Then we'd tee off and play, and then we'd have lunch.

The final farewell for Zech-san was going to be on a Tuesday morning, and so was the arrival of a typhoon. So they were tracking that typhoon more closely than I was, but they were doing it because they didn't want it to mess up the golf tournament. [Laughter] I did it because I had ships out there. So the day before, it looked like the typhoon was going to hit just about the time we were going to start playing, and my chamber of commerce industry friend sent his Man Friday, like an EA, over to see me, and he said, "Kosano-san [his name was Kosano] does not want to cancel tournament for Zech-san. Any suggestions?" [Laughter]

I said, "That typhoon is coming, and there's nothing I can do to stop it."

"Well," he said, "would you agree to go over to Atsugi in case it doesn't hit?" [Stillwell laughs.]

So I agreed to that, called all my guys who were going to go. They were the subordinate commanders and a couple guys from my staff, my chief of staff, and my ops officer, and I said, "We're going to go over, go by car. We won't helo over," because that's an iffy thing to do. It was about a 15-minute trip by helo, which we normally did, and about and hour and a half by car in the morning.

So we got in the cars very early, drove over there. Light rain. We had breakfast, rain got a little heavier. Kosano-san said, "Look okay to me."

Zech said, "Well, if you want to do it, we'll do it." So we went out. We didn't have rain gear. We had some plastic ponchos, and we teed off. The balls went out into the wind and came almost straight down. [Stillwell laughs.] And we played five holes. The fifth hole ended up back near the clubhouse, and Kosano-san looked up at the sky and said, "I think we quit now." [Laughs]

So we went in, had coffee and had an early lunch, and that was it, but we did it. We saved face. We had the farewell ceremony and farewell luncheon, and everything was fine.

Paul Stillwell: Interesting how important saving face is.

Admiral Trost: Very important. Very important.

Paul Stillwell: I guess you didn't have enough pull with the weather gods. [Laughter]

Admiral Trost: I did not. I did not. And that typhoon didn't hit, went right up the spine of Japan, and it wasn't the most severe one that we had while we were out there, but a lot of rain.

Paul Stillwell: Did your staff routinely keep in touch with ships that were possibly in danger?

Admiral Trost: Oh, yeah, very definitely. That was a major caution, and especially if it was an exercise that would add emphasis to it. But we didn't have any severe damage to any ships while I was out there. We had some facilities damaged on Okinawa at the Marine base, and we toppled something, I forget what, some kind of tower at the air station in Okinawa, and that's the only real serious damage I recall. Subic was hit but not damaged, and those were my big concerns. Basically, we had enough warning to get ships off the expected path of the hurricane, so we didn't end up with any problems.

Paul Stillwell: And presumably the ships would be looking out for themselves as well.

Admiral Trost: They would be, but we made sure they had up-to-date weather information and predictions, and the weather predictions were pretty good out there. Matter of fact, a lot of countries relied on our weather reports. They would check in if we had an embassy. They'd check with the embassy, get Seventh Fleet weather reports, which we did because it's a good way to build friendships, and it worked out very well.

Paul Stillwell: You were collecting it for your own purposes, but it could also have other uses.

Admiral Trost: Yes. We had the information available, so it was just so that we had much better information on typhoon predictions than the Japanese Navy did, for example. And having their fleet headquarters in Yokosuka made it very easy to keep them informed on what we knew and as far as getting what they had. So a working-relationship operation was very close with them.

Paul Stillwell: How much did you emphasize public affairs in that job?

Admiral Trost: Quite a bit. Quite a bit.

Paul Stillwell: What examples might you give?

Admiral Trost: Well, for example when we had major operational exercises with the Japanese fleet commander and a couple of ships, he and his flagship, I and my flagship, and usually about two destroyers from each Navy operated together around Japan, cruised once a year. We left Yokosuka, went north, went up into the northern ports, went into Hokkaido. We went into port there, had a port visit there for usually two or three days, came back down the west coast of Japan. Had a port visit—and I can't tell you the name of it anymore—across from Korea, with their major west coast naval base, came around to southern Japan, went into Sasebo with all the ships. And at every one of those things, we had open house for visitors, and generally as we went by the major Navy installations, we had exercises with them. But that worked out fine. It was, as a matter of fact, much looked forward to by the Japanese, and it gave them status within their own operating force because they were operating with us, and it's something neither the Army or Air Force did. So we had a very close relationship.

Paul Stillwell: I would expect that the Japanese sailors and officers had a better command of English than the Americans did of Japanese.

Admiral Trost: Indeed. By far, by far. Also had a better capacity for sake. We had a reception in Sasebo where both flagships were there, and we had a reception on *Blue Ridge*, but the reception I looked forward to was the one on the Japanese flagship because they could serve sake. Obviously we couldn't. So it was very popular. And, God, they put out hors d'oeuvres spreads that wouldn't quit, and our guys never managed to match it.

It was interesting. It was a good relationship. Our officers from the two ships got to know each other. I don't really know how extensive the crew relationship was, but it was there. But the officers we saw at all the receptions and that became a very close relationship, and it carried on after we got back to Yokosuka, which was the good thing about it. So we had some enjoyable moments.

Paul Stillwell: Good. Did you and your wife get to do any touring and sightseeing in Japan, such as Kyoto?

Admiral Trost: We did. We did. We went to Kyoto, as matter of fact, and extensively in Tokyo, Sasebo, and went up to Hokkaido on two occasions. There was a businessman up there who owned a major Japanese wood-processing business on the West Coast of the U.S., was one of the most pro-U.S. guys I've ever met overseas anywhere. He was the organizer behind the Olympics. I've forgotten when the winter Olympics took place there, but it was before I was over there.[*] The facilities were all still basically intact. Well, you don't tear down a ski jump. They were using them, and I think they used them to train their own Olympic teams. As a matter of fact, I'm sure they did. But Yoshi was a big, big gun there. He insisted, when we went up there for an official visit while I had Seventh Fleet, that we stay with him and his wife and his daughters. They had a very nice home on Hokkaido. I'm trying to think what the—is it Sapporo?

Paul Stillwell: Yes, that was the winter Olympics.

Admiral Trost: Yes, it was Sapporo. I guess that's the capital of Hokkaido. There was also a major naval base on the west coast, and I've forgotten. We went in there every time we were up there. It was Sapporo where he was living. I've got his address in the other room. Anyway, very pro-American, and when you went into his house, it emulated an awful lot of conveniences you'd expect. You'd think you were in a Western home. And we'd stayed in regular Japanese homes where Japanese bathrooms and the bed—the one couple in southern Japan, mayor—and I can't think of what his name was now. I visited a number of times, but he was the big gun in the area. But his place was built with Japanese bathrooms. He had an American bathroom which had a bathtub, which they sometimes had. The big thing was the multi-headed shower in a glass enclosure, which he was very proud of. The kitchen was sort of a combination Japanese and American. The American side of it looked like what you might expect in a—not necessarily a diner, but a place with commercial equipment, and you could cook anything, and he did, as a matter of fact. Big businessman down there. I can't remember the name of that place. You're 20 years too late for me.

---

[*] The XI Winter Olympic Games were held from 3 February to 13 February 1972 in Sapporo on the island of Hokkaido, Japan.

Paul Stillwell: Well, we're getting what we can. Some of those Japanese toilets were holes in the floor. [Laughs]

Admiral Trost: You're right, and we had a number of those. But this one I was talking about—well, both the two I was talking about were conventional, like a U.S. toilet. Matter of fact, I'm not sure they weren't U.S. brands, as a matter of fact, but they were very convenient, very good.

Paul Stillwell: How much interaction did you have with Taiwan?

Admiral Trost: Almost none. We had sort of severed the relationship that existed shortly before I went to Japan, and we were no longer permitted to make port visits. Taiwan had been—I'm trying to think what I had there. Part of my support was in Taiwan. I know what it was. War reserve ammunition stores were on Taiwan. I had met the chief—what was he? He was probably the Chairman, Joint Chiefs equivalent in Taiwan while I was the Deputy PacFlt. When I got to Japan, I got a message from him saying he was sorry he couldn't invite me to visit, assured me that my ammunition stores were safe and we could, as agreed, start removing them, taking them to the Philippines and to Okinawa to alternate storage areas, which was good, because all my war reserve was in Taiwan. I think this was a Jimmy Carter initiative to pull out of Taiwan.[*]

Our relationships during my time out there were very good, even though our personal interface was off the island. We met in Tokyo one time to talk about the what-ifs of contingency operations and what we would hope we could get from them and he would hope to be able to provide. So we had a good relationship, but I never got to Taiwan, nor did any of my staff. So we put a lot of load on our naval attaché in Taiwan. He basically was unofficially my rep, but that was limited mostly to communications, and he'd keep an eye on things and was my liaison with their Chairman, Joint Chiefs. So that

---

[*] The United States officially recognized the People's Republic of China (mainland) on 15 December 1978 and severed diplomatic ties with the Republic of China (Taiwan), though both countries maintain quasi-official representation with each other.

worked out.

Paul Stillwell: Well, that was a watershed change when the Nixon administration tilted toward the People's Republic. For example, the U.S. Navy used to have a three-star in Taiwan, the Taiwan Defense Force Commander.

Admiral Trost: That's right.

Paul Stillwell: That had been downgraded considerably by your time.

Admiral Trost: Yeah.

Paul Stillwell: What do you remember about relations with the Philippines?

Admiral Trost: Very good with the Philippine Navy. I met with President Marcos on two occasions, both was very friendly, but also reminding you of his status and of his ego.[*] First time I called on him, I walked in and there he is sort of on a stage that was a couple of feet high, sitting behind his desk.

Paul Stillwell: Kind of like a throne?

Admiral Trost: Like a throne. And you sat down here in a couple of chairs and talked to him up there. [Laughter] So that was my memory of the imperial Marcos, and he was. The head of their Navy and the guy who was the Chairman of Joint Chiefs there, I believe was a West Pointer when I was out there. The number-two guy in the Navy was a U.S. Naval Academy graduate. So our military relationships were outstanding. I was invited by Marcos, for example, to go out to Corregidor, both to sightsee but to evaluate how defensible it was in the case of some contingency, which we didn't expect unless the

---

[*] Ferdinand Marcos was President of the Philippine Islands from 30 December 1965 until 25 February 1986.

Russians decided to take us on out there. He provided his presidential yacht, to take me out, rather than my simple barge from my flagship. They basically facilitated anything we wanted to do. We were a very important part of their economy. Up the coast was the Clark Air Force base. We were a very major impact on those economies.

The mayor of Subic was a guy named Dick Gordon, whose wife was a beautiful Filipina.[*] They both spoke fluent English, very pro-U.S. And Subic, of course, depended for very much of its local business income from the U.S. sailor, and his job was to keep it controllable so I didn't put it off out of bounds, and he did a good job of that.

I told somebody recently about my experience taking Pauline and our two daughters out into Olongapo. He had absolute control of the businessmen in that community, because they depended on his good graces, and if they got in trouble or caused a problem, they were out of business. So he was very pro-American.

Paul Stillwell: Well, the other side of the coin is that Subic Bay was a very important support base for the Seventh Fleet.[†]

Admiral Trost: Oh, yeah. Oh, absolutely. And when we lost that, we lost a lot of capability. We lost an operating shipyard, an operating supply center. They were our two principal ones of each out in that area.

Paul Stillwell: And a carrier base.

Admiral Trost: And a carrier base and a good airfield. So it was important. Local community relationships were good because they were so dependent on the income from the U.S. Navy. When we got booted out, the local business community there I thought

---

[*] James Leonard T. Gordon was the first elected mayor of Olongapo City, from 30 December 1963 to 20 February 1967. He was born on January 17, 1917 of an American father, John Jacob Gordon, and a Filipina mother, Veronica Tagle Gordon. His son, Richard J. Gordon, born in 1945, was mayor of Olongapo from 1980 to 1986 and from 1988 to 1993.

[†] Subic Bay is a protected anchorage on the island of Luzon in the Philippines. It borders the Bataan province and is about 35 miles north of the entrance to Manila Bay. During the Vietnam War, Subic had a strong role as a support base for the U.S. Navy. Included were a naval air station, piers, ship repair facility, supply depot, and recreational outlets for ships' crews. It was closed in 1992.

was going to go into a riot status. They demonstrated against their own government for doing that, and they were economically put out, basically.

Dick Gordon—I don't know if this is before or after he became a member of the Senate in the Philippines, but he had lured into Subic Bay two Japanese companies, and I don't remember what they were doing. They were on the western, northwestern end of the harbor of Subic Bay. He had managed to get them there because he foresaw problems with the U.S. for some reason, and got those businesses started before we pulled out. One was ship repair, as I recall, and, of course, we had a hell of a good shipyard there, skilled workers and a good shipyard, and a major supply center. So it hurt us to lose it.

Paul Stillwell: Things change.

Admiral Trost: And the Singaporeans tried to move into the gap for port visits and ship repair, but they were behind the curve for that, but that's built up considerably in the last 20 or so years.

Paul Stillwell: What do you remember about war planning vis-à-vis the Soviet Union?

Admiral Trost: I remember that they were the major potential enemy, not discounting North Korea, and that they figured very heavily in our contingency plans and we tracked them very carefully.

Paul Stillwell: Was there much interaction, their ships and ours?

Admiral Trost: Not much, not much. In fact, they tended to avoid us, and we tended to track them and leave them alone, made sure they knew we were there. They sent a submarine out, and he didn't stay undetected for very long or very often. So they knew we were alert to them, and every once in a while would, I guess, try to see how alert we were by sort of flushing somebody out of one of the ports and see what our reaction would be.

Paul Stillwell: What was your relationship with the U.S. submarines that were doing intelligence against the Soviet Union?

Admiral Trost: I'd say more of keeping advised. Their tasking came outside my realm. I always kept advised as to who was where, if they had special instructions, what they were, what their operating areas would probably be, so we were alert to what they did, and we had a fair amount of knowledge of who was where and what they were doing, but no opcon. Well, I say that. It varied, because I had Sub Group Seven out there, headed by a Navy captain, and I've forgotten how that working relationship was. I don't think he reported to me. I'm not sure. After 30-some years, you'd think I'd remember. I don't remember that.

Paul Stillwell: Were there any problems with U.S. nuclear-powered ships going into Japanese ports?

Admiral Trost: No problems. Complaints from time to time. We'd keep them advised, and they knew we were alert, they knew our operational controls, and there were always members of the Diet who made themselves known, and peacenik spokesmen who complained every time somebody came in. The Japanese Navy welcomed them. I don't know if it was symbolic as much as anything else, but they showed their support by supporting visits of nuclear ships. We didn't flaunt it. We were very careful. I wasn't worried at all about incidents unless somebody did something very carelessly, and if they did, they knew their ass was in a sling. So they were pretty darn careful.

Paul Stillwell: Any connections with Australia, New Zealand?

Admiral Trost: Australia, yes. New Zealand, no. New Zealand had put out an edict that said that any ship coming into a New Zealand port had to declare whether it had nuclear weapons on board, which was contrary to our national policy. So I was specifically uninvited to visit New Zealand. I had been there when I worked for John Warner and we went to the South Pole from there, as matter of fact, and we spent a couple of days, visited military installations there when I was a Navy captain, and visited Wellington, head of government, and Auckland. Auckland is the major port. When I was there, they specifically—I've forgotten when it was during the time I was Seventh Fleet—they specifically uninvited any port visits from U.S. ships who wouldn't declare, and, of course, we wouldn't declare. So my relationships with them were none.

My relationship with Australia was two visits a year, because we made major use of Western Australian ports, and I also went to the capital on a number of occasions, went to Sydney several times. We used Sydney as a relief valve for ships deployed out there. We used Western Australia frequently for port visits. We had a communications station in northwestern Australia to support our ships in the Indian Ocean. It was a joint-usage station, jointly manned, and we eventually turned that over after I left out there, I think to the Australians. I'm not sure how complete that was. We pulled out our own people, but what we did with it, I don't remember. But I think it's still operational. I'm trying to remember the name of the port. It was the place where U.S. submarines came down at the start of World War II.

Paul Stillwell: Brisbane? Fremantle?

Admiral Trost: Fremantle. The relationship with the Aussies was outstanding. They pulled a trick on me on one visit, and I may have told you this before. My travel conveyance when I was going anywhere on an official visit or anything else, other than just flying out to a carrier, was a P-3 based on Guam. It was a P-3 Alfa with Bravo engines, which gave us better range, better fuel economy. Had the mission gear stripped out, was used as a bounce bird for the VQ guys on Guam who flew the EP-3s, I guess, I'm not sure which.[*] Anyway, it was their training airplane, and it was kept available as a logistics support bird for the Indian Ocean and for Seventh Fleet travel. The area behind the right copilot seat was—I think the navigation station was on the port side. On the right side, they had built in two facing sets of good-sized seats, regular seats, not jump seats or anything, and a table, a working table, and bookshelf behind the after thing, that I could use as a working space when I was traveling.

---

[*] VQ – electronic warfare.

The Australian Air Force, my host, when we landed in Canberra for a visit, thought that was a pretty—what did they call it? Not the "Decrepit P-3," but something similar, because what they'd done up there, since it wasn't an operational bird, it got corrosion control, but they would paint the places where things were starting to—not decompose, but where you get corrosion on the skin. They'd clean it off, they'd put the undercoat on, but they didn't put the finish paint back over it. So it looked like an airplane with smallpox. [Stillwell laughs.]

So they gave me a hard time when I came to Canberra for the first time with that airplane, and when we came back out two days later to depart, they had a sign on the side of it. I think they called it the "Decrepit P-3" or something like that. And when the door was opened into the rear area, you didn't see anything. When you closed the door, a big kangaroo painted on the door. [Laughter] So our kids got a kick out of that. They were great to work with. They were really outstanding to work with and provided outstanding support.

Went to Western Australia, and I'm trying to remember what the capital of western Australia is now. The governor of Western Australia was very supportive, and we had ship visits. We got good support, good control. We had a visit of a carrier and part of its battle group. I guess that's Fremantle. I think Fremantle's the port.

Paul Stillwell: It's the port for Perth.

Admiral Trost: Perth, yeah. Okay, it's Fremantle then. There was a place between Perth and Fremantle with a very popular bar with the Australian Navy, and they introduced our sailors to it. They had an argument between the two sets of sailors and tore the place up, and the first I knew of this, even though I was the fleet commander, was a call from a woman diplomat on the staff in Perth saying, "Do you know what your Navy has done?"

Well, first of all, I didn't know her from Adam, didn't know Adam either, didn't know who she was. [Stillwell laughs.] I said, "Why are you calling me?"

So she described herself, her excellent position. She was responsible for diplomatic relations in Western Australia. She really wasn't the boss, but she was responsible for it. So she told me that my sailors had torn up this bar, and it was going to cost, I don't know, a couple hundred thousand dollars to repair.

Paul Stillwell: Wow. [Laughs]

Admiral Trost: So they apparently totaled it. So I was directed by CinCPac to go to Australia to meet with their senior diplomat in Perth and go out and meet with this owner and tell him, "We're prepared to reimburse you for that."

I did all of the above, my last visit being with the owner, who was very congenial, retired Australian Navy.

"I'm prepared to offer you a check. I'd like to know what your cost of repair was."

He said, "Offer me a check?" He says, "Best damn fight I've ever had." And he wouldn't take money. He repaired the place, went back to business. [Laughter]

Now, my people, my U.S. government diplomats in Western Australia, were pissed off at me because I didn't negotiate a deal, and that was their instructions. The fact that we left with a relationship was irrelevant.

Paul Stillwell: And you saved money.

Admiral Trost: The estimate of the damage was like a quarter million dollars, and he said, "Nah. Worth every bit of it."

Paul Stillwell: What do you remember about your principal staff members and their contributions?

Admiral Trost: Well, my chief of staff, Lew Chatham, came in.* He was relatively new at the time, former commander of the Blue Angels, carrier aviator, very bright, very hard worker, and was outstanding. I guess he made flag and went off. My ops officer was a

_____

* Captain W. Lewis Chatham, USN, was Seventh Fleet chief of staff from March 1980 to October 1981.

guy named Jim Taylor, who was an F-14 pilot.[*] Jim was on my staff the whole time there. When I came back to Washington, I came back as the Director, Program Planning, and a couple months after I took over, I needed an EA, and I got Jim Taylor back to be my EA. He did a great job there, made flag. I think his final assignment was Chief of Naval Reserve. He's retired, living down in Southern Virginia, just at the river, as a matter of fact, and good people.

My intel officer was a guy named Ted Sheafer, who later became the Director of Naval Intelligence.[†] I remember some people, but I don't remember the names exactly anymore. I had a good group. My aide was Larry Pearson, an F-14 pilot who later commanded Blue Angels, retired Navy captain.[‡] He was relieved by a guy who had been his backseater in F-14s, named Lee Mason, who was in Washington when I became CNO, volunteered to be my naval aide and was for, I guess, the last three years, great guy.[§] He retired as a Navy captain because he was a backseater, not nuclear trained. I tried to talk him into nuclear training, he could go into nuclear school, go into a carrier exec job, deep draft, then a carrier, and he was a shoo-in for flag in my book. But retired as a Navy captain because his aviators talked him out of the nuclear power program, to my regret.

But I had good people, really good people. I was trying to think who my—I did have an initial chief of staff before Lew Chatham, and I can't remember who it was. Had a good staff. We communicated well. I believe in staffs talking. If you're the ops guy, that's fine, but you'd better be talking to the plans guy if he's screwing up, and other guys ought to know what's going on. Certainly the intel guy's got to be very tied in with both of them. So I kept the staff, how shall I say, in each other's faces. It wasn't an antagonistic relationship of that sort. It was a work together, meet together every workday, and so everybody was on step about what was going on. I found that helped, because we got good input from guys that weren't the ones responsible for the particular item being discussed, and so it helped, gave us good variety.

---

[*] Commander James E. Taylor, USN. Later, as a rear admiral, he was Chief of the Naval Reserve from 1989 to 1992.

[†] Commander Edward D. Sheafer Jr., JAGC, USN. As a rear admiral he was Director of Naval Intelligence from 1991 to 1994.

[‡] Lieutenant Commander Larry G. "Hoss" Pearson, USN.

[§] Lieutenant Commander Lee C. Mason III, USN.

That's about all I remember about the staff. They were good people.

Paul Stillwell: We mentioned briefly the Desert One hostage refugee rescue attempt, and that it was highly compartmented.[*] Anything else to add on that one?

Admiral Trost: No, except Bob Kirksey, who was my senior carrier group guy and who was one guy cleared after I left PacFlt.[†] They told me when they briefed me, because my boss was out, that was the only reason I got briefed on it, was that Kirksey was going to be briefed, and he was, fortunately. He was also given the word to make sure he could get out to the carrier, which wasn't an alert to anybody because he went out there very frequently to ride the deployed ships.[‡] So he was out on scene on the carrier that launched the helicopters that went in and recovered them. So it was fortunate that we had one very, very competent operational commander on there, but also a guy who was briefed in what was going on and who made the right calls and saved that helo full of people. He probably should have gone to four stars.

I forget what he did as a three-star.[§] He came back. He got at cross breakers with John Lehman.[**] If you were a favorite of Lehman's, you were a favorite of Lehman's. If you weren't, he didn't support you. Kirksey was one of the guys he didn't support, because he didn't kowtow to him. So I'm of the judgment I had Kirksey on my list to go to three and then four stars, because I think he was that good. He retired as a three-star, unfortunately. But that happened to a couple other people, and when I complained to some of my contemporaries, they said, "Well, that's the name of the game. You win some, you lose some." But some people have an undue influence sometimes I don't think they should have. Well, he should have because he was Secretary of the Navy, but that

---

[*] In an effort to rescue American hostages held in Iran, on 26 April 1980 six Air Force C-130 cargo planes and eight Navy RH-53D helicopters flew to Iran with a joint-service commando team embarked. The aircraft rendezvoused at Desert One, a site 200 miles from the Iranian capital of Tehran. Because of helicopter problems, the mission was canceled. Several servicemen were killed in the futile rescue attempt.
[†] Rear Admiral Robert E. Kirksey, USN, Commander Carrier Group Five/Commander Carrier Striking Force Seventh Fleet (Task Force 77).
[‡] USS *Nimitz* (CVN-68) was the carrier involved.
[§] Kirksey's final active duty billet was as Director, Space Command and Control.
[**] John F. Lehman Jr. served as Secretary of the Navy from 5 February 1981 to 10 April 1987.

was one of the points of disagreement we had, and there were many.

Paul Stillwell: A lot of it as you get that high depends on who's in what places and the timing of it.

Admiral Trost: That's right. That's right. Well, if Lehman had had his way, I wouldn't have been CNO, because he didn't want me. And I could understand why he didn't want me.

Paul Stillwell: What do you recall about ship readiness in that era? I know there were problems in the Atlantic Fleet.

Admiral Trost: When I commanded the Seventh Fleet, I tied up two destroyers in Subic after they deployed to WestPac because they weren't ready operationally. They weren't either manned or trained to be safe on the gun line, in my view. So we tied them up and started school of the boat, to use a submarine term, for the one guy about a month spent alongside the pier—classes, demonstration, exercises, drills, because they were not safe to send out. So we had a need for a more professional force than we had during part of the Vietnam War. Ace Lyons was my surface warfare guy down there, and he's the one who I had tie them up and direct the training.[*]

Paul Stillwell: Right. There were a lot of long deployments to the Indian Ocean after the Iranians took the hostages.

Admiral Trost: Yeah, that's the time frame when we had one of our Norfolk-based carriers came out, was en route to the Mediterranean, diverted to go around Africa and come up through the North Arabian Sea, spend five months before it got a five-day port visit in Singapore, the only port visit in a six-month deployment, and that was the norm for my carriers coming from the East Coast.

---

[*] Rear Admiral James A. Lyons Jr., USN, Commander Naval Surface Group Western Pacific.

Paul Stillwell: Anything else to mention about the Seventh Fleet job?

Admiral Trost: No, except it was one of the most satisfying things I've done. I think of all the jobs I had, I enjoyed that the most.

Paul Stillwell: Why do you say that?

Admiral Trost: I say that because I was in the Western Pacific, my boss was in Hawaii, I was the senior Navy guy west of Hawaii, and my realm went from Hawaii to the Persian Gulf—the coast of Africa, really. Well into Africa, because actually Seventh Fleet negotiated with the then-president of Kenya for Mombasa access and more airplane access. So I had a widespread realm of responsibility. It was interesting; it went from potential Korean conflict to actual operational confrontation in the Persian Gulf. I was the senior military diplomat in most of my areas of responsibilities. So I met a couple of presidents, I met senior diplomatic people on both sides, theirs and ours, and had responsibility, and I enjoyed that. So you were sort of your own boss in many respects.

In Japan, there was nobody in Japan other than Mike Mansfield, who was the ambassador, who could really tell me what to do, and that was kind of nice.[*] It also gave you the responsibility to watch what you did and to be careful. I had a good working relationship with Mansfield. The first time I walked into his office to pay a courtesy call early in my tour, he said, "How do you like your coffee?" He had his own way of brewing coffee, and he went and hand-brewed each of us a cup of coffee. I forgot what his secret was, something that he insisted made the coffee taste better, anyway. I didn't challenge him. But he was a very easygoing guy. I thought Mansfield, being where he's been, I think he'd been the Speaker—not Speaker of the—

Paul Stillwell: He was Senate Majority Leader.

---

[*] Michael J. Mansfield, formerly a U.S. Representative and U.S. Senator, served as Ambassador to Japan from 10 June 1977 to 22 December 1988.

Admiral Trost: Senate Majority Leader, that's the title. And I thought, "Boy, this guy's going to be hard to get along with." He was a prince of a guy to work with. He'd pick up the phone and dial me himself, not the secretary. I'd pick up, and, "This is Mike, and I want to talk about the following with you." It was great. He always greeted me with a cup of coffee when I came up to call on him. I stopped to see him every time I went to Tokyo, just about, and the relationship there was good.

My relationship with several of the Japanese members of the Diet was very good, and they were very helpful. So I had a responsible job, a good staff, friendly people around. It was great. I didn't want to leave.

Paul Stillwell: Especially going to the Mixmaster of OP-090.* [Laughs]

Admiral Trost: That's right. When he called me to tell me I was going to be relieved, Staser Holcomb, my classmate, had been 090 for two years. Tom Hayward, who was then CNO, had been 090 for two years, and said to me, "It's inhumane to keep anybody there longer." So I spent four years there.

Paul Stillwell: That's twice as inhumane. [Laughs]

Admiral Trost: That's twice as inhumane, yeah. And I thought it was a dead end. Well, I was the senior three-star in Washington, and then I figured that's where I was going to die. But I never worked more than seven days a week.

Paul Stillwell: Good. [Laughs]

Admiral Trost: That was an interesting job. In retrospect, I enjoyed more flexibility in that job, in terms of influence, than I could have in any other job there, except for the CNO and the Vice Chief. Both CNOs I worked for, if the Vice Chief was out of town, I was in town, including getting recalled twice from leave because the Vice Chief was

---

* OP-090 was the designation of the Director, Navy Program Planning, the chief budgeter.

going to go on leave or on a trip or something. And so that didn't sit too well, especially with Pauline.

Paul Stillwell: Especially. Please describe the nature of the 090 job.

Admiral Trost: Well, responsible for all aspects of Navy program development and planning, all budget support to carry out that program, changes involved in the execution. I had the control of the Budget Division, the Systems Analysis Division. I guess that was it. Everybody who wanted anything had to come through my organization, and the ultimate responsibility for getting CNO and Secretary decisions was mine, meaning brief properly, prepare briefs, do the briefings in some cases. It was a job where you were into it. I didn't have to go work to testify before Congress because the CNOs decided that was compromising my—what do you call it?

Paul Stillwell: Objectivity?

Admiral Trost: Objectivity, my independence. If I was over there supporting the budget on the Hill while I was developing the new budget or the new plans, that struck them as a conflict, and it was. I can tell you that when I was CNO, when it was still all 090, not N-8 yet. But I continued that. There were times when Congress, in particular committees, knowing of the 090 organization, would, as one member said, "I want to hear it from the horse's mouth."

I said, "That's me. My three-star stays over there because he works for me, and anything you need, I'll provide to you."

He eventually accepted that; reluctantly, I might say. But it's kind of hard. As I put it, you were straddling the railroad track with one foot on each side, and trains were going in opposite directions. You can't win.

Paul Stillwell: That's quite a metaphor. [Laughs]

Admiral Trost: That's the way I felt about it. [Laughs] But I was lucky because my congressional committee chairman was Senator Sam Nunn during much of my time, and he was a prince to work with, and Ike Skelton on the House side, similarly.[*] So it was good relationships there, and I must admit I kind of cultivated their senior staff guys, except for Nunn's, who was a Marine Reserve officer named Arnold Punaro.[†] Arnold and I never got along. Arnold was a one-star Marine, and he knew he was senior to four-star Navy guys and tried to exercise accordingly.

Finally, I told Nunn, "When I come over to call on you," which I did frequently, both voluntarily—or he'd call me and say, "I want to talk to you about so-and-so," and Arnold would always sit in. What we talked about was out of the building before I was, and that just didn't go. So I told Senator Nunn that, "When we meet, I can't meet you if Arnold's in the room," and told him why. So Arnold stopped being there, so I earned the undying enmity of Arnold Punaro. We never did make up. But except for him, most of the staffers over there were pretty decent guys, and he was very smart, very powerful guy, because he controlled what Nunn saw, and that wasn't always good.

Paul Stillwell: I still see his name in the paper frequently. He stayed involved.

Admiral Trost: Yeah. He's quoted periodically. He's a retired two-star, I believe, now, and he's with some organization, defense group.[‡] I read about it probably within the last two or three years. But he was not my favorite guy to work with.

Paul Stillwell: How much of what you did involved extending current things and how much was going beyond, thinking outside the box in the 090 job?

Admiral Trost: In the 090 job, very much involved in current when there was a need for budgetary adjustments or a programmatic change, even though I didn't have the authority

---

[*] Samuel A. Nunn, a Democrat from Georgia, served in the Senate from 8 November 1972 to 3 January 1997. He was chairman of the Senate Armed Services Committee from 1987 to 1994. Isaac Newton Skelton IV, a Democrat from Missouri, served in the House of Representatives from 3 January 1977 to 3 January 2011.

[†] Arnold L. Punaro was staff director for the Senate Armed Services Committee.

[‡] Punaro is CEO of the Punaro Group and IronArch Technology.

to do, but my boss did. As far as future, almost total control of what went to the CNO and the Secretary for decision. If it was current year, they'd already approved of the program. If we did variations, they'd need that briefing. For the downstream stuff, we briefed status periodically. They were pretty well cut in on what we were thinking or what we were asking or what we were recommending be adjusted.

In terms of control, you have reaction control. You don't have control of what happens to you necessarily, but you have to respond responsibly to what's happened to you and then figure out where you have to make your adjustments for the future, and there always are adjustments. It's amazing. My final year budget was 101 billion, I think, and that included support of the Marines but not the total Marine budget, and that was about, my recollection, about 8 or 9 billion short of what we thought we needed at the time. So you do an awful lot of adjusting and trimming and reacting.

Paul Stillwell: Well, the thing that stuck out, and I think this was about 1980, a little before you got there, but there was an oiler in the Atlantic Fleet.[*] The skipper said, "We're not capable of going to sea." And this sort of demonstrated that there was a hollow Navy in terms of support.

Admiral Trost: There was, because I got to Seventh Fleet in 1980, I guess it was, and when I got out there, I had ships sailing from the West Coast that were declared unready to sail by SurfPac for various reasons, maintenance primarily, deferred maintenance that had not only been deferred but it had been labeled as critical for deployment.[†] Had no choice but to deploy ships anyway.

I remember, well, even before that, when I was the Deputy PacFlt, we sailed guys from the West Coast. If they made it halfway to Hawaii, we kept them coming. If they broke down before they got to the halfway mark, they were towed back to San Diego. We were undermanned, especially in the engineering ratings, for some reason at the time. I remember we had a group of about three destroyers that we sailed from Hawaii for Subic

---

[*] On 10 April 1980 the Navy announced in Washington that the fleet oiler *Canisteo* (AO-99) had temporarily suspended operations because of a shortage of experienced boiler technicians and machinist's mates. See *The New York Times*, 11 April 1980, page 14.
[†] SurfPac – Naval Surface Forces, Pacific Fleet.

with the word, "Do whatever you can to get into Subic so we can fix them. In the meantime, we'll see if we can get volunteers from ships already deployed out there to transfer to these ships for the balance of their deployment to make sure they're fully manned."

So it was kind of grim, and it's the kind of thing where what scared me most was that we were building up for something bad to happen, something catastrophic with personnel injuries and so forth, with no control over what we have to do to fix it. Fortunately, we didn't have any serious problems, but I attribute that to some very hardworking sailors and officers on those ships, because they scratched like hell. When they came from Pearl, we sailed some of them a little further north than normal so they'd go within the vicinity of Guam. In case they broke down, there was a ship repair facility in Guam. And if they made it past Guam, man, they were going to make it Subic, and then we could really fix them up. But manning was another issue.

Paul Stillwell: It's ironic that Jimmy Carter, a Naval Academy graduate, was so parsimonious on defense.

Admiral Trost: He really was. Well, I have some very good friends, and these are very senior retired friends, who said Jimmy Carter was the worst President we've ever had. He should have known more about the Navy. He really didn't. He was still a JO when he left the Navy and experience was limited. He considered himself an international expert. He really wasn't. It was kind of sad. But in the Navy he had the reputation for being anti-Navy, and I think it was probably true throughout defense.

Paul Stillwell: I think he vetoed a carrier in one budget.

Admiral Trost: Yeah, he did. He'd make decisions and you'd hear grumblings, "presidential decision." Was it you or was it this morning? Jimmy Carter didn't make his ceremony for distinguished graduate here. He was selected in 2002, and the process—just stop me if I've told you this.

Paul Stillwell: No, you haven't.

Admiral Trost: I've forgotten who was supposed to call me, either the president of the selection board that selected the new crop of distinguished grads or the chairman of the Alumni Association. I think it was the former, because when I was chairman, I did not make the calls. I called people to notify them, and it was supposed to be when we started out, 2002, when he was selected, was the third selection. First one was this one guy, Tom Moorer, and the next one picked up Staubach and astronaut, class of '52, Jim Lovell.[*] I've forgotten who was all in the group.

The next group was honored in 2002. Jimmy Carter and I were two of the four, and the others were Charlie Minter and John Ripley.[†] Carter didn't respond to the phone call, and so there as a lot of discussion: "How do we get to Jimmy Carter? Well, Bill Crowe is class of 1947 and knows him well, so we'll ask Bill to make the call."[‡]

Bill got through to a Carter aide and passed the word and said, "Jimmy has to say yes or no, I accept or don't accept." Still nothing. They finally persevered and got a response saying he'd accept.

Then the recognition ceremony and dinner were to be such-and-such a date. Indeterminate whether he was going to be there or not. He wasn't. I don't know if he notified anybody he wasn't coming or not. There was a guy out of class of '57, Bob Rositzke from Northern Virginia, who made up a little film, clips, bios on everybody.[§] The one on Carter featured an interview with Carter where he talked about himself as the senior officer in the *Seawolf* pre-commissioning detail. He had orders to *Seawolf* via the prototype in upstate New York, Schenectady, and it was whatever the GE prototype was. He was at that plant qualifying when his father died, and he resigned from the Navy. So he never got to *Seawolf.*

---

[*] Admiral Thomas H. Moorer, USN (Ret.), former CNO and Chairman of the Joint Chiefs of Staff. Roger Staubach, who won the Heisman Trophy in 1963 and graduated from the Naval Academy in 1965, later played professional football for the Dallas Cowboys from 1969 to 1979. Captain James A. Lovell Jr., USN (Ret.), was commander of the moon mission that was dramatized in the Tom Hanks movie *Apollo 13*. Lovell himself played a cameo role in the film.

[†] Vice Admiral Charles S. Minter, USN (Ret.), was former commandant and superintendent of the Naval Academy. Colonel John Ripley, USMC (Ret.), earned a Navy Cross for combat exploits in Vietnam.

[‡] Admiral William J. Crowe Jr., USN (Ret.), was a former Chairman of the Joint Chiefs of Staff and a Naval Academy classmate of Carter.

[§] Commander Robert H. Rositzke, USN (Ret.). His company is Empire Video, Inc.

My former CO, Yogi Kaufman, was the exec of the *Seawolf* commissioning, after command of a regular diesel boat, and Dick Laning was commanding officer.* And I thought to myself, "Laning and Yogi would have been surprised to hear that Jimmy Carter was a senior officer of *Seawolf* detail, since they were respectively a commander and a lieutenant commander and he was a lieutenant." Anyway, that sort of ticked off a few people. I have no respect for the man. I have respect for him as a humanitarian soul, and he's done a great job there, but when he's in foreign policy or defense, he's out of bounds. I think he's way off. He's done a lot of great things in his life and continues to do good things for people.

Paul Stillwell: He does. Well, just as a side trip, I interviewed Dick Laning, and what a character he was.

Admiral Trost: He was.

Paul Stillwell: Did you have any interaction with him?

Admiral Trost: I met him. I knew him. Yogi was later my CO in *Scorpion*, and so I met Laning after the fact as well as before, while he was a PCO. I was in *Swordfish* pre-comm detail. I met him after he'd had command, after he'd retired. Interesting guy.

Paul Stillwell: He's a character. [Laughs]

Admiral Trost: He's quite a guy.

Paul Stillwell: How did you put together the building blocks of the budget each year?

---

* USS *Seawolf* (SSN-575), commissioned 30 March 1957, was the Navy's second nuclear-powered submarine. The first, USS *Nautilus* (SSN-571) had a pressurized water reactor. The *Seawolf* served as a test bed for a reactor cooled by liquid sodium. The latter was not deemed a success, so the *Seawolf* was later equipped with the pressurized water type. For the first skipper's view, see Richard B. Laning, "The *Seawolf*'s Sodium-Cooled Power Plant," *Naval History*, Spring 1992, pages 45-48.

Admiral Trost: Well, you get input from everybody, including the major claimants like fleet commanders, heads of bureaus. It gets scrubbed by their OpNav sponsor to make sure that they're in agreement with it. We get all of that together and then take a look and do our own analysis of anything we had questions on, both operational and budgetary, and then start seeing how much we could fit into whatever the size boot is we've been given.

It's a continuous, I'd say, repetitive—I'm not sure that's the right term—process until you finally shake it down. And in the process of the program and in budget development, you have briefings for the senior people, the CNO and the Secretary, to get their input and guidance on things that they might want, and make sure they're aware of any congressional interests and push, which we had to either—"fend off" is not the right term, but stop from trying to control our internal workings and come up with a budgetary program that could be fit within the budget. Interesting process. Only took seven days a week to do it.

Paul Stillwell: How long were those days?

Admiral Trost: My days started at 7:00 in the morning, and I got out of the office by 6:00 in the evening when I could. My predecessor had 5:30 heads of divisions meetings every day, Monday through Friday.

Paul Stillwell: This was Admiral Holcomb.

Admiral Trost: Yeah, it was. And those meetings went to 6:30 or 7:00, so people who came in at 7:00 or 7:30 in the morning were there till 12 hours later. I don't work that way, never have. So I came in around 7:00, mostly for traffic purposes, and I left at 5:30, and that got my people out on the road with the evening traffic, but got them out of the office anyway. Some of the offices, we'd bring somebody in at 7:00, tell them to go home at 4:00, or we'd bring them in at 8:30 and say, "You're staying till the end of the day." That was more popular.

I couldn't stay out of the office on Saturday because I'd be either on call for the Secretary or the CNO, and some of my people, a lot of my people, were in also on Saturday. Sunday I worked at home, and I worked at home every Sunday, I think, of my tour. My wife used to say she knew she'd see me for Saturday and Sunday meals, and she did, and for breakfast. It was tough on the family. Our youngest daughter, Kathleen, was a senior in high school when I first took the job, and then the kids went off. Steve came to the Naval Academy. Laura Lee had graduated from college. Carl had dropped out of college. So we had them scattered around.

I used to spend some Saturday afternoons and Sundays, when Steve was a midshipman, which he was for much of that time—"entertaining" is not the right word, but meeting with Steve and his buddies, who, if they had a weekend or a day off, a day Saturday free, they'd come over and come to the observatory, where they knew they could get a good dinner.* Well, they'd get a good dinner back here, too, but they'd come over and we'd tell sea stories and talk to them about the Navy and Naval Academy.

Paul Stillwell: So even relaxation was dealing about the Navy.

Admiral Trost: Yeah, it really was. Sunday morning, we did go to church. We went to the chapel out on Nebraska Avenue, near American University. That was a fully functional chapel, and that's where we went. So we were close enough to get there and back without spending too much of my Sunday, and then generally I'd work till dinnertime, then take the evening off. It was trying. It was full-time. My EA used to show up sometimes middle of Sunday afternoon, unwelcome, with a bunch of stuff that had to be done before morning, and so it was tough on those kids, too, who served with me.

What we did when I was CNO was stagger our working hours for the inside staff. I had a chief yeoman who, I found out after I'd been there a couple months, lived down south of Fredericksburg. He left home at 2:30 in the morning because he was the office opener. He'd get in. By 4:00 o'clock he had the morning intelligence papers and the *Early Bird* and other stuff that people were going to read and I was going to read, and

---

* The living quarters for the Trost family were on the grounds of the Naval Observatory, just off Massachusetts Avenue in Washington, D.C.

sorted the messages, had everything ready for the EA, who got there at 6:00 o'clock, ready for me, who got there at 7:00 o'clock. And I told this chief, "You know, Chief, since you're coming in so early, why don't you leave about 1:30 in the afternoon?"

"Oh, I can't do that," he said. "Who's going to wrap things up?"

I said, "One of the 10 or 12 people who are still in the office can wrap things up."

So he started doing that. He said, "Guys, it's a whole new world out there." [Laughter]

But, you know, it's inhumanity imposed by people who are very humane. To illustrate that, when I was a captain working for John Warner, Bobby Inman was the EA to the Vice Chief, who was Mickey Weisner.[*] Bobby came down one Friday afternoon about 1600 and said, "Is Secretary Warner going to be in tomorrow?"

I said, "Tomorrow is Saturday. He doesn't come in on Saturday unless there's something really hot going on."

He said, "Well, how do you keep him informed?"

I said, "He takes a package of stuff with him Friday night, gives it back to me Monday morning."

He said, "Hmm. And you close the office?"

I said, "We close the office."

And, "Hmm."

What triggered this, turns out, was Weisner's comment, "Find out if Warner's going to be in tomorrow," because he was planning to be there. And when Bobby went back, he told the Vice Chief, "He's not going to be here tomorrow." The Vice Chief was Acting CNO also.

Weisner said, "Well, what difference does it make whether I come in or not?"

Bobby said, "Well, I have checked. There are about 1,000 people at OpNav who will come in if you're in who won't come in otherwise."

Weisner said, "Hmm." So Weisner didn't come in. That started an avalanche of three-stars who didn't come in when they didn't have to.

---

[*] Admiral Maurice F. Weisner, USN, served as Vice Chief of Naval Operations from 1 September 1972 to 1 September 1973.

Every once in a while people stop and think, "The world's going to go on whether I'm there or not." [Laughs] So I tried that when I was CNO. I tried not to go in on Saturday when I didn't have a meeting, and I'd work at home, and my EA had to pick up the slack. He and the writer had to package things up and get them out to me and get them back, but that worked out pretty well and gave people time free.

The same with Sunday. There are people who used to catch up Sunday in the office, which is fine if you've got highly classified stuff to work on, but why didn't you do that during the week? And it was also fine, in my case; I had top secret courier and storage capability in my quarters, so I could work on anything that came up. But when I worked on it, it was just me working on it, not an office full of people waiting to see whether I coughed or called or what I did. It's doable. It's doable.

Paul Stillwell: Depends on the individual and his personality and habits.

Admiral Trost: Yeah, it really does.

Paul Stillwell: How much interaction did you have with your counterparts in the budget shops of the other services, including the Coast Guard?

Admiral Trost: With the Coast Guard, yes. With the other services, not too much, unless we had a program that was funded by multiple inputs. We provided certain funding support for the Coast Guard, so my organization had a fair amount of interface. I talked to Paul Yost, who was the Coast Guard Commandant all my four years as CNO, and so we met periodically on items of mutual interest or responsibility.[*] But the other services, not too much.

Paul Stillwell: Well, I would think you would have to have some interface with the Marine Corps.

---

[*] Admiral Paul A. Yost Jr., USCG, served as Commandant of the Coast Guard from 30 May 1986 to 31 May 1990. His oral history is in the Naval Institute collection.

Admiral Trost: Oh, very definitely, we had a lot of interface with the Marine Corps, because, first of all, 090 has a Marine on the staff on the OP-90 staff for Marine program interface. Also the Navy funds Marine aviation, Marine ordnance, and amphibs, of course. So you have a lot of interface with the Marine Corps.

Paul Stillwell: Your time in OP-090 and CNO was the time of the barons, the DCNOs for Air, Surface, and Submarines. What do you remember about refereeing among those three individuals?

Admiral Trost: My run-ins with the DCNOs were more while I was OP-090 and, before that, Systems Analysis. My biggest problems with Systems Analysis time frame was not with the three platform-specific guys; it was OP-06, the political/military guy. It was specifically Joe Moorer when he was there. He used to accuse me of getting into his business. Now, that's a fair accusation if it's true, but 96 was allocator for an awful lot of programs.[*] I told you previously about his calling me down when I sent Lieutenant Greg Johnson to chair a meeting.

In my career, Systems Analysis was a very unique billet. And Staser, who was my predecessor, had open access to the CNO, as had Zumwalt when he took over the job. It was just the name of the game. You were working for them and you reported to them without having to go through somebody, and that bends a lot of egos.

Paul Stillwell: What do you remember about working with Admiral Hayward when you were Program Planning?[†]

Admiral Trost: When I was Program Planning we had Hayward and then Watkins, CNOs. Hayward knew the job very well and used it very heavily, I'd say.

---

[*] OP-96 was the Systems Analysis office.
[†] Admiral Thomas B. Hayward, USN, served as Chief of Naval Operations from 1 July 1978 to 30 June 1982. His oral history is in the Naval Institute collection.

Paul Stillwell: Because he had been in the job himself.

Admiral Trost: Yeah, and knew what kind of capabilities were on call, and so he'd ask for input at times that would surprise me, but he just wanted to be more informed of things. It was Hayward who taught me the value of impatience on the part of the CNO. I had my first briefing as CNO in the PEC, Program Evaluation Center, up on the fourth floor of the Pentagon. It was a briefing room, and that's where most of the briefings of SecNav and CNO took place, and it accommodated maybe 40 people. And my first meeting up there, which was some programmatic topic, I don't remember what it was, but it was like, let's say, 9:00 o'clock in the morning. So my aide and I walked up at 9:00 o'clock in the morning. The room was about half full, and the sponsor who was there said, "Gee, I'm sorry, Admiral. We're not ready yet."

I said, "Nine o'clock."

"Well," he said, "yeah, people have a tendency to wander in."

I said, "Is your briefer here?"

"Yes, sir."

"Start the briefing." All that had a remarkable side effect.

Paul Stillwell: I'm sure it did. [Laughs]

Admiral Trost: After that, briefings started on time and people showed up on time. [Laughter] And I wasted a lot less time than I otherwise would have.

Paul Stillwell: So Admiral Hayward taught you that one.

Admiral Trost: He taught me that one. And meetings started on time.

Paul Stillwell: What do you recall about Admiral Watkins as CNO when you were in that Program Planning job?*

---

* Admiral James D. Watkins, USN, was Chief of Naval Operations from 1 July 1982 to 30 June 1986.

Admiral Trost: Well, Watkins, by background and jobs, was not familiar with the 090 organization, and so he pretty well left me alone except when I was there in lieu of the Vice Chief, when my duties generally had things other than 090 business to do. He was pretty much hands-off with respect to me, and I think he trusted me. I think that was really the key to it, and I got lots of assignments, as I said, some of which had nothing to do with 090.

Paul Stillwell: What would be an example?

Admiral Trost: I was trying to think. "Look into so-and-so," like maybe a ruling on personnel on what it means to us, because he had been CNP, and he knew I'd been in the personnel business for that one tour. When he had programmatic questions, he'd often pose those personally rather than ask the questions in a briefing, and get up to speed himself before he went in, which I think was as much to make sure he knew what he was talking about when he asked questions than anything else. He did his homework very well.

Of course, he was fighting John Lehman, as was Hayward, which was one of the reasons Lehman didn't want me as CNO because for four years I'd been the thorn in his side being sent in after the CNOs left so I could tell Lehman why he screwed up, and he didn't like that very much at all. He sometimes gave in sometimes. So I was not the popular person.

Paul Stillwell: Do you recall any of that you won with him?

Admiral Trost: Some that I don't remember. I don't remember the specific issues. I remember one time his comment was, "Goddamn it, all you do is come in here and tell me what I can't do."

I said, "No, I tell you what you can do legally." And he pushed the envelope on a lot of things where the question of legality or likelihood of being able to do it without being challenged was there, but he pushed the boundary. He pushed the envelope all the time.

Paul Stillwell: This was the era when the so-called Maritime Strategy was evolving. Did that affect your work?[*]

Admiral Trost: To a degree, making sure we supported it. Watkins used me as a sounding board to more of what was doable, what was not, and that was kind of the stretch of my responsibility until I became CNO when I inherited it. And since I'd worked with him on it, and lots of others, I sort of felt comfortable with it. My discomfort, if any, was that it wasn't widely enough promulgated or understood by a lot of senior Navy people, and so sometimes we had opportunities where we could have made some good points clearer with Congress, but the person being asked the question wasn't sufficiently conversant to really make the points. It was interesting being involved with it. Watkins was adamant on some aspects of the strategy, and I credit him with awakening the Soviets to the fact that they had a more serious challenge than they realized, and a determined challenge rather than just words.

Paul Stillwell: Well, and that was reflective of President Reagan's approach as well.

Admiral Trost: Yeah. Reagan very strongly supported it.

Paul Stillwell: Well, ideally, your strategy would be supported by your programs.

Admiral Trost: Yeah.

Paul Stillwell: Well, my recollection is that the money became more available after the Reagan administration took office.

Admiral Trost: Money became more available. That's right.

---

[*] By the early 1980s, the U.S. Navy had developed what it termed the Maritime Strategy, which was a controversial concept built around forward offensive operations by carrier, amphibious, and attack submarine forces.

Paul Stillwell: What kinds of things were you then able to do?

Admiral Trost: Well, Reagan was a strong supporter for the first couple of years. We had more flexibility in operational spending, which he supported very strongly, and the final couple of years when I became CNO, we were really living off the advantages made early in the Reagan administration in the first four years and the next two years when I was there. We were basing programs on a flow of money which would have been justified and in a large measure obtained in the early part of his first administration. Bush, of course, had served as two terms as Vice President under Reagan when he came in as President.[*] He was basically carrying on in his first administration, his only administration, much of what had been established by Reagan, but which was being eaten away by congressional action. So it was a time of internal turbulence created by uncertainty because of congressional action but also uncertainty in what the budget levels were going to be and what programs were going to survive and what was going to have to be axed to fit within the total pot.

Paul Stillwell: Well, the "600-ship Navy" became a rallying cry and a slogan and justification.

Admiral Trost: Yeah, and do you know when I retired, we had 594 ships. Today we have 280. Matter of fact, we had 596,000 active duty Navy personnel. Today we have 320, 000 or 310,000, so just over half. The level of certainty that the budgetary machinations are injecting into the system now did not exist then, and it was a combination of a very determined President with policies that were supported by enough of Congress to be supported.

I'm not very happy with what's happening right now, for example. Well, first of all, we're stretching our active forces too thin, not only the Navy. This arbitrary cut with the Army, for example, is reflective of national policy, or following national policy, and

---

[*] George H. W. Bush was Vice President of the United States from 20 January 1981 to 20 January 1989. Bush then served as President from 20 January 1989 to 20 January 1993.

yet we're continuing to wander down the street, reeling from side to side, trying to decide what we're really going to do. We take half-hearted actions internationally. We take no action because we have no policy on a lot of things. I could go on.

Paul Stillwell: Well, back in the '80s, the presumed enemy was a lot more clear-cut and easily defined. It was the Soviet Union.

Admiral Trost: But we have chosen now not to define the enemy, and we take actions which don't seem to be correlated or part of a policy. I am glad I'm not a member of the Joint Chiefs or I'd go crazy.

Paul Stillwell: What do you recall about Admiral Small and working with him as VCNO?[*]

Admiral Trost: He was an interesting guy. Our relationship was fairly good. He was a bright guy and had strong opinions on a lot of things, but he was a good operator and very smart guy. I thought he was easy to work with. We had our occasional disagreements. [Laughs] Bill was a good guy, he had good fleet experience, and he understood the programmatic job and basis for it, so he was easy to work with in that sense.

Paul Stillwell: What about Admiral Hays, who succeeded him, another aviator?[†]

Admiral Trost: Hays I found easy to work with. We had a very easy working relationship, and he relied on me heavily when I was 090, for programmatic questions and answers. I would say, to his credit, to the credit of anybody who's in that job, if he didn't understand something, he got a briefing before he went in to a meeting that was going to require a decision. Or if something came up that he wasn't clear on, he'd ask me to come in and fill

---

[*] Admiral William N. Small, USN, served as Vice Chief of Naval Operations from 1981 to 1983.
[†] Admiral Ronald J. Hays, USN, served as Vice Chief of Naval Operations from 1983 to 1985.

him in to the extent that I could, which usually worked out pretty well. So we had a good working relationship, and that continued when he was CinCPac and I was CNO.

Paul Stillwell: Was there a special category for strategic weapons and money for them in the system?

Admiral Trost: It wasn't fenced. It had to compete for money, but it had a higher priority than some other things. So a special category, probably in that—there probably was a push. I don't remember that now, no. It was part of the process.

Paul Stillwell: What do you recall about the 095 admirals, McKee and Baggett, and their relationship to program building?[*]

Admiral Trost: It was often advisory and helpful. It was sometimes adversarial when they wanted something and we couldn't fund it. But generally they were pretty smart guys and they understood the problem, and I thought they did a good job of balancing what their requirements were. Three very competent guys.

Paul Stillwell: Then Admiral McKee took over from Admiral Rickover in that period.[†]

Admiral Trost: Oh, very well, very well. The naval aviation supporters were pushing hard to get a former carrier CO in line to be McKee's replacement. Certain aviators were pushing Lehman to get rid of McKee, put an aviator in. We didn't think there were any as qualified as the submarine candidates available.

When I was CNO, Kin and I talked. He agreed that he'd be willing to cut his eight-year term by a year or so to force a decision earlier so Lehman wouldn't make the decision at the end of Kin's tour. He and I decided that as the two senior nukes, we were

---

[*] Vice Admiral Kinnaird R. McKee, USN, served as Director, Naval Warfare, OP-95, from 1979 to 1982. Vice Admiral Lee Baggett, Jr., USN, served as Director, Naval Warfare, OP-095, from August 1982 to April 1985.
[†] Admiral Kinnaird R. McKee, USN, served as Director, Naval Nuclear Propulsion, 1982-88.

going to try to influence the relief, and we decided that Bruce DeMars, who was then a three-star as OP-02, senior submariner—was the guy with the tickets and the demeanor to take over from McKee.[*] So we talked to Bruce, asked, "If you were asked, would you be a volunteer?" Because that's not a job everybody aspires to. And he said, "Yes." So that worked out right from my perspective. It worked out well because Bruce did a hell of a job and was good continuity. And McKee didn't mind being shorted. That's a tough job, and I don't know if he was feeling the demands or not, but for the good of the Navy, he was willing to step down. Now, most of what I've told you isn't written down anywhere and isn't known to anybody except McKee, who's dead, and DeMars.

Paul Stillwell: I've gathered that Admiral Watkins played a role when Rickover was moved aside.

Admiral Trost: Yeah, he did. Rickover listened to Watkins. It was an interesting time.

Paul Stillwell: Well, I've also gotten the impression that President Reagan thought it was going to be a nice pat-on-the-back departure, and it was anything but.

Admiral Trost: It was, that's right. I think he called him in to thank him for a good job, and something along the line in the conversation pissed Rickover off, apparently. He is said to have turned on his heel and left the office, gone back to his own office, business as usual.[†]

Paul Stillwell: During that period, I wrote a letter to Admiral Rickover to ask if he would do an oral history, and he said, "I'm not ready yet, but check back with me in 50 years." [Laughter]

Admiral Trost: Wouldn't it be great if we had one? I'll tell you what.

---

[*] Admiral Bruce DeMars, USN, served as Director, Naval Nuclear Propulsion from 1988 to 1996.
[†] For an account of the Rickover-Reagan meeting, see John F. Lehman, Jr., *Command of the Seas* (New York: Scribner's Sons, 1988).

Paul Stillwell: Well, I think the best substitute for that was Frank Duncan, to whom he would pass information, and then Duncan would print it under his own name. He's written one of the good biographies of Admiral Rickover.[*]

Admiral Trost: I haven't read that.

Paul Stillwell: You talked about this buildup in funds, and then came the Gramm-Rudman-Hollings law that went the other way.[†] How did that affect your work?

Admiral Trost: Well, it affected it rather markedly because we had to change a lot of our programmatic planning and try to fit a few more pounds into a shrinking bag, and that wasn't easy. A lot of work.

Paul Stillwell: CNET was relatively new at that time.[‡] How much did you work with it?

Admiral Trost: Quite a bit, because things changed. I had a claimancy issue. Earlier, as PERS-4, I didn't have much interface with CNET, but I did as OP-090 and then as CNO. I had interface mostly on claimancy and who was responsible for what. CNET, at the time I was working with them, had a very bad habit, in my view, of gold-watching things. CNET had gotten a say about Naval Academy funding. I took it away from them when I was 090 because they'd put something in, the budgets pass, and all of a sudden that money disappears to one of the admiral's pet projects or one of his things that I didn't think was as high a priority as other requirements. So we had at it now and then. When you have four years in a job like that, there are not very many people around, except your full-time civilians, who have the background you have and know what's happening under the sheets on claimancy issues. So you become effective and dangerous and sometimes effectively dangerous. [Stillwell laughs.] But it's interesting. CNET momentarily—I say

---

[*] Francis Duncan, *Rickover: the Struggle for Excellence* (Annapolis: Naval Institute Press, 2001).
[†] In 1985, when the national debt was increasing steadily, Congress enacted the Balanced Budget and Emergency Deficit Control Act. This law was known as Gramm-Rudman-Hollings because of the Senate authors of the original bill (Phil Gramm of Texas, Warren Rudman of New Hampshire, and Ernest F. Hollings of South Carolina).
[‡] CNET – Chief of Naval Education and Training.

momentarily because I don't remember how long anymore—got control of the budget for the Naval Academy and for the Naval War College and, for a while, the PG School at Monterey. I took it away from them because they were doing some dumb things.

With the CNO's knowledge. I made my case and knew I had the backing before I did something dumb, but we basically got the CNO back into the claimancy line. Things had to be approved by the CNO to be effective. These things were important and they put a lot of money in, but the impact of cutting dumbly, and some of these cuts were dumb, and it could have been disastrous. Because somebody says, "It's my claimancy, and I can see from here to the edge of my base and that's it. I'm not worried about the rest of that stuff out there." So that's an indictment of senior people, but a proper indictment.

Paul Stillwell: How much interaction did you have with CNET as far as policy setting?

Admiral Trost: My major interactions were making sure they knew whom they worked for and worked as independent policymakers. That sounds a little bit cruel, but that really was my case. I had a problem with—how should I put this? As I said, I had a problem with claimancy of educational institutions. Most of my discussions with CNET, for example, were on budgetary issues, on what I wanted supported better than he was supporting.

Paul Stillwell: You used the term "gold-watch."

Admiral Trost: They'd take something they knew I was interested in and not fund it, figure out how to find money somewhere else so that they didn't have to take it out of their pot of money.

Paul Stillwell: That's an old trick. [Laughs]

Admiral Trost: That's an old trick, and it's alive and well, was alive and well during my time there.

Paul Stillwell: Do you remember any specific instances?

Admiral Trost: I can't tell you the specific budgetary items anymore, except that there were things that they knew I was interested in, and, therefore, I would undoubtedly fund them if they didn't. Sometimes I did, but usually they did, not voluntarily.

Paul Stillwell: I remember interviewing Admiral Yost, and he said one year he put in a budget that had no funding for the Coast Guard yard in Curtis Bay, and immediately he heard from Senator Mikulski of Maryland.* [Laughter]

Admiral Trost: I can imagine he would. I imagine he would.

Paul Stillwell: Were you getting inklings that early about Goldwater-Nichols going to be coming along?†

Admiral Trost: I don't remember specifically. I remember Goldwater-Nichols coming in, and people saying, "We're finally going to get the Joint Chiefs under control." I don't know what that meant. I don't really recall.

Paul Stillwell: Well, I gathered it boosted the stature of the operational commanders and gave them some more input on the budget side.

Admiral Trost: They had a pretty good input before. I'm not sure. I have never done an analysis of that or thought about that, but that could well be.

Paul Stillwell: Anything else to mention about that job, Program Planning?

---

* Barbara A. Mikulski, a Democrat from Maryland, served in the House of Representatives from 3 January 1977 to 3 January 1987; she was a member of the Senate from 3 January 1987 until her retirement on 3 January 2017. See the Naval Institute oral history of Admiral Paul A. Yost Jr., USCG (Ret.).
† The Goldwater-Nichols Defense Reorganization Act of 1986 went into effect on 1 October of that year. It mandated a good deal more in the way of joint-service relationships than had been the case up to then. For details, see "DoD Reorganization," *U.S. Naval Institute Proceedings*, May 1987, pages 136-145.

Admiral Trost: No, just that it's a killer. I'm trying to remember the conversation I had with Frank Kelso shortly after he relieved me as CNO.[*] He thought it was too powerful, had too much say and too much programmatic stuff, and he wanted to increase control, that is, put the lid on 090, I thought. He didn't discuss that till after the fact. He called me and asked me to come in at 5:00 o'clock one morning to have breakfast with him to tell me about his reorganization of OpNav.

I said, "Gee, I'd be happy to work on that with you, even though I'm retired."

He said, "No, I knew if I approached you with that, you'd disagree with me, so I didn't tell you until I was done."

Paul Stillwell: Why 5:00 o'clock in the morning? [Laughs] You're shaking your head. You don't know?

Admiral Trost: That beats the shit out of me. [Stillwell laughs.] I never went into the Pentagon for a 5:00 o'clock breakfast except that one time. I don't know. Maybe because there was no one else around to say, "Why didn't you invite so-and-so?" I don't know.

I privately think Frank was upset when Lehman nominated him to be CNO, but I became CNO instead. I think that bothered him. He relieved me down in Norfolk and spent four years down there as a four-star.[†] He did a good job, and I think he wanted the job when first nominated, and I didn't. But hard to tell.

Paul Stillwell: Well, you did get promoted to four stars when you went to the Atlantic Fleet.[‡]

Admiral Trost: Yeah, I did.

---

[*] Admiral Frank B. Kelso III, USN, served as Chief of Naval Operations from 29 June 1990 to 23 April 1994. His oral history is in the Naval Institute collection.

[†] Admiral Kelso served as Commander in Chief Atlantic Fleet from 30 June 1986 to 4 November 1988. He then served as Supreme Allied Commander Atlantic and Commander in Chief Atlantic Command from 22 November 1988 to 18 May 1990.

[‡] Admiral Trost served as Commander in Chief Atlantic Fleet from 4 October 1985 to 30 Jun 1986.

Paul Stillwell: How did that job come about?

Admiral Trost: That's something I've never found out. Well, first of all, it came about because the decision was made to split the triple-hatted four-star down there, the SACLant/CinCLantFlt.[*] The fleet job is a full-time job to begin with. It's Fleet Forces Command now. But that decision apparently was made, and by whom, when, I don't know. I was not aware of it until all of a sudden I was told I was getting orders, getting a fourth star, and came out of the blue to me, and on, I might say, pretty short notice. So I don't know who was involved in this. Wes McDonald was the senior guy before the split.[†] He was my immediate predecessor in the fleet part of it. Then Baggett relieved McDonald, and three years from that time I would be eligible for the big job down in Norfolk for three years.[‡] Then I'd reach 62, the mandatory retirement age. So when I got those orders and got promoted to four stars, I had it all planned out. Not very smart. Didn't get there. [Laughter]

Paul Stillwell: Well, it's interesting that Secretary Lehman, whom you didn't get along with, would presumably have a vote on this.

Admiral Trost: That's what happened. I just thought it was unlikely that he would. I expected to retire as a three-star, and I didn't think Lehman would ever have a hand in anything that would promote me.

Paul Stillwell: I would guess that Congress had a role in splitting up those billets.

---

[*] For a number of years prior, one four-star U.S. admiral simultaneously held the posts of Supreme Allied Commander Atlantic (SACLant), a NATO billet; Commander in Chief Atlantic Command (CinCLant), a joint-service U.S. billet; and Commander in Chief Atlantic Fleet (CinCLantFlt), a Navy-only U.S. billet. In 1985, the commands were divided, with one four-star admiral serving as SACLant and CinCLant and another four-star admiral as CinCLantFlt and Deputy CinCLant.

[†] Admiral Wesley L. McDonald, USN, served as Supreme Allied Commander Atlantic, Commander in Chief Atlantic, and Commander in Chief Atlantic Fleet from 30 September 1982 to 27 November 1985.

[‡] Admiral Lee Baggett Jr., USN, served as Supreme Allied Commander Atlantic and Commander in Chief Atlantic Command from 27 November 1985 to 22 November 1988.

Admiral Trost: Could have. Well, I'll tell you what. It's not that it was unmanageable. It was not fully controlled, let me say. When I took over as LantFlt, that was a full-time job. The big four-star was a very busy guy, too, and I was his Deputy CinCLant. My CinCLant involvement was really more staying informed and attending meetings than anything else. My real job was Atlantic Fleet, which needed programmatic and budgetary input and expertise that it didn't have. It might have something to do with my going. I don't know. But we did not have it.

Paul Stillwell: Well, since you were surprised at getting the job, you probably didn't have a ready-made agenda for what you would do.

Admiral Trost: I did not. I did not. My agenda was made up in about the week before I took over.

Paul Stillwell: What did that then become?

Admiral Trost: Well, that became my program, and we lived with the reduced budgets and tried to find workarounds, tried to prioritize maintenance, tried and were successful in cutting back some deployments.

Paul Stillwell: But there's a much smaller Navy now and not that big a reduction in commitments.

Admiral Trost: Much smaller Navy. As CNO I had 15 deployable carriers, and today there are ten. I had the 15th air wing being stood up. Now we have ten. So you can't do things with units you don't have, and we are maintaining the same basic commitments today as when we had a full-sized Navy. Our President talks a lot, and I don't know what he's going to do where.* It's not clear at all. But things that require forces get forces, even though they don't exist in sufficient numbers to provide rotational base, and that's biting us already in terms of retention. And what's hurting more than anything else, we're

_____

* Barack Obama was President at the time of this interview.

losing officers, I'm told, in the 5- to 12-year time frame. These are guys who everybody expected to stay around, and they're leaving, and that's the experience drain that's hard to replace or make up for.

Paul Stillwell: Because you can't just go put out a want ad and go hire somebody. [Laughs]

Admiral Trost: Right. You can't hire somebody who's a trained OOD or a trained maintenance officer. They don't come off the street.

Paul Stillwell: One of Secretary Lehman's initiatives was the Strategic Homeporting Plan. What were your views on that?

Admiral Trost: I don't remember specifics.

Paul Stillwell: Well, the idea was rather than have such huge concentrations in, say, San Diego and Norfolk, you would have more home ports, such as Staten Island, Corpus Ingleside, etc.

Admiral Trost: Well, the problem was getting the money to provide the infrastructure to support another station or another port. What we expended in places like Jacksonville, the basic infrastructure was there, the underlying support, so you could add to that. Staten Island, nothing. We did expand our Northwest U.S. presence. There were a lot of facilities there already. Bremerton was there, both shipyard and supply facilities, and later on, the Bangor facilities, and there was a torpedo station up there, so there was infrastructure.

Paul Stillwell: And Everett came in.[*]

_____

[*] Naval Station Everett, Washington is on Puget Sound, about 25 miles north of Seattle. It opened in 1994.

Admiral Trost: Everett came in. So it was an idea whose time was hampered by the lack of facilities and the lack of money to provide the facilities.

Paul Stillwell: And, of course, the argument is if your fleet decreases in size, you don't need that many homeports.

Admiral Trost: Well, that's true. If your needs are such that you don't need the fleet size, it's irrelevant. But I didn't see that we had any excess homeports with the 500-ship Navy or 600-ship Navy. But we don't need them anymore, don't need a lot of them.

Paul Stillwell: Well, Admiral, I've come to the end of my list of questions for today, so I look forward to the next time.

Interview Number 11 with Admiral Carlisle A. H. Trost, U.S. Navy (Retired)

Date: Tuesday, 29 September 2015

Place: Admiral Trost's apartment in Ginger Cove, south of Annapolis, Maryland

Paul Stillwell: During our last visit, we talked about your stint as OP-090, Director of Navy Program Planning. Yesterday I looked through Admiral Hayward's oral history, and he said you did a better job than he did as OP-090.

Admiral Trost: I certainly did it longer than he did.

Paul Stillwell: Well, longer in terms of years, shorter in terms of days. How did you manage to do it in shorter days?

Admiral Trost: Well, I had a dislike of late afternoon meetings, and when I took over, my executive assistant, who was a carryover for about a month, scheduled my daily meeting with my staff for 5:30 in the afternoon. I said, "That's the time I go home." Having been there since 7:00 in the morning, that didn't seem to be unreasonable to me. And I found that I had people working for me who waited around later than they had to and after their day's work was basically done because they had to meet with me, and I thought it was kind of stupid and against my preference, so I just cancelled that evening meeting and said, "If we're going to have a meeting, we'll have it at 4:30 in the afternoon. If anybody needs to see me in the interim, come see me." So that sort of caught hold and prevailed for my four years there.

Paul Stillwell: He said that he got maybe four or five hours of sleep a night when he was in that job.

Admiral Trost: I got probably seven or eight.

Paul Stillwell: Oh, great. Others who had those high-pressure jobs in the Pentagon said they would take a break at noon, go down to the gym and exercise. Did you do that?

Admiral Trost: I did that.

Paul Stillwell: What sorts of things did you do as workouts?

Admiral Trost: Well, I went down, I did calisthenics, I did sit-ups, pushups, and runs in place, and occasionally I started trying to play squash, but I found I wasn't fast enough or alert enough, I guess, to be a good squash player, so I gave that up. Just general physical workout, get my blood flowing, sweat a bit, be ready for a shower, and back to work.

Paul Stillwell: Did you get some exercise on weekends?

Admiral Trost: I did, but that was at home. I was usually walking, running. We lived in the Observatory, so I had a nice area to get out and do things.

Paul Stillwell: There was a story—and I'm not sure where it fits in the timeline—where you took over some quarters from Admiral Gravely.[*] When was that?

Admiral Trost: That was at the start of that job. It was Quarters C in the Naval Observatory.

Paul Stillwell: Did you have any interaction with him?

Admiral Trost: I knew him before that. Our only interaction was that he and Alma, his wife, took us through the house and showed us everything. They were there about a week into my job. I think we stayed with my in-laws just outside of D.C., as a matter of fact. So the interaction with the quarters was being shown around and showing the idiosyncrasies of an old house, and it was an old house and had not been well kept. The Navy has had spotty records on maintaining senior quarters, because it depends on who's in charge and

---

[*] Vice Admiral Samuel L. Gravely Jr., USN, served as Director, Defense Communications Agency from September 1978 to July 1980. He retired in August 1980. It was his final active duty assignment. Admiral Gravely's oral history is in the Naval Institute collection.

they don't want to spend money that's visible as something they've done. So a couple times I've moved into quarters where that was the case. This was one of the cases. And it wasn't Gravely. I guess it was the CO of the Naval Observatory, who was responsible for those houses. I think he didn't want to spend money on quarters, because he'd have to appear before a House subcommittee to justify, and he didn't want to do that. So we inherited, among other things, an almost dysfunctional kitchen stove, which was probably about 25 years old, and Sam Gravely said, "You want to get rid of that, but you're going to have to push hard to get it done." A week after we got there, we got it done.

Paul Stillwell: Were there other things you were able to remedy?

Admiral Trost: Well, there were, as a matter of fact. We had a problem with a raccoon in the third-floor attic, and the raccoons came up from Rock Creek Park, which was just a couple blocks away. They liked to forage in the garbage cans in the quarters on the Observatory, and we knew that. So I clamped my garbage can lids down. When I did that, they found their way somehow up and through a hole just below the eaves on the back of our quarters. We didn't know a hole was there. We heard scratching at night up above us in our bedroom, and when I went up to look there, there was stuff all around. There were leaves, and there were needles from fir trees up there. The guy had a little nest up there, had pulled some insulation up, a nice comfortable little pad for himself there. [Laughter] We found the hole. I managed to block the hole from the inside, but then they tried to trap this thing, never did get it. So we had a few things that had to be done.

Paul Stillwell: Were you able to persuade the head of the Observatory to boost the support?

Admiral Trost: To a degree. I did some of the repair work for that hole, for example, myself, by borrowing one of their ladders and putting some of their workmen to shame when I was on the outside on a weekend hammering away and covering it up with a piece of plywood. [Laughter]

But it was a nice place to live. It was a great place to live, very convenient, and it took me, gosh, 15-20 minutes to get to work in the morning. I just left the Observatory, went down through Rock Creek Park, and I came out down by the Lincoln Memorial and across the river from the Pentagon.

Paul Stillwell: On a substantive side, the Coast Guard Chief of Staff then was Admiral Paul Yost, later Commandant.[*] In his oral history he characterized the relationship between the two of you as sort of a zero-sum game on funds. He said he thought that you were wary of him, that he was trying to pick your pocket.

Admiral Trost: He was. [Laughter] He was. Paul and I were good friends, but Paul would testify—and he used the Yost-Trost name-alike to confuse people. This was primarily later, when he was Commandant. He wanted more support. The Navy supports a lot of stuff for the Coast Guard. The military capabilities of a Coast Guard cutter are paid for by the Navy. He was constantly trying to parlay that into other things, using that as the basis for his requests, and on occasion he'd kind of fuzz Trost and Yost as saying, "Trost approves this." It was Yost who brought it up, and it was Yost who approved it, and he got caught a couple times. So we had sort of a friendly, confrontational relationship in some respects.

Paul Stillwell: I imagine he won some and you won some.

Admiral Trost: He won a few that he got behind my back.

Paul Stillwell: What would be examples?

Admiral Trost: Well, examples would be support funding for certain of his ships, which weren't my responsibility to support, and he'd get money transferred from my operations or maintenance funds by the staffers on the Hill, and especially in the House Armed

---

[*] Admiral Paul A. Yost Jr., USCG, served as Commandant of the Coast Guard from 30 May 1986 to 31 May 1990. His oral history is in the Naval Institute collection.

Services Committee. I accused him of a lot of cock and bull that he fed them in order to get the money transferred over. And these guys were not necessarily as conversant with what the division of funds was as I was, because I'd been 090 and I knew what he got and what he was supposed to have from my budget and what he shouldn't have. He won a few of those.

Paul Stillwell: Well, the comparative budgets were so disproportionate . . .

Admiral Trost: Oh, they were.

Paul Stillwell: . . . he had to scratch for whatever he got.

Admiral Trost: And he was not getting support from the Department of Transportation that he should have. It was a low-priority thing.

Paul Stillwell: That seemed to be perpetually the case with the Coast Guard up till 9/11.*

Admiral Trost: It has been. It has been. And I'm not sure it still doesn't persist to a degree, because we need icebreakers, we need to repair old icebreakers, and we're not putting the money into it. That's a national disgrace, I think. Of course, when the ice coverage in the north receded, that was used as an argument against more funding for the Coast Guard. "You don't need as many icebreakers." That, I think, is a national disgrace. It's a fatal oversight for the future.

Paul Stillwell: There was a story on "NBC News" a couple weeks ago pointing out how few icebreakers the U.S. has and how many Russia has.

Admiral Trost: Yeah, the Russians have an awful lot. Of course, the Russians have a greater need from the standpoint of strategic use because they have a lot of those northern

---

* On 11 September 2001 terrorists hijacked commercial airliners and crashed them into the twin towers of the World Trade Center in New York City and the Pentagon in Arlington, Virginia.

ports which are not ice-free year around, so they use their icebreakers more heavily for local commerce than we do. But we still have a need.

Paul Stillwell: You told me last time about being picked as CinCLantFlt, even though you had expected to retire as a three-star.

Admiral Trost: I don't remember how it came about. I guess Jim Watkins, who was CNO, called me in and said, "We're thinking of splitting LantFlt off from the triple-hatted SACLant/CinCLant/CinCLantFlt, and establishing it as a stand-alone command, but there will be no increase in manning to reflect the split off. And you're being considered as the guy."

So I heard that, and about two weeks later, I was called up for hearings and had a hearing on my fitness, I guess, to be LantFlt.

Paul Stillwell: With Congress, that is?

Admiral Trost: Yeah. And I was nominated and approved, sent down there, and told, "Okay, you're now the fleet commander. You don't have a staff. You don't have any people assigned to the Atlantic Fleet. That's a separate entity." So my executive assistant was an assistant intel officer on the big staff. He came over temporarily to be my EA, knew nothing about being an EA, but he was a good worker.

Paul Stillwell: Who was that?

Admiral Trost: He was a commander, and I don't remember his name. Ruth Miller, who was a lieutenant, was the protocol officer. She was pulled over to my staff as my protocol officer and assistant EA. She was a lieutenant. They assigned a chief of staff, because there was none for that side of the job, who came from Washington, came down, and in the interim, I had a guy who later became Sixth Fleet, an aviator. Can't think of his name offhand. I fired him as Sixth Fleet.

Paul Stillwell: Admiral Moranville.[*]

Admiral Trost: Ken Moranville. He was my interim. And then retired three-star now, who was an idea guy, communications expert.

Paul Stillwell: Admiral Tuttle?

Admiral Trost: Jerry Tuttle came down when they were renovating and actually adding to the command center, building an addition to it.[†] Jerry Tuttle turned out to be the perfect guy to be the oversight for that. He knew what he was talking about, communicated well with people, including the workers who were putting stuff in as well as the staff. So Jerry became my chief of staff, stand-alone, so I had him all for himself.

For an EA, I got Tom Paulsen. Tom had worked for me in Seventh Fleet as my surface ops officer. Pauline, my quiet, demure wife, said, "I know you're worried you need an EA. Do you have anybody in mind?"

I said, "I have a couple people in mind, but they're all in jobs."

"Well, who would you like?"

"Well, I'd like somebody like Tom Paulsen, but he's got the following encumbrances."

She called Mar Beth Paulsen, Tom's wife, from Norfolk to Yokosuka and said, "Mar Beth, here's the situation. Do you think Tom would like the job?" [Laughter]

Mar Beth said, "Yes."

The next thing I got from Tom was, "I'd hate to give up my sequential command,

---

[*] On 20 August 1988 Vice Admiral Kendall E. Moranville, USN, was relieved as Commander Sixth Fleet. He had been under consideration for another three-star job until 19 August, when he received a letter of reprimand as the result of an admiral's mast. He was charged with improprieties involving travel claims and for being accompanied by an unauthorized female Italian civilian while flying U.S. military aircraft when he was Commander Sixth Fleet. As Chief of Naval Operations, Admiral Trost forced Moranville to retire as a rear admiral, one level below his highest active duty rank.
[†] Rear Admiral Jerry O. Tuttle, USN, served as deputy CinC and chief of staff.

but if you want me, I'll come."

I said, "I want you." So I got him.

Paul Stillwell: That was generous of him, giving up a command.

Admiral Trost: It was. And because he was a diesel submariner who'd surfaced, had a destroyer coming in, so he was a contender for flag, theoretically, in the surface community, but major command followed by sequential major command would have been the icing on the cake for him, so he was giving that up. He later made flag. He came in as my EA, and I had a good, strong guy there. Then when I went to become CNO, I took him along to be my EA up there. So I didn't harm him.

Paul Stillwell: That says a lot for loyalty in both directions.

Admiral Trost: Yeah, well, he was just a very capable guy, and he worked two years in Washington, made flag, went to his flag job. He's a great guy.

Paul Stillwell: Did Admiral Watkins give any explanation why he had picked you for the job?

Admiral Trost: No, no, did not.

Paul Stillwell: What was the rationale for splitting off the fleet?

Admiral Trost: The fleet was a busy enough thing that it was taking too much of the attention of the unified and NATO commander, who had the other two hats, and the thought was that the fleet needed focus and didn't have it because it was the third of three hats and it was the junior of the three hats. I was also the Deputy CinCLant, but I didn't spend much time in that hat. Mostly it was the fleet, and it did need time and attention, just a lot of things that had been left go due to the lack of attention, lack of priority being focused on it. So it was a proper move. It was a good move. Why they waited that long to do it, I don't know. Should have been done years ago.

Paul Stillwell: Well, the number of four-star billets was quite limited.

Admiral Trost: Probably a factor, yeah.

Paul Stillwell: After the recorder was turned off last time, you told me about Admiral Tuttle and devising JOTS. What was that?

Admiral Trost: Well, actually it stands for J.O. Tuttle System, and it was a system that restructured fleet communications, to make them more logical, more user-friendly, and I'd say more prompt and responsive. It was the right thing to do, again. He was the guy who was smart enough to think up what to do. Nobody else ever thought of it. Jerry was an interesting guy. He was controversial. He spoke what he believed, and he was not the suave, smooth admiral. He was a get-it-done admiral and did a great job.

Paul Stillwell: Well, he had a great operational background also.

Admiral Trost: Yeah, he did. He did. He used to say, "If it's bullshit, it's bullshit. It's not worth paying attention to." [Laughter]

We had a great relationship, and that continued later on when he became our head communicator for the Navy. He was a guy to whom I could say, "Jerry, I need the following job done."

He said, "Yes, sir. Aye, aye, sir," and that was the last you had to worry about it. It got done. He was just that kind of guy.

Paul Stillwell: Well, that's the ideal way to get it done.

Admiral Trost: Yeah. Now, he ruffled a few feathers in the process. He upset some flag officers, but that was okay.

Paul Stillwell: What were examples of that?

Admiral Trost: I'm trying to think. He shook up—oh, who in the hell was it? I've forgotten the guy's job. He didn't think the flag community in Norfolk, which is a pretty big bunch of guys overall, was cohesive enough. So he asked if he could kind of pull these guys together periodically and talk over what was happening so they each would know what the other was doing. He did that, and turned out to be a very effective thing to do and smart thing to do.

But he had an ability to get people who might have thought at the outset, "This guy's crazier than a coot," all of a sudden he had them doing exactly what he wanted. He was not the smoothest operator in the world, but one of the most accomplished operators in the world. So, a great guy to work with. I could give Jerry a job and forget about it, and the next time I knew it, he was reporting it was finished. So that's the kind of guy you want lots of.

Paul Stillwell: Yes. That was the era when personal computers were just coming into vogue. How much did you get involved in that?

Admiral Trost: Not very much, because I was computer-illiterate. My naval career was always just ahead of the next innovation for which I wasn't prepared. [Laughter] I say this. When I went to Washington for the first time as a commander, I could type about 70 words a minute on an IBM Selectric, and that was from high school training. And I'd done a lot. As a matter of fact, as exec on my first submarine, I typed all the classified patrol reports for the operations, because my yeoman wasn't cleared for it, for especially the code-word stuff that we had to type.*

So I was adept as a typist and a new commander going to Washington. I reported in to the Deputy Secretary of Defense's Office, I had an assigned secretary, me alone— actually me and my co-guy, the Air Force colonel. She could type faster than I could dictate, and she took dictation as fast as I talked. So I spent three years with that capability. I didn't have to type anything, didn't do anything.

---

* In 1962-63 Trost was executive officer of the submarine *Scorpion* (SSN-589).

I became Warner's EA, same thing. I had my own secretary, she was very fast, she typed, took dictation, was very good. Now, in this time frame, they started bringing computers in at a very basic level. I didn't have to. I didn't. Then when I moved next door with him to the Secretary's office, personal computers were starting to be used, but not very much.

When I came back to Washington, personal computers were *the* thing, and I didn't know how to use them, so I was computer-illiterate for almost the balance of my Navy career. But I had good people. I had flag writers who knew how to use a computer, knew how to type, knew how to take dictation. So I can't say I took the easy way out. I took the fast way out by using the tools at hand.

Paul Stillwell: Have you become computer-literate since then?

Admiral Trost: Very basic, and it's going away. I have my computer sitting here. I use it to read emails. I just changed my Windows from Windows 7 to Windows 10, I think. It was a free offer, and I'm not sure who from. But, anyway, so I downloaded, which I was told by my boys was okay. And it's changed a bunch of the displays and other things, so now there are things I used to know how to do that I can't anymore. For example, I need help when I want to print something out to my printer. I used to be able to do that myself, but there's something different in this system that I haven't mastered, and I haven't asked them for the time to sit down and help me, teach me.

Besides that, I've got lots of help here. I've got a couple of neighbors, one neighbor who when I wanted to type a recommendation, I wanted a nice piece of paper, nice document, she said, "I can type that for you." She took my computer and she took my handwritten scribbling notes, and about 20 minutes later came back with a finished letter for me to sign and send in. So I'm leaning on helpers.

Paul Stillwell: Well, I'm reluctant to get Windows 10 myself for just the reasons you cited.

Admiral Trost: Well, it's changed the display. I used to be able to put my computer in the sleep mode. I don't know how to do that anymore. It's different. Well, there are a couple things I can't do anymore that I used to, so I'm waiting for a time when one of my daughters is here for the weekend and has some time to sit down and show me how dummies do it. [Laughter]

Paul Stillwell: Different is not necessarily better.

Admiral Trost: No, and I've got all the computers this and that *For Dummies*, but, you know, those books, they're probably well written, but they don't really help the dummy get to where he wants to go. Basic questions aren't answered. So that's my excuse.

Paul Stillwell: Okay. Moving right along, the person who came in to relieve Admiral McDonald as SACLant/CinCLant was Admiral Baggett. What are you recollections of working with him?

Admiral Trost: Well, we'd been friends for a number of years and we'd served together. He was SurfPac when I was Deputy PacFlt, for example, so we talked probably five days a week and had a lot of interface there. I'd known him in OpNav, so we knew each other there. So when he came in, it was a very easy adaptation, I should say, for me, because I knew him well, he knew me. He didn't tell me how to do my job, and I gave him all the support I could, and so the relationship was a good one.

Frankly, my goal when I told Weinberger I didn't want to be CNO was because my plan was to be CinCLantFlt for three years and then relieve Lee Baggett, who was going to retire at the end of his three years.[*] I thought that's what the Navy trained me for. So I was probably a dummy, but I had a motive in my dumbness.

Paul Stillwell: Well, let me ask a stupid question then. Were you disappointed that you didn't get to carry out that plan?

---

[*] Caspar W. Weinberger served as Secretary of Defense from 21 January 1981 to 23 November 1987.

Admiral Trost: At first, yes. Ultimately, no, because I think I had a good influence on the Navy in my tour, and I think I had skills that wouldn't have been as utilized as a fleet commander. I thought of myself as a operational guy, and I think I was, but I had worked with Congress as a flag officer long before I became CNO. I'd worked with congressional staff, so I knew the organization in Washington, including the other services and the joint setup. So I probably had skill sets that were more ready utilization than they would have been had I stayed down there, and I was able to get some things done that I wouldn't have been able to do down there unless I got the CNO's concurrence.

In retrospect, and I'm not saying this in disrespect, but Frank Kelso and I had different ideas on certain issues. As I watched him after he took over, there were things he did that I would never have gone along with. And had I come up with certain initiatives, he would never have supported me. We just didn't see eye-to-eye on a number of things. So in retrospect, I think it was the right thing for me and for the Navy.

Paul Stillwell: What are some of the examples of things that you got done that you might not have?

Admiral Trost: Well, I'm thinking, first of all, I got, as a result of my time in Norfolk, which was brief, I got all 21 of the—oh, what was that—the 1907 big—

Paul Stillwell: The Exposition houses?[*]

Admiral Trost: Yeah. I got all 21 of the buildings renovated; they were not all residences. Some of them were really badly in need of it. Kelso wouldn't support that. He was angry, because when he relieved me as the fleet commander, he had to wait six months to get into Missouri House, which was my quarters, because to prove the pudding, I started with Missouri House because—having lived there less than a year—I knew its shortcomings

_____

[*] The most senior U.S. naval officers in Norfolk live in houses that were built for the Jamestown Tricentennial Exposition of 1907. It celebrated the 300th anniversary of the establishment of the Jamestown colony in 1607.

and knew what it needed. So I started with that on the renovation system, which meant he had to wait six months to move in.

Paul Stillwell: And you started this when you didn't know you were going to leave shortly.

Admiral Trost: That's right. But I managed to nail it shut as CNO when I didn't get support from down there in their budget, so I just put it in the budget myself. So that's kind of a minor thing in some respects, but these were places where quarters occupied by two-star, that you had to be careful where you walked in the attic so you didn't put your foot through the broken floorboards and through the ceiling down below.

Paul Stillwell: How valuable or how useful was Missouri House as a place to entertain and just to live?

Admiral Trost: Well, as a place to entertain, fine, except when your systems crap out when you had a houseful of people, but they were very useful, by and large. I complain. I'd like to think I left them better than I found them, and that really was a case of emphasis. I was concerned in Norfolk about the status of quarters because we weren't doing anything to maintain them. One night that I remember vividly, we were in Missouri House, asleep. And if you look at the house, the master bedroom is on the right side, two back. There's a guest bedroom in front and then the master bedroom, with a bathroom in between the two, accessible for me at the side. I was awakened sometime during the night, I don't remember the time, by a very loud noise and a crashing sound and then total silence. So I looked out the window. I didn't see anything out there. I looked out front. I didn't see an accident out front or anything else.

It wasn't till about two days later that I discovered the problem. I was outside and walked over to the one side of the house, which was the blind side from another set of quarters, but also it had no windows in our direction, and we had no lower level—we had one lower level window in that direction. Next to the house I saw all this debris, including bricks outside. When these houses were built, they were built as showplaces, not to be around for a long period of time. We had a brick-veneer house, but the bricks were not full-depth bricks. They were half bricks. So it was just a two-inch sheet. There was a big section of wall about twice the size of that end wall here, and it was bare. The bricks were all lying on the ground; they had just fallen away. Now, that wasn't structurally significant, but it was weather-resistance significant, and that was one of the first things I saw when I looked. We knew we had other problems and that these places haven't been maintained. I don't know what that looked like before because I hadn't gone out and checked the siding on the house. I was living there. I wasn't paying any attention to it. [Laughs]

There were some quarters that had just things that were totally dysfunctional and discomfort for the occupants, and we just hadn't paid any money to maintain them. Some of the buildings were buildings that were used for other purposes, not residences. They were part of that era, that vintage exposition.

I think I remember there were either 19 or 21 buildings, most were quarters, and I don't remember what the others were. One was over toward the base. There were several in that area. There were other buildings which were used daily but hadn't had any maintenance for years. And it was across the board. It was the plumbing, air conditioning, physical condition of the exterior walls.

We had the house—I forgot what it was called. As I recall, it was a duplex. Missouri House was on a corner, then there was a set of quarters, and then Virginia House, which was the big quarters, "the Big CinC."* That house across from us, I remember—who was it? A two-star who was deployed to the Mediterranean, his wife called me one evening and said, "I hate to bother you with this, but I need somebody to look. I think I've got a major plumbing problem." And she *had* a major plumbing problem. They found that a section of drain line under the house had just collapsed, because the straps holding the pipes up had rusted out and finally the thing just fell in. So she had a problem. The water was draining under the house. No basement, obviously. None of those places had basements. So, little things like that, just total lack of maintenance, not even inspection to determine whether or not there were problems.

---

* The house was the quarters for SACLant/CinCLant.

And I remember the Virginia House itself—oh, God, I don't remember the problems. We had a whole legion of Navy public works guys in the backyard. He had all sorts of stuff. I don't remember what all the problems were, but we decided just to fix this place and make it a little more livable. I can't blame anybody for neglect. I'll just say they weren't maintained, and no money was ever put toward them until we got the first real money after I left. But I'll take credit for it because I'm the one who put myself on the line with the CNO and said, "We've got to do something," when he said, "I'm not putting money into those old places." But those old places had served, at that point in time—

Paul Stillwell: Almost 80 years.

Admiral Trost: Yeah, and we needed them, we were using them, there were no substitutes for them. It was either send these high-priced flag officers out in town to find a place to live or put them in a little house on base.

Besides the problems with the bricks falling off Missouri House, I was the big-shot fleet commander, and the hot water heater didn't work. We found that out one night when we were entertaining 21 people for dinner. And it was things like that. The kitchen was totally dysfunctional because it was so goddamn old, obsolescent. It was little things. Bathroom fixtures didn't work. When I moved in, we had one guest bathroom which actually served two bedrooms, where the john worked sometimes. And I said, "Well, I want it replaced."

"Nobody ever said anything about it." That was a little thing. That's maintenance.

One night we had a dinner party for Christmas. I had my entire family down there, and the heat stopped. The furnace broke. So when I called public works, the duty public works guy said, "Oh, we're not supposed to do anything other than emergency jobs over the holidays."

I said, "To me, this is an emergency. I'm freezing my ass off." [Laughter] So they finally managed to get a couple guys who were designated to be on call, for the very purpose to come to the base because the guy asked them if they'd like to, even though they were on the list. It was little things.

I don't piss off too easily, but when I do, it's pretty intense, and there were a few things down there about quarters and public works that I had some real problems with. Matter of fact, I fired the public works officer who, when my hot water heater quit and I said, "I've got a houseful of people and I need hot water," he said, "That's not my problem."

I said, "You are the public works officer." A month later, we had a new public works officer. And this guy had been the deputy to the—what did we call the guy—the senior Seabee in the Navy, facilities commander, something like that. So I wrote a special fitness report, and the public works officer told me, "You can't do that. You're not my reporting senior."

I said, "Check your orders, which I have done, and you're here, you're assigned here, and you're on orders to the commander of the naval station," or naval base, whichever it was, "and your temporary duty assignment is to LantFlt. And I'm the senior guy in Norfolk, other than Baggett, and you work for me." So his challenge got him retired a little earlier than he planned to.

Paul Stillwell: So how much longer did he work for you? [Laughs]

Admiral Trost: About three months till we got a replacement. And, Paul, I'm not a vindictive person. I didn't do that out of vindictiveness. I did that because of lack of performance. He was a guy who was sitting back in his rocking chair, retired in place, convinced, however, that he was going to be a flag officer. So he didn't make it.

Paul Stillwell: What can you say about Admiral Baggett's personality, his working style?

Admiral Trost: Well, as I said, we had a very good relationship. Straightforward, honest guy, considered by some to be a little brusque, impatient with people who didn't get results, nothing you wouldn't have expected. He was a very professional guy, and I think from the people who worked for him that I knew, he was a good guy to work for. He was a very, very competent guy. Matter of fact, we had a very good relationship for those eight months that we overlapped.

Paul Stillwell: How much interaction did you have with him?

Admiral Trost: About once a week we'd sit down and go over what was going on, and I kept him cut in on anything with the fleet that I thought he needed to know.

Paul Stillwell: What were the types of issues that you did discuss with Admiral Baggett?

Admiral Trost: Mostly upcoming operations, any problems I had with budget execution, sometimes when we were in the process of formulating budget, which I did only one time in that job, but mostly operational issues, exercise results, readiness to do different things. We were under an operations maintenance funding shortfall.

The week I relieved, I was told I had a 15% cut in my operations and maintenance budget for the year, which had already begun, the fiscal year, being on the first of October, and so we had to accommodate that 15%. If you have an O&M shortfall, where you take it out is flight training, ship maintenance, and miscellaneous stuff, that is small potatoes. So we were very heavily engaged in getting down, cutting back on certain operational aspects, which I had to share with my boss so he'd know that certain exercises weren't going to be run, and participation in other things, including workups for deployment, which he had a very big interest in, were going to be affected by it. Those were probably some of the key issues that we dealt with. I guess that's primarily it.

Paul Stillwell: Admiral Train said that you achieved a higher degree of fleet readiness than some of your predecessors.[*] Where did that fit in with this budget cutting?

Admiral Trost: Well, I think it fit in with the fact that, first of all, I was, let's say, educated on budget matters, and I knew where I could cut and where I could steal more money from another pot to get it. I also focused heavily on fleet operations, and not having had a separate fleet CinC before, I think that attention focus helped readiness,

---

[*] Admiral Harry D. Train II, USN, served as Supreme Allied Commander Atlantic, Commander in Chief Atlantic, and Commander in Chief Atlantic Fleet from 30 September 1978 to 30 September 1982. His oral history is in the Naval Institute collection.

frankly. I don't know that I had any more skills than anybody else in doing it, but I was there. I was the guy on scene. So now you've got a four-star who's focused only on this subject, so it should have improved.

Paul Stillwell: Admiral Yost had the view that you were more of detail oriented than others who were more big-picture.

Admiral Trost: That's interesting. [Laughs] Maybe that's because I spent four years as 090, and you had to be detail oriented. I would have thought that my reputation in Seventh Fleet, Deputy PacFlt, and the other operations jobs I had, would be more the big-picture type. Maybe that's ego speaking. It might be. I thought particularly when I had Seventh Fleet, every ship at sea from Hawaii to the coast of Africa was under my opcon. I think that took a fair amount of breadth of focus on fleet operations.

Paul Stillwell: That was just a perception. [Laughs]

Admiral Trost: Yeah. Well, it's interesting.

Paul Stillwell: Admiral Yost was the Atlantic area commander also.[*] Did you have interaction with him in that job?

Admiral Trost: Not too much, not too much.

Paul Stillwell: What about the maritime defense zone?[†] Did you concentrate on that?

Admiral Trost: There again, we talked, but I really basically got input from what they were doing, what kind of cooperation they needed, and coordination was really the only thing I got involved in.

---

[*] Vice Admiral Paul A. Yost Jr., USCG, served as Commander Atlantic Area, 1984-86. The oral history of Yost, who retired as a four-star admiral, is in the Naval Institute collection.
[†] The maritime defense zones, a collaboration between the Coast Guard and the Navy that was begun in 1984. Both the Atlantic and Pacific have MDZs.

Paul Stillwell: Admiral Yost was so eager and ambitious, he wanted to do inshore things, and found out that maybe the Navy was better at those after all. [Laughs]

Admiral Trost: He was ambitious. He was ambitious. The guy I worked with more than Paul Yost in many respects was the guy who was the fellow up in New York on Governors Island. I had met that guy. He was our host for the Fleet Week July 4th of the year I took over, 1986, and Pauline and I were his houseguests.* So we developed a rapport that I think Paul was a little jealous about, because we talked without going to a "Mother, may I?" before we got on the line, and that may have had something to do. The Eastern Sea Frontier matters, he and I talked directly on an awful lot, and that may have been a little bit of an annoyance to Paul.

Paul Stillwell: Did you develop an agenda once you got into that CinCLantFlt job?

Admiral Trost: Well, my agenda was, first of all, learn how to live within the budget and maintain maximum readiness, and the second thing was to get the fleet accustomed to having a boss who was available to talk to them and from whom they were going to get guidance on a regular basis. It was almost like CinCLantFlt didn't exist before, even though it was a hat for the other guy. So it was establishing the fleet as an entity in charge because I took all budget control and I took all operational control of fleet units, when that had been sort of an "Oh, by the way" of the big CinC. So I think that probably there were people who had to come in and report to me who never reported to anybody, through default, basically, because the big boss was busy. He was not focused on this stuff, and now they had a new big boss who was not as big, but was focused on it. They had, for example, the three-stars who reported to me, like AirLant, specifically AirLant, were unaccustomed to having anyone tell them what to do and how to do it, and that was my job. And also I knew more about budgetary matters than they did.

---

* Captain Robert E. Kramek, USCG, served as commanding officer of the Support Center, Governors Island, New York, from July 1984 to July 1986. He was later Commandant of the Coast Guard from 1994 to 1998. His oral history is in the Naval Institute collection.

Paul Stillwell: So that sort of reduced their autonomy.

Admiral Trost: It did. It did, very definitely. When I took over, the distribution of aviation, flight-hour funding, and maintenance funding, AirLant three-star aviator and the Marine Corps guy, who was Al Gray at the time, would decide how to divvy up the funding for flight hours.* Well, I had a financial guy who'd never gotten into it, so I said, "We're going to get into it. That's our job," not these guys saying, "I'll give you this if you give me that," type thing. So in a sense, I was probably an interferer as much as anything, but I was the boss.

Matter of fact, Al Gray—I've reminded him of this—came in one morning to my morning briefing, and I said, "Al, you're the most insubordinate son of a bitch I've ever known."

"Sir, that's a compliment." [Laughter] And that, in a sense, sort of marked our relationship when he became Commandant of the Marine Corps. We got along, but I got along better with his subordinates than I did with him.

Paul Stillwell: Interesting. What do you remember about Admiral Dunn at AirLant?†

Admiral Trost: Very competent, very good. We had a good working relationship. He later came up to be OP-05.‡ The only problems, the only disagreements Bob and I ever had were on funding splits. He had gone to the Hill as OP-05. He was up there campaigning to kill an approved submarine program to get more money for flight hours. Pissed me off. And also it was wrong. It was an approved budget he was messing with, trying to get money shifted from the budget year to the now-year funding. So that's the only big disagreement. He's a very bright guy, very competent guy. When I retired, he gave me a

---

* Lieutenant General Alfred M. Gray, Jr., USMC, served as Commanding General Fleet Marine Force Atlantic Fleet from 1984 to 1987. As a four-star general served as Commandant of the Marine Corps from 1 July 1987 to 30 June 1991.
† Vice Admiral Robert F. Dunn, USN, served as Commander Naval Air Force Atlantic Fleet from 8 December 1983 to 23 December 1986. His oral history is in the Naval Institute collection.
‡ Vice Admiral Dunn served as OP-05, Deputy Chief of Naval Operations (Air Warfare) from 15 January 1987 to 25 May 1989. The title changed from Deputy to Assistant Chief on 1 October 1987.

little thing that told me I was an honorary aviator for my support of aviation programs.

Paul Stillwell: Sounds like no hard feelings.

Admiral Trost: No hard feelings, no. And we're still good friends. He's a very capable guy.

Paul Stillwell: What do you remember about Admiral Cooper at SubLant?[*] What do you remember about your relationship?

Admiral Trost: Well, we had known each other for quite a few years and had worked together. When I was 090, he was the budget officer, so I knew him quite well, so our relationship was always a very close one and very good one. Still is, matter of fact. Very competent guy.

Paul Stillwell: What do you remember about control of the SSBNs, targeting and operations? Was that a CinCLantFlt billet?

Admiral Trost: CinCLant. CinCLant, J-43 or something like that was the code, and that's something that we at the fleet level did not get into.

Paul Stillwell: What do you remember about relations with other American navies? South America?

Admiral Trost: Had a very close relationship throughout my CinCLantFlt and my CNO time with the South American Navy chiefs. When I became CinCLantFlt, we were getting together every other year with the commanders of the South American navies. We eventually brought in the Central American guys and the Canadians, and we had biannual meetings. I was one of the promoters of that program. I don't know if it still exists or not. It did exist through my time at CNO, and we had that, South, Central, and American—the

---

[*] Vice Admiral Daniel L. Cooper, USN, served as Commander Submarine Force Atlantic Fleet, 1986-88.

American Navy is really what it was, our biannual conferences. We were involved in the around- South America cruises.

Paul Stillwell: UNITAS?

Admiral Trost: UNITAS. I think it may have been started before then. As a matter of fact, I'm sure it was, had to be. But we formalized the program and we got the South American CNOs and their staffs involved in the scheduling, including our scheduling going around where they'd have suggestions for exercises and things would get through that would show our flag and provide them with support, and that worked very, very well. That was a good one. And they became more active participants in the international sea power symposiums up in Newport as a result of that, I think. We had a good relationship.

Paul Stillwell: Are there any of those navies you would single out as especially capable?

Admiral Trost: From the standpoint of capability and operations, I'd say Chileans were probably the most professionally capable and most amenable to interoperability exercises. Brazilians were cooperative. The Argentineans varied. I probably knew the Chilean and the Brazilian CNOs best.

The Peruvian I got to know quite well, but he couldn't invite me to Peru because he couldn't guarantee my safety. I might not live. And I didn't like that idea. [Laughter] But he was very frank about it. He said, "I cannot guarantee your safety." And we had occasions where we did exercises. For example, our diesel submarines from the West Coast, operating with them in an exercise, did not go into certain ports because they couldn't guarantee the safety of the ships, not the crews so much as the ships.

The Chileans were probably the most open in terms of all-embracing operational aspects. Brazilians were very good at the Navy level. The head of the Navy was frustrated by lack of cooperation from his government on occasion, and I can't tell you where or what the focus was or why. But he and I and our wives became very close. The Peruvian came to a formal visit to the States, but as I said, he couldn't invite me back.

The Chilean came up to the States a couple of times, and our relationship was a very good one. Matter of fact, that beautiful seascape over there is a gift from him to me.

Paul Stillwell: Displayed prominently.

Admiral Trost: Yeah. I like it. There's no detail on it other than water, and I like it.

Paul Stillwell: Were there any lingering hard feelings with Argentina after the Falklands War?[*]

Admiral Trost: Yes, yes. It was interesting. The relationship with the Navy cooled considerably, and that was our principal interface with them from a military standpoint, but they came through in their use of the southern Argentinean port that we used to help support the operations down at the South Pole, and I've forgotten what the port is, but we used it for port visits and U.S. government support, as a matter of fact, and for air support, and that worked pretty well. I don't know how close the relationship was. That was always there as sort of an irritant.

Paul Stillwell: A shadow?

Admiral Trost: Yeah, it was still there.

Paul Stillwell: Because the United States had tilted toward the British in that war.

Admiral Trost: Yeah, openly, openly. There was still a carryover then. They had a dented pride. My Navy counterpart, I don't know how to describe him personality-wise. I think he was probably a very professional guy, very political guy, and wore his ego on his sleeve; my take. Pauline felt the same way about his wife, frankly. She was, "You can be

---

[*] The event that triggered the 1982 Falklands War was the Argentine occupation of South Georgia Island on 19 March 1982, followed on 2 April by the occupation of the Falklands. The British then mounted a long-range expedition that made an amphibious assault on the islands and recaptured them. Argentina surrendered on 14 June.

CNO, you can be Mrs. CNO, and you can think yourself above it all. You're not." And when you behave that way, people react that way to you.

Paul Stillwell: Did that diminish the enthusiasm of the Argentines' participation in UNITAS?

Admiral Trost: I would say to a degree, yeah. No question.

Paul Stillwell: Did you have opportunities to get on board ships while you were CinCLantFlt?

Admiral Trost: Yeah, I made opportunities to get on ships, and made a point of visiting all my bases, all my homeports, all my ships. I didn't get aboard every ship, but I got aboard a lot of them.

Paul Stillwell: There are lots of them. [Laughs]

Admiral Trost: Yeah, there were a lot then.

Paul Stillwell: What was the level of concern about the Soviet Navy during that period?

Admiral Trost: Well, they were clearly a very capable organization. We had the results of Reagan's "stand firm" presidency, so we were geared up to be strong and make sure they saw it, so operations would be designed in many cases to reflect our capability to do things that kind of told them, "If you're going to do something, you'd better have this in mind." And that was true of our operations in the North Atlantic, the Norwegian Sea, and we never pulled back from anything because of concerns about what the Soviets might think. We wanted them to know we were capable and ready. We wanted to know we'd be there if the balloon went up, and I think we were successful in that.

Paul Stillwell: Well, this dovetailed with the Maritime Strategy that was being propagated.

Admiral Trost: Yeah.

Paul Stillwell: Any specifics you remember about the forward presence?

Admiral Trost: We debated long and hard about fleet operations and, again, in the Norwegian Sea predominantly, about the liability and validity of air interceptors, where they'd launch a bunch of Backfire bombers and we'd intercept them, show them we could. Some of those airplanes that we intercepted came from Norwegian airfields, some came from Iceland, some came from aircraft carriers.* So there was a variety of capabilities that we made sure they understood we had.

Paul Stillwell: So that was getting into the NATO area also.

Admiral Trost: Yes, yes.

Paul Stillwell: What do you remember about emphasis on ASW?

Admiral Trost: Heavy emphasis on ASW throughout, and across the board, all aspects of ASW-capable units, a lot of focus. Now, we'd had the Incidents at Sea Agreement and the follow-on, you know, about Soviets wanted us to tell them where our submarines were. Sure they did, because they couldn't find them.

Paul Stillwell: What do you remember about mine warfare as part of the fleet?

_____

* The Tupolev Tu-22M Backfire was a long-range, high-performance bomber that was flown by Soviet Strategic Aviation and Soviet Naval Aviation. The Backfire-B, which entered service in 1975, had two jet engines, a cruise speed of 560 miles per hour, and a range of about 3,000 miles. It could be armed with either bombs or missiles.

Admiral Trost: Underfocused, underappreciated, underfunded, in need of modernization, in need of more forces, more priority. That's what I remember. I'm not sure that's changed.

Paul Stillwell: Right. 'Twas ever thus. [Laughs]

Admiral Trost: Yeah. And I can't say that I did a hell of a lot to improve it.

Paul Stillwell: It's usually at the back end of the funding priorities.

Admiral Trost: Yeah, it was, and it's at the back end of the funding priorities for the people who should have been supporting it, who owned it. Now, that doesn't excuse me or people like me from pushing a stronger emphasis on it. I probably didn't do enough. Hard to tell.

Paul Stillwell: Well, later the fleet did get more mine countermeasures ships.

Admiral Trost: Yeah.

Paul Stillwell: What do you remember about the growing role of Military Sealift Command? It was taking over more underway replenishment and the towed sonar arrays.

Admiral Trost: Well, we used that as a way of basically saving money or shifting money, priorities for funding. It was a less expensive way than supporting with Navy ships the capabilities that they provided. I think their capability really came into focus with the Gulf War, which was after I retired, right after I retired.

Frank Donovan was the Sealift commander. Frank and I were good friends. Matter of fact, I had put him in that job. He invited me to be in for a briefing about a month after I retired, and showed me he had 110 ships at sea involved in support of the

Gulf War on one day.[*] And he showed me the map. They were scattered all the way across the Atlantic through the Med, through the canal, and I couldn't believe it. But that was probably the height of it. So it was a very major effort on his part there, but they were also supporting us in the Pacific and at sea in the Atlantic. Ships under his opcon included Russian ships, Russian commercial ships used as bottoms to haul freight in support of our own forces in the Middle East.

Paul Stillwell: I did not know that.

Admiral Trost: I didn't either till he briefed me on it. And they were chartered, chartered on the open market. But when you looked at his plot and his charts, it was just like drawing a line, and it's a line of ships all the way across and through.

Paul Stillwell: So he was a substantial operational commander.

Admiral Trost: He was a very substantial operational commander.

Paul Stillwell: There were a number of events during that brief period in the Mediterranean, the *Achille Lauro* seizure.[†] Did you have anything in that, other than monitoring?

Admiral Trost: Monitoring predominantly.

Paul Stillwell: Would that also be the case with the attacks on Libya in 1986, Operation

---

[*] In January 1991 U.S. and Allied Coalition forces attacked Iraq to get it to retreat following its August 1990 invasion of neighboring Kuwait. The holding action in the meantime was Operation Desert Shield. The conflict itself became known variously as Operation Desert Storm and the Gulf War. Coalition forces won the war in February 1991.

[†] On 7 October 1985 four armed Palestinian terrorists hijacked the Italian cruise ship *Achille Lauro* in the Mediterranean, in the vicinity of Egypt. The hijackers demanded that Israel free 50 Palestinian prisoners. The terrorists killed a disabled American tourist, 69-year-old Leon Klinghoffer, and threw his body overboard with his wheelchair. The terrorists finally left when granted safe passage, but their plane was intercepted by Navy F-14 fighters and forced to land in Sicily.

El Dorado Canyon?[*]

Admiral Trost: And I think that was before I took over as CNO.

Paul Stillwell: It was.

Admiral Trost: Yeah. And did I have direct involvement? No, but a lot of my ships were over there.

Paul Stillwell: In these attacks on Libya, there were bombers coming out of England and through the Strait of Gibraltar.

Admiral Trost: Yeah, I know what you mean. We couldn't get permission to overfly France, as I recall, yeah. I do remember that.

Paul Stillwell: Anything on terrorism in general from your time as fleet commander?

Admiral Trost: God, I can't think of anything offhand. Paul, I'm getting old. You know what I mean? You're asking me to pull out things that are 40 years old. [Laughs]

Paul Stillwell: I never know when the question will spark something, and so I've got to keep asking.

Admiral Trost: Okay.

---

[*] On 5 April 1986, a bomb exploded in a discotheque in Berlin frequented by U.S. service personnel. Intelligence indicated that Libyan terrorists were involved in the bombing. On 15 April, the United States retaliated by attacking Libyan military installations in Benghazi and Tripoli. The attacks were made by U.S. Air Force FB-111 bombers and carrier-based attack planes of the U.S. Sixth Fleet.

Paul Stillwell: What about the Walker spy ring? That was very big news.[*]

Admiral Trost: Oh, yeah, yeah, it was big. Arthur Walker, who was the lower-profile brother, was a neighbor two doors over when I was in Norfolk.

Paul Stillwell: Oh, gee. [Laughs]

Admiral Trost: That was when I was on the SubLant staff between my FBM command and coming back to Washington to go to work for John Warner.

Paul Stillwell: Did you know him?

Admiral Trost: I met him. He was a lieutenant commander. I was a new captain and I was on SubLant staff. He was a submariner. We chitchatted a couple times when we were out mowing the grass. We were on a cul-de-sac. We were at the end of it. Next door I had Esther Powers and—what was her husband's name? Anyway, the Powers, good friends of ours, and stayed friends. Next to us, Arthur Walker, and then there was somebody up on the corner; don't remember.

Paul Stillwell: It's amazing how a few bad apples can ruin a whole barrel.

Admiral Trost: Yes. And interestingly, he was not an outgoing neighbor. He did keep his kind of low profile, which I understand now, or did after it broke.

Paul Stillwell: Well, his brother John was really the ringleader and mastermind.

---

[*] On 20 May 1985 Chief Warrant Officer John A. Walker, Jr., USN (Ret.), was arrested and charged with selling classified information to the Soviets. He ran a spying organization that included his brother Lieutenant Commander Arthur J. Walker, USN (Ret.); son, Seaman Michael L. Walker, USN; and a friend, Senior Chief Radioman Jerry A. Whitworth, USN (Ret.). For details, see James Bamford, "The Walker Espionage Case," *U.S. Naval Institute Proceedings*, May 1986, pages 110-119.

Admiral Trost: The brother was the ringleader. He was a provider of information. I don't really recall what else he did other than provide information, and I don't remember what his job was at the time.

Paul Stillwell: I thought he was in communications in Norfolk.

Admiral Trost: He was in Norfolk for sure, in a headquarters assignment.

Paul Stillwell: Did you institute added security measures after those disclosures?

Admiral Trost: I think the sense of awareness was raised considerably. It's kind of like closing the door after the cat's out. The sense of awareness and security processes were changed, because these were people who were inside the hen coop, and they were chopping the necks off the hens, so it was closing the door after the coop's been violated.

Paul Stillwell: But you didn't want any further violations.

Admiral Trost: That's right. So there was a lot of tightening of access, primarily, a lot of rechecking of security clearances and background. But it's a kind of thing that's hard to detect, because you're faced with actions on the part of people which are intentional. They're competent people, know how to live like normal lives while they're doing what they're doing, and there's nothing to alert you to it unless your system is so tight that in many cases it hampers your operations.

Paul Stillwell: I think the disclosure came from the wife of one of the Walkers.

Admiral Trost: It did. It might have been Arthur. But John even pulled his kid who was in the Navy into the thing, and I don't know how you counter guys like that.

Paul Stillwell: No. What was your role vis-à-vis the Second Fleet Commander and the Sixth Fleet Commander when you were CinCLantFlt?

Admiral Trost: I was the provider of forces for the Sixth Fleet trained by the Second Fleet, the provider of Second Fleet forces for anything to do in the Caribbean, South American, or Atlantic Command, basically.

Paul Stillwell: And I presume you had regular measures of effectiveness that you went by.

Admiral Trost: We did. We did.

Paul Stillwell: Inspections and what have you.

Admiral Trost: We had inspections, exercises. Well, exercise oversight, basically, some participation in designing the exercises and dictating the types of exercises that should be run. Second Fleet Commander had a fair amount of autonomy in the training process, and we were the monitors, basically, of his exercises and the approvers of them, of course. But I don't recall getting too directly involved except when foreign forces were involved in our exercises, and I'm trying to remember what my role as fleet commander— sometimes the exercise sponsor, always the exercise evaluator, but no real direct involvement on my part in fleet operational exercises.

Paul Stillwell: And I'm guessing you stayed in touch with the fleet training groups on readiness.

Admiral Trost: Oh, yes.

Paul Stillwell: There was one active battleship then, the *Iowa*. How did you use her as fleet commander?

Admiral Trost: You know, I don't remember what we did with *Iowa*. I'm trying to think. We used battleships, *New Jersey*, I remember, possibly *Iowa*, off the coast of Iran when things were getting hot over in the Persian Gulf, and I don't remember time frame.

Paul Stillwell: That was later, when you were CNO.

Admiral Trost: Okay. Yeah, I guess you're right. You have a better memory on this than I do.

Paul Stillwell: But I've been looking things up recently. [Laughs]

Admiral Trost: You know, so much of that time frame sort of runs together. Did I do it then or then? You've got a cheat sheet.

Paul Stillwell: That's right. It's right there on the table. [Laughs]

      Anything else to say about your CinCLantFlt tour?

Admiral Trost: No. I made a point when I first became fleet commander of visiting every fleet base wherever they were and supporting bases like Iceland, obviously—-oh, God— outside the U.S. but north of Maine. What's up there across the St. Lawrence Strait?

Paul Stillwell: In Canada?

Admiral Trost: Canada, yes, but Newfoundland. Places that don't see senior officers very frequently.

Paul Stillwell: Argentia.

Admiral Trost: Argentia. And, of course, Iceland, I made a point of not only visiting the base because it was so key, much more key than it is today, but visiting the base, visiting the local people, because we were using the airfield as an Icelandic commercial field as well as a P-3 support base, and going up to the capital and meeting with their senior government people, who were very congenial and very supportive. So we wanted to salvage that relationship. That got me an invitation to go salmon fishing about five years after I retired, but I couldn't do it. [Laughter]

Paul Stillwell: That's a long way to go for fishing.

Admiral Trost: It is that. It is. You have to be a better fisherman than I ever was.

Paul Stillwell: Well, how then did you evolve into being Chief of Naval Operations, despite your desire to stay as CinCLantFlt?

Admiral Trost: Well, I've told this story several times recently. I was just trying to remember whether it was you I told it to or not. I got a phone call one day from the Vice Chief's Office saying, "You're going to get orders to come up tomorrow to Washington from Norfolk to see the Secretary of the Navy and the Secretary of Defense, and you are to stop and see the Vice Chief of Naval Operations, one Ron Hays, on your way into the Pentagon."[*] The Vice Chief said, "You're to go see Lehman, and it's about the CNO's job."

Well, what I didn't know at the time was filled in by them then, was that Lehman had submitted Kelso's name to the White House. What he did was draw up a nomination for CNO, which normally would go from him to the Chairman of Joint Chiefs, to the Secretary of Defense, to the White House. Lehman sent a nomination directly over, hand-carried over to a Marine colonel who was on the White House staff, who got it on Reagan's desk somehow. And the story—now, this was related to me after the fact. The story is that Reagan called Poindexter, who was the National Security Advisor there, and said, "I've got a nomination here for a new CNO. Doesn't have your chop on it. What's your comment?"[†]

John said, "Haven't seen it. Didn't know anything about it."

"Find out how it got on my desk."

---

[*] Admiral Ronald J. Hays, USN, served as Vice Chief of Naval Operations from April 1983 to September 1985.
[†] Vice Admiral John M. Poindexter, USN, was National Security Advisor to President Ronald Reagan from 4 December 1985 to 25 November 1986.

Well, they somehow or other finally found out how it got on his desk. So Reagan said, "Send it over to Bill Crowe and Cap Weinberger to see what they think."* He did that.

What I'm telling you now is related to me after the fact by Crowe, Weinberger, and Poindexter, all at various times. So Weinberger and Crowe got together, and for reasons unknown to me, they decided I was their nominee. So Weinberger called the Chief of Naval Personnel and said, "Draw up a nomination for CNO Trost and don't staff it. Draw it up in your office, send it directly to me by hand," which they did.

Weinberger and Crowe signed off on the thing and then hand-carried it to Poindexter in the White House to give it to the President, who signed it.

I, in the meantime, had been called up to Washington, went in to see the Vice Chief to tell me I was going to see the Secretary of the Navy and the Secretary of Defense. I don't recall whether he said what it was for.

So I went in to see Lehman, whose first words were, as I walked in the office, "You don't want the job."

I said, "What job?"

And he told me. Well, when he said I don't want it, I thought, "Well, maybe I do." [Laughter]

Then I went on down to see Weinberger, who told me why I was there, and didn't tell me any of these background details, and said, "Do you want the job?"

I said, "Not especially," and I told him what I'd told you before. I told them my eyes looking ahead six years.

And he said, "That's nice. So I'll let you know."

I went back down to Norfolk. I heard nothing until I got a phone call from Weinberger in his airplane, having just left Brussels for a NATO Defense Ministers' meeting and saying, "The President has signed your nom and sent it forward, and we'll be in touch." So that's how I got the word.

Paul Stillwell: Did you gradually warm to the idea?

Admiral Trost: Well, didn't have any option. Pauline didn't like the idea at all, because she was just getting Missouri House shaken down and she didn't like the idea of moving. She liked Norfolk.

So we had then a relatively short time to get the LantFlt nominated. They nominated Kelso, and he and I never did have a turnover down there. We never had a face-to-face turnover because the time frame was so compressed.

Paul Stillwell: He said it was a telephone change of command.

Admiral Trost: It was. It was. I was already in Washington and he called, basically, and said, "I got it." I don't remember what briefings he had beforehand, but I know he got briefed. So that was it.

Lehman made it very clear from the outset that he didn't want me, wasn't happy with me because I'd been his nemesis as a proxy for Watkins and Hayward before that, when I was 090, because whenever they had a disagreement on programmatic stuff, I'd get sent in after the meeting to explain to Lehman why he was off base or wrong or other unpopular terms. So I was not viewed very favorably by him, and that was for four years. He was SecNav the entire time I was 090. So our relationship started off basically with an "I don't want you," made it clear we were not going to get along, and we didn't for the next nine months till he left. But that's how I got there.

Paul Stillwell: What do you recall about the confirmation hearings?

Admiral Trost: Piece of cake, as I remember. It was very, very easy. All this never came up. Now, I called on the chairman, who I think was still the gentleman from Georgia—

Paul Stillwell: Sam Nunn.

Admiral Trost: Sam Nunn. I had met with and briefed Nunn as 090 a number of times before that, so I didn't feel like a stranger walking in the office. So I made my courtesy call on him and others, but I don't remember who they were. My confirmation hearing was brief, innocuous, and I was there.

Paul Stillwell: So this necessitated another move.

Admiral Trost: Yeah, it did, necessitated another move. And Pauline didn't like the thoughts of the Navy Yard for two reasons. If you have children coming in and out, that's not a good place to be. Kids were all in or out of college, so that wasn't a problem. She had a Chrysler convertible, her pride and joy, which we'd bought in Norfolk just less than a year before, and she was afraid to drive that with that soft top down in the neighborhood of the Navy Yard, and you can understand that. So she wasn't very happy, and she never drove it with the top down, always worried that somebody was going to come slit her top and get in the car. The region down there, by the way, is much tamer today than it was back then.

Paul Stillwell: Well, there's been a great revitalization of Eighth Street. Barracks Row, it's called.

Admiral Trost: Yeah. There was a place on Eighth Street, a restaurant, that you almost needed an armed guard to get to when we lived there. We went there, oh, about two years ago, I guess, and totally different atmosphere, people sitting out at tables on the sidewalk and lots of people with kids in the restaurant, a totally different environment. She liked to shop at the Eastern Market on Seventh Street near Pennsylvania, but she wouldn't walk out there.

Paul Stillwell: My son used to live right near the intersection of Eighth and I, and he felt pretty safe with the Marine Barracks across the street. [Laughs]

Admiral Trost: Yeah, I can understand that. But if you got three or four blocks from Eighth and I, you might be in trouble.

Paul Stillwell: What do you recall of publicity when your selection as CNO was announced?

Admiral Trost: Well, before I was sworn in, an interview with *Navy Times* took place. I knew Lehman was pushing, along with senior aviators, to reinstate the khaki uniform, which Mike Mullen eventually did.[*] Lehman said, "It looks sharp and the aviators want it." Well, it had been abolished for years. I had worn it as a midshipman and as a JO, I guess probably through commander. It's hot in the summertime. Instead of wearing tropical white or tropical khaki, you're wearing a long-sleeved cotton shirt, you're wearing a blouse buttoned down the front. It's hot, so I didn't like it. So this chief who was interviewing me had prepared a bunch of questions, and one of the questions was "How do you feel about service dress khaki?" And he asked me and I told him, and he printed it.

The next day Lehman called me. This was just the day before I was sworn in, and he said, "You son of a bitch. You cut the rug right out under me," or something like that. [Laughter] And I thought, well, it had been something if I'd taken it on after it was approved, but it was never proposed, nor was it approved. So that was one of our problems.

Paul Stillwell: That was not exactly a friendly "Welcome aboard." [Laughs]

Admiral Trost: It wasn't adhered to. And a lot of things were liberalized, too much so, including uniforms, I thought. No, I was not his friend, I was not his choice, and he made that clear. We worked together only nine months, fortunately. But I'm not a Lehman fan. Lehman is not, in my view, an honest person. He's a self-server, likes to be in charge. He was a lieutenant commander in the Naval Reserve, after all, and here he was telling admirals what to do.[†]

---

[*] The service dress khaki uniform went away in the 1970s. Admiral Mike Mullen was CNO from 2005 to 2007.
[†] Lehman was promoted to Naval Reserve commander during his tenure as Secretary and in 1989 promoted to captain.

Paul Stillwell: We were talking before on the selection regime about extracurricular shenanigans that didn't get into the fitness reports. My sense is that now those things do get noticed earlier.

Admiral Trost: Yeah, I think we're more sensitive to it, and it's been the result of several instances of guys getting fired for shady behavior, let's just say. Senior officers are expected to live with their wives, not with a woman in their deployment area. Senior officers are expected to set an example of behavior for their people, not be misleaders. I think that's a tighter requirement today than it has been at times in the past. I do know that when you fire a vice admiral in a very senior position, you get a lot of shit, and that happened once with me.

Paul Stillwell: You're speaking of Admiral Moranville?[*]

Admiral Trost: Yeah. He had a remarkable number of supporters, and I took a lot of gas. And part of it was "When this gets out, it's going to give the Navy a bad eye."

I said, "Yeah. It already has from the people who know about it, and a lot of those people who know about it are sailors. And, more importantly, *I* know about it, and I'm supposed to be the moral leader of the Navy officer corps. So this is what I do."

Paul Stillwell: And I would guess that your action had a deterring effect, in addition.

Admiral Trost: I would hope so. I would hope so. Well, the good ol' boy club rose to defense, and, "How could you do such a thing?"

Paul Stillwell: Well, another trend I've noticed is that the *Navy Times* has become much more sensationalized.

---

[*] On 20 August 1988 Vice Admiral Kendall E. Moranville, USN, was relieved as Commander Sixth Fleet. He had been under consideration for another three-star job until 19 August, when he received a letter of reprimand as the result of an admiral's mast. He was charged with improprieties involving travel claims and for being accompanied by an unauthorized female Italian civilian while flying U.S. military aircraft when he was Commander Sixth Fleet. As Chief of Naval Operations, Admiral Trost forced Moranville to retire as a rear admiral, one level below his highest active duty rank.

Admiral Trost: Oh, yeah.

Paul Stillwell: It reports a lot of these cases now that were sort of off the record before.

Admiral Trost: *Navy Times* today, compared to what it was when I became CNO, is a rag. We had a couple of retired chief journalists, as I recall. I know there was one who interviewed me when I became CNO, and I can't think of his name. But we had a couple guys over there who I think maintained the balance: "We're an information publication, not another rag sheet." And I think they maintained the balance. But *Navy Times* is not under the same ownership. I think—was it *Army Times*? I don't know who bought them, but they were bought.

Paul Stillwell: They're all under the same umbrella.

Admiral Trost: Yeah, they're under the same umbrella, and I think they were independent during my time and they were cooperative. I'd get calls from *Navy Times*. One of the chiefs over there and one of the editors called me on several occasions and said, "We have the following information. We'd like to either have you confirm or deny ideally, but tell us whether it's something we should print or should hold." And a couple of occasions what they had was sort of half-truths and sensationalism stuff that might have made a good story in a rag, but not in an information document.

Paul Stillwell: I suspect those calls don't get made now.

Admiral Trost: I don't think so. I stopped my *Navy Times* subscription after retirement, matter of fact, about, let's see, post-2000, I think. And I got a call, "Gosh, you've been a subscriber for so many years. What caused you to stop your subscription?"

    I said, "The truth."

Paul Stillwell: Good answer. [Laughs]

Admiral Trost: And I never heard back. I was offered a free trial subscription for a year if I'd sign back up, and I chose not to, and, you know, I haven't missed it. Maybe it's of value to the sailor in the fleet, but I don't think so, because they can provide some information that's misleading, and sensationalism is more important than fact. You might know I'm biased.

Paul Stillwell: Everybody is.

Earlier this week, I had an exchange with Vice Admiral Bob Dunn because *Navy Times* had a five-page article about a helo incident on board the USS *William P. Lawrence* in which two pilots were killed.[*] Admiral Dunn said he was just livid about the article because it didn't portray that it was poor seamanship on the skipper's part that permitted that accident to happen.

Admiral Trost: Well, I would go by his judgment. Bob Dunn's one of the finest guys I've worked with, and I've worked with him in two jobs. His retirement job I also worked with him a little bit. He's a four-square guy.

Paul Stillwell: I have a great deal of admiration for him.

Admiral Trost: He's a fine gentleman. He's a good leader and one of the best aviators I've known, best naval officers I've known.

Paul Stillwell: Yes. What do you remember as priorities for you as you settled into the job ass Chief of Naval Operations?

Admiral Trost: My priority was people and readiness. We were deploying people for eight, nine, ten months, and I had talked to a lot of people on ships, and that was clearly a sticking point in retention issues and morale in general. So I had tried to get Watkins to

---

[*] USS *William P. Lawrence* (DDG-110) suffered a fatal accident while operating in the Red Sea on 22 September 2013. A high-speed turn broke the chains holding down an MH60S helicopter on the ship's fantail, and the helo fell into the sea. Killed in the accident were the two pilots, Lieutenant Commander Landon L. Jones, USN, and Chief Warrant Officer-3 Jonathan S. Gibson, USN.

issue a Navy-wide edict on shorter deployments. We had a lot of ships compared to today, for example, but accepting the fact that the shorter deployments meant more frequent deployments. But when you're on a three- or four- or five-year cycle, it's not that big an increase in frequency.

So I had, where I could with LantFlt, cut the op tempo. For example, have a guy who deployed, say, to the Mediterranean and for presence purposes, we'd send him to the Indian Ocean at the end of his six-month deployment and make a couple of port visits in the Indian Ocean, come around South America and home, adding two months to his deployment. And I cut back on those. I tried to get Watkins to shorten deployments Navy-wide. He would not, and I understand it. The rationale was clear. We have a requirement, we have a commitment, and here's what happens when you shorten deployments, more people deployed, etc. So I decided to bite the bullet and I put out a Navy-wide edict limiting deployments to six months, and we used about three months to phase that in. That may have been my most controversial foot in the water, but I did it, and it worked. It helped. We increased retention noticeably. I won't say markedly. I'll say noticeably.

Fleet readiness, I thought, had been underfunded, because we had that year that I had on LantFlt with the 15% deficit, and so I put an emphasis on getting more funding for readiness and sending more people to the Hill, pestering more congressmen about the importance of funding readiness, and we got some relief.

So my priorities were readiness and people, and that's where I had most of my focus, and I had enough budgetary knowledge and programmatic knowledge to be able to see what was happening and interfere with them, or I'd like to say give them guidance, keep that going. So I kept that focus throughout my four years and tried to get organizational efficiency improvement without putting a lot of money against it.

I found, for example, that when we added up the number of man-days needed to respond to congressional requests for information, it became an astounding amount percentagewise of OpNav manpower utilization. So I went to see the committee chairman and told him, "You know, you're telling us we ought to be cutting back there and cutting back here, and here's what you guys are doing." A couple of them listened to me. Ike Skelton on House Armed Services took that aboard and did something about it. Nunn, while he was there, did something about it. They were the two key guys for me at that time.

So we got results, not always as much as we wanted, but we got results. I tried to reduce the adverse influence of guys like Byrd of West Virginia.[*]

Paul Stillwell: Who had been there for a long, long time.

Admiral Trost: Oh, yes, he had.

Paul Stillwell: And paved West Virginia in the process.

Admiral Trost: Yes. My experience with him, I was told, "Well, you'd better call on Senator Byrd, because he's a very influential guy." And I called on a number of other members of the Senate, guys I hadn't worked with before. So I made an appointment through my Office of Legislative Affairs, and it was to be at 1:30 or 2:00 o'clock—I think 2:00 o'clock—on something like a Tuesday or Wednesday afternoon. So my OLA escort and I showed up a half hour early, and a secretary said, "Well, have a seat, and he'll see you shortly."[†]

Well, if it was 1:30 for the appointment, it was 2:30 by the time I was sitting there cooling my heels, and my escort kept asking the secretary about the time. She said, "He's very busy." Nobody went in or out of his office in that time frame.

Finally, after an hour-and-a-half wait, after the appointed hour, I was told, "He'll see you now. Go on in."

I walked in. His greetings to me are [in southern accent], "What have you done for West Virginia today, son?"

I stopped, I said, "Well, Senator, I'm afraid I haven't done anything today for West Virginia."

[In southern accent] "Well, son, come back and see when you done something for

---

[*] Robert C. Byrd, a Democrat from West Virginia, served in the Senate from 3 January 1959 until his death on 28 June 2010.
[†] OLA – Office of Legislative Affairs.

West Virginia."

I walked out the door. The secretary said, "Should I make another appointment?"

I said, "Don't bother." And I went back to my office. I never saw the son of a bitch again. [Laughs]

Paul Stillwell: Deliberately rude.

Admiral Trost: Oh, arrogantly rude. And I never did anything else. He got a lot of things done, got a lot of Navy money for things that didn't help Navy readiness in the process. But there were a few guys like that. I tried to avoid them, and, by and large, was successful. But we ended up, the guys that were my heroes were the guys like Sam Nunn and Ike Skelton, who worked with you well and were helpful to the Navy, to the military.

Paul Stillwell: What was the role of the Office of Legislative Affairs? How much did you depend on that office?

Admiral Trost: Heavily, to make sure the right people were aware of what we wanted to do, to give advanced notification to people who needed to know, who would be helped by having information that would be useful to them and help them help us. I also put a priority on manning, which Tom Hayward had done before me, and Watkins never changed it.

When I got there to the job, my Chief of Legislative Affairs was a guy Lehman had picked. He'd been the CO down at Patuxent.[*] He was a tall, slender aviator, a real ass. He would show up at my morning lineup, which was supposed to be at 7:15 in the morning, to brief me on Legislative Affairs, along with about six or so other guys who came in. He was invariably late, invariably unprepared. He'd have papers that an aide, one of his guys, had stood outside of CNO Office in the corridor with a sheaf of papers to hand him. Well, he hadn't even read them, so he couldn't very well brief them. But he was a Lehman buddy, and I couldn't get rid of him. So he was of little help, but under

---

[*] Rear Admiral Edward J. Hogan, USN, served from December 1982 to October 1985 as Commander Naval Air Test Center and from November 1985 to September 1987 as Chief of Legislative Affairs.

him, his deputy—and I don't remember who that was now, except it was somebody who was handpicked and was a good guy, and I interviewed everybody who went into that office from that point on and made sure, first of all, they knew I had an interest in the office, I could give them general guidance, and they knew I was going to be watching. So that helped the quality of performance immensely.

Paul Stillwell: Well, they presumably knew that they had your support as well.

Admiral Trost: Yeah. By and large, we did well, and when we got rid of that head guy and got a good guy in there, we did even better. But he was basically disengaged. I wish I could remember his name.

Paul Stillwell: But essentially these were the Navy's lobbyists.

Admiral Trost: They were. They were. And they were the guys who advised me when and whom to call on when a particular issue came up, so you were really dependent on them for effectiveness on the Hill. And somebody would say, "Gee, you know, So-and-so's aide asked me some questions. He really doesn't understand."

I'd say, "Send So-and-so over to brief him." And you depended on that. You depended on those guys to do that.

Paul Stillwell: So it's an educational function too.

Admiral Trost: Yeah, really is. And if the people you've got representing you—and then there's some guys who are over there all day every day, not back at the Pentagon plotting or planning, and so those guys are really critical, and they see very little of the day-to-day real life in the Pentagon or the real Navy. So they've got to be able to think for themselves, know when to ask questions and whom to ask them of, so they're critical.

Paul Stillwell: Well, this was during the period with the 600-ship Navy as a goal. Did you still push toward that?

Admiral Trost: Yeah. When I retired, we had either 594 or 596 ships and we had 594,000 or 596,000 people, one or the other. I've forgot which it was, but both in that 595 area. We kept pushing because Lehman kept pushing. We were on track to get there or nearly there, and Lehman's successors wanted to keep going on. Because, you know, we really today, we don't need 280 ships; we need double that number of ships. And we're deploying people for eight months, nine months. I just read something, an article—oh, of all things, the wedding announcements in the *Capital*, an article about two lieutenants junior grade, male and female, academy grads, same class, who either just got married or are about to get married. She had finished a tour on a destroyer, and I've forgotten what his job was, and they're now both shore assigned. They just got married. Now, why was I telling you this? Deployment. She just came off an eight-month deployment aboard the destroyer. I have made a five-month destroyer deployment and shorter destroyer deployments. Eight months is inhumane.

I've told the story of my briefings on a carrier in the Mediterranean when I was CNO. I flew aboard on a Sixth Fleet visit, and they had set up a hangar briefing for as many troops as could attend. I briefed about—I think there were 2,100 or 2,500 sailors and some officers in the hangar deck, and I opened up to Q&A and got some good ones. At that time, I was still waiting for an evaluation of the shorter deployments. They were coming off an eight-month deployment, and that's before the whole thing took effect. I said, "What's the difference hypothetically between eight months, six months, ten months?" I said, "What the difference between ten months and six months?"

This guy pops up in the front row, first-class petty officer, and he said, "If you've got kids, about two years." And he's right. They are away from their kids. We have people today who come off of deployment and see for the first time a child which was already in the incubator when they deployed and has been born since they deployed, and they see this kid who's nine months old. We don't have to do that in peacetime. If we do, we've got more obligations than we have forces.

The other concern I had was about was unnecessary paperwork. I mentioned the congressional workload that we had. But I was always annoyed by requirements to submit certain reports that made absolutely no sense. You read it, you said, "Now, what the hell does anybody get out of this? What's its value?"

So one of the things I did the first week I was CNO was signed out a NavOp, a directive to the Navy, directing a review of all Navy instructions and notices. They're all categorized and they're all listed for utility. God, did I get a swamp of responses. I had the guys in OP-96, the Systems Analysis Division, as the focal point to collect all these, collate them. The first shot, we cancelled over 1,000 directives. I don't know how many there are all told. There are a hell of a lot more than that. But when I looked for the rationale for cancellation, it was no value added, and there were instances of people would have to gather data that I saw no utilization for, things not defensible and of no utility to the Navy. Ultimately, I think we cancelled something like 1,800 or 1,900 directives that were Navy-wide, that were taking people's time and energy to fill out and send back. And where do they go? In a file. So things like that, I had a chance to satisfy my desire to get rid of a lot of crap that had pissed me off for a lot of years.

Paul Stillwell: Good to be in a position to do so. [Laughs]

Admiral Trost: It was nice to be in a position to do so.

Paul Stillwell: Were you able to reduce some of the commitments to facilitate shorter deployments, such as the carrier in the North Arabian Sea, the presence and demand?

Admiral Trost: Not very successfully, because there was such pressure on commitments. There was more pressure to add than there is to take away. So not substantially. The only thing that reduced commitments was losing ships, and that didn't start till after I retired, not because I retired, I hope.

Paul Stillwell: Please tell me about your direct interaction with the Soviets.

Admiral Trost: Marshal Akhromeyev, who was then their Chairman Joint Chiefs, went through World War II as a sergeant, Soviet Army, was badly wounded, apparently was a real hero in World War II. He came over for the first time in 1987, and by then he was the senior marshal in the Soviet military.* He got in for his meeting with the Joint Chiefs, and he was going to give a briefing. But the first thing he did was point to me and say, "You and your goddamn submariners are the problem. We need to know where those submarines are." He said, "Right now I know where my submarines are. I see where your P-3s are flying, but we don't know where yours are. That's destabilizing."

I said, "Yes, sir." And then we left it at that.

Paul Stillwell: Admiral Crowe developed a good relationship with him.

Admiral Trost: He did, a very good relationship. They got along well together. They spoke well together, they respected each other, and Crowe was the first to be invited back. Marshal Akhromeyev came back the year after the first visit—that would have been '88—when we signed something with the Russians. He was a senior person in their delegation, as I recall.

Bill Crowe had a reception for him, and I don't remember whether it was the first visit or a second visit, and as we were going through the receiving line, he was there with Bill and Shirley Crowe. I got there, Pauline was introduced, and he greeted her very nicely. When I was introduced, he said, "You and your goddamn submarines. You're the problem." [Laughs] That was translated for me. The roughness in his tone was not, but I got that first time through, and it was really fascinating.

My favorite Akhromeyev story from his visit was when he went down to Camp Lejeune.† They lined up a Marine honor guard, and he walked down and said something to every guy in the front row, stopped at one guy and said, "What do you think of my visit?'

The young guy, through the interpreter, said, "I think it's a good idea. We need to know each other better to get along better."

Akhromeyev thought that was a very diplomatic, smart answer. He said, "If I had

---

* Marshal of the Soviet Union Sergei Fyodorovich Akhromeyev was the last Chief of the General Staff of the Soviet Union, serving 1984-88. He visited the United States for the first time in 1987.
† The name of Marine Barracks, New River, was changed on 20 December 1942 to Camp Lejeune in honor of General John A. Lejeune, USMC (Ret.), who died on 21 November 1942. He had served as Marine Corps Commandant from 1920 to 1929.

asked one of my guys in ranks a question, he'd have frozen, he'd have been afraid of me, and he wouldn't say anything," which I thought was interesting. But he was impressed by the people he met.

Paul Stillwell: I remember Admiral Crowe and he were on "60 Minutes," and Crowe took him down in a missile silo.*

Admiral Trost: Yeah, and Crowe took him to the plant where they changed—what was it? They had a Farmall tractor mounted thing, and they put cotton-picker fronts on them. As they were driving into this plant down in Oklahoma, Akhromeyev saw all these cars parked in the parking lot and said, "You told me they were making cotton-pickers. They're making cars."

Bill said, "No, those are our workers' cars." He would not believe him, wouldn't believe those were workers' cars, and admitted that at a dinner party for him before he left, that he was surprised at that.

Paul Stillwell: Admiral Crowe had a great crack about the "60 Minutes" show. After that show aired, he said, "One of my friends called me and he said, 'Bill, I had heard that you were two-faced, but now I'm convinced you're not, because if you had another face, that's the one you would have used on TV.'" [Laughter]

Admiral Trost: Bill Crowe was a great guy to work for, and I never saw him mad in the vindictive sense. I've seen him mad as things were happening, something we did that he thought was pretty dumb, but he was a great guy to work with, and I had him for, I guess, over three and a half of my four-year tour, and so I had the best guy. The nice thing about it was you had open-door policy. If a chief of service walked into his outer office, he was ushered in without, "What do you want? What do you need?" or anything else. He was ushered in to see Bill because that was his policy. So it was a pleasant operation.

_____

* "60 Minutes" is a "magazine"-style program that has aired for years on the CBS television network.

When Akhromeyev was here, they had agreed on that second visit that Bill would go over and make an exchange with the Soviets. So in '89 Bill went over as the first senior military guy to make an exchange visit, and he spent a week in the Soviet Union.[*]

Then we followed that up with all of the four service chiefs on both sides making visits, staggered down the line. The Army was to be the initial one, because obviously they're the senior service. But for reasons I never did find out, the Army Chief's visit was cancelled, and instead of our Army Chief going, I was to go. So I spent a week in the Soviet Union. My visit was the last one during my time as CNO, and the others didn't resume.

The next one I remember is my Russian counterpart, who was to visit six months after I visited them. He got here two years after I visited them, and he went to Norfolk. He had me shown through one of their nuclear submarines up north in Murmansk. He had them show me a Victor III, which was at that time their latest nuclear attack sub, on the proviso that I show him one of our SSNs when he came over to the U.S.[†] They showed me the ship, and, matter of fact, the ship deployed that week to the Mediterranean. So we not only had seen the ship, been through it with my EA, Captain Dan Oliver, who was a U.S. naval aviator, a P-3 pilot and pretty astute.[‡] I had another guy with me. I've forgotten who the commander was. He was a submariner. So we had two submariners' eyes going through.

We had agreed to show that admiral through our propulsion plant, because they knew our ships were quiet, didn't know why, and somehow they were going to find out. Well, they were amazed to find out that we sound-mount everything, including turbines, which is one of the reasons they're quiet. They do things in bulk. They hard-mount their equipment but then have a dead space filled with foam to keep the sound from going through the hull.

Paul Stillwell: Did you get into the reactor compartment in the Soviet submarine?

---

[*] Admiral Crowe made a ten-day visit that concluded with a news conference on 21 June 1989. A summary of his news conference remarks appeared in *The New York Times* the following day.

[†] Soviet Victor III-class nuclear-powered submarines first went into service in 1979; 25 of them were produced between then and 1991. They were quieter than previous Soviet submarines. They were designed to launch torpedoes, cruise missiles, and mines.

[‡] Captain Daniel T. Oliver, USN, later vice admiral.

Admiral Trost: Walked through it, but, of course, first of all, they were critical, so I walked through the space outside, through the tunnel. We didn't take him inside our reactor compartment. We took him through the machinery spaces, and he was amazed at how thoroughly everything was shock-mounted, including the pipes and everything else.

The other thing that was interesting was the damage control on the submarine, which I was especially attuned to. We have emergency air-breathing masks. They're throughout the ship in lockers, and you have the lines throughout the ship that you plug into and uncap. You turn the thing and the cap drops off and you plug in so you've got instant clean air. They had stations where you could plug something in, but you had to find them and there weren't very many of them, and they were mostly in critical areas, which is smart, but we have them in key operation areas, but also where people might have to gather who are not on watch and not helping fight the problem, but they've got to breathe. And I didn't see that there. If you happened to be in a place where there was one, you were in luck. So it was interesting.

Paul Stillwell: Anything more on the Soviet situation?

Admiral Trost: I don't think so. It was interesting with Chernavin, who was my host.[*] He was my opposite number when I went over. He was a nuclear submariner. One of the things he said to me during our initial discussion was, "Well, you know I'm a submariner too."

I said, "I know."

"Okay," he said, "I expect you to know that." He said, "I had command of a nuclear submarine."

I said, "I know."

"I went under the ice."

I said, "I know."

He said, "I commanded a November-class nuclear submarine."

I said, "I know."

---

[*] Fleet Admiral Vladimir Nikolayevich Chernavin was Commander in Chief of the Soviet Navy from 1985 to 1992.

He said, "What don't you know about me?" [Laughter] We got along extremely well.

Paul Stillwell: Well, there was a common bond.

Admiral Trost: Yeah, it really was. And what did he say? Oh, I know. His parting message to me when I called on him the last morning was interesting. We had a breakfast and there were seven types of liquor on the breakfast table in the BOQ with the members of their group that had escorted us at various times on the trip, and my staff and me and Pauline. I knew I was going to call on my counterpart, my host, and also the ambassador, and I didn't want to be bombed-out. They kept saying, "Have some of this."

So I'd pretend to take a sip.

When I had the session with the ambassador, he said, "How'd they do?" And I told him what we'd done. He said, "You know, they were more open with you than they have been with anybody on my staff, things they'd shown me and places they'd taken me." Then he said, "Well, okay, and you're going to go see the admiral?"

I said, "Yes."

Chernavin's parting words to me were, "Let's stay in touch and let's keep talking to our respective Congresses about our enemy, because that's the only way we're going to get enough money to survive." [Laughter]

I thought, "He's a realist." But we had a great rapport.

As a matter of fact, when he came to the U.S. two years later, I got a call. Kelso invited him down to Norfolk to see that submarine I had promised him. He got a call, gave me his impression of Norfolk, what an impressive naval base that was, his impressions of the submarine, how well treated he'd been, respectfully and with questions answered and all when he came to the Washington area, and how much he appreciated that.

So we had a good rapport, and he wrote to me a couple times later. He was one of the guys who started a group of retired Soviet military officers whose goal was to improve relationships military-to-military between the countries as step one. He got derailed somewhere along the line. That outfit is no longer in existence. They got disbanded, which was a shame, but in keeping with Putin, I think, and his philosophy.[*]

Paul Stillwell: A quite different one.

Admiral Trost: Yeah.

Chernavin was great with the workers. He'd just strike up a conversation with a guy who'd be standing there, asked him all sorts of questions, and focus on what the guy's doing, listen to him.

So Frank Kelso made good on the tour. I don't know what happened with the other services. I'm sure they had an exchange, but I wasn't privy to it. This was after I retired. But it was interesting, the two tied together. That first visit prepared me. I'd seen a lot of their installations, saw their installations in Leningrad. When I went back, we spent a day, part of it touring that base, and they made no overt attempt to hide anything from me. One of the comments made by the flag officer over there, who was my host, was that, "We have shared things with them that tells them that we know things they didn't know we knew, so it's okay to show me." [Laughter]

They also had me address their Naval War College, I guess it was there, in Leningrad, which was interesting, because they hauled everybody who was a flag officer in the area in, and they came in. I got a chance to make a presentation in English, which my interpreter simultaneously interpreted, so we knew that they were getting what I was saying and not what their interpreter was saying. We had a Q-and-A session, lasted about an hour and a half. It was fascinating, because these guys were mostly commanders and captains in the Soviet Navy, and they seemed to be very open or willing to be very open. They'd ask me a question, I'd give them an answer, and I'd ask them a question, and they'd respond. So it was a good visit. It was a good time.

Paul Stillwell: You said that the things they showed you, they figured you already knew about. Were there things that you didn't really know about that you learned?

---

[*] Vladimir V. Putin is President of the Russian Federation. He previously served as Prime Minister.

Admiral Trost: They showed me on that visit an amphibious ship with a big bow that opened up, when I was on the Black Sea. We knew they had something. We had no idea what it looked like, what its capacity was, or anything else. The skipper of that thing came up and briefed me on it and told me what it was, what its capacity was—I don't remember, but I reported it—and how many people they carried, how many vehicles they could carry. It was big, it was impressive, and it was fast. I don't know if they have a lot of them or not. I never did follow up on that.

They took me up and showed me a Backfire bomber, which was still current at the time, and that was in the Crimea also. The admiral in charge down there, a four-star, took me up to this Backfire base and showed me this airplane. It's a dual cockpit-type thing, and as I remember, there was one guy in the front and one guy in the back. And I said, "Well, I don't know much about airplanes. How about Captain Oliver, my EA, can he climb in?"

"Oh, sure, sure." He was a P-3 driver and knew P-3 equipment and said this was, by comparison, outdated or prehistoric by comparison. He said the cockpit was less up to date than the P-3 cockpit, which was saying something. And the second seat, the equipment operator seat, he thought was—I forget what term he used, but obsolescent, basically, which was the first internal look we'd had at a Backfire bomber. So they were showing us things we had not seen.

Now, what we did see on that Backfire bomber were tires that were worn down to almost no tread. I wouldn't want to be in there landing at high speed, but it didn't seem to bother them. They took us aboard—I think it was *Slava*, one of the first of a class of cruiser that we'd seen for the first time on a visit to Malta that they made.[*] They took me aboard a number of different ships. I'm trying to think. Except for that nuclear submarine, that was the only submarine. They took me aboard a new cruiser down in the Black Sea, which was very, very nice. We knew about it, but nobody had ever been aboard one. I went aboard, and my biggest impression was all the paint topside was wet. They had just painted that sucker stem to stern for my visit. [Stillwell laughs.] So we

---

[*] The Soviet guided missile cruiser *Slava* went into service in 1982. The class was conventionally powered and intended as a less expensive version of the nuclear-powered *Kirov* class battle cruiser. The *Kirov* went into service in September 1980.

hadn't seen that.

They took me to Yalta, the place in the Black Sea where the Presidents met. They took me by boat, by fancy boat, a couple hours' ride over to Yalta and showed me all the rooms. They'd preserved everything just as it was in 1945, a very impressive place. What it was like in the winter of '45, I don't know. But it was well painted and well preserved, I remember that.

Paul Stillwell: So you got pretty far north and pretty far south.

Admiral Trost: Got all the way north. Another thing that was interesting, I don't think I told you, when the Northern Fleet Commander, actually the deputy commander, took me through, he took me through *Kirov*, the first of their nuclear cruisers, that was the flagship up in the North Sea Fleet, and we went out on deck, actually on the bridge, and looked across the channel. I think it's about, seems to me, three or four miles across. It's a major fleet anchorage by the time you're down at the base. He said, "And, of course, as you know," which was an interesting preface, he said, "we have submarine pens in the cliff." When you look across, you look at high cliffs.

I said, "Yes, I know." Now, we had speculated on that for years. He confirmed it, unknowingly. [Laughter]

They took me through the cruiser, wouldn't take me into the power plant because it was nuclear, took me into their damage control central, which was basic, and I thought, "God almighty, is this really damage control central?" They had a number of piping systems and all, but not very much, not what I expected in a cruiser. So I asked if I could see some of the damage control equipment. They did take me down into a berthing space, and they have what I call a P-3 fire extinguisher, which are things that are about this big. I have them. I don't have one here. I had one in my house back in downtown Norfolk and I have them in my place down in Sandbridge. They're the little ones about this big that's used in a house.

Paul Stillwell: Foot and a half long.

Admiral Trost: Yeah. One of those in a berthing space that had bunks for about 40 guys. So I wasn't too impressed by the damage control focus.

Paul Stillwell: Better have a small fire. [Laughs]

Admiral Trost: Yeah. And the visiting flag quarters, which they assigned to me during my brief time up there, had a nice walk-in room that was outfitted with a dining table and chairs and sofas and big, big bedroom, and everything in there was flammable, including the wooden trim. The stairs in the officer country, wooden railings and wooden trends. So their damage control was questionable, but it was spit-and-polish clean.

Paul Stillwell: Did you have any concern when you were over in the Soviet Union that your room might be bugged?

Admiral Trost: Oh, yeah. They were. They were. One of my staff was a master chief radioman who, among other things, was trained in detecting things that shouldn't be there. Pauline and I were in an official guesthouse, and I don't know if—it probably doubled as a BOQ. Our bathroom—there was one—was bugged. Our bedroom was bugged. Our living room was bugged. Our kitchen was bugged. [Stillwell laughs.] Hank is an expert in looking for stuff like this, but they were detectable. Now, in the bathroom, he had to take down a lampshade to find the bug in there, but it was there, and they kept tabs on us.

Paul Stillwell: So what precautions did you take to counteract those?

Admiral Trost: We didn't do any inside business, and Pauline and I were very careful about what we talked about and didn't talk about, "Did you see what that dumb guy did?" [Laughter] Nothing like that.

She became very conscious of bugs when we made a trip to China in '88. They bugged everything, including some very obvious stuff, like we had a bathroom with a long counter along one side. The shower was over here, the toilet was here, and under the sink was a mirror. There was a mirror all the way across the top too. And I saw like a sliding curtain thing down one end, so I pulled it all the way across. The next time we were in the bathroom, the curtain was pushed back. I said, "You know, I'm going to check outside." So I went outside in the corridor, sure enough, there was a little narrow door about where the bathroom should be or next to the bathroom. When I opened the door, it was unlocked, and there was glass. You could look through into the bathroom and monitor what was going on. And they had that place heavily bugged.

Paul Stillwell: Did you get out to see any normal Soviet citizens around Leningrad?

Admiral Trost: We saw some people. We didn't have any intercourse with them, except for the ones at the museums, and they were there. They were very businesslike. The head of the museum was our tour guide and both of them were there with a delegation when I was there.

The hotel staff was staffed for an international hotel and very helpful, spoke English, nice people. I'm trying to remember the name of the hotel. We spent a night in what turned out was a major tourist hotel when Pauline and I were there—as a matter of fact, the night we were all there. I think it was the same hotel. So they were very hospitable, but also very interested in knowing what was going on by bugging everything.

Our guides all spoke English, spoke pretty good English. Our guides all had a great interest in the United States, like tourist-level interest, and "What do you do? How do you do such-and-such? And do you have this?" So it was interesting.

Paul Stillwell: Was Hermitage the museum you went to in Leningrad?

Admiral Trost: Yeah.

Paul Stillwell: See any Fabergé eggs?

Admiral Trost: I, matter of fact, did. Pauline was with me on this trip, and so she got to tour the Hermitage. The first time I was there and my official visit there, the first time when we were there as a delegation, saw Fabergé eggs, saw things, including paintings, that were unprotected, that were left to the elements, and the atmosphere in the area where the art was displayed was terrible. Humidity was high and there wasn't any good ventilation. That was amazing. They have national treasures, just invaluable things that couldn't be reproduced because you don't find the people who did it originally. They're all dead. So it was interesting.

Paul Stillwell: What were your experiences in working with the two men who were Presidents during your CNO tour, Reagan and Bush?

We heard an awful lot about Reagan being out of it, you know, not paying attention to things. I was in my new job As CNO for three months when we had our first meeting of the President with the Joint Chiefs. They were supposed to take place quarterly but hadn't for three quarters. Then I was told that we were going to meet with the President. He was coming over to the Tank, the Joint Chiefs' conference room in the Pentagon. And he came over, very congenial.

Then it was time for the return about over in the White House Cabinet Room, and that was attended by SecState, SecDef, the National Security Advisor, I don't know, enough people to fill a table that's about as long as from here to that door over there, and with the President being in charge, obviously. So I that day drew the short straw, so I was the first service chief to give my eight- to ten-minutes' pitch, and I started talking and I talked for about four minutes and looked over at him. He was sitting in the middle of table, and I was down at the end. All of a sudden, he put his hand on his chin. and I thought, "Oh, shit, I put him to sleep." [Laughter]

Paul Stillwell: I've got to describe. You showed yourself nodding off, in imitation of him.

Admiral Trost: Yeah. His head dropped, his chin dropped, and his eyes were closed, and he was not moving, and he was not asking me any questions. So my eight minutes, ten minutes, whatever it was, were up. I looked over at Bill Crowe, who was sitting halfway down the table across from the President. Crowe kind of shrugged. I stopped talking, sat down. Reagan's eyes opened up, and he started asking me questions. So he wasn't sleeping. [Laughter] He was wide awake, but he was there with his eyes shut. And that threw a lot of people, I think, in the time he was President, because people used to say, "Oh, he doesn't pay attention to things." I think he paid attention to everything he wanted to.

Paul Stillwell: Did that give you a sinking feeling when you saw that?

Admiral Trost: Oh, God, I thought, "Oh, shit. That's it." [Laughter] But he was an interesting guy, and I had a couple one-on-ones with him on Navy subjects when he came over, and he was always very open, asked good questions. I liked the guy. Matter of fact, I was lucky; I had two years with him and two years with George Bush.* And they were two great guys to work with.

Bush, on his first Saturday as President of the United States, invited the Joint Chiefs and their wives and the Deputy Secretary of Defense, because SecDef was out of town, up to Camp David for Saturday.† We heloed up there out of the Naval Observatory, with wives, and got up to Camp David. Barbara Bush took charge of the wives, and we had a session with the new President for him to ask questions and get a briefing from Crowe on things that were hot.

The wives came back in, we all had lunch, very relaxed, congenial lunch. Then we reconvened for another four hours. I don't know what the wives did, but they went off with Barbara again. And that's the way he started off his presidency, said he wanted to get to know the people and wanted to know what was hot. So that relationship started off really good. The relationship with him was more relaxed than with Reagan, but they were both very businesslike. So two good men to work for.

Paul Stillwell: And President Bush had the benefit that he'd been in the Navy, so there

---

* George H. W. Bush was Vice President from 20 January 1981 to 20 January 1989 and President from 20 January 1989 to 20 January 1993.
† Camp David is a secluded presidential retreat near Thurmont, Maryland.

was that connection.

Admiral Trost: That and he'd been the Vice President for eight years. We had the advantage of living in the Naval Observatory for four of the years he was the Vice President. We got to know him personally to the extent that we lived a block away, just outside of his fence, as a matter of fact. He had at least two or three social functions a year that we got invited to. He always had a Fourth of July picnic, and the guests for the Fourth of July picnic and the Christmas party were his mess specialists, all Filipino, their moms and grandmas and kids, and he catered. There's a caterer in Washington, a very well-known outfit. They would cater the function, and the MSs were all given the day off so they and their family could enjoy the party.

Paul Stillwell: What a nice touch.

Admiral Trost: A really nice touch.

Paul Stillwell: And I gather he was unpretentious in his dealings with you.

Admiral Trost: Very unpretentious, very unpretentious. Barbara was a very gracious hostess, a little less relaxing than the President was. She was obviously in charge and that was clear.

Pauline recalls the time she was chewed out by Mrs. Vice President, because there was a beautiful picture in the dining room, a painting, and Pauline was explaining the painting, which she had seen before, to one of the other guests, and she put her hand out like this, and Barbara thought she was touching the painting. Well, she was a good six inches away from the painting, but, "Ta ta ta, Pauline, don't do that." [Laughter] She never forgot that. But they got along.

We had dinner with the Bushes in the private dining room in the White House up on the second floor with them on, I think, two occasions, where he said, "We just want to get reacquainted." What he really wanted to do was get me off to the side by myself and pump me for some information I don't think he wanted to ask Bill Crowe about.

Paul Stillwell: That's interesting.

Admiral Trost: So it was interesting. It was a congenial evening, very much of a social evening, but there was a little business mixed in, sort of like, "What do you think of so-and-so or this idea?" or something like that.

Paul Stillwell: That's the kind of informal setting to foster that.

Admiral Trost: Yeah. And he was very informal at those events, but he was all the time, an easy guy to work with and very congenial. He liked coming over to the Pentagon for his meetings with the Chiefs, because then when we brought briefers in, they just walked into the briefing room and then went back to work, and so it was very casual in that respect, but all the information was there. Easy guy to work with.

Paul Stillwell: What do you recall about the process of flag slating in your role as CNO?

Admiral Trost: A lot. I was asked one time how much of my time did I spend on it. My estimate was about 15% of my time on flag matters. Well, I spent a lot of time with the Chief of Naval Personnel, primarily him and my Vice Chief, on deciding. I think it's one of the more important priorities to any CNO, because the effectiveness of today and tomorrow's Navy is dependent on flag slating. I emphasize "tomorrow" because you're building, you always have to look a couple of—for example, Chief of Naval Personnel. You have to look ahead about two guys when you're planning to make sure you've got somebody that's going to meet the requirement.

I took Mike Boorda from one to three stars to make him Chief of Naval Personnel.[*] Reason, he was the best prepared, even though he'd never been that senior, to be Chief of Naval Personnel, and was one of the better ones. I'd say he and Bud Edney,

---

[*] Vice Admiral Jeremy M. Boorda, USN, served as Chief of Naval Personnel from 9 August 1988 to 6 November 1991. He was later Chief of Naval Operations, 1994-96.

who was later my Vice Chief and later SACLant/CinCLant.[*] Anyway, they were the two guys that were seen a lot as being among the best that I saw. But you always have to be looking ahead a couple of jobs on the key jobs that you had.

The two-star force commanders, fleet deputies, and so forth are sort of brought up to that point by their communities. Then you have to decide which one of these guys is going to go further, and what he might need to be qualified to go further, like a numbered fleet command. You want a variety of backgrounds for him. If you're nominating for a fleet commander, he'd better have a wide spread of jobs in his career time. And in my case, I also have a thing about the individual's—what do I want to say?—his reputation or what kind of person is he, and that's why I think I mentioned to you I fired Admiral Moranville, a fleet commander, for moral turpitude, basically, and he didn't see anything wrong with what he was doing.

Paul Stillwell: So you were grooming people for the eventual four stars.

Admiral Trost: Yeah, three- and four-star guys. You had to be looking ahead, including your own relief. You need to make sure there are preferably at least two guys that you personally think are qualified, and it would be nice to have even more, have a couple more. But there are people who sort of get sifted out, sifted through the top. The way it normally works is sift down, but they rise like cream.

Paul Stillwell: The cream rises. [Laughter]

Admiral Trost: And I was lucky they were a couple of people that I considered qualified for the job. When it was my term, I had my favorite, and I didn't get him, but that—

---

[*] Vice Admiral Leon A. Edney, USN, served as Chief of Naval Personnel from 9 October 1987 to 8 August 1988. As a four-star admiral, he was Vice Chief of Naval Operations from August 1988 to May 1990 and Supreme Allied Commander Atlantic and Commander in Chief Atlantic Command from 18 May 1990 to 13 July 1992.

Paul Stillwell: Do you want to identify him for this purpose?

Admiral Trost: I could. He's dead. Dave Jeremiah. Dave was the PacFlt commander, and I had worked with Dave at various jobs over the years at the Pentagon. I knew him well, and he and I had the same philosophy on a lot of things in fleet matters, people, and I selected him for PacFlt and got him into PacFlt, and I liked the job he was doing very well. He took over on short notice from Ace Lyons, who got fired, and just did a good job and was very highly regarded throughout the flag community.[*]

I did, as my predecessors had, put out a thing to all four-stars—I guess I did three- and four-star—requesting their thoughts on who should relieve me. There was no obligation whatsoever to abide by that, but it's sort of interesting to see how people sit with the three-stars, for example. "This guy's your leader. How's he doing?" And I got some good inputs. But the two guys who were the most favored by the three- and four-stars to me were Jeremiah and Kelso. My favorite person was Jeremiah.

Colin Powell took over as chairman in October of '89, and Crowe retired.[†] The law had come out and changed the status of the JCS. The Chairman is now the one and only voice. There are no service chiefs as acting chairmen when he's out of town. There's a Vice Chairman who is the acting Chairman when he's out of town, which is fine. That's a good system. Colin, in a private session about two months after he took over, said, "Who do you have in mind for your successor?" Because I had, at that point, a little over six months to go in my tour.

I said, "Dave Jeremiah," who was currently PacFlt.

He nodded his head, and a new subject came up.

The next thing I found out was that Bob Herres, Air Force general, Naval Academy grad, was retiring in February, and Dave Jeremiah was now to be his relief.[‡] [Laughs] So Colin got my favorite nominee and took him away from me.

---

[*] Admiral James A. Lyons, Jr., USN served as Commander in Chief Pacific Fleet from 16 September 1985 to 30 September 1987. Admiral David E. Jeremiah, USN, served as Commander in Chief Pacific Fleet from 30 September 1987 to 1 February 1990.
[†] General Colin L. Powell, USA, served as Chairman of the Joint Chiefs of Staff from 1 October 1989 to 30 September 1993. In 2001 he became the first black person to serve as Secretary of State.
[‡] General Robert T. Herres, USAF, served as Vice Chairman of the Joint Chiefs of Staff from 6 February 1987 to 28 February 1990. Admiral Jeremiah was Vice Chairman of the Joint Chiefs of Staff from 1 March 1990 to 28 February 1994.

Paul Stillwell: So Admiral Jeremiah got a good job out of the deal.

Admiral Trost: Yeah. Well, Dave did a good job with that job.

Paul Stillwell: He had been the battle group commander for those raids on Libya in early '86 when Admiral Kelso was the Sixth Fleet Commander.

You mentioned Admiral Boorda. What qualities in him did you admire?

Admiral Trost: Well, obviously, his rising from seaman recruit to admiral. I'd known him as a captain onward, I guess, primary expertise being personnel, and he was damn good at it. He was a one-star surface warfare guy when I was briefly CinCLantFlt, so I saw him operationally in that job, which he did very well, and had a good reputation, a reputation for integrity. He was Watkins's EA at BuPers, and I worked with him quite a bit at that time because I was in Washington, and he was always very straightforward and honest with me. So I was favorably impressed with the guy and the job he did.

I've forgotten the sequence of Chiefs of Naval Personnel, but Mike was a one-star, second or third job, I guess, as a one-star, one or two, and I needed a Chief of Personnel who knew the business, and he knew it better than anybody else. So I nominated him for three stars, got no opposition from anybody, and made him Chief of Naval Personnel. I don't know who bumped him up after that. He came to the attention of President Clinton because of his seaman-to-admiral progress, which I think is the basis for his having been nominated for a fourth star. I think it's consensus—I know it is of Jim Holloway and me—that we felt he was nominated to a job where he felt he was over his head. He used to tell me, as his confidant, how tough it was. This was after I retired.

Paul Stillwell: When he was CNO, that is?

Admiral Trost: Yeah. We talked. Well, Boorda called me periodically when he had a question or wanted to share something with me or wanted advice, which he did on occasion. And same thing with Holloway. Holloway and I went to a retired CNO session which CNOs used to hold every six months, and after that session, he said to the two of us—we were standing side by side talking—"I'd like to call each of you privately to discuss something with you."

Well, he called me, and what he discussed with me was basically how I handled certain things and advice. And Holloway confided in me after Mike's suicide that his conversation started of with, "This job is hard," and then asked a few "How did you handle such-and-such?" which I thought was the purpose of the calls to start with.[*] But Jim said that Mike told him, "This job is tough. I never realized how hard it was." And Jim Holloway's take on it was that Mike just didn't feel up to the challenges of the job and that that and personal problems with his son and—probably his son. He had a son who, I don't know what the malady was, but he was disabled mentally, and that was a burden on Mike and his wife. And his wife probably wasn't cut out to be a senior officer's wife, and I say that not because she wasn't a nice person, but because she couldn't cope with a lot of the challenges that everybody faces when they get senior, and then she had the burden of this son who required constant attention.

So I think his suicide was probably caused by a feeling of inadequacy which was foreign to him, because he had always been so successful, and, I think, demoralizing to him, but that's just a personal evaluation. But I knew him probably as well as some of the other flag officers would have, and felt sorry for him because he was so bent on doing the right thing that any feeling of inadequacy on his part would be demoralizing to him, I could see. But that's truly sort of private information. I don't know what you want to do with it.[†]

Paul Stillwell: Well, he was getting some criticism, which probably he had not had a lot

_____

[*] Admiral Jeremy M. Boorda, USN, committed suicide on 16 May 1996 while serving as Chief of Naval Operations. Among the several reasons cited as possible causes was that he was about to be interviewed by news media representatives about whether he was entitled to combat devices on his service ribbons received during the Vietnam War. See Nick Kotz, "What Really Happened to Admiral Boorda," *Washingtonian*, December 1996.

[†] Admiral Trost did not delete the section on Admiral Boorda when he edited the transcript, so it is here as part of the historical record.

of up till then, including the Stan Arthur nomination for CinCPac.[*]

Admiral Trost: Yeah, but I would defend that nomination because I worked with Stan Arthur, one of the most competent flag officers I've ever known. But we all have our opinions.

Paul Stillwell: Anything to add about Admiral Arthur?

Admiral Trost: Well, as I said, I worked with him on a number of occasions, a number of jobs, very capable, *very* conscientious. He went to work for Lockheed Martin in Florida. I knew someone, and I don't remember who, who worked for him down there, a civilian, no military background, didn't know Stan as a military officer, who sang his praises as a businessman, handling of people, grasp of issues, common sense. That's what I would say about Stan, a great guy. So we can have different opinions. I'm sure there were people would think I was a real shithead and that's all right too. Doesn't bother me.

Paul Stillwell: What do you remember of your relationship with your VCNO, Admiral Busey?[†]

Admiral Trost: What do I remember? First of all, very professional, nominated him for the job in Naples, very reliable. He was an ideal Vice Chief, capable, professional, handled people well, totally trustworthy and competent as a Vice Chief, and did a good job over there, I thought. So I'm high on Jim Busey.

Paul Stillwell: How did you divide the issues? Who would deal with which ones?

[*] Stanley R. Arthur, USN, the Vice Chief of Naval Operations, was slated in 1994 to become Commander in Chief Pacific. There was a concern that his Senate confirmation would be a protracted one at a time of increasing tensions in Korea and Admiral Arthur agreed to retire. Senator David Durenberger (Republican-Minnesota) had placed a hold on the nomination to pressure the Navy for information on the case of Lieutenant Rebecca Hansen. Durenberger expressed concern that Hansen had been washed out of helicopter flight training as retaliation for charging sexual harassment on the part of an instructor. Admiral Jeremy M. Boorda, USN, Chief of Naval Operations at the time, was heavily criticized for not having given Admiral Arthur stronger backing. Boorda later said that his failure to be more supportive was the biggest regret of his tenure as CNO.

[†] Admiral James B. Busey IV, USN, served as Vice Chief of Naval Operations from 1985 to 1987.

Admiral Trost: I don't know that we divided them as much as we worked together. Of course, he gets first shot at just about everything that comes to the CNO, and if he had a problem with something and wanted to discuss it, we discussed it. And if I had a problem with things, I'd see him, I'd ask him to come up. I sought his opinion on a lot of things, aviation matters, certainly, and operational because he had a different perspective than I did. And a good people guy. So we talked a lot and met one-on-one quite a lot. I had good Vice Chiefs. He was great. Bud Edney was great. Bud Edney was unbelievable. And Hunt Hardisty.* Those three guys, and I couldn't have asked for three better guys, frankly. Probably the best was Edney.

Paul Stillwell: Why do you say that?

Admiral Trost: Deepest thinker, broadest experience, very capable guy. And Bud Edney, in addition to being a strong leader, was a perfect number two. He was there to support you. You knew you were going to get his opinion, even if you didn't ask for it. If he felt strongly about something, he'd come in and talk to me about it, and I welcomed that. That, to me, is loyalty. And if he thought I made a bum decision on something, normally he'd have been advised of any decision that was pending before I made it, but if I did something that he thought maybe was on the wrong tack, he'd come tell me about it. And everybody's not like that, especially when they're senior and maybe looking to get more senior. Now, he was already a four-star, but he had one more job coming up, and he didn't know that at the time. He was very, very capable and very straightforward.

Paul Stillwell: It sounds as if all of them apparently served as sounding boards for you.

Admiral Trost: Yeah, they did. They did. And you have to have that, and you have to listen. That's the big thing. I used to talk to all my three-stars in OpNav, and they were not only invited, they were demanded to see me at least every two weeks, and if they had something else, anytime they wanted to come in.

---

* Admiral Huntington Hardisty, USN, served as Vice Chief of Naval Operations from 1987 to 1988. Admiral Leon A. Edney, USN, served as Vice Chief of Naval Operations from August 1988 to May 1990

But I was influenced in part by two retired two-star flag officers who came to see me early in my tour. They both said, "We were in OpNav as two-stars. We never saw the CNO. We were never invited in to brief him or talk to him."

I thought, "What a shame." First of all, what a lack of morale opportunity for them, but what a sort of tossing aside expertise that could help you. So I made a point of making sure every OpNav flag officer saw me at least once a month, and every two-star every two weeks, even just stop by and say hello. "But if you've got something on your mind, come and see me." And I think that paid off. I think I found out about some things I'd have never heard of otherwise.

Paul Stillwell: Do you remember any ideas that germinated from those kinds of meetings?

Admiral Trost: I don't specifically, but we're talking about 30 years ago.

Paul Stillwell: Right. Do you remember any things that the VCNOs talked you out of?

Admiral Trost: I can't think of anything right offhand. Generally by the time I had made a decision on something, I had input that had come via them, so if I had a disagreement with them, we talked it out. I didn't have many controversies with my staff people, because I kept them cut in.

I had good EAs. Tom Paulsen was one and Dan Oliver was the other, and I couldn't have asked for two better guys. Norb Ryan, who has been running MOA for years, was the assistant EA my first two and a half years.[*] Matter of fact, his brother, John, who was supe here at the academy. They were twins, and I had met John, but Norb was working for me.[†] I walked into my office one morning, and there was Commander Ryan, but he had captain's insignia on. I said, "Norb, who the hell promoted you?"

He said, "I'm John." [Laughter] And I saw Norb Ryan every day many times, and

---

[*] Vice Admiral Norbert Ryan, USN (Ret.), was CEO of the Military Officers Association of America.
[†] Vice Admiral John R. Ryan, USN, served as superintendent of the Naval Academy from 4 June 1998 to 7 June 2002.

mistook the two.

Paul Stillwell: Well, they were jointly very successful.

Admiral Trost: Yes, they were. Judy Ryan, Norb's wife, told Pauline when Norb was working for me, that she dated Norb, they got married. She said, "In high school, I dated the Ryans and I never was quite sure which one I was dating." [Laughter]

And there was a girl who thought that somebody—I think it was John—was really sweet on her, and the next time he went out with her, he was cool. The next time she went out with him, it wasn't him. [Laughter] So I got a kick out of that. And their parents were jewels. Their parents were nice people.

Paul Stillwell: You indicated there was a bit of discomfort working with Admiral Kelso when he was CinCLantFlt and CinCLant. How did that work out?

Admiral Trost: Well, it worked out. I think he was an accomplished person. He wanted to be seen as his own man and not subordinate to anybody and didn't like to be second-guessed. I didn't do much second-guessing. If my wife were here, she would say, "He's annoyed because you became CNO when he didn't," the first time around, so that may be a factor. I don't know. But I don't say that to people. He was a very capable guy, didn't like to be told what to do, didn't really solicit other people's opinions, at least senior people. So I don't know.

Paul Stillwell: Well, a lot of us are like that. [Laughs]

You've mentioned Admiral Lyons before. Anything else to add about him?

Admiral Trost: I don't know anything good about him, so I won't say much. [Stillwell laughs.] Oh, he just got some sort of award. One of our either current or retired members of Congress was the speaker at some function recently. I saw something in the paper. Matter of fact, I got an invitation to this event, an evening event, where the member of Congress was the speaker, and an award was being given to Admiral Lyons. I don't know what the hell anybody would give him an award for, but he had an award for something. He's very low on my totem pole of people I respect, so, no, nothing more about him.

Paul Stillwell: You've already talked about Admiral Jeremiah, so evidently things went well after the change of command in which he relieved Admiral Lyons.

Admiral Trost: They did. They did. Things changed completely, and so did staff morale out there, so that didn't hurt.

Paul Stillwell: How much, as CNO, contact do you have with the operational commanders?

Admiral Trost: Not a whole lot. You're kept advised of operational things at your morning briefs. The CNO's morning would start always with the immediate staff and the people like the Chief of Legislative Affairs, my executive assistant, head of the CNO Executive Panel, so they would know what's going on. So when I tasked them to write something, they could do so intelligently because they knew what the background was from the morning sessions. Had the Legislative Affairs, the immediate staff, EA. I'm trying to remember who was all there.

Paul Stillwell: Probably the public affairs officer.

Admiral Trost: Public affairs officer was there. It was a small group, about half a dozen people. That's about it, I guess.

Paul Stillwell: Anything you remember specifically about public affairs involvement, media coverage?

Admiral Trost: Yeah, I do, but I don't remember who he was. And the JAG was there. My initial public affairs guy, I don't remember who he was. He worked for Jim Watkins, who was very high on him. My personal opinion of him was very low, both from professional confidence and he was an ass-kisser, and I don't see that as a road to success when you're supposed to be a professional. So I wanted a replacement, and I asked a couple of people for input. Tom Jurkowsky was then a commander, captain's billet, name came up a couple times. I checked on Tom. He was out at AirPac as the PAO out there. So I called AirPac, and I don't remember who it was now, and asked them, got big up-checks, told them I had in mind interviewing the guy, and if he was successful at the interview, he'd be my PAO. Well, instead of fighting the loss of a good man, he said, "He's the kind of guy you need."

So I called Tom back. He had been out there part of the tour, and so I called him back for an interview. He was very frank. Yes, he wanted the job, but he didn't want the job, because his wife, Sally, was happy in San Diego, and they hadn't been there that long and didn't really want to move the family around again.

So I finished talking to him and said, "Well, Tom, let me think about it. Stay in town for another night." So he did.

I called him in the next day and said, "Sorry, but you're it." [Laughter] And he did an excellent, spectacular job. He was just good. He was very good.

Paul Stillwell: Went on to become Chinfo.*

Admiral Trost: Yeah, and he became the Naval Academy guy because Chuck Larson, as CinCPacFlt, I guess it was at the time—yeah, it would have been fleet. Chuck was so impressed with the job he was doing at PacFlt after he left the CNO assignment, that he took him on out there, and then when he came back for a second tour as supe here, he brought Tom here, because he needed a good guy then.† Tom's probably the most competent and, because of his competence, believable public affairs officer I think I've ever known, and there was no braggadocio in his makeup and a lot of common sense.

Paul Stillwell: I remember last year after Admiral Larson died, Jurkowsky had a nice

---

* Rear Admiral Thomas J. Jurkowsky, USN, was the Navy's Chief of Information from 1998 to 2000.
† Admiral Charles R. Larson, USN (Ret.), served as superintendent of the Naval Academy from August 1994 to June 1998. This was a rare instance in which a retired officer served as superintendent.

article about him in the *Evening Capital*.

Admiral Trost: He was a great guy—is a great guy. I still talk to Tom periodically. He calls every once in a while with a "What do you think about so-and-so?" [Laughs] And it's usually the same thing that's got me shaking my head.

Paul Stillwell: What do you remember about the impact of the Goldwater-Nichols law that came in just during that period?

Admiral Trost: Well, it came in during my CNO time.* The biggest impact was on the JCS structure and the fact that we were no longer a group of equals. We were subordinate to the Chairman. Bill Crowe, interestingly, fought it, fought it publicly, disagreed publicly in testimony.

I think the establishment and acceptance of the Vice Chairman as a full-time guy who keeps up to speed and who can step in and take over was a good move, so I think that restructuring was smart. In that sense, I liked the idea. When I was in OSD for three years as a commander, I would see the changes in—the Chairman is out of town, and today it's the Chief of Staff of the Air Force. You never knew whom to call, and that was detrimental to the efficiency of the whole organization.

I'm sure the SecDef and Deputy Secretary who had to work with this were probably a little bit annoyed by it, because they didn't know who they were going to talk to, and they would sometimes be dealing with the Chairman, who was Bus Wheeler, who was very highly regarded. Sometimes it would be with Rivets Rivero as the Vice Chief of Naval Operations, who had a tendency to get very excited when he briefed something.† I sat in on some of those briefings, and he could get quite excited. When the *Liberty* attack took place, he was the acting Chairman, and his initial—I don't know what to call it—

---

* The Goldwater-Nichols Defense Reorganization Act of 1986 went into effect on 1 October of that year. It mandated a good deal more in the way of joint-service relationships than had been the case up to then. For details, see "DoD Reorganization," *U.S. Naval Institute Proceedings*, May 1987, pages 136-145.
† Admiral Horacio Rivero, USN, served as Vice Chief of Naval Operations from 31 July 1964 to 17 January 1968. His oral history is in the Naval Institute collection.

posturing, advice, could probably have gotten us into a full-fledged war with the Israelis.[*] Of course, it wouldn't have been much of a war at that time, but he was ready to go mount carrier strikes, which maybe they deserved. I think they did deserve it, because I lost a classmate as exec of *Liberty*, a good guy, and we lost a lot of sailors.[†] So kind of hard to tell. I think the current structure is the right structure. Specifically having a professional Vice Chairman there to pick up the load and provide your continuity, I think is the right thing to do.

Paul Stillwell: Did the new law diminish your power noticeably?

Admiral Trost: It probably did, but I lived under that with Colin for about seven months, eight months, and I can't say it particularly bothered me except when he got into my business and did it without telling me. He did an early 1990 Plan for the Future Navy and submitted it to the Secretary of Defense without my getting a sniff at it, and it was describing the future of *my* Navy, things that were *my* responsibility under law, which I kind of got pissed off about and chewed on him about it. Didn't make any difference; he did it anyway. So that's just a professional difference of opinion. That and the fact that he stole my relief. [Laughter]

Paul Stillwell: You talked about planning in terms of flag officers and grooming them. What about planning for the future of the Navy? What organization and philosophy did you have there?

Admiral Trost: Well, planning for the future was largely in the 090 organization, but with inputs of the fleet. I sat down with my fleet commanders and senior OpNav guys twice a year, usually offsite outside of the Pentagon. My favorite spot was Pensacola because they had just built a new auditorium down there, it was a good briefing theater, and right

---

[*] On 8 June 1967, during the Six-Day War between Israel and Egypt, Israeli aircraft and torpedo boats made a number of attacks on the U.S. communications intelligence ship *Liberty* (AGTR-5). Of the ship's crew of 297, 34 were killed and 171 wounded. Israel claimed that the attack on the *Liberty* was a case of mistaken identity and apologized. Many in the ship's crew were skeptical of the claim.
[†] Lieutenant Commander Philip M. Armstrong, USN, was executive officer of the *Liberty*.

next to it is a BOQ, and about a block down the street is visiting flag quarters, main BOQ, not the extension, and so we had room. I could bring the guys in, and it was basically since most of the people coming from out of town were flying on an airplane that was designated for their command, the four-stars, they could bring their wives at no cost to the government. They'd pay for their meals. My OpNav flag officers who were also invited down could fly down with me or the Vice Chief, and so we weren't costing the government a lot of money, but it was a lot more, let's say, efficient to get everybody together who should be in on planning for the future and without costing a whole lot of money.

So, as I said, Pensacola was my favorite spot. We used Jacksonville one time because they had an outstanding BOQ complex there and visiting flag quarters again and accommodations that could take care of everybody who came. We used Newport coincident with the International Seapower Symposium on several occasions. That worked out. Newport also had great facilities.

So we got together offsite where there was more time to focus and less interruption, and we had full communications coverage anyway. That worked out well, and that's something I have recommended to my successors. I think most of them have done that. The new guy says he's going to do that. The new CNO—this is an aside—John Richardson's father was a shipmate of mine in *Scorpion* when I was exec of *Scorpion*.[*] His father was a lieutenant, class of '59, Naval Academy. He was a lieutenant commander in Naples when I was a captain on SubLant staff and when Joe Williams, another seaman-to-admiral guy, to three-stars, Joe Williams was chief of staff, I was the N1. He got me and the N3, two junior captains. "You guys are going to go to Naples to do a command inspection of Sub Group 8," which was the NATO submarine command. "Oz Osborn [who at that time was a flotilla commander in Charleston] is going to be on leave in Europe.[†] I'm calling him back to active duty for two days to be the critique officer after you guys finish your five-day inspection, and he'll come and be the referee

---

[*] Admiral John M. Richardson, USN, was nominated as Chief of Naval Operations shortly before this interview. He took office 18 September 2015. His father is Captain William E. Richardson, USN (Ret.).
[†] Rear Admiral James B. Osborn, USN, Commander Submarine Flotilla Six. As a commander Osborn was the first skipper of the blue crew of the USS *George Washington* (SSBN-598) when she was commissioned on 30 December 1959 as the Navy's first Polaris submarine.

when you debrief."

So the two of us hopped on an airplane and went to Naples for five days. On the second or third night there, Bill Richardson invited the two of us out to his house. He was renting a house in Posillipo or something like that. Why I remember that name I don't know, but it was a suburb of Naples. And there was young ten-year-old John, who talked about the Navy, wanted to go to the Navy, and young John went in the Navy, graduated from the Naval Academy in '82. His father is a retired Navy captain. I saw the father, for the first time since Naples, at the change of command here two weeks ago. And young John has been brought up the right way, good guy, surprised that he'd been the head of Naval Reactors organization for three years, and that's an eight-year term by statute. So he was a little surprised. He headed up two investigation boards for the Secretary of the Navy. He's a pretty sharp guy when you consider him, because I think he was a dark horse. Well, he would have been anyway because of that eight-year thing. So John spent about four hours here a couple weeks ago milking my brain on things that were successful and things that I'd rather not do again.

Paul Stillwell: Well, that's useful. Do you remember any ideas that came out of these CinC conferences that you had in Pensacola or elsewhere in planning for the future?

Admiral Trost: Oh, boy. Well, we had a lot of focus on size of the fleet, deployment lengths, organizational structure, and what are we doing that's nonproductive. And we briefed him on what we're doing in personnel policies, what's happening on the Hill, so everybody got the same base of understanding on what's going on. I found that to be— well, to me, that was very important, keeping my subordinate commanders advised of what was going on, because if you're out in the field and you don't know what the hell the thinking is back in the head shed, you could do something that would be detrimental to the Navy's future planning without even realizing it. I don't mean that people are going to do bad things. I'm saying they're doing things that aren't quite in sync with what the roadmap is, and so the guy who's responsible for the planning ought to be sharing that planning and getting the input. The more important thing to me was to listen to what they had to say not only about our plans and programs, but in response to a two- or three-star briefing him on his area of interest and what they would recommend happen or should happen and what would be helpful. You have to get a team, and you don't get a team spirit without participation, and so I put a lot of emphasis on that.

Paul Stillwell: And obviously, you have a lot of unknowables the farther out you get.

Admiral Trost: Yeah, and, you know, just because you're CNO doesn't mean you're the smartest guy in the world or that you think of everything or you think of the right things. It's an interesting job. It's a satisfying job. You get pissed off a lot of times at both internal Navy and external influences on the Navy. You think sometimes, "How could those dumbshits do that, and how could they ask us to do this?" But sometimes that's—I like to call it educated bias.

Paul Stillwell: What were some of the things that pissed you off?

Admiral Trost: Well, getting dumb guidance from the Hill in testimony, having to put up with people like Patsy Schroeder of Colorado on the House Armed Services Committee, who burst in on one of my testimonies before the committee.* We were about an hour into the session, and she came popping in the door and interrupted the chairman, who was Ike Skelton, "Oh, Mr. Chairman, Mr. Chairman, sorry to interrupt, but I've been in another meeting and I've got another thing. I can't stay for this meeting. I have just a few questions I'd like to ask the admiral. I wonder if I could just ask those questions now."

Well, I guess other than appearing as a shitbird, what's he say? "Well, okay, okay."

So she asked a bunch of questions which I'll classify in memory as inane, because most of what she had to say was inane. She asked me her questions, which she read off a sheet of paper, stuck it back in her briefcase, got up, and left.

She's one of my least favorite people. She testified about air conditioning the Naval Academy Bancroft Hall. That place was un-air conditioned until Larson was in

---

* Patricia S. Schroeder, a Democrat from Colorado, served in the House of Representatives from 3 January 1973 to 3 January 1997.

either the first or second tour as the supe. So for all those years, and it got pretty goddamn hot in the summertime and freezing in the wintertime, and we had in our budget—I don't know if I was 090 or CNO at the time, probably 090, and she objected to air conditioning Bancroft Hall. Her son went to one of the New England universities, might have been Princeton, and didn't live in an air-conditioned dormitory. I don't know if anybody asked her how hot it got in the summertime in New England, or in Princeton, New Jersey, really, but she voted against it, and it was killed that year, as a matter of fact, because of that. So she's not my favorite person. She fought the Alumni Hall, which basically got—I think we paid for most of that with contributions from alumni, which is why it's Alumni Hall. I don't remember what the split was.

Paul Stillwell: My recollection, it was 50-50 appropriated and nonappropriated.

Admiral Trost: It might have been that. I know we put in a substantial amount of alumni funding to get it, and I know also that Ross Perot offered to put in four or five million dollars if he could name it.* He actually wanted to name it after Jim Stockdale, which I don't think anybody had a big objection to, but the fact that he said, "I'll pay this much if I control this," stuck in the craws of the Alumni Association. But it's good. It's Alumni Hall, and that's how it should be, and it's a very utilitarian structure.

Paul Stillwell: That was really Admiral Larson's vision during his first term as supe.

Admiral Trost: He is the guy who really swung the Congress to the final approval, and I don't remember whether it was first or second. It must have been first term.

Paul Stillwell: It was the first, yes.

Admiral Trost: Yeah, it was the first. Its flexibility and utility were demonstrated by this

---

* Midshipman H. Ross Perot, USN, was president of the Naval Academy class of 1953. He resigned from the active Navy in 1957 and became a successful businessman. He founded Electronic Data Systems (EDS) in 1962. In 1992 he ran unsuccessfully for President.

just recent CNO command change. We went in and they had the near end, the front end, curtained off so it's an auditorium with a stage, and speeches were all made there. The change of command took place there. Honors for the departure were done there. Then we went around the curtain, and the inside's set up for the reception and it can easily handle 1,000 or more people, and it did. So it's very utilitarian, and it can be used for basketball.

Paul Stillwell: It might have enough seats to accommodate the entire brigade.

Admiral Trost: Yeah, and that's the beauty of it.

Paul Stillwell: Were there things within the Navy that pissed you off and frustrated you?

Admiral Trost: There probably were. [Laughter] There probably were. I can't think of anything right offhand. Well, anytime you're in charge of results and don't get the results, you get annoyed, but specifics, I can't think of any right offhand.

Paul Stillwell: Well, another piece of legislation from that era was Gramm-Rudman-Hollings, which was cutting back on budget.* What was the impact at your level?

Admiral Trost: Make work. It made a lot of work for us. I don't remember the specifics anymore, I just remember things being chopped in, and what I guess was the philosophy. When people who are not held responsible for the results do things that influence or direct the results, you're bound to have a bad deal. When Congress gets into directing things that impact operations or ways of doing business that have been changes to what you've always done, not that what you've always done was right, but you should ask the question "What can we do to improve this?" rather than directing change by people who are not knowledgeable of the system or of what the outcome might be. And that's been my longstanding gripe about congressional interference, and we are dependent on them,

---

* In 1985, when the national debt was increasing steadily, Congress enacted the Balanced Budget and Emergency Deficit Control Act. This law was known as Gramm-Rudman-Hollings because of the Senate authors of the original bill (Phil Gramm of Texas, Warren Rudman of New Hampshire, and Ernest F. Hollings of South Carolina).

and they do interfere and they are critical and they are bossy, sometimes good. We had some real stalwarts. Again, my favorites are Skelton and Sam Nunn and people like that, some really good people in Congress.

Some real bums. I mean that. They're there, they're self-serving. This guy Byrd from West Virginia, one of them. He asked, "What have you done for West Virginia today?" that was his credo. "What have I done for West Virginia today?" He did a lot, including that airport in I've forgotten what city it was, it's his town, big airport that can accommodate all sorts of people who never fly there, expansion of the Army or Guard facilities there that are superfluous when it comes to need. He'd just get it to get it and get the money—

Paul Stillwell: And he kept getting reelected.

Admiral Trost: Yeah. Oh, yeah.

Paul Stillwell: Well, I guess an eventual result of Gramm-Rudman was that you'd been building up to this number of ships and then started going down in fleet size.

Admiral Trost: Yeah. Today's fleet—of course, we don't have foreign policy either. That's why I was going to say today's fleet doesn't support national needs, but if you say each area is going to be fine if I do nothing, you don't need much of a fleet, and if you could deploy them for nine or ten months, so these guys get out of the Navy, we'll get more, we've got lots of people in this country, and that's sort of what I see as the philosophy today. I'm glad I'm not on active duty. I think had I been CNO during the current administration, I'd have been fired, because there are things that happened that I couldn't sit tight for, and as a member of the JCS, I'd have felt an obligation to speak out, and I'd have been fired, which might not have done much for the Navy but would probably be for the personal satisfaction of the people I work for. [Laughs]

Paul Stillwell: How would you describe the atmosphere of Tank meetings when you were CNO and Admiral Crowe was Chairman?[*]

Admiral Trost: Very professional, collegial. Is that the right term?

Paul Stillwell: Yes.

Admiral Trost: Crowe never opened up with, "I have decided that—." Whatever the subject was, we always discussed, he got everybody's input. If he'd already made up his mind, he'd tell you, "I've already decided, and here's what I'm going to do." So we had an input and we knew we had an input, and we were expected to do our homework for the meeting, if there were advanced paperwork, briefing papers, and we did, and it worked quite well. And it was pretty well we came out of things, out of discussions pretty much of a mind that resulted in concurrence on most things. We very seldom had a real— we had some arguments, but they were generally resolved and had no problem.

Paul Stillwell: Do you remember any of the arguments?

Admiral Trost: I don't. I don't, but, my God, we had several topics of discussion just about every meeting. I don't.

Paul Stillwell: Well, presumably that was a way to stay up to date on the other services as well.

Paul Stillwell: Yeah, we did, and kept us up to date on each other, and there was a lot of—"chitchat" is sort of a mild term to use about the discussion between the service chiefs, one-on-one on things that impacted us both. Most of mine were with the Air Force, because Larry Welch and I served from the same day to the same day.[†] Of course, there were points—we conflicted on division of responsibility for aircraft usage and

---

[*] "Tank" refers to the room in the Pentagon in which the Joint Chiefs of Staff meet on a regular basis.
[†] General Larry D. Welch, USAF, served as Air Force Chief of Staff from 1 July 1986 to 30 June 1990.

money and roles and missions and get out of my box to play in. But that usually got resolved pretty well.

Monroe Hatch was the Vice Chief of the Air Force.[*] He's class of '55 Naval Academy, and he was the number-two guy in the Air Force. Then we had Herres later on, class of '54 Naval Academy, as the Vice Chairman. So I always felt we had two guys whose heart was in the right place, even though they wore a different color uniform. [Laughs] But they were good people. They were very broadminded guys and deserved the jobs they had. Actually, the camaraderie was pretty good.

My biggest problem, frankly, was with Al Gray as Commandant of the Marine Corps. I think Al would disagree with me for the sake of disagreeing. And even though we paid for an awful lot of the Marine Corps stuff, like their airplanes, their ammunition, and things, he liked to control what we did in the budgeting business, which was centered within the Navy staff but with his people on my staff. He once said, "Give me it all and I'll be satisfied." [Laughter]

Paul Stillwell: So did the negotiations work out?

Admiral Trost: Sometimes when he negotiated. Sometimes he kept trying to go around me to the Secretary, who was Jim Webb.[†]

Webb was not the Navy's choice, would not have been my choice. Very difficult guy to work with. I'll tell you how I found out about his departure as Secretary, his resignation. We were both in Corpus Christi for the Navy League. They had a dinner on a Saturday night. Both Webb and I were to speak at the dinner, and there were more than 2,000 people there, so I think it was the Navy League National Convention.

The next morning, we would go up to the north side of Corpus Christi, or the bay, to the dedication of the new NRF base that was going to homeport three new Reserve Force destroyers and the training carrier from Pensacola, and we were going to build this new base on the Texas coast, south of Houston—Ingleside.[‡] And there was to be a

[*] General Monroe W. Hatch Jr., USAF, was Vice Chief of Staff of the Air Force from 1987 to 1990.
[†] James H. Webb served as Secretary of the Navy from 1 May 1987 to 23 February 1988.
[‡] Naval Station Ingleside, Texas, is on the north shore of Corpus Christi Bay. It opened in 1992.

ceremony following a luncheon hosted by the Texas delegation, actually hosted by the mayor of Corpus Christi.[*] So the two of us, we had the two C-140s that Navy staff had, one of them painted Marine colors at Lehman's request.

Paul Stillwell: At Webb's request, probably.

Admiral Trost: Well, I don't recall whether it was painted yet at that point in time or not. It could have been Webb's request. Anyway, they were both on the tarmac at Corpus Christi, at the air station. I was supposed to fly up to Houston after Webb got up there, be met by the mayor, and the congressman from the area, and they were going down and they were going to do some things in Ingleside before the luncheon. I was supposed to arrive in time to be at the luncheon and to say a few words.

So we got out in the morning about a half hour before we were due to take off and go. Parked next to my airplane was Webb's airplane, which was supposed to have been off the ground a half hour ago. So we asked around. Nobody knew anything about the Secretary. They hadn't heard from the Secretary or his staff that morning. So I kept watching my watch, and I said, finally, "Hey, we've got to get going or we're going to be late. To hell with the Secretary."

So we flew to Houston and were met there. Everybody was saying, "Where's the Secretary?"

"We don't know."

So finally the mayor got increasingly nervous because part of our congressional delegation was going to show up. So we got down there, we got to the hotel, motel, whatever it was, where they had the luncheon set up, and no Secretary, no contact with the Secretary or anybody on his staff, nobody answering any phones. So we went ahead, and the congressman was now pressed into being the luncheon speaker, which he volunteered to do. We had a luncheon, he spoke, then I was asked to say a few words.

Then we went out to the site where the new base is going to be. And no Secretary. So I became the Navy speaker, and the congressman spoke and the mayor spoke, and we had our ceremony.

---

[*] The groundbreaking for the new naval station was on 20 February 1988.

We got back to Houston, to our airplane to fly back to Andrews and we heard, "No, we haven't seen anything of the Secretary, haven't heard or had any cancellation or anything else. He's still expected."[*]

Well, by this time, it was hours after the expected time, so we took off and headed for Andrews. We landed at Andrews, pulled into our regular parking spot. The next spot was filled with the other airplane. And I said, "When did the Secretary get in?"

"About 2:00 o'clock this afternoon."

I said, "Did he come directly from Corpus Christi?"

They said, "That's our understanding." So I was scratching my head.

I went home, spent Sunday night, got in the next morning, and we got the *Early Bird*, which was a compilation of the early morning press clippings, along with the intel briefs and all. My aide came in with the *Early Bird*, and it said "Secretary of the Navy to Resign." And that's how we found out that Webb was going to quit.

We had an inside passageway between the two offices, so I went in the office, and he was sitting behind his desk. I said, "Jim, what the hell is this?"

"I quit."

I said, "With no notice?"

He said, "I'll announce it officially this morning, but I'm tired of this shit."

What "this shit" was, was not specifically stated, but it was clear something was bothering him, and that was it, end of his official duties, and he signed a few more papers and quit.

Paul Stillwell: He didn't last in that job very long.

Admiral Trost: A year. Wasn't happy in the job, made that clear. Why not? I don't know. Did a number of things, put out a couple of edicts, things he didn't like the way things were being done, and changed them. And, of course, the things that people didn't like didn't last long, because Will Ball came in to relieve him, and Will applied the common sense approach and cancelled some of the secretarial edicts that had just been come out in

---

[*] Andrews Air Force Base, located approximately ten miles southeast of Washington, D.C., in Prince George's County, Maryland.

the last year.[*] Will Ball was a great Secretary of the Navy, although brief because of his connection with John Tower. When Tower got into some kind of trouble—I've forgotten what it was—I think he was up for confirmation to be Secretary of Defense or something.

Paul Stillwell: Yes.

Admiral Trost: And Tower got across the breakers on something, I've forgotten what it was, that he was criticized for.[†] Will was asked by the administration to come over and speak in defense of it, because Will had been, I guess, his aide or his EA or something at one point in time, been one of his senior staffers. And that got him ousted as Secretary of the Navy, just by being a good guy and being an honest guy, but his tour while he was there was very good. Then Garrett came after him.[‡] Garrett was a good Secretary. So they were both guys who did their job and did it very conscientiously, in my book. But Webb was—I can't say least favorite because Lehman was my least favorite, but Webb was not an easy guy to work with.

Paul Stillwell: What about him made that the case?

Admiral Trost: Snap judgments, judgments made while annoyed at somebody or something. He was very opinionated and very demanding of, "If I say do it, I want it done now." And I thought his judgment on personnel policies was poor. He was obviously a great combat leader and a very capable guy, great writer. I just didn't like his judgment, and he knows that because we had our share of arguments.

Paul Stillwell: Do you remember any of the issues?

---

[*] William L. Ball served as Secretary of the Navy from 28 March 1988 to 15 May 1989.
[†] After George H. W. Bush was elected President, he nominated former U.S. Senator John G. Tower to be Secretary of Defense. On 9 March 1989, the Senate voted 53-47 to reject the nomination. Among the factors cited were Tower's drinking and womanizing.
[‡] Henry L. Garrett III served as Secretary of the Navy from 15 May 1989 to 26 June 1992.

Admiral Trost: I don't, I don't, except that he'd challenge my and other senior officers' judgments on things. Rather than using us as advisors, he challenged what we did or what we were recommending. Not that that's bad. That can be healthy. I just didn't like his judgment compared to mine, so I was obviously biased.

Paul Stillwell: Did he interfere in the flag slating that you had intended?

Admiral Trost: Very active in flag slating, yeah, but not to the detriment of the Navy, I'd say that, but he had opinions on everybody and everything.

Paul Stillwell: Well, that's bound to be the case.

Admiral Trost: Yeah.

Paul Stillwell: Any specifics with Secretary Ball that you remember?

Admiral Trost: That he was a very easy guy to work with, yeah, I remember that, and outside of that, no controversial things with him.

Paul Stillwell: So that must have been a refreshing change.

Admiral Trost: It really was. It really was.

Paul Stillwell: Did the level of communication step up when he came in?

Admiral Trost: Markedly, markedly. Webb did not communicate with senior people. Matter of fact, he might challenge me, but I'd say he demonstrated disdain for senior officers, like, "I'm here, I'm younger, but I'm senior and my judgment goes."

Paul Stillwell: Any specifics on Secretary Garrett?

Admiral Trost: No. Good to work with. He'd been the general counsel of the DoD, so he knew the organizational structure, a very conscientious guy, good guy to work with. By and large, we had no policy differences and I enjoyed working with him. Matter of fact, he and Ball were both very good guys to work with. They listened, they sought input, they took input. Well, Larry and I had some differences where he saw a legal reason not to do what we were proposing but never, never illegal, but just if we do that, he was always looking downstream, what's the impact of doing such-and-such, and that was healthy. So I had good guys to work with toward the end there.

Paul Stillwell: Admiral, I've got a bunch more questions, but we've been at it for nearly three hours, so let me reserve those for another session, please.

Admiral Trost: That sounds good to me.

Paul Stillwell: Thank you for another fantastic interview.

Admiral Trost: Well, I hope it's worthwhile, Paul.

Paul Stillwell: It is. I've learned a lot.

Admiral Trost: You're not a fiction writer, are you? [Laughter]

Paul Stillwell: No.

Interview Number 12 with Admiral Carlisle A. H. Trost, U.S. Navy (Retired)

Date: Wednesday, 7 October 2015

Place: Admiral Trost's apartment in Ginger Cove, south of Annapolis, Maryland

Paul Stillwell: Admiral, last time we were talking about your time as Chief of Naval Operations. Two of the great educational facilities for the Navy were the Naval Academy and the Naval War College. I'd be interested in your relationship with each of those during your time as CNO.

Admiral Trost: Well, I spent a lot of time attending Naval Academy functions, including giving occasional lectures, talking to people at the academy, talking to the superintendent about the policy changes that he proposed.

With the Naval War College, I took a very close interest because I participated in the International Sea Power Symposium. I also spoke there on several occasions. I guess they were lectures in a sense in that they were formal presentations on different topics of interest to the student body. We gathered my senior officers up there about every other year to go over potential policy changes, recommendations from the folks in an environment where we, one, had secure facilities, and, two, everything was very professionally done and supported.

Paul Stillwell: Admiral Hayward had been very interested in the Strategic Studies Group up at Newport.[*] What are your recollections of its achievements?

Admiral Trost: Well, I continued the emphasis that he and Jim Watkins after him had on the group. I personally interviewed the proposed candidates. I personally tasked them or drew up the tasking, or my 00K organization, to have them do what I thought was necessary for the future of the Navy.[†] I also kept in mind that these guys were there for a purpose other than just to serve me. They were there to develop their own capabilities as

---

[*] Admiral Thomas B. Hayward, USN, served as Chief of Naval Operations from 1 July 1978 to 30 June 1982. His oral history is in the Naval Institute collection.
[†] OP-00K was the designation for the CNO's executive panel.

future leaders of the Navy. So I stayed involved without interfering, I think. I think.

Paul Stillwell: Do you remember any people or ideas that came out of that group?

Admiral Trost: I remember people, but it's so long ago that, no, I don't.

Paul Stillwell: One who went through that program—this may have been a little earlier—was Admiral Snuffy Smith. What do you recall about him?

Admiral Trost: Well, I recall a number of things about him. He was a very active guy. I think he was probably a captain when I met him. And as a flag officer, I, of course, had responsibility for approval of the detail for him. I can recall specifically a time when he was a senior guy in the Mediterranean, a carrier group commander, and looking forward to moving on.[*] He was a very active guy. At the completion of that job, I sent him to EuCom staff as a two-star Navy guy in a Navy billet there.[†] When I saw him, he protested mightily, "I'm not a staff guy." "Staff weenie," I think was the term. "I'm an operational naval officer. I was happy where I was. I thought I was doing a good job where I was."

I said, "That's exactly why you're going where you are." I needed somebody with good operational expertise on that EuCom staff to represent Navy interests better than the incumbent in the job at the time. I needed an aviator on the EuCom staff, an aviator flag officer with balls. So he went, under protest. Of course, he got a third star out of that job, and eventually his fourth star, so it really hurt him mightily, career-wise. [Laughter]

We, by the way, became very close personal friends, and he likes to tell the story about my visit as CNO to the EuCom staff. Our wives went shopping rather than go to lunch with us, so we decided to have a sandwich, at his invitation, in his quarters. He fixed a sandwich, we had our sandwich, a glass of milk. I got up from the table, as is my

---

[*] Rear Admiral Leighton W. Smith Jr., USN, served as Commander Carrier Group Six from December 1987 to July 1989. His oral history is in the Naval Institute collection.
[†] Smith served from August 1989 to June 1991 as J-3 (operations director) on the staff at U.S. European Command headquarters, Stuttgart, Germany,

habit here at home, picked up my dishes, took them to the sink, and started rinsing the things off.

He said, "What the hell are you doing? A CNO in uniform in a two-star's quarters, and you're washing the dishes." [Laughter] He's never let me forget that, matter of fact, as recently as this last year.

I got to know him quite well. We served together quite often, and he preceded me as the chairman of the Naval Academy Alumni Association, and then stayed on by a change in ruling and philosophy both, stayed on for another three years to ensure good carryover on that staff. So I know him quite well.

Paul Stillwell: Well, he and CinCEur/SACEur formed a really close bond, so he was the operations officer and really dictated a lot of things that happened in that theater.[*]

Paul Stillwell: Yeah, he did. He did a great job.

Admiral Trost: We've talked about Systems Analysis when you were heading it in OP-96. What do you remember about its role when you were CNO?

Admiral Trost: Gosh, much the same. Again, I'm dragging memories that are more than 25 years old. I remember using them. I don't remember that we lessened their role or their influence, and I used them very much as I had when I was running it, so they had good access. They had very good access. I'm right now at a loss for who was running it when I was CNO. I don't remember. But I guess that's probably one of the few things I— well, there are a lot of things I don't remember. But I remember them being active players.

Paul Stillwell: Dr. Tom Hone has written a chapter about your term as CNO and the interaction with Secretary Lehman, and he had set up a program management proposal to be administered through the Office of Program Appraisal. How did you deal with that change, some of the power going over to his office?

---

[*] General George A Joulwan, , USA, was NATO's Supreme Allied Commander Europe, 1993-1997.

Admiral Trost: I think I resisted it mightily, and I don't remember it ever happening. He did try to duplicate what my Systems Analysis Group was doing by putting a good two-star in, but I don't remember who it was. We were at odds on most things, but, fortunately, we only overlapped for nine months when I was CNO, which was good.

Paul Stillwell: Another thing that happened on his watch was dissolving the Naval Material Command, which had functioned in the CNO chain of command. Do you have a recollection of that change and its impact? It had been a four-star billet.

Admiral Trost: It had been a four-star billet. I go back to Lehman's having installed Steve White as the Chief of Naval Material while I was OP-090.[*] I recall specifically because White took over, and one day—maybe the day after—my hotline to that job, that guy's desk, disappeared. Jack Williams had been the Chief of Naval Material.[†] We talked several times a week and usually on the hotline for its convenience. When I called the Chief of Naval Material's office to note that my hotline wasn't working, the executive assistant said, "It's not working because I was told to disconnect it. Admiral White doesn't speak on the hotline to junior officers."

Paul Stillwell: What? [Laughs]

Admiral Trost: I was the senior three-star in Washington at the time, and White got his fourth star. Lehman and Mel Paisley, Assistant Secretary for R&D—I don't know if "courted" is the right term.[‡] They selected White for the job, very heavily influenced what he did and how he did it. He was very much a member of their camp. So we had difficulties in our relationship.

---

[*] Admiral Steven A. White, USN, served as Chief of Naval Material from 1983 to 1985. On 6 May 1985 the command was disestablished.
[†] Admiral John G. Williams, Jr., USN, served as Chief of Naval Material from 1 July 1981 to 31 July 1983.
[‡] Melvyn R. Paisley served from December 1981 to March 1987 as Assistant Secretary of the Navy (Research, Engineering, and Systems). In October 1991, a federal judge sentenced Paisley to four years in prison and fined him $50,000. Paisley admitted receiving more than $3.3 million in kickbacks from various corporations for steering Navy contracts their way during his time in office.

Paul Stillwell: What was the structure that took its place after it was dissolved?

Admiral Trost: There was no structure that took its place, really. It was more the individual bureaus reporting to the Secretary directly, bypassing the CNO's office or the CNO organization. That's about all I remember.

Paul Stillwell: So that would be another bone in your throat.

Admiral Trost: It was. It was.

Paul Stillwell: What was the role of the CNO Executive Panel while you were the CNO?

Admiral Trost: I used them as sort of a special think tank to evaluate different programs, different approaches. I used them almost exclusively for developing my testimony before Congress, and that started with my first posture statement, which had inputs from everybody. I described it as the lowest-common-denominator document I'd ever seen. It was garbage.

So I tasked the CNO Executive Panel staff, which was headed by a captain, gave them guidance on what I wanted to talk about and said, "Develop a statement for me with these items as items to emphasize." They did, and I liked the product and that's what I used. I upset my senior three-stars because they felt bypassed. I told them, no, I hadn't bypassed them. I'd read everything they gave me, and it was garbage, and so I treated it accordingly. And it was the lowest common denominator. Everybody agreed. When everybody agrees, it mustn't be very good, and it wasn't.

Paul Stillwell: Do you remember any of the things that you substituted in the posture?

Admiral Trost: No, I just put my philosophy in, rather than what people were pushing as their favorite programs, and my programs were not necessarily the favorite programs, although I didn't denigrate what they were giving me. I just used 00K where I had some very smart people who could think, who could follow guidance on what I wanted to emphasize, and give me a statement that put those things forth. Now, I used 00K for quite a few things. The captain in charge attended my morning briefings in CNO office before the day began to make sure he knew what was current, what I was thinking about, so they were very much involved in my day-to-day thinking, philosophy, statements.

Paul Stillwell: I would guess that two of the emphases were on executing the Maritime Strategy or being ready to execute it and building toward the 600-ship Navy.

Admiral Trost: That's right. Both very much so. The 600-ship Navy was one of the areas where Lehman and I agreed on, so a bigger Navy, not necessarily 600 ships, but that was a good target, good goal.

Paul Stillwell: The great irony, as we talked last time, is that the purpose of the forward strategy was to deter the Soviets and, if necessary, to win the war against them, and it was so successful that the Soviet Union dissolved, and then the number of ships went down precipitously after that.

Admiral Trost: They did that. Now, I should emphasize that the 600-ship Navy and the Maritime Strategy really preceded my time there as CNO. I'd have to give Hayward and Watkins credit for the concept and for the philosophy, with Jim Watkins being perhaps the strongest pusher.

Paul Stillwell: But certainly you were pushing that during your term as well.

Admiral Trost: Oh, yeah, but I was pushing it as a supporter of them as 090 and as CNO.

Paul Stillwell: One of the operational events during that period was Operation Earnest Will, which involved escorting reflagged Kuwaiti tankers in the Persian Gulf out through the Strait of Hormuz.* What do you remember of CNO's role in supporting that?

Admiral Trost: The thing I remember is that we used the battleships off Iran when they threatened to close the straits. They put this installation in on the Iranian side—I've forgotten what that area is called, but down where ships have to come through the Strait of Hormuz. They had this thing that had a capability of running missile launchers out from a cave, and they could threaten somebody 12 or so miles out. But they were within battleship range. We deployed a battleship and an Aegis cruiser over there, because these crews are 1,000 yards behind and could shoot any missiles down before they could hit. The Iranians were warned that if they ran their missiles out, the battleship would be sitting out there, off the coast, close in, in international waters. It would engage any Iranian ship or missile that was out there.

Paul Stillwell: Well, the Iranians also had the Silkworm missiles with the range to reach that area.

Admiral Trost: Yeah, that's right. And that's why they were sitting out there.

Paul Stillwell: I managed to get over to the Persian Gulf for that operation.† That was fascinating.

Admiral Trost: I'll bet. I'll bet.

Paul Stillwell: I went through the Strait of Hormuz one night on board a supply ship, and you can sleep with the noises of a ship. But she lost the load in the strait, and I woke up instantly because of the silence. We saw the convoy moving away from us, but fortunately the engineers got the plant started quickly.

---

* In the early months of 1987, during a war between Iran and Iraq, each side was attacking tankers in the Persian Gulf. In order to protect the flow of oil in the gulf, the United States re-flagged a number of Kuwaiti commercial tankers to provide them U.S. registry. That enabled the U.S. Navy to escort the tankers in an operation labeled Earnest Will.

† In January 1988 the interviewer was recalled to active duty as a reserve officer and sent to the Persian Gulf and the Gulf of Oman to conduct interviews with participants in Earnest Will. The interviews were done on behalf of the Naval Historical Center, now the Naval History and Heritage Command.

Admiral Trost: Did you see any small boats go buzzing.

Paul Stillwell: No [laughter].

Admiral Trost: I remember persuading the JCS of the viability of putting a battleship off the coast of Iran when they were threatening to shoot these guns that roll out of the caves and stop traffic going through. When the battleships sat out there with an Aegis cruiser to shoot down any missiles that came their way, the Iranians pulled the guns back into the caves and left them there. So, yeah, we got involved with that.

Paul Stillwell: And they didn't shoot any Silkworm missiles.

Admiral Trost: No.

Paul Stillwell: What do you recall of your relationship with General Crist, who was CentCom?*

Admiral Trost: Sometimes controversial, and that was personality-related, I think. George and I didn't see eye-to-eye on everything. Specifics elude me.

Paul Stillwell: What do you remember about the reaction to the *Stark* incident when she was hit by Iraqi missiles?†

Admiral Trost: Well, I remember, first of all, the damage that was done, and what I

---

* General George B. Crist, USMC, served as Commander in Chief Central Command from 27 November 1985 to 23 November 1988.
† On 17 May 1987, while she was operating in the Persian Gulf, the guided missile frigate *Stark* (FFG-31) was hit by two Exocet air-to-surface missiles fired by an Iraqi Mirage F1 fighter. One of the two missiles exploded, resulting in heavy damage and fires. Of the *Stark*'s crew, 37 men were killed and 21 injured. For details, see Jeffrey L. Levinson and Randy L. Edwards, *Missile Inbound* (Annapolis: Naval Institute Press, 1997).

would call very heroic efforts to save the ship. The performance of the crew was absolutely marvelous. I remember the incident, but not many of the specifics anymore.

Paul Stillwell: Well, I interviewed Admiral Hal Bernsen, who was Commander Middle East Force, and he was disappointed, to say the least, that the skipper had allowed the plane to get that close to be able to shoot the missiles.[*]

Admiral Trost: I'm trying to think. Was *Stark* the ship that was hit and nearly sunk?

Paul Stillwell: Yes, and then later *Samuel B. Roberts* ran into a minefield.[†]

Admiral Trost: Okay. I guess maybe I'm thinking more of *Roberts* than I was of *Stark*. I am. I remember one that was very heavily damaged and almost sank, and the damage control was outstanding and they saved the ship. It was probably *Roberts*.

Paul Stillwell: That probably applied to both of them.

Admiral Trost: It could have. It could have. But *Stark*, I do remember *Stark*. But things run together.

Paul Stillwell: What do you recall about getting mine warfare assets out there to deal with the mines?

Admiral Trost: Well, I remember we had insufficient assets out there at the time, and I'm not sure we could ever have had enough to guarantee control if they'd had a concentrated capable mine warfare effort on the part of the Iranians and all that. First of all, we really

---

[*] Rear Admiral Harold J. Bernsen, USN, served as Commander Middle East Force from July 1986 until February 1988. His oral history is in the Naval Institute collection.

[†] On 14 April 1988, the frigate *Samuel B. Roberts* (FFG-58) incurred extensive damage when she ran into and set off an Iranian naval mine in the central Persian Gulf. It took hours of effort on the part of the crew to save the ship from sinking. She received temporary repairs in Dubai and was later returned to the United States for rebuilding. For details see Bradley Peniston, *No Higher Honor: Saving the USS Samuel B. Roberts in the Persian Gulf* (Annapolis: Naval Institute Press, 2006).

didn't have enough assets on scene. It took a long time to get a buildup out there because they're small ships, they have to get out there, have to transit, and that in itself takes time.

Paul Stillwell: I thought they were towed.

Admiral Trost: I think they may have been. I don't remember. But little things like that, going across that distance of ocean, we're not very mobile.

Paul Stillwell: I've seen pictures that showed you out in the area in the fall of 1987. What do you remember from your visit to the theater?

Admiral Trost: Well, I don't know which visit that was. I was out there several times, I think. I believe that's the one where I visited—what was that floating platform we had up in the north?

Paul Stillwell: Well, they had a couple of barges. One was called *WimBrown* and one was *Hercules*.

Admiral Trost: Yeah. I remember visiting them and talking to the people.

Paul Stillwell: I know you were on board the *Missouri* during part of that trip.

Admiral Trost: Yeah, went aboard *Missouri*. I remember being there. I remember going up on the barges. I remember being impressed by how much capability they had managed to put into a barge, and how upbeat the crew was on there. "Hell, we can handle everything. We can do this. We can do that."

I remember also being told by Middle East Force that I was putting myself in danger by flying in a helicopter from Bahrain up to the barge. [Laughs] I figured if I was putting myself in danger, the guys I had up there sure as hell were in danger because they were there 24 hours a day.

Paul Stillwell: They had a bunch of SEALs and small boat units as well.

Admiral Trost: Yeah.

Paul Stillwell: What are the logistics of getting a CNO from Washington to the Persian Gulf?

Admiral Trost: Well, pretty simple, really. I used the P-3 that was assigned to me to fly to Bahrain, and then from Bahrain, I went by SH-3 helo up to the barges. As I remember, they were north and off maybe roughly on parallel with the southern part of Iraq.

Paul Stillwell: They were up by Kuwait.

Admiral Trost: Yeah. It was by Kuwait, obviously to the east of Kuwait. We were pretty far north, and I thought we were abreast of islands off to the east. That's about all I remember of it now.

Paul Stillwell: Did you have extra security for that trip?

Admiral Trost: No.

Paul Stillwell: Did you have any extra bodyguard or security during your tenure?

Admiral Trost: No.

Paul Stillwell: What was the communications capability when you were away from the office?

Admiral Trost: Paul, I had it and I don't remember it. I had an ability to, I guess, to tie in, but I don't remember the specifics. I find my brain is wilting after 25 years, 20, almost 30 years, you know.

Paul Stillwell: There must have been a secure voice connection.

Admiral Trost: I had secure voice capability. I'm trying to think how I tied in. We had a capability of being reached and being able to tie in and talk to people, but I don't remember the specifics.

Paul Stillwell: Was there any frustration in not being an operational commander in that scenario, since the operational commander was CinCCent?

Admiral Trost: We talked, we communicated, and I wasn't there to take over his job. I was there to observe and as a visitor from the Joint Chiefs.

Paul Stillwell: And presumably to support his needs as best you could.

Admiral Trost: Yeah, but really to become more knowledgeable of what was there, what the problems were, who was doing what. Our relationship with the Bahrainians was quite good, and my interest in going to Bahrain, other than the need to go there to travel onward, was primarily to maintain the relationship. I had a good personal relationship with the Bahrainian government because I went with John Warner when he was Secretary on visits to Bahrain, met the Sheikh and met him again when he came to the U.S. for a visit. So I felt sort of a personal tie with the then-Sheikh.[*] We had a good working relationship, good supporting relationship.

Paul Stillwell: You talked about the Joint Chiefs' meetings. How often did you meet in the Tank with your counterparts from the other services?

Admiral Trost: It least weekly, sometimes more frequently. We usually had a weekly meeting.

---

[*] Sheikh Isa ibn Salman Al Khalifa was the first Emir of Bahrain; he served in that capacity from 2 November 1961 until his death on 6 March 1999.

Paul Stillwell: And I presume that you took the opdeps with you, the OP-06 to those meetings.

Admiral Trost: The opdeps always went with me. Right.

Paul Stillwell: How much would you confer with them before you went into a meeting?

Admiral Trost: Well, usually we met the morning of the meeting. If it was a 1400 meeting or something like that, we'd meet in the morning, go over the issues, go over the proposals. Sometimes when it required a paper to be developed, have a position ready, we met several times before the JCS meeting. He had a very major input to the agenda. Matter of fact, I was challenged one time by my Air Force counterpart, General Welch, on driving the agenda in directions that focused on the Navy, and if that's the case, so be it.

Paul Stillwell: I don't know that that's a shortcoming on your part. [Laughter]

Admiral Trost: Yeah. Well, I think it was a challenge to him. Our relationship was generally good. It was sometimes confrontational, but usually where it came to the Navy taking a stronger role than he would have liked because he'd like the Air Force to be more dominant in policy matters. I'm sure that if you asked him the question, he'd say I got into his business or I tried to drive agendas. Sometimes I did.

Paul Stillwell: Sounds a little bit like your relationship with Admiral Yost.

Admiral Trost: Oh, yeah, it was. [Laughs]

Paul Stillwell: Did you have any part in Navy working with Coast Guard on drug seizures, law enforcement?

Admiral Trost: Not other than providing support that they needed, but, no, not for policy development or anything else.

Paul Stillwell: What do you recall of your relationship with Secretary Weinberger?

Admiral Trost: Very good, very good. Weinberger would have his service meetings, and very often I was the Navy rep at those meetings as 090, and so I guess I got a lot more face time than a three-star normally would have with Weinberger. So I felt I knew him pretty well because I often, after one of these meetings in the SecDef conference room, would be asked to stay behind, and he'd have questions that he wanted answers to but didn't want to toss them out for the whole room. So I felt very comfortable with the man. Good relationship.

Paul Stillwell: What about Secretary Carlucci?[*]

Admiral Trost: I knew him well, again, good relationship, less so than with Weinberger just in terms of closeness of contact.

Paul Stillwell: How about Secretary Cheney?[†]

Admiral Trost: Very good. I had met him when he was a member of Congress. I don't recall the occasion. I remember being in Union Station at a function, and that's where I met him. I still remember the area. Went in the front entrance of Union Station, way off to the right was a room that they used for functions, and I remember talking with him some length that day.

Then when he was named as SecDef, I called on him after he came in. I remember specifically his saying that the most significant thing was the size of the staff. He said, "I've never in my life had a staff bigger than about six people, and now I've got this

---

[*] Frank C. Carlucci served as U.S. Secretary of Defense from 23 November 1987 to 20 January 1989.
[†] Richard B. Cheney served as U.S. Secretary of Defense from 21 March 1989 to 20 January 1993. From 2001 to 2009 he was Vice President of the United States.

whole department." I remember we talked quite some length about that. I'd had three years in OSD as a commander in the Deputy Secretary's Office, so he invited me to give him observations, which observations from a once commander to the new Secretary was a little bit of heady stuff.

But we had a good relationship. Matter of fact, that relationship continued. His wife, Lynne, and I were fellow directors on the Lockheed and then Lockheed Martin board, so I continued to see him at Lockheed Martin functions after I retired from the Navy, during that time frame, and we had a good relationship.

Paul Stillwell: You talked about presenting the posture statement and testifying. Any specific recollections of your congressional testimony?

Admiral Trost: Wow. Specific topics? We covered the gamut of what the Navy was doing, where we were going. I don't remember specifics.

Paul Stillwell: Do you remember murder board sessions before the testimony?

Admiral Trost: More briefing sessions, more when I present the following, what are some of the pitfalls of my encounter, and what did people who dealt regularly, like the congressional liaison people, what were they hearing, what did they see as the focus of the members, things of that nature, are they getting advanced?

Paul Stillwell: Well, that's useful to be prepped on what they're likely to ask.

Admiral Trost: Yeah, and this would focus on what are they talking about, what are the staffs asking you in advance of the hearings, and we'd get some information on that.

Paul Stillwell: And I would guess that money was the frequent topic time and again.

Admiral Trost: Money was a very frequent topic, the dominant topic. Money, more than what do you need the money for, interestingly.

Paul Stillwell: Well, and a number of the congressmen have their own pet projects that may or may not align with the Navy's wishes.

Admiral Trost: Generally it did not. Generally it did not.

Paul Stillwell: Trying to support contractors in their districts.

Admiral Trost: Yeah.

Paul Stillwell: Well, money was another topic in your dealings with the barons, who got somewhat downgraded during your tenure as CNO. What do you remember about Admiral DeMars as head of Submarine Warfare?[*]

Admiral Trost: I remember DeMars, a very strong guy. I had known him for a number of years and knew he was very alert, intelligent, and a fighter for his programs. As a matter of fact, I supported him to relieve McKee when McKee retired from the Rickover job.

Paul Stillwell: You mentioned that earlier.

Admiral Trost: I must say he was one of my favorites to work with, sort of a droll sense of humor backed up by a lot of brainpower, so a good guy.

Paul Stillwell: And a lot of operational experience in submarines.

Admiral Trost: Yeah, yeah.

---

[*] Vice Admiral Bruce DeMars, USN, served as Deputy Chief of Naval Operations (Submarine Warfare), OP-02, from November 1985 to October 1988. His oral history is in the Naval Institute collection.

Paul Stillwell: What about Admiral Dunn in aviation?[*]

Admiral Trost: Well, first of all he was AirLant during my brief tour as CinCLantFlt, so I chose him to come up and be the OP-05, the DCNO (Air Warfare). We had a good relationship, except when he tried to shoot down certain things I had approved in the program, specifically submarine-related, and tried to substitute submarine money for more airplanes. [Laughs] So we had an occasional tiff over that. I usually won.

Paul Stillwell: I wonder why. [Laughs] How about Vice Admiral Joe Metcalf in surface?[†]

Admiral Trost: Feisty, good friend. We'd worked together in BuPers and I knew him quite well, good professional relationship, very good.

Paul Stillwell: What do you recall about your relationship with the Naval Reserve?

Admiral Trost: It was good and became—I don't know if I should say "better" or not. Jim Taylor became the head of the reserve.[‡] He was not a reserve himself; he was a line officer—F-14 pilot, as a matter of fact. Jim had worked for me as my deputy for operations in Seventh Fleet, so I'd known him. He came to Washington, and I brought him in when I was 090, as my executive assistant, where he served for several years. So I'd known Jim quite well, and I don't recall specifics of his getting that reserve job. I don't remember whether I had a voice in that or not. I obviously had a voice of approval because he was on my staff. A very capable guy. Jim was a very, very professional guy. When he got an assignment, he did his homework like nobody I'd ever seen and just dug in, learning everything he could about everything. So I think he did a strong job. I don't know how the reservists felt, quite frankly. I don't recall any big controversies during that time frame.

---

[*] Vice Admiral Robert F. Dunn, USN, served as Deputy Chief of Naval Operations (Air Warfare) from 15 January 1987 to 25 May 1989. The title changed from Deputy to Assistant Chief on 1 October 1987. His oral history is in the Naval Institute collection.
[†] Vice Admiral Joseph Metcalf III, USN, served as Deputy Chief of Naval Operations (Surface Warfare) from September 1984 to December 1987.
[‡] Rear Admiral James E. Taylor, USN, was Chief of the Naval Reserve from 1989 to 1992.

Paul Stillwell: What do you recall about the value of the reserve in supporting the active forces?

Admiral Trost: Well, I've always been a supporter of the reserves because there are a lot of things where we need support and don't have the talent necessarily in the active force to provide that support, and that talent does reside in the reserves in many cases. So I was a proponent of having reserve input, reserves on staff. I saw, for example, when I was LantFlt, the value of reserves. I found out, after I'd been there about six months, that the guy who ran my operations briefings every Saturday and Sunday was a Naval Reserve captain, not in a paying billet, who flew down from New York City every weekend and put in his reserve time because he wanted to.

Paul Stillwell: That's dedication.

Admiral Trost: That's dedication. So we got good strong reserve support. Matter of fact, some staffs, like LantFlt staff, wouldn't have functioned without the reserves on the weekends because they basically carried the load, and a lot of those guys were volunteers in nonpaid billets. So I'm a reserve proponent.

They helped me in Great Lakes when we got into a tiff because we didn't have the money to do facilities improvement and they could no longer hire some of the local contractors who had very strong reserve support but needed to get work done. And by talking to the senior reservists out there and using them as lobbyists, in a sense, I got to use Seabees sometimes on weekends, bring Seabees in to do construction projects out there that we didn't have the money to get done. So they were useful in many, many different ways, and I think my relationship with them was quite good.

Paul Stillwell: I remember a specific example from your tenure as CNO during the escort of convoys in the Persian Gulf. Military Sealift Command had the naval control of shipping organization in the reserve, and they were the ones who worked with the convoys.

Admiral Trost: Yeah.

Paul Stillwell: How much of a social obligation did you have as CNO?

Considerable. My advice from Jim Watkins when I relieved him was, "Try to limit yourself to five nights a week," and we tried. Some weeks we didn't make it. We tried to keep Saturday night for personal stuff or personal entertainment, if that. Sunday we tried just to stay for chapel and catch-up on my part, and not entertaining, although we didn't always succeed there.

We hosted ten visits a year by foreign CNOs, and that meant three nights in Washington. Then we'd send them off for about a week to various things, depending on who they were, where they were from, what their interests were, and then they'd come back. We'd have them generally for another two nights, one night of which was theirs, to entertain. A reception was one of the first three nights. So from a social perspective, we averaged five nights a week.

Paul Stillwell: That seems like a lot.

Admiral Trost: It's a lot. I was blessed with good people working for me. When we were entertaining at home, I tried to get home 15 minutes before the event to have time to shave and change clothes, which is about what it took me. I'd get home and come down smiling, looking clean and refreshed, and greet my guests as they came in the front door. Again, staff was all-important, because they just did a great job.

Tomorrow for lunch I'm hosting a guy named Luke McCollum, class of '83 Naval Academy. I'm going to promote him on Friday to rear admiral (upper half) reserve. He's a vice president for Walmart, has been for a number of years. He was what was called the junior aide, the house aide, a few other not so complimentary terms. He was the second guy the last half of my CNO time. His responsibility was quarters, including maintenance, the staff, the four MSs, the yard people who worked for the base but got their guidance from him, social functions preparations, making sure everything was set up, we had enough people to help and enough people drawn in from outside as necessary.

He got to make an occasional trip, but basically he was there working in the Navy Yard, responsible for the CNO barge, which we used for entertainment, and the barge crew, which was four guys. He was stuck with the quarters most of time, a very important job, not a glorious job, not a big high-visibility job unless something went wrong.[*]

Paul Stillwell: But certainly necessary.

Admiral Trost: Very necessary. He and the lieutenant, who was the protocol officer in the CNO office, were the two people on whom entertainment depended. They made sure all the arrangements were taken care of. They made sure I could do what I just said, come home, change clothes, shave, and come down and greet guests and look like I was all set to reign over the evening. It made my life a lot easier. I had two of the finest lieutenants, and when I think about it, they were also known as the SLJO, Shitty Little Job Officers. And I didn't coin that phrase.

Paul Stillwell: No.

Admiral Trost: Because I'll tell you, without those guys, you couldn't function. But Luke, I don't know how long Luke stayed on active duty. I'm going to ask him that tomorrow.[†] We heard from him for a number of years, and then he suddenly sort of dropped off my scope and I couldn't find out where he was. Then somebody said, "Well, he's working for Walmart."

Then I found out two years ago that he has a daughter at the Naval Academy. He came to the Naval Academy from time to time and had called several times when he was coming in, but for some reason we couldn't connect. So I'm looking forward to the next couple of days and see him. A fine gentleman.

So my world was supported by some very good people. Ten of 5:00 was my standard awakening time during the week and sometimes on Saturday. If I went in on

---

[*] Tingey House, Quarters A, was the CNO's residence in the Washington Navy Yard from 1978 to 2005. It was built around 1804.
[†] Luke M. McCollum left active duty in 1993. In September 2016 he became Chief of the Navy Reserve as a vice admiral.

Saturday, it was my Saturday time also. I'd get up, get shaved, showered, dressed, get down by 6:00. At least one MS was already there. He had breakfast ready for me. My driver was there. He had the pouch with the classified briefing stuff, the intel, and message traffic for the morning. So I could sit down, do my reading, do my eating, and by 6:30 we'd get in the car and head for the Pentagon.

My morning there would start with the rest of the briefing material that they hadn't gotten yet before he went to pick it up in the morning, and then my 7:00 o'clock in-house staff meeting, and then I guess 8:00 o'clock was the regular intel brief.

So it was a regular routine, except for Saturday, and I tried not to go in on Saturday unless somebody senior to me had scheduled a meeting and I couldn't get out of it. I told you the story about the response of Holloway about how many people come in, "I will not come in if you don't come in." The answer was about 1,000, and I never forgot that, and I think it as true. Because when I didn't go in, an awful lot of people didn't have to come in, and not only didn't have to to respond to me, but to cover their ass, which was what most of them were doing. And that didn't make sense.

So I'd have the stuff delivered out to me on Saturday morning. I'd spend Saturday morning working, tried to spend Saturday afternoon with my wife and do things that didn't have anything to do with the office. Sunday, I did my reading, and usually I'd wait till about 8:00 o'clock Sunday morning to get that stuff, because I could finish that and then get to chapel by 10:00, and took Sunday afternoon off and did other things. So it was a full schedule.

Paul Stillwell: What role did your EA play in all this?

Admiral Trost: He put the things together, came out Saturday morning usually to work with me when we had papers that needed attention, but he also lived on the Navy Yard, which helped. So he could go in if he'd want, and he could also stay home and have stuff delivered, and then he just had to walk down the street a block to get to my quarters.

Paul Stillwell: Some EAs would listen in on extension during phone calls, take notes, and then move out with action items. Was that your practice?

Admiral Trost: Depended on who it was. Sometimes yes.

Paul Stillwell: What would be the bulk of your day at the Pentagon?

Admiral Trost: Meetings, briefings, paperwork, something needed attention, but reading was a very major part of it, keep up to speed on things and keep current if there'd be something that needed guidance. That was the bulk of my day.

Paul Stillwell: Then a very important person in that process is whoever decides what gets to you.

Admiral Trost: Yeah, and that's the EA, and I had an assistant EA. The EA was a captain till he made rear admiral, and the assistant was a commander. Matter of fact, my two EAs were Tom Paulsen, who I'd brought up from Norfolk, and I think I mentioned him before.

Paul Stillwell: You did, yes.

Admiral Trost: Tom left the office as a two-star. His assistant was Norb Ryan, who left the office as a captain, retired as a three-star. The second EA was Dan Oliver, who retired as a three-star and then went out and ran the Postgraduate School, got into a flap, got relieved on something I've looked into since then, which was a bunch of crap. It was jealousy on the part of some people that he didn't give their head to. Anyway, that's another subject.

But they were two outstanding guys whom I had making that decision on what I saw. Three guys, really, because Norb was very much there. Now, I'm trying to remember who relieved—somebody relieved Norb before I left, because we transferred him, I think to Barbers Point to run the P-3 organization for the Pacific.

Anyway, had some very good staff members, had good yeomen, very good yeomen. I had a flag writer for all four years, same guy, who was just very quiet. He was, in terms of an office presence, the guy who was there because you see the product, never hear from him. He was just a quiet worker, great guy. And you needed that kind of staff support.

My protocol officer was a lieutenant, female, very capable. Protocol, they took care of the social schedule and the entertainment schedule, traveled with me as a companion to my wife, as well as running the schedule when we traveled overseas or anywhere else, for that matter. And had an assistant protocol officer who was a female chief petty officer yeoman. Had the senior aide, who was a commander. Had a Marine aide. They were responsible for travel and office support, basically. They were like the division officers for the enlisted staff. That was a pretty big immediate staff, but they were pretty busy people too. And I think I told you about the senior chief yeoman who I found out left his house at 2:00 in the morning to get to work, and stayed all day.

Paul Stillwell: What about your own stamina? You talk about getting up before 5:00 in the morning, working all day, and then having these evening social events.

Admiral Trost: You learn to live with five or six hours' sleep at night, which I did, and when I retired, I learned *not* to sleep for only six hours. [Laughter]

Paul Stillwell: I'm guessing that wasn't a very steep learning curve.

Admiral Trost: Well, I was helped by the fact that I retired on a Friday so we wouldn't have to get everybody—you know, you muster hundreds of people at the Naval Academy for the change of command, and these were done in front of Bancroft Hall until this most recent one. I retired on a Friday, even though Saturday was my last official day. Saturday was the last day of June. I don't remember what I did. I probably loafed. But I remember getting a call at midnight from the duty watch officer in the command center saying, "I'm calling, and I know it's a quarter of 12:00, but I normally call you at quarter of 12:00 on Saturday night to give you an update of what's happening, and it will be my last report for the weekend." And he said, "I figured you'd like to know what's going on before you officially retire." [Laughter]

So 15 minutes before I retired officially, I got this call. Sunday, I wasn't feeling well, and Monday morning, sometime Monday we were going to move out after the change of command because the quarters were going to be renovated. They were going to be offline for six months, and they weren't going to start for a week after I moved out. So I wasn't rushed to move out.

So Sunday I was getting paperwork together, primarily, and we were getting stuff organized a little better than we had at that point in time, and that afternoon I couldn't urinate. And I went down—there was a little dispensary there on the Navy Yard—and the duty corpsman said, "I'm going to have to send you out to Bethesda. I don't know what to do."

So they took me out to Bethesda. In the meantime, I was sitting there, I had to go, but I couldn't. I got to the emergency room and they plopped me down and called for a urologist. The guy said, "You've got a blockage and I don't know what it is."

But in the meantime, my abdomen had swollen up and I was in real discomfort. They took me to an operating room, and I have a place right here with an indentation where he took a thing and plunged it into my abdomen, into my bladder, and urine squirted about three feet in the air all over him. [Laughs] They got a bag connected. I put out about a gallon of urine in that bag.

Paul Stillwell: Oh, my God.

Admiral Trost: And I suddenly could breathe again. But I spent, I guess, about three days in the hospital, and they put me on medication. My problem was an enlarged prostate, and it had just choked off my ability to urinate. So I spent about a week at the hospital in bed while poor Pauline had to take care of most of the move. I got over there for a couple hours a day. So that's the way my retirement started.

Paul Stillwell: I'm guessing that you made CNO history. That experience was probably unique in CNO retirement annals.

Admiral Trost: It probably was. It probably was.

Paul Stillwell: Well, speaking of your wife, what role did she play in this overall social life?

Admiral Trost: Very much of a role, and I might say she was not one who sought social life. She wasn't a nerd. She was a very personable person, but she didn't like gadding about. We had to do a lot of entertainment, but she had this junior house aide and the protocol officer and the staff of four mess specialists. And what she had to do was tell them what to prepare, and they took care of it, getting stuff ready, and they took care of any side arrangements that were necessary. For example, we always did a couple of lawn parties every summer, and that required coordination with the people who did the lawn care who belonged to the Navy Yard staff and whatever. Well, we needed tents and stuff set up and things like that, and there the aides would pick up and take care of that. Her job was to be Mrs. Hostess, smile sweetly even when she didn't want to, and greet people and host them, and she did that real well. I used to get a kick out of her and the stories they told about her when we had foreign visitors. The foreign visitors—I may have told you this one before.

Paul Stillwell: I don't recall.

Admiral Trost: The foreign visitor would come to town. Day one, we would lodge them in the Navy Yard flag quarters on the other side of the gate from the last set of quarters before Tingey House. The night they arrived, I would greet them, but then we got out of their hair, because they were generally tired from having traveled all day. We'd make sure they were accommodated, then we took the rest of the evening off.

The next day would start with a formal arrival ceremony out at Leutze Park, which is the parade area out in front of Tingey House, and we'd have a small arrival parade with an honor guard, a welcoming speech by me and arrival speech by the foreign guest. Then he and I would go to the Pentagon and start our formal talks.

Pauline would take the wife and anybody in her party to the house for coffee and to talk about what they were going to do, what the schedule was going to be, go over the schedule with them. The fixed part of the schedule was going to be a formal arrival dinner that night and then a return invitation from them the following day, and then maybe a third night.

Paul Stillwell: Would this be at that country's embassy in Washington?

Admiral Trost: The third night would be, yeah. They arrived one night, they were at the house one night, and we're at their embassy.

She and the protocol officer would sit down with the lady and any aides she had and decide what we were going to do. Now, we were always getting advance messages, "Mrs. So-and-so likes museums, likes art, likes to do things." By the time they left the house, Mrs. So-and-so would like to see Walmart, different discount stores. That's basically what they did, then some sightseeing. [Laughs] Then by evening, they were good friends. They were feeling at home, Pauline was happy with them, they were happy with Pauline, and we were having a very delightful evening.

I always got a kick at this transition, and it was invariable—with one exception in four years. By that evening, the guy and I had spent most of the day together. He was, hopefully, feeling comfortable. The wife was quite comfortable. She was very happy with things and had done things she liked. So we would have a very congenial evening, and we were good friends.

Pauline had a talent for making people feel at home. I'd say that was her forte, and she enjoyed it. As I said, she's not a big social butterfly, but she enjoyed that and she made a lot of good friends. So we generally invited them, and they would invite us in return. Sometimes it went the other way around. When it went with them coming to the U.S. first, the visit on the other end was always very congenial, because they were happy. Sometimes the wives came back alone, sometimes with a daughter, to see Pauline and to shop.

The Egyptian CNO's wife was interesting. We visited Egypt first in the process. My job was to try to wean them from the Russian Navy influence. At the Egyptian Naval Academy, the cadets still had to learn Russian. Russia provided their books and all their stuff. When we left over there, I had agreed to provide a lieutenant commander from our Naval Academy, who was an experienced instructor, to them to head up a transition team of Egyptian officers to convert their Naval Academy to the model of our Naval Academy, which they couldn't do totally. That worked successfully.

We got an agreement where he could send selected officers to ride our ships through the Suez Canal and talk with our people, get a tour of the ship, find out a lot of professional things that they hadn't been exposed to. The CNO and I stayed good friends until he died, which was shortly after he retired, but the wife liked her first visit to the U.S. so much that about a month later, Pauline got a call, an overseas call, saying, "Would you be free on such-and-such dates? I'd like to come to Washington and visit and bring my daughter," who was in her early 20s.

Pauline said, "Sure." So we set up a visit. They came. Put them up in the visiting guest quarters, and if that would have been occupied, we could have accommodated them in our house. But they stayed great friends. There's a lamp from her over there. She said, "I'm bringing this present." She carried it with her on the airplane coming over, because she didn't want to give it to Pauline, because she knew we had to turn everything in and didn't mean we got to keep everything we turned in either or even get it back. So she gave that as a personal gift rather than as an official gift, which is funny. But that relationship was really unique, almost.

Our first visitors were the Australian head of the Navy and his wife. He'd been fleet commander when I had Seventh Fleet, so we'd known each other for quite some time, and that relationship started off very great. He was our first official guest. I was his guest about two months later in Australia, and we went back out to Australia later on again for his retirement.

But those visits were very important to working relationships. We had good working relationships with some people who were not our friends before, and it worked out. Matter of fact, as a result of my working relationship with the Pakistani Navy, Pauline and I had lunch with President Zia and his wife. I may have mentioned that to you. It happened about a month before he was assassinated. Zia was a retired Army general who became the head of government, effective, sometimes controversial, effective in his own country, but controversial because he brooked no nonsense, and the politicians didn't like him and were probably the ones behind his assassination.

But relationships, by and large, were quite good. Matter of fact, I can't think of any that were bad. My Greek relationship was not warm, friendly, and I don't know the reasons for that, I really don't. I never figured that one out. It was sort of a cool relationship.

Paul Stillwell: Do you remember substantive achievements that came out of these meetings?

Admiral Trost: By and large, an increase in port visits. The Egyptian Naval Academy transformation. A transfer of ships to the Pakistanis that were decommissioned U.S. destroyers. I think we had a couple of other ships that we gave to the Pakistani Navy. Of course, that's walking on a very fine path because the Indians didn't like us giving things to them, but we helped the Indians with their building programs as well. Indians are very, very proud people. My relationship with the Indian Navy was a very good one, two CNOs. The Eastern Sea Fleet commander and I had a personal relationship that included correspondence and conversations and some mutual visits, were quite good.

My relationship with the Europeans was very strong. We had a very good Navy-to-Navy relationship with the French, the Germans, the Danes, the Swedes, the Spaniards, the Italians. So we covered it, with the exception of the Greeks. Turks was very strong. A lot of those were, I think, the results of personal interchanges in both directions.

In Germany, I actually testified before the Bundestag in Bonn, at their request, about Navy issues, arranged by my German counterpart, and it was an interesting experience. I testified in German. I could in German at that time. I couldn't do it anymore.

Paul Stillwell: That made a hit.

Admiral Trost: That made a hit. Then I had a press conference after the testimony, in German, and got good coverage, so that worked well. And I lectured at the German Navy

College in northern Germany in German, so, fortunately, I still had the capability, but by the time I retired, I don't think I could have done it.

Paul Stillwell: How were the language things handled during these meetings with foreign CNOs?

Admiral Trost: Usually with an interpreter.

Paul Stillwell: Who provided those?

Admiral Trost: They did. But very often it was done in English. For example, the Greek CNO spoke English quite fluently. It just wasn't the warm, fuzzy environment, and, why, I never did figure out. Pauline thought the wife of the CNO just didn't like Americans, and she was treated rather coolly.

The Turks, in English, very warm relationship during my—I made one official CNO-to-CNO visit with Turkey, but I made another visit that was just Navy-to-Navy, not considered a formal exchange. On the formal one, we met in Istanbul, the capital of Turkey, but also in Ankara. We had our formal meetings in Ankara, met in Istanbul for Navy-to-Navy and cultural exchange. They flew me down to Gölcük Naval Shipard on the sea south of Istanbul, on the opposite side of the channel. It was their main Navy base. When I walked into the shipyard, I had been to our Philadelphia Naval Shipyard on two occasions, the three-month destroyer overhaul and the beginning of a diesel submarine overhaul, so I was familiar with the yard. I felt I was walking into Philadelphia Naval Shipyard. Their shop numbers were the same. Every label was in English. They had simply built their own Philadelphia Naval Shipyard.

I had a formal meeting down there with their CNO and with their fleet commander, and the CNO said, "We're going to have a lunch aboard one of my destroyers." He said, "You'll recognize it because it was one of yours."

So I said, "Fine."

So we drove down to the shipyard for lunch. It was in the shipyard, moored there. It was kind of a shipyard Navy base, and here was a ship alongside the pier. We pulled alongside, and I looked at it. It was a FRAM destroyer.[*] Are you familiar with the difference?

Paul Stillwell: Yes.

Admiral Trost: Okay. It was a FRAM destroyer. I walked aboard the quarterdeck and there was this big U.S. brass plate, USS *Robert A. Owens*, which was my first ship as an ensign, but it wasn't FRAM'd then.[†] It was one of two of a kind. The *Owens* and *Carpenter* were built from the keel up as DDEs, and this is my ship. And we had lunch on board. They took me for a tour. They said, "Anything special you'd like to see?"

Well, I was the only Naval Academy graduate when I reported aboard the ship of 24 officers, and so the captain automatically assigned me as the engine room weekly inspector, so I went through the engine rooms every week. The XO was the former engineer of the ship before he became exec, and he had said when he was relieved as engineer, "Last time I'm going down in those spaces." So I became the engineering inspector.

So I said, "I'd like to see your forward engine room." They took me down, and I have to say it was cleaner than it ever was when I served aboard it. [Laughter] It was dry bilge, just clean, wiped bilges, beautiful shape. So I had sort of a soft spot in my heart for the Turkish Navy.

When we turned over some submarines to the Turkish Navy, I was aboard a diesel boat in Norfolk at the time. So I was the liaison officer. They turned the boat over in Groton, and brought their crew in and did some training in New London, and then came down to Norfolk, where I was based, and so I was the liaison officer, not because I spoke the language, but because I was on board a ship of the class that they were getting.

I went out to sea one time on their indoctrination cruise. They got some new crewmen who came down to Norfolk and joined the ship for the first time. So I had some

---

[*] FRAM is an acronym for the fleet rehabilitation and modernization program. Under this program many U.S. destroyer-type ships of the 1950s and 1960s were substantially modernized by extensive rebuilding that incorporated later technology than that available at the time of original construction.
[†] The USS *Robert A. Owens* was decommissioned on 16 February 1982 and transferred to the Turkish Navy. There she became TCG *Alcitepe* (D-346) and served until 1999, when she was scrapped.

exposure to the Turkish Navy, and it was interesting, because my response to "How did you feel about being out at sea with them?" I said, "In a word, their laxity surprised me." [Laughs] They were lax operators compared to our guys. The things they didn't do prior to a dive, for example, took a lot for granted. "Somebody's done that, obviously, so I don't have to worry about it," which surprised me.

We had several guys who rode the ship as liaison officers in case they had a problem going across. I met with them after they came back, and they said felt better in our submarines, felt a lot safer in our submarines from an operational perspective. So it was sort of an interesting aspect of my submarine experience.

Paul Stillwell: Well, as Yogi Bera might have said, going in that engine room of the destroyer, "It's like déjà vu all over again." [Laughs]

Admiral Trost: It was. Unbelievable. It really was interesting. But they were very proud of that ship. And it wasn't just the engine room; the whole ship shone. If it was brass that was supposed to be polished, it was. It was clean. And I'd been led to believe otherwise, and maybe otherwise was standard, but not on that ship.

Paul Stillwell: When you were on these trips, did you have an arrangement that the VCNO had to be in Washington to handle things?

Admiral Trost: Yeah, yeah, VCNO. And when I was 090, I had to be in Washington when the CNO or VCNO was out of Washington. So with both Hayward and Watkins, I had to be in the Pentagon, but I was the senior three-star, so that made sense. But also I was responsible for any admin stuff that came up. As a matter of fact, I attended the JCS meetings in their stead, which was really unusual. They let me sit quietly and silently. [Laughter]

Paul Stillwell: You talked last time about General Akhromeyev coming to the United States. Last time you described your visit to the Soviet Union. Is there anything else to you recall about your trip to Russia while you were CNO?

Admiral Trost: It was a very, very interesting trip. First of all, Chernavin, who was the Russian CNO, and I were both submariners, and we had a very, very good relationship.[*] He understood English, would speak a few words, would depend on the interpreter, who for most of our meetings was my interpreter, who was a native Russian who had come to this country many years ago, worked for the State Department officially, was SecState's interpreter when SecState traveled overseas, was his interpreter when the Russians came to the U.S., and obviously very capable, and also obviously very trusted by our folks as a real legitimate immigrant who was here and was really an American. So it was quite good. But Chernavin insisted on my interpreter being present all the time. As a matter of fact, on our final meeting, his interpreter wasn't there. He used our guy—not my guy—the whole time. We had very frank and open meetings.

Paul Stillwell: I'm sure you were well briefed before you went.

Admiral Trost: I was well briefed. Akhromeyev had retired.[†] Was he still alive? He might not have been alive. He was the former Chairman who had been over here. His relief was a young Army general.[‡] I say "young." He was younger than me, gave me the impression of being a young hotshot, and kept probing. I didn't like his air of superiority because I knew his background. I didn't think he had enough, as one of my friends would say, "warts on his belly" to behave the way he was behaving. So he and I had a formal meeting, but it wasn't a very good meeting, and he kept trying to sort of, in a sense, trying to one-up me on everything.

Paul Stillwell: Was he trying to bait you?

Admiral Trost: I don't know. I don't know. I know he pissed off my interpreter, and he

---

[*] Fleet Admiral Vladimir Nikolayevich Chernavin was Commander in Chief of the Soviet Navy from 1985 to 1992.

[†] From 1984 to 1988 Marshal of the Soviet Union Sergey F. Akhromeyev was Chief of the General Staff of the Soviet Armed Forces. In 1991, following the disintegration of the Soviet Union he was involved in a failed coup and committed suicide.

[‡] Akhromeyev's relief as Chief of the General Staff was Colonel General Mikhail Moiseev, who was born in 1939.

had his interpreter present also, which was fine. They normally did that.

I told you before about being with Dan Oliver when we saw the Backfire bomber. They were very open showing us this place, and they also had a MiG-28. It was their newest, latest fighter at that time. They claimed it was comparable to the F-14 or the F-18, I've forgotten which. Anyway, they had this young captain who briefed me, spoke fluent English, and kept saying, "I can outfight anything you can put in the air."

I said, "Well, you've survived so far, so I guess you haven't put that to a test." He didn't like that. I have his wings. He took his wings off and gave them to me, which I have in a box in there. A very pleasant guy, though, very professional.

So they showed me that. They showed me their naval installations in the Crimea. They showed me this airbase entirely, including their weapons storage areas. Of course, I didn't learn anything from it, so they probably knew I wouldn't. So it was a very good visit, very congenial visit.

Paul Stillwell: It sounds as a reciprocal of what Admiral Crowe showed the Soviets when they came to the United States.

Admiral Trost: It really was. Now, Crowe had been back in the Soviet Union ahead of me. He was the first visitor in June of the year when I came over in October, and they had showed him a lot of things then, including one of their missile submarines of the Northern Fleet, and I'm not sure I recall what else, but he sort of laid the groundwork.

Paul Stillwell: Probably Leningrad.

Admiral Trost: It might have been Leningrad still. Might have been St. Petersburg, back to St. Petersburg.[*] I'm not sure. I've been there under both names. They took me around the base, which had been off limits to Americans forever, and I think our attaché said that was the first time he'd been to the base. I think he was arrested once when he sneaked aboard a bus in civilian clothes that picked up sailors and took them in. They nabbed him inside and booted him out, literally booted him out. [Laughter]

---

[*] The city's name was changed back to St. Petersburg in 1991, following the collapse of the Soviet Union.

Anyway, that was a good visit, professional from the standpoint of the war college thing. They took me up to Northern Fleet Headquarters, took me aboard the *Kirov*, the first of their nuclear cruisers. They took me through that ship, took me down into their damage control spaces where everything had been erased from the boards, so I didn't really learn anything. At the Northern Fleet the guy went across the cruiser's bridge, pointed across, and on the other side of the area where the naval base is are these high bluffs, and he said, "Of course, as you know, that's where our sub pens are."

I said, "Yes." I didn't know, but we suspected they were there, and he confirmed it. [Laughs] They were bored into the mountainside. So we picked up one bit of intelligence anyway.

But the deputy fleet commander—fleet commander had been called, along with all the other senior guys, to Moscow, and we think it was for a debrief from Chernavin about my visit and our pending meeting the next day, which was the last day. We went from there back down to Moscow. We were hosted by the U.S. Embassy that night. He was the guest of honor, and we had a very pleasant, very congenial evening.

The next morning, we had a breakfast in the Russian guesthouse where we were staying with the people that they assigned to be our aides, our assistants on the trip there, and we had breakfast. We had breakfast. I counted seven different alcoholic beverages on the table. They started with a couple of toasts with vodka, and we had some of everything, and I was being very careful since I still had a formal meeting with my host.

About 10:00 o'clock that morning, we had our session, just he and I and my interpreter, which was interesting. We had a very good session. He was talking about the things he hoped we would show him when he came to the U.S. So we had a very congenial meeting, and departed after what I thought was a very good session, very good week, as a matter of fact.

Pauline enjoyed the visit, except that they assigned the wife of a three-star officer on the staff to be her escort. She'd do things like come up behind Pauline and pull a woolen cap over her head, saying, "It's cold. You should have your head covered." She was bossy as hell, and Pauline doesn't like somebody grabbing her and guiding her somewhere. [Laughs]

So other than that, we had a good visit. The U.S. hosted a formal evening the night before. My last visit with him was very, very congenial. It was like being in the States and having a visit with friends, and he had a great time.

Paul Stillwell: Was the nuclear plant in the submarine pretty much similar in types of equipment to what you'd known in the U.S. ones?

Admiral Trost: Yeah, it's what I would have expected, and, as a matter of fact, it's about what we had surmised it was. So my notes and debrief coincided with what we thought we knew about them. As a matter of fact, that ship deployed to the Mediterranean a week after I was aboard. We sound tracked it in the Norwegian Sea, and it came out just about where we expected, what our guys had expected. So, learned very little except that I thought the submariners were a very professional bunch. They seemed to be pretty much on their toes. The ones I met were sharp. The skipper was a real sharp guy.

The other thing we picked up was that the hull had sound-absorbent coating. Dan Oliver, my EA, had a coughing fit while we were on deck. What I didn't know at the time was he came up with a handful of sound-dampening material from the hull, which he dug out, broke a couple fingernails in the process, but got a sample of the stuff and stuck it in his pocket, basically unseen by the Russians who were standing right next to him.

Paul Stillwell: Was the coughing to cover over what he was doing?

Admiral Trost: Yeah. He coughed and dropped to his knees. [Laughter] I didn't think he was down that long, but he was down long enough to grab and tear out a handful of this stuff, and we had no idea what composition it was or how thick it was until they got that sample.

Paul Stillwell: Were there any revelations from the analysis?

Admiral Trost: Just standard sound-dampening, absorbent material. But it confirmed that.

Paul Stillwell: What was the substance of your discussions with Admiral Chernavin?

Admiral Trost: We talked about operations. Incidents at Sea was the topic of discussion. He understood that they want to know where our submarines were and we weren't going to tell them, and he understood our forward deployment and the philosophy that we're going to be forward deployed in a crisis situation, and they're not going to have a free ride in what they think are their home waters. Understood that perfectly.

Paul Stillwell: Well, Admiral Gorshkov had always claimed that they had a defensive Navy.

Admiral Trost: Yeah, yeah. Well, and they would have be even more defensive than they thought they were going to be when Watkins started publicly briefing our strategy.

Paul Stillwell: Well, that's the essence of deterrence. [Laughs]

Admiral Trost: Yes, that's deterrence. And right now if we had more ships, we could probably enforce that deterrence, but we don't have ships.

[Telephone interruption. The remainder of the interview was not recorded.]

Interview Number 13 with Admiral Carlisle A.H. Trost, U.S. Navy (Retired)

Date: Tuesday, 6 June 2017

Place: Admiral Trost's apartment in Ginger Cove, south of Annapolis, Maryland

Paul Stillwell: Admiral, it's a pleasure to see you again, as always. We're on an auspicious anniversary date. June 6 was the invasion of Normandy in 1944. The purpose today is to fill in some blanks from our previous interviews and make up for the fact that my lack of skill in digital recording let some of our conversations go up in the air unrecorded, so that we can fill in.

Admiral Trost: Okay.

Paul Stillwell: One of the things that you told me that did not get recorded was about Yogi Kaufman and the sit-up contest. So if you could recall that, please.

Admiral Trost: We were on a deployment, and it was time for the annual physical fitness test they were having at the time.

Paul Stillwell: Was this in the *Scorpion*?

Admiral Trost: In *Scorpion*. Yogi was CO. I was exec. So he decided to make life a little more interesting. We were deployed; we were at sea for 70 days underwater. To make life interesting he decided to challenge any combination of two crew members for total scores in sit-ups—what were they? Sit-ups, runs-in-place, I think, but certain different exercises. And if they beat him, they'd get some basket leave. You know what basket leave—

Paul Stillwell: That's where you have a vacation but don't get charged for it.

Admiral Trost: You don't get charged; that's right. So the crew was all up for it. So on the appointed day, I was the scorekeeper and referee. We went up to the forward torpedo room, which has a nonskid metallic plate deck, which is not very easy on the skin if you lie on your bare back and do sit-ups, which was one of the exercises.

So he would take on any combination of two, any team of two members of the crew, and if they beat him, they got this basket leave for I think it was a week, and if he beat them, nothing. So the crew went through, the crew took this on in a big way, and a couple of the guys did really well. So Yogi, as I remember, did pushups and then sit-ups and runs-in-place for the third item, as I recall. He was doing quite well, but when it came to the sit-ups, which were the last thing, he had to do quite a bit to up his score numerically to beat these guys. So he did, and he beat them, but because they'd done so well, he granted them basket leave anyway.

Then we got back into the wardroom and he said, "Step into my stateroom," which was just forward of the wardroom, and he pulled his shirt up and dropped his shorts. His tailbone was bone red, just as red as could be; he had a little bit blood seeping out back there. He said, "We're going to have to fix this up. I don't want anybody to know about this. I've got some bandages in my medicine cabinet. I want you to bandage me up, and don't you dare tell anybody what happened."

So I bandaged him up, and, of course, the guys got their basket leave anyway, but he wouldn't admit to anybody that he'd hurt himself in the process. He was just an absolute physical fitness nut. So the crew was happy, the guys got their basket leave when we got back in, and that was Yogi.

Paul Stillwell: And now after all these years, the secret is out. [Laughs]

Admiral Trost: Well, I haven't told many people about it, but nowadays it's okay. Yogi's dead, so I think he'll forgive me.

Paul Stillwell: Yes, I think so. I have seen a film of him doing pushups with somebody lying on his back.

Admiral Trost: Yeah. I don't know if you ever knew Dick Lumsden.

Paul Stillwell: No.

Admiral Trost: Dick was class of 1952. I knew him well. He was in my company. Dick was also a shipmate, and Lum was a wrestler, stocky build, about 5-feet-10, probably weighed at the time under 200 pounds, but very, very solid citizen physically.[*] We had a pushup competition in the wardroom one afternoon, and Lum lost to Yogi, and Lum said, "I'll bet you can't do pushups with me on your back."

Well, Yogi couldn't pass up a challenge, so he said, "Okay." So he did—I don't remember the number, but some unheard of number of pushups with this big guy on his back. Lum was probably, I'd say, 30 pounds heavier than Yogi at the time.

Paul Stillwell: Yogi was not a big man.

Admiral Trost: No, he was not, but he was a strong man.

Paul Stillwell: Oh, yes. [Laughs]

Admiral Trost: The only time he was physically one-upped was when he was standing inside the wardroom door. You never stand on the inside of a door where somebody might come through. And Jim Patton, who was a young jaygee at the time, charged around.[†] He never went anywhere slowly. Yogi was leaning against the wardroom door, the door burst inward, with Patton behind it as a propelling force. He knocked Yogi off his side into the cabinets that were on the after deck at the bulkhead of the wardroom, and bloodied his nose. [Laughter]

Paul Stillwell: Oh, no.

Admiral Trost: So Patton was persona non grata for a while, told, "Don't come through that door again without knocking," which he didn't. Except that a couple weeks later,

---

[*] Lieutenant Commander Richard E. Lumsden, USN.
[†] Lieutenant (junior grade) James H. Patton Jr., USN.

Patton was the junior officer of the watch, and there is a stairway coming from the bridge, from the control room area, right down into the wardroom. Let's say this was the wardroom here. That was forward, and here was the door coming out from the stairway. Yogi was standing here. The stairway door opened this way. The stairway door exploded and hit Yogi in the face, knocked him backwards. Young Jim Patton came down riding the handrails with his feet up and kicked the door open so it had a lot of momentum.

Paul Stillwell: Oh, no. [Laughs]

Admiral Trost: And it knocked the skipper right back against the back. [Laughs] So it was a big joke to us, but not to him.

Paul Stillwell: Not to Yogi. [Laughs]

Admiral Trost: Not to him.

Paul Stillwell: There were a couple of Jim Pattons who were submariners, and one of them was the technical advisor for *Hunt for Red October*.[*]

Admiral Trost: That would have been our Jim.[†] This Jim was in the class of 1960. He's up in Groton as a retired captain. He's an advisor to a British firm that does research on submarines, among other things. He's a good writer.

Paul Stillwell: He has written for *Proceedings*.

Admiral Trost: Very good. Yeah, he's a good writer and very bright. I think the term Yogi used was "obstreperous."

---

[*] *The Hunt for Red October*, a movie released in 1990, starred Sean Connery as the commanding officer of a Soviet submarine crew that attempted to defect to the West. The film also includes scenes on board a U.S. submarine.
[†] It was indeed the same James Patton who served as advisor to the movie. See Patton's article, "The Making of Hunt for Red October," *U.S. Naval Institute Proceedings*, January 1990.

Paul Stillwell: That would fit. That would also fit Yogi. [Laughter]

Admiral Trost: Oh, yeah, it would. But he loved to challenge the crew on things that were physical in nature. I think once a quarter or once every six months, I forget what we had to do for the fitness test, and we knew that a lot of our fellow submariners said, "The hell with it. They'll never know." But to him it was a challenge, and so we did it.

Paul Stillwell: I would guess he challenged the crew professionally as well.

Admiral Trost: Yeah, he did. They'd team up. When they had a two-on-one on skipper, that was a challenge, especially when there was a good prize at the end of it.

Paul Stillwell: Well, moving along to the mid-'70s, you were the Director of Systems Analysis, OP-96.

Admiral Trost: Right.

Paul Stillwell: That was from 1976 to 1978. Who directed the studies that were to be done by your outfit?

Admiral Trost: Well, the CNO, sometimes the Secretary, sometimes self-generated when we saw something. We had a lot of flexibility. I worked for Jim Holloway during that time frame, and he gave me tremendous leeway. I think my predecessors had it as well. But if I saw something in the programmatic area that I thought needed research, I was authorized to start my own studies and did them in-house. And then Joe Moorer—

Paul Stillwell: He was OP-06.

Admiral Trost: Yeah, he was OP-06 and at the same time. And I think I may have told you before about the incident where he called me in.

Paul Stillwell: You did, yes.

Admiral Trost: Yeah. So except for that kind of challenge and except for John Lehman sometimes who didn't like the outcome of a study, we did pretty well.

Paul Stillwell: Well, that would have been when you were OP-090.

Admiral Trost: That was later, yeah. That was later.

Paul Stillwell: How much personal interaction did you have with Admiral Holloway?

Admiral Trost: Quite a lot. Red Dog Davis was OP-090, my boss, for most of that time, and my instructions were, "When Holloway calls, go directly in and debrief me," and that's the way we worked it. Holloway was a heavy user. For example, I did all the programmatic briefs during my time as 090 rather than my boss, who was a three-star, doing them, so had a lot of leeway and good support.

Paul Stillwell: I remember V/STOL aircraft were among the issues back then.[*] Did you study that?

Admiral Trost: Yeah, we did. We did.

Paul Stillwell: Any other cases you recall?

Admiral Trost: God, Paul, this is 1970-something. [Laughter] Do I recall? Not really. We got into everything, and I had a very bright bunch of guys who were basically handpicked by the detailers. They'd give me their very best talent. If I wanted a lieutenant, that lieutenant was probably, in terms of value added, the equivalent of a commander, because they'd pick their very best guys, smart guys with good imagination.

---

[*] Vertical Take-Off and Landing.

Paul Stillwell: Well, you told me about Greg Johnson, for example.

Admiral Trost: Yeah, Greg was a good example.

Paul Stillwell: How big a staff did you have?

Admiral Trost: I want to say about 40. It was, I'd say, about 40, yeah.

Paul Stillwell: How much computer support did you have in that era?

Admiral Trost: We had fairly good computer support. I was not a real computer-literate guy, so I read the results, not necessarily the blueprint for what to do. I would call one of these young bright lieutenants in and say, "I want to study the following. How do we do it?" And they would tell me how they would do it. I was smart enough to let them do it.

Paul Stillwell: Someone like Jon, who has the technical expertise.[*] [Laughs]

Admiral Trost: Yeah. Well, Jon, you know, if you're smart, when you get senior in any organization, you recognize that you're not smarter than the talent that's working for you, and when you realize that, you get a lot more done.

Paul Stillwell: We've had our parable, our lesson for today. [Laughter]
Please tell me more about your relationship with Admiral Davis in that job.

Admiral Trost: It was a very good relationship. Frankly, I liked the man as a boss. He was the kind of guy who told you what he wanted done, didn't tell you how to do it, and then told the results. Our relationship was one of "If the CNO called, go see him, debrief me later," and that's the way we worked. He gave me very little guidance on what to do. "Do what the CNO wants." That was guidance.

---

[*] Jonathan Hoppe of the Naval Institute staff did the audio recording of this interview.

Paul Stillwell: So he didn't have much in the way of specific tasking for you.

Admiral Trost: No, no. And we had a very good working relationship. If I had a problem, I'd go talk to him. He was always available. Red Dog Davis was a very common-sense guy. He used to say, "I ain't the smartest guy in the world," and maybe he wasn't, but I worked for him there and I worked for him as his deputy out in Hawaii. He had more common sense than most human beings I've known and was just damn good.

Paul Stillwell: Do you have any examples of his common sense?

Admiral Trost: Oh, God. That's a tough one. He knew what he knew, he knew what he didn't know, knew his own shortcomings, never tried to tell me how to do something, told me what he wanted. If he didn't like the result, he called me in and told me what he didn't like, either "Go redo that," or, "That's ready to go. Go tell the CNO." A great guy to work for.

Paul Stillwell: That's the best kind of boss.

Admiral Trost: Boy, I tell you, he was great. Out in Hawaii, I was his deputy for nominally about a year and a half, a little under a year and a half, and he called me in when I first got there and said, "Your job is to keep me honest." Well, I thought he was a pretty honest guy to start with. But what he really meant was, "You're the guy who has to tell me if I'm screwing up." And the beauty of working for a guy like that is when you see something, if you're right—and you'd better be right—he accepts it, so it's a very satisfying position to be in.

There was a door between our two offices, between Chester Nimitz's office and mine next door.[*] It was Nimitz's old office and there was a door in between. Every once in a while, the door opened—it never just opened; it exploded outward and it'd be Red

---

[*] Admiral Chester W. Nimitz, USN, Commander in Chief Pacific Fleet and Pacific Ocean Areas, 1941-45. In December 1944 he was promoted to fleet admiral, a five-star rank. From 1945 to 1947 he was Chief of Naval Operations, and from 1949 to 1953 worked with the United Nations.

Dog with something. And sometimes he was pushing somebody to say, "You go talk to the deputy and see what he says," when he didn't want to deal with something.

So he was an enjoyable guy to work for. Then I went out to Seventh Fleet and he was still my boss. There was only one time we ever got across the breakers. I believed in doing what my people had to do, so I got a ride in every airplane that was flying off a carrier, except the F-14. For the F-14, you had to go through a hyperbaric chamber test at the Air Force base in Okinawa, and so I said, "Okay, I want to fly in an F-14." My aide, who was an aviator, made arrangements for me to go to Okinawa, or we stopped in Okinawa, whatever it was, anyway, to take this test.

About two days before I was due to take the test, I got a call from my boss. The words were something to the effect of, "What the fuck do you think you're doing?"

I said, "What do you mean?"

"What's this Okinawa shit?"

"I'm going down to take the hyperbaric chamber test so I can fly in an F-14."

"Look, goddamn, Seventh Fleets are a dime a dozen. Let somebody else fly in the goddamn airplanes. It's not your business." [Stillwell laughs.] So my flight got cancelled. I never did fly in the F-14, but I flew in every other airplane off the carrier.

He was a great guy to work for, just tremendous. He was a guy who even when he was in Hawaii and I was Seventh Fleet, I was the senior guy west of Hawaii, basically, in a Navy uniform. He called, kept me cut in, got my opinion whenever he felt he needed it, and a very satisfying guy to work for. So it was a good tour.

Jim Watkins relieved Red Dog, and Jim was a more hands-on guy in that he didn't want anything to happen that he didn't know about, so we had a lot more conversations than I had with Red Dog. But Red Dog was an interesting guy to work with.

Paul Stillwell: It sounds like a great relationship of mutual respect.

Admiral Trost: It was a great relationship, and he was a practical guy. Red Dog was a very common-sense, practical guy. One of his aviators—and I won't mention his name— who I think was jealous of him because he passed him and became more senior, said,

"He's dumb." He was like the fox, dumb like a fox. He was just very, very pragmatic and everything was common sense.

Paul Stillwell: People said that about Junior McCain also.

Admiral Trost: Yeah. And what I liked, both those guys, when they asked you an opinion, they didn't ask lieutenant or commander or captain; they asked *you* for your opinion no matter who you were. McCain shook up my boss when I was on the West Coast as a submarine group commander, and that was Frank McMullen, who was SubPac at the time.* I was having lunch in the outdoor BOQ in Hawaii, whatever it's called, not the mess, but it's like an outdoor café. I was sitting there with McMullen, and I don't remember who else, but McMullen was the one who counted because he was my boss. I was visiting from the West Coast, and I heard a car pull up behind me, and the driver came over and tapped me on the shoulder and said, "Please join Admiral McCain, who's in the car" and had been driving around, wanted to talk to me about something. I don't remember what it was, had nothing to do with Submarine Force. Because I suddenly got pulled out of the foursome having lunch and disappeared in a car. When I got back to my visiting flag office, there was a message: "See the admiral." [Laughter] It was probably totally innocuous. It wasn't anything he could chew me out about, but he was pissed off that his boss snapped up his JO, his junior flag officer, without even an acknowledgement. [Laughs] But McCain was a great guy to work with, I thought.

Paul Stillwell: Also very pragmatic.

Admiral Trost: Oh, yeah, very, very.

Paul Stillwell: Well, getting back to OP-96, you described the toxic atmosphere that existed in the '60s with the Whiz Kids. What was your relationship like with OSD in the '70s?

---

* Admiral John S. McCain Jr., USN, served as Commander in Chief Pacific from 31 July 1968 to 1 September 1972. His oral history is in the Naval Institute collection. Rear Admiral Frank D. McMullen, USN, served as Commander Submarine Force Pacific Fleet from 1972 to 1975.

Admiral Trost: With David Chu in the early '80s, it was every bit as bad as it ever had been. He was the Systems Analysis Division guy who, interestingly enough, before he got hired he was sent to me for six months to find out what Systems Analysis Division did, and then he came down. Of course, David has an ego bigger than the Empire State Building, and when he came there, he listened and didn't say very much, but you'd have thought he was an expert in everything, and when he became the Assistant Secretary, he was really brilliant.

I can recall, along with Lee Baggett, who was one of the senior three-stars on OpNav staff. Lee and I were invited to see David Chu after he's taken over and been in the job for a couple months, and he's got a document that we had submitted for something. He said, "I reject this." He points to a bookshelf about like that one; it was full of things. "When you guys have completed as many studies as I have on that shelf, I'll read your paper." And I thought, "You arrogant son of a bitch."

Paul Stillwell: You said that to him?

Admiral Trost: No, I didn't say it.

Paul Stillwell: You thought it.

Admiral Trost: I thought it, and I wanted to say that to him.

Paul Stillwell: [Laughs] Yeah, I'll bet.

Admiral Trost: He and I had a very bad relationship. We got into arguments. I was the senior Navy rep for all the budgetary and programmatic meetings hosted by SecDef and normally chaired by SecDef, and so I was the Navy spokesman. David and I did not get along at those meetings because he'd say something. I can remember one time saying, "David, that's pure bullshit and you know it."

The Secretary of Defense turned to me and said, "Tell me your version." [Stillwell laughs.] Boy, that really pissed him off.

Paul Stillwell: This was Weinberger?

Admiral Trost: This was Weinberger. Weinberger and I had a very good relationship because I was the Navy spokesman. Both the CNO and the Secretary said, "If Weinberger calls, you go see him and debrief us," and that's what I did. And if it was programmatic or budgetary, Weinberger called me up to brief him, which was good because I knew more about it than my bosses did anyway. So we had a very good working relationship, and I think David was always sort of annoyed by that. David and I never got along, just never got along.

Paul Stillwell: Well, that condescension is really strange in that you had always bright people working for you and all the operational experience, which he didn't have.

Admiral Trost: And he did a part-time six-month internship with us before he ever got the job, and he did not have a background, didn't have a legal background, did not have a systems analysis background when he took the job. But he was expert in everything.

Paul Stillwell: So he thought. [Laughter]

Admiral Trost: Yeah.

Paul Stillwell: What relationship did you have with the Center for Naval Analyses when you were in that job?

Admiral Trost: A very close one. They worked for us at the time, and I basically did the tasking. My organization did the tasking for them. I spent about probably a day every other week with them, being debriefed on studies or study progress that they were working on, things that we had tasked that they were doing. A very close relationship.

Paul Stillwell: Did you find them to be a useful adjunct to your work?

Admiral Trost: Very, yeah, very at that time.

Paul Stillwell: What kinds of things would they work on?

Admiral Trost: Well, they did independent studies on programmatic issues. If we had something that was controversial, they were generally the guys who did the academic research to provide the material for the briefings that we gave the CNO and Secretary. So it was a very close relationship with my organization. I wasn't the only guy there. We had a very close relationship, so it was not unusual to see guys from CNA or in my work area meeting with my guys or sitting and working on a project with my guys, or vice versa. Our guys went over there to provide briefings and participate in studies. So it was a very close relationship at that time, I think perhaps closer at that time than it has been since. I don't know what it's like now.

Paul Stillwell: Was there a lot of mathematical modeling involved in these studies?

Admiral Trost: A lot of mathematical modeling, yes, but only as an adjunct to just common-sense studies, doing the research, coming up with conclusions on a topic that was controversial.

Paul Stillwell: Well, I've heard that OP-96 was established really to deal with OSD and the PPBS so that you could speak the same language to answer their questions.[*]

Admiral Trost: That's right. And really I think in the early days when Zumwalt was there, for example, it was to get a leg up on the guys in OSD who really weren't that coordinated until Chu came in to head that up, and then, of course, it became a power center in OSD, answerable, I would say, to no one, but obviously the Secretary.

---

[*] OSD – Office of the Secretary of Defense. PPBS – Planning, Programming and Budgeting System, which was started in January 1961 by Secretary of Defense Robert S. McNamara. For details, see Gordon G. Riggle, "Looking to the Long Run," *U.S. Naval Institute Proceedings*, September 1980, pages 60-65.

Paul Stillwell: Do you think that the planning, programming, and budgeting system was a useful tool to add discipline and rigor to the budgeting process?

Admiral Trost: Absolutely, absolutely. And we went a step further. The CNO Special Studies Group was a spinoff standalone reporting directly to the CNO.

Paul Stillwell: Is that OP-00K?

Admiral Trost: 00K, yeah. And Zumwalt actually started that, and the idea was to have a totally independent organization answerable only to the CNO that would study specific areas and provide input without influence from the OpNav three-stars, for example, because it was headed up by a Navy captain, and the staffers, a small group—a couple of lieutenant commanders, a couple of commanders, headed by a captain.

Paul Stillwell: Chuck Larson had that job for a while.[*]

Admiral Trost: He did have, yes. And when I became CNO, I was familiar with the organization and I used him. My first posture statement, for example, was a collage of inputs from all the different OPs. I called it the lowest common denominator paper I'd ever read. So I pulled all the inputs from the OpNav guys, gave them to 00K, and said, "Here is a one-page of topics I want to cover in my posture statement. Write me a posture statement." They did. I did it over the objection of my senior three-stars, who said, "You don't have our input." I said, "Your input was given to the people who wrote this stuff, and I've got your input, just not your words." So I used them very heavily that way. I think the CNO needs an input that is totally nonparochial in its content, and that's the way to get it. I don't know what the current setup is, but I think it's still working.

Interestingly, I had Jay Donnelly, a young submarine officer who eventually became a three-star and ComSubLant before he retired.[†] I think they're still in the area. I know he gets his hair cut by the same woman who cuts mine. [Laughter] He was a

[*] Rear Admiral Charles R. Larson, USN.
[†] Vice Admiral John Jay Donnelly, USN, was Commander Submarine Force Atlantic Fleet, 2007-2010

lieutenant commander when he reported to that 00K organization, made commander while I was there, and retired as a three-star. But he was an example of a young guy who thought very clearly, wrote very well, and just kept going.

Paul Stillwell: My sense was that 00K also had a long-range planning function.

Admiral Trost: They did. They did. They had whatever CNO tasked them to do, and we got very bright young guys, not necessarily guys with programmatic backgrounds, just good naval officers who were good writers, good thinkers, most importantly, and they did a great job.

Ann Rondeau, the woman who was later the head of the National Defense University as a three-star, was a commander in that 00K organization when I was CNO, one of the best writers I think I've ever encountered, very, very good.[*] I got a kick out of her. She had a cousin who was an Air Force colonel on the air staff. They used to have dinner together once a week. Neither one was married, apparently. She came in one morning—I had one rep from that outfit sit in on my early morning conference every morning, and she was the duty OOK rep this one morning. She said, "I have to tell you what happened last night." She'd had dinner with her Air Force cousin, and she said, "He got chewed out yesterday by Larry Welch," who was the Air Force Chief of Staff. "He said, 'You goddamn guys are being paid to make sure I'm smarter than anybody else in the room, and the Navy is eating our lunch. Find out what the hell is going on.'" [Laughter]

Paul Stillwell: You told me you had a competition with him throughout your time as CNO.

Admiral Trost: I may have told you this before too.

Paul Stillwell: I had not heard that particular story.

_____

[*] Vice Admiral Ann E. Rondeau, USN, served as president of the National Defense University from July 2009 to April 2012.

Admiral Trost: Larry Welch didn't like my organization. He didn't like the Navy.

Paul Stillwell: And Admiral Yost liked the Navy only as a source of handouts. [Laughter]

Admiral Trost: That's right. Somebody he could steal from.

Paul Stillwell: Well, moving on from there to the Deputy CinCPacFlt job, I'm going to guess that Admiral Davis asked for you for that spot.

Admiral Trost: I assume so. I assume so.

Paul Stillwell: What was the division of labor between the two of you when you were in Hawaii?

Admiral Trost: Well, he was the big policy guy and the boss. I did the admin work for PacFlt. I shouldn't say I did it; I was responsible and I signed off a lot more documents than he did. He signed the policy things, I signed programmatics, routine day-to-day business. I met with the type commanders, but he did too, had a meeting with me before they went to see him, to see what was hot.

I had an EA who was a junior captain at the time, who was just really a jewel on putting his finger on what was important and what wasn't. So we got all the routine day-to-day stuff, and I met with the assistant chiefs of staff on day-to-day business and left the boss alone. I cut him in on what we were doing and what I did, so it was a good relationship. It was very enjoyable from my perspective, because I was sort of the boss, I could think independently, I could take action on things. It was a satisfying way to do business. And he kept his finger on all the policy issues, gave general guidance, so it worked out well.

Paul Stillwell: It sounds like you were essentially the executive officer and chief of staff.

Admiral Trost: Basically, yeah, basically.

Paul Stillwell: What were some of the policy issues he was confronting?

Admiral Trost: Oh, God.

Paul Stillwell: Well, Korea is always an issue.

Admiral Trost: Korea was always an issue. God, I don't know. We were the operational command for everything into the Persian Gulf, all the way around and in. As I said, as Seventh Fleet I was the senior naval officer from Hawaii to the Persian Gulf, so our relationship with Okinawa and the Okinawan government, I got involved in that. There was always the issue about bases, and our airplanes make too much noise when they take off from the big airbase which is almost downtown Okinawa. And the Marines' presence, which they wanted the money but they didn't want the Marines. Then, of course, Okinawa really wasn't too much—Kadena was Air Force, and they were busy. We had a very good working relationship with them. I spent more time working on the Philippines than I did on anything else out there. Our relationship was good because the local mayor was very pro-U.S. His father had been mayor of Olongapo. The son followed Mom as a mayor of Olongapo.

Paul Stillwell: Dick Gordon.

Admiral Trost: Gordon. Dick Gordon. Dick was a tremendous guy to work with. And Dick was the reason that relations with the Philippines were good, even with Marcos, who was a piece of work.

Paul Stillwell: That's an understatement. [Laughs]

Well, back to Okinawa. The reversion to Japan had already taken place at that point. I remember when I was there in the late 1960s, the American greenbacks were the legal tender and cars drove on the right side of the road.

Admiral Trost: When I went there, I flew into the airbase, which was downtown and the source of a lot of their gripes. I would go to Navy headquarters, which were down there. I spent more time with the Marines who were over on the east coast and played golf on the Marine course, tried to play golf. I never really played it, but I tried a lot, though. I spent more time with the Marines than anything else there. The Marines, of course, had the—was it Iwakuni in Japan?

Paul Stillwell: Yes.

Admiral Trost: Iwakuni. Their air headquarters were in Iwakuni. I did not much spend much time in Iwakuni. I went down about every three months or so, spent a day, flew through Okinawa quite often, quite a lot. Usually we flew in a—I don't remember the name of the airplane now, twin-engine turboprop, which refueled on Okinawa, Japan to Okinawa to the Philippines, but a one-stop hop down. So we got into Okinawa sometimes only just for gas, a couple hours, and on down.

I had a good relationship with the three-star Air Force guy in Okinawa, who really was the senior military guy there. And the Marines—the Marines actually worked for me under my opcon, and so the Marines there and the Marines in Korea, I had about 33,000 Marines working for me, so which I think was a bone of contention with Marine headquarters. They didn't like all their Marines under somebody else's opcon, but that's the way it was.

Paul Stillwell: And you had FMFPac there in Hawaii to work with.[*]

Admiral Trost: Yeah.

Paul Stillwell: During the Vietnam War, for political reasons, our ship could not go directly from Japan to Vietnam, so we always had to stop in Okinawa, create some kind of fiction that Japan was not supporting the Vietnam War. [Laughs]

---

[*] FMFPac – Fleet Marine Force Pacific Fleet.

Admiral Trost: Yeah. Well, our relationship with Okinawa was good, very good at the time, although we were getting things like one drunk Marine is the equivalent of about a platoon of Marines here in Annapolis if they do one thing wrong, and I'd hear about it right away.

Paul Stillwell: Well, I remember Admiral Macke lost his job as CinCPac because of an incident in Okinawa.[*]

Admiral Trost: Yeah. It was never an easy relationship while I was out there. But they were—how shall I say it? They were really pushing for their independence from Japan, and the way to start is to get rid of the Americans.

Paul Stillwell: What was a typical day for you as Deputy CinCPacFlt?

Admiral Trost: Well, mostly administrative stuff. The day would start with morning intel brief and operations brief, that was generally good from about 7:15 to 8:15, 8:30, and then the lineup of the assistant chiefs of staff came in and we had our morning session. Then paperwork, receiving calls from visiting flag officers. Basically that's it. And I tried to get down to the waterfront about three times a week and visit all the visiting ships and homeported guys as well, and went down to talk to the senior guys down there, fleet commander, base commander. Kept pretty busy.

Paul Stillwell: What do you recall about the impact of the Iran Hostage Crisis in 1979?[†]

Admiral Trost: Well, it was an interesting one.

---

[*] In November 1995, while serving as CinCPac, Admiral Richard C. Macke, USN, made insensitive comments to reporters about the case of U.S. sailors and a Marine accused of raping a 12-year-old Okinawan girl. He said that a prostitute would have been less expensive than the rental van used in the attack. The comment produced an outcry in Japan, and Macke was removed from his post shortly afterward. He retired from the Navy 1 April 1996 as a two-star admiral.

[†] When the Shah left Iran in January 1979, the Ayatollah Ruhollah Khomeini seized power and declared the nation to be an Islamic republic. On 4 November 1979 Iranian militants seized the U.S. embassy in Teheran and took the staff members there as hostages. The hostages were ultimately released on 20 January 1981.

I was on the fringes. I was told, "There will be a time when you lose communications." And when I lost communications, that's a real hot-shit item. They said, "You won't have any radio communications. Don't ask any questions."

Then one day a guy in civilian clothes came out to brief me. I didn't know who he was or what he was. He was a JCS rep. I never to this day knew whether he was civilian or an Air Force officer in civilian clothes. He briefed me on the fact that on a certain time out there—this is a hostage rescue attempt—"You will lose Seventh Fleet communications." Now, that's a battle stations-type thing if you lose comm. He said, "You won't be able to talk to anybody. You won't be able to talk to any of your subordinate commands. You won't be able to reach Hawaii by phone, and that's as much as we're going to tell you right now."

Then Red Dog called me because Bob Kirksey was a two-star, my senior forward-based aviator.

Paul Stillwell: He was CTF-77.

Admiral Trost: That's right. Kirksey now was out riding a carrier in the Indian Ocean as routine, but he was on board the carrier.

Paul Stillwell: I think *Nimitz* was the one that launched the helicopters.

Admiral Trost: If it was *Nimitz*, that's what it was. Anyway, Kirksey was briefed on what was going to happen, I was not, and that's sort of where we were.

When the whole thing happened, I found out about just about everything after the fact. I got a phone call—I don't remember who from; somebody in Washington to tell me that the landings had taken place, the helicopters were on the ground. I got another phone call saying, "We have a problem out there." And then I got another call saying, "Thank God the carrier moved in and saved all those guys in helos," because apparently Bob Kirksey, when he heard of the problem, went balls-for-the-wall for the coast, and had he not done that, we'd have lost helicopters full of people. So he saved the day. But then I got debriefs after the fact, got my comms back after it's all over, and that was sort of my involvement. I was a real bystander.

Paul Stillwell: Well, one of the criticisms of that Desert One operation was that it was too highly compartmented and you didn't get inputs from people who could have made useful contributions.

Admiral Trost: And we might have had a better backup plan in case something went wrong. There was no backup plan.

Paul Stillwell: That's right.

Admiral Trost: I was told this story by a Marine captain who I happened to know. His Marines walked aboard the helicopter, having never been aboard that type of helo before, and part of the problem with that helicopter that burned up had duffel bags and equipment bags being stacked behind the cockpit on heaters, on heater panels that were— I don't know what the layout is, but that's what started the fire and that was the problem. These guys had never been briefed. They hadn't been in that kind of helo before. They were just loaded aboard and hauled in. So it was too tightly compartmented. Not enough people of the right nature knew about it. Kirksey's staff, I don't think any of them, if maybe one or two guys, were briefed, but this was so closely held. And this was an administration directive, "Nobody is to know about this."

Paul Stillwell: President Carter.

Admiral Trost: Yeah. So we're lucky we didn't lose a whole bunch of people, a whole bunch of people.

Paul Stillwell: Well, that had become a personal obsession with him.

Admiral Trost: Yeah.

Paul Stillwell: And ultimately the Iranians got great theater in releasing the hostages the day that Carter left office.

Admiral Trost: Oh, yeah.

Paul Stillwell: Well, the other great impact from that was the buildup of deployments to the North Arabian Sea. What was the impact at your level on trying to provide those resources?

Admiral Trost: Well, I drew on the Mediterranean. Middle East Force. Middle East Force chopped to me on a classified secret chop, and I don't remember when that took place. It was while I was Seventh Fleet. So the buildup required assets. We had at one point in time five carriers out there in that time frame, and they deployed from the East Coast for five or six months without a liberty port. I remember the fight we undertook to get—I don't remember which one of the big guys—into Singapore, because you were going to send them all the way across the Indian Ocean. They'd been at sea five months, and we're going to send them all the way across the Indian Ocean.

My big success with Sri Lanka, Colombo, was getting the President to agree to carrier visits. We hadn't had any there for a long, long time. And I made a trip there, told them very frankly, "I've got a problem. I've got ships out here, they're doing a job. They're not doing you a direct input, but you're benefitting from it, and I'd like to be able to bring a carrier in every six weeks."

"I'll have to think about it." He thought about it. Before I got on my plane to leave, he said, "Okay." So we started getting carrier visits in there, which was half the distance to Singapore, basically.

I went to Mombasa, and actually went into Kenya to Nairobi and met with the Kenyan—what was he, President at the time, I guess? I had indications from our embassy there that he was prone to listen to possibly opening Mombasa to carrier visits. So I went and got an audience with him. He was, as I recall, a retired Army general, I think. Anyway, he listened, said, "You make a good case. Let me look into it. When are you leaving?"

I said, "Tomorrow morning."

"You'll have an answer."

The next morning before I left, I had an answer, "Yeah, start sending ships into Mombasa. Send one every five weeks, every six weeks." One carrier a quarter could make a port stop for five days. So we got in, we got some break, but, boy, those kids were going out there, they were deploying from Norfolk for five and a half and six months without a port visit.

Paul Stillwell: Well, just feeding that many people is a challenge.

Admiral Trost: Yeah, it was.

Paul Stillwell: You're talking, what, 5,000 people a carrier?

Admiral Trost: Yeah.

Paul Stillwell: That's 25,000 plus support ships.

Admiral Trost: Yep. We had a good logistics effort going. We had a very productive one, fortunately.

Paul Stillwell: And Diego Garcia was a real key.

Admiral Trost: Oh, God, was it ever. Diego Garcia, without it we couldn't have done anything we did out there. Well, we couldn't have done most things we did out there. And the people in Oman were extremely helpful. There's an airbase north of the capital, it's their principal airbase, and we started out out there with one overnight a week. I got that to five overnights a week for P-3s. That let us fly up into the Gulf, remain overnight, and come back out rather than having to turn around and go back to Diego Garcia.

And then we got the—I think I mentioned to you before, we got the access to Pakistan, thanks to the Pakistani CNO who had been a friend of mine from Seventh Fleet days and stayed a friend afterwards. On one of my visits, he arranged with his Air Force counterpart for my P-3s to drop in without advanced notice to an airbase that was north of the main seaport on the west coast. The head of the Air Force said, "Have your P-3s declare a fuel emergency and land. We won't shoot them." And they did. And so the P-3s then would leave Diego Garcia, fly their mission, declare fuel emergency, land in Pakistan, spend the night, refuel, fly the return mission, and we did that once a week, so it really improved our coverage considerably. So it was an interesting time, a challenging time.

Paul Stillwell: As Seventh Fleet, how much did you work on keeping war plans updated, or were you too occupied with current ops?

Admiral Trost: We worked on war plans. As a matter of fact, the war plan review was part of every quarterly CinCs' conference out there. So did we do a lot? We didn't have to do a lot. We kind of looked, made sure everybody was briefed on what they were supposed to do, had about a two- or three-hour session, had our quarterly meetings, and that was it.

Paul Stillwell: I remember talking to Admiral Steele, who was one of your predecessors.[*] He said that when he took over, it was just as Vietnam was ending, and all the action was geared toward Vietnam, and he had to focus it now on the Soviet Union.

Admiral Trost: Yeah.

Paul Stillwell: Anything else to mention about Seventh Fleet?

Admiral Trost: I'd say one thing, it's a great job. It was a tremendous job. The relationships with the Japanese were really based on personal contact. They were very good when I was out there. The relationships with the Koreans, again, personal contact,

---

[*] Vice Admiral George P. Steele, USN, served as Commander Seventh Fleet from 28 July 1973 to 14 June 1975. His oral history is in the Naval Institute collection.

but the Korean Navy chopped to Seventh Fleet under the U.N. contingency plans. I think I told you I had an office in the Korean Navy Headquarters and went there. I went to Korea once a month, usually to Seoul, every about four months to their Korean headquarters, which was south on the coast. My memory of names now is slipping. The Korean headquarters are on the southeast coast.

Paul Stillwell: You mentioned Chinhae.

Admiral Trost: It's Chinhae. And that kept the relationship with the operational people, the fleet commander. The Korean CNO and I met about every month or six weeks in Korea, and the Chairman, Joint Chiefs was an Army general who later became the Korean Ambassador in Washington and was in that job when I came back to Washington. I've forgotten his name. I've forgotten a lot of names.

Paul Stillwell: Did you ever have to eat kimchi?

Admiral Trost: Once.

Paul Stillwell: And that was that.

Admiral Trost: Once. It was terrible. [Laughter] I thought I was going to choke. I was there on my birthday in April '81. I was visiting a Marine base on the east coast. Unbeknownst to me in planning, they were having a birthday luncheon for me. I ate kimchi without knowing what it was in advance. I almost choked. I thought I'd kill myself. I never tried it again.

Paul Stillwell: Well, moving on to your brief tenure as CinCLantFlt, we talked about the type commanders before, and we did not discuss Admiral McCauley, who was SurfLant.[*] What do you recall of him?

---

[*] Vice Admiral William F. McCauley, USN, served as Commander Naval Surface Force Atlantic Fleet from 1984 to 1987.

Admiral Trost: Very bright, very pigheaded when he disagreed with you, but a damn good naval officer and good friend.

Paul Stillwell: I think he had been commandant at the academy for a while.

Admiral Trost: He had been. He had been. Scott and I got to know each other quite well, very professional, very professional, and a tiger. My problems with LantFlt were with the future Commandant of the Marine Corps, Al Gray, who was FMFLant at the time, and considered himself subservient to no one, certainly not the fleet commander who wore a Navy uniform. [Stillwell laughs.] And that continued throughout our three-year overlap as heads of service.

Paul Stillwell: One of your friends you told me about from earlier days was Jake Laboon, and then a ship was named for him. Did you have any connection with the ship?

Admiral Trost: I had a lot to do with the ship.[*]

Paul Stillwell: Please tell me.

Admiral Trost: Well, I've forgotten who made the recommendation that we name a ship after Jake Laboon. I talked to the Secretary of the Navy, told him what Laboon had done and why he warranted to have a ship named after him, and it happened. I think it was probably Larry Garrett. And we made it happen.

Similarly, we have a new submarine that's going to be named USS *Columbia*.[†] I think it's the lead of this new bunch. And Columbia happens to be my hometown in Illinois, and it happened to be the hometown of—

---

[*] Lieutenant John F. Laboon Jr., CHC, USN, had graduated from the Naval Academy in the class of 1944 and served as a line officer before becoming a chaplain. He died in 1988, while Trost was Chief of Naval Operations. The guided missile destroyer *Laboon* (DDG-58) is named in his honor. The ship was commissioned 18 March 1995. Three of Laboon's sisters served as sponsors.

[†] USS *Columbia* (SSBN-826) will be a nuclear-powered ballistic missile submarine. She is scheduled to begin construction in 2021 and enter service in 2031.

Paul Stillwell: Blackie Weinel?

Admiral Trost: Back in Illinois, yes. But Will Ball was from Columbia, South Carolina, and we got a naming package that came forward via me to him one day, and they were having problems coming up with a name. There was controversy about the name. There was a real peeing contest between two names, as a matter of fact. And Will said, "You're from Columbia, Illinois."

I said, "That's right."

"I'm from Columbia, South Carolina. Why don't we name it *Columbia*? With the two towns together, there are enough people population-wise," to meet whatever the population criteria was. [Laughter] So we named the ship *Columbia*.[*] Now the second one's going to be named *Columbia*. My hometown when I left, it was 1,800 people.

Paul Stillwell: Columbia, South Carolina, is a little larger.[†]

Admiral Trost: A little bit larger, a little bit larger. But I think then we had to have a quarter million people or something like that was the criterion.

Paul Stillwell: So most of them aren't from your hometown. [Laughs]

Admiral Trost: No, no.

Paul Stillwell: I just saw Will Ball three days ago at the Naval Historical Foundation meeting.

Admiral Trost: Did you? How's he doing?

Paul Stillwell: He seemed to be fine.

---

[*] USS *Columbia* (SSN-771) is a nuclear attack submarine named for Columbia, South Carolina, Columbia, Illinois, and Columbia, Missouri. The *Columbia* was sponsored by first lady Hillary Clinton and commissioned 9 October 1995.
[†] The 2017 population of Columbia, South Carolina, is 129,272.

Admiral Trost: We had planned a luncheon. It hadn't taken place because of my hospitalization last year, and I'm not very mobile anymore, so we haven't gotten together in Washington for lunch.

Paul Stillwell: He still looks the same as he did way back when.

Admiral Trost: He was a grand guy to work with, and as you probably know, he lost his job because of his relationship with John Tower, called in to defend Tower when Tower had the problem. But he was a great Secretary of the Navy, very, very people oriented and had common sense.

Paul Stillwell: Well, moving on to your tenure as CNO, I wonder how much input, how much conversation did you have with your predecessors.

Admiral Trost: Well, I worked with Jim Watkins, with him and for him, and my relationship with him, I had the every-six-month retired CNO conference, attended at the time by Tom Moorer, Jim Holloway, Watkins.[*] I think that was all. And they were great, quiet, private advisors, and I looked forward to that every six-month thing, as a matter of fact. And we did a thing socially as well.

Hayward was a regular contributor.[†] He was also at those meetings. So I got good, thoughtful input from those guys without being obtrusive or bossy. They'd been there, they knew what the problems were, and I got some good advice. What we did was meet in the morning, generally. We tried breakfast, and it turned out to be too early for Holloway, so we dropped breakfast and started at 8:00 o'clock and had coffee and doughnuts and went through the morning, had lunch. In the afternoon we used about three hours to update them, give them a very comprehensive intelligence update and get their input on whatever I wanted to get their input on. So we did that every six months

---

[*] Admiral Thomas H. Moorer, USN, was CNO from 1967 to 1970; Admiral James L. Holloway III, USN, was CNO from 1974 to 1978; Admiral James D. Watkins, USN, was CNO from 1982 to 1986.
[†] Admiral Thomas B. Hayward, USN, was CNO from 1978 to 1982.

and it worked out quite well. That has not been the way it's gone since I retired. Kelso very seldom did that.[*]

Paul Stillwell: Well, you said there was some friction between the two of you.

Admiral Trost: Yeah. Well, I think mostly because I became CNO when I did, and Lehman had nominated him, and, of course, he worked for me at one time too. When I was fleet commander, he was the submarine CO and then—well.

Paul Stillwell: And did Admiral Zumwalt take part in those meetings?[†]

Admiral Trost: He did, yeah. He did. Zumwalt was basically pissed, I told you before, I think. Zumwalt, I think, got annoyed with me. He was very helpful to me when I first came to Washington. He was Nitze's EA when I went down to OSD as a brand-new commander, never been to Washington before. Been to the Pentagon one time. And I think when he wanted me to become 00K and I went to work for Warner instead, I pissed him off, and that never stopped. And I told you also when my name showed up on the flag selection list, he told me, "You just proved anybody can make it." I made it.

Paul Stillwell: Well, he had those who were very loyal to him personally, and then there was everybody else.

Admiral Trost: Yeah. Well, and this comment came within a couple of months of my having put the kibosh on his bypassing the Secretary to SecDef by hand-carrying things down to OSD and having them put on the desk of the Secretary of Defense, things that were policy issues that Warner hadn't any idea of. So I was in the shits for that.

Paul Stillwell: And you made CNO anyway.

---

[*] Admiral Frank B. Kelso II, USN, was CNO from 1990 to 1994.
[†] Admiral Elmo R. Zumwalt Jr., USN, was CNO from 1970 to 1974.

Admiral Trost: Made CNO anyway. Made flag.

Paul Stillwell: That's right. [Laughter]

Admiral Trost: Right after that, as a matter of fact. [Laughter]

Paul Stillwell: What value did you get from the system of the three-star warfare barons?

Admiral Trost: Let's say that three-star warfare barons and OP-090, for example, were organizationally at odds because you got the guy who's the keeper of the keys to the budget and the programmatic basis, who's sitting in judgment of guys who, by and large, in my case were senior to me, older to me and senior to me. And so they would try to bypass me and always get the papers returned to them.

My most cantankerous guy, frankly, throughout my time in Systems Analysis, OP-096, was Joe Moorer, who really was very much so. Ed Waller was OP-95, and he and I got along extremely well.* Lee Baggett, when he was in that job, and I got along extremely well. So Moorer was really the guy I had problems with. And Jim Doyle, when he was OP-03 and I was OP-96, did not get along.† As he said one day, he didn't like a junior flag looking over his papers. But his papers would be sent to me for comment before the 090 would take action, so he had no option but to like it. If you're doing your job, you're going at times be at odds with the people that submitted things.

Paul Stillwell: Well, I was thinking also of your time as CNO. What was their value to you?

Admiral Trost: Good advisors. I told you the story about Tom Paulsen. I'm trying to remember what that was about. There was the time one of the three-stars came to see Paulsen, who was my EA at the time, and said, "I heard that CNO said umpty-ump about this. I want to go in and challenge him."

---

* Vice Admiral Edward C. Waller, USN.
† Vice Admiral James H. Doyle Jr., USN, served as Deputy Chief of Naval Operations (Surface Warfare) from August 1975 to September 1980.

Tom said, "Well, go ahead, but, yes, he did say that. I heard him say that." The guy never came to see me. [Laughter] But it was something he didn't like on his program. So being CNO, being OP-090 are not jobs that you win friends and influence—you influence people, but you don't win friends.

Paul Stillwell: And each one of those barons wanted the biggest piece of the pie.

Admiral Trost: Oh, yeah, oh, yeah, and didn't like to be second-guessed, and the 090 organization is the second-guesser for the CNO, so not much you can do about that.

Paul Stillwell: Who was 090 for you?

Admiral Trost: Bill Smith was one.*

Paul Stillwell: Okay. Bright person.

Admiral Trost: Very. And Dan Cooper was another.† Two very bright persons. Caught a little flak because both were submariners and I was a submariner, but both had been OP-90, which was a programmatic job under the 090 organization. Both, before they were 090, had all the basic work that they could have had in preparation. It's almost like they were trained for the job. So they were logical choices for me, and that's such a key job. You know what I mean? First of all, you need the relationship with the CNO and the Secretary, although with Lehman that was difficult. That's one of the reasons he didn't want me as CNO, which is fine.

Paul Stillwell: Well, moving to an entirely different subject, what do you remember about the retirement of John D. Bulkeley, who was an institution by that point?‡

---

* Vice Admiral William D. Smith, USN.
† Vice Admiral Daniel L. Cooper, USN.
‡ Rear Admiral John D. Bulkeley, USN, began serving as president of the Board of Inspection and Survey in 1967, continued after his age-mandated retirement in 1974, and remained until he finally left active duty in 1988 and was promoted to vice admiral.

Admiral Trost: Well, John wasn't ready to retire.

Paul Stillwell: He never was. [Laughs]

Admiral Trost: And told me so. "There must be something I can be useful for." He lived right down the street from me in the Navy Yard. I saw him quite often, both socially and he'd come over and call on me quite often. I love the guy. He's a font of wisdom and common sense. And he didn't want to retire, but he didn't fight it. As a matter of fact, those were his words, "I don't want to retire, but I'm not going to fight it." He said, "You could fire me."

I said, "I know I can," but that would have been a sin, I think.

Paul Stillwell: He'd been on active duty for more than 50 years.

Admiral Trost: Oh, yeah, he'd been on active duty forever, and he still had a lot of common sense, a lot of pragmatism. People were worried about him saying, "Health and age are one thing. You know, the guy's getting old, and does he still have the smarts and the common sense?" Well, his advice was still good, so I thought he did, but it was time for him to retire, and basically we didn't have another job for him. Had he been younger, he could have been promotable, but he wasn't.[*]

[Telephone interruption]

Admiral Trost: That's Steve, Naval Academy class of '85, nuclear submariner, surprise Naval Academy applicant to us. I may have told you we were in Japan, he'd graduated from high school, aboard *Midway*. He rode *Blue Ridge*, my flagship, down to Hong Kong and back. We were sitting on a Thursday evening or a Wednesday evening in our quarters in Yokosuka having dinner. "Well, Mom, that was good. I'll be leaving in the morning,

---

[*] Midshipman John D. Bulkeley, USN, born in 1912, graduated from the Naval Academy in 1933 but was not commissioned until a year later. He received the Medal of Honor for his service in command of PT boats in the Philippines early in World War II.

so I don't know what you're going to have tomorrow." That's when we found out that he applied for the Naval Academy, been turned down, but offered NAPS.[*] [Stillwell laughs.]

This is my number three of four. He's class of '85 Naval Academy. He was, I would say, a wild-ass teenager. [Laughter] He was a character. He left active duty after eight years, was a nuclear submariner, is a retired reserve commander, was a very active reservist and keeps close tabs on me.

Sorry.

Paul Stillwell: No, that's interesting. You sweetened the pot for Admiral Bulkeley by giving him a third star.

Admiral Trost: Oh, yeah. But not a job with it.

Paul Stillwell: No.

Admiral Trost: And getting that through the system and through Congress was easy.

Paul Stillwell: After all he had done.

Admiral Trost: After all he'd done. Just a remarkable guy.

Paul Stillwell: Well, now, another personnel assignment—and this is the other end of the age spectrum—was giving Paul David Miller the Seventh Fleet when he was pretty junior.[†]

Admiral Trost: He was very junior, and he became Seventh Fleet over my strenuous objection. He didn't have the experience for the job. I thought it was pushing him because he was Lehman's buddy, and I thought he needed another sea assignment before he was even considered for that. I was overridden.

---

[*] NAPS – Naval Academy Preparatory School.
[†] Vice Admiral Paul David Miller, USN, served as Commander Seventh Fleet from 9 December 1986 to 21 October 1988. He was born 1 December 1941 and thus 45 years old when he took command.

Paul Stillwell: How did he do as Seventh Fleet?

Admiral Trost: Well, I don't recall any problems. Paul's a very bright guy, and I just thought we were pushing him too fast and pushing him out at the top too fast. Now, when he was in Norfolk as a four-star, he was controversial.[*] He had a tendency to act without talking to either his senior subordinates or cutting anybody else in on what he'd do. He just did it, which is okay, but that ain't the way to do business. You miss a lot of input.

Paul Stillwell: Well, he told me he had an interview with Secretary Weinberger for the job, and Weinberger also brought up his youth, and he said his answer was, "Well, I'm getting older as fast as I can, sir." [Laughs]

Admiral Trost: Paul was very, very bright, no question of it.

Paul Stillwell: Lots of enthusiasm.

Admiral Trost: Yeah, very much so.

Paul Stillwell: What do you recall about the involvement in the Panama thing with Noriega, who just died here recently?[†]

Admiral Trost: Oh, quite a lot, and I notice he's certainly a hero, it says in the newspapers. Wasn't a hero to me. When we decided to go in—well, first of all, he—I don't remember the background. He had a sort of disagreement with George Bush. I don't remember what the occasion was or what the thing was, but he did something that

---

[*] Admiral Paul D. Miller, USN, served as Supreme Allied Commander Atlantic and Commander in Chief Atlantic Command from 13 July 1992 to 31 October 1994.

[†] Manuel Noriega was de facto ruler of Panama in the early 1980s and in August 1983 promoted himself to general. Relations between the United States and Panama deteriorated in the late 1989. Following harassment of U.S. service personnel in Panama, on 23 December 1989, the United States invaded Panama. Noriega surrendered to U.S. forces on 3 January 1990. He was subsequently convicted in U.S. federal court and imprisoned. He died 19 May 2017.

caused us to want to get rid of him, and I've forgotten what it was, even though I was there.

I got a call on a Sunday from Colin Powell saying, "We're going to take Noriega out, and all the services should be represented. You've got a carrier heading for the Mediterranean. Do you want to turn it around and send it to Panama as your contribution?"

I said, "Shit. What contribution?"

"Well, we might need airplanes."

Well, we had a base somewhere north of Panama City. "We've got Air Force airplanes there now."

"Well, I just thought you'd want a Navy part in it."

So I declined, and the Chiefs voted to tell the President, "Let's go in." I've forgotten what the occasion was or what the circumstances were where we went in and did very well.

I don't think much of Noriega as a human being, and when I read something the other day that sort of glorified him, I thought, "Jeez, wrong guy." But I just remember a weekend conference with the Chiefs on to the President about getting rid of Noriega.

Paul Stillwell: Well, it sounds like sending the carrier there was kind of an artificial deal to make it seem more joint than need be.

Admiral Trost: Oh, it was. It was. Very definitely an artificial deal in terms of jointness. Everybody would get a piece of the action.

Paul Stillwell: Did you have an opinion on the reversion of Panama, the Canal Zone part, to the Panamanians?

Admiral Trost: I did, but I didn't have a voice.

Paul Stillwell: I assume you wanted to keep it.

Admiral Trost: I wanted to keep it. I wanted to keep operational control of it because Noriega was such a shifty son of a gun that I never knew what he had in mind.

Paul Stillwell: Well, and Torrijos before him.

Admiral Trost: Yeah. So I thought the canal itself is so vital to our interests, and we were talking at the time about the widening project, which made sense to me. What was it? The carriers had eight inches on either side or something like that going through the locks.

Paul Stillwell: That was the *Essex* class.* The current ones could not.

Admiral Trost: That was the old ones. The current ones had to go around, yeah. I went through the canal one time. It was in *Swordfish* going from the East Coast to Hawaii for homeport.

Paul Stillwell: Oh, right, when the dependents were left stranded.

Admiral Trost: That's right. That's right. And Joe Fuller and I alternated as ODs going through, approaching and going through the canal, and, of course, for a submariner, the *Skate* class was small anyway, and we had plenty of room going through, although you really had to be on your toes because you were dependent on some Panamanian line handlers on the docks. And our guys knew what they were doing. They were neophytes, I thought, but I was told that because we were such a small ship, we took up so little of the canal, so the span of lines was so big, they had trouble with them. But Joe and I steered for the center channel and went through. But my total exposure to Panama was two days on the Panama City side after we got through the canal, and then I visited twice when I

---

* USS *Essex* (CV-9), lead ship of her class, was commissioned 31 December 1942. She had a standard displacement of 27,100 tons, was 872 feet long, 93 feet in the beam, an extreme width of 148 feet on the flight deck, and had a draft of 29 feet. All told, 16 ships of the class were in combat in World War II.

was CNO. I was not for reversion.[*]

Paul Stillwell: Another personnel issue, what do you remember about the relief and retirement of Admiral Lyons as CinCPacFlt?[†]

Admiral Trost: I remember it well. I was on a three-day leave in our place down in Virginia Beach, Sandbridge. I got a call from Cap Weinberger saying, "Fire Ace Lyons," who was PacFlt.

I said, "What's the problem, Mr. Secretary?"

"Fire the son of a bitch. He's going to get us into a war with Russia."

It turned out Lyons had been telling Crowe one thing, me another thing, and something different to Weinberger when challenged, and he, among other things, had laid out an exercise plan that started at the Aleutians, assembled from various sources a major task force, including several carriers, and steam balls-for-the-wall for Kamchatka to see what the Russian reaction would be. Weinberger's comment was Russia's reaction would be to start a war because they would think we were about to.

So I called Ace, said, "What the hell is going on?"

"None of your fuckin' business."

Paul Stillwell: Gee.

Admiral Trost: I said, "What do you mean?"

He said, "I briefed you on this."

I said, "On what?"

"I briefed you that I was going to do an exercise off the Aleutians."

---

[*] On 7 September 1977, President Omar Torrijos of Panama and President Jimmy Carter of the United States signed a new Panama Canal Treaty. It specified that the United States would transfer full control of the canal to Panama on 31 December 1999. The treaty did away with the Panama Canal Company, the Canal Zone, and its government as of 1 October 1979. The Panama Canal Commission then operated the canal during the 20-year transition period that began with the treaty.

[†] Admiral James A. Lyons, Jr., USN served as Commander in Chief Pacific Fleet from 16 September 1985 to 30 September 1987. Lyons had been a close associate of Secretary of the Navy John Lehman, who by September 1987 was no longer in office.

I said, "Yeah, you told me you were thinking of an exercise off the Aleutians. You didn't tell me what kind of exercise."

"Well, I briefed Bill Crowe."

So I called Crowe, and he got the same different story. Ace told Weinberger that he had briefed us both and gotten our okay. So Weinberger said, "Fire the son of a bitch. I want him out of there in three days."

So I came back to Washington, called Ace, and said, "Ace, I'm calling to tell you you are relieved as of tomorrow and you will be retired. And to save a lot of explanation to members of Congress, you're going to be retired as a four-star. If you want to challenge that, you're going to be retired as a two-star."

The response was "Fuck you."

So, anyway, I came back, started the ball rolling, and issued retirement orders, which my Chief of Personnel said, "God, if he's got buddies on the Hill, you're going to be in trouble."

I said, "Okay."

So Ace retired. Now, not on the record is the fact that Ace sent an airplane to WestPac to pick up some of Rene's most recent purchases for her store in northern Virginia, wherever they had their house, and sent another airplane back from Hawaii with a mess specialist on board, carrying highly classified material to be entrusted to an OP-06 buddy, which he had no business—first of all, that guy wasn't cleared for anything, and this whole thing was all screwed up. So I've been ever after in Ace's target crosshairs, which suits me fine.[*]

Paul Stillwell: I figured it would. [Laughs]

Admiral Trost: He called me one time to tell me—I think the words were "Fuckin' son of a bitch."

I said, "You made your bed. Lie in it." And that's what I can tell you about Ace Lyons.

---

[*] When Admiral Trost edited the transcript, he opted not to delete this paragraph.

Paul Stillwell: Well, I talked to Admiral Crowe, and he had some interesting things to say also.

Admiral Trost: Well, he was claiming to have briefed Crowe, claimed to have briefed me, to each other. But Ace, not my favorite person. To use the words of a classmate of his from the Naval Academy, "I was surprised when he made four stars, but I was more surprised when he made commander." [Stillwell laughs.]

Ace was the surface group commander based in Subic Bay when I had Seventh Fleet. He was an insubordinate son of a bitch. I got a phone call from him one day saying, "You've got to do something about Mombasa." He was in Kenya.

I said, "What the hell are you doing in Kenya? I didn't see any movement order on you." Supposedly he worked for me and he didn't go out of area without my okay. I didn't know he was in Kenya. I thought he was in Subic.

On another occasion, I called Subic to talk to him about something because CNO had called and said, "Where's Lyons?"

I said, "In Subic."

"You'd better check. He's going to be in the Secretary's office tomorrow to talk to Lehman."

So I called down. The yeoman said, "The admiral can't talk to you now."

So I called the chief of staff, Jack Beaver.[*] We'd been friends since we were commanders. I said, "Jack, where's Ace?"

"I'm not allowed to tell you."

I said, "Jack, you work for Ace but you also work for me, and I can fire you if I want to. Friendship is only so far."

"If you call Manila International Airport and have him paged, you might get a response."

So I did. Ace got on the line, "Who the fuck told you where I am?"

I said, "That's immaterial. Where are you going?"

"I'm going to Washington."

---

[*] Captain John T. Beaver Jr., USN, chief of staff to Commander Naval Surface Forces Western Pacific. Beaver, like Trost, was a submariner.

I said, "I didn't see anything about a movement or anything else." And supposedly he needed my okay to travel.

"Well," he said, "you don't outrank John Lehman."

"No, I don't." I said, "But you don't outrank me."

So he hung up, left on an airplane, went to Washington. He and Lehman were going over new flag moves, so he was invited by Lehman on flag moves, which is none of his goddamned business. So we are not friends.

Paul Stillwell: But then Lehman was gone when the problem came up with the Kamchatka operation.

Admiral Trost: Was he? I don't know. But he was not in the loop, I know that. Matter of fact, I'm sure he was gone. I don't know who the Secretary would have been. Would probably have been Webb.

I know he pissed Pauline off by causing me to cancel the only leave I'd had in a long time. [Laughter]

Paul Stillwell: What do you recall about the *Iowa* turret explosion in 1989?

Admiral Trost: Well, I read about it.* I still think that the guy who was killed, the second-class petty officer, was responsible for the explosion, and I base that on having gone into great detail with both the paperwork and the people on the *Iowa*.

My successor, Frank Kelso, was CinCLantFlt. Kelso held that this guy was framed, that he really wasn't guilty. He responded to the female congressman from Ohio from whose district this kid had come, who raised quite a stink in Washington about the whole thing, and I didn't bend to her, despite her threats to have me fired if I didn't knock off the investigation and so forth.

---

* On 19 April 1989, an explosion occurred in the center gun of turret two on board the USS *Iowa* (BB-61) during firing operations off Puerto Rico. As a result of the accident, 47 of her crew members were killed. The Navy's initial investigation of the turret explosion on board the *Iowa* found that Gunner's Mate Third Class Clayton Hartwig had killed himself and his shipmates by placing a device in the breech of a 16-inch gun. Subsequent tests determined that the explosion could have been caused by over-ramming of powder bags into the gun, and the Navy withdrew its claims that Hartwig had been responsible.

So what I recall about it is Kelso and I were on opposite sides of the fence. I still think the guy was instrumental in the explosion. All the background on him was shady, even though he was a second-class petty officer, and I think Frank was happy not to have this woman from Ohio on his ass and was willing to sweep it north and out of his bailiwick. So that's my biased opinion.

Paul Stillwell: We'll never know for sure.

Admiral Trost: Never know for sure. Never know for sure. There were enough questionable things, but all the eyewitnesses were dead.

Paul Stillwell: And so, it turned out, was the forensic evidence, because the Navy is so meticulous about cleaning up ships.

Admiral Trost: They swept everything over the side. Matter of fact, I read the statement of a kid who manned the fire hose to wash stuff off the deck and stuff that had been thrown out of the turret so it wasn't recoverable.

Paul Stillwell: Well, I think that was a big blow to the battleship program.

Admiral Trost: It was, it really was.

Paul Stillwell: And they were all then decommissioned on Admiral Kelso's watch.

Admiral Trost: Yeah. We'll never know.

Paul Stillwell: What do you remember about the incident in which the USS *Vincennes* shot down the Iranian Airbus? That was in the summer of 1988.[*]

---

[*] On 3 July 1988, Iran Air flight 655, an A300 airbus en route from Bandar Abbas Airport to Dubai, United Arab Emirates, was destroyed by two SM-2 Standard missiles launched at a range of nine miles by the Aegis cruiser *Vincennes* (CG-49). All 290 persons on board the civilian airliner died.

Admiral Trost: What do I remember about it? I talked to the skipper when it happened.[*] Based on his recollections of things that happened, I might have done the same thing. He thought the guy was coming in on an attack. We had reason to believe that they were talking about some sort of incident, but we didn't know what it was, in the near future. So when this guy came in and started dropping altitude without communicating, was he bent on hitting us or what was the story? And I can say I can see the skipper's point of view. He's got a big, expensive ship and he's going to defend it, and if he waits much longer, it's too late.

Paul Stillwell: Well, the mindset went back a year before to when the USS *Stark* got hit by the Exocets.[†]

Admiral Trost: That's right.

Paul Stillwell: And then the prevailing idea was defend your ship.

Admiral Trost: Yeah.

Paul Stillwell: So it was unfortunate in both cases.

Admiral Trost: Well, I stood in defense of the skipper, because I thought his action was appropriate. He thought he was under threat and this thing was not flying normally, not communicating.

Paul Stillwell: As did Admiral Crowe.

---

[*] Captain William C. Rogers III, USN, commanded the Aegis cruiser *Vincennes* (CG-49) from 11 April 1987 to 27 May 1989. He and his wife Sharon wrote a book titled *Storm Center: A Personal Account of Tragedy & Terrorism* (Annapolis: Naval Institute Press, 1992).

[†] On 17 May 1987, while she was operating in the Persian Gulf, the guided missile frigate *Stark* (FFG-31) was hit by two Exocet air-to-surface missiles fired by an Iraqi Mirage F1 fighter. One of the two missiles exploded, resulting in heavy damage and fires. Of the *Stark*'s crew, 37 men were killed and 21 injured. For details, see Jeffrey L. Levinson and Randy L. Edwards, *Missile Inbound* (Annapolis: Naval Institute Press, 1997).

Admiral Trost: Yeah.

Paul Stillwell: What was the division of labor between you and your VCNOs?

Admiral Trost: Well, I don't know how to answer that. [Laughs] I kept my VCNOs cut in. I had several. I had Busey. I had Edney. I had Huntington Hardisty.

Admiral Trost: I had a good working relationship. I used them—if you asked me why and what kinds of things, I really don't remember, Paul. It's been a few years.

Paul Stillwell: But was it the same kind of sounding-board relationship you had with Admiral Davis out in PacFlt?

Admiral Trost: It was, yeah, very much, very much. I kept them cut in on everything that was going on. I sought their advice. I had some pretty smart guys there, and they gave good advice. They were very useful. So when we had a problem, I talked it over with them and took their input. It's not much of an answer, but—

Paul Stillwell: Well, that's what it is. Is there anything else we need to talk about from your period on active duty?

Admiral Trost: Well, we've talked about the fact that Lehman and I did not get along. Other Secretaries, Larry Garrett and Will Ball were my two favorites. Jim Webb was not. Jim Webb did not communicate. Jim Webb behaved like a guy who didn't like his job, and he obviously didn't. It was not a collegial relationship. As a matter of fact, I'd hear about things, go up to see him. "Oh, yeah. I didn't think you needed to know about that."

"It's my Navy as well as your Navy, you know."

Paul Stillwell: What were the satisfactions of being the top-ranking officer in your service?

Admiral Trost: Well, the most satisfying was that I had for many years been pissed off at the amount of paperwork generated by what I thought were unnecessary directives. So when I took over, I directed a complete review. I don't remember now how much stuff we eliminated, but we eliminated more than 10% of the directives that were outstanding at the time in the fleet. I think it ended up being more than that. But that was one of my early satisfactions, getting rid of crap that caused people to spend time on nonproductive issues.

The other was being able to do what you thought was right. If people challenge you, they damn well better be right or you disregard them. The other thing was I enjoyed my relationship with Weinberger and with Carlucci because it came at time, both when I was 090 and then CNO, when Lehman was not having a good relationship with them personally but still directing what the Navy input was on various programs. Lehman stayed clear of budget issues at the talking stage with the Secretary of Defense. He never, to my knowledge, attended one of those meetings. The other service secretary sometimes did, sometimes didn't. But the Air Force Secretary tended to be there, Army about half the time, and I'd be the senior Navy rep. So I enjoyed that. But Lehman was a great second-guesser. He, "Well, I disagree with that." Well, that didn't surprise me because I generally disagreed with him.

Paul Stillwell: Were there things you accomplished as CNO that would not otherwise have gotten done?

Admiral Trost: Wow. I'd have to think about that. Let me think.

Paul Stillwell: Well, shorter deployments is one thing you've talked about.

Admiral Trost: Shorter deployments, but that's out the window now because we don't have the ships. I think the deployment was one of the things. I told you the sea story about being aboard a carrier in the Med and the young guys' response about length of deployment.

I guess what I really felt best about was I think I was an honest broker, even during Lehman's time, and did what I thought was best for the Navy. I consider myself a people-oriented guy, I always have, and I think during my term, people knew that people mattered, by the things we did on their behalf and to them and for them.

Well, of course, we maintained a big, strong Navy, which went "bloop" not too very long thereafter.

I was proud of my relationship with Bill Crowe, with Reagan and Bush both, with Colin Powell my last eight months, roughly. To me, the Chairman, no matter what the law says today, is the leader of a group. Colin was a one-man show. I don't know how the other Chiefs felt. I felt cut out of the picture when he took over. When I found out about a program, a Navy program that he put together for the next four years and gave to the Secretary of Defense without a word to me, pissed me off, and I told him. "Well, I'm simply acting within my prerogative under the new law," which says the Chairman is one, not one of five or whatever.

Bill Crowe's argument was, "I need the input from the other Chiefs because I don't know everything about all the services, and so I need the input." Colin, whether it was ego or what, I don't know—I suspect that—was very much his own guy. I wasn't the only Chief who got cut out of the system.

So I enjoyed being the guy who'd say, "Do this because it makes sense, do this because it's the right thing to do, even if people don't like it." So I guess I enjoyed being my own man. Now, that could be a fault too. [Stillwell laughs.] I think I had a reputation for being a people person; at least I tried to be. I think that's important.

Paul Stillwell: You had a reputation for being a straight shooter also.

Admiral Trost: Well, I'm not a bullshit artist. I told you, I think before, that I was proud of the fact that in my first part of my tour, we got rid of an awful lot—I think we got rid of like 10% of the Navy directives in the first month, and that's just crap people don't have to worry about, you know. I guess I got a chance to correct some of the things that annoyed me during my Navy career.

Paul Stillwell: That's a neat feeling.

Admiral Trost: Yeah, it's a good feeling. And I have to admit I enjoyed being in charge, so is that ego? Maybe. But I never tried to take on anything I didn't think I could handle. And on the fun side, I enjoyed pissing off Larry Welch. [Laughter]

Paul Stillwell: That's not part of the job description.

Admiral Trost: We were sworn in together and we retired the same day, and we worked together, obviously, four years. But he had a thing about the Navy. Our very presence annoyed him. He wanted to take over Navy air, and I told him, "I'm used to going underwater, but when you take that on, I'm fighting you all the way." [Stillwell laughs.] And he was giving me all their reasons, they were going to save all this money, and I didn't think they were going to save anything.

Paul Stillwell: That battle had been decided long before.

Admiral Trost: Oh, yeah, but he was reopening it. And he didn't like the idea of the three-star Navy guy out in Omaha as the senior guy on Joint Strategic Planning Staff. He approached me, wanted to eliminate that billet. I told him, "That billet is approved by Congress, and you're going to have to go through. The Navy will be asked for an input, and I'll give an input, and I don't think you'll get it."

Paul Stillwell: Isn't it ironic that since then four-star Navy admirals have been StratCom?* [Laughs]

Admiral Trost: I know. I know. I went out to Omaha about once a year when I was CNO. I always got VIP, VVIP treatment out there, and I used to get a kick out of it because I thought, "These guys are bending over backwards for the head of the Navy, when their boss really is pissed off." [Laughter] So strange sense of humor.

---

* StratCom – Strategic Command, which controls the use of U.S. nuclear weapons.

Paul Stillwell: Well, you told me about your retirement and the medical emergency you had. What sorts of things did you do after you left active duty?

Admiral Trost: Well, I served on a number of boards. I served on Louisiana Land and Exploration. I served on General Dynamics board. I served on Lockheed and then Lockheed Martin. General Public Utilities, which became First Energy when they moved out to Ohio. It was a New Jersey-Pennsylvania company, bought by an Ohio company. They ran Three Mile Island when they bought it.[*] I think they had two nuclear plants and we had three, so they ran five nuclear plants, which is why I went on the board. And who else was I with? Briefly with McDonnell Douglas, very briefly. I've forgotten the details of why I was invited to join the board. Something happened that—

Paul Stillwell: Must have been your aviation background. [Laughter]

Admiral Trost: Yeah. My aviation background is what got me on Lockheed board. Dan Tellep was the CEO of Lockheed, and Dan was a senior advisor to OP-05, the Navy, and I used to brief that board every six months when they had to go to the Pentagon.[†] And he decided that even though I was a submariner, I knew enough about airplanes to be of use in advising them on things to do with the government, how to do business.

So I served on ten boards. I'd have to stop and write them down to remember what they were. Then I was chairman of the Naval Academy Alumni Association board of directors for six years.

Paul Stillwell: Please tell me more about that.

Admiral Trost: I was also chairman here for six years.

Paul Stillwell: Here at Ginger Cove.

---

[*] On 28 March 1979, at the Three Mile Island commercial nuclear power plant near Middletown, Pennsylvania, a partial meltdown occurred and released radioactive material.

[†] Daniel M. Tellep was chief executive officer and chairman of the board of the Lockheed Corporation from 1989 to 1995 and subsequently CEO of Lockheed Martin Corporation following the 1994 merger.

Admiral Trost: Yeah. Alumni Association, I was the chairman from I want to say about '98 till '04, something like that, or '06, maybe, '06. That involved semiannual meetings and running the Alumni Association headquarters through a president over here in Annapolis, a meeting, served as a go-between between alumni and the superintendent and the Naval Academy and the policy guy for Alumni Association and so on. It was a frequent meeting because I lived here in Annapolis and could get over there very easily. I can't remember how often our board met. Quarterly, I think. And had a lot of interface with the superintendent on policy things he wanted to go forth with. He used me as a sounding board. And got good seats at games. [Laughter]

Paul Stillwell: Well, the Alumni Association became much more robust in fundraising around that era.

Admiral Trost: It did, and that was intentional. Really Jim Holloway was responsible for being a spark plug for that. He really got things going. That's when he headed the Foundation. Matter of fact, I give him credit for the robustness of the Foundation and the Alumni Association today. He really put a lot into it, had some good ideas, some good push, highly regarded, of course, and common-sense guy, so he was the right man for the job, did a great job.

Paul Stillwell: When I first came 40-some years ago, the Foundation had a little office on Maryland Avenue.

Admiral Trost: That's right.

Paul Stillwell: And its role was to raise funds for prep school for prospective athletes.

Admiral Trost: And they still have that office and we support about 39 to 40 plebes each year from prep school into the academy. It's a good source of input. People say, "Oh, you're just recruiting athletes." Yes and no. A lot of women who are not athletes, they're students. They've got to be students first. But we get some good people of real character who lack the funding to do much on their own who need the prep school support, and the families can't afford it. I've been a trustee for over 50 years, and I know an awful lot of kids who have been graduates of that program, and they're damn good kids.

Paul Stillwell: I remember there was a submariner named Elliott Loughlin who ran that for a number of years.[*]

Admiral Trost: Yeah, yeah, he did. My first meeting was in 1966, I think. I'd been in Washington about a year. Tom Blount, who was an early to mid-'40s alumnus from the academy was running the fundraising side.[†] I was in OSD. And they had a paper they wanted to get through SecDef, a policy paper that basically established their legitimacy. So here I am, I'm working for the Deputy Secretary. So Tom invited me to lunch one day and said, "We'd like your assistance, like to make you a member of our organization, and ask for your help in getting this document through." It sounded good to me, so I signed up and got the document signed, and they became an official entity.

The first meeting I attended was up Route 15 north of Frederick, up there in the Catoctin Mountains. The big Capitol Cadillac guy was the head of the Foundation. He was not a naval officer, I don't think. He owned Capitol Cadillac, and I used to remember his name.[‡] He was the kingpin. Elliott Loughlin was the local guy. We had these meetings up in the Catoctin Mountains. This guy owned a little retreat off Route 15, and you drove up this road through the trees in nowhere, and all of a sudden you came to a couple of open shed-type buildings, cookout things, and I think there was a cabin there that this guy owned, and that's where we had our semiannual meetings, and then a quarterly one in Washington or Annapolis area. And that was my first introduction to the foundation, and they've been going strong ever since.

Paul Stillwell: Probably not too far from Camp David.[§]

---

[*] Rear Admiral C. Elliot Loughlin, USN (Ret.). His oral history is in the Naval Institute collection.
[†] Commander Thomas E. Blount, USN (Ret.), class of 1941.
[‡] Capitol Cadillac, Greenbelt, Maryland.
[§] Camp David is a secluded presidential retreat near Thurmont, Maryland.

Admiral Trost: Not far from Camp David, that's right. Very pleasant place, and it was a rich man's hideaway. Nice little cabin where he spent time, and great cookout and barbecue facilities. Like the grill is not the grill; the grill is a fireplace with grills that fit in various places, and fixed steaks for 50 people.

Paul Stillwell: And then do the good business.

What do you recall about your role as president of the Naval Institute? This was when you were CNO. It was ex officio.

Admiral Trost: Oh, that was interesting. Of course, it's abolished because along with the fact that flag officers cannot serve on boards, I also spent four years as a member of the USAA board.* I was on the board here at the Naval Institute, as chairman, by virtue of being CNO. I found it interesting. I found that people listened. We had an operator input. One of my prime duties was to keep Lehman from taking over the Naval Institute to be his organ, what I call his propaganda organ, which he really tried hard to do.

Paul Stillwell: I did not realize that.

Admiral Trost: He wanted to take over the Naval Institute and have a guy on his staff who okayed every article that would appear to be submitted for the *Proceedings*. And he wanted veto authority over the *Proceedings*, and we withstood it; let's put it that way. So I found it interesting. I got to read articles that were submitted that never got published, some pretty interesting controversial ones. So it was sort of a fun job and entertaining.

Paul Stillwell: And you read some that did get published.

Admiral Trost: Yeah, yeah. But it was pretty good.

Paul Stillwell: Well, moving on to your family life, what do you recall about living with Pauline in Annapolis and then her passing?

---

* USAA – United Services Automobile Association, an insurance company.

Admiral Trost: Well, first of all, she was born and raised 29 miles from Annapolis, so she had an affinity for the area, and her parents lived in that house where she was raised until they died.

She came over here for the first time my second year, and I was—well, she and two girlfriends came over. They all had dates, including Pauline. One of the guys had watch on Saturday, which terminated at 1800, started the night before and went for 24 hours, so he couldn't take his girlfriend out during the day on Saturday, so I was recruited to substitute. That's where I met Pauline, and she was dating another guy. And I've forgotten how I ended up being the only escort for these three women for Saturday afternoon.

Paul Stillwell: Oh, darn. [Laughs]

Admiral Trost: It was just before Christmas, so they wanted to Christmas shop. I wanted to Christmas shop because I didn't have enough money to buy a pair of gloves for my dad, and I wanted to walk out to State Circle to that little place on the corner there and buy the gloves I'd seen and hadn't had the money as a youngster.

So I had a great afternoon, and at 1800 I reluctantly turned over my charges to their boyfriends, and that's when Pauline and I met. She then dated a guy, upperclassman in my company, for about a year and a half afterwards. I used to see her. We had the hops every Saturday night in Dahlgren Hall, and I went to them because I liked to dance, and used to dance with her every Saturday night, even though she wasn't my date.

We did not date until the George Washington birthday weekend of my last year. My roommate was dating a girl whose husband and sister lived in Silver Spring, Washington suburb, the northern side, inside the beltway. The couple had invited my roommate and their sister for the weekend, told them if they had any close buddies that wanted to bring their dates, they would arrange the sleeping accommodations and be the chaperones. So I invited Pauline and she said yes. So we spent a very, very nice weekend, went over to Great Falls on Saturday and went sightseeing and had a nice dinner and pleasant evening listening to music, and we went to church on Sunday morning and had lunch on Sunday, then returned the girls to their respective homes and us to the Naval Academy.

From that point on, I thought, "Gee, I really like this gal," and I'd gotten to know her pretty well. So I asked for a date. "Nope." [Laughter] For three months or four months, three months, up until June Week, she said no.

June Week, my parents and my sister were coming, and I called her and I said, "Would you come over for June Week and stay with my parents? My mother said it'd be fine; she's got room for you." She was working the first three days, could take off Thursday and Friday, said yes for Thursday and Friday. That was our first real get-together.

Saturday morning, my parents and I were invited to the wedding of a company mate just outside of Philadelphia, and we were leaving Sunday morning. My mother, bless her life, fell in love with Pauline in the two days she'd known her and said, "Pauline, why don't you come with us?" I found out later on Pauline initially said no because a Marine lieutenant was coming up from Quantico, had a date on Saturday evening, and she jilted him, which was something that she never got over, and said yes. And that was our first real time together, that week.

By the end of the weekend, my parents had stayed over for the weekend, and, of course, I had graduated, so my mother had invited Pauline to come to Illinois, and since I was coming back for a wedding of a classmate coming through Washington, she could take the train back with me and wouldn't have to travel alone. All this worked out.

So about ten days after graduation, I was in Norfolk for a wedding, picked up Pauline in Washington, we rode the train out to Illinois, an overnight trip in seats in a coach, and she spent either a week or ten days out in Illinois. By the time the week or ten days was over, I was totally smitten and came back through Washington on my way to my first ship down in Norfolk. And we stayed in touch; we dated. I went immediately to Key West to Sonar School for eight weeks. She and two girlfriends came down to Key West and spent about four days in Key West. I fixed up the other two gals with dates with fellow ensigns, and we had a good four days. Thereafter, we stayed in touch, and I would come up from Norfolk, particularly from time to time on weekends for the month after I got back.

Then I deployed, stayed in correspondence while I was in the Med for five months, and came back, resumed dating. I proposed to her maybe a month into my return, and she reluctantly said yes. [Laughter] And three months later we got married.

Paul Stillwell: And there's somewhere a former Marine who's been weeping ever since.

Admiral Trost: You know, the bad thing about it was Pauline and her two girlfriends, both of whom I knew—one of whom has died too—they stopped in Parris Island to see the fiancé of one of these girls, and at the club the night their one night there, they ran into this guy—

Paul Stillwell: Oh, no! [Laughs]

Admiral Trost: —who Pauline says, "He not only didn't talk to me, he didn't acknowledge my presence." I can understand that.

Paul Stillwell: Yes.

Admiral Trost: So, anyway, but he came up for the day, and Pauline's mother wouldn't open the door because she didn't want to talk to him. [Laughter]

Paul Stillwell: Well, please tell me about your life here in retirement, first on Compromise Street, then at Ginger Cove.

Admiral Trost: Well, we moved over here in 1999 after I'd been retired, and enjoyed life. Of course, I was at that point involved with the Alumni Association, so I was busy with that, and in 1999 I was still serving on about seven or eight boards. So I had a pretty busy life, spent a lot of time in and out of BWI and on the train to New York, as I had two boards in the New York area, one in New York, one in New Jersey, and stayed busy really with the Alumni Association and with the Naval Academy as sort of an informal advisor to the supe.[*] I knew all those guys and would meet with them about monthly for whatever they wanted to talk about.

We enjoyed life in Annapolis, liked that. Pauline always said she wanted to move to Annapolis someday, and I couldn't early on because I was traveling so much that I really needed the travel facilities out of Washington. I was going on the Metro to New York twice a month and I was flying. I was just off the USAA board. I went down early on from Washington, but not from here. I flew out to the West Coast for my first five years of retirement, and that was Lockheed, and then Lockheed Martin moved to Maryland. Thereafter, I had a five-minute drive when I was living back in my old house back in Potomac.

So stayed busy here, mostly Naval Academy related, and Pauline worked with the Officers' Wives Club, was pretty active with them, and the Society of Sponsors. She was a ship sponsor, so she stayed active with them.

Paul Stillwell: Which ship?

Admiral Trost: *Pasadena*, submarine.[†] And we were active with the *Columbia*, as I told you. I stayed active with them for a number of years and haven't done anything really with *Columbia*. Their ship is about to be decommissioned after 30 years, either is about to or is, and one of the new missile submarines is going to be *Columbia*. So I'm happy with that. And my little hometown of 1,800 when I left, 13,000 when I retired, and now it's 23 or something like that. It's more an agricultural community and a St. Louis bedroom community because it's across the river and 20 miles south, so there's a lot of people working in the industrial region of East St. Louis and in St. Louis. So I've lived an easy life.

Paul Stillwell: Please tell me about her passing.

---

[*] BWI – Baltimore-Washington International Thurgood Marshall Airport, in Linthicum, Maryland, outside of Baltimore.

[†] USS *Pasadena* (SSN-752), launched 12 September 1987, when Trost was Chief of Naval Operations.

Admiral Trost: Well, she started having problems with nerves in one leg about two years, two and a half years before she died, and they tried various medications, some of which eased the pain and let her sleep but also caused pain and caused her some sleepless nights. About her last year, she was in pain most of the time and on heavy medication that had side effects that were not pleasant. Matter of fact, she slept by herself in our guest bedroom for about her last three or four months, because when she rolled over next to me or I rolled over next to her, it bothered her legs. So I'd get up with her, I got up with her about two or three times a night. She needed help to go to the bathroom. She needed help to roll over sometimes, so she had a painful time through the years.

She was going into the hospital for a series of checks to see if they could determine more of what was causing this problem. She was admitted to Anne Arundel on a Sunday or Monday night. We took her in. The bed wasn't ready, the—not emergency room, but the care room.

Paul Stillwell: ICU?

Admiral Trost: ICU.[*] So she got admitted finally about 9:30 at night, and I guess it was Monday night. And the next morning we had a snowstorm, so I couldn't get over there right away. Got over there about 9:30, and when I got to the hospital, she was not feeling well and she was in pain, and they didn't know what was causing it, but her legs were bothering her. Her one leg was sort of semi numb. So she wasn't talkative, wasn't communicating, which was very unlike her, and she said, "Why don't you go down and get a couple papers and sit and read the paper." So I did, and I was sitting there reading the paper, and all of a sudden, a nurse came in, swatted the paper away from me, grabbed me off the couch and hauled me out of the room. I said, "What the hell's going on?"

A swarm of people came in. Pauline had a heart attack, and when I came back in, she had a mask on and a fibrillator or whatever, I don't know which. But she was in bed with an oxygen mask and something that kept her heart pumping. What's that thing called?

---

[*] ICU – intensive care unit.

Paul Stillwell: Pacemaker?

Admiral Trost: Pacemaker. But external. So the doctor was there, starting to make his rounds. He was an outside doctor. So he just sort of stuck there, and they decided she needed—first of all, he said to me, "Have you all decided what would happen if you're unable to recover your health?"

I said, "Yes, we have." And our decision had been we don't want life-sustaining actions be taken.

So he talked to her. She couldn't talk, but she could squeeze a hand, and told her about our conversation and said, "Do you still feel that way?"

And, "Yes."

So she was unable to communicate for that day. I called the kids. All the kids and the grandchildren got here. She went downhill and was finally on—well, she was on assisted breathing and assisted heartbeat. And about 9:00 o'clock at night, the doctor said, "You know, she's either going to be a vegetable or have life-sustaining equipment full-time." And he said, "She doesn't want that."

I said, "She made that clear," and she did that in writing to him before. So they kept her on oxygen, which she needed to be sustained. She saw her kids, all her grandchildren, and about 9:30 at night she went like this to me, and I said, "You want this pulled?" She said—

Paul Stillwell: You're making a motion with your hand across your throat.

Admiral Trost: Yeah. So cut off the oxygen. She died about five minutes later.[*]

Paul Stillwell: What a terrible thing to go through.

Admiral Trost: Yeah. I guess I'm still emotional about it. [cries]

Paul Stillwell: Well, there's been a hole in your life ever since.

---

[*] Pauline Trost died 7 January 2015 at Anne Arundel Medical Center in Annapolis.

Admiral Trost: Yeah. Excuse me. Has been. She raised four great kids, no complaints.

Paul Stillwell: Well, please bring me up to date on those four children.

Admiral Trost: Well, the eldest son—two boys, two girls, boy girl, boy girl. Oldest is a sound technician for NBC, works in Washington.

Paul Stillwell: This is Carl.

Admiral Trost: That's Carl. Shifting from NBC in Bethesda downtown across from the Capitol. I think that's going to be a permanent move. It just takes place this week, as a matter of fact.

Laura Lee is the oldest daughter, married, three children, and living in northern New Jersey. Husband is a CPA, partner in his own firm and introduced, as a matter of fact, by his aunt, who is a classmate's wife whose memorial we attended last this Memorial Day. She was the one who introduced John, my son-in-law, and Laura Lee.

And then there's Steve, who's Naval Academy class of '85. He's a retired commander reserve, spent—nuclear submariner—eight years' active duty and the rest reserve time. I think he had 23 years total.

Then Kathleen, who's the youngest, is 50 and she's a special ed teacher in an elementary school in Chesapeake, Virginia, about two years from retiring on 31 or 32 years.

All are great kids, two married, two not, and to which I have to give my wife credit because she spent a lot of time raising them alone, and a good mom, great wife. Used to bemoan the fact that she didn't have a college education because she had to go to work right out of high school, smarter than most people I know.

Paul Stillwell: Admiral, do you have any final valedictory to sum up this productive life of yours?

Admiral Trost: You know, I was lucky. I got good breaks. I had a good education. I had a good elementary education, went to the Dupo High School, which was a good move on my part. Had my year of college, was saved by the Naval Academy because I didn't have any money left and didn't, until I got sworn into the Naval Academy, know I had a full-on scholarship. I stayed on active duty and enjoyed every minute of it—almost every minute of it.

Paul Stillwell: [Laughs] Fate is really an interesting companion as you go through life.

Admiral Trost: Yeah, it really was. And I worked with some good people. My first skipper, my first two skippers, never saw them again, and that was fine with me. I was asked—and I don't remember who it was—I had a call from somebody representing the daughter of that skipper Jack English that I didn't like at all on the *Owens*, and said, "I was given your name by so-and-so. Would you submit to an interview about Captain English?" [Stillwell laughs.]

I said, "No, I would not, because it would be negative, and I'm not going to do that." And so I didn't. But he was one of the biggest asses I ever met, in a category with John Lehman.

Paul Stillwell: Admiral, it has taken us a long time to get this done, but I am profoundly grateful for your cooperation.

Admiral Trost: I am very grateful for your patience. I would think it would be boring as hell. And Laura Lee, the oldest daughter, says after all these years, she's looking forward to reading about me. [Laughs]

Paul Stillwell: Well, other people will be as well, and this will be a resource from now on.

Admiral Trost: I hope it was helpful. I hope it is.

Paul Stillwell: It is.

Admiral Trost: Good.

Paul Stillwell: And it has been a pleasure to work with you, sir.

Admiral Trost: I've enjoyed it. I've enjoyed it. And I'm glad you were back on the case.

Paul Stillwell: Great. Thank you, sir.

Admiral Trost: Okay. You're welcome. My pleasure, and thank you.

Index to the Oral History of
Admiral Carlisle A. H. Trost. U.S. Navy (Retired)

Problems on board the nuclear submarine *Scorpion* (SSN-589) in the early 1960s were handled by senior enlisted men rather than a captain's mast, 257-259

Dixon, USS (AS-37)

In the early 1970s served as flagship for Commander Submarine Group Five at Ballast Point near San Diego, 379, 381-382, 390, 423-424

Initial group of women crew members in the mid-1970s included a lesbian, 423-424

Dolphin, USS (AGSS-555)

Small deep-diving submarine used for experimental work in the early 1970s, 383

Dominican Republic

U.S. Marine landing in April 1965, 289

Donnelly, Vice Admiral John Jay, USN

In the late 1980s served on the OP-00K panel, later was ComSubLant, 647-648

Donovan, Vice Admiral Francis R., USN (USNA, 1959)

Commanded Military Sealift Command, 1990-92, 405, 538-539

Doyle, Vice Admiral James H., Jr., USN (USNA, 1947)

In the late 1970s objected to the possible assignment of Dennis Blair as XO of a fleet destroyer, 417

Drew, Christopher

Coauthor of controversial submarine book *Blind Man's Bluff*, published in 1998, 395-396

Drugs

Changes in the ComSubLant drug policies in 1969-70, 342-344, 349

Dry Docks

In the early 1970s Submarine Group Five had a floating dry dock at Ballast Point near San Diego, 382, 387-388

Dunn, Vice Admiral Robert F., USN (USNA, 1951)

Served as ComNavAirLant in the mid-1980s, later as OP-05, 532-533, 552, 614

Dwight D. Eisenhower, USS (CVN-69)

Visited Singapore in the early 1980s during a respite from operations in the North Arabian Sea, 431-432

Earnest Will – Operation

Use of battleships to protect the escort of reflagged Kuwaiti tankers in the Persian Gulf in 1987-88, 603-605, 607

Issues with mines in the gulf, 606-607

Fuller, Lieutenant Joe Ed, USN (USNA, 1951)
Member of the first crew of the nuclear submarine *Swordfish* (SSN-579), commissioned in 1958, 225, 229
Conned the *Swordfish* through the Panama Canal in 1959, 669-670

Garrett, H. Lawrence III
Served from 1989 to 1992 as Secretary of the Navy, 595-597

Germany
Some citizens of Western Illinois spoke German regularly in the 1930s-40s, 34-35
German prisoners of war did farm work in Illinois during World War II, 33
Interaction between the Trosts and Germans while he was an Olmsted Scholar in 1961-62, 237-239, 241-247
Trost's involvement with the Federal German Navy when he was CNO in the late 1980s, 625-626
The Berlin Wall was erected in 1961 and taken down in 1989, 241-242

Goldwater-Nichols Defense Reorganization Act
This 1986 law affected allocation of resources to the Navy, 506
Trost viewed a beneficial effect that of creating a Vice Chairman of the JCS, but it diminished the power of the service chiefs, 583-584

Goodpaster, General Andrew J., USA (USMA, 1939)
Trost's favorable assessment of, 311

Gordon, Richard J.
Served in the 1980s-90s as mayor of Olongapo City, Philippines, 475-476

Gorshkov, Admiral Sergei G.
Visited in Moscow in 1972 by U.S. delegates to the Incidents at Sea negotiations, 370-371

Gravely, Vice Admiral Samuel L., Jr., USN (Ret.)
In the late 1970s-early 1980s occupied flag quarters on the grounds of the Naval Observatory in Washington, 513-514

Gray, General Alfred M., Jr., USMC
Served as Commanding General, Fleet Marine Force Atlantic, from 1984 until 1987, when he became Commandant, 532, 592, 659

Great Lakes, Illinois, Naval Training Center
Problems with deteriorating physical plant in the mid-1980s, 414
Problems with the quality of officers assigned in the late 1980s, 413
Role of Naval Reservists in doing construction projects in the late 1980s, 615

Greece
Visit by the destroyer *Robert A. Owens* (DDE-827) in the mid-1950s, 142, 157-158

Gregg, Captain Otis C., USN (USNA, 1927)
Headed the aviation department at the Naval Academy in the early 1950s, 111-112
Commanded the aircraft carrier *Princeton* (CVA-37), 1953-54, 111-112

Grenada
U.S. occupation in 1983 after the overthrow of the island's government, 410-411

Griffiths, Commander Charles H., USN (USNA, 1946)
Advised Trost in 1954 how to get into Submarine School, 188
In 1962 detailed Trost as executive officer of the nuclear submarine *Scorpion* (SSN-589)

Guantánamo Bay, Cuba, Naval Base
The destroyer *Brownson* (DD-868) trained there in the summer of 1950, 89-90

Gunfire Support
Simulator that provided training at the Naval Academy in the late 1940s-early 1950s, 72-73
Simulated near Virginia Beach by the destroyer *Robert A. Owens* (DDE-827) in 1954, 172

Guppy Program
In the late 1940s the submarine *Sirago* (SS-485) got the GUPPY modification, 203

Hanson, Captain Carl Thor, USN (USNA, 1950)
In the early 1970s served as executive assistant to the Secretary of the Navy, 364

Harlow, Captain David L., USN
Served in the late 1970s as executive assistant to the Vice Chief of Naval Operations, 427

Harvey, Ensign Andrew C., USN
In 1953 reported for duty on board the destroyer *Robert A. Owens* (DDE-827), 120

Havana, Cuba
Liberty visits in the 1950s, 120-121, 200

Hawaii
Family life for the Trosts in the Pearl Harbor area in the late 1950s and late 1970s, 233-234, 436-437
In 1978-80 the living quarters of the Deputy CinCPacFlt were useful for entertaining and often helped accomplish things with local leaders, 440-443

Iskenderun Bay, Turkey
Visited by the destroyer *Robert A. Owens* (DDE-827) in the mid-1950s, 142-143

Italian Navy
Participated in NATO exercises in the Mediterranean in 1953-54, 138-139

Italy
Site of port visits by the destroyer *Robert A. Owens* (DDE-827) in the mid-1950s, 138, 140-142, 181-182

Japan
Yokosuka served as a valuable base for Seventh Fleet ships in the early 1980s, 447-450, 465-466
Trost's interaction with the Japanese Defense Minister, 448-449
Role of Commander U.S. Naval Forces Japan in the early 1980s, 467-469
Trost and his wife were tourists in Japan, 471-473
Position toward U.S. nuclear-powered ships in the early 1980s, 477
Michael J. Mansfield cooperated with Trost while serving as U.S. Ambassador to Japan in the early 1980s, 484-485

Japanese Maritime Self-Defense Force
In 1955 sent students to the U.S. Submarine School as a prelude to receiving U.S. diesel submarines, 199, 466-467
In the early 1970s acquired two diesel submarines from the U.S. Navy, 377-378
Joint exercises with U.S. warships in the early 1980s, 470-471

Jeremiah, Admiral David E., USN
Was Trost's choice to become Chief of Naval Operations in 1990 but became Vice Chairman of the JCS instead, 573-575

Johnson, Lieutenant David E., USN
Member of the first crew of the nuclear submarine *Swordfish* (SSN-579), commissioned in 1958, 226

Johnson, Admiral Gregory G., USN
In the late 1970s did outstanding work in OP-96, 429-431

Johnson, President Lyndon B.
Brief telephone interaction with Trost in the mid-1960s, 288

Johnson, Captain Willard E., USN
In the early 1970 served as chief of staff to Commander Submarine Group Five, 386, 390

Joint Chiefs of Staff
Impact of the Goldwater-Nichols Defense Reorganization Act of 1986, 506, 583-584

In 1982 relieved Admiral Hyman Rickover as Director, Naval Nuclear Propulsion and served in that billet until 1988, 502-503, 613

McMullen, Rear Admiral Frank D., USN (USNA, 1947)
Served 1972-75 as Commander Submarine Force Pacific Fleet, 385-386, 643

McNamara, Robert S.
Working style as Secretary of Defense from 1961 to 1968, 282-283, 287, 309
Involvement in Vietnam War policy, 291-292

McNitt, Rear Admiral Robert W., USN (Ret.) (USNA, 1938)
Naval Academy dean of admissions, 1972-85, 60

McWilliams, Captain George Randolph, USN
Served in the early 1970s as Trost's aide and later as U.S. naval attaché in Japan, 330, 383-384
Role as flag lieutenant, 384
Reconditioned old automobiles, 383-384

Medical Problems
Shady dentists dealt with plebes who reported to the Naval Academy in 1949, 54
Cases of venereal disease among the crew of the destroyer *Robert A. Owens* (DDE-827) in 1953-54, 179, 183-184
An enlisted man on board the *Robert A. Owens* deliberately shot himself in the foot in a vain effort to go see his girlfriend, 182-183
In 1968 Trost needed treatment in Charleston after cutting his bare feet on oyster shells, 323-324
In the summer of 1980, Trost had a problem with an enlarged prostate gland, 621

Merritt, Lieutenant Glen C., USN
Member of the first crew of the nuclear submarine *Swordfish* (SSN-579), commissioned in 1958, 226

Metcalf, Vice Admiral Joseph III, USN (USNA, 1951)
Served in BuPers in the 1960s, 404, 410
Commanded the Second Fleet during the Grenada operation in 1983, 410-411
Served in the mid-1980s as DCNO (Surface Warfare), 411

Metzel, Commander Jeffrey C. Jr., USN (USNA, 1947)
Executive officer of the first crew of the nuclear submarine *Swordfish* (SSN-579), commissioned in 1958, 221, 225, 228
In the mid-1960s was the first commanding officer of the Gold crew of the ballistic missile submarine *Von Steuben* (SSBN-632), 261-262

Superintendents in the late 1940s-early 1950s, 74-77, 80

Social life for midshipmen, 99-100, 103, 111-112

Trost as class vice president and brigade commander in his first-class year, 78-83, 112-113

Graduation June Week for the class of 1953, 83-84, 99, 107-108

Ross Perot, class president, later made financial donations for structures at the academy, 294-295

Value of the Naval Academy experience, 109-110, 113-114

Change over the years in professional training/academics balance, 114

Concern in the 1980s about air conditioning in Bancroft Hall, 587

Role over the years of the Naval Academy Alumni Association and Foundation, 681-683

As superintendent in the early 1980s, Charles Larson spearheaded the idea of creating Alumni Hall, 587-589

Naval Academy Preparatory School, Newport, Rhode Island
Trost's son Steven attended in the early 1980s, 61

Naval Education and Training, Chief of
See: Chief of Naval Education and Training (CNET)

Naval Institute, U.S.
Trost as ex-officio president, 1986-90, 683

Naval Material Command (NavMat)
Secretary of the Navy John Lehman's dissolution of this command in 1985, 601-602

Naval Nuclear Power School, Idaho Falls, Idaho
Curriculum in 1957, 214, 218-221

Naval Nuclear Power School, New London, Connecticut
Curriculum in 1957, 213-218

Naval Observatory, Washington, D.C.
In the 1970s-80s had sometimes-substandard quarters for senior naval officers, 513-515

Naval Reserve, U.S.
Officers and enlisted were compelled to leave active duty following the end of the Korean War, 177-178

In the early 1970s reservists did useful repair and maintenance work on a floating dry dock near San Diego, 387-388

Role of during Trost's tenure as CNO, 1986-90, 614

Panama

For the invasion of Panama in 1989, Trost declined the opportunity to supply an aircraft carrier, 667-668

Panama Canal

Trost and Lieutenant Joe Fuller conned the nuclear submarine *Swordfish* (SSN-579) through the canal in 1959, 669-670

Trost opposed letting the Canal Zone revert to the nation of Panama, 668-669

Patton, Lieutenant (junior grade) James H. Jr., USN (USNA, 1960)

In the early 1960s served in the nuclear submarine *Scorpion* (SSN-589), 636-637

In the late 1980s was technical advisor for the movie *The Hunt for Red October*, 637

Paulsen, Captain Thomas C., USN

Former diesel submariner who did well after transferring to surface ships and later became Trost's executive assistant, 315, 348, 421, 518-519, 579, 619, 663-664

Pensacola, Florida, Naval Air Station

In the late 1980s was the site of planning meetings involving the CNO and principal subordinates, 584-587

Perot, Midshipman H. Ross, USN (USNA, 1953)

President of the Naval Academy class of 1953, 76, 78, 83, 101

Made a number of financial donations for structures at the Naval Academy, 294-295

Personnel

Reserve officers and enlisted men were compelled to leave active duty following the end of the Korean War, 177-178, 183

Peruvian Navy

A midshipman from Peru attended the U.S. Naval Academy in the late 1940s-early 1950s, 56-57

Trost could not visit Peru in the 1980s because of concerns for his personal safety, 534

Philadelphia Naval Shipyard

Overhaul of the destroyer *Robert A. Owens* (DDE-827) in 1954, 172-179

Philippine Islands

Seventh Fleet Relationship with this nation in the early 1980s, 474-475

Subic Bay provided support to the Seventh Fleet for many years, 475-476

Pirie, Captain Robert B., USN (USNA, 1926)

Commandant of the Naval Academy, 1949-52, 76

Poindexter, Vice Admiral John M., USN (USNA, 1958)
Involvement in the process by which Trost became Chief of Naval Operations in 1986, 545-546

Point Loma, California
Site of a submarine support facility for Submarine Group Five in the early 1970s, 184-185

Polaris Missiles
Training in missiles in the mid-1960s at Dam Neck, Virginia, for those reporting to Polaris submarines, 263-264

Portsmouth Naval Shipyard, Kittery, Maine
From 1956 to 1958 built the nuclear submarine *Swordfish* (SSN-579), 213, 219-222, 224-225

Pounders, Lieutenant Jerry K., USN
In the mid-1950s was chief engineer and later executive officer of the destroyer *Robert A. Owens* (DDE-827), 125, 151-152, 156, 161, 187

Powell, General Colin L., USA
As Chairman of the Joint Chiefs of Staff in 1990, chose Admiral David Jeremiah to be his deputy, 574-575
Developed a plan for the future of the Navy without consulting Trost, 584
For the invasion of Panama in 1989, Trost declined Powell's suggestion to supply an aircraft carrier, 667-668
Trost's assessment of, 679

Prisoners of War
Germans did farm work in Illinois during World War II, 33

Program Appraisal, Office of (OPA)
Secretary of the Navy John Lehman's use of the office to counter the OpNav systems analysis shop in the 1980s, 600-601

Program Planning, Navy
Navy budget issues, 1981-85, 485-507, 512-513

Promotion of Naval Officers
As Secretary of the Navy in the 1980s, John Lehman had a large influence on flag officer promotions, 482-483
As CNO, 1986-90, Trost spent a lot of time on flag officer assignments and promotion, 572-577, 599

Propulsion Plants

Crewmen made coffee in the engineering spaces of the destroyer *Brownson* (DD-868) in 1950, 95-96

Top-notch engineering spaces in the destroyer *Haynsworth* (DD-700) in 1952, 186-187

Engineering setup on board the destroyer *Robert A. Owens* (DDE-827) in 1953-54, 154-157, 187

In the late 1940s the submarine *Sirago* (SS-485) got the GUPPY modification, 203

Reliable diesels in the *Sirago* in the mid-1950s, 187

The submarine *Wahoo* (SS-565) had troublesome "pancake" diesels in the 1950s, 205

Nuclear plant in the submarine *Swordfish* (SSN-579) in the late 1950s, 227

After being decommissioned in 1989, the former ballistic missile submarine *Sam Rayburn* (SSBN-635) served as a training ship for nuclear plant operators, 273

Sturdy plant in the battleship *Wisconsin* (BB-64), 91-92

Pueblo, USS (AGER-2)

Lack of U.S. support after the ship was seized by North Korea in January 1968, 313-314, 362-363

In 1969 Secretary of the Navy John Chafee directed that the commanding officer, Lloyd Bucher, not be court-martialed, 362-363

Racial Issues

In the 1930s-40s, a local ordinance prevented black citizens from being in Columbia, Illinois, after dark, 35-36

Black midshipmen at the Naval Academy in the early 1950s, 56

Areas of Annapolis, Maryland, were segregated in the late 1940s-early 1950s, 98-99

Raffaele, Captain Robert J., USN (Ret.) (USNA, 1953)

Naval Academy classmate of Trost, 55

Read, Vice Admiral William L., USN (USNA, 1949)

As a junior officer in the destroyer *Haynsworth* (DD-700) in the late 1940s-early 1950s, 406

Served in BuPers in the mid-1960s, 404, 410

Military assistant jobs as a flag officer, 406

Reagan, President Ronald W.

In the early 1970s, as California's governor, toured the Mare Island Naval Shipyard and the ballistic missile submarine *Thomas Edison* (SSBN-610), 391

Served as President of the United States, 1981-89, 391, 499-500, 503, 569-570

Met with Admiral Hyman Rickover in 1982 on Rickover's retirement from active duty, 503

Involvement in the process by which Trost became Chief of Naval Operations in 1986, 545-546

Redelsheimer, Lieutenant (junior grade) Sigmnd, USNR
Served in the destroyer *Robert A. Owens* (DDE-827) in the mid-1950s, 153

Religion
Frequent church attendance by the Trost family in the 1930s and 1940s, 18-20, 34

Replenishment at Sea
By the destroyer *Robert A. Owens* (DDE-827)in the Mediterranean in 1953, 152

Reserve Officer Training Corps (ROTC)
Army ROTC at Washington University in the late 1940s, 46-47
Service obligations of NROTC-trained officers in the early 1950s, 133
Ivy League universities shut down ROTC units in the 1960s, 162

Richardson, Admiral John M., USN (USNA, 1982)
The son of one of Trost's former shipmates, he became Chief of Naval Operations in 2015, 585-586

Richardson, Captain William E., USN (Ret.) (USNA, 1959)
As a junior officer, served in the nuclear submarine (SSN-589) in the early 1960s, 585
Was on the Submarine Group Eight staff in Naples around 1970, 585-586
Attended the change of command when his son became CNO in 2015, 585-586

Rickover, Admiral Hyman G., USN (Ret.) (USNA, 1922)
In 1957 interviewed Trost for the Navy's nuclear power program, 211-212
Experiment in accepting an individual who was not a technical major, 216-217
Drafted some individuals into the program in the 1950s, 217-218
In 1958 visited the pre-commissioning detail of the nuclear submarine *Swordfish* (SSN-579) at Portsmouth Naval Shipyard, 213
In the mid-1960s took part in the sea trials of the ballistic missile submarine *Von Steuben* (SSBN-632), 267-269
In the mid-1960s asked Trost to track down a document stalled in the Defense Department, 312-313
In 1968 presided over a prospective commanding officer course that included Trost, 317-320
In May 1968 reflected on the loss of the nuclear submarine *Scorpion* (SSN-589), 320
In the late 1960s mistakenly made a call to Trost about the ballistic missile submarine *Sam Rayburn* (SSBN-635), 334-335
In 1973 attended Trost's frocking ceremony for rear admiral, 375-376
In the early 1970s kept tabs on submarine work in various shipyards, 378-380
In the mid-1970s tried to influence selection boards, 418-419
In 1982 was retired from active duty over his objection, 503-504

When commanded by Trost in the early 1980s, was prepared to prevent incidents comparable to the 1968 seizure of the intelligence ship *Pueblo* (AGER-2), 314-315, 363

Trost's travels to various nations as fleet commander in 1980-81, 431-433, 433-434, 443-447, 451-455, 457-461, 474-480, 650-652, 655-658

Yokosuka, Japan, served as a valuable base for Seventh Fleet ships in the early 1980s, 447-450

Connections with Western Pacific nations in the early 1980s, 461-463, 470-476

Quarterly scheduling conferences in the early 1980s, 462-463

Monitoring of weather conditions in the area of operations in the early 1980s, 469-470

Interaction and planning concerning the Soviet Navy in the early 1980s, 476-477

Principal staff members in the early 1980s, 480-482

Unreadiness on the part of some Seventh Fleet ships in the early 1980s, 483-484, 488-489

Shear, Admiral Harold E., USN (USNA, 1942)

In the 1960s kept tabs on the operations of the ballistic missile submarines, 428-429

Had piles of paper all over his office when he was relieved as Vice Chief of Naval Operations in 1977, 427-428

Ship Handling

In the destroyer *Robert A. Owens* (DDE-827) in the mid-1950s, 129, 148-152, 170-171

In the nuclear submarine *Scorpion* (SSN-589) in the early 1960s, 254-255

In Charleston's Cooper River for the ballistic missile submarine *Sam Rayburn* (SSBN-635) in the late 1960s, 324-326

Sicily

Crew liberty and voyage repairs to the destroyer *Robert A. Owens* (DDE-827) at Palermo in 1953, 134-137, 142

Simcoe, Lieutenant (junior grade) Richard O., USNR

Served in the destroyer *Robert A. Owens* (DDE-827) in the mid-1950s, 153-155

Simulators

Used for training students at Submarine School in 1955, 189-190

Singapore

Site of port visits by U.S. aircraft carriers during respite from operations in the North Arabian Sea in the early 1980s, 431-432, 464

Richard Kneip, the U.S. ambassador to Singapore from 1978 to 1980 was a neophyte concerning the Navy, 431-432

Trost visited in the early 1980s when he was Commander Seventh Fleet, 453-454, 459

CPSIA information can be obtained
at www.ICGtesting.com
Printed in the USA
BVHW08*0804050818

523412BV00012B/62/P

9 781682 473689